D0886691

an anthology of KOKUGAKU SCHOLARS 1690–1868

an anthology of KOKUGAKU SCHOLARS 1690–1868

translated and annotated by

JOHN R. BENTLEY

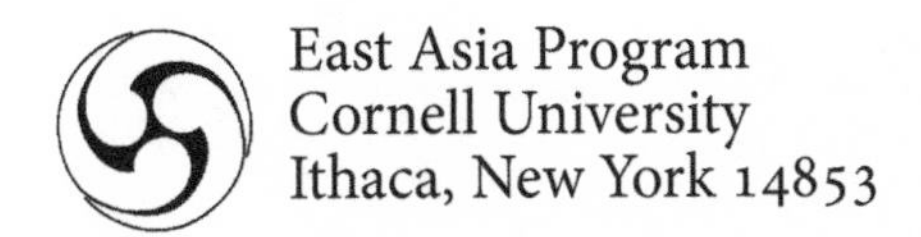

East Asia Program
Cornell University
Ithaca, New York 14853

To Chiemi

The Cornell East Asia Series is published by the Cornell University East Asia Program (distinct from Cornell University Press). We publish books on a variety of scholarly topics relating to East Asia as a service to the academic community and the general public. Address submission inquiries to CEAS Editorial Board, East Asia Program, Cornell University, 140 Uris Hall, Ithaca, New York 14853-7601.

Number 184 in the Cornell East Asia Series

ISSN 1050-2955
ISBN: 978-1-939161-64-2 hc
ISBN: 978-1-939161-84-0 pb
ISBN: 978-1-942242-84-0 ebook
Library of Congress Control Number: 2017941814

Cover images: Shutterstock vector ID 428458120 and stock illustration ID: 1924476

CONTENTS

Part Two VIEWS ON LITERATURE

Part Three VIEWS ON SCHOLARSHIP

Part Four VIEWS ON JAPAN/RELIGION

ACKNOWLEDGMENTS

At an early stage of research on *Kujiki* I was exposed to the writings of Motoori Norinaga, and discovered there were a number of his works I would need to have access to further my study. In the spring of 1985 I was fortunate to find the 21-volume set of *Motoori Norinaga zenshū* at a secondhand bookstore. I was fascinated by Norinaga's breadth and depth of knowledge of texts, history, linguistics, and literature. As my work began to trace his sources, I was led to the essays of Kamo no Mabuchi and Keichū. Their research into *Man'yōshū* issues was insightful and at times surprisingly accurate, considering the severe limitations these early scholars operated under. Over time I felt that an anthology of the works of these men in one volume would be beneficial.

The journey from start to finish for this anthology has taken almost a quarter-century. The prose in the original Japanese of many of these works is dense and difficult to understand at times. When I would get eye-sick of translating Edo-era prose, my attention would turn to another project, not returning to the anthology for months or years. Another hindrance to the completion of this work was that many of these Kokugaku scholars assumed their reader would have a vast knowledge of earlier work that we cannot assume of most of our modern readers. This forced me to provide rather heavy annotation.

As always, such a long journey inevitably results in a number of people who have assisted me along the way. Michael Cooper, then editor of *Monumenta Nipponica*, was an early supporter of my work. He often provided witty criticisms that kept me going. Steven D. Carter was also very supportive of me when I was a green graduate student at BYU. There were times I would say something odd or strange, and he would respond, "You have been reading too much Norinaga." Robert N. Huey at University of Hawai'i was instrumental in helping me better understand Nara and Heian poetry. Alexander Vovin and Leon Serafim, also at University of Hawai'i, deepened my appreciation for Classical Japanese and its grammar. Paul Varley (1931–2015) was very kind to me, and helped me appreciate ancient Japanese history.

I am sincerely grateful for the comments from three readers who carefully and thoughtfully read the manuscript and provided a wealth of information and advice. Part of that advice was to reconsider the incredible length of the manuscript. I ended up going back through and deleting about a hundred pages of text from the manuscript to make it more affordable. I also express my gratitude for a substantial subvention from Northern Illinois University to bring down the cost of the work.

Other colleagues and friends who have been kind and helpful are David Ashworth, Katharina Barbe, Anne Birberick, Blaine Erickson, Bjarke Frellesvig, Doug Fuqua, Yutaka Kuroki, Samuel Martin, Marc Miyake, George Perkins, Robert Ramsey, Barbara Riley, Kerri Russell, Robert Russell, Linda Saborio, Moriyo Shimabukuro, Rumiko Shinzato Simonds, and John Whitman.

I am also very grateful for the hard work and effort of Mai Shaikhanuar-Cota, Managing Editor at the Cornell East Asia Series at Cornell University and Sheryl Rowe, formatter for CEAS. Any errors that remain are my responsibility.

My children, Jennifer, Michelle, and Stephen have always been supportive of everything I have undertaken. My granddaughter, Cailin Fritsch, has provided tremendous comedy relief. Finally, Chiemi, my wife and the love of my life, has been the pillar of everything I do. I dedicate this work to her.

INTRODUCTION

In the December 1934 inaugural number of the academic journal *Kokugaku,* the eminent Japanese linguist Yamada Yoshio (1875–1958) contributed the opening article, aptly titled "What Then Is Kokugaku?" There he notes that most people in the present do not know what Kokugaku actually means or what is included under the umbrella term (1942:31). He states that if you look through Ōkawa Shigeo and Minami Shigeki's massive *Kokugakusha denki shūsei* (1904, expanded by Ueda and Haga in 1934) and examine the contributions and works of the 680 people they claim are associated with the Kokugaku tradition, you notice that the central criterion for inclusion appears to be that these people composed *waka* (poetry written in Japanese) or wrote in Japanese (as opposed to Chinese). Yamada (1942:32–33) then affirms, "Looking through *Kokugakusha denki shūsei* it is evident that in the Meiji period Kokugaku declined and people even forgot what the appellation 'Kokugaku' meant. . . . As there was no defined field of Kokugaku before the petition [for a native school] by Kada no Azumamaro, those scholars and people belonging to branches of schools [established before Azumamaro] should not strictly be labeled as 'scholars of Kokugaku.'"[1]

It is interesting that this article was written as a foil for an article composed thirty years previously by Haga Yaichi; both articles have the same title (see Haga 1904). Also, the first half of Haga's two-part essay appeared as the opening article in the January issue of *Kokugakuin zasshi.* Having studied in Europe, Haga experienced how philology underpinned the study of culture and civilization in the West, which must have caused him to remember the philological work of Kamo no Mabuchi and Motoori Norinaga. Haga made a robust argument in 1904 that the study of Kokugaku in Japan equaled philology in the German sense, grounded in a tradition inherited from Greece and Rome. Based on this European system, he then attempted to bring Kokugaku back into focus for the Japanese by redefining

1. It needs to be pointed out that the term *kokugaku* is not without its own inherent problems. As Nosco (1981:76) notes, "As a term, however, it has been used to describe a broad range of scholarly and ideological endeavors. In its broadest sense [Kokugaku] refers to all learning and scholarship which took Japan as its focus instead of China."

it, describing three main pillars of the field: the ideology of the Japanese, the Way of Japan, and the special character of the national polity. In this way, Haga deleted the poetic and literary interests of Kokugaku, perhaps returning to the earlier thought of Kada no Arimaro, who found that poetry was mainly an artistic endeavor and was of little use in the sphere of politics.

Three decades later Yamada took an insular turn, and refuted the need for a connection with the civilizations of Greece or Rome (or even Europe), arguing that Kokugaku was specific to the Japanese, so no other country on earth could create the same type of discipline. To him Kokugaku did not match the Western idea of philology. Perplexed by Haga's reformulation of the basic ingredients of Kokugaku, Yamada (1942:33) quotes from *Wakun no shiori* (finally published in its entirety in 1887) by Tanigawa Kotosuga (1709–76), where he states, "Kokugaku is the study of Japan. It is the study of the *kami*, and the study of poetry." Yamada goes on to qualify this definition, contending that Kokugaku is the study of the indigenous religion of Japan, as well as the proper appreciation of poetry, not simply its [proper] composition. Kokugaku started as a study of *waka*, and Yamada argues that the Japanese should return to Kokugaku's origins. After all, no other people on earth were endowed with the ability to produce *waka*.

In the beginning days of 1937 the prominent ethnologist Orikuchi Shinobu (1887–1953) wrote an article for the Ōsaka *Asahi Newspaper* titled, "What Is Kokugaku?" He writes that recently he had begun to believe that Kokugaku was actually the study of the "fortitude" (気概) of the Japanese people (1956a:278). He goes on to write that he was greatly exasperated that some people labeled scholars of Chinese history and culture as "scholars of Kokugaku," even though they had but a faint connection with Japan through interdisciplinary research. He wanted his readers to clearly recognize that Kokugaku was grounded in Japanese culture, specifically poetry (1956a:278–79). To demonstrate this, the reader finds that he has sixteen different poems sprinkled among his article.

Over an almost four-decade period these three scholars confronted the same issue: the general public in Japan struggled to relate to the nebulous label of "*kokugaku*," unclear as to what it actually represented. Rather than fault the general public for this gap in their knowledge, the responsibility actually lies with the multifaceted movement, which morphed into different iterations with the establishment of each new school founded by Azumamaro, Mabuchi, Norinaga, Atsutane, and others. As a movement to demonstrate that the Japanese identity transcended status, occupation, or locale (Burns 2003:2), Kokugaku was clay in the hands of different but equally zealous potters. Almost a century later, Japan is searching again for its identity. Current events in the world are causing groups in Japanese society to revisit this sense of identity. There is a modern movement to greater insularity in Japan, reminiscent of prewar Japanese society. It is as if we are straddling the same "moment of truth" dividing line Yamada and Orikuchi faced some eighty years ago. To better understand this important movement it is critical to hear from a variety of voices from the past. This anthology is compiled to let these people speak.

* * * *

The term "kokugaku" was originally rendered into English as "National Learning," the literal meaning of the characters 国学; however, in the last several decades or so it is often given in English as "nativism." I eschew both translations for reasons noted below. Nosco's dissertation (1978) contained the term "nativism" in its title, and Harootunian (1988:1) prefers the word to the more traditional and literal translation. Flueckiger (2010:233, n1) uses the term "nativist" for all Tokugawa individuals engaged in purifying "Japanese culture of foreign influences, whether or not they belong to what is normally labeled as 'Kokugaku.'"

The difficulty is in defining what the term means, as well as mapping such a term on the vast and varied field that Kokugaku covers. The term tends to have a slightly different hue according to which school of thought one studies. In the present we are still confronted by the same conundrum as Haga, Yamada, and Orikuchi. While we could claim that Kokugaku meant whatever each individual scholar wanted it to mean, there are enough commonalities among the schools to demonstrate that in many cases the focus of study was α and not β. Thus, this fuzziness of meaning and subject is what makes Kokugaku so interesting, and yet so demanding.

In a review article, Mark Teeuwen (2006:227) makes the important observation that not all nativism is Kokugaku, and not all Kokugaku is nativism. This stance forces us to view Kokugaku as it was (a nebulous, multifaceted force), not as it has been received and mirrored by later Japanese scholars, especially during the tumultuous decades before the Pacific War. One purpose of this anthology is to put on display the tapestry of Kokugaku, strengths as well as weaknesses, from its vague, nascent articulation by Keichū through time until the dawn of the Meiji Restoration. Part of the modern problem is that many scholars are wont to talk about Kokugaku from afar, via secondhand knowledge mingled with snippets of quotes, but not based on the fuller context of the actual texts. Hirata Atsutane's habit of eclectic discourse, where he freely wove information from the tripartite scriptures of Japan (*Kojiki*, *Nihon shoki*, and *Kujiki*), as well incorporating material from Chinese and Dutch works, which tended to blur the lines of different narratives, was carried on by any number of later scholars, amplifying the fuzziness surrounding Kokugaku.

In his review article of two recently published works on Kokugaku, Teeuwen claims, "Burns's focus on interpretations of the *Kojiki* naturally … leads her to stress this aspect of Kokugaku, but, *of course*, only a minority of Kokugakusha were interested in studying this text, and still fewer wrote about it" (2006:231, my emphasis). While work on *Kojiki* was important in its own right (fourteen different Kokugaku scholars continued to write about it after 1822), the focus of the movement continued to be about a cultural shift (or transformation), where classical poetry and literature provided tools to school the feelings of the Japanese (see Flueckiger (2010:6–7). As Yamada rightly notes, most of the so-called Kokugakusha after Norinaga and Atsutane continued to focus on poetry and literary concerns. This fact supports the main thrust of Teeuwen's review, which is to pull the definition of Kokugaku back to its roots in poetry (2006:238).

Yamada Yoshio is called "the last Kokugakusha" by a number of scholars.[2] In his influential article, Yamada (1942:41) expands the definition of Kokugaku to include teaching about the imperial *kami*, elucidating the ancient meaning of the native language, and the ancient Way. Not long after Yamada penned his article, Matsuo Sutejirō (1936:16) wrote a small essay on Norinaga included in *Motoori Norinaga kenkyū*, where he offers a concise definition of Kokugaku:

> Generally, Kokugaku is divided into three parts. One, the research into the ancient lexicon and poetry; two, research into history and ancient courtly customs; three, the elucidation of the ancient Way. Men like Keichū, Nariakira, and Kageki concentrated on the first category. People like [Ban] Nobutomo and [Oyamada] Tomokiyo mainly worked within the second category. And people such as Reisei and Atsutane specialized in the third category. Azumamaro, Mabuchi, and Norinaga did not lean toward one category, but worked in all three areas, striving to clarify the ancient lexicon, read the ancient records, and comprehend the ancient Way.

In the West, an important dissertation came from Peter Nosco (1978:39), who pointed out that Kokugaku took the idea of historicism and ethnocentrism from the Zhu Xi school. The other major contributor to Kokugaku

2. Furuta Tōsaku ends his *Encyclopedia Japonica* entry on Yamada with this label (1973, 17:651). Shimizu Yasuyuki's entry in *Nihon daihyakka zensho* makes the same statement (1994).

was the Japanese school known as *Kogaku* "Ancient Learning." *Kogaku* sought for the true essence of what Confucius had said by looking into the actual words of the master, abhorring someone else's interpretation. *Kogaku* scholars' main goal was to have people return to the fathers, abandoning the practice of relying on the commentaries of later scholars. One of the most influential individuals of this school was Ogyū Sorai (1666–1728). Sorai's important contribution, according to Flueckiger, was in "his views on the relationship between human nature and social norms, a relationship in which poetry [was] a vehicle in educating rulers in the emotions of those they govern" (2010:11).

Nosco (1978:45) lists three ways in which the Ancient Learning movement influenced Kokugaku. One was a highly systematic philological method to analyze ancient texts. Second was an attack on the Zhu Xi school (this was an indirect barb against China), leading to an affinity for things Japanese. Lastly, and most importantly, *Kogaku* weakened its own foundation by showing that Neo-Confucianism ultimately was not suitable for the Japanese, creating a space for the establishment of a purely Japanese school. From these methodological and spiritual seeds sprang the philological drive that constituted the heart of Kokugaku, which continued till the end of Norinaga's career.

Harootunian (1988:2–3) attempts to draw a line connecting language and culture, basing his analysis on the reading of the original texts. His purpose is to "examine how the nativist discourse functioned ideologically" (p. 3). Harootunian examines the evolution from the Hirata school into the Meiji Restoration. He demonstrates how Kokugaku was pulled down to the level of the commoner as a group, which resulted in the weakening of the ruling shogunate. In other words, through Hirata and his disciples, Kokugaku turned from a private, personal affair into a public, activist-group movement with its sights on the nation. In her review of Harootunian, Nakai (1989:225) makes a case that some parts of Harootunian's analysis are not as cogent as he claims. For example, Hirata's eclectic analysis is much like Arai Hakuseki (1657–1725), and is not actually a break from a Kokugaku tradition as much as a remanifestation of an earlier trend. However, I believe that Harootunian makes a strong case for poetic politicization within the movement that many modern scholars have tended to overlook because they have been too quick to mislabel these poetic endeavors as lacking an understanding about what poetry or literature should be.[3] He argues, "This strategy [of a self-determining system of po-

3. Flueckiger (2010:7) states that "the central contention of [his] book is that we need to take seriously the ways in which writers of this time combined poetry with cultural and

etics] created a space for a subject that could be mobilized for ideological contestation against the received authority and its form of representation" (1988:49). It is thus important for readers to see *waka* within the framework of Kokugaku as more than just an artistic endeavor. Fleuckiger (2010:1) begins his work by noting that many of the writers of the eighteenth-century "saw poetry ... as the purest form of ancient language, making the study and composition of such poetry a crucial component of philological training. They valued such language not only as a scholarly tool, but also for how it embodied aesthetic qualities and cultural forms that could put people ... in touch with normatively correct cultures from the past."

Traditional teaching of Kokugaku as a subject tends to give the impression of a linear progression of ideas; thus, when people speak of Kokugaku, there is a tendency to offer the view, inadvertently, that the work of these scholars was unified behind a common goal, fighting a common "foreign" enemy. It should be understood, however, that the various schools of Kokugaku during the late Edo period were more like flowers dispersed in a field. As Wachutka (2013:1) has described, scholars who were trying to shepherd "Japanese things" out of the shadow of Chinese culture and literature were diverse and often strongly divided in material and methods.

Recent work by Burns (2003) and McNally (2005) reach for similar aims: to demonstrate that Kokugaku should be examined and understood as a more multifaceted movement than most typically understand it, an attempt to remedy the common focus on the "four great men": Kada no Azumamaro, Kamo no Mabuchi, Motoori Norinaga, and Hirata Atsutane. McNally's work demonstrates that after the death of Norinaga the Norinaga school fractured, and conflict developed between two factions, those who saw the school's main focus on literary tools, and those who desired a greater inclusion of religious and cosmological thought (2005:242–43). As the literary group began to suffocate, the religious group became more narrowly defined, until the mantra became "state Shintō."

Here is the textbook example: After the death of Norinaga, the *Sandaikō* debate erupted. Two senior members of the Norinaga school, Norinaga's adopted son, Ōhira (1756–1833), and Suzuki Akira (1764–1837) both

intellectual pursuits that to the modern reader lie outside the rubric of 'literature,' rather than dismissing such efforts as evidence of these figures' failure to grasp some purported essence of what poetry or literature should be." Wilburn Hansen (2013:288) also argues, "In essence, the academic tendency for contemporary scholars to describe intellectual events as either pre-modern or modern leads to biased judgments on the relative importance of the event."

wrote scathing critiques of Hattori Nakatsune's small cosmological work, *Sandaikō*. McNally (2005:113) writes that these two men disagreed with Nakatsune's use of Dutch scientific knowledge to uncover facts about Japanese "mysteries," stating that Western knowledge "was inappropriate to the task of studying Japanese antiquity."[4] McNally (2005:114) continues, "Ōhira and Akira agreed on one major point: Nakatsune's interpretation of Yomi was unacceptable."

Jumping into this debate came Atsutane. He wrote *Tama no mihashira* in 1812 to support Nakatsune's position and to create a pivot point so he could lead the school in a new direction. McNally (2005:116–17) argues that Atsutane created "a platform from which he could declare that eschatology took precedence over philology." Thus, Atsutane paid lip service to textualism even as he emphasized that a knowledge of the afterlife was of greater importance. This emphasis allowed Atsutane to argue for the prominence of cosmological studies over anything literary. The importance of the Hirata school thus comes from this break with the textually based *waka* tradition of the previous century of Kokugaku.

In order to demonstrate what Kokugaku embraced as well as its varied emphases, I have constructed the anthology along a chronological axis, demarcated by themes to illustrate the diversity of thought as well as the evolution of the various schools. Because of the importance of poetry in the birth and development of Kokugaku, the selections begin with this theme. This anthology contains works from thirteen influential Kokugakusha, locating their works within one (or more) of four main themes: Views on Poetry, Views on Literature, Views on Scholarship, and Views on Japan/Religion. I provide a synopsis of each author below, listed in chronological order of their deaths. A summary of each work is included at the beginning of each title.

* * * *

KEICHŪ (1640–1701)

One of the forerunners of this movement was a Buddhist monk of the Shingon sect named Keichū. Keichū was born in Amagasaki in Settsu Province. At the age of eleven, he took Buddhist vows. He was fond of poetry and this interest led to a bond of friendship with Shimokōbe Chōryū (1626–86). Chōryū was well known as a *renga* poet, and under the guid-

---

4. In contrast to this position, Hansen (2008:208) writes that Atsutane referenced "the power of Western scientific method and often used Western knowledge himself to discredit and ridicule the unscientific minds of his opponents and detractors."

ance of his master, Kinoshita Chōshōshi (1569–1649), he began studying the text of *Man'yōshū*, partly to use as a weapon against the established poetic circles. Chōryū's strong desire to concentrate on the essence of the poetry in *Man'yōshū* influenced Keichū, and his prominence in Man'yō studies at the time cannot be understood without acknowledging Chōryū's influence. Thus, Donald Keene (1976:308) stated, "Chōryū, perhaps more than any other scholar, should be credited with the revival of *Man'yōshū* studies."

Chōryū worked on gaining the original essence from poetry by studying the usages and words of the poems themselves. News of this work reached the ears of Tokugawa Mitsukuni (1628–1700), who was daimyō over the province of Mito. Mitsukuni requested that Chōryū compile a new commentary on the poetry contained in the laborious and cryptic anthology *Man'yōshū*. Chōryū began work on the anthology, but later withdrew from the project due to health concerns. In his place appeared Keichū, who after much dedicated work completed *Man'yō daishōki*, one of his most outstanding works. *Daishō* in the title refers to the fact that he was completing the work on behalf of another scholar (Chōryū).

Keichū also compiled commentaries on other poetic anthologies as well as literary works. Nosco (1978:115) argues that Keichū felt there was a divine essence in Japanese poetry. Keichū also believed that if one wished to gather information concerning the roots of the Japanese mind, then it would be more profitable to search for that information within *waka* than within the bland Chinese-based histories. This motivation came from Keichū's belief that poetry acted as a mirror of the human heart. He also believed that the essence of the human heart was buried in the much badgered indigenous religion. In spite of this indigenous-looking resolve, Keichū's own methodology borrowed much from Chinese traditions, and he was not prepared to declare that Chinese influence should be avoided outright. While Keichū did not feel that Chinese learning was problematic, or that a person should emulate *Man'yōshū* poetry, or even that Japan should return to its former divine glory, his greatest contribution was the fundamental philological methodology that later gave birth to such outstanding works as Kamo no Mabuchi's *Man'yōshū-kō* and Motoori Norinaga's *Kojiki-den*.

ANDŌ TAMEAKIRA (1659–1716)

Andō Tameakira was born in Tamba Province to Andō Bokuō (Sadatame), who served at the Fushimi Palace, being a descendant of the princely family associated with that area in Kyōto. Bokuō studied Confucianism and poetry, and these interests rubbed off on his son. Tameakira later studied Confucianism under the tutelage of Itō Jinsai (1627–1705), which explains why he is often labeled "a Confucian scholar." After some time he entered the service of Tokugawa Mitsukuni and helped with the compilation of *Dai Nihonshi* and *Reigi ruiten*. *Dai Nihonshi* is a comprehensive history of the successive reigns of the emperors in 397 volumes, while *Reigi ruiten* is an encyclopedic collection of information gleaned from historical records, compiled in 515 volumes. These two projects exposed Tameakira to a variety of historical data, providing him with a global view of history that few other scholars had at the time.

Mitsukuni also assigned Tameakira to work on *Man'yōshū* under the guidance of Keichū. Keichū had a strong influence on Tameakira. In early 1700 Tameakira took the completed manuscript of annotated *Man'yōshū* poems to Mitsukuni, who asked Keichū to appear before him, but he respectfully declined. With the death of Keichū, Tameakira turned his attention to other works, specifically looking at *Genji monogatari* and issues regarding its reception and interpretation. He completed this work, *Shika shichiron*, in 1703. One of the most important parts of the work is where Tameakira discusses the basic intention of the author, Murasaki.

KADA NO AZUMAMARO (1669–1736)

Kada no Azumamaro came from a family of hereditary priests at the Inari Shrine. He was born in Fushimi in Yamashiro Province. His parents loved poetry and literature, and his interest in these subjects began at a young age. He was a gifted poet, and became the personal tutor of Prince Myōhōin, a son of Emperor Reigen (r. 1663–87). After a short term as tutor, he resigned, and at the age of thirty-one, moved to Edo. He opened classes and taught poetry, mainly concentrating on *Kokinshū*. His studies, however, gradually moved away from just poetry toward the ancient records, from which he attempted to glean evidence for ancient Shintō.

Since Azumamaro's family held hereditary positions at the Inari Shrine, it is only natural to recognize his great interest in Shintō studies. Nevertheless, Azumamaro did not attempt any far-reaching changes; rather, as Nosco (1990:79) points out, it was Azumamaro's "concern with scriptural authority and his stated intention of applying the methodology of philological analysis to ancient texts in order to elucidate the archaic roots of his faith and creed" that motivated his study.

One reason most scholars label Azumamaro one of the founders of the Kokugaku movement is because of a letter of petition he supposedly sent to the shōgun (Tokugawa Yoshimune) in 1728 asking for permission to establish a school within which students could concentrate on the studies of ancient Japanese literature.[5] The stimulus for this idea is said to have come from Azumamaro's experience while he was in Edo when the government asked him to check and arrange the Shogunate Library. Many scholars, though, are convinced that this letter is not what others believe it to be.[6]

In a review of Nosco's work, Bob Tadashi Wakabayashi (1990:373) voices his displeasure with scholars suggesting that Azumamaro should even occupy a place in the hierarchy of Kokugaku founders, "First, the author's appraisal of Azumamaro as one of *kokugaku*'s founding fathers owes too much to Atsutane and prewar Japanese scholars." The crux of the problem hinges on *when* the petition was written. Saigusa Yasutaka's *Kokugaku no undō* offers this view of the events (1966:105), "The first time anyone recognized the significance of the 'School Petition'—written by a student of Azumamaro's—was by Hirata Atsutane, as everyone knows."

Saigusa thus denies that Azumamaro wrote the document, but stresses that it at least was written by a student of Azumamaro's, thus reflecting the thoughts and intentions of the master. Saigusa (1966:106) even claims that the copy of this student's manuscript still exists in the present. If we can actually take this chain of events at face value, then perhaps the document still has some value, its late date notwithstanding. To be fair, I have included the document in the anthology.

Azumamaro's chief textual interest was *Nihon shoki*, forming the linguistic foundation for his ideal restoration of pure Shintō. From this work he studied the "divine age" (神代), trying, like Hirata Atsutane would later do in *Koshi seibun*,[7] to amalgamate the varied and variant myths. He studied this text trying to gain an understanding of the state in which the

5. Hirata Atsutane was the first to advocate the importance of this petition, his beliefs recorded in *maki* 9 of *Tamadasuki*. It is important to note that many scholars do not share Atsutane's enthusiasm. There is also some evidence that the petition is not what Atsutane claimed it was. However, since the publication of Ōkubo Tadashi's work on Edo Kokugaku (1964:83), more scholars are willing to entertain the idea that the petition at least represents Azumamaro's intention, even if he did not actually write the letter.

6. Nosco states, "Azumamaro's 'Petition to Found a School' is a remarkable document. It contains the most concise statement of Azumamaro's academic and institutional goals and aspirations, and the most articulate definition of the new field of National Learning as he envisioned it" (1990:90).

7. I believe William George Aston's analysis of *Koshi seibun* is the most accurate, most articulate of any. "It (*Koshi seibun*) is an attempt to harmonise the myths of the *Kojiki*, *Nihongi* and other ancient books in a continuous and consistent narrative, written in the archaic dialect of the *Kojiki*. As these old stories differ very considerably among themselves, Hirata was naturally obliged to do them violence in order to make them agree, and scholars will prefer to go to his originals rather than accept his version of them" (1972:339).

divine age had occurred. But as Nosco (1978:116–26) points out, one of Azumamaro's faults was that he chose the wrong work. He should have chosen *Kojiki* instead of *Nihon shoki*. Though the exact prominence of Azumamaro is difficult to gauge, he is one of the first to have openly declared that he believed Japan was superior to China, opening the door to the xenophobia for which later Kokugaku would become well known. Azumamaro said in *Nihon shoki montōshō*, "The teachings of our country are the ancient teachings from the divine age, existing in one path, including things not seen in Confucianism and unknown to Buddhism. Our land is called the divine land and the Way—the Way of the *kami* and the teachings—the teachings of the *kami*."[8]

Regardless of this somewhat optimistic and positive portrayal of the man, I think we should temper our appraisal of Azumamaro by taking Saigusa's assessment of him to heart (1966:106), "Azumamaro did say, 'You should study the true Way from the divine age in *Nihongi*, learning the exhortation from the good and evil actions of those deities, searching after the doctrine of rewarding good and punishing evil.' Thus, the influence of Confucianism was strong in Azumamaro and he viewed literature with a strict moral eye."

KADA NO ARIMARO (1706–51)

The next influential figure was a nephew of Azumamaro's, Kada no Arimaro. He was born in Kyōto to Kada no Takakore, the younger brother of Azumamaro. When Azumamaro's health began to fail in 1728, Arimaro advanced to become heir to the school. With the death of Azumamaro in 1736, Arimaro took control of the school. Due to the prestige coming from being designated head of the school by Azumamaro, Tayasu Munetake (1715–71) put Arimaro in his employ. In 1738, Arimaro was sent to the old capital to study about the ancient enthronement ritual of the emperor. He returned to Edo and published his findings as *Daijōe bemmō*, "A Treatise on the Festival of the First Fruits." He published this work under the auspices of the Bakufu, but later privately published a revised version, which incensed the government, and this resulted in his arrest, an event that caused his employer, Munetake, great embarrassment.

A few years later, in 1742, Munetake—who was a devout Confucian—asked Arimaro to set his ideas about poetry down on paper. Arimaro naively did just that, and unwittingly wrote a controversial essay known as *Kokka hachiron*. Arimaro's greatest mistake was to boldly write that poetic composition was to be valued for its aesthetic and artistic significance. He

8. Quoted in Saigusa (1966:102).

unwittingly announced that he stood on the other side of the ideological river, as Munetake saw political power in poetic composition, and he blanched at the frivolous idea about poetry's artistic value. Arimaro's ideas incited Munetake to anger, and he wrote a rebuttal, *Kokka hachiron yogon.* Wishing to add support to his camp, Munetake then requested that Kamo no Mabuchi compose a rejoinder. To this request, Mabuchi contributed *Kokka hachiron yogon shūi.* In the end, Arimaro lost the debate, and was obliged to resign. Most scholars now believe, however, that the impetus for Munetake's request for a poetic treatise from Arimaro came from the embarrassment resulting from his arrest; Munetake thus was laying a trap to force Arimaro out of his service.

Arimaro's ideas and research methods were still in a pioneering stage of the Kokugaku movement, confined mainly to the old Japanese lexicon (linguistics) and ancient Japanese customs. Therefore, Arimaro originally declined Munetake's invitation to compose a poetic treatise, feeling that it was not his field. With much prodding, however, Arimaro accepted and set his idealistic thoughts on paper. Fortunately, Kokugaku received its first electric jolt of life through this debate surrounding poetry. Keichū and Azumamaro concentrated on poetry, and poetry formed the center of the early movement. Donald Keene (1976:314) belittles Arimaro's essay, claiming that it "contains only a handful of provocative statements set in a tissue of placid and conventional reiterations of the lofty purposes of poetry."[9] Needless to say I disagree. It was an energizing essay that, for better or worse, crystallized the fluid thoughts of juvenile Kokugaku. To the scholars of Kokugaku, the essence and purpose of poetry was a critical issue.

KAMO NO MABUCHI (1697–1769)

With the resignation of Arimaro, Kamo no Mabuchi became the head of the school of thought founded by Azumamaro. Mabuchi's more effective role was his guidance of Kokugaku from a loosely organized field of poetic thought to one concentrated on an ideology grounded in a literary text. Mabuchi was born in Hamamatsu. His parents, especially his father, were fond of poetry, and this influenced him as a youth. Early in his life, Mabuchi studied briefly under a physician also engaged in Confucian studies named Watanabe Mōan (1687–1776), from whom he received his first philological training. Later, Mabuchi enrolled in Kada no Azumamaro's school, where he proved himself a diligent student.

9. To be fair to Keene, he does go on to say that the debate stirred up by Arimaro's honest assessment of poetry aroused "the most celebrated controversy over the nature of the Waka" (1976:314).

When Arimaro resigned his post to Munetake, Mabuchi became the head of the school. Mabuchi's greatest gift to the movement was a clear definition of native scholarship. More than his predecessors, Mabuchi realized that the reader could not taste the fruit of the ancient trees if he could not distinguish the fruit from the blossoms. Mabuchi saw in the poetry of *Man'yōshū* the original essence of the Japanese, the so-called naive and sincere nature that the Japanese had inherited from the *kami*. Thus, to Mabuchi, *Man'yōshū* was the key to the pursuit of ancient Japanese learning. Mabuchi recast Azumamaro's rudimentary ideas of Japanese being distinctly different from Chinese, and emerged with a narrative of foreign defilement from the introduction of Chinese thought in earlier Japan. As he further analyzed the typological desecration inherent in foreign philosophy, he also provided an escape route from the disaster of ancient Sinification. His goal was to influence the heart of those "infected" in the present by re-creating the "pure" past within them. Thinking of this from a medical perspective, rather than taking a homeopathic attitude toward correcting this infection—an attitude typical of some of his peers—Mabuchi took an allopathic approach, where creation of a condition different from the disease is believed to have the effect of curing the illness. This was a radical break with tradition where the student learned, in a sense, how to return to the Garden of Eden.

Mabuchi believed the student could return to the past, and rekindle or recapture that ancient glory because the essential element of ancient Japan still resided in the hearts of the Japanese by virtue of their birth. He believed this was possible because of the divine parentage of all Japanese. The critical step was for the student to rid the dust from his heart (Mabuchi uses the example of a dusty mirror being unable to clearly reflect), and he could restore that sincere state. This was Mabuchi's main weapon against Arimaro who thought that poetry had no outward merit except to cause enjoyment. Mabuchi refuted *Kokka hachiron* by saying that poetry was an outlet for strong and violent emotions, thus allowing people to find peace. This in turn made the country easier to govern; it also allowed the ruler a view into the hearts of his subjects. Mabuchi proposed a concrete link between these ancient texts (and their inherent essences) and the present situation. This belief required that poetry be taken out of the hands of so-called trained poets (mainly the Dōjō poetic circle),[10] and given back to the average person.

In order to accomplish this, it was critical that the student be able to

---

10. A group of poets who composed and critiqued *waka* according to standards that mirrored the poetry of Fujiwara Teika (Nosco 1990:106, McNally 2005:144).

read and digest the ancient text of *Man'yōshū*, so Mabuchi put together a commentary on the confusing and obscure epithets of the poetry in *Man'yōshū*, titled *Kanjikō*, a work finished in 1757. Three years later he started his greatest contribution, *Man'yōshū-kō*, a commentary on the same poetic anthology. This work was finally completed around 1768, and became one of his chief claims to fame.

From 1762 till his death in 1769, Mabuchi wrote five essays collectively called "The Five Treatises" in which he elaborated on his major ideas. It is these essays that help us see and feel what Mabuchi believed. The master dealt with literary texts from two fronts, a linguistic one and a literary one. The purpose of his work was to restore the original word, and then elucidate the original meaning of that word (found in *waka*). After Mabuchi laid this foundation, the student of ancient Japanese could theorize about the original state of ancient society. Conclusions reached from this research led him to theorize that the original heart was sincere, straightforward, and masculine.

ISE SADATAKE (1717–84)

Ise Sadatake (貞丈, also read Teijō) was a *hatamoto*, a samurai directly under the service of the Tokugawa shogunate. With the death of his older brother at age thirteen, the Bakufu confiscated the land and property of the Ise family, but some officials later regretted the approaching demise of a well-known family like the Ise, so Sadatake was made the heir at age twelve (a deception concocted by the government officials, as Sadatake was still only ten years of age). With an heir established, Sadatake and the family received a three-hundred-*koku* parcel of land (from among the larger holdings). As he became an adult, this status allowed Sadatake to focus on scholarship. Most of the influential people of Sadatake's early life (his father, Arai Hakuseki, and Ogyū Sorai) were dead by the time he came of age, so he conducted much of his study on his own. In this respect he was a self-made scholar.[11] His family had a rather substantial library of texts, so Sadatake began to catalog these works, organizing these by topic. Along with this work, he began copying manuscripts of works that had a connection with works already in possession of the family library. Based on his study of these varied works, Sadatake began writing treatises in a question and answer format in relation to customs and instruments surrounding

11. Much of this description comes from Nihon koten bungaku jiten henshū iinkai (1986:78).

both the court and samurai culture. He also authored reviews and critiques of the works of other writers.

By the Meiwa era (1764–72) Sadatake had sufficient confidence to begin writing works based on his own learning and ideas. He wrote about the court, samurai culture, and Shintō. The fame of his writings spread throughout the country quickly, and his work became "must read" material for students of samurai culture. Sadatake wrote *Sansha takusen-kō* around 1784 and argued that *Sansha takusen* "The Oracles of the Three Shrines," was a spurious work, one grounded in Buddhist belief. He was suspicious of the work because of his knowledge of the earlier histories, and he realized that the term *sansha* "three shrines" did not appear in any early work from the Nara era.[12] Another influential work, *Shintō dokugo*, was written in much the same spirit, being an attempt to show that what people considered to be "Shintō" was a muddied amalgamation of a variety of thoughts and creeds. He argued, however, that vestiges of original Shintō could still be found in festivals connected to various shrines.

MOTOORI NORINAGA (1730–1801)

Mabuchi took the Kokugaku movement to greater heights, but it was Motoori Norinaga who guided his own school of Kokugaku to a pinnacle where poetic and textual issues were examined as never before. Born in Matsusaka[13] to a well-to-do merchant, after he annulled his adoption into the Imaida family, Norinaga's mother suggested that her son choose a profession other than the family business. Norinaga went to Kyōto to study medicine, and it was there that he obtained a copy of Mabuchi's *Kanjikō*. He read it repeatedly till he felt convinced of the truthfulness of the author's ideas.

Norinaga's interest in poetry started from an early age, and he appears to have been a voracious reader. His trivial pursuits while in Kyōto appalled his mother, who quite forcefully wrote him, demanding her son mend his ways. He remained in the old capital for five years, and returned to Matsusaka to practice medicine. Having read a great deal, Norinaga also began to answer questions from others less well read. He opened classes and taught people about poetry and literature. This resulted in his writing commentaries on *Genji monogatari* and other literary works.

---

12. From *Shintō jiten* (1999:575).

13. Many have transcribed 松阪 as *matsuzaka*, including this author, but a reader informs me that local residents are very quick to correct this error in pronunciation. Even Google Maps makes it clear the name is *matsusaka*.

In 1763, at the age of thirty-three, Norinaga had his only personal meeting with Mabuchi at an inn in Matsusaka. According to Norinaga's personal account, Mabuchi suggested that the young scholar pursue his work elucidating *Kojiki* only after he had mastered the textual complexities of *Man'yōshū*. The more likely story appears to be that Norinaga went to ask for the master's permission (recognition) to work on *Kojiki*, but Mabuchi chastised him, saying that such a work could not be undertaken until the young Norinaga had mastered the difficult usages of ancient Japanese in *Man'yōshū*. The nuance may be that though Mabuchi noticed the intellectual talent of this young man, he felt compelled to ground (Norinaga's) young scholarship in the Mabuchi school first.

Whatever the actual events, Norinaga joined Mabuchi's school and studiously applied himself to *Man'yōshū* and just about every other literary work still extant from ancient Japan. His knowledge was vast, and though he sometimes damaged his own theories through an overzealous adherence to Shintō tradition, much of his work is still valuable for the student today.

Norinaga's magnum opus was *Kojiki-den*, a colossal annotation of the rather thin text of *Kojiki*. Norinaga set about to establish a critical (authorial) text for *Kojiki*, and much of his work has given us the present text. In his commentary on this oldest of Japanese works, Norinaga expounded upon every worthy word in the work, adding criticism and interpretation here and there, taking Mabuchi's work a step further by solidifying the ideology of the ancient Japanese Way. Norinaga believed the deities so prominent in the ancient legends had actually existed; thus, the Japanese were by birth inheritors of that divine heritage, a sacrosanct legacy of such import that ignorance was inexcusable. It was imperative that the commoner know about his background, and thus break the shackles of Chinese culture and learning. From his reading of *Kojiki*, Norinaga concluded that the only tool to break the shackles of Chinese learning was to pray to the *kami* of rectification, "Naobi no mitama."

Norinaga loudly proclaimed that the sun goddess, Amaterasu, had actually existed and was in fact the very globe shining down upon Japan as well as the rest of the world. This attitude led Norinaga to declare that Japan not only excelled China, but was superior to all nations in the world. Granted, the major pollution in the heart of people in Japan had come via China, but all foreign ideas defiled the Japanese spirit (an idea Mabuchi was fond of using). What the Japanese individual had to do was put a stop to the foreign pollution resulting from the importation of Buddhism and Confucianism. In much the same way that Mabuchi had advocated, Norinaga stressed the importance of gaining a knowledge of the past. One way to do this was to compose classical poetry or write prose in classical Japanese. By following carefully articulated hints from ancient texts, the student could be guided to recapture the ancient spirit.

Though Mabuchi and Norinaga stressed similar points, Norinaga took this idea a step further by bringing in defilement from the evil deity, Magatsubi. In other words, some tragedy and some pollution was unavoidable. This is how it was originally, and the answer for such problems lay in pure (original) Shintō. Therefore, Norinaga placed the indigenous religion out in the open, and though his theology was greatly lacking in areas, he advocated the return of Shintō as the inherent belief of the Japanese.

In spite of Norinaga denigrating the thinking and philosophy of Buddhism, he never abandoned the religion himself, and his will specified in what manner his Buddhist funeral was to be carried out. Rather than a paradoxical sense of hypocrisy, as some scholars disparage the man, it is perhaps more equitable to see this bifurcated philosophy as something completely characteristic of Norinaga, who advocated change, but not revolution (cf. Matsumoto 1970:163–64). Compared to Hirata Atsutane, Norinaga took a careful (almost outright passive) stance within his own thinking. He did not confront the Bakufu government with certain problems, and though he advocated reform, he did not burn his bridges as Atsutane would later do.

After thirty-two years of work, Norinaga completed *Kojiki-den*, assuring himself a place in history. What made Norinaga so well known, and so worthy of our notice even now, is that he attacked the field of Japanese scholarship from so many angles. He elucidated Japanese grammar (*Kotoba no tama no-o*), tried to clarify the ancient Japanese vocalism (*Kanji san'onkō, Ashi kari yoshi*), explicated the ancient Japanese lexicon (*Kojiki-den*), developed a literary approach ahead of his time (*Shibun yōryō*), and essentially became the father of beautiful Japanese prose, ushering in an era where classical Chinese was not the only literary format for the educated. Norinaga was a hard worker, his fame spreading throughout Japan. At his death almost five hundred students were enrolled in his school, from which sprang other notable scholars like Ban Nobutomo, Kurita Hijimaro, Fujii Takanao, Motoori Ōhira, Suzuki Akira, and Hirata Atsutane.

UEDA AKINARI (1734–1809)

Ueda Akinari was born in Ōsaka. He came from a complicated family, and was abandoned by his mother in his fourth year, according to his own account. Ueda Mosuke, a proprietor of a paper and oil establishment in the Dōjima section of Ōsaka, adopted the young boy, and he was called Senjirō.

The following year he contracted smallpox and lost the use of several of his fingers. As his adopted family had the financial resources, Senjirō was fortunate to receive a good education. He began to compose *haikai* verse and later made this a serious effort. His life seems to have taken several parallel paths. He was gifted in writing, and is well known for two literary works, *Ugetsu monogatari* (1768) and *Harusame monogatari* (ca. 1808). About the time he was writing *Ugetsu monogatari* he came in contact with Katō Umaki (1721–77), a disciple of Kamo no Mabuchi. Under Umaki's tutelage he applied himself to the study of *waka* and earlier Japanese literature. He also became interested in *Man'yōshū* as well as historical relics such as the famous gold signet found on Shikanoshima (Fukuoka), with its evidence suggesting that the ancient polity of Na (奴 Nu) had diplomatic ties with the Han empire.

Another claim to fame is Akinari's bitter rivalry with Norinaga, demonstrated by the exchange contained in *Ashi kari yoshi* (or *Kagaika*). Some believe Akinari should not be labeled a scholar of Kokugaku (cf. Teeuwen 2006:229–30), but it is difficult to ignore his scholarly output, which matched that of other Kokugaku scholars: he wrote a work centered on Mabuchi's *Kanjikō*, edited the poetry of Mabuchi, wrote five volumes on *Man'yōshū*, and produced an annotated version of *Ise monogatari* (like Mabuchi). It is clear that while Akinari had a literary talent that roundly outshone his scholarly ability, his scholarship still provides important evidence of how multifaceted the new movement was.

HATTORI NAKATSUNE (1757–1824)

Hattori Nakatsune was born in Matsusaka as the oldest son of Hattori Tokinaka, a samurai of the Wakayama clan. As Nakanishi (1998:557) points out, Nakatsune's ancestors could trace their lineage back to the Kitabatake family, which had a connection with Oda Nobunaga. In 1785 Nakatsune joined the Motoori school, influenced by his grandfather who already was a student of the school. Nakatsune was interested in cosmology and history, and Norinaga's dabbling in cosmology stimulated his own ideas. Nakatsune asked if he could take home a copy of Norinaga's *Tenchizu* "Diagram of heaven and earth." The master acquiesced, and in 1789 Nakatsune wrote a draft called *Tenchi shohatsu-kō* "A Treatise on the beginning of heaven and earth." After further discussions with the master, Nakatsune went back and expanded his draft and titled it *Sandaikō*.[14] The title refers to the "three great concepts" in Shintō cosmology, those being the concept of

14. McNally (2005:106) argues that Norinaga was more than just passively involved in the writing of both the draft and the final version.

heaven, earth, and Yomi, which Norinaga believed was a representation of the afterlife. In imitation of human birth, Nakatsune's theory established three spheres to represent these three *places*, each connected by an umbilical cord. As time progressed, he theorized, the cords broke and resulted in the current separation of heaven, earth, and the afterlife. While this work is not very long, it had a penetrating influence on other scholars, such as Motoori Ōhira, Suzuki Akira, Hirata Atsutane, Uematsu Shigetake (or Shigeoka), and Suzuki Masayuki.

KAGAWA KAGEKI (1768–1843)

Kagawa Kageki was born in Tottori. Around the age of twenty-five he took his wife and left for Kyōto. There he studied poetry under the tutelage of Ozawa Roan and Kagawa Kagemoto. In 1796 he was adopted by Kagemoto and made heir to Kagemoto's poetic school. It was around this time that he began studying poetry under Roan. Roan's teachings of simplicity, with poetry written in common, everyday themes ran counter to the conservative style of the Nijō school of Kagemoto. The ideas Roan taught about the intersection of the poet and the poem resonated with Kageki. Frustrated with the shackles put on poetic composition by the Nijō tradition, he left the school in 1806. Kageki found the clash between his ideas of poetry and that of the Nijō school too great to overcome, but he kept the surname of Kagawa, perhaps as a token of gratitude for what Kagemoto had done for him. His decision to leave the school caused him to endure competing criticism from both the poets in Kyōto and Edo. Kageki founded a school later known as Keien. He was one of the most able *tanka* masters of his time, and his school wielded great influence.

Kageki's desire to compose poetry that reflected the true feelings of the poet mirrors that of Norinaga, but this philosophy was contrary to that espoused by Mabuchi. Having read Mabuchi's work on poetry, Kageki felt it necessary to respond, so he wrote *Niimanabi iken* in 1811 as a criticism of the style of poetry that Mabuchi and his school espoused, especially as it related to the idea of melody or rhythm (*shirabe*). This demonstrates that while Norinaga's school was growing in influence, the Mabuchi school and its students still wielded considerable authority. Kageki also wrote a work titled *Kogaku* "Ancient Learning" in a question and answer format with Rai San'yō (1780–1832), where he recorded a discussion about Japanese and Chinese poetry.

HIRATA ATSUTANE (1776–1843)

Atsutane enrolled in Norinaga's school a month before the master passed away. Due to Norinaga's absence (he was in Kyōto), Atsutane was never able to meet the man he believed his thinking most closely reflected. Atsutane was born in Akita to a retainer of the Akita daimyo. When he turned twenty, he left for Edo, and later was adopted by Hirata Atsuyasu, a retainer of the Bitchū daimyo.

Atsutane revered Norinaga and allied himself closely to his dead master, a ploy that helped to gradually increase his own influence and prestige. He took responsibility for instructing students in the workings of the Shintō ceremonies. Though he initially attempted to traverse the same ground as his master, working with poetry and literature, the strength and influence of his scholarly output ran off in a sharp tangent, following his theological ideals. In Hirata one branch of Kokugaku took a sharp turn to the right, barreling down the hill toward xenophobia based on cosmological beliefs.

Through the pedigree of Kokugaku scholars, we can see an evolution at work. Whereas Keichū, Azumamaro, and Mabuchi concentrated on poetry, Norinaga broadened the path, adding a new dimension to the field; he expounded deeply upon the Way. Atsutane took another step down this path, shifting the emphasis from poetry to cosmology and theology. If Azumamaro and Mabuchi were poets, then Atsutane was a theologian.

Previous Kokugaku scholars often employed poetry (with its ancient lexicon) to discover a lost past in Japan, and create a political foundation where Japan could return to its former, pristine state. Atsutane discarded the telescope of the past and brought in a microscope. Mabuchi and Norinaga had endeavored to discover the ancient creature. Atsutane brought minute scrutiny of the creature to the fore, and drew ultranationalistic conclusions.

Hirata Atsutane took the literary folds of Kokugaku and gave them a theological hue. To Atsutane, the true heart seen from ancient poetry was not enough; philology was an impotent tool to peer into the afterlife. He believed there had to be a link, a bridge, coupling the past with actual life, a real life connected to a real death. What happened to the dead? How did the *kami* interact with mortals? These questions were of critical importance to Atsutane. Since these ideas are representative of Hirata's scholarly output, I have included two of his most influential works, *Kodō taii* "An Outline of the Ancient Way" and *Tama no mihashira* "The True Pillar of the Spirit."

The most important aspect of scholarship to Norinaga was the word, the simple morpheme containing the essence of the true heart of the ancients in its linguistic pocket. He also saw Yomi, the afterlife, as a cul-de-sac for the dead spirits, a dumping ground filled with defilement. Hirata did not see it this way. He saw existence as a by-product of the *musubi* "binding" deities, from which all creation had sprung. This deity-oriented Genesis opened up a path through which Hirata could address the greatest failing in Motoori's scholarship: What can the average man do about death and salvation? Norinaga had not been able to answer this question to the satisfaction of someone wishing for more than the idea that after death his spirit when to Yomi. End of discussion.

Atsutane's theology was nothing short of brilliant. He did with Shintō in the Edo era what Buddhism had done in the seventh century—he gave native theology to the masses. Buddhism offered salvation to everyone, regardless of status. The common man viewed Shintō as a courtly, imperial, close-quartered cult under Buddhist and other influences. Hirata turned the divine origin of the imperial family on its head. If the imperial line descended from the sun goddess, then the rest of Japan descended from the sons of Susanoo, the brother of Amaterasu. Everyone in Japan was a descendant of the deities; thus, direct interaction with the deities was still possible. And it created a divide between the people of Japan and the rest of the world.

Atsutane taught that because deities went to a specific, though concealed, place after death, so would the offspring of the deities, the Japanese. He argued, however, that the spirits of the dead did not go to Yomi to be forgotten, but remained in this sphere, unseen. The Japanese creator-deities formed heaven, so the Japanese had a specific place set aside for them. The residents of Japan were not dependent on a foreign theology, written in an alien tongue, describing a strange afterlife. Atsutane, in a word, stated that the Japanese would take care of themselves in the proper manner inherited from the deities. While this gave the masses hope, it also carried the seeds to create a caustic environment in relation with foreign countries.

KAMOCHI MASAZUMI (1791–1858)

Kamochi Masazumi was born in Tosa Province into the Yanagimura family, and his father subsisted at the bottom of the feudal hierarchy, though his own family tradition related how his distant ancestor was Minister Fujiwara Masayasu (Ogata 1944:31–33). Around the age of eighteen he began studying Kokugaku from Miyaji Nakae. This was a fortunate teacher to have, because the father, Miyaji Haruki, not only was a student of the Norinaga school he also studied under Tani Mashio (d. 1797), a student of Mabuchi. This allowed an influence from both schools. As a young man Masazumi was known as a voracious reader.

Fukuoka Takanori, one of the elders of the domain, noticed Masazumi's ability and his remarkable memory, so he opened the domain's storage room and allowed Masazumi access to the library (Oagata 1944:70–71). He read Norinaga's *Kojiki-den*, and then read *Man'yōshū ryakkai* by Katō Chikage (1735–1808). As his knowledge increased, he began giving lectures to small groups of interested friends and people, and in 1819 officials in the feudal domain in Tosa appointed Masazumi a teacher in the domain school.

Greatly influenced by Norinaga's thorough work on *Kojiki*, a desire to attempt the same detailed work on *Man'yōshū* grew in Masazumi. He spent the rest of his life putting the manuscript together, but did not live to see it published. The manuscript was reported lost for several decades, until researchers located it. It was published as *Man'yōshū kogi* in 1891. As his detailed introduction makes clear, he viewed *Man'yōshū* much as Mabuchi did: it was more than a literary text. It was the portal to gain access to the Way of the ancient Japanese.

SUZUKI MASAYUKI (1837–71)

Few scholars have paid much attention to Suzuki Masayuki, perhaps because he only lived thirty-five years. However, his works, especially *Tsuki sakaki* are worthy of notice. Masayuki was born in Shimōsa Province. As a youth he studied *waka* and helped his family with farming. In 1865 he divorced and joined the school of Kamiyama Natsura (d. 1882) to study poetry. Later he left his home village and appears to have wandered, until he arrived in Furushiro Village, where he met Hirayama Shōsai (1815–90), an important official in the Tokugawa government who also was a student of Kokugaku (Katsurajima 1992:130–31).

With the advent of the Meiji government, the blueprints for the Daikyōin "the Great Teaching Institute" were drawn up. The institute was created to begin the restoration of the imperial family (and by extension Shintō) to where it had been in the Nara era. This meant a joint education policy by Shintō and Buddhist scholars. Inō Yorinori, who met Masayuki at Kamiyama's school, recommended the young scholar as an instructor in the soon-to-be completed institute, and the government officially appointed him in 1870. However, as fate would have it, Masayuki passed away before he could fill this post (cf. Kanamoto 2013:144).

Masayuki's scholarship evolved during a time when Kokugaku was changing from a text-based movement to one of activist ideology. This pull away from textual or philological studies was spearheaded by students of the Hirata school (Katsurajima 1992:107). Katsurajima (ibid. 109) argues that while Masayuki did not break completely from the Hirata school's ideology, his work opened a path allowing Motoori Norinaga's influence to survive the attempt to smother it by the work of Atsutane's disciples. This is seen in Masayuki's work, where he is not afraid to quote from either *Kojiki* or *Nihon shoki*, but he returns to the actual texts (including *Kogo shūi*) and avoids arguments based on an amalgamation of traditions. Masayuki wrote works on both *Kojiki* (*Kojiki shakkai*) and *Nihon shoki* (*Nihon shoki meibutsu seikun*), as well as a number of liturgies (*Amatsu norito-kō* and *Amatsu norito setsuryaku*).

In *Tsuki sakaki*, Masayuki develops his own ideas of the purpose of this life and the afterlife, based on *Sandaikō*; however, he does not shy away from correcting perceived errors in Motoori Norinaga's earlier teachings. I have included *Tsuki sakaki* as the final chapter to the anthology to function as a signpost demonstrating where a faction of Kokugaku could have proceeded if it were not for Masayuki's untimely death.

NOTES ON THE TRANSLATION

The eminent Chinese professor, Burton Watson of Columbia University, notes that when translating, the question one always encounters is how much annotation to include. He notes that "annotation, while desirable in the ideal, should be kept within bounds that are practicable for the scale and purpose of the particular translation project" (1995:352). I agree with this statement and have tried to keep my annotation limited to pertinent information, such as prominent people, written works, and areas that aid the reader in comprehension.

One of the fundamental principles of Kokugaku is "the word" as found in earlier states of the Japanese language. This was part of the focus of scholars who zeroed in on works like *Man'yōshū* and *Kojiki*. Thus, when representing the romanization of earlier Japanese forms, especially in poetry, I have used a modified version of *Kunreishiki*, based on the system used in my translation of *Tamakatsuma* (2013:10). In other words, I have used two different systems based on whether the word belongs to Old Japanese or Middle Japanese. The two methods are: (1) when written in *man'yōgana* or *kundoku* from the Asuka or Nara eras I have used **bold**; (2) when written in *kana* or *kanji* from the Heian era or later I have used *italics*. The following chart demonstrates this:

Text	Old Japanese	Text	Heian-era Japanese
阿米都知	**ametuti**	天地	*ametuti*
國造	**kuni no miyatuko**	はじめ	*fazime*

However, I have not followed this principle when representing titles of works, and well-known Japanese terms that have entered our scholarly, English vocabulary. Two terms are worthy of note here. *Kami* "spirit, deity" is, as Norinaga himself argued, a complex term that defies definition. I have left the term as is, in italics. The other is *tennō* "emperor," which is not gender specific. I have used the term "emperor," regardless of the gender of the individual, as long as they reigned. Also, when representing Chinese I have relied on *pinyin*, and for Korean I have used McCune–Reischauer.

Abbreviations:

GSS	*Gosenshū*
HAZ	*Hirata Atsutane zenshū*
KJK	*Kojiki*
KKS	*Kokinshū*
KKWS	*Kinkai wakashū*
MNZ	*Motoori Norinaga zenshū*
MYS	*Man'yōshū*
NKBT	*Nihon koten bungaku taikei*
NKBZ	*Nihon koten bungaku zenshū*
NKT	*Nihon kagaku taikei*
NS	*Nihon shoki*
NST	*Nihon shisō taikei*
SKKS	*Shin Kokinshū*
SNKBT	*Shin Nihon koten bungaku taikei*
SS	*Shūishū*
ST	*Shintō taikei*

Part One
Views on Poetry

MAN'YŌ DAISHŌKI

Keichū | 1690

[Keichū began working on Chōryū's unfinished manuscript in 1683, and completed his work by 1690. The word *daishō* 代匠 in the title appears in a number of Chinese works, notably *Lunheng* and *Wenxuan*, and refers to work begun by one skilled person later being finished by another person. This is clearly a nod to the work of Chōryū. Keichū viewed the poetic anthology *Man'yōshū* as having been corrupted over time by so many hands having been involved in its transmission that he determined to go back in time, as it were, and restore the anthology to its original state. His purpose was to elucidate the true state of the poems in *Man'yōshū*, a work difficult to read. Keichū wanted people to be able to appreciate the poetry, not someone else's interpretation of it.]

Our court belongs to the divine country. Therefore, in the official histories and public documents, divine affairs have priority over temporal ones. In ancient times, the sovereigns governed the country solely according to Shintō. Nevertheless, not only were the people primitive, but they lacked writing, so they transmitted everything orally, resulting in a lack of didactic criticism in the indigenous religion, but found in the Confucian Classics and Buddhist works. The works *Kujiki*,[1] *Kojiki*,[2] and *Nihongi*[3] are ancient, but these only record public events at court from the divine age. It is testimony to the divine beginning of poetry (*waka*) that though it weakened through the successive reigns, undergoing a variety of changes, our form of poetry never died out.

Susanoo[4] originally was ruler over the land, and because he lamented

1. A work with a fraudulent preface trying to make it appear that the work was compiled by Shōtoku Taishi and Soga no Umako; in the Edo era from the time of Tokugawa Mitsukuni it was labeled a fraud, though Motoori Norinaga noted that some parts are ancient and authentic (MNZ 1976.9:14–15). As time went on, however, this stance softened so that most researchers consider it to be a derivative work having relied on *Kojiki* and *Nihon shoki*. For a patiently laid out argument that attempts to date the text, see Bentley (2006).

2. Presented at court in AD 712 by Ō no Yasumaro. It is written in a mixture of Classical Chinese with phonograms inserted to assist in accurate recitation.

3. Normally called *Nihon shoki*. It is the first official history of the Japanese court, written in beautiful Classical Chinese. It was presented to the court in AD 720.

4. Susanoo was the younger brother of Amaterasu, and committed crimes in heaven and

and mourned for his mother, Izanami, who had already gone off to the nether world [world of spirits], his father, Izanagi, told him to do as he pleased and cast him out. Because Susanoo was of a violent nature, green mountains become desolate. If his nature was this way, how was he able to become the father of our tranquil form of poetry?[5] The limited knowledge of man cannot comprehend the good and evil workings of the *kami*. The thirty-one syllables of Japanese poetry belong to the *yang* element,[6] and within the upper and lower halves of poetry reside all the elements of heaven and earth, *yin* and *yang*, master and subject, father and son, husband and wife. The upper half of poetry consists of three stanzas of 5-7-5 and this equals the *yang* element [seventeen syllables, an uneven number], and three stanzas is also *yang*. The fourteen syllables of the lower half constitute the *yin* element. Also, two stanzas [an even number] fits the *yin* pattern. The five stanzas taken together also form the *yin* element.[7] This is also apparent since the upper stanza is longer than the lower stanza. Because the structure of poetry comes from divine intention, human poets cannot comprehend its profundity, and surely they will compose poetry using ordinary emotions when allotting words into the *yin* and *yang* sequence, but the poetry will spontaneously spring from the principle of the way things should be. Our court exists in the middle of the eastern sea, so it is a *yang* country. When *yang* is distinctively superior, it surpasses resoluteness. The sun goddess used the virtue of perseverance to come down [to this land] and establish the earth, so later she was able to also defend that resoluteness. This is all demonstrated in the fact that Susanoo was not able to obtain the right to rule the country because of his violent nature, so he left us the inauguration of this poem. …

Japanese poetry (*waka*) is like a fine golden ring refined one hundred times. Not only does it coincide with the principle of the way things should be discussed above, but it also suits the human emotions of society. The poetic preface written by Fujiwara Arikuni says, "Poetry is to be used by officials at court. People in the provinces should also use poetry. Words

---

was banished to earth where his son, Ōkuninushi, is said to have had so much control that Amaterasu commanded her own son to go down so that the royal family would keep (regain?) control over Japan.

5. Susanoo was long believed to have been the founder of Japanese poetry because his *Yakumo tatsu* poem is the first poem in *Kojiki* and *Nihon shoki*. For an explanation of this poem, see *Kokka hachiron*.

6. The Chinese believed that odd numbers were *yang* and even numbers were *yin*.

7. This is no doubt a mistake for *yang*, since five is uneven and *yang* is the uneven element.

used in poetry composed at banquets and expressions of joy are pleasing as well as soothing. Poems of lamentation and of [sadness about] demotion in court rank or banishment bring feelings of anxiety and sorrow. Poetic stanzas depicting parting of company before a journey cause one to feel regret and vexation. …"

Let us set aside for a moment the discussion about such events, and focus first on poetry being like a jeweled broom that sweeps away the vulgar filth within one's breast.[8] I do not know who composed it, but I remember having seen the following didactic poem a long time ago in a vulgar collection of one hundred poems:

renga sezu	I did not write linked verse
uta wo mo yomanu	and did not even compose a poem.
sono fito no	Indeed, the reason
sa koso nezame no	that person awoke was
kitanakarurame	because he could not stand it.

The usage of *nezame* is amusing. There are people who wake up in the middle of the night filled with thoughts, and the man with a poem in his heart longs for the time when the snow, moon, or blossoms are at their height. There are people who yearn for friends with whom they had played the *koto*, composed poetry, or drunk *sake* together. There are those who wait like the cuckoo for the moon to peak through the clouds,[9] or upon hearing the cricket near his pillow, creates an illusion to awakening from an ephemeral dream.[10] Preparing a torch for those remaining in this limited world, and feelings move within their hearts and are expressed out-

---

8. A reference to MYS 4399, a poem by Yakamochi about a ceremonial broom decorated with bells attached to a string, which rang out by simply being touched. This later morphed into a story of an old monk from Shiga Temple who visited Kyōgoku no Miyasudokoro, and when he touched her hand, his heart is said to have resounded, like the bells on the broom.

9. Allusion to SKKS 237:

samidare no	Ah that cuckoo!
kumoma no tuki no	Waiting so patiently
fare yuku wo	for the moon to appear
sibasi matikeru	behind the bank of clouds
fototogisu kana	during the rainy season.

10. Allusion to SKKS 518:

kirigirisu	The cricket chirrups
naku ya simo yo no	on this evening of frost.
samusiro ni	In the bamboo box

side, then there is the voice of the pines singing, and the sound of the bell is refined. …

Though one studies Confucianism and searches the Buddhist commentaries, a person who does not set his heart on poetry wades through the vulgar filth of the world, making it difficult to seek after the ten thousand mile journey of the sages, easily overcome with weariness when hindered in his search for the many stations of the Bodhisattva. …

The "Canon of Shun" in *Shangshu* says, "Poetry is the expression of earnest thought; singing is the prolonged utterance of that expression; the notes accompany that utterance, and they are harmonized themselves by the standard tubes."[11]

Liji records, "Confucius said, 'When you enter any State you can know what subjects [its people] have been taught. If they show themselves to be warm and kind, gentle and good, they have been taught from the *Book of Odes*.'"[12]

It further states, "The failing that may arise in connection with the study of the poems is a senseless simplicity. … If they show themselves men who are warm and kind, gentle and good, and yet free from that senseless simplicity, their comprehension of the *Book of Odes* is deep."[13]

The Analects records, "Ch'en Kang asked, 'Have you not been taught anything out of the ordinary?' 'No, I have not. Once my father was standing by himself. As I crossed the courtyard with quickened steps, he said, "Have you studied the *Odes*?" I answered, "No." "Unless you study the *Odes* you will be ill-equipped to speak."'"[14]

The Analects also records, "Why is it none of you, my friends, study the *Odes*? An apt quotation from the *Odes* may serve to stimulate the imagination, to show one's breeding, to smooth over difficulties in a group, and to give expression to complaints. 'Inside the family there is the serving of one's father; outside there is the serving of one's lord; there is also the acquiring of a wide knowledge of the names of birds and beasts, plants and trees.'"[15]

The Zi Xia preface to *Book of Odes* says, "Poetry is the product of earnest thought. Thought in the mind becomes earnest; exhibited in words, it

---

koromo katasiki	will I sleep alone tonight
fitori kamo nen	with my robe spread for one?

11. Legge (1960:34).
12. Slightly altered version of Legge (1967, 2:255).
13. Slightly altered version of Legge (1967, 2:255–56).
14. Lau (1979:141).
15. Ibid., p. 145.

becomes poetry. The feelings move inwardly, and are embodied in words. When words are insufficient for them, recourse is had to sighs and exclamations. When sighs and exclamations are insufficient for them, recourse is hard to prolonged utterances of song. When those prolonged utterances of song are insufficient for them, subconsciously the hands begin to move and the feet to dance. The feelings go forth in sounds, when those sounds are artistically combined, we have what is called musical pieces. The style of such pieces in an age of good order is quiet, going on to joyful—the government is then in harmony. Their style in an age of disorder is resentful, going on to the expression of anger—the government is then in discord. Their style, when a state is going to ruin, is mournful, with the expression of [retrospective] thought—the people are then in distress. Therefore, correctly set forth the success and failures [of the government], to move heaven and earth, and to excite spiritual beings to action, there is no readier instrument than poetry. The former kings by this regulated the duties of husband and wife, effectually inculcated filial obedience and reverence, secured attention to all the regulations of society, adorned the transforming influence of instruction, and transformed manners and customs. Thus it is that in the [*Book of*] *Odes* there are six classes: first folk songs, second rhapsodies, third metaphorical pieces, fourth allusive pieces, fifth metropolitan pieces, and sixth eulogies."[16]

Huainanzi says, "Warmth and kindness, gentleness and goodness are the teachings of the *Odes*."[17] The reader will realize that the merit of *waka* follows from this evidence. The *Kokinshū* preface uses the basic objective of the preface to *Book of Odes*. The [Mana] preface of *Kokinshū* says, "The world in general cares only for material prosperity; it takes no interest in poetic composition. What a pity! What a pity! Even if a man combines the offices of Minister of State and Major Captain and amasses inordinate stores of wealth, his name will disappear from society before his bones rot in the earth. The people whose names happen to be known to later generations are all poets, because the language of poetry enters the human ear easily and the spirit of poetry reaches the *kami* themselves."[18] How true these words are.

The names of poets and writers remain long in society, but when we address the beginnings of Japan's own literary tradition, we do not hear of

16. Legge (1960:34).
17. Major (2010:808).
18. McCullough (1985:258).

anyone other than Hitomaro[19] and Akahito.[20] In middle antiquity,[21] we do not hear of anyone rivaling Tsurayuki[22] or Mitsune,[23] or Sadaie[24] and Ietaka[25] after them. We hear of no one else like these poets. This state of affairs has nothing to do with the skill of their poetic ability. It is related to whether there was divine intercession or not.

Mencius said, "Therefore, those who explain the *Odes*, may not insist on one term so as to do violence to a sentence, nor on a sentence so as to do violence to the general scope. They must try with their thoughts to meet that scope, and then we shall apprehend it. If we simply take single sentences, there is that in the ode called 'The Milky Way'—'Of the black-haired people of the remnant of Zhou, There is not half a one left.' If it had been really as thus expressed, then not an individual of the people of Zhou was left."[26]

Since this section deals with poetry, it started with the words "Those who expound upon the *Odes*." In reality, we should apply this to all works. Even those who compose poetry should keep these words in mind. …

Scholars must use works that existed before *Man'yōshū* to elucidate this

---

19. Dates unknown. Nothing is seen of Hitomaro's court appointments in either *Nihon shoki* or *Shoku Nihongi*, suggesting that he was a low-ranking courtier. According to headnotes in *Man'yōshū*, Hitomaro was active during the reigns of Tenmu (r. 673–86), Jitō (r. 687–97), and Monmu (r. 697–707). His poetry is marked by a sensitive and strong ability to portray the human condition through verse.

20. Dates unclear. Nothing appears of Akahito's being granted rank in *Shoku Nihongi*, suggesting that he was a low-ranking courtier. All chronological information comes from headnotes in *Man'yōshū*. His most powerful poetry is descriptive and scenic in nature, much like Chinese poems that depict scenery through verse.

21. I have translated 中世 as "middle antiquity." An anonymous reader kindly pointed out that "middle ages" sits within a modern context our Kokugaku scholars did not have. As the general tendency was to see time along a tertiary line: ancient, middle, and recent time, I have opted for middle antiquity.

22. Ki no Tsurayuki (868?–945) was one of the main compilers of *Kokinshū*, and wrote the Kana preface to the anthology. He was a low-ranking courtier, but much of what we know about him is based on *Tosa nikki*, a quasi-anonymous account of a governor returning to the capital.

23. Ōshikawachi Mitsune. His dates are uncertain. He was one of the compilers of *Kokinshū*, along with Ki no Tsurayuki. He was a low-ranking courtier who also had his own personal anthology of poetry.

24. Better known as Fujiwara Teika (1162–1241). Sadaie was a multifaceted, prolific, and influential poet and courtier. He is known as one of the four greatest poets of Japan and was a poetic influence at the courts of Emperors Gotoba and Juntoku.

25. Fujiwara Ietaka (1158–1237) was also a distinguished poet from youth. He was a student of Teika's father, Shunzei.

26. From Legge (1970:353).

work's [*Man'yōshū*] text. Nevertheless, nothing else remains other than two or three works like *Nihongi*, so we find ourselves with few choices. A few other works include: *Kaifūsō*, *Shoku Nihongi*, *Kogo shūi*,[27] *Kanke Man'yōshū*, and *Wamyōshō*.[28] *Ruijū kokushi* is also a rare work in society that one must examine.

There are many parts of the *Man'yōshū* text we cannot elucidate simply by relying on the essays and commentaries of our predecessors. We should select works from which we can reconstruct the original meaning from the text. We know that people in later eras found *Man'yōshū* poetry baffling because many of the Man'yō poems quoted in *Shūishū* are plagued with errors. For example, many categorize poems in Book 15 of *Man'yōshū* attributed to the ambassador to Silla as having been composed by Hitomaro.[29]

The composition of these poems occurred in Tenpyō 8 (736), but Hitomaro lived long before this era. The three poems the ambassador to Silla composed recorded [in *Shūishū*] have Hitomaro as the poet. Not only that, but *Shūishū* has a head note: "written while in China." We can guess the rest of the actual situation from this small sampling. If we believe things written later about *Man'yōshū*, then what can we safely doubt?

Kiyosuke[30] Ason was not only a gifted poet, but was allowed to oversee the study of poetics as a professor. After he wrote his poetic treatise, *Ōgishō*, poets everywhere kept copies of this work near their pillows. Inspecting the last section of this work, the segment that has become part of the secret poetic traditions, the reader finds that these people have made glass their pearls. The student may know the truth of this if he reads the work on his own. You will also find a section on *Man'yōshū*.

When Man'yō poets composed poems about famous sites around Yamashiro, many wrote that they were near Yamato. People in later ages were living in present-day Kyōto and could not take themselves out of the present, and because of this misjudged the location of things.[31]

---

27. This is a small personal history of the Imibe family compiled by Imibe Hironari around AD 806–7.

28. Officially known as *Wamyō ruijūshō*, it is one of Japan's first Chinese–Japanese dictionaries, having been compiled in AD 930.

29. Poems such as MYS 353, 478, and 493.

30. Fujiwara Kiyosuke (1084–1177). He was the son of Fujiwara Akisuke, compiler of *Shika wakashū* (1151). Kiyosuke was a famous poet of the late Heian era. More than poetry, though, he concentrated on the study of poetics. He wrote the famous poetic commentary *Okugishō*. He also compiled *Zoku shikashū*.

31. Motoori Norinaga deals with this problem in *Tamakatsuma* in relation to the Tatsuta or Minase Rivers (cf. Bentley 2013:21–23, 67–69).

If we deal metaphorically with the poetry in *Man'yōshū*, then it would be like building a mountain. The person could make it high and mighty, and yet, the appearance is far from stunning. And though the plants and trees are strong, it is as if the person undertook the planting without putting his heart into the task. Comparing the height and breadth of *Kokinshū* poetry with *Man'yōshū*, the poetry is interesting, the trees and foliage planted carefully.[32]

The elegance of later poetry is like the phrase, "I wish to fall from a high peak into the bay."[33] The elegance comes through when the poet desires to write sophisticated poetry, regardless of the skill of the poem. Do you not think that the depth of poetry is like when the cultivator takes great care in the planting of trees and herbs and the arranging of the rocks?

The poetry in *Man'yōshū* contains divine utterances mixed with traces of the ancient days. Compared with Chinese poetry, the make-up of the majority of these poems resembles poetry from the Six Courts era more than it does poetry from the Han–Wei era.

The key to understanding Man'yō poetry is to possess the forbearing and clear heart of a mother trying to listen to the mumbled, half-finished words of her baby. Naturally, this is not the case in reality, but I have given you a metaphor so you will realize that listening to Man'yō poetry with contemporary ears means you lack sufficient vocabulary, and it sounds as if it is missing syllables. When reading *Man'yōshū*, the reader must put himself in the shoes of the ancient poets, and forget his own contemporary feelings.

Do you think Shintō was ever replaced by either Buddhism or Confucianism? The answer lies in *Nihongi* and other ancient books. The reader should open and read them. Confucianism came to our country during the reign of Emperor Ōjin.[34] Buddhism came here during the reign of Emperor Kinmei. After this time, sovereign and subject alike used these two philosophies together to rule the country, and there were disciplines that were

---

32. Keichū is referring to *Man'yōshū* poets composing naked, strong feelings, packed with emotion, but the words themselves were not planted (selected) carefully.

33. A poem by Li Zhi (李質, dates uncertain); she is known as one of the three great female poets of the Tang dynasty. This poem appears in Book 5 of *Santi Tangshi*. The first two stanzas are: 古木疑撐月、危峰欲墮江 "I doubted my eyes, as if the old tree was holding up the moon—as if it wants to fall into the bay from the steep mountain."

34. Keichū is referring to the line in *Nihon shoki*, "Sixteenth year of Ōjin, spring, second month. Wang Ren came to the court. The Crown Prince, Uji Wakiiratsuko, studied various works with Wang Ren as his teacher." The assumption is that he studied the Confucian classics.

suitable and others that were not. People who read poetry should make Shintō their foundation, avoiding a biased frame of mind where one keeps Confucianism but throws off Buddhism.

This anthology [*Man'yōshū*] does not properly employ Chinese characters [orthodox forms versus abbreviated forms]. Even if a reader refers to a recent Chinese character dictionary, it is still very difficult to grasp the meaning of the poetry.[35] Since many ancient character dictionaries have been lost, we should not engage in fanciful debate. The poetic text also employs Japanese characters at times.[36]

Eastern dialect songs in Book 14 of *Man'yōshū* can be understood by converting the song back to central Japanese as employed at the court, as the five vowel sounds correspond with each other. There are many voiced sounds, so the reader should be careful. Various frontier guard poetry in Book 20 of the anthology should be treated in the same manner as the eastern dialect poetry mentioned above.

One must be alert to the phenomenon of crasis. For example, the phrase 吉野在・吉野有 *yosino naru* "in Yoshino" should be read with the particle *ni* inserted [as *yosino ni aru* > *yosino naru*]. The two syllables *ni-a* coalesce into one syllable *na*, and this is signified by the characters 在・有 "to exist, to be in," which has the interlinear reading of *naru* attached. It is as if the character 有 "to be" was read as 成 "to become." Originally there was no reason to read this as *naru* "to become," and you should follow this logic when you see the text glossed as *naru*, though the characters want it read as *ni aru*. This all goes without saying, but I have made a note of it here for the greenest of beginners. If you understand this fact, then you will benefit much from regular poetry.

In China they put description ahead of content, but in our country we put content ahead of description. Thus, when you read Chinese works you have to read it with these two ideas reversed.[37] For example, in Japanese we say 花を見、月を待つ, but in China they write 見花、待月, so if you do

---

35. This is the greatest barrier for a reader trying to gain access to the text of *Man'yōshū*. It is also the heart of the seed from which Kokugaku sprouted. Scholars starting with Keichū delved into the ancient past to unearth the original meanings of words. One unresolved problem spilling over into the present is the lack of sufficient textual criticism to produce reliable readings for Chinese characters employed in the text in forms other than phonograms.

36. These are Chinese characters the Japanese invented that do not exist in China. An example is MYS 40, where *otome* "maiden" is written 媙嬬. The character 媙 appears to have been invented by the Japanese.

37. He is pointing out that in Japanese the object comes before the verb, but is reversed in Chinese.

not reverse these, you get *miru fana* and *matu tuki*, so with every Chinese character you need to create a predicate. If you do not do this, then it will not sound grammatical when you read out loud. When you place phrases like *omofikiya* "I had expected . . ." in the first stanza of a *waka*, the meaning of the poem works backward, but the first stanza sends it onward.

Anciently there were various theories about *Man'yōshū* being an imperially decreed anthology, which emperor gave that decree, and what person actually compiled the poetry. On this subject, *Shūgaishō*[38] says, "Fujiwara Teika states, 'There was contention between contemporary poetic sages concerning the era of *Man'yōshū*.' Looking at the places in the anthology mentioning compilation, we see that Books 17 on do not contain any old poetry. Poetry in Book 17 was composed between Tenpyō 2 [730] and Tenpyō 20 [748].[39] Book 18 contains poetry composed between the third month, twenty-third day of Tenpyō 20 and first month, second day of Tenpyō Shōhō 2 [750].[40] Book 19 contains poetry written from the third month, first day of Tenpyō Shōhō 2 until the first month, twenty-fifth day of Tenpyō Shōhō 5 [753].[41]

"Generally Japanese and Chinese documents often record the era of compilation somewhere in a note. Why is it that the note of compilation[42] has been lost, and people simply rely on information from other works?[43] Analogous to the extreme lack of information concerning the date of compilation, there is also no definite theory about the compiler. *Eiga monogatari* records, 'During the reign of the Takano emperor, a sovereign had instructed Minister Moroe to present *Man'yōshū* to the court.'[44] But there are many poems written after Tachibana Moroe died, and some commentators

38. This is a work recording the theories of Kyōgoku Chūnagon Nyūdō, better known as Fujiwara Teika. Tradition held that it was compiled by Tōin Kinkata (1291–1360), but as the title of the work appears in the bibliographic lists of *Honchō shojaku mokuroku* (1294), it must have existed in some form before Kinkata was born. It is plausible that Kinkata took the basic text and expanded it, leading to his name being associated with authorship.

39. Keichū adds the following note, "The last poem in this chapter was composed in the spring of 749."

40. Keichū adds, "Upon investigation, I found there was poetry composed from the fifth day of the first month until the eighteenth day of the second."

41. Keichū comments, "Upon investigation, this should be second month, twenty-fifth day. I suspect that it is a copyist's error."

42. Referring to a note in the colophon, or perhaps referring to the loss of a preface.

43. Keichū states that "other works" points to both the Japanese and Chinese prefaces in *Kokinshū*.

44. Cf. McCullough (1985:79). I have slightly altered the translation to account for Teika's text.

state that Minister Yakamochi compiled the rest of the work. This is very strange."

This is what Teika believed. Minister Moroe died on the sixth day of the first month of Tenpyō Shōhō 9 [757]. Therefore, Book 20 of *Man'yōshū* contains poetry composed around the fourth day of the third month of the same year [757], with poem 4481 composed by Ōhara Mabito, till the end of the book. Looking through the work of Teika, and carefully considering the range of poems within its covers, I think that the work was not an imperially ordered anthology, nor was it the work of Moroe. It was compiled by Yakamochi with a few years worth of privately composed poetry, which he had recorded. The work up to Book 16 was compiled between the years 744 and 745, when he was about 27 or 28 years of age. The poems up to the fifth day of the fourth month of Tenpyō 16 [744] were picked up later and added to Book 17. Poems dated from the first month of Tenpyō 18 [746] until the end of Book 20 resemble a poetic diary, lacking arrangement by topics. These were gradually gathered and in Tenpyō Shōhō 3 [759] these became one part of the collection. I will now select certain points to provide as proof of my reasoning.

Book 2 says, "A poem composed when Ōtomo Sukune proposed to Kose Iratsume."[45] This Ōtomo Sukune is called Major Councilor Yasumaro in the Kanbon manuscript.[46] Generally, the practice in the text is that the real names of persons of the rank major councilor and higher are not recorded. That is why in Book 4 we see this same person recorded as "Major Councilor General Ōtomo"; this is the reason his name is not written. The reason that we presently do not record the name of low-ranking courtiers is because we pay respect to the ancestors of these people recorded in private anthologies. If the work was an imperially decreed anthology, then protocol would have obliged Yakamochi to record his name when he presented the document.

Book 3 records, "A poem composed by command at the end of spring when Middle Councilor Ōtomo went to the old palace in Yoshino. He also composed a short poem here."[47] This is Major Councilor Tabito when he

45. Headnote to MYS 101.

46. This text was so named because Keichū had copied it from Tokugawa Mitsukuni's library. Thus it was called the "government manuscript" (官本). Interestingly this text has a note after this headnote, "Another text states, 'Ōtomo Sukune, his real name was Yasumaro. He was the sixth son of the Minister of the Right of the Naniwa Court (Kōtoku) Minister Nagatoko of the Great Purple Rank.'" He passed away as major councilor and general during the reign of the Heijō Court (Genmei) (Abe and Taira 1972:482).

47. Headnote to MYS 315.

was still holding the rank of middle councilor. His name is not recorded out of respect for his father. The reader can glean the truth of my words from looking at other poetry in the same book, such as "A poem written by Middle Councilor Abe Hironiwa," or another place where it simply says, "A poem by Abe Hironiwa."[48]

There is also the line, "A poem composed by Isonokami Maetsukimi." A note after the poem says, "Concerning the aforementioned poem, perhaps this Maetsukimi is Isonokami Ason Otomaro who went to Echizen as governor."[49] Since Otomaro lived until at least Tenpyō Shōhō 2 (750), and if this was an imperially ordered anthology, then there would not be anything amiss. In the same book, we see the words, "In the sixth month, summer, Tenpyō 11 [739] Ōtomo Sukune Yakamochi composed this poem to mourn his mistress who passed away."[50] After this it says, "To this poem, Yakamochi's younger brother, Fumimochi, composed thirteen poems in reply."[51] This was written by Yakamochi himself. In the second month of Tenpyō 16 [744] Imperial Guard Ōtomo Yakamochi composed six poems when Prince Asaka passed away. Yakamochi also wrote the note following these poems. The court made Yakamochi an imperial guard in Tenpyō 12 [740]. This is seen in Book 6. In the codes[52] it says that people are promoted to the rank of imperial guard when they reach the age of twenty-one. So in Tenpyō 16 Yakamochi was about the age of twenty-six or twenty-seven. There are no poems composed in Tenpyō 17 in the anthology, so as these poems appear here, I believe that the anthology up to Book 16 was compiled in Tenpyō 17. In the same book, after the poem composed by Takahashi Ason who lamented the death of his wife, a commentary note says, "These three poems were composed on the twentieth day of the seventh month of Tenpyō 16, but his name is unknown. However, it is said that he was the son of the head of the Imperial Kitchen."[53] If the compilation of this anthology was ordered by Emperor Shōmu,[54] it would be suspicious not to know the names of lower courtiers.

48. Referring to MYS 302 and MYS 370, respectively.

49. MYS 368.

50. MYS 462.

51. MYS 462–74.

52. It is unclear which set of codes Keichū has reference to, though it is likely he is relying on *Ryō no shūge*, an annotation of the Yōrō codes, including quotes from some of the earlier Taihō codes.

53. In reference to MYS 481.

54. Who reigned 724–49.

Book 4 records, "Iratsume was the daughter of Major Councilor Saho."[55] This line points to the fact that she is still living, but because she was the aunt of Yakamochi, that explains why there is this note recording her name as Iratsume. For example, even if Yakamochi presented the anthology to the court, he would not be able to write such intimate notes unless this was a private collection. We can guess as much from other usages like "Tamura Ōiratsume, sister of Sakanoue Ōiratsume."[56]

In the same book there is the sentence, "A poem composed by the emperor and presented to Princess Unakami."[57] This is proof that the work was not decreed by Emperor Kōken, due to the way that Yakamochi treats the currently reigning emperor [Shōmu]. This much we can glean because throughout Books 6, 8, and 18, as long as Emperor Shōmu reigns, the previous ruler, Genshō [r. 715–23], is called Dajō Tennō "Abdicated Emperor," but when the reign changes to that of Emperor Kōken, Yakamochi changes his usage so Shōmu becomes the abdicated emperor, while Genshō is now known as Sendaijō Tennō.[58] In the note directly after the poem we see, "Having considered the aforementioned poem, the poet composed it in imitation of ancient poetry. Perhaps because the feelings of this poem fit the circumstances perfectly, the emperor presented this poem to the Princess."[59] This was not decreed by Emperor Shōmu, but is proof of private compilation.

There is also the line, "A poem composed by the emperor when he yearned for Princess Sakahito."[60] Also, "Princess Yashiro presented this poem to the emperor."[61] "This poem was presented to the emperor."[62] "Two poems presented to the emperor."[63] These were not compiled according to the decree of Emperor Kōken. This is also proof of private compilation at the time. The note after poem MYS 649 says, "Sakanoue Iratsume is the daughter of Major Councilor Saho." After poem MYS 667 there is the following note, "The mother of Ōtomo Sakanoue Iratsume." There is more than sufficient evidence in this book to show that these poems were not

55. Referring to MYS 525–28.

56. MYS 756.

57. Headnote to MYS 530.

58. *Dajō Tennō* refers to the father of the emperor, while *Sendaijō Tennō* refers to the grandfather or grandmother. In this case it points to Shōmu's aunt, Genshō, who reigned directly before him.

59. Note after MYS 530.

60. Headnote to MYS 624.

61. Headnote to MYS 636.

62. Headnote to MYS 721.

63. Headnote to MYS 725.

compiled by imperial decree. Since these poets are all relatives of Yakamochi, [we must conclude that] these chapters were compiled privately. …

In Book 5, other than notes explaining the meaning of poems with explanation for certain terms, the poetry exhibits a mixture of styles, showing that the anthology does not even have the overall structure of a compilation put together by imperial decree. …

Book 6 contains a poem with a note that says, "A poem composed when the emperor presented *sake* to the military overseers. A short poem was attached."[64] This is also proof that someone compiled the poetry during the reign of Emperor Shōmu, and that Emperor Kōken did not issue a decree for the compilation. A note after a poem says, "The aforementioned poem was the composition of the abdicated emperor."[65] This abdicated emperor points to Emperor Genshō. This note shows that this part is from a private anthology. If this [actually] was an imperially ordered anthology, then there should be no confusion here. …

Book 7 contains a note after these seven poems,[66] which states, "These seven poems are the composition of Minister Fujiwara. The dates are unknown." This should be Fujiwara Kita, but perhaps the character 北 *kita* has been dropped,[67] and that is why this note was attached. Minister Kita is Fusasaki who lived until Tenpyō 9 [737], so if this anthology were compiled by imperial decree, the compilers would know the dates.

Book 8, in the Miscellaneous Autumn poems, after the seven poems composed at the banquet at the house of Minister of the Right Tachibana [Moroe], we have a set of Naramaro poems from the same banquet, with this note attached, "These poems were compiled from compositions at the banquet held by the Minister of the Right Tachibana at his old villa on the seventeenth day of the seventh month, winter."[68] These compilations were not ordered by the court, and this provides evidence that Minister Moroe is not the compiler. There are two poems composed by the emperor.[69] Later we find, "Prince Sakurai, Governor of Tōtōmi, presented a poem to the emperor … and the emperor replied with a poem."[70] As noted above, these

64. Headnote to MYS 973. Military overseers (Jpn. *setsudoshi*) were sent to various parts of the country to overseer the establishment of military outposts. These were sent out in 732, and abolished in 734.

65. Headnote to MYS 974.

66. There is confusion in Keichū's text. His text would have the seven poems as MYS 1189–95, but in our current texts, these seven are divided up as 1218–25, 1194, and 1195.

67. So named because he was the founder of the northern branch of the Fujiwara family.

68. Headnote to MYS 1591.

69. Referring to MYS 1539–40, two poems by Emperor Shōmu.

70. Headnote to MYS 1614 and 1615. The emperor is Shōmu.

words provide further proof that Emperor Kōken did not order this anthology compiled. In the Miscellaneous Winter poems, there is one poem from the abdicated emperor, followed by one poem by the emperor with this note, "According to what I have heard, these aforementioned poems were composed at the residence of Minister of the Left Saho at a banquet he sponsored."[71] This is the usage of a privately compiled anthology, and not one compiled by an edict. The headnote after the one poem composed at the banquet held on the western side of the pond says, "It is unclear who the poet of this poem is. Rather, this poem was heard and recorded by a page, Abe Ason Mushimaro."[72] Again, these are the words of a privately compiled anthology. The empress during the reign of Emperor Kōken would have had her titled altered to empress dowager.

In Book 9, after the poems written on "Thinking of a certain maiden," we see the note, "The three aforementioned poems are found in the poetic collection of Tanabe Sakimaro."[73] Also the note, "One poem composed when the poet saw a corpse while crossing over Ashigara Hill."[74] A note after these seven poems claims the poems came from the poetic collection of Tanabe Sakimaro. This note is the same as that after the mention of Tanabe Sakimaro's private collection seen in Book 6.

In Book 12, a note after the *onore yuwe noraete* poem says, "According to Heguri Fumiya Ason Masubito, 'I heard an old tradition, where the aforementioned poem was composed after Princess Ki was severely chastised for having improper sexual relations with Prince Takayasu.'"[75] These are not the words of an imperially ordered anthology.

At the end of Book 14 there is a note, "From these previous poems, we cannot figure out the name of the province, or the names of the mountains and rivers." Considering this, if this anthology had been compiled by imperial edict, do you not think they could have figured out these things?

The beginning of Book 15 states, "On the twenty-eighth day of the sixth month, summer, Tenpyō 8 [736]. … After these [145 Silla poems] we have Nakatomi Ason Yakamori's poems." Considering the record in the reign of Shōmu [in *Shoku Nihongi*], we see in the record that the court ordered a great amnesty in the sixth month of Tenpyō 12 [740], and while Hozumi Asaon Oyu and others were recalled to the capital, Isonokami Otomaro,

71. Headnote to MYS 1638.

72. Headnote to MYS 1650.

73. Headnote to MYS 1794.

74. Headnote to MYS 1800.

75. Headnote to MYS 3098. Keichū abbreviates most of the note but I have quoted the first part to provide context.

Nakatomi Yakamori, and others remained outside the limits of the amnesty.[76] Yakamori was banished to Echizen in Tenpyō 11 [739], which is considered "near banishment," but he was never pardoned. Considering he was not directly involved in the rebellion [of Fujiwara Nakamaro], what harm would there have been to pardon him? This book starts with a concrete date, but does not contain any more dates, which probably shows the circumstances of the time. Regardless, this is more proof that the anthology was not composed by edict from Emperor Kōken.

Book 16 has a note after the Asaka Yama poem, saying, "According to an oral tradition, the aforementioned poem was composed when Prince Kazuragi was dispatched to Mutsu Province, and the reception from the staff of the provincial office was terribly negligent."[77] Prince Kazuragi was the original name of Minister Tachibana Moroe. More proof that this minister was not the compiler of the anthology.

The poetry in Book 17 dates from the eleventh month of Tenpyō 2 [730] to the fifth day of the fourth month of Tenpyō 16 [744]. So after the anthology up to Book 16 was compiled, perhaps the compiler collected more overlooked poems. Thus, Book 3 contains an elegy dated Tenpyō 16, Book 4 has correspondence dated by notes, Book 6 has miscellaneous poems composed between Yōrō 7 [723] and Tenpyō 16, while Book 8 has a variety of poems on the four seasons dating up to Tenpyō 15 [743]. Now Book 17 has none of these types of poems, so perhaps the compiler was searching for material during summer between the sixteenth and seventeenth years. ...

Book 19 says, "Twenty-second day of the tenth month. Three poems written at a banquet held at the residence of Major Controller of the Left Ki Iimaro."[78] Two notes after the first two poems read, "The aforementioned poem is a version of the 'when I was in the national capital' poem orally transmitted by Minister of Justice Prince Funa," and "The poem on the right is a version of the 'when I was in the old capital' poem orally transmitted by Middle Controller of the Left Nakatomi Ason Kiyomaro." These are commentary notes from Yakamochi when he first had returned to the capital, and all are proof that this is a privately compiled anthology. ...

Book 20 also contains both examples of Yakamochi's poetry and commentary, like the others just mentioned. We see humility in the words at-

---

76. This appears in the edict dated the fifteenth day of the sixth month of Tenpyō 12 (740).

77. Headnote to MYS 3807.

78. Headnote to MYS 4257.

tached only to the poetry of Yakamochi. By this you may know that this anthology was compiled by none other than Yakamochi. …

Question: Though your new theory is well founded,[79] since we received our training in the old theory, we find it difficult to convert. The reason for this comes from the line in *Shinsen Man'yōshū*,[80] which says, "This *Man'yōshū* is comprised of poetry composed in the old style. … This anthology is not only a compilation of verse presented to the throne by the order of the blue sash and the coffin rope [imperial decree], but it also contains song transmitted orally, comprising several tens of volumes. [I] have added ornamentation, and placed [the text of *Man'yōshū*] in a large box and await criticism."

The origins of this work were modeled after the preface of Ban Gu's Rhapsody on Two Capitals in *Wenxuan*, which says, "Another source says that rhapsodies were an old genre of poetry." Li Shan's commentary [in *Wenxuan*] says, "The preface to Maoshi says, 'Poetry has six principles, and the second is called rhapsody, because it is a genre of old poetry.'" Therefore, do you not think that the intent of Sugawara Michizane's preface is that the work was compiled according to the imperial command of the Son of heaven, Daidō?

In *Kokinshū*, in Book 18, there is a poem composed in the Teikan era [859–77] in reply to the question, "In what era was *Man'yōshū* compiled?" The reply was:

kaminatuki	This is an ancient work
sigure furi okeru	coming from that palace whose
nara no fa no	name is the same as
na ni ofu miya no	the *nara* tree[81] whose leaves
furugoto zo kore	are drenched in the tenth month.

[KKS 997] Fun'ya Arisue

In the preface of the same anthology, it says that our poetic tradition is ancient, but the poetic tradition did not gain popularity until the reign of the Nara Court. … Poetry composed before this era was collected and the work was titled *Man'yōshū*. …

79. From here Keichū engages in the common practice of setting up supposed questions and giving his answers. "New theory" points to Keichū's argument refuting the older idea that *Man'yōshū* was compiled by imperial decree by Tachibana Moroe.

80. Also known as the Sugawara Family *Man'yōshū*. The quote above is from Michizane's preface. The ellipses appear in the original.

81. The Japanese oak. This is a pun on the capital, which was at this time in Nara.

In the Mana preface of *Kokinshū* it says, "A sovereign of the past, Son of Heaven Heizei, commanded certain of his attendants to compile *Man'yōshū*.[82] ..." Minamoto Shitagō's collection says, "When Shitagō of the Pear Jar Circle read old poems from the Nara capital and compiled these. ..." In the eleventh volume of *Honchō monzui*, in the headnote to the poem composed by Fujiwara Arikuni where he praised the twenty-eight *varga* of the *Lotus Sutra*, it states, "Perhaps it was compiled by edict [and those in charge] collected and recorded poems old and new, or perhaps with this intention they collected new and old, from the time of *Man'yōshū* till the anthologies of the various houses, and so there are already many bound volumes, and truly this is the prosperous origin of poetry. ..."

There are various other theories about *Man'yōshū* that are like orchids and chrysanthemums [it is impossible to tell which is superior]. Do you propose that all these theories are mistaken? We ask you to deliberate on this subject and recognize our old ideas. Take this evidence to heart and rid yourself of future doubts.

Answer: There is no need to wait for further evidence, for it is clear which is correct. Why is it that you cannot make up your minds? Public opinion is in Buddhist scripture. We do not need to adhere to this or that theory because So-and-So said it; we should rely on objective evidence. There must be one error among a thousand ideas of a wise man, much as even a fast horse will stumble once. And there must be one inspiration among a thousand ideas of a fool,[83] like a dull sword has times when it will cut. But though the dull sword might cut something, the famous swordsmith, Gan Jiang, would not believe that it is sharp. And though a gifted horse may stumble, the skilled horseman, Po Le, would not say that the beast is slow. Even good scholars are prone to error.

Nevertheless, a fool will want to sprout feathers and cover his mistakes, while he looks for the small faults in others. Why would this be the desire of our ruler? It would be wise to understand the maxim of the monkey's wasted effort in trying to capture the moon reflected in the water,[84] or the

---

82. Slightly altered version of McCullough 1985:258.

83. Keichū has quoted from the *Biography of Marquis of Huai-yin* in *Shiji*, "I have heard that there must be one error among a thousand ideas of a wise man, and there must be one inspiration among a thousand ideas of a fool" (translation from Nienhauser 2008.8:83).

84. This analogy is found in *Mohe sengqi lü*, a Buddhist text. The work in question says, "Buddha proclaimed to the various monks, 'In a previous world, there were five hundred monkeys at Vārānasī City. Below a certain tree was a well, and within the well they could see the moon. Holding on to the branches of the tree, linking their tails and hands, they entered the well to capture the moon, but the branch broke and they all died.'"

bark of a dog makes a lot of noise [but accomplishes nothing else].[85] Then you can quickly stop pulling the robe of the nobleman, Qian Lou [and make a fool of yourself].[86]

Pondering on these things, in spite of the period between Tenpyō Hōji [757–65] and Keiun [767–70] being full of events at court, causing the people's hearts to be unable to find rest,[87] did the court cease to raise their voices in poetic composition? Emperor Kōnin was a wise ruler, and since he was not especially fond of Japanese poetry, there is not a single poem from him in *Man'yōshū*, regardless that he did compose poetry as Prince Shirakabe, and there are poems in the work from other sons of Emperor Tahara.[88] These poems are not seen in later works, and that is why I doubt this. Did not Minister Moroe find this fact disturbing himself? A few reigns after the reign of Emperor Kanmu, this poetic practice died out.[89] Among these reigns, Emperor Saga was fond of poetry, so he composed poetry until he reached the Kamo Retreat. Therefore, because courtiers did not compose Japanese poetry for such a long time, its transmission ceased, so the wise men of ancient days were bound to make mistakes, receiving blind and incorrect traditions. These people did not conduct thorough investigations into *Man'yōshū*, foolishly determining that: it was compiled by imperial decree; the compilers worked by moonlight or the darkness before dawn, never recording who the compilers were. And the preface to *Kokinshū* influenced the theories of later scholars. There are many places in this preface of which I am suspicious, so I will set that aside for the time being. I only have respect for the theory of Teika, adding nothing else to my commentary.

[NST 39:309–28]

---

85. This appears in *Qian fu lun*, "A proverb says, 'If one dog starts barking, a hundred other dogs will join in the barking.'"

86. This appears in *Lienu zhuan*, "[The body of Qian Lou] was dressed in a padded robe with no upper garment over it. He was also covered with a cloth quilt that did not completely cover his head and feet. When it was moved to cover his head, his feet were exposed, and when it was moved to cover his feet, his head was exposed" (Kinney 2014:38).

87. It was during this period, especially from 761 to 764, when Fujiwara Nakamaro and the priest Dōkyō fought for power. Nakamaro raised troops against Dōkyō and paid for it with his life.

88. Emperor Tahara, a posthumous title, was the father of Emperor Kōnin.

89. Meaning that Chinese poetic composition became the vogue.

KOKKA HACHIRON

Kada no Arimaro | 1742

[Written at the request of Tayasu Munetake, Arimaro wrote down his feelings about *waka*, and inadvertently placed himself at odds with his master, Munetake. He categorized poetry into eight theories, hence the title. The section that incited the most controversy was "The Significance of Poetry," where Arimaro declared that poetry was not suitable as a tool to govern society or people. He saw the endeavor of poetic composition worthy according to how artistic the poem was; to him it had no didactic value. Nosco (1981:77) has argued, "On the surface, the Kokka hachiron controversy appears to have been a literary dispute. It was, in fact, at least as political and ideological as it was literary, and it had a determinant influence on the emergence and future development of National Learning. It also brought into focus what was, perhaps, the most compelling issue in quondam intellectual circles, namely, whether the Way ... was a product of nature ... or of human invention."]

THE ORIGIN OF POETRY

Poetry is where our words are lengthened and made rhythmical, and our hearts are comforted.[1] Thus, [as mentioned in the preface to *Kokinshū*], "Poetry comes into being from feelings aroused by what one sees and hears,"[2] is an inadequate explanation. The words of Izanagi and Izanami, "What a delightful lad!" "What a delightful maiden!" which appear in *Kojiki* and *Nihon shoki* and other works are feelings from the heart that have been verbalized. However, the record calls these words *spoken* and not *sung*, because these were not drawn out and had no rhythm. The following words of Susanoo were sung from the heart,

yakumo tatu	Endowed with power,
idumo yafegaki	a twofold multiwoven fence—

1. The recitation of poetry is almost an act of singing in which words are drawn out when sung.

2. This is from the Kana preface of the *Kokinshū*, "Japanese poetry has the human heart as seed and myriads of words as leaves. It comes into being when men use the seen and the heard to give voice to feelings aroused by the innumerable events in their lives" (McCullough 1985:3).

tuma gomi ni	To conceal ourselves
yafegaki tukuru	I have built a twofold fence.
sono yafegaki wo	Yes, within that multiwoven fence![3]

[KJK 1]

While these words were also thoughts of the heart, Susanoo gave them rhythm and *sang*. Also, the younger sister of Ajishiki Takahikone, Takahime, sang,

ame naru ya	In the heavens
oto tanabata no	the jewels strung upon
unagaseru	the string hung around
tama no misumaru	the neck of the weaving maiden,
misumaru ni	upon that string,
anadama wa ya	are very beautiful—
mitani	like the beauty
futa watarasu	of him who shines over two hills
adisiki	it is the *kami*
takafikone no kami so ya[4]	Ajishiki Takahikone!

[NS 2]

These words appear in *Nihon shoki*, sung to announce the name of Takahikone to those who had gathered together.[5] If there was no intention to sing, then those who had gathered would not have understood the name within the context.[6] That is why we know that it was sung. When we look at Chinese verse, the same thing is true. The songs created by beating on one's belly and stamping one's feet do not appear in any verifiable historical

3. This is the first poem in the *Kojiki* and *Nihon shoki* and long has been said to be the birth of Japanese poetry. Needless to say, this poem is most likely from the Suiko-Tenchi era. The interpretation of this poem is difficult, and my translation has been done only after much difficulty. *Yakumo tatu* is usually translated as "many rising clouds," but as Inoue Mitsusada and others point out, this is metaphorical for "great power" (NKBT, *Nihon shoki*, 1:123, n18). Naturally this is only fitting for Susanoo, a powerful *kami* who resided in Izumo.

4. This last character was not intended to be read as a *man'yōgana ya*. It is the copula *nari*. However, Arimaro believed it to be *ya*, and I have followed his text.

5. The story went that Ame Wakahiko had died, and Takahikone, being a friend who greatly resembled the dead individual, had come to console the family. However, at the funeral the family mistook Takahikone for Ame Wakahiko, which insulted Takahikone.

6. Because his name is in the song. In other words, he used song to announce his name of Takahikone.

work, and so I set these aside for the time being without discussion.[7] Even the songs of Emperor Shun and his minister Gao Tao, contained in the Yiji section of the *Book of Documents*, are seen for the first time within the Six Classics of Confucianism, and it is clear from the Yiji section that these poems were sung.[8]

And truly, if one does not sing, then his heart is not comforted. In singing, words should be drawn out and given rhythm. Thus, in our country as well as in China, poetry was precisely the act of singing. One composed poetry because s/he wanted to sing, and so it was impossible to employ the same words used in everyday speech. Also, it appears that the syllables per stanza were not necessarily set, but [in our country] by repeating roughly five and seven syllables, the poet created a desirable rhythm with song made up of long and short breaks, much the same way that poetry in ancient China employed four characters per stanza. Nevertheless, as the concluding stanzas of Takahime's song contain stanzas of six, nine, ten, and four syllables, the repeating length of these stanzas is uneven, making it inferior to the *Yakumo tatsu* poem, or any of the other poems recorded in the divine age. Thus, this type of poem was called *hinaburi*[9] in the *Kojiki* and *Nihon shoki*. Then, during the time of Hohodemi, we have exchange poems between him and Toyotama Hime. Since these are exchange poems, perhaps we cannot call these songs, because they were not sung. But exchanges within society at that time should not be considered love exchanges between men and women seen in later eras. These were songs produced and sung out loud to clear up one's feelings. The words to that song likely were then sent to the individual the person longed for. When the person's feelings were simply written down, and not sung, then the person should be able to use everyday words to relay what s/he wanted to say. It was not necessary to add extra expressions. I believe that the use of phrases like *siratama no kimi* or *okitudori kamo* were used because the poem was intended to be sung when it was composed.[10] Other poems in the *Kojiki*, *Nihon shoki*, and other old records were likely all sung. Within these poems,

7. This refers to a state of tranquility in the land, where people have full bellies and pound on them like drums, and stamp their feet on the ground and clap their hands as a form of rejoicing for their peaceful and prosperous circumstances.

8. The preface to these poems uses the verbal 歌曰, "to sing, saying."

9. There is some discussion on exactly what *hinaburi* constituted. *Furi* meant to sway or dance, and *fina* is believed to have pointed to the provinces. What is clear is that ancient poetry was divided into several classifications.

10. The two phrases mentioned here appear in poems that were sent via a messenger and therefore were not actually sung. Arimaro is thus saying that the use of these extraordinary phrases is due to the poets having originally intended to sing these.

there are some with regular alternating stanzas [of 5–7 syllables], and some with an irregular meter. Even among the poems with a regular meter, there are some places where the sequence of sounds is poor and the rhythm is choppy. Among irregular-meter poems, we see some that have smooth sequences and a clean rhythm.[11] At this time [*Kojiki* and *Nihon shoki*], the world did not amuse itself with flowery words, and society did not produce songs dealing with elegance or scenery. If we were to discuss the superiority or inferiority of poetry, then we should label as superior those poems with a regular meter and rhythm while those with an irregular meter and choppy rhythm are inferior; however, we do not see any such literary criticism in the ancient records. The ancients just let the poem flow from the mouth of the singer and recorded it as it was sung.

However, with the artistic nature of literature in China blossoming earlier than Japan, from the period of the *Book of Odes* on, we see that the Chinese amused themselves with flowery speech, and by the time of Li, who ruled the Tang court, Chinese verse had reached its apex. The beginning years of the Tang emperor, Gao Zu, coincides with the reign of our [ruler] Suiko. The height of the Tang period coincides with the reigns of Genmei and Genshō.[12] During that time in our country, Prince Ōtsu produced the first Chinese poems, and the composition of Tang verse has continued ever since, done in imitation of Tang poetry. Perhaps during this time the style of Chinese verse composed by Japanese gradually changed from the *Book of Odes* style to the Tang style, and our poetry was judged on this new standard; for the first time, our people were amusing themselves with flowery speech—the poetic words gradually becoming like blossoms.[13] This means that even though the thirty-nine imperial reigns from Emperor Jinmu till Emperor Tenchi represent a passage of over thirteen hundred years, there is little difference between the poems in the divine age and the following poem from Emperor Tenchi, saddened at the death of Saimei:[14]

---

11. What Arimaro means is that there are songs that sound nice and songs that do not have a pleasant sound, but this is not necessarily because of a strict adherence to the number of syllables per stanza.

12. The Tang period is usually divided into four stages: early, high, middle, late. Arimaro is talking about the second stage.

13. This is in reference to the Kana preface of the *Kokinshū*, "Because people nowadays value outward show and turn their minds toward frivolity, poems are mere empty verses and trivial words" (McCullough 1985:5).

14. Emperor Kōgyoku (r. 642–45), also known as Saimei (r. 655–61), was Tenchi's mother.

kimi ga me no	I dock and stand here
kofosiki kara ni	because I long for a glance
fatete ite	of my highness's eyes!
kaku ya kofimu mo	How I long for a look—
kimi ga me wo fori	a look into my highness's eyes.
	[NS 123]

Among those songs from these thirty-nine imperial reigns, there are some with a tight structure, being very close to poems from later eras. Then there are some songs with a choppy rhythm, being unlike anything from later eras. Of course, this represents the varying degrees of skill in the poets, as well as the circumstances surrounding some of the production of these poems, so we should not judge indiscriminately. The newer and older poems included in the *Kojiki* and *Nihon shoki* are all basically straightforward in tone, and it can be said that the structure changes little through time.[15] The time from Emperor Tenchi to Daigo consists of twenty-one reigns, and occupies less than three hundred years, but things gradually changed, and analogous to the style seen in *Kokinshū*, poetic expression and content became more elegant. There is no other explanation than this: There is a difference between singing naturally and amusing oneself by composing a poem using flowery speech. Within the *Man'yōshū*, there are only four or five poems from the time of Nintoku to Yūryaku, and Kōgyoku to Saimei; all the rest of the Man'yō poetry comes from the time between Tenchi and Kōken. Thus, the *Man'yōshū* poems are more advanced in expression than those in the *Kojiki* and *Nihon shoki* and yet have more substance than the *Kokinshū* poems after it. Within the twenty books of *Man'yōshū*, one can see a gradual change in style between Books 1 and 2, and 19 and 20.

Now, when we look at *Man'yōshū*, we naturally see poems sung vocally during the time of Ōtomo Yakamochi; at the introduction of a banquet at Yakamochi's house, we notice that there are poets reciting new poems and others reciting poems [based on] ancient poems. There were times when the person who recorded these poems did not know whether a certain poem was considered new or old, and so he wrote, "It is unclear whether this poem is new or old." Had poetry not have been sung at this time, then

15. Naturally, this statement cannot be taken at face value. A poem like the Uda poem (NS 8) in *Nihon shoki* may be archaic in nature and meter, but it is complex in structure with the employment of apparent exotic words to give the poem a foreign or sophisticated air, and with the employment of a high level of variation in the *man'yōgana*.

there would not have been *old* poetry to sing. Furthermore, *Man'yōshū* records a large number of poems from frontier guards in the various provinces. Since it was a different era from our time, if the poet only employed flowery expressions in his poetry, then people who were base and common like the frontier guards should not have enjoyed composing poetry. Thus the frontier poems probably are much like the popular folk songs enjoyed by youth in the present. However, we know from the *Man'yōshū* that not every poem was sung during the time of Yakamochi. As the poets tried earnestly to employ flowery speech within those poems that were not sung, we can here discuss the superiority or inferiority of these. Yet the poems in the *Man'yōshū* were simply written down upon being heard, and there is no poetic selections like those within the *Kokinshū*.[16] Within some of the songs composed by the frontier guards in Tōtōmi and other provinces south of it in the last book of the anthology, we see where a headnote states that some of the poems were not recorded because they were inferior. Likely these poems included words from a dialect or vulgar speech and would be hard for the people in the capital to understand. However, there is also the poem written by Ōtomo Yakamoch when he was at the residence of Prince Hayashi,

sirayuki no	Thinking about you,
furisiku yama wo	my life-string seems about to break—
koyeyukamu	my beloved who
kimi wo zo moto na	is crossing over those
iki no wo ni omofu	mountains covered with snow.

[MYS 4281]

A note from the minister of the left [Tachibana Moroe] mentions that he took this poem, and tried to change the last stanza [*iki no wo ni omofu*] to *iki no wo ni suru*. By this time there was an attitude of polishing poetry, so poetic deftness was supplanting poetic clumsiness. As I have already mentioned, the songs of the *Kojiki* and *Nihon shoki* and other records were generally composed as song and were not enjoyed because they employed ornamental speech; thus, we should not judge the skill or clumsiness of the expressions within these poems. The poems of the *Man'yōshū* include poems that were sung and others that were not. Poems that were not sung were generally enjoyed because of their ornamental phrases, and we should

16. The Kana preface says, "He addressed [the compilers] and caused them to present him old poems missing from *Man'yōshū*, and also with compositions of their own ... also, miscellaneous compositions unsuited to seasonal categories" (McCullough 1985:7–8).

judge these poems on their artistic level. There are even poems sung found within *Man'yōshū* that should be considered for literary criticism.[17]

When we come to the era of the *Kokinshū*, we no longer see composition of any of these old types of poetry aside from poetry from the folk music department, and eastern songs. By the Kokin era, the literary world had reached a period of vibrancy. Generally, in dealing with poetic skill, it is clear from the *Kokinshū* preface that we are dealing with poems that were selected for their refined elegance. And from the Kokin period until the present, because people compose poetry as a way to enjoy flowery speech, some poems have a deep sense of beauty, some are deeply lyrical, others describe scenery, others employ difficult topics, while some poems offer clever, repetitive word association puns. The standard of judging poetry on its elegance has not changed from the era of *Kokinshū*. However, the style of poetry has changed gradually from that time, and with the Shin Kokin period, poetic splendor reaches its height. From that time forth, the essence of poetry has slowly moved to expressing the plain feelings of the heart. Since this poetic transition is common knowledge, there is no need to describe it in detail here.

THE SIGNIFICANCE OF POETRY

As poetry is not one of the six arts a person should learn,[18] it originally had no effect on the ruling of a country, and offered no assistance in everyday life.[19] The words in the *Kokinshū* preface, "Poetry moves heaven and earth" or "inspiring the spirits and gods"[20] was written because the compilers believed these senseless ideas. Even though poetry may soothe the heart of the brave warrior to a certain extent, how could it approach the effect of music? And though on the one hand it may improve relations between men and women, it has also become the medium for adultery on the other. Therefore, poetry is not highly esteemed in society. But when one reads poetry of profound beauty, being deeply lyrical, having repetitive word as-

17. Arimaro thus divides poetry into three groups for criticism: ballads, experimental poetry that was written down, and poetry composed at banquets that were sung and then recorded.

18. The "six arts" refers to subjects every cultivated man should know, as found in the *Rites of Zhou*: proper conduct, music, archery, government, writing, and math.

19. This has reference to a line from the Mana preface to the *Kokinshū*, "Poetry did not seek to please the ear or eye, but served solely to instruct" (McCullough 1985:257).

20. This is from the Mana preface, "Japanese poetry as a means to moving heaven and earth, stirring the spirits and gods" (McCullough 1985:256).

sociation, or describing scenery, then do you not also feel that desire swell in your breast to compose a good poem? If I am able to produce a good poem, then I am pleased. For example, it is the same feeling when one is drawn to a good picture, or when one has won a game of *go*.

[While poetry has its personal joys] there is also a reason for scholars to take interest in poetic composition. That is, Japan is the country of our imperial family, which has reigned for a myriad generations, but because literature blossomed late [in relation to China], our ancestors had to rely upon Chinese script; they employed Chinese etiquette, laws, codes, dress for court officials, and tools; everything has been based upon Chinese models. Only Japanese poetry was based on the natural sounds of our language, and there are no Chinese usages included in the least.[21] Concerning epithets and plays on words in Japanese poetry, they are superior to the Chinese usages, and we can feel proud because they are genuinely Japanese.

However, court nobles from middle antiquity on saw their power to govern the state usurped by military families. With time on their hands, they earnestly engaged solely in poetic pursuits, and finally came to call it "Our Poetic Way of Shikishima."[22] Not only does this show that these courtiers knew little about the origins of poetry, but they did not even comprehend what constituted "a Way," which is not really worth refuting.

THE CHOICE OF WORDS IN POETRY

As I have said above, when scholars are attracted to Japanese poetry because it is truly indigenous to our land and amuse themselves with it, should they still use ancient words without any thought for poetic styles that have changed as eras have come and gone? We can say that by using these traditionally transmitted ancient words [in our poetry] we prevent these from vanishing. Truly there is logic in this one principle. But the origin of poetry is in the very act of singing. Anciently, even high officials composed verse to comfort their hearts. Presently, only children raise their voices and find amusement in singing. The very act of singing can please the ear of an adult [even if s/he were to raise her/his voice] whether it be in

21. Again, this is wishful thinking. I have already mentioned that there are some foreign influences in some of the poetry in *Nihon shoki*.

22. Literally the *Way of Shikishima*. Shikishima was a place name in Yamato, and thus became a synonym for Yamato that pointed also to Japan in general. Later this came to refer to Japanese poetry.

refined or lewd music. But even if the words are made up by the singer and added to any tune the singer likes, is it true that the more one sings the more this person's heart is put at ease? Of course not. Thus, even if one were to ignore the origins of poetry, it is best to amuse oneself by using ornamental words current in society. If one wishes to amuse himself with flowery words in poetry, then he must select a poetic style, and poetic conjunctions for each stanza. However, because ancient words are simple and sincere, there are some words within the ancient lexicon that are now jarring, apprehensive, or tedious to us, and if you use these then the poem produced lacks elegance.

Thus, after the era of emperors Tenchi and Jitō, the use of clumsy words gradually disappeared, and poetic word usage became more elegant. For example, in Book 1 of *Man'yōshū*, we have a poem from Nakatsu Sumera Mikoto:[23]

tamaki faru	The horses are arrayed
uti no ofono ni	on the large plain of Uji
uma namete	where the ruler
asa fumasuramu	at dawn has trodden the grass.
sono kusa fukeno	That deep grass in the large plain.
	[MYS 4]

First, this poem was not one of deep emotion. Also, the words are not very elegant. The lines *tamaki faru uti no ofono ni* are words that may be used even now, and need not be avoided. However, the fourth and fifth stanzas of this poem are very choppy, employing an unnecessary epithet.[24] Obviously this was added to fill out the number of syllables. Poems produced by ancient poets are clumsy. Even the line *uma namete* later became *koma namete*. The meaning is basically the same, but *uma* has a flat accent, and putting *namete* with it makes the line choppy. *Koma* has a rising accent, and it flows with *namete*. And that is why poets changed *uma* to *koma*. The words *asa fumasuramu* are choppy and cluttered, because there must be some particle, like *te*, *ni*, *o*, or *fa* after this word *asa*. The stanza *sono kusa fukeno*[25] is also choppy. By adding the unnecessary word *sono*, a particle [*te, ni, o, fa*] must now be added. Needless to say, by placing this

23. Some believe her to be the daughter of Jomei and wife of Kōtoku. Others say she is actually Saimei. The poem in question is MYS 4. Omodaka (1983, 1:55) follows Kada no Azumamaro's theory that this is really Empress Hashihito, wife to Jomei.

24. The apparent reference is to *tamaki faru*.

25. There is a difference of opinion as to whether this is *fukano* or *fukeno*. Most modern scholars agree that *fukano* seems to be the more natural reading.

stanza last in the poem, it loses its elegance. Also, in the same book of the *Man'yōshū*, we have a poem by Prince Nakada:

aki no no no	In the golden field cutting grass,
mikusa karifuki	we thatched the roof with it
yadorerisi	and spent the night there.
uti no miyako no	How my thoughts return to
kari ifo si zo omofu	that hut by the Uji Palace.

[MYS 7][26]

This poem was not originally composed with any profound meaning, and it even lacks in elegance. The two lines *aki no no no mikusa karifuki* should not be looked down upon, but may be employed even now. However, the stanza *yadorerisi* does not suit the tone perfectly. Later eras certainly would have ended the poem with *yadorituru*. The meaning is the same, but *yadorerisi* just does not sound proper. *Kari ifo si zo omofu* uses nine syllables instead of seven, and this is extremely unbefitting because it is too long. Yet, we do not even know now if the author originally intended it to be read *karifo si zo omou* or *kari ifo si omofu*. But either way, it is unsuitable.

If we delete the unsuitable, cluttered and choppy words from these two poems, then we would have:

kusa fukaki	The horses are arrayed
uti no ofono ni	on the large plain of Uji
koma namete	where the ruler
asakiri nagara	has trodden down the grass
fumiyawakuramu	while in the morning mist.

aki no no no	I have oft stayed in
tikusa karifuki	a hut thatched with grass cut
yadorituru	from an autumn field.
uti no miyako fa	How can I ever forget
wasureya fa suru	the capital of Uji?

And in this way, the poetry itself now uses the style of poetry from middle antiquity on. Nevertheless, because there is no elegance, if one were to enjoy poetic composition by employing ornamental words, then he

26. Arimaro has apparently relied on a variant reading of the text. The standard reading of the last stanza is *kari ifo si omofoyu*.

would of necessity have to avoid these simple, sincere words from ancient days.

WORDS TO AVOID

As I have touched upon above, if one wants to preserve the elegance of a poem, simple and unornamented words must be avoided. Among these "simple words" are some that that have a complex accent, are cluttered or choppy. If it were not for this complex, cluttered, and choppy nature, poets would have continued to use these ancient words until now. Even with words used after the time of the *Kokinshū*, there are some that sound strange and thus should be avoided. These include words like *beranari* and *sika fa aredo*.

Let me say concerning all the ornamental words in poetry, that since these words are poetically used and have nothing to do with everyday life, they have no relation with laws or regulations. There are no poetic regulations such as: "Poetry should be read this way"; "Poetry should not be read in this manner"; "Poetry should use these words"; "Poetry should not use these." Therefore, no one is critical about what words are used or in what way poetry is to be produced. However, since we are talking about enjoying producing poetry by employing flowery words, there are standards about which words should be discarded in order to produce something of elegance, and this should be left up to the judgment of each poet. Now there is the danger that the budding poet will do as s/he pleases in selecting words, or the poet may lack judgment. Therefore, s/he should inquire and learn what usages his elders have chosen and avoided. But I am not arguing that the contemporary poet select poetic vocabulary in exactly the same way that earlier poets did.

Even now there are some words that, while not jarring, apprehensive, or tedious, should still be avoided. For example, in the five-stanza *Yakumo tatu* poem, *yakumo tatu* is used as an epithet for Izumo, and is an elegant usage. However, this is Susanoo's well-known "fence of Izumo" poem, but not only that, it is a divine poem, and a poet should avoid this kind of usage in the first stanza of his poem [out of respect for the divine]. From the beginning, no one would have hesitated to use it in the middle of a five-stanza poem, because it does not resemble any other poems. Nevertheless, based on the idea that one would avoid using *yakumo tatu* at the beginning of a poem, there is also a theory that a poet should avoid *sode fidite* at the beginning of a poem. Are they saying that Tsurayuki's *sode fidite musubisi midu no* poem[27] should be elevated [to the divine]? It is not *that* worthy. Theories like this are what I mean by improper judgments and should not be followed.

Also, there is the teaching of "forbidden words" among poetic scholars of the current Dōjō school.[28] For example, there are some twenty or thirty forbidden words like *kasumi kanetaru* and *uturu mo kumoru.*[29] It is unknown who was the first to name the forbidden words, and it is completely unclear what the limits of the usage of these forbidden words are. Words like *kasumi kanetaru* or *uturu mo kumoru* were popular in their own day, and many of these added vigor to the fourth stanza of a poem, and became the key element. And yet, when this phrase is used in the present, it is like stealing the glory from the person who first produced it. Thus, avoiding the usage of phrases like this can readily be said to be proper. These kinds of phrases should be avoided. But within these twenty or thirty forbidden words, words like *ame no yufugure* or *yuki no yufugure* are not key elements to new stanzas, and thus it is not proper to declare that these should be avoided even now. Also, words that form the key element of a new stanza within a poem of deep emotion should be avoided though they are not included in this group of forbidden words. For example, I am talking about phrases like sixteenth-century Sanjōnishi Sanetaka's *arashi wo somete.* It is up to the people of later times to decide whether phrases like this are to be avoided or not.

EMENDING ERROR THROUGH LOGIC

As has been noted above, the words that are used at the time of composition do not necessarily have to be words from a certain era. As long as the

27. That poem is:

sode fidite	Perhaps the wind of
musubisi midu no	this first day of spring will be
koforeru wo	melting the iced water
faru tatu kefu no	that soaked the sleeves of my robes
kaze ya tokuramu	when I scooped it up with my hands. (KKS 2)

28. This was a school of court nobles who took their name from the *dōjō* status, which meant that these people were able to appear before the emperor in person. This school of thought followed the Nijō school, and hoarded so-called secret teachings of poetry. Arimaro denigrates these poets because they stifled the tradition.

29. Fujiwara Teika argued that certain couplets should be avoided in poetic composition. This "list" was expanded upon by his son, Tameie, in a work called *Eiga ittei* (ca. 1270). An unknown hand reworked *Eiga ittei* to create a list of forty-four types of couplets that should be avoided by poets.

jarring, apprehensive, and tedious words are avoided, a poet may use words from ancient times or from middle antiquity. Chinese words and slang usages should be avoided from the start. Therefore, even though producing a poem appears easy, it is not. In other words, the possibility of completely avoiding mistakes within a poem produced by someone who does not completely understand poetics is rare. Here there is no need to correct the mistake by saying that So-and-So is the poetic father, or some other figure is the poetic founder.[30] The problem generally can only be corrected through an investigation into the principle of the way things naturally should be.[31]

Investigating into the principle of the way things naturally should be, for example, can be demonstrated with poems from the collection called *hyakunin isshū* "One Hundred Poets, One Hundred Poems," written on the paper screens of the mansion in the Saga Chūin and now enjoyed by women and children. One poem reads:

aki no ta no
karifo no ifo no
toma wo arami
wa ga koromo de fa
tuyu ni nuretutu

The mats of the roof
of the autumn storage hut
are coarsely woven—
the sleeves of my robes have been
completely soaked from the mist.
[GSS 302]

It is not clear what kind of unfounded stories the editors of the *Gosenshū* have passed on, but they have included it in the anthology, claiming that this poem was written by Emperor Tenchi. Is this poem written in the poetic style of Emperor Tenchi's day? We need not debate that here, as it clearly is not. Looking at *karifo no ifo* in the second stanza, why did the poet use these words? One theory states that *karifo* means "cutting stalks of rice," but there is no way that someone would construct a small hut out of cut stalks of rice. Another theory states that *karifo* is a temporary hut, and that 廬 "hut" is a double repetitive word. This is better than saying "cutting rice stalks." However, in ancient times they did not use repetitive words like this. These so-called repetitive words are like *akita kari karifo wo tukuri* (MYS 2174) or *siga no kara saki sakiku aredo* (MYS 30). The first *kari* above comes from "to cut," while the second *kari* means "temporary." Also, the first *saki* means "cape" [of land] while the second means "happiness." And

30. A popular figure Arimaro may be alluding to is Fujiwara Teika.

31. "The principle of the way things naturally should be" is a translation of 当然の理, which is a Chinese phrase 当然之理 from Zhu Xi thinking. It appears that the word was coined by Zhu Xi (1130–1200) himself, as found in his commentary on Mencius. See Huang (2001:185). Thanks to an anonymous reader who suggested this translation.

this is how the words are repeated, using different meanings. If the first *karifo* is "temporary hut," and the latter *ifo* is 廬, then we have the repetition of the same meaning. There is no known example of repeating two synonymous words. This type of stanza should not be used in poetry. Also, in the fifth stanza we have *tutu* from *kasumi ni nuretutu*. What does this represent? From ancient times, *tutu* has been represented by the character 乍 "while." So *nuretutu* became the word *nurenagara*. It does not make sense to have *nurenagara* modify the previous stanza adverbially. The stanza simply terminates. *Tutu* also has the meaning of "earnestly,"[32] but it does not make any sense to say that one earnestly wets their sleeves. In any case, this *tutu* is different from the particles *te, ni, o, fa*.

Also, there is the poem

faru sugite	Spring has come and gone;
natu kinikerasi	it feels as if summer is here.
sirotafe no	It has been said that
koromo fosu tefu	robes white like mulberry bark
ama no kagu yama	are hung on Mount Kagu.[33]

Because the second and fourth stanzas of this poem do not match the original poem in the *Man'yōshū*, the editors of the *Shin Kokinshū* either misread the *man'yōgana* of the original, or they altered the ancient poem, creating a new poem written in the style of the Shinkokin era. The fourth stanza is variant from the *Man'yōshū* [MYS 28], which is written *koromo fositari*; the phrase *koromo fosu tefu* is hard to comprehend. *Tefu* means *to ifu* "to say." When *to ifu* is run together, it becomes *tifu*, and that is why there are many *tifu* usages seen within the *Man'yōshū*. All of these are *to ifu*. After the *Kokinshū* era, all of these were written as *tefu*. Perhaps *tifu* became *tefu* because *tifu* did not sound proper, though they are based on the same pronunciation. *Tefu* seen in poetic works after the *Kokinshū* period all come from the original phrase *to ifu*. Making the fourth stanza *koromo*

32. Arimaro's text has また「つつ」といふにひためての心なるもあり, but there is no such word as *fitamete*. I have followed the NKBZ editors who see this as a mistake for ひたすら (Hashimoto et al. 1975:550, n5).

33. Arimaro quotes this from the *Shin Kokinshū* (175), but a slightly different version is seen in MYS 28:

faru sugite	Spring has come and gone;
natu kitarurasi	it feels as if summer has arrived.
sirotafe no	Upon Mount Kagu
koromo fositari	the white robe is hung out to dry,
ame no kagu yama	white like paper mulberry.

foso to ifu in the *faru sugite* poem makes no sense. This means that the *Shin Kokinshū* editors did not understand the word *tefu*, and this usage [of *koromo fosu tefu*] is thus a mistake. The noble Minister Fujiwara Ietaka and others also read poems like *tuki ni fosu tefu fatu kari no kowe,* "the sound of the first wild duck when they say to hang things out under the moon."[34] Now there is the theory from the Nijō family that *tefu* was just a meaningless appendage, and perhaps the editors of *Shin Kokinshū* understood *tefu* that way. In any event, using *tefu* here in this poem is a mistake.

I have argued thus, criticizing things based on investigating things through the principle of the way things naturally should be. Even if Hitomaro and Akahito together were to praise a poem, and Tomonari and Tsurayuki were to applaud and glorify that same composition, if there was something that needed to be examined and criticized through the principle of the way things naturally should be, then the poem would still be inferior. Also, even if Hitomaro and Akahito were to mock a poem, and Tomonari and Tsurayuki shook their heads and condemned it, if there was nothing wrong with the poem, then we should recognize it as superior. In criticizing good and poor poetry, there is nothing as urgent as criticism based upon the principle of the way things naturally should be.

ORTHODOX COURT POETS

In spite of this urgent need, high court nobles presently do not discuss things based on the principle of the way things naturally should be, but only engage in silly discussion on simple and complex rhythm within poetry, desiring complete simplicity within their own verses. To these courtiers, a simplistic style means a weak rhythm, while strong means a complex, inelegant style. These poets consider a poem with a strong style and weak rhythm to be the apex of artistic poetry. However, as they suggest, if it is difficult to produce such a poem, then it is better to produce a weak, simplistic poem. So who was the first person to use the phrase "mainly earnestly weak"? Looking at the high court nobles of today, we see that two or three of them will produce a powerful, error-free poem. But the remaining twenty or thirty poets idly make weak poetry their objective. Upon looking at the poetry produced by these poets, we find that it lacks aesthetic elegance, weak like the branches of the weeping willow. What

34. No such poem is known of in the present.

pleasure is there in producing this kind of poetry? Even though I have a stubborn and opinionated sentiment, this type of verse—written on the spot as soon as the brush has been put into the hand of the poet—numbers in the hundreds. Nevertheless, sometimes these poets who idly engage in producing weak poetry will produce a powerful poem, and then they will declare, "This is written in the style of the commoner! It isn't a poem!" "This is *haikai*! This isn't poetry!" And people who hear this, not knowing that their own poetry is superior to these courtiers, sit and think, "I'll never be able to attempt *good* poetry like the people of the Dōjō school." And these people then have no doubts with which to begin debating about poetry. If it is said that things that only look like poems are not poetry, then they cannot use the principle of the way things naturally should be to criticize the superiority of poetry. They do not develop their argument that far, and this is how the majority of the high court nobles who recklessly use the title *dōjō* are revered by the commoner.

The difference between high court noble and low courtier (now the so-called commoner) was originally decided by the courtier's post. Before middle antiquity, when the court noble actually had tasks to perform, low-ranking courtiers, though they were not called "high court nobles," had access to the palace chamber as hall men or workers in the Ministry of Central Affairs. Also, the eight ministers (starting with the minister of ceremonies) were called high court nobles, but they did not have the privilege of entering the palace chamber without imperial permission. Those who entered the palace were not necessarily highly respected men. Also, it is not necessarily true that those who could not enter the imperial presence were commoners, either. For example, it was like the simple distinction of private and public between the various servants of the military class. Thus, Great Minister Arihira[35] was only allowed into the imperial presence a total of six times in his life. Of these six times, one was as a Chūnagon and one as a Dainagon when Minister Minamoto Shigemitsu was a councilor. These two times are also seen in the popular text of *Kinpishō*. But down to the present, those who had access to the palace chambers always had their children introduced into the imperial presence, and these were called the families of the Dōjō. Those who were denied access to the palace chambers naturally could not gain access for their children either, and these became the *jige*.[36] The manner in which the courtiers of the Dōjō look down upon the *jige* is harsher in nature than how freemen view bondsmen. The chil-

35. Fujiwara Arihira (891–969).

36. Low-ranking officials, who later had the same status as commoners.

dren of the Dōjō who have no title and no post treat *jige* of the same status as shogun or feudal lords with the third rank or higher as if they are their own servants. And the title of *jige* itself is looked down upon as if the holder is not even human. Exactly in which book of amendments to the codes is the enactment of this distinction recorded?

Moreover, because these courtiers do not know about the origin of poetry, they label poetry a product of the Dōjō, which is beyond the comprehension of the *jige*. The distinction of *dōjō* and *jige* is a product of a later era, but even if it came from ancient times, how should we then look upon Hitomaro and Akahito, who are revered as the fathers and founders of poetry? Even though *Man'yōshū* does not record Hitomaro's rank, we know that he was perhaps in the ranks of the secretaries, clerks, or messenger boys of the government in the province of Iwami. Since his death is written with the character 死 instead of 卒,[37] it is clear that his status was below that of the sixth rank. Akahito's rank is not recorded in *Man'yōshū* either. If he held status above the fifth rank, his appointments would have been seen in the national histories. If his appointments are not recorded because he lived before the era of the histories, at least his death would be seen in *Shoku Nihongi*[38] if he held the fourth rank or higher. Since we do not see Akahito's name anywhere, even if he was of the fifth rank, he never made the fourth rank. Therefore, both of these poets were either low-ranking courtiers, or people of no rank at all. And even among the compilers of the *Kokinshū*, we see Ōshikōchi Mitsune, a minor clerk in the government of Kai, and Mibu Tadamine, an assistant guard of the Right Gate. Are not both men of the lowest ranks of the court? How can it be said that low-ranking people should not attempt poetry? Also, the distinction between *waka* and *haikai* is in the emotions being sought after, not in the words themselves. You can see this by looking at the *haikai* sections of the *Kokinshū*. Do the high court nobles fail to comprehend the structure of *haikai*? Whenever they see a poem with any vitality, they label it *haikai*, because it does not resemble their own poorly composed verse.

---

37. According to Article 15 of the Statute on Mourning and Funerals in the Yōrō codes, the deaths of certain classes of people were to be recorded with different verbs. When the ruler, or a divine entity, has passed away, he is said to have "divinely departed" (崩 *kamuagaru* "divine-rise up"). Royal princes and courtiers of the third rank or higher are said to have "passed away" (薨 *kamusaru* "divine-leave" or *miusu* "lose one's body"). Courtiers of the fifth rank or higher are said to have "expired" (卒 *mimakaru* "body-retire"), while those below the fifth rank down to commoners have simply "died" (死 *sinu* "die").

38. Compiled around AD 797 after being reedited. It covers the years from AD 697 till 791. Akahito's death is unknown, but it is believed he died around 736–40.

ANCIENT LEARNING

It is not true that one cannot compose poetry without knowing about ancient verse. However, without some understanding of ancient poetry, a poet becomes like a man standing before a high wall [he is unable to learn, unable to progress], being in the worst possible position. Studying ancient poetry is called *kagaku,* "poetics." As our country's examination system weakened, poetry flourished, imperial-ordered anthologies were compiled, and the national histories came to an end. Therefore, originally it was exceptional that a person who amused himself with poetry was talented in Chinese literature. Thus, poetics was considered a trifling field of learning, and there was no one who carefully dealt with the origins of poetry.

There is nothing older than the *Man'yōshū* among poetic collections.[39] A person's studies cannot be called poetics without studying *Man'yōshū.* Because it contains poems written up to New Year's Day of AD 759, we know roughly about the date of compilation, and it is also clear that Ōtomo Yakamochi compiled these poems because it is recorded inside the work. However, we see the following recorded in Book 18 of the *Kokinshū,* "During the reign of the Jōgan Emperor [Seiwa], the question was asked, 'When was *Man'yōshū* compiled?' Fun'ya Arisue then produced the following poem in reply,

kaminatuki	This is an ancient work
sigure furi okeru	coming from that palace whose
nara no fa no	name is the same as
na ni ofu miya no	the *nara* tree whose leaves
furugoto zo kore	are drenched in the tenth month."

[KKS 997]

Thus, did even Emperor Seiwa fail to read the *Manyōshū*? Even if he had read it, since he did not know who compiled it, could he have thought it a product of a later generation? And though Arisue gave his answer as *nara no fa no na ni ofu miya*, it is nothing but a vague reply. The capital was in Nara from the era of Genmei till Kōnin, and because this spans seven reigns, Emperor Seiwa should have asked in what imperial reign was the work compiled. When we look at the *Kokinshū* prefaces of Tsurayuki and

39. It seems clear that he is basing his argument on the fact that *Man'yōshū* is the oldest *extant* collection. The *Man'yōshū* itself mentions Yamanoue no Okura's lost *Ruijū Karin*, and other older works called *Kokashū,* "Old Poetic Collection," which predated the anthology.

Yoshimochi,[40] we see that the names Heijō Palace and Emperor Heizei have been confused, and have become "the reign of Emperor Heijō." As the Kana preface states, should we take Hitomaro and Akahito to be figures from this vague Nara period? This is extreme nonsense. That is not the only blunder, but we also see *chōka,* "long poems," included in the *Kokinshū* labeled as *tanka,* "short poems"; not only that, but even though the *Kokinshū* preface says that the compilers selected poems that were not included in the *Manyōshū*, we actually find *Man'yōshū* poems in the work! Because the sentence in the Kana preface that mentions that Hitomaro and Akahito lived during the reign of Emperor Heizei does not agree with the Mana preface, and makes Hitomaro of the third rank, it is probably a later interpolation. It is impossible to infer whether the inclusion of *Man'yōshū* poems in the *Kokinshū* is also a later addition or not; however, the mistakes about the *Man'yōshū* being a product of Emperor Heizei's reign and calling a *chōka* a *tanka* cannot be ignored. Therefore, we conclude that even Tsurayuki did not read *Man'yōshū*, and even if he had, he could not have understood it.[41] How very strange.

After that, up to the reigns of Emperor Gotoba and Tsuchimikado [when Minister Teika appeared on the scene], down to the present, court poets have revered Fujiwara Teika—for some unknown reason—as the poetic sage. But we do not see where Teika learned about poetics. This means that like the Jitō poem mentioned earlier, Teika has not fully comprehended ancient poetry. We see mistakes in the use of ancient words in Teika's poetry and writings. Because there is much work still to do, I ignore any examples of these mistakes. But let me say the Japanese sounds of *o* and *wo*, *we* and *e*, *i* and *wi,* are different sounds. And the sounds that occur as suffixes or particles, like *fa* and *wa* are not the same. *Fi* is not the same as *i* or *wi. Fu* is not the same as *u*. And *fe* is not the same as *we* or *e. Fo* is different from *o* and *wo*. These kinds of syllables are never once confused in the twenty or thirty times that they appear in *Kojiki*, *Nihon shoki,* or *Man'yōshū*. What is informally called *kanazukai* is extremely accurate. Since *Kokinshū* is written in *hiragana*, and the scribes who copied the text were not careful in their copying, we now cannot tell exactly what the character content in the original text was.[42] However, we do not see one poem that misuses a

40. Referring to both the *kana* and *mana* prefaces.

41. Arimaro brings up an important point here, because a careful look through *Kokin waka rokujō* (ca. 950), which contains a great deal of *Man'yōshū* poetry, appears to have been an easy-to-read version of popular poems from *Man'yōshū* that Tsurayuki and his Pear Jar circle may have studied.

42. This is criticism aimed at Teika's attempt to regulate earlier spellings. Arimaro is as-

character. Teika [clearly] had read *Man'yōshū*, but he does not appear to have taken notice of its consistency in *kanazukai*. Thus, we see many mistakes of *kana* usage in the texts that he has left. The worst examples are writing plum (*ume*) as *mume*, and horse (*uma*) as *muma*.[43] And sometimes in his poetry there are poems with mistaken characters. But later people revered Teika, and made his incorrect usages the standard. People who sometimes notice that Teika's usage does not follow that of *Kojiki*, *Nihon shoki*, or *Man'yōshū* think that anciently there were no rules for the usage of certain characters, and that this standard started with Teika. Because people negligently revere Teika, we now have this type of great inaccuracy. Because people do not understand character usages, they always misinterpret the old poems or old words. We must remember that Teika did not understand poetics. Not only that, but later people forged works in Teika's name, and these contain hideous lies. Most people, however, do not expound upon which works are genuine or fraudulent. Teika has been recklessly revered for several hundred years, and even his words have been used as evidence for arguments, more so than the national histories and poetic works like the *Man'yōshū*; people do not realize that they need to research into the periods before Teika. And this is the reason why poetics is not conducted properly in the present.

Time passed, and we come to the recent past, when there occurred a movement called *Kokin denju*.[44] In order to understand a text, there is no other method than searching for exemplification and comparisons of usages, along with adding some of your own intellectual work as required. Thus, there should be no such thing as secret teachings in poetry. And what is more, *Kokinshū* is just one anthology among many, so why should it have been compiled with some ulterior motive? And even after middle antiquity, there was no such distinction within poetics as "instructions to

---

tute to notice that Teika's main error was in selecting a text that still did not make a consistent contrast between many of these syllables.

43. The word *muma* appears in MYS 4372. Since both horse and plum are believed to have come from China or Korea, the original pronunciation is hard to ascertain. However, Arimaro's thesis and criticism must be taken with a grain of salt, though the basic charge is correct.

44. Some students were taught secret interpretations relative to *Kokinshū* poems by their masters. These teachings were transmitted orally, or sometimes on strips of paper, in an attempt to prevent wider circulation. These teachings tended to focus on commentary regarding the interpretation of difficult words and minute grammatical points in *Kokinshū* poems. Over time these teachings devolved into insipid debates about minute details of some poems.

understand the *Kokinshū*."[45] Perhaps this tradition is based upon a fraudulent work of Tō no Tsuneyori[46] later spread by the poet Sōgi.[47] Sōgi, who is said to have inherited the *Kokin denju*, produced a commentary on the commentaries of *Ise monogatari*, *Hyakunin isshū*, and *Eiga taigai* by Hosokawa Yūsai[48] and also wrote a commentary on *Kokinshū*. But there is not a comment among Sōgi's that is worthy of praise. His commentaries are entirely ignorant and shallow, and it is clear from a quick glance at them that we need not trouble ourselves arguing about a reckless belief in unfounded theories. The reader should look into these works himself, then he will see how those who have accepted these secret teachings of the *Kokin denju* actually know nothing about poetry! Therefore, even now, there are people who have talent, and though they are the children of the fathers of these secret teachings, they cannot be compelled to accept them, but want out of the tradition. Recently Konoe Iehiro[49] and Nomiya Sadatoshi[50] are two examples of people denying these secret teachings. Also, there is the governor of Chikuzen, Kada no Nobutsuya (a relative of mine). He served the abdicated emperor Goyōsei. The abdicated emperor was pleased that Nobutsuya was fond of poetry, and with the imperial brush he corrected several hundred poems of Nobutsuya's; along with this, he participated in discussions regarding these secret traditions about *Kokinshū*. These discussions and the corrected poetry are now at the house of another relative, Nobuya, governor of Dewa. And because of this, I have been able to listen to these secret discussions in their entirety, but because these events are of recent memory, I refrain from discussing these here.

Some people of recent history, or even of the present time, are erudite, and though there are people who do nothing but memorize the various imperial or private anthologies, it is regrettable that they do not concentrate their intellect on the ancient works. Because there is no criticism conducted on these ancient works, the current state of poets worshipping

45. This is a loose translation of *Kokin denju*.

46. Tō no Tsuneyori (1401–84). Originally a warrior, he lost his territory during the Ōnin civil war. He moved to Kyōto and studied poetry. He is said to have promulgated the *Kokin denju* through Sōgi. He was prolific and has left three poetic collections, as well as treatises on poetry.

47. Sōgi (1421–1502) was a Zen monk who later turned to *renga* "linked verse." He is known as one of the greatest *renga* poets in Japan, and because of his ability he had a large following. He also wrote commentaries on *Ise monogatari* and *Genji monogatari*.

48. Hosokawa Yūsai (1534–1610) was originally named Fujitaka. He spent most of his life as a warrior, and only during the latter years of his life did he devote himself to poetry.

49. Konoe Iehiro (1667–1736) was Sesshō Dajōdaijin.

50. Nomiya Sadatoshi (1702–57) was a minor official.

Teika is much like the high reverence paid to the belief in Zhu Xi learning, and people are not able to rid themselves of lifelong traditions. Because of this, poetics has not been enlightened even in the times of middle antiquity nor in our era. From the successive eras, only a few people like Fujiwara Kiyosuke and Akiharu have produced commentaries on word usage.[51] It cannot be said that these two mastered poetics, however. In recent times, a bonze named Keichū[52] from Ōsaka in Tsu has written a few commentaries starting with *Man'yōshū* and *Kokinshū*. And though there are a few areas in his research that are not well thought out, he has dealt with many old works, and has put a temporary halt to the old misinterpretations. Also, my stepfather, Azumamaro,[53] loved to learn about ancient Japanese things as a child, and in the end he produced many new theories, and corrected many of the faulty observations of poetic scholars. His opinions tacitly agree with some of Keichū's. There are differences and agreements, and yet they have never met each other. They have walked alone since middle antiquity. In spite of this, prudent scholars who hear these teachings accept them while the ignorant scholars reject them and try to interfere. If three people hear these teachings, two will reject them as heresy. Nevertheless, in this tranquil period, we live our days in flourishing civilization, and during these last few years, half the scholars have accepted the teachings of Keichū and Azumamaro, with people now copying the works of Keichū. There are people who find joy in this work and have realized that Teika should not be blindly followed on everything. The nature and essence of poetics is finally about to change; is this not exciting?

POETIC STANDARDS

Of those many eras between the compilation of the *Kokinshū* and the present, what era should be called the height of poetry, and who should be made the standard of poetics? Those people who trust the scholars of the

---

51. Kiyosuke wrote *Okugishō*, and Akiharu wrote many commentaries, such as *Shūchūshō*.

52. Originally named Shimokawa Kūshin (1640–1701). He changed his name to Keichū around the age of thirteen.

53. Kada no Azumamaro (1668–1736). He was one of the few followers of what later became Kokugaku who was an adept poet. He petitioned the shogun to open a school in which ancient works could be studied and learned. Though Arimaro was his heir, Kamo no Mabuchi successfully inherited the movement, because of the perceived victory of his refutation of *Kokka Hachiron*.

Dōjō school say that the present is the pinnacle of poetic style, and there is nothing left to add. However, this is because people believe that they cannot produce poetry like the high court nobles; poetry in the present has neither wit nor style, so those concerned are not satisfied with it. Then there are those who take the *Kokinshū* and make it the standard of appearance and substance and the unchanging model. But my own unworthy opinion is that the time of *Kokinshū* has passed, and I see it as anything but flourishing. Many scholars view the *Shin Kokinshū* as overexcelling in elegant expression and weak in substance.[54] Nevertheless, flowery phrases originally esteemed the blossoms, and literature values beauty. But I cannot understand the phrase "overexcels in elegant expressions." I believe the pinnacle of poetry is that found in *Shin Kokinshū*. But since this is my own personal opinion, we should not call on others to conform to it.

When we criticize ancient poets, we should not force our opinions on others either. The poetry of Hitomaro and Akahito is like specially selected beautiful blossoms from their own era. Upon comparison, we see that their own blossoms are excellent, but we should not use these as a standard for today. Tsurayuki is truly a rare gem of wit and style. But since his time was still relatively close to the ancient period, we find that though his substance is superior, his style is lacking. Now, if one produces poetry like Tsurayuki, it cannot be said that this is the art of perfection. On the other hand, every poem of the Regent Yoshitsune[55] is superior, and every stanza is like gold. Upon reading the feeling of the poem, the listener is instantly pierced with emotion, and he feels as if the scenery being described is floating before his very eyes. The style is elegant and has vivacity to the very end, with the stanzas flowing together smoothly. There are no gaps in the stanzas. In reality, this is the epitome of ornamental versification, but because people have spent so much time worshipping Teika, Yoshitsune's poetry is ranked below Teika's. Which of Teika's poetry is excellent and profound? Which of his poems are extremely well done? This should be examined. When people engage in Utaawase,[56] and Teika's and Yoshitsune's poems are compared, more of Teika's poems lose than Yoshitsune's. When Yoshitsune is compared with his father, Toshinari,[57] there are weaknesses. My own private

54. Meaning that *Shin Kokinshū*, like the blossoms of the trees, is beautiful, but weak in lasting substance.

55. Fujiwara Yoshitsune (1169–1206). He has seventy-nine poems in the *Shin Kokinshū*. He was minister of the left, and then Dajōdaijin. He was renowned as a poet.

56. An entertaining, almost sportslike event where two poems from differing poets are compared and their merits and demerits are debated.

57. Fujiwara Toshinari (1114–1204). A famous poet of the late Heian era. He compiled

opinion is that Teika is far from being above Emperor Gotoba or Minister Ietaka. And because it is my own opinion, it should not be forced upon others. It is only that a person believes what he feels, and I believe and follow what I feel.

You should not force people to follow you in relation to the style of poetry. During the time of Teika, emphasis was placed on Toshinari's flowing elegant style, Ietaka's four-stanza poetry, and Saigyō's[58] flowing rhythm; the style of each of these three men varies greatly. However, all of these men were elegant and superior poets, and should be respected even now. If you take Toshinari's style as wonderful, then must we conclude that Ietaka's and Saigyō's is not? Or if you take Ietaka's style as your model, does that make Toshinari's and Saigyō's unworthy? And making Saigyō the standard yields the same problem. Style is what a person delights in. Recommending my own preferences to someone else is like a lover of wine forcing his wine on someone who does not drink.

Written on the fourth day of the eighth month of Kanpo 2 [1742]. I have written the thoughts of my heart upon the request of a friend.[59] Being hastily written, and lacking a chance to reread it, I will attempt to make corrections at a later date.

Kada no Arimaro
[NKT 7:81–98]

©

the anthology *Senzai wakashū* (ca. 1188). He was one of the most famous poets of the time, with thirty-five poems in *Kinyō wakashū*, eleven in *Shika wakashū*, thirty-seven in *Senzai wakashū*, and seventy-two in *Shin kokin wakashū*.

58. Saigyō (1118–90). A very skilled poet. His private poetical collection is called *Sankashū*.

59. Tayasu Munetake (1715–71) was the second son of Tokugawa Yoshimune. He was an influential poet and gave Mabuchi much-needed financial support.

KOKKA HACHIRON YOGON SHŪI

Kamo no Mabuchi | 1742

[After Arimaro had written his honest feelings about poetry, Tayasu Munetake wrote his own rebuttal, and then invited Mabuchi to contribute his ideas to the debate. Mabuchi produced this response in 1742. The current manuscript we have appears to be a draft, as it does not conclude as a completed manuscript should. For example, it only contains seven treatises instead of eight. Mabuchi's ideas mirrored those of Munetake, and he argued that poetry constituted "a Way," which allowed students to be schooled and molded, making government easier. Mabuchi argued that poetry accomplished this in three ways: one, people become governable through poetry's power to change behavior; two, poetry creates a window through which a ruler can know the hearts of the people; three, poetry provides a vent for pent-up emotions. With this, Mabuchi defeated Arimaro who then lost his employment with Munetake. Mabuchi took Arimaro's place, and this essay marked Mabuchi's rise in prestige and authority.]

THE ORIGIN OF POETRY

The preface to *Kokinshū* records that poetry originated from the time that heaven and earth were created. This refers to the event in *Kojiki* where Izanagi said, "What a beautiful maiden," and then Izanami replied, "What a delightful lad." Though we cannot look upon these first divine words as poetic, in one of the variant quotes in *Nihon shoki*, we see the characters 唱和 "bid and reply poetically." It appears that the *Shoki* compilers considered this some form of poetry. Tsurayuki appears to have followed *Nihon shoki*'s reasoning.

In *Kojiki*, when Emperor Jinmu asks for Princess Isukeyori's hand in marriage, the poem produced between this princess and Ōkume has no ornamental words, with only three stanzas and an irregular meter.[1] And in the reign of Emperor Suinin[2] as recorded in the same work, the record says,

1. Poem KJK 17. The poem is as follows:

ametutu	Like the swift,
tidori ma sitoto	the wagtail and the plover:
nado sakeru tome	what big eyes you do have.

2. This song actually appears in the Keikō section, not Suinin.

fasikeyasi	How delightful!
wagife no kata yo	Clouds are on the horizon
kumo itati ku mo	in the direction of home.

[KJK 32]

This is a fragmentary poem.

From these types of poems, we can infer that during the [early] era of men, the ancient Japanese labeled this type of poetry "fragmentary poems."[3] The poetic vocabulary was plain, since the poet sang what he felt in his heart. Poetry in the beginning of time had few words. Thus, shall we not call the honorable words mentioned above [from Izanagi and Izanami] the origin of poetry? These are my personal feelings.

Now, in poetry there are epithets at the beginning of a poem like *yakumo tatu idumo yafegaki*.[4] There are stanzas employing allegorical phrases like *ana tama waya mitani futa watarasu*.[5] There are stanzas that compare the subject with something else, like *famatu tidori yo*.[6] And some stanzas continue on like *okitudori kamo tuku sima*.[7] Taking this all into account, we should say that these are the first songs seen in the ancient poetic anthologies, but I find it difficult to call these poems the origin of Japanese poetry. There are many poems from the era of Emperor Jinmu onward composed by various people that appear older than some of the poems in the divine age, and though I have my doubts, it is wiser to leave the debate as it is without attempting any conjecture.

Poetry was sung. As far as singing, it was proper to have rhythm consisting of five and seven syllables. Most Chinese as well as Japanese poetry follow this pattern. Now, much of ancient China's poetry consisted of four-character stanzas. In Japan, much verse originally contained a rhythm of four syllables. When the poet draws out his voice in singing, he guides his voice through inhalation. This preserves the rhythm of five and seven syllables. With the *Yakumo tatu* poem, one does not need to arrange his voice to preserve the 5–7 syllable rhythm. He can raise his voice as he wants and the meter remains regular.

Though it seems that this occurs without any conscious effort, as I

3. Jpn. *kata uta*, literally "part of a poem." These were generally the first or last half of a poetic sequence, though it is possible this is an archaic poetic form that was later categorized based on a newer standard.

4. KJK 1. "Endowed with power, this double Izumo fence."

5. KJK 6. "Like jewels strung upon a thread, he crosses over two valleys."

6. NS 4. "Ah! The plovers on the beach."

7. NS 5. "Birds in the offing, ducks gather on the island."

stated above, one cannot make proper connections between the stanzas without great mental effort. By the era of Emperor Jinmu, poems employing allegorical imagery turned into *chōka*. Because of this technique, people composed what they felt. Perhaps this explanation will give the reader a better understanding of poetry.

THE SIGNIFICANCE OF POETRY

Originally poetry was the singing of feelings in one's heart. Whether the person sang to himself, or to another person, the poet sang with sincerity from his heart, using elegant words to express sadness or delight. In proportion to the poet's voice this essence of delight, sadness, or lamentation did not only soothe the feelings of the poet, but caused the hearer to feel emotion also. The general reason behind people's expressions is that while it tends to make the hearts of people submissive, there are few people where these feelings actually sink into their hearts to make them submissive. There are many instances in the past and present where a person listened to poetry, and there was a feeling of attachment without a depth of profundity.

Nevertheless, since immediate endearment means quick forgetfulness, the great organ of government naturally respects the uplifting of the people. Therefore, the sages in China who ruled the country debated about those situations where logic and precept did not penetrate, so they established music. Music was used in the home as well as at the national level. It changed the mind of the people and soothed their hearts. Those of noble birth have not seen or heard how worthy this idea is, nor about how the state of the world or country should be. Also, those above do not understand the human heart very well.

Zhuang Zhou[8] said that poetry enhanced human feelings. Poetry compresses the feelings of the human heart into one poetic verse. From this laudable departure, events and people within the world can be governed, so is it [poetry] not a wonderful act?

These meritorious and grand human feelings cover all creation and include all human desires for fame and fortune. There have been many people who have published works on diminishing this influence, but it is a rare person who has heard these theories and rids himself of these desires. This entity we call poetry will trammel these desires of the human heart. If one

8. Born 369 BCE, Zhuang Zhou's death is unknown. A contemporary of Mencius, Zhou was a philosopher who continued to spread the ideas of Confucius.

becomes too attached to poetry, however, then that person forgets about his daily duties he has charge over, leaves the inheritance from his parents for no reason, and oblivious to himself he even turns into someone who enjoys wasting time.

This is a terrible turn of events, but among the many people it is clearly a burden. Regardless of whether noble or base, these people are influenced by this practice, but if they would enjoy composing poetry, like the ancient poem says about putting one's hearts at ease, then the desire to fight over status and gain would naturally decrease.

Emperor Shun composed his southern song and ruled the empire.[9] He did not leave for the palace, but ruled from the Wei castle. This was nothing unduly outstanding. In spite of this, society abandoned the longstanding tradition of poetic composition for a time, and struggled over giving names to things that were especially wondrous; thus, in the end, even the homes of poets lost poetry they had received from previous generations, while other people continued to hand down the traditions of ancient events.[10] Yes, poetry is the seed of the heart and should be in every home. When we examine people who have abandoned poetic composition, we find that they know nothing about ancient things. These people have truly had evil designs since the beginning.

The works of Kiyosuke and Toshinari are also seen in the work of Kamo no Chōmei.[11] Teika's intentions are found only in things said by Koshibe Zen'ni. People born into these families were forced into poetic exercises so the tradition would not die out. Moreover, they hid the mistakes of their fathers, and there are many places where they have corrected their fathers' mistakes to deceive people. How can the people receive these traditions blindly? The people belonging to these poetic schools ignore these facts.

Concerning the great period of time when our country has been governed, there have been people from time to time who have enjoyed studying the ancient things and imitated ancient poetry, and their compositions are

9. A reference to the legend where Emperor Shun supposedly created a five-stringed zither. He then sang songs accompanied by this instrument, and sang about virtues such as discipline and loyalty. Thus, these virtues allowed him to successfully govern the empire.

10. Mabuchi argues that abandoning poetic composition not only causes harmony to vanish from among humans, but it causes people to look down on poetry.

11. Kamo no Chōmei (1155–1216). He was born the son of a priest at the Kamo shrine. His father died when he was rather young. Natural and man-made tragedies of his day appear in his most famous work, *Hōjōki*. It appears that some of Chōmei's work went up in flames with the capital in the great fire of 1177. Mabuchi here has reference to Chōmei's work, *Mumyōshō* (ca. 1212).

peerless. Nonetheless, a person whose soul lacks energy finds it hard to do anything for people. How can someone who uses this lofty practice [of poetry] avoid becoming a more sensitive person? Therefore, the ancient poetry of China also laid the foundation to teach the common man, and it is proper to produce poetry from this frame of mind.

While this is true, even one stanza, even one short *waka* is good if you have put your true feelings into it. In Japan, *chōka* was certainly written with the intent to teach, and some poetry in *Man'yōshū* tries to instruct people. If one poem does not contain your true feelings, then it accomplishes nothing, but this principle is far-reaching, and people who do not compose poetry realize this when they hear the poem. The proper form and vocabulary of poetry is difficult to regulate consistently. If you have the proper attitude when composing poetry, then is this not like the mind of the ancients?

If you preserve this mental state, then you will feel their feelings when you deal with ancient poetry. When you enter this path [of poetry], then you should try to adorn rather than amuse yourself with verse, as noted above. Your poetry will become great teachings, and this will develop into the ingredients for superior composition.

THE CHOICE OF WORDS IN POETRY

Poetry is not only for composition. Poetry is not composed carelessly, or even casually, and to do so will not refresh the person's heart. To compose poetry carelessly means the words do not flow freely from stanza to stanza. Thus, the poet must carefully choose his words. There are some words society believes are proper, and sometimes these are judged to be improper. It is hard to group these words into one standard, but when we look at the vocabulary contained in *Man'yōshū*, we find that people did not hesitate to speak things casually. The reason for this is clear. These phrases are like the babbling of little children. And the words flow together nicely. Since all poetry fits this description, we should accept that this was the condition of society in those days. And since these words sounded properly then, we must conclude that those words were viewed as proper in that era.

Are there not also words in this anthology that people in later eras felt were proper that the ancients did not? There is Princess Nukada's poem:

aki no no no	In the golden field cutting grass,
mikusa karifuki	we thatched the roof with it
yadorerisi	and spent the night there.

udi no miyako no	How my thoughts return to
kari ifo si omofoyu	that hut by the Uji Palace.

[MYS 7][12]

This poem also appears in *Shin chokusen wakashū*,[13] where the compiler changed the second stanza to *wobana (ni maziru)*, but this was a poor choice. The fifth stanza, *kari ifo si zo omofu*, does not grate on people's ears in the present. This stanza has nine syllables, and that has made it sound all the more elegant. On the other hand, I think that the ancient poets would not have composed it thus, writing *ifo* as "five hundred," but when a stanza like *akita karu karifo no yadori*, "the small hut where we stay while we cut the autumn fields" in *Man'yōshū*[14] is changed to *karifo no ifo no* "the small hut from where we guard the autumn fields" in *Gosen wakashū*[15] just sounds wrong. Some may think that this is merely a misspelling, but in *Kokinshū* there is the stanza *yamada moru aki no kari ifo ni oku tuyu fa* "The dew that lights upon the hut guarding the mountain field in autumn,"[16] and this refers to a small hut used to guard the fields during harvest. Therefore, anciently people were accustomed to saying *karifo*. There are many places in *Man'yōshū* where a line says one thing, but should be read by association; thus, though the word is represented with the characters 五百 "five hundred" [representing the word *ifo*], it should be read *fo*, as there are many examples where the sound *i* is nullified by syncope with the previous vowel (here *-i* of *kari*). And the verb *omofu* should be read *mofu*. In the poem in the Saimei record of *Nihon shoki* there is the stanza, *wakaku ariki to a ga mofanaku ni* "I do not consider myself to be young"[17] and *Man'yōshū* also has examples where *omofi* becomes *mofi*, so we know that the first syllable was often abbreviated, and a reading of *karifo si zo mofu* is proper.

When we hear stanzas like this now, they sound poorly written, but the ancients thought syncopated syllables as proper. In Prince Shōtoku's verse

---

12. A note affixed to this poem quotes from Okura's *Ruijū karin*, saying that this poem was written around 648. Cf. Takaki et al. 1974:13–15.

13. Perhaps this is merely a misspelling for *Shin gosen wakashū*, *go* accidentally becoming *choku*, but I have checked three surviving manuscripts, and all have the same mistake. It would appear that Mabuchi has reference to poem 316 in *Shin gosen wakashū*, which starts *aki no no no / wobana ni maziru*.

14. From MYS 2100.

15. Compiled around 958 by Kiyowara Motosuke, Fujiwara Koremasa, Minamoto Shitagō and others. The poem in question is 302.

16. KKS 306, composed by Tadamine.

17. NS 117.

contained in the Suiko record,[18] the stanza *ifiniwete* "starving to death," appears twice in the same poem, and the poem in the Kōgyoku reign reads *ware wo fikirete* "inviting me into the grove."[19] Many examples like this are also seen in *Man'yōshū*, where the poet abbreviates syllables when written phonetically. If we said it now, it would be *ifi ni uwete* "starving to death," which sounds very elegant. Because examples like this are different from the past, a later compiler wished to write *karifo si zo mofu*. Even if a poet thinks a certain word came from the ancient period, when he uses it in a modern poem, it belongs to the modern period.

Speaking of elegant words, there is little difference between words in middle antiquity and the present. And yet words like *fogara fogara* '"brightly," *medetaki* "splendid," and *beranari* "it is like" were later avoided. *Bera* came about in the early era, but there are people who did not use it because they did not like the sound.[20] *Fogara fogara* and *medetaki* are not really inferior when used for transitions between stanzas, but when one group finds them disagreeable people become stubborn. As I have thought about such an obstinate attitude, I realized that poets of later generations have composed very exceptional and skillful poems, and among them are some that sound interesting; however, since the poet has put these clever words in his poem, the listener knows in advance that the poem will turn out this way. In the end, the poem turns out to be trite, so one must be careful not to imitate this form.

There are many examples of poems using *kasumi kanetaru* "piles of morning mist," *uturu mo kumoru* "the moon that shines through the clouds,"[21] and *tuyu no soko naru* "the bottom of the dew."[22] In the era of composition, these phrases were very splendid, and reached a point where later people even designated them as forbidden words, but when you compare these phrases contained in these ancient, good poems, one gets a trite, tedious feeling. If a poet uses only these kinds of clever phrases in his poetry, versification becomes an impotent act.

The Kamakura minister of the right[23] composed a poem:

---

18. NS 104, known as the Shinateru poem.

19. NS 111.

20. Nearly all usages of *bera* in the early poetic corpus belong to male poets. It appears that women writers found the word to be grating to the ears and avoided it.

21. A new type of phrase using contradiction. This first appeared in *Shin Kokinshū* (ca. 1205) in poem 57.

22. First seen in *Shin Kokinshū*, poem 474.

23. Minamoto Sanetomo (1192–1219). He became the third shogun of the Kamakura Bakufu at the age of 12. He had a love for the culture of the Kyōto capital and was active in

mononofu no	Elegantly arranged,
yanami tukurofu	the fletchings in the quivers—
kote no ufe ni	Here on Shinohara
arare tabasiru	with my hand on an arrow,
nasu no sinofara	hail has come gushing down.
	[KKWS 348]

The second and third stanzas are taken from ancient poetry, but the sound is not harsh. The poet has done a wonderful job of composing a poem about the bravery accompanying those in battle who experience sadness. People in the present study transparent, worthless poetry, but do not learn how to employ the *kiratsu* style.[24] Looking through ancient poetry and following what you read will allow you to compose strong poetry as well as subtle verse. And though this style [*kiratsu*] is something poets employ seldom, with that aside, this poet [Sanetomo] enjoyed many forms, even the form in *Man'yōshū*. He did not rely only on *Man'yōshū* vocabulary [but used other types], and composed poetry tranquilly, and this attitude suits the ancient heart of Japan.

People in the present have heard many things that are rare; therefore, setting aside words in *Man'yōshū* that are very different from those in the present, people should mix vocabulary from later imperial anthologies in their poems. Cautiously learning to compose poetry in the ancient style, a person acquires two types of vocabulary and enjoys the familiarity of these words.

WORDS TO AVOID

Forbidden words and words avoided out of respect for the original poet is a philosophy that was not favored in the beginning because of the obstinate attitude of other poets, so tradition states that these words should be avoided in your own poetry. Among these forbidden words, stanzas like *ame no yufugure* "a rainy dusk," *yuki no yufugure* "a snowy dusk," or *towo*

---

poetic composition. A private anthology of his, *Kinkai wakashū*, still survives, compiled around 1213, but there is some doubt about its authorship.

24. This was a style taught by Fujiwara Teika. It was a form that demanded strict adherence to form and word usage, evicting a strength and dread. Teika's *Meigetsushō* says, "The *Kiratsu* style cannot be mastered except after great difficulty, but why should a student not be able to compose poetry like this after sufficient practice? He will be able to. It is simply too complex for a beginner to compose in this style" (Hashimoto et al. 1975:514–15).

no siragumo "a far-off white cloud," are the pearls of each poem, so you are warned not to use such a stanza in a new poem. Nevertheless, even if you should avoid all such forbidden phrases, what remains for you to express your thoughts in your poetry? There are too many forbidden words, and in recent years there has been a movement called the *Te-ni-wo-fa* tradition, which addresses the issue that the majority of people certainly avoid these forbidden words. I have heard something of this tradition, but it does not deal with the ancient use of the particles *te, ni, wo, fa*. Since this poetry is using a tradition five hundred years in the past as its evidence, there are many mistakes to be found.

Among these, phrases like *omofikiya* "I had never thought," *naka naka ni* "thoughtlessly," and *wa ga kofi fa* "as for my love," are not in the least bit difficult to comprehend. Anyone can understand these stanzas. And though the phrase *miwataseba* "gazing out upon" is readily apparent and should not be forbidden, it is important to remember that in ancient poetry it only meant to look at something, and the idea of a second, subliminal object being viewed is a later phenomenon. *Nagamureba* "staring at [something] for a long time" anciently was a usage everyone knew, referring to the act of staring silently at something for a long time. It is a mistake to interpret this to mean "look forward to the afterlife." This is also clear from the preface in *Kokinshū* which said, "viewing the lower leaves of the autumn bush clover."[25]

And placing *kana* at the end of a stanza is the same as *kamo* seen in *Man'yōshū*, it being the particle showing doubt, but also showing mourning. *Mo* is an auxiliary particle. The *kamo* showing mourning is what we currently mean when we say *kana*. This word came about in the Kōnin era (810–23). One printed manuscript of *Man'yōshū* glosses the Chinese characters 欲得 "wanting to obtain" as *kana*, but this is a mistake. The editor did not know that he could not use such a reading. Using *tutu* "while" to close a poem means the same thing as *nagara*, and is written in *Man'yōshū* with the character 乍 "suddenly," and means that two things are happening together.

For example, as you walk down the road you stare at something. This can be expressed as *mitutu yuku* or *minagara yuku*, because they mean the same thing. Originally, they were the same word.[26] Every word has a history, some deeper than others, and one should not judge a word by the

25. There is no such poem noted in the preface to *Kokinshū*, but it does appear that Mabuchi is making a reference to KKS 220. Cf. McCullough (1986:56).

26. This is one of the interesting aspects of Old Japanese grammar. Both Old Japanese

newest meaning. If you think about these words from the most important meaning, then the various other meanings will gradually become clear. Later tales that use flowery, ornate vocabulary were written by people who did not understand the lexicon and have made mistakes in usage.

The grammatical set *no-ramu* is a case in point. *Kokinshū* records:

fisakata no
fikari no dokeki
faru no fi ni
sizu kokoro naku
fana no tiruramu

On this springtime day,
when the celestial orb
diffuses mild light,
why should the cherry blossoms
scatter with unquiet hearts?

[KKS 84][27]

This poem's structure is supported from the beginning, and the auxiliary *ramu* is not interrogative, but means something like "Why?" This is used to show contrast between the upper half of the poem and the lower. The pivotal stanza [the third stanza] connects to the upper half with the particle *ni* (it could have been *wo*) and ends with *ramu*. In just *Kokinshū* there are over ten poems that use this kind of particle, most using *ni* and *wo* to connect the lower stanza to the upper, and then ending with *ramu*. Among these is the following:

wa ga mi kara
uki yo no naka to
nazuketutu[28]
fito no tame safe
kanasikaruramu

To label this world
"a world of bitterness"
is my own fate.
So why should I lament
the fate of other people?

[KKS 960][29]

The last stanza does not operate like the *no-ramu* in *fana no tiruramu*, *tori no nakuramu* "Why does the bird sing?" or *fito no ifuramu* "Why do the people talk?" because there is no connecting word between the upper and lower segments. The upper segment of the above poem opens with an interrogative and closes with *ramu*. There is naturally a feeling of doubt

---

nagara and *tutu* have the same meaning of "a parallel or continuous action" (Vovin 2005, 2:908, 916). This suggests that one of these is a loan, perhaps from the language of Paekche.

27. Translation from McCullough (1985:30).

28. One text of Mabuchi's has *nagekitutu*. Yamamoto Yutaka's text has *nakekitutu* (1942:12). I have left the poem as it is in *Kokinshū*.

29. Translation from McCullough (1985:210).

contained in the particles *te, ni, wo, fa*, and it would be improper to add a word of question here. Therefore, the reader should carefully examine old poetry, and when you select things to incorporate into your own poetry, do not concern yourself with avoiding certain words. Poetry is the vehicle of the citizens of the state, and having one or two groups of people control how it operates is highly suspicious.

LEARNING POETRY[30]

Aside from the sages, it is usual for a person to have only one gift. From ancient times, it has been viewed as evil to exchange one's talent with someone who does not have that same talent.[31] Nonetheless, in later eras, the status of certain families changed, and though they did not have a specific talent nor did they abandon their original station, these families usually went in search of something better. Among things they sought for, these families obtained one or two things especially reserved for royalty, they themselves being nothing but commoners. The lot of a ruler is to bless those below him. If the ruler were to become prejudiced, then one group would receive blessings, while the other group lost its blessing.

Therefore, a person surely would not be particular about insignificant avocations, but he should not abandon them, either. When I see endless debates, those people surrounding the ruler appear very wise. Among these people are those who selfishly think that the path of medicine is to help those people right before their eyes. And though these people cannot remain unlearned, the ruler of the people would never think about abolishing people with specific skills. So a group should not abandon its own station. It is much more so for the commoner.

Regardless that poetry appears to have no use in relation to things immediately before us [society in general], poetry spontaneously clears the fears of the human heart and soothes the individual. A person who employs these benefits assists the government, so why would someone fail to make use of poetry? Needless to say, if an important person likes poetry, then those below him will naturally like it. If those above compose verse by

30. Arimaro's fifth section was labeled "emending error through logic," a section dealing with the proper reading of poems and how to establish that reading.

31. This goes back to Hohodemi and his older brother, who each had special hunting tools. Hohodemi and his brother exchanged them for a day, but neither could catch anything. Mabuchi is thus saying that ancient precedent shows that exchanging (or coveting) someone else's talent is injurious.

using the vocabulary of the ancients, those below will also return to the ancients. The sages have said that if your words lack elegance, then virtue does not go far.[32]

If there are mistaken words employed in the poetry used now to spread the virtue of the ruler, then the commoner will become skeptical of the ruler. Because of this, the ruler of men should not worry about things. To clearly elucidate all the ancient words is much like obstructing the great path. Therefore, if these things were known to the commoner, would the ruler have the servant correct these things? If a base knave could obtain the Way, able to lead one hundred or one thousand people in its teachings, then one word from this wise man would be worth that of the mountain echo and its thousand voices. Does not the proverb about being modest include even these types of events?

When one learns the vocabulary of ancient poetry, he should make his heart his master, and since the feelings of one's heart become clearer when put into words, a person who has studied the ancient poetic lexicon will see his own feelings much more clearly. While the world is ruled by reason and grows closer to that logic, people's countenances appear to show signs of obedience, but they are not obedient from their hearts. If a person becomes familiar through poetry, then the people will follow without any lingering doubts. If a person wonders why this is so, it has nothing to do with a second sphere of reason that transcends the principle of the way things should be. It only deals with lofty and gentle feelings of the heart. And I believe that someone once said that poetic composition is infantile. This is exactly the case. No matter how wonderful an event, it is very unreasonable to force a person to listen to it. For example, if a person found it inevitable to send a poem and thought nothing of it, then the final product of such a custom would be viewed as childlike, as if a person had composed nonsense like someone who was puerile; nevertheless, he sent the poem because he was touched. Ancient poetry operated on this simple principle.

Later generations added ideas of logic and their poetry functioned like sermons. If the poet does not have a humble, gentle attitude, then he sounds as if his petition is nothing but an argument. A person should not learn poetry like this, for this is learning to quarrel.

---

32. A reference to a line in the Zhenglun-jie "An understanding of the correct argument" chapter of *Kongzi jiayu*, "If your words have no elegance, then [proper] behavior does not go far [does not penetrate into the heart]."

DISCERNING THE DIFFERENT ERAS OF POETIC PROSPERITY AND DECLINE

The respectful debate is clear. How many generations have passed since the reason was given that poets lost the original intention of poetry when they had poetic contests? After that time courtiers did not accept topics of beauty. In reality the teachings about establishing the Way of poetry clearly came from the thinking of men. From among these ideas, there were those who inevitably became obsessed with composing verse in poetic contests, and during the Kanpei [889–98] and Engi [901–23] eras, it was difficult for anyone to determine that such practices were detrimental. When we examine the gentle and sincere prose and poetry written by Tsurayuki, I do not think that the ancient Japanese feelings had weakened by that era. From the Tenryaku era [947–57] on, these original Japanese feelings began to weaken considerably.

Some poetry originally seen in *Man'yōshū* also appears in *Kokinshū*, *Gosenshū*, and *Shūishū*, but there are many mistakes in word usage, as well as in entire stanzas, but these are not all copyist errors. In *Gosenshū* there are blatant examples where poets have updated the word usage of *Man'yō* poems. Concerning poetic sages, there is a trend to label all sorts of strange things as "sages," and this custom came from China into our country in a later era. Examining the poetry of Hitomaro in *Man'yōshū* there is nothing that could be misconstrued as "teachings" in later eras, but the word usage does resemble that of later didactic poetry. Though poetry does not become teachings for people around the poet, there was no one before or after the era of Hitomaro and Akahito to lay the groundwork for the rules of this poetic Way, though it [poetry] was performed widely in society. So there is likely no harm in tentatively praising these poets as "sages."

Also, it is not clear whether it is correct to call Li Taibo[33] a poetic sage or not, but such appellations come from respect for poetry. Imitating the custom of calling Du Zimei[34] "the grass sage," the preface to *Kokinshū* calls Hitomaro a poetic sage. In reality, however, there were no people in the

33. Li Taibo (701–62). He is more commonly known as Li Bai. He is renowned as one of the great poets in China. He and his friend Du Fu took Tang era poetry to new heights, and this period is called the Golden Age of Chinese Poetry.

34. Du Zimei (712–70). More commonly known as Du Fu. He originally wanted to serve his country as a civil servant, and when this did not work out, he devoted himself to poetry. He ranks with Li Bai as one of the greatest of Chinese poets.

ancient eras who composed only poetry like Hitomaro and Akahito, because of the mysterious skill in their poetry. Because of this skill, elegant poetry increased in later eras, without regard for the topic in question. The use of the label "sage" is out of respect for the Way of poetry. This is clearly an argument about respect.

EMENDING ERROR THROUGH LOGIC

I wonder when I was able to collect paper upon which Master Mabuchi had scribbled down various ideas, things I unexpectedly came into possession of. Among these was this manuscript, *Kokka hachiron yogon shūi*. It was such a rare but pleasant event to come into possession of this manuscript, and I have recopied and corrected the text, and recorded the six arguments seen above. Lastly, I found the seventh heading, "Emending Error Through Logic," but there was no text below. I believe there was text here, but as far as I know, this manuscript does not exist anywhere else. When (and if) the text does appear, it must be added here. Also, I have thought about the fact that Lord Tayasu's[35] *Kokka hachiron yogon* consisted of eight themes, just like Kada no Arimaro's essay, meaning that this manuscript is missing two sections. Since this essay is done in imitation of the others, it necessarily should follow the pattern of "eight."[36]

[NKT 7:116–26]

ଓ

35. Tayasu Munetake (p. 68, note 59).

36. Thus ends the manuscript edited by Shimizu Hamaomi (1776–1824). For comparison, Mabuchi's later essay, *Kokkaron okusetsu*, has the first part of the text as, "The argument in *Kokka hachiron* is proper. Yet, I do not think that the meaning of *tuyu in nuretutu* in the poem Arimaro quoted is difficult to comprehend. And the issue is not just about correcting mistaken words. It is also a great mistake to change older words to [newer words] used in the present."

KAIKŌ

Kamo no Mabuchi | 1760[1]

[It appears that Mabuchi felt that *Kokka hachiron yogon shūi* served a different purpose than what he wanted his students to glean from his ideas on poetry, which ideas had matured somewhat since the Kokka Hachiron Controversy. Thus, he wrote this short essay for the instruction of his students. In spite of this desire, it is unclear why this manuscript was never disseminated to his students. Arakida Hisaoyu, a student of Mabuchi, worked to publish a variety of "draft" manuscripts that his teacher had written, but apparently had never distributed. In this essay Mabuchi instructs students how they can polish their innate "mirror" through the composition of ancient poetry, allowing their *magokoro* "true heart" to shine, and return to a paradisiacal past.]

PREFACE

When one climbs a high mountain and looks down upon the foothills, he can clearly see the bends in the peaks and the innermost corners of the valleys. But when one gazes up at a high mountain from a hill, it is hard to distinguish many features of the mountain. Here, I take the five discourses of thought concerning the study of antiquity[2] of my master, Agatai no Ushi.[3] This discourse on poetry [*Kaikō*] is still in rough draft form, and though I am not fully satisfied with it, it discusses the sincere and profound poetry of antiquity compared with the narrow-minded and constrained verse of recent eras. Realizing that we should earnestly follow the poetry of the ancients is like finding the entrance to the pass of that high mountain; however, scholars of late who follow the path of poetic learning[4] now teach that later poetry is better. Using this kind of flattery, they have discarded the ancient style of poetry.[5] How sullen and regrettable this state is, but

1. The end of his treatise mentions that the work was completed in 1764, but internal evidence suggests that the work was essentially finished in 1760, and Mabuchi only engaged in slight editorial work afterward, completing this four years later. I thus leave the date as 1760.

2. Those five discourses are *Kaikō*, *Bun'ikō*, *Kokuikō*, *Goikō*, and *Shoikō*.

3. Kamo no Mabuchi's scholarly name.

4. Pointing to the Norinaga school.

5. This barb is aimed at Motoori Norinaga, who disliked the *Man'yōshū* but was fond of the much later *Shin Kokinshū*.

nothing can quench this desire I have to tell the world about my Master's teachings; thus have we put this incomplete manuscript forward for publishing.

Seventh month of the twelfth year
of Kansei [1800], Arakida Hisaoyu[6]

KAIKŌ

How profound! How moving was the earnest and sincere heart of men in ancient times. Because the ancient heart was earnest, there were few tasks to be done, with few tasks there were few words. Because of this condition, when an emotion struck the ancient's heart, he would lift his voice and put these feelings into words to sing, and that appears to be the reason ancient Japanese called poetry *uta*.[7] This kind of singing was done earnestly from a frankness of feelings, the words having integrity, employing everyday, unornamented words in the song strung together without concern for connections, having no set pattern. With this, singing was simply the form of expressing one's feelings; therefore, anciently, there was no distinction between a poet and a nonpoet. Near the end of the reign of our distant, successive imperial rulers who have ruled endlessly for fifteen hundred generations, philosophies and vocabulary from Paekche and India entered our country and mingled with our realm's culture and language. Due to this, *magokoro* "the true heart" became wicked like the swirling wind, and the words themselves, too, have become corrupted and divided like the crossroads, overly complicated. Therefore, as we come to the present, the emotions and word usage of contemporary poetry, even ordinary words, are different from those of antiquity. What people now call poetry forces a *waka*-type image on the hearer, proposing a selected [restricted] vocabulary, imitating the old poetic traditions without expressing the real thoughts and emotions of the poet. The emotions contained within these poems are like mirrors covered with dust—nothing is reflected clearly. Or these poems are like flowers growing amidst pollution, their stamens fouled and sterile. It is filthiness for people of later eras to try producing poetry while

6. Arakida Hisaoyu (1746–1804). He was a priest at Ise Shrine. He joined the school of Mabuchi in 1765 at the age of twenty. He was greatly interested in *Man'yōshū* and wrote poetry in the tradition he learned from his master.

7. *Uta* "song," is related to the verb *utau* "to sing," and later came to refer also to the production of poetry.

their hearts are in this confused and polluted state. Should I then keep my mouth shut concerning this state of affairs while I grieve for the fallen state of poetry? Of course not.

Magokoro was reflected in the shape of the mirror Ishikori Tobe made for the sun goddess, and the undefiled language of Japan resembled the blossoms Idakeru created. All this has been forgotten. The sincere heart and undefiled language still exist today [preserved] in classical literature, but people have forgotten these things, having become accustomed to living in filth. People now exist in a state where they do not even know that their lives are polluted, and they have lost that natural ability to recall the past.

Truly, considering that heaven and earth continue unchanged, and the birds, beasts, plants, and trees have not varied from their condition in ancient times, then why should humans differ now from what they were in the past? So-called human beings are sadly troubled by arrogant wisdom, naturally learning wickedness to the extent that they fight with their enemies, and society declines. If a person believes this present condition of society is corrupt, why does he not try to return to the straight and sincere state of ancient times? People should awaken themselves and become familiar with ideas that resemble those objects from the ancient past in color and shape; like looking into the imperial Yata mirror every morning and coming into daily contact with the pure flowers of ancient times.[8] With this desire let us compose poetry and write prose in the same straightforward spirit, with the same natural beauty, as the ancients.

Because the body of man is the same as it was in the past, the more one tries to return to the past, the more he can polish the mirror of his heart, uncovering that which is sincere. Then the words of that person will seem as if they had come out of the thicket, being able to behold the blossoms far off on a high mountain—everything will be clear and undefiled. In all respects, people desire a revival of the past, so should we not change the idea of respecting the government of the sages[9] in which the ruler successively changes, and revert to the noble government of the unbroken lineage of the heavenly rule of the golden age? Is it proper to cherish the present that resembles a river cascading out of the mountains?[10]

Poets who say that we should determine the form of poetry by the cur-

8. Here Mabuchi is using two metaphors, where the Yata mirror is the heart of man, a reflection of what he thinks. The flowers refer to his words, a metaphor often used in Japanese poetry.

9. The Confucian (or ultimately Chinese) idea of governing.

10. That is, headed only downward.

rent style are extremely self-righteous. Thus, regardless that these poets are corrupt, the traditions of our land of the ancient *kami* are undeniably still there to be found, and those who long for the old ways are surely more than a few. And yet, when one reads the ancient literature of our lofty past, there is no erudite method for understanding them, like a path into steep mountains hitting a dead end. This is because the contents are deeply mysterious and boundless. Some of the contents of these works are like the spring moon passing through the misty sky,[11] while some are like various kinds of leaves blown together by the autumn wind.[12] Many people through the ages have become lost in the mists, embracing mistaken ideas, while others have been enticed by unfathomable, foreign ideas, forgetting what the state of our ancient country was like. Only ancient poetry composed by those of antiquity, containing the ancient words and emotions, remains unchanged, like the cycles of the moon and sun. And like the beautiful blossoms or autumn leaves in nature, the beauty of ancient poetry has the same effect on people in the past and present. If poets concentrate on the poetic style of the resplendent reigns located in the capitals of Fujiwara and Nara [the poetic style seen in the *Man'yōshū*], poets would gradually abandon and forget the current vulgar poetic style, which is like the hideously colored umbrellas of mountain woodcutters.

As time goes on, the more one reads *Man'yōshū* poetry, the more he is naturally impressed by it, and the realization opens up to him that the ancient hearts of the people were earnest, their words straightforward without the slightest taint of defiling, ornamental dust, their disposition lofty and masculine. After this, when one reads many literary works, in the end, he is like a man who has lost his way, crossing through deep mountains, finally arriving home to his village, or like a man crossing the deep ocean till he reaches his home. Life in this world is not a Way constructed from the ideas of men who comprehend the mischievous heart; society cannot be built up or constructed, forced, or taught. Society must conform to heaven and earth, and governed thus. It is the poetry of the ancients that helps us understand the reign of the divine age when the country was at peace. My poetry resembles theirs.

When I was a young man, my mother had many ancient poems in her collection. Among those poems were such like:

---

11. Perhaps a reference to *Kojiki*, alluding to the blurry image one gets when reading the mythological story, which was so foreign to people in Mabuchi's time.

12. Perhaps a reference to *Nihon shoki*, alluding to the mixture of foreign ideas among truly Japanese ones.

About Mount Kagu—

inisfe no
koto fa siranu wo
ware mite mo
fisasiku narinu
ame no kagu yama

I do not know anything
about ancient happenings,
but it seems a lifetime
since I have set eyes upon you,
Mount Ame no Kagu.

[MYS 1096]

A poem given to a son by his mother when he was about to be sent to China—

tabibito no
yadorisemu no ni
simo furaba
wa ga ko fagukume
ama no turumura

If there should be frost
on the grass of the field
where wayfarers bed,
with your wings, protect my son,
you flock of cranes in the sky.

[MYS 1791]

A poem written when a man's wife went to Ise on an excursion, and was there reunited with her Lord—[13]

nagarafuru
yuki[14] fuku kaze no
samuki yo ni
wa ga se no kimi fa
fitori ka nuramu

On this cold evening
with the falling snow
scattered by the wind,
does my beloved husband
have to sleep all alone?

[MYS 59]

A poem written by Ōtomo Tabito[15] as he was parting with a woman whom he had spent the night during his return to the capital from Tsukushi—

13. Written for the abdicated emperor, Shōmu.

14. Mabuchi's text has *tuma fuku kaze no*, which appears to be an emendation by Arakida. The original text has 流経　妻吹風之, and Arakida felt that 妻 "spouse" was a mistake for 雪 "snow." I have followed Omodaka's text because of his exposition of the verb *nagarafuru*, which means to "be blown about by the wind." Having spouse (*tuma*) as the object of this verb is difficult to comprehend (1983, 1:379–80).

15. Ōtomo Tabito (665–731). Most scholars agree the woman in question was a prostitute.

masurawo to
omoferu ware ya
miduguki no
miduki no ufe ni
namida nogofamu

Should I be wiping
my tears as I stand upon
the moat embankment—
this person who thought himself
someone one of dignity?
[MYS 968]

Topic unknown—

sita ni nomi
kofureba kurusi
kurenawi no
suwetumu fana no
iro ni inu besi

What anxiety—
only I have fallen in love.
Like the safflower
with its bright colored petals,
should I show my true colors?[16]

From a story—

aru toki fa
ari no susami ni
katarafade
kofisikimono to
wakarete zo siru

When we are together
I find myself much at ease
and I forget love.
When we part, I then remember
how much I long to be with you.[17]

A trip—

nagufasiki
inami no umi no
okitu nami
tife ni kakurinu
yamato simane fa

The isle of Yamato
is hidden in the waves of
the offing of the sea
with the beautiful name—
the sea of Inami.
[MYS 303]

afadi no
nusima ga saki no
fama kaze ni

The wind from the beach
of the cape of Nushima
on Awaji island

---

16. This is an unknown poem, though it resembles that in KKS 496. The NKBT editors believe that Mabuchi has dovetailed two poems from the *Kokin waka rokujō* together, poems 496 and 968 (Nakamura 1966:420). It is also possible, though difficult to prove, that this is a variant of MYS 1993.

17. From *Kokin waka rokujō*, vol. 5, no. 2805.

imo ga musubisi	is causing it to flutter,
fimo fukikafesu	that string my beloved tied to me.
	[MYS 251]

Upon reading these, my mother would say, "I am not educated and cannot comprehend the poetry you young people imitate when you compose verse amongst yourselves lately. Nevertheless, I find ancient poetry easy to understand, and it leaves a deep impression upon me. The rhythm is smooth, peaceful, and elegant. Why do you think this is so?" I pondered her question, not really agreeing with her feelings, but I thought there was much that was good in the poetry produced from hard work by these famous poets of later eras. Though we could not understand the poetry yet, I believed there was a good reason for imitating those famous poets of later eras. I held my tongue, and then my father came in and said, "Most people feel like your mother does. Wise men in the past taught that if a person wishes to study some subject, he should return to the past."[18] I did not comprehend these words right away, but I retired with, "I understand, sir." At any rate, the years passed, and I always felt that my parents said such things because they had never officially studied poetics. My parents have already passed away, but every time I read something poetic, I recall their words, and have asked my teachers the essence of many of the old literary works. With my limited knowledge, I then poured my soul into ancient poetry, and naturally came to the realization that I should make the ancient literature my model. And for a long time now I have been a champion of the restoration of ancient poetry. Thus, when I think about it, those arrogantly wise scholars who were my seniors were leading me into far-off, crooked, and corrupted paths. Even ignorant people, if they search candidly, can find the proper path to follow. People who do not compose poetry, like my father and mother, can differentiate between sincere old poetry and thoughtless newer verse, because they are straightforward. Now I finally feel that I have distanced myself from the *kami* of deceit.[19]

Starting one's studies of antiquity in an awkward fashion would prove to be unfortunate. When one learns a myriad of corrupted foreign methods,[20] then his mind becomes set, and he loses his original Japanese spirit. Afterwards, he will sometimes hear theories coming from the proper di-

---

18. An unknown reference. Consider that the following appears in *Lun heng*, "Why call a teacher a man who knows neither ancient nor modern times?" (Forke 1962, 2:77).

19. This *kami* is mentioned in *Konjaku monogatari* (vol. 27, story 42). He leads people into strange paths so they become lost.

20. Mabuchi has reference to Chinese or Confucian styles of learning.

rection, but by then it is too difficult for him to enter the sincere and undefiled path of a thousand ages. Figuratively speaking, it is like trying to climb a high mountain; one has to force his way through the thickets at the base of the mountain [in an attempt to find the entrance to the pass leading upward]. Then there are tree trunks and half-buried boulders that you must climb over. The climber is covered in sweat as he pants along the path, finally reaching the top. Having reached the top in this manner, the climber looks down at the hills, and can see to the ends of the land that he could not clearly see while he was climbing. Now, the climber's heart is swept clean of doubts, and he feels as if he has seen the whole world in a different light. Nevertheless, it is the tendency of the human heart to be dissatisfied with being at the top. The climber wonders why he cannot go even higher, riding the clouds and the wind. He then attempts difficult theories and strained conclusions. If one learns the strange ways of the hermit, and feels that he has mastered these doctrines of learning, then the climber becomes proud of his distinguished accomplishments, and spends the rest of his life laughing to himself. At that point, he suddenly finds that though he had wished to jump and ride the clouds, he invariably must come back down to earth. He has wished to ride the wind, but everything has its limits. When one notices the mistakes in his own thinking, it is as if the climber has returned to square one, the base of that high mountain.

Now, when the climber's mind has become calm, he will realize how impulsive he has been. Upon reaching this point in time, it is like awakening from a long dream at dawn [to find that everything is clear]. At this moment, when one looks at the old records again and tries to compose poetry [in the ancient style], he finds that he has departed from that strange Chinese methodology and has returned to the bottom of the mountain. Now the person can think calmly again. When that occurs, one is able to realize that the heart of the ancient man was sincere and honorable. Thus, giving respect to this Way of our awe-inspiring imperial ancestors, one comes to an understanding of the heart and soul of antiquity that ruled in tranquility for fifteen hundred generations. And when you talk to someone who has studied the ancient history of China, you realize there were many sincere aspects about China before the advent of Confucianism. Nonetheless, when one has gone through this long process, he finds that he has but few years left to his life, and he is helpless. No matter how young a person is, he must have strong resolve, concentrating his energies on reading the ancient works and reciting the ancient songs, reading and writing in the old tradition. Then you will surely learn and understand the spirit of the ancients.

Man'yōshū now consists of twenty books, but the poetry we are sure Prime Minister Tachibana Moroe[21] selected and compiled consists of only Books 1 and 2. Also, the texts for Book 2 are fraught with mistaken character usages and incorrect readings for some of the passages. There is evidence to make me believe that Books 11, 12, 13, and 14 were compiled next after Books 1 and 2. The reason for this is because the names of the poets appear in these two books, and the poetry is composed in the court style. The poetry in Books 11, 12, and 13 consist of old poems written by anonymous poets, but we do know that the poets were courtiers. Also, because the sources for this poetry are titled *Anthology of Old Poetry*, I believe these sections to have been compiled by someone other than Moroe.[22] The compiler, however, surely did not compile one or two books of a known poet's poetry and then ignore all the anonymous poetry. Now, concerning Book 13, it contains very old poetry of an ancient, elegant style. Also, since there are many *chōka*, we can theorize that Book 13 was the third volume of the original compilation, and Books 11 and 12 were the fourth and fifth of the Moroe compilation.[23] Book 14 contains Eastern songs and many provincially based poems. Even in the ancient poetry of China there were songs in a provincial style,[24] showing that originally poetry was a form of communication from one's heart. With that as a pretext, why should the anthology only be arranged with poetry composed at the court when provincial poetry let the politicians know how the masses felt? Thus, someone compiled these Eastern songs and placed them at the end [in the fifth book] of the work. Ōtomo Yakamochi compiled the frontier poems now contained in Book 20, but Book 14 contains Eastern songs that are older than those in Book 20. I believe that this section was compiled after the fifth book, and these should be included with the fifth book.

21. Tachibana Moroe (684–757). There is a tradition that argues Moroe was one of the compilers of the *Man'yōshū*. Many once believed that he was the principal compiler, and Mabuchi is trying to correct this idea.

22. Many scholars take this usage of *kokashū* (古歌集 "Anthology of Old Poetry" as seen in MYS 89) as a proper noun. More likely, it is a common usage for what was probably a profuse amount of common poetry, something like "an old poetic anthology."

23. Mabuchi is proposing that what Moroe had originally compiled in five books was rearranged when *Man'yōshū* passed through the final stages of editing. Moroe died in 757, but the last poem in the *Man'yōshū* is dated 759, suggesting that final compilation was done after Moroe was dead. Due to the carefully arranged nature of Books 1 and 2, many suspect this part of the anthology to have been compiled under imperial auspices, something Moroe may have been able to achieve.

24. There were provincial poems recorded in China's oldest poetic anthology, *Shijing* or *Book of Ones*, in the first section, 国風 "folk (provincial) songs."

Also, Yakamochi compiled many of the sections after Book 3. Yamanoue no Okura compiled the actual fifth book [the current Book 5] of *Man'yōshū*. Books 7 and 10 are much the same, apparently compiled by the same person from private poetic collections stored at his house. From this, we see great diversity in the compilers and a lack of continuity in many of the books. Also, there are some offensive poems, poems lacking balance from beginning to end, and poems with elegant upper stanzas, but poor concluding ones. Therefore, if one wishes to use the *Man'yō* style as his model, he must carefully select his poems. Because this task of selection is difficult, it is no simple matter for someone to choose his model.

Only poems with a smooth flow, easy to comprehend contents, modestly elegant style, and sincere words from the heart should be selected. The student should automatically avoid any poem that is even the slightest bit hard to listen to or feels stifled. Of the forty-three hundred poems in *Man'yōshū*, there are many poems the student may select because of their clean rhythm.[25] There have been people who have not understand these concepts, believing that all the poems were the same as the various books themselves are, the entire anthology composed in the so-called *Man'yō* style. They then declare that this style of poetry was not suitable for later ages.[26] It was Kamakura minister of the right, Minamoto Sanetomo, who understood what I have discussed above, and knew the elegant styles within *Man'yōshū*. In *Kinkai wakashū* one sees poems from the early, middle, and later eras of poetry. The later era style found in this collection has been especially well selected, and it would be well for the student to imitate.

On the other hand, one should be careful of poems composed by women. Among the poems of the *Kokinshū*, Nara era poets composed the anonymous poems during a period after the compilation of *Man'yōshū* till the establishment of the capital in Heian. When the student studies these poems compared with poems composed in the Engi era [901–923],[27] he finds that these anonymous poems cover a broad area of subjects, and their emotions are elegant and rich, inheriting its clean rhythm and rich literary tradition from *Man'yōshū*; surely women composed these poems. Since men were brave and masculine during the era before *Man'yōshū*, their poetry was of the same nature. But during the era of the *Kokinshū*, men com-

---

25. The actual number of poems is different from manuscript to manuscript. Currently, counting every poem whether it be a repetition or not, *Man'yōshū* consists of 4,516 poems.

26. People like Kada no Arimaro were of this general disposition.

27. When *Kokinshū* was compiled.

posed poetry in a feminine style, and the distinction between male and feminine styles blurred. This means that it is sufficient for women only to study *Kokinshū*, but the Kokin tradition has declined, and now the feminine style has become such that poets are so interested in poetic devices that their literary expressions have become illusions; the style has naturally grown unpleasant, turning into an annoyance to the heart. We must learn about the sincere, lofty, straightforward hearts of the ancients by studying the time of *Man'yōshū*. The student may study about *Kokinshū* later. People have forgotten this human principle [sincere, straightforward hearts], studying *Kokinshū* as the model of poetry, but I have never heard of a person who could produce worthy poetry like *Kokinshū*. Also, there is not a person who deeply understands the essence of the *Kokinshū*.

When a person views the world from the bottom up, he cannot see through the clouds and mist—thus, nothing appears clear. If one obtains the method to climb to the top of the mountain, and grasps the proper methodology, then he can study about climbing higher. With this task accomplished, the student should then look at the bottom. As I have already stated, if you will look down at the world from a high mountain, you will see everything clearly. Even in the essence of things, the commoners find it hard to fathom the minds of statesmen, but it is easy for a statesman to understand the minds of commoners. What we learn from this is that it is good to proceed with one's poetic studies from the ancient eras forward. The people of China have taught us this in the past.

Written by Mabuchi in his old age
in the beginning of the Meiwa era [1764]
[NST 39:347–56]

ꕥ

MAN'YŌ KAITSŪSHAKU TO SHAKUREI

Kamo no Mabuchi | 1749

[This little-known work of Mabuchi's examines a variety of issues in relation to *Man'yōshū*, its history, text, and interpretation. It demonstrates Mabuchi's high level of skill and insight into diverse problems surrounding *Man'yōshū*. It is easy for scholars and students in the present to underappreciate Mabuchi's insight because we have so much knowledge at our fingertips today. In this essay Mabuchi tries to answer the question of authorship and also to guide students through orthographic and grammatical pitfalls by providing ample examples.]

[1] The meaning of the title *Man'yōshū* is "a collection of a myriad leaves."[1] The [Kana] preface to *Kokinshū* says, "Poetry takes the human heart as the seed, and produces a myriad leaves."[2] This is proof that the phrase *kotonofa* definitely is a reference to the two characters in the title (万葉). Again, in the Mana preface to *Kokinshū* we find, "People presented various volumes of private poetic collections along with old poems from long ago, and a work called *Man'yōshū continued*."[3] There is evidence of an anthology first called *Man'yōshū continued*, so we can say that both prefaces of *Kokinshū* have reference to the same work. (However, it appears that the Kana preface was created first, and the Mana preface was written later, so it is necessary to consider that the Kana preface has reference to *Man'yōshū continued*. I intend at a future date to argue that the Mana preface was written at a later date. Someone once claimed, "The title *man'yō* refers to a myriad reigns." While it may be true that there are many examples where 万葉 is used to refer to "a myriad reigns" in both Japanese and Chinese poetry, in this case it is a barren and groundless theory to say the title means this. If this later had been called *Man'yō wakashū* that would be one thing, but *waka* refers to Japanese poetry in contrast to Chinese poetry, and appears for the first time in Book 5 of the anthology, but here it appears to have meant "a poem written in reply." That is why I discard the theory

1. It should be noted that Mabuchi often wrote the word *kotoba* "word" as こと葉, demonstrating his belief that the anthology was a collection of leaves (葉), where leaves = words.
2. See McCullough (1986:3).
3. See McCullough (1986:258).

that the title means "a myriad of reigns" and claim that it means a myriad leaves.)

Concerning the time when *Man'yōshū* was compiled, Minister Teika says,

> In relation to when *Man'yōshū* came about, in recent years there are many theories among the poetic sages, and this results in fights and arguments [but there is no consensus]. Looking at internal evidence, Book 17 onward has the composition of a commentary, including the date of composition, the reason, setting, and other information. So Book 17 contains poetry from Tenpyō 2 [730] down to Tenpyō 20 [748]. Book 18 consists of poetry composed on the twenty-third day of the second month of Tenpyō 20 down to the second day of the first month of Tenpyō Shōhō 2 [750]. (From what I have been able to tell from my own inspection of the manuscript, this book ends with a poem dated the eighteenth day of the second month. There is a poem before this dated the second day of the first month of the second year of Tenpyō Shōhō, so perhaps Minister Teika did not see the last poem.[4])
>
> Book 19 contains a poem dated the first day of the third month of the same regnal period and ends with a poem dated the twenty-fifth day of the first month of Tenpyō Shōhō 5 [753]. (This must be a mistake for the second month.) Book 20 contains poetry dated from the fifth month of Tenpyō Shōhō 5 and continues till the first day of the first month of Tenpyō Hōji 3 [759]. ... In general there are many cases where we can figure out the date of composition of poetry, be it Chinese or Japanese, because headnotes are attached. However, it is a circuitous method to determine the date of composition of poetry by relying on the preface of some other work. Now, concerning the compiler [of *Man'yōshū*] there is no consensus. However, in *Yotsugi monogatari*[5] it says, '*Man'yōshū* was presented to the throne by Minister Tachibana Moroe in the reign of Takano. ...'[6] However, there are many poems included in the anthology that were composed after the death of Minister Moroe; perhaps Minister Yakamochi came into possession of these poems in some way.

This is a very insightful theory. If we follow *Shoku Nihongi* Minister Moroe passed away in the first month of Tenpyō Hōji 1 [757], but within the anthology there are poems dated the first month of Tenpyō Hōji 3, so these cannot be the work of the minister. There is also proof that [the last part of the anthology] is a private collection of Minister Yakamochi. Also,

---

4. The poem Teika has reference to is MYS 4136. It is possible that the last two poems of Book 18 (4137–38) were on the next leaf of the manuscript and Teika did not see this, as Mabuchi theorizes. It is also possible, though impossible to prove, that Teika's manuscript lacked this last leaf, period.

5. This is another name for *Eiga monogatari*.

6. As McCullough and McCullough (1980:79) point out, Emperor Takano was first called Emperor Kōken [r. 749–58] and later reascended the throne as Shōtoku [r. 764–70]. Tachibana Moroe passed away two years before the last datable poem in the anthology.

names of poets are not recorded unless they were of the status of major councillor or higher, but this standard is broken only for Yakamochi's father, Minister Tabito, who at the time he composed his poetry, was only a middle councillor, as mentioned in the headnotes. Among the twenty books of this anthology, there are poems by poets with humble titles, but there is not a single time when a name is given.[7] We find in the final books of the anthology the words "composed with my humble thoughts" only connected with Minister Yakamochi's poetry, using words of self-deprecation. I think based on this we can conclude that [the latter part of] the anthology is based on the private compilation of Minister Yakamochi. Especially from Book 17 onward there is clear evidence of this. There is also other evidence but I will address it later. In the quote above from Teika we find the words, "The anthology appears to have been annotated by Minister Yakamochi," but Teika never says that Yakamochi was the compiler. This gives one the impression that he might have believed the anthology to be based on a private collection. I believe that this provides great weight to the theory that *Man'yōshū* is based on the private poetic collection of Minister Yakamochi.

[2] In relation to this issue, Kada no Azumamaro said the following,

> Following the theory of Minister Teika, there is much evidence that Minister Yakamochi was the compiler of *Man'yōshū*. But my own thoughts are that scholars still need to examine the old anonymous poems and one or two more points in relation to who compiled Books 1 and 2, and Books 10 through 13, before we conclude that these were put together by Minister Yakamochi. It is plausible that poems from the private anthology of Minister Yakamochi were later included into an anthology originally compiled by Minister Moroe. However, the ancient definition of a "private anthology" meant that only poems composed by the poet were included. When Yakamochi was dispatched as an official to Etchū Province, he also recorded in his private anthology poems he heard about from the capital, so he appears to have recorded old and new poems in his private anthology in a chronological order, and when he reached his own period, he included poems he had composed. Thus, in *Man'yōshū* ancient poems appear first and then heading chronologically to the present he included poems of his own composition at the end. There is no problem with seeing Minister Yakamochi's private anthology comprising Books 17 till the end.

I, Mabuchi, heard about this theory, but because I was already convinced from the beginning that the anthology was the compilation of Yakamochi I did not pay any special attention. But as my research has pro-

7. This refers to the practice of people giving themselves titles or labels lower in status than the person actually held, which was a practice of self-deprecation.

gressed over the years, recently my thoughts on this issue have changed; I believe that the theory of Azumamaro is correct. Examining the overall makeup of Books 1 and 2 clearly this is the work of a different compiler. Books 10 to 13 appear to be a compilation of anonymous poems. Book 16 starts with poems written on specific themes, then next playful poems, but there is only one poem from Yakamochi in this book. Considering the context, there was only a few months in time between poems in this book and the next, so it is difficult to imagine he only composed a single poem. This part of the anthology was composed of playful poems, giving one the impression that someone composed this book, finding one playful poem from Yakamochi.[8] Thus, Book 16 also was the work of someone else. Perhaps it is the work of Okura. If it is the work of one person then the same poem should not appear several times, but based on the fact that we do see the same poem more than once, this makes me believe that Azumamaro is correct.

Adding my own thoughts, Book 1 originally was a compilation of miscellaneous poems, many of which were travel poems. Book 2 starts with Love Poems and ends with elegies. Book 3 contains miscellaneous poems, travel poems, allegorical poems, and elegies. If these were the work of the same person then the Yūryaku poem, the Jitō poem, and the other poems from the ancient period found in Books 1 and 2 should all have been placed within the same book. Thus, Book 3 should be considered a separate compilation. The anthology is not just a mixture of Minister Moroe's compilation with the work of Minister Yakamochi, but is a complex mixture of the poetic anthology of Okura and many other poets. A careful examination of the succeeding books of the anthology will make my point evident.

Keichū originally believed that "someone compiled this anthology from the work of Okura and other collections with the intention to make a great anthology, but some unknown event prevented the completion of the anthology, and it remained uncompleted." Aside from Books 1 and 2, the other books demonstrate evidence that a variety of people were involved in the compilation, so perhaps a poetic anthology from Minister Moroe also existed. There is no reason to deny the existence of the work of Moroe. (Even in Book 1, by the end there are many pieces of evidence suggesting that other people's poems were mixed in, or some kind of confusion resulted. There is still room to debate who Emperor Taikō refers to.[9])

8. Mabuchi's reasoning here is that if Yakamochi had been the compiler of Book 16, surely he would have had more than one playful poem to include.

9. Emperor Taikō first appears in the headnote to MYS 71. Taikō is a term used when an

[3] Concerning the difference between *Man'yōshū* and the description of the anthology in the preface to *Kokinshū* Priest Keichū has the following opinion:

We should listen to Minister Teika concerning the date of compilation of the anthology. ... The phrase "words in the preface" has reference to both the Kana and Mana prefaces of *Kokinshū*. During the time of the abolished emperor [Junnin, r. 758–64] and Emperor Shōtoku there were a lot of things happening at court, and the Way of poetry was in decline. Emperor Saga [r. 806–09] only had interest in Chinese poetry, and at court both princes and princesses diligently applied themselves to the composition of Chinese poetry, and the Way of poetry waned, and various strange theories cropped up [regarding the origin of *Man'yōshū*]. No one paid attention to this anthology. Later the Way of poetry made a comeback and people began to compose poetry again, and these people accepted these ridiculous theories without any serious investigation into the origins of the anthology, and even in regards to the answer to the emperor in the Jōgan era's question or the Engi edict of compilation,[10] important events that happened later, people left a record of vague answers [as an explanation]. Because the answers to these questions about *Man'yōshū* came from the great poets of the time there was no one at court who would doubt them. Later Minister Teika appeared and studied the anthology deeply, and put forth his theory as I have noted.

(After this Keichū presents evidence for this argument that Minister Yakamochi is the compiler, but I have abbreviated it here, because it is in most points the same theory as most other scholars.)

Keichū also said,

It is strange that during the fifty-year span from Tenpyō Hōji 3 [759] until the Daidō era [806–10] of the Nara emperor there is not one person or one poem included in any anthology. Also, even the poems from when Hitomaro left Iwami Province to head back to the capital as a servant of the court and later when he was on his way home, his wife Yosami Otome heard about his death and was sad, these poems are all included in the era of the Fujiwara Palace, so it is clear when these were composed. And of course the poem composed by Prince Hozumi when Princess Tajima passed away in the sixth month of Wadō 1 [708] also falls into this era. Emperor Genmei moved her capital [from Fujiwara] to Nara in Wadō 3 [710], so it

---

emperor has passed away, but has not yet been granted a posthumous title. Kamochi notes that this title points to Monmu [r. 697–707]; cf. Kamochi (1891, 1.6:79a).

10. This is in reference to the headnote to KKS 997, which says that the emperor had asked when *Man'yōshū* was compiled, and the answer was, "from the capital bearing the same name as *nara* oaks" (cf. McCullough 1985:218). Thus, the vague answer is "during the Nara era." The Jōgan era spanned two reigns, Seiwa [r. 858–76] and Yōzei [r. 876–84]. Most scholars believe the question was asked by Emperor Seiwa. The reference to the Engi edict appears to mean the compilation of *Kokinshū*.

appears they called that previous reign the Fujiwara era. If this is accurate, then the period when Hitomaro went to Iwami and then later died would have occurred between the end of Emperor Monmu's reign and the beginning of Emperor Genmei's reign.

I, Mabuchi, believe that Keichū must have believed that either Hitomaro's family was originally from Iwami, or that he was a gifted man brought to the capital from Iwami. But there is evidence in the anthology that Hitomaro originally was a court attendant to Prince Takechi [654–96], so it is more probable that he was from the capital. It would appear that he was assigned to serve in Iwami as a matter of official business. It appears that he shuttled between Iwami and the capital as a messenger with the rice tax receipts.

In Book 10 there are many *Tanabata* poems, and among these is this poem:

amanogafa	On the sandbar
yasu no kafara ni	of the Yasu River of the Milky Way—[11]

The headnote to this poem reads, "This poem was composed in a *kanoe tatu* year. These poems appear in a poetic anthology of Kakinomoto Hitomaro." This would appear to be a poem from Hakuchō 9 [680] of Emperor Tenmu, and there is some evidence that Hitomaro is still in Iwami and has not yet returned to the capital. Also, there is evidence in the anthology that there were other anthologies from other people involved, where an anthology is noted in the headnote with a name, but that does not mean that all poetry contained in there is from this no specific poet. People during the reign of Emperor Heizei [r. 785–806] wrote down the wild claim that Hitomaro served the courts of Jitō [r. 686–97] and Monmu based on other evidence without carefully searching this anthology. Also regarding the rank of Hitomaro, there is the idea that he was of the "great lord" rank.[12] In general there are two methods to differentiate between upper-class and lower-class. The usual one is that those of the fourth rank and lower are lower-class individuals, while those of the third rank and higher are upper-class. Hitomaro's rank is not recorded

11. MYS 2033. The final stanzas, 定而神競者磨待無, are of unclear reading or meaning. The full poem is:

amanogafa	On the sandbar
yasu no kafara ni	of the Yasu River of the Milky Way—
sadamarite	the *kami* are engaging in a contest
kami arasofu fa	to settle the question.
maro matu naku ni	How I cannot wait.

This is a basic interpretation to a difficult poem. I have followed Omodaka (1983, 10:255) who sees 磨 as scribal error for 麿 *maro*, a humble form of "I."

12. *Ofokimi no kurawi* refers to the senior third rank. This theory that Hitomaro held such a high rank first appears in the preface of *Kokinshū*.

in the anthology, meaning he did not hold a sufficient rank worth noting. In relation to a person's death, this anthology and other old documents make a distinction between people by recording their rank when they were still alive. In the two places in the anthology where Hitomaro's death is mentioned, it is written as 死. This graph was used for the death of people holding the sixth rank down to commoners, and by this we may know that he did not hold such a high rank while alive. …

Concerning this same issue, Azumamaro stated,

Tsurayuki's opinion about *Man'yōshū* and the era in which Hitomaro lived appears in *Kokin wakashū*, but this opinion is incorrect. Proof of this is clearly found in *Man'yōshū*. Minister Teika made mention of information in the *Kokinshū* preface, saying, "Poetry has been handed down from ancient times thus …" This preface lines up Kakinomoto (Hitomaro) and Yamabe (Akahito) in the same reign of Monmu. But all of Hitomaro's poetry was composed in the Fujiwara era, while Akahito's poetry is confined to a period between Jingo 1 [724] and the Tenpyō era [729–49]. While these two eras are not that far apart, there is no reason to make them appear to have served in the same reign. From the time of Taihō 1 [701] in the reign of Monmu until Engi 5 [905] consists of 205 years and eighteen imperial reigns. Even though it is the Nara era, there are twenty-four years in the reign of Shōmu (which time frame spans the reigns of both Genmei and Genshō). The preface calls this era the reign of Emperor Heijō (Kenshō attached this). During the time of the Daidō era [806–10] there were no people who collected Japanese poetry [for an anthology]. It is suspicious to call poetry composed after the reign of Emperor Shōtoku the period of Emperor Heijō. The same [*Kokinshū*] preface also glosses over poetry composed before this period. There is something unnatural about the headnotes, noted times of composition, and the length of periods being written carelessly, where a poem composed during the Tenpyō Shōhō era is only labeled as "a poem from a time before this."

This quote includes the thought-provoking insight, "One cannot gauge the events of the people in *Man'yōshū* from the information in the *Kokinshū* preface." Every time I ponder on the information in the Kana preface, especially from the sentence, "Poetry has spread ever since the Nara period …" to the statement, "There have been only one or two people who knew [the ancient songs] and composed them," I realize that there is a misunderstanding, for the sentences do not appear to be those of a literary artist. Now, let me try my hand and take out the problematic sections:[13]

---

13. Mabuchi believes that the preface was corrupted later by someone who added information about early *Man'yōshū* poets that was incorrect. What follows is his attempt to return this particular section of the *Kokinshū* preface to its supposed uncorrupted state. My translation is based on McCullough (1985:6), though I have altered it according to the version Mabuchi writes.

> ... that presently smoke no longer rises from Mount Fuji, or that the Nagara Bridge is built anew; it was only when people heard these words that their hearts were consoled. Poetry has been handed down from ancient times thus, and among these poems is Kakinomoto Hitomaro, the poetic sage. Also, there was the poet Yamabe no Akahito, whose poetry was supernal and splendid. It is difficult to place Hitomaro above Akahito, nor is it easy to place Hitomaro below Akahito. Aside from these two poets, other superior poets had a reputation that continued unbroken, like twisted twine. Since then there have been only one or two people who knew how to compose [ancient songs]. However, each poet had strengths and weaknesses. We will discuss the ones who have excelled, omitting those of exalted rank and office as a matter of discretion.

I believe that the preface originally ran this way, and likely later-era people added parts based on their logic. Other than this, there are still one or two points that are suspicious, and if we delete these then I think the paragraph runs smoothly. The Kana and Mana prefaces begin in similar ways, but they part ways in the middle. If we focus on the context and the preface to *Poems from the Sovereign's Excursion to the Ōi River*, then we realize that Master Tsurayuki wrote his Kana preface to *Kokinshū* first and later the Mana preface came about, and at that point there was some editing in word usage. Furthermore, it seems plausible that people in later eras read both prefaces and noticed that additions in the Mana preface did not appear in the Kana preface, so they added these supposed omissions to the Kana preface. There are many places where phrases from the Kana preface have been inserted into the other preface. (The literary style is not artful, using phrases like "since that time," "during that reign." The juxtaposition of the Tatsuta River and Mount Yoshino is poor because the rhythm does not match. Furthermore, the attribution to Hitomaro of the poem about doubting the sight of clouds is baseless. And it feels like someone recklessly added the words "since then." And the phrase "had strengths and weaknesses" should refer to the six poets mentioned previously. If this is true, then the phrase "since that time" becomes unnecessary. The phrase "people who knew and composed [ancient songs]" feels verbose. I will omit other minute details, but what has been presented above are the difficulties in the literary style of the preface. More than this, there are grave errors that exist, as pointed out by Minister Teika and Keichū. Thus, we should gather these problematic sections and reexamine each.)

If one does not compose poetry well he cannot communicate information about the style of ancient poetry. This is also true of literature. It is difficult to talk about literary styles unless one has a profound knowledge of our literary style, and is able to discern between native Japanese words and Sino-Japanese words, and can write in the masculine style in imitation of this preface, and the ancient texts like the liturgies and *Kojiki*—not in the feminine style such as the tales. Azumamaro also said in jest, "I believe Master Tsurayuki and have confidence in what he wrote. If I were a member of his household, I would likely be praised for being loyal to my master."

[4] In relation to the categorization of each book of *Man'yōshū*, Keichū said,

> The books [of this anthology] can be divided into six categories. The first is miscellaneous poems, which is the same as the miscellaneous category seen in the successive imperially ordered anthologies. The second is correspondence poetry, consisting of poems sent back and forth between people where they confess their feelings for each other. This category is later labeled "love poetry," but it is not consistent. Some sixty or seventy percent are related to feelings between men and women, but the remaining poems are feelings expressed to their ruler, lord, father, son, brother, or friend. The third category is elegies. These are later called lamentation poems. The definition from *Yu pian* says, "挽 is read *wan*. It is 'to pull.' It is the same as 輓 'draw, pull.' In the custom of China, during a funeral, people took the rope wrapped around a coffin and pulled it while they sang dirges like "Xielou" and "Haoli."[14] Based on this song of distress, this was called an elegy. The fourth category is metaphorical poems, where the poet describes his feelings compared to things or events related to his circumstances. There are many of these poems in Book 3, where a variety of feelings are compared to an assortment of things. A number of love poems also include metaphors, so I have set up this category provisionally. The fifth category is poems written on the four seasons. If one were to divide each season into its own category, then there would be eight categories. The sixth category is love poems related to the four seasons. These are found in Books 8 and 10. If one were to divide each of these into its own category, then you would have twelve categories. If you collapse this last category into a larger category of "love poems," then you would only have five categories. This anthology places great value on love poems, so poems dealing with seasons but not love were called "miscellaneous spring" or "miscellaneous summer" poems.

[5] Next, concerning the division of each book, Keichū goes on to say,

> It seems that each book of *Man'yōshū* was compiled around a fairly well established standard, but the text we currently have is a draft version exhibiting some disarray. Book 1 is compiled around a theme of successive imperial reigns, but the latter half consists of just miscellaneous poems. Book 2 follows the same pattern as Book 1, with love poems first and ending with elegies. Book 3 is divided into three sections. First it lists anonymous poems composed after the reign of Emperor Jitō, then lists metaphorical poems, and ends with elegies, starting with the poem com-

14. People sang the dirge Xielou at the funerals of nobility, while people sang Haoli at the funerals of lower-ranking people.

posed by Shōtoku Taishi. Book 4 starts with a poem to his younger sister and the succeeding poems are all love poems, descending in order of status of the poet. Book 5 starts with "A poem in response to a prophecy of death through divination, written by Minister Ōtomo, Governor of Dazaifu" and ends with Yamanoe Okura's love poem, "Longing for the boy named Furufi, one long poem with short poems." This book contains miscellaneous poems composed between the beginning of the Jingi era and Tenpyō 5 [733]. This book likely is based on the private anthology of Okura with later additions from Minister Yakamochi. All the poems from the beginning down to Okura's [block of poems] written "In humble response to the feelings about Kumagori"[15] were composed in Tsukushi, with some exchange poems from the capital mixed in. It also appears that the poem "Exchange poems regarding extreme poverty"[16] was composed in Tsukushi, but this is not certain. The poems after the two poems with the headnote "Praying for a Prosperous Departure and Return"[17] were surely composed by Okura when he was at the capital. This book also includes Chinese poetry. As there are also poems written on the topic of plum blossoms one is tempted to categorize this as spring, and there are quite a number of elegies. However, Okura gathered together all the poems composed at Tsukushi into one collection, so I have categorized the whole book as miscellaneous.

Book 6 is miscellaneous poems, composed between Yōrō 7 [723] and Tenpyō 16 [744]. Book 7 consists of three sections. The first is miscellaneous, starting with the topic of heavenly phenomena and earthly principles, and including a variety of topics. Next is metaphorical poems, including many poems written on the topic of a variety of things. The final section is elegies. This book is a collection of poetry from anonymous poets from unknown periods. Book 8 consists of poems written on the seasons, listed in order of spring, summer, autumn, and winter. Love poems are also mixed in, and all other poems are categorized as miscellaneous. However, these last poems are not anonymous. Book 9 also consists of three sections: miscellaneous, love, and elegies. Most of the poets are difficult to figure out as the headnotes simply list them with their ancient name.[18] These are surely notes from the compiler. Book 10 has the exact same makeup as Book 8, but it is different in that this book does not include the names of the poets. I believe that the order of Book 9 and Book 10 should be swapped. Both Books 11 and 12 are like the love and travel poems found in *Kokinshū*, divided into a Book 1 and Book 2. The compiler collected a variety of anonymous poems like those found in other books of this anthology, but he appears to have also compiled poems where he knew the poet and the period of compilation into one book [with the anonymous poems], so both books have been treated as works of unclear composition and date. In Book 11 we find metaphorical poems also included in Book 13. ... Book 14 contains "Eastern" poems, divided according to the province, then categorized as miscellaneous, love,

15. MYS 886.

16. MYS 892–93.

17. MYS 894.

18. This includes names such as Yamanoe, Kasuga, Takechi, Gan'nin, Kinu, Shimatari, and Maro. In some cases we *could* conclude that Takechi was Takechi Furuhito, or Yamanoe was Yamanoe no Okura, but there is no firm proof.

and metaphorical poems. Near the end, there are poems where the province is unclear, but these again are divided into miscellaneous, love, *sakimori*,[19] metaphorical poems, and elegies. The *sakimori* poems in Book 20 should have been included here, but during the middle of Book 17, Yakamochi was dispatched to Etchū as governor, so that is the reason for the placement. Book 15 contains 145 new and old poems composed during the sixth month of Tenpyō 8 [736], when poems were composed in honor of the voyage of the envoy about to be dispatched to Silla, and sixty-three poems composed when Nakatomi Ason Yakamori was banished to Echizen Province, for a total of 208 poems. The setup of this book resembles that in Book 5. Book 16 is truly a collection of miscellaneous poems, as its opening headnote says, "a collection of poems as about relations and miscellaneous poems." All these poems have some connection to ancient traditions. There are also many *haikai* poems. Book 17 contains poems composed between Tenpyō 2 and the first month of Tenpyō 20. However, these poems are not arranged in chronological order; they were collected as Yakamochi saw or heard them, and then added poems that had been lost at a later date, which we can infer from the present arrangement of having ten poems from Tenpyō 2 followed by the *Tanabata* poems from Tenpyō 17 [745]. And then the poems composed in the fourth month of Tenpyō 13 poems to the fourth month of Tenpyō 16 follow immediately thereafter. Minister Teika said, "Poems from Tenpyō 2 till Tenpyō 20," but it actually only conintues until the eighth month of Tenpyō 18 [746] after which Yakamochi was dispatched to Etchū as governor, and he did not separate these poems. It is as if he kept a diary of these events. Thus, up to the eighth month of Tenpyō Shōhō 3 [751] he composed these poems while in Etchū, and at that time people who came up from the capital brought poems composed by the emperor or nobility, and other old poems that Yakamochi had not heard before. He then immediately wrote these down, "recording things as they occurred." In the middle of Book 19 he records that he returned to the capital and by the seventh month of Tenpyō Hōji 2 [759] Book 20 was completed, and the book is crowned with a poem written at the banquet to celebrate his appointment as governor of Inaba on the first day of the first month of that third year.

The above words of Keichū are generally accurate, but, there are a few places where he has overanalyzed things. I will give detailed criticism when I discuss each book. Keichū's comment that "Minister Yakamochi had a hand in the compilation of the entire anthology" as I have noted above, is not satisfactory. First off, clearly Books 1 and 2 are not the compilation of Minister Yakamochi. The other books exhibit the same tendency, so as I have already argued, the compilers must have been Lord Moroe, Okura, including a mixture of poetry from other anthologies. It is not the work of

19. Written as 防人 "a defense person." *Saki* likely is based on the meaning of "in front," and appears to have had an extended meaning of "frontier." These were "border guards," men sent to Kyūshū, or the islands of Tsushima and Iki to protect the archipelago from a possible invasion from the continent. Poems from these men appear in *Man'yōshū*.

one person. Thus a number of problems appeared, and by the reigns of the Jōgan era the origins were not clear, and that is why the question was addressed to the emperor.[20] Regardless of which anthology came to be included in *Man'yōshū* the answer is that both were products "of the palace named after the *nara* oak tree." Some criticize this answer, but poetry was the vehicle to articulate things beyond everyday words, so naturally this poetic answer is a bit vague. There is proof that Japanese poetry had declined before the period of this reign [in the Jōgan era]. Proof appears in the congratulatory words of Emperor Nimmyō's fortieth birthday, where it says that a Buddhist monk from Kōfukuji presented a *chōka* in the ancient tradition, and only this priest knew the ancient poetic tradition, as found in *Shoku Nihon kōki*.[21]

[6] The [current] texts of *Man'yōshū* were collated by Sengaku alone. Among these the majority simply add readings in the margins. There is a printed version of the text without readings added, and the critical text for this was that of Sengaku, but there are many typos in this text, so it is better to use a woodblock print instead. It is also quite enlightening to have several different woodblock prints so you can compare the differences. One of the old handwritten manuscripts that Azumamaro was able to obtain as well as *Koyō ryakuyō*, a text that has made a selection of poems from *Man'yōshū* in possession of the priestly family at Kasuga Wakamiya,[22] are convenient in supplying correct readings for corruptions in the woodblock prints. I have come into possession of a number of old handwritten manuscripts of *Man'yōshū* and would like to create a critical edition, but as I noted in the beginning all the ancient manuscripts are lost and there is no value in continuing. There are also some manuscripts where [the original *man'yōgana*] has been converted into later [cursive] script. Perhaps these texts were changed so that women like queens and princesses could read them. When it comes to the readings in ancient texts, they are generally trustworthy, but they should not be used as a gold standard. This is espe-

---

20. Referring to the question mentioned in the headnote to KKS 997.

21. This event appears on the twenty-sixth day of the third month of Kashō 2 [849] in *Shoku Nihon kōki*. Various Buddhist objects were presented for the prayer for the emperor's longevity, and then a *chōka* was presented. The text quotes the poem. The comment about Japanese poetry on the verge of disappearing appears after the poem.

22. Mabuchi writes this as 古葉略要, but the full (and correct) title is *Koyōryaku ruijūshō* (古葉略類聚鈔). It was compiled around 1250. Authorship is unknown, but Nishide Naho (2010:302) argues that it was compiled by Nakatomi Sukesada (中臣祐定, 1198–1269). The work arranges poems from *Man'yōshū* according to topic, but only five books of the original manuscript survive in the present.

cially true of *Man'yōshū* where many poems have erroneous readings added, so there is no way to have correct readings by simply converting these poems into *kana*. There are also many examples where people have altered the order of poems based on information in prefaces from other works and information about the poets. This is illogical. In general even if there are mistakes in ancient texts, overall the texts are correct, so it is best to simply write your opinions in the margins. Characters you might consider mistakes may be considered correct by people in later eras. And problematic works that I have mentioned earlier will write about having suspicions about things that are decisively right, and claim that something is decisively correct when it is spurious. The reader must study the poetry in *Man'yōshū* to improve his poetry. Did not Minister Teika and those after him say the same thing? Therefore, there is no value in downplaying the difficulties in this text for the benefit of the beginner. Convenience is fraught with perils. I have used the technique of convenience in this essay, but if I only used vague words from the ancient lexicon then it would have been difficult for the reader to understand me, and it is not my intention to give the impression that the subject at hand is trouble-free.

[7] In order to understand *Man'yōshū* the reader should not be satisfied with texts where readings have been added, but he should read through the text five times. Having done this the reader will naturally obtain a basic understanding of the readings and meanings based on context. Next the student should read one more time, examining what he reads to understand the meaning. Later the student can compare what he reads with the printed text, writing down mistakes in characters in the margins and give readings to places where there is no reading [in the handwritten texts]. In the beginning, there will be times when it is very difficult to know the reading and times when a reading from some other poem will come to mind. When you cannot remember the reading, then you may look at the printed text. Doing this, you will come to the realization that you can read the poems fairly well. After reading several volumes, then you can read old works from *Kojiki* down to *Wamyōshō*. After you have read *Kojiki*, *Nihon shoki*, the various kinds of liturgies, and the successive reigns of imperial edicts, when you then go back to the unannotated text of *Man'yōshū*, you will find that in general you will know how to read sections you earlier have found unclear. At the same time you will be able to critically analyze the various manuscripts, and you will see that this should be read thus, or this is a skillful play on words, or this section was not understood well. You will also be able to tell where characters have been miscopied or dropped altogether. Even if you had doubts, this does not mean that you will be able to

solve all the problems by yourself. But if you carry a million doubts in your heart, then you may be able to come up with solutions to problems not only with some works, but also dialects and slang usages from the various provinces. …

[8] People in later eras who have tried to study ancient works should separate themselves from the customs of later eras and take an open-minded attitude. They should also study the Taihō Statutes and be familiar with laws observed in our land for over a thousand years. It appears that these instituted statutes were modeled after the Tang Statutes, but in reality these statutes are based on ancient laws already in place in our country, but were written down in the Taihō era using the characters and terminology from the Tang Statutes. So the characters are Chinese but there are many cases where the spirit of the statute is Japanese. When studying the ancient past these practices are of great use. Next, the student must have some familiarity with *Kojiki* and the events from the divine age. As *Kojiki* is written completely in Japanese[23] and a study of this text will allow the student to see the origin of words, he can then compare this with *Man'yōshū*. After this, the student should study *Nihon shoki* and the successive histories, as well as *Engi shiki*, *Wamyōshō*, and other miscellaneous works after the Engi period. "Miscellany" includes *Kaifusō*, *Kogo shūi*, *Shōryōshū*, and other words.[24] Having studied these, the student can then proceed to look into *Man'yōshū*. There are no other works than these suitable for preparing the student to understand human emotions and our customs, to become discerning of the ancient lexicon, and to understand the ancient texts. It is the same as knowing the *Book of Odes* for understanding China. Also, being familiar with the liturgies will allow the student to understand the texts from successive eras. These texts came about in the Asuka and Fujiwara eras and continue down to the Engi era. My ideas here go starkly against the theories of people in society. For proof of my stance, please read my other works. Asuka and Fujiwara were the height of this period, and poetry began to weaken in the Nara era, and from the time the capital was moved

---

23. On the surface this appears accurate, but Mabuchi uses the word 和文, which generally is used in opposition to 漢文, or texts written in Chinese. *Kojiki*'s text is actually a *kundoku* text with phonograms added to aid in proper reading or recitation.

24. *Kaifūsō* is Japan's oldest extant collection of Chinese poems written in Japan, compiled in 751. *Kogo shūi* is a small edited history of Imibe Hironari's (dates unknown) family within the larger framework of mythology and legend. It was presented to the court in 807. *Shōryōshū* is the shortened title for *Henjō hokki shōryōshū*. It contains poetry and other writings of Kūkai (774–835). The date of compilation is unknown, but likely during the late 830s after his death.

to its present location [Kyōto] literature has become shallow. By studying the liturgies one can see the change in literature. This is also true of *Man'yōshū*, for during the Fujiwara court Hitomaro appears and he was peerless. Akahito belongs to the Nara period, but his style is a bit weaker than Hitomaro's. And this becomes clear when one has read both the liturgies and *Man'yōshū*, and you will become attached to those works that you enjoy, and the titles mentioned above will naturally become your resources.

Focusing on *Man'yōshū*, you must first have a good grounding in the laws and organization of the times, including the rites, ranks, costumes, the people of the various provinces, the *sakimori*, the capital versus the provinces, the mountains and sea, the dikes and villages, the barriers and markets. …

[9] There is a great amount of confusion regarding the readings in the current text. If one character is misread in a poem, the entire meaning is lost. Because the editors could not get one poem correctly, it casts doubt on other poems. For example, in Book 1 there is a *chōka* with the headnote, "A poem composed by Kakinomoto Hitomaro when Prince Karu took lodging on the Aki Moor," and the *hanka* afterward reads:[25]

真草苅	**makusa karu**	It is only a wild field
荒野二者	**arano nifa aredo**	where people cut hay,
葉	**momidiba no**	but it is now a memento
過去君之	**suginisi kimi ga**	to our lord who has passed on
形見跡曽来師	**katami to so kosi**	in the autumn of his life.

[MYS 47]

One book adds the character 二 to this poem. The editor has not noticed that the character 黄 "yellow" has been dropped from before 葉 "leaf" [in the third stanza]. The current printed text reads the three final stanzas as *sugiyuku kimi ga katami no ato yori zo kosi*, which does not make any sense. If we add the character 黄 then we can read these stanzas as *momidiba no suginisi kimi ga katami to zo kosi*. Comparing this with the following poem, we then have Prince Karu (the childhood name of Emperor Monmu, who was the son of Prince Kusakabe; Prince Kusakabe was also called Prince Hinamishi) who composed a poem when he came to the place where his father had before hunted. The falling of autumn leaves is generally used as a metaphor for death, but it can also be used to show the changing of the seasons. In an elegy in Book 2 we have 黄葉乃 過伊去等

25. Mabuchi quotes a number of poems and includes both the original orthography and includes readings. I have thus given both here.

momidiba no sugite iniki to "(my wife) passed away like autumn leaves. …"[26] In Book 3 we find 黄葉乃 移伊去者 **momidiba no uturi inureba** "He passed away like autumn leaves … ."[27] In Book 9 we find 黄葉之 過去子等 **momidiba no suginisi kora to** "my wife who passed away like autumn leaves. …"[28] In Book 13 we have 黄葉之 過行跡 **momidiba no sugite iniki to** "He journeyed on (to the next life), like autumn leaves falling. …"[29] Also in Book 4 we find the following poem:

松之葉尓	**matu no fa ni**	The moon has changed
月者由移去	**tuki fa yuturinu**	into the leaves of the pine tree.
黄葉乃	**momidiba no**	My heart has changed
過哉君之	**sugure ya kimi ga**	like the autumn leaves,
不相夜多焉	**afanu yo no ofoki**	will there be many nights without you?
		[MYS 623]

There is also this example found in Book 10:

黄葉之	**momidiba no**	Like autumn leaves
過不勝兒乎	**sugikatenu ko wo**	I cannot overlook that girl;
人妻跡	**fitoduma to**	shall I continue to see her
見乍哉将有	**mitutu ya aramu**	as the wife of someone else?
戀敷物乎	**kofisiki mono wo**	Though I miss her so much.
		[MYS 2297]

These examples demonstrate that for the word glossed as *momidiba*, we must insert the character 黄 into the text.

Also in Book 10 there are thirteen poems written on the topic of wild geese. The first poem reads,

秋風尓	**akikaze ni**	The sound of the call of
山跡部越	**yamato fe koyuru**	wild geese that fly over
鴈鳴者	**kari ga ne fa**	Yamato on the autumn wind
射矢遠放	**iya tofozakaru**	slowly become fainter,
雲隠筒	**kumogakuritutu**	while they become hidden in the clouds.
		[MYS 2128]

26. MYS 207.

27. MYS 459.

28. MYS 1796.

29. MYS 3344. Mabuchi only quotes these two stanzas, but it appears likely that his reading is corrupted. Current scholars believe the reading should be *momidiba no sugite iyuku to*.

The second poem in the sequence reads,

明闇之	**akegure no**	Calling out as they fly,
朝霧隠	**asagirigomori**	hidden in the morning mist
鳴而去	**nakite yuku**	in the fleeing darkness at dawn,
鴈者言戀	**kari fa a ga kofi**	you wild geese!
於妹告社	**imo ni tuge koso**	Take this message to my wife.
		[MYS 2129]

The third poem is:

吾屋戸尓	**wa ga yado ni**	The geese that
鳴之鴈哭	**nakisi kari ga ne**	called out at my house
雲上尓	**kumo no ufe ni**	are now calling out
今夜喧成	**koyofi nakunari**	tonight above the clouds.
國方可聞	no reading	???[30]
遊群	Playful flock	
左小壮鹿之	**sawo sika no**	When the stag
妻問時尓	**tumadofu toki ni**	calls after his mate
月乎吉三	**tuki wo yomi**	and the moon is proper
切木四之泣所聞	**kari ga ne kikoyu**	you can hear the call of the geese.
今時来等霜	**imasi kurasimo**	I think they are coming now.
		[MYS 2131]

In this way, after the third poem is a new heading, "playful flock," making it appear that the next poem [MYS 2131] was composed on a new topic, but again it is written on geese. In Tang poetry we have topics such as "the playful elaphure and stag," or "the herd of deer," so this heading "playful flock" can be interpreted in a variety of ways, but none of these explanations make sense. My own personal opinion is that these two characters actually belong to the final stanza of the previous poem [MYS 2130]: 國方可聞遊群, read **kuni fe kamo yuku** "heading off to their homeland." A copyist must have mistakenly put this on the next line, separating it from the poem, and whoever arranged the list of poems later at the beginning of Book 10 made it a separate heading. People who did not understand this poem read the truncated version as *kuni-tukata kamo*. Who would not

30. MYS 2130. I have not attempted to translate the last stanza, because the printed text Mabuchi has reference to has truncated the final two characters, 遊群, and made it the headnote for MYS 2131. Mabuchi correctly identifies the problem and provides his correction on the next page.

know the direction to his homeland when he is on a journey? The reader should doubt that the geese are calling out above the clouds "Is this the direction home?" Claiming that some old poems are difficult to understand and this is an example of that is jumping to conclusions. The meaning of the first two poems is that the geese who were calling out here have now journeyed off, hidden in the clouds, hinting at the geese heading off to Yamato, where the poet's thoughts are, and he wants the geese to give a message to his wife who is at home. Thus, the geese are calling out close to where the poet lives and tonight they have taken flight and are hidden by the clouds. The poet is on a journey, but his thoughts are headed to his homeland, perhaps they will go with the geese. *This manner of interpretation is not that difficult [when comparing different texts], but people who are only familiar with the printed text with readings added could not figure out the correct reading. The reading of* kunitukata kamo *does not fit the context of the other poems, making the poem disagreeable.* This opinion belongs to me, Mabuchi. Azumamaro seems to have thought this way also, but Keichū did not understand what was going on. Other examples follow this pattern.

[10] To gain an understanding of the ancient lexicon, the student must have a firm understanding of the fifty sounds of Japanese. However, other scholars have already expounded on the phonology of Japanese with facts about dentals, labials, and the lightness or heaviness of the four tones. You must have an essential understanding of these things, but at present the study of phonology is not a pressing matter. However, you must understand elision, syllabic lengthening, and voicing of the ancient words based on ancient precedent. The evidence for these things is not explained in everyday Japanese books, where they only scratch the surface by talking about the five places of articulation[31] and *kana* contraction, but to understand the ancient lexicon these things are insufficient. I will give one or two examples.

Elision and syllabic lengthening refer to *kana* contraction. There are a variety of examples. First, an example of elision is where *kuniuti* "in the province" is shortened to *kunuti* where the two sounds *niu* elide to just *nu*. *This is also known as* niu *being sliced and respliced as* nu. *However, to make this discussion easier to understand, I will simply state that xy elided.* Also, *siduko* "child of a lower-class family" elides to *sugo* in the same way that *sidu* elides to *su*.

31. This is based on traditional Chinese phonology, where sounds were described as being produced in one of five areas of the mouth: lip sounds (labials), tongue sounds (laterals), tooth sounds (dentals, palatals), back-tooth sounds (alveolar), and throat sounds (pharyngeals and glottals). See Pulleyblank (1999:115–17).

Examples of syllabic lengthening are found when *miru* "to see" becomes *miraku* "seeing." Where the sound *-ru* is lengthened to *-raku. So the sliced and respliced example of* raku *is* ru.[32] Another example is *kuefaya* "kick swiftly," which is a lengthening of *kue* "kick." *The elision of* kue *would result in* ke. This elision is the same phenomenon as lengthening, where a word is reduced and rearranged or lengthened and rearranged, so it is important to make both distinctions.

Also voicing occurs with both elision and lengthening. *Wagaimo* "my beloved" becomes *wagimo*, where *gai* elides to *gi*. There are also examples where *zoa* shortens to *za*, so *mono ni zo arikeru* contracts to *mono ni zarikeru* "it was such." Lengthening follows the same pattern. Every example of voiced syllables will remain voiced regarding of the process it undergoes. Voiceless syllables often change to voiced when undergoing syncope, but there are no examples where a voiced syllable changes to a voiceless one. Thus, most cases are easily discerned because of the presence of a voiced syllable.

There are also cases where several words strung together undergo elision and become one word. This includes examples like the one that appears in the divine age, where *turifari* "fishing hook" contracts to *ti*.[33] There are also cases where one word is lengthened into several words. In the songs in *Kojiki* we find an example where *fure* "to fall" is lengthened to *furabafe* in the stanza **fotue no uraba fa nakatue ni otifurabafe** "the leaves on the top branches fell on top of the leaves of the middle branches. ..."[34] *Thus* bafe *shortens to* be, *and* -rabe *is later shortened to* re, *resulting in* otifure. *The lengthened form is* otifurabefe. ...

There are also cases of contraction. In *Man'yōshū* there is the phrase *yukutifu* meaning "to go" but here *to* and *i* have contracted to just *ti*. In another place we have *yuku tofu*, which has the same meaning as the case above, but here the *i* of *ifu* has elided. Thus, in the text there are cases of 有云恋云 that are glossed as *aritofu* or *aritifu*. But in the present printed text these are glossed as *kofi tefu* and *ari tefu*. The meaning is the same, but there is no case in this anthology where anything is read *tefu*, although there are cases of *tifu* and *tofu* written in phonograms. There are also no other ancient texts that write *tefu*. After the Kōnin era people became more ornate and tried to make their writing more flowery, so they altered the *ti*

32. This demonstrates the rather primitive understanding of linguistics at the time. There is no phonological change at work here, but the addition of a verbal suffix, *-aku* which nominalizes the verb.

33. Phonologically this is a stretch. It is better to see *ti* as a word for hook with a different etymology than *fari* "needle."

34. KJK 99.

in *tifu* to a similar sound, and made it *tefu*: *kofisu tefu* "love is ..." and *kado saseri tefe* "they say the gate is overgrown with weeds. ..."[35]

There is a standard for voiced and voiceless syllables. Among the fifty sounds of Japanese, twenty of these are voiced. If we group these together with voiceless syllables, then we can say there are fifty sounds, but if we make this a separate category, then we should say there are seventy sounds. Let me give an example. The sounds *ba bi bu be bo* are related to *ma mi mu me mo*, so we say Mount Kamunabi but we can also say Mount Kamunami, for "lonely" we say *sabisiki* or *samisiki*. There is also an example in *Nihon shoki*, in the reign of Kenzō where **midu yukeba** "according to the flow of the water" is written *midu yukema*,[36] or where **asobasisi** "journeying for the hunt" is written *asomasisi* in the Yūryaku record. ...[37]

[11] Originally the meaning of the ancient poems and literature was clear and straightforward. These were adorned with numerous epithets, prefixes, and suffixes. There were many epithets *called* makurakotoba, numbering upward of five hundred. These have existed from the very ancient past, and there are many that are not interpreted correctly. As it is not easy to correctly interpret these I wrote a work titled *Kanjikō*.[38] Thus here I will have occasion to abbreviate some things, or where there is much debate, I will write "recorded in another work" [referring to *Kanjikō*].

[12] Regarding *chōka*, in the ancient times people wrote down their feelings immediately, but from the time of the Asuka Kiyomigahara Palace [Tenmu] it seems that a standard for these poems took shape. During the time of the Fujiwara Palace, Master Hitomaro appeared on the scene, and the *chōka* he composed was supernal, and he demonstrated skill as seen in shorter poems [*tanka*]. While these *chōka* had many more stanzas, one can clearly discern a difference in the use of stanzas employing techniques superior to any other poet, like hidden meanings, repetition, persuasion,

---

35. It is possible that this clause is another example where Mabuchi appears to have dovetailed two different poems together. He has taken the opening line from *Kokin waka rokujō* 3955 and stuck the last stanza from 3018 to it. However, as a poetic clause it does not seem to work, so I interpret this as two examples of *tefu* (with one in the evidential form) listed together.

36. Mabuchi quotes 寐逗喩凱麼, where the character 麼 is read *ma*, but while the *go-on* reading is *ma*, the *kan-on* reading is *ba*. The poetry in *Nihon shoki* is primarily based on *kan-on*, so the reading of *yukema* is a ghost. However, Mabuchi is correct that –b– and –m– are interchangeable in a number of words in Japanese.

37. Mabuchi quotes this stanza as 阿蘇磨斯志, but the original appears to have been 阿蘇麼斯志, so textual work debunks this example.

38. Written by Mabuchi, and completed in 1757. It explains the meaning and usage of 326 epithets found in *Kojiki*, *Nihon shoki*, and *Man'yōshū*, arranged in the Japanese a-i-u-e-o order.

pulling back, and conclusion. Poets after this, like Ōtomo Kanamura, Okura, Takahashi Mushimaro, composed poetry that was unsophisticated and strong yet elegant, displaying a style older than that of Hitomaro. It is not that these poems are chronologically older than Hitomaro's, but they exhibit less skillful techniques. When we reach the time of Minister Yakamochi, the value of his poetry begins to decline, having less skill. In relation to *chōka* he displayed the habit of writing notes in the margins. Master Akahito was not very skilled at *chōka*, but when it came to *tanka* his are peerless. Compared with the *tanka* of Hitomaro, Hitomaro's poetry is tragic and classical, while Akahito's poetry is free and unfettered, more up-to-date than Hitomaro's. It has been said you cannot value one above the other, but a difference in era is evident. Other than this there are many other poets who were superior but their names have not been recorded. I will write about this at a later date. Other than that, Minister Tabito's poetry is superior to Lord Moroe's, and by the time of Lord Okura, his *chōka* are superior to Akahito's, but his general reputation is not as high. As far as the reputation and value of this anthology, scholars who should be trustworthy and have a reputation for valuing things despise it. They cannot turn away from earlier misinterpretations, and they have a habit of rejecting a new interpretation *a priori* when it is announced. Azumamaro said that we aspire to the logic of bettering our own development. Minister Teika once said, "There is no teaching in poetics. The only teacher is the ancient poems." These words originated from a sage in a different country, but has led the hearts of people in the proper direction. These words refer to all things, not just poetry.

Even if these are the words of our master, if they do not suit the ancient meaning found in the ancient texts, then there is no shame in altering it. Minister Teika's argument about *chōka* and *tanka* in *Man'yōshū* was different than the opinion of his father, but scholarship is a public affair. It is not the work of one family. Even if some someone puts forth a twisted theory, it does not mean that it will continue on indefinitely. Scholarship is not a private affair. Minister Teika does not appear to have been deeply involved in ancient scholarship, but through his natural ability and talent he came to this conclusion. For a long time, I, Mabuchi, have believed in these words and have studied the ancient texts, and I have been able to detect one or two things that were incorrect. There are been many times when I have found his theory to be incorrect. This was the intention of Minister Teika's words. I beg people to stop being suspicious of things when they read this.

[Yamamoto 1942:190–215]

ꕤ

ASHIWAKE OBUNE

Motoori Norinaga | 1756

[Written when Norinaga was only twenty-six, he sets forth his feelings on poetry, which remain rather constant throughout his life. Framed in a common question and answer format, Norinaga articulates that poetry is written from feelings found in the heart of all creatures. When people put on airs, they begin to stifle the heart, which leads to poetic composition losing its emotional effect. Flueckiger (2010:185) notes that this essay centers on "the complexity of the notion of genuineness" in one's emotions expressed through poetry.]

Question: *Waka* is something that aids in governing the state, not something that should recklessly be used as entertainment. And that is why the preface to *Kokinshū* says much the same. What do you think of this reasoning?

Answer: Your reasoning is mistaken. The essence of *waka* is not to aid the government, nor govern the individual, but is nothing more than expressions of thoughts in the heart. There are some poems that may aid the government, and others that may become precepts for an individual's life. There are also some that harm the government, and others that are perilous to the individual. That is because all poetry is produced according to the emotions of the poet.

Poetry can be used whenever one wants: for evil, for good, for pleasure, for anxiety, when inspired, when overjoyed, or when angered. If the poem expresses well the feelings of the poet, and uses profoundly rich words, then it moves the spirits and *kami* to emotion.

If one twists the interpretation of the meaning of the preface of *Kokinshū*, then you can reach the conclusion noted [in the question], but the preface should not be interpreted to mean such. The phrase in the preface, "Anciently the hearts of the people were unsophisticated, and they only used poetry to govern the individual"[1] does not explain the original essence of song. It merely describes the hearts and minds of the ancient people. The author thought that people [in that day] used poetry only for love, so he phrased it that way, lamenting the decline of Japanese song, it having become a tool for people to use only for *amour*.

1. McCullough (1985:256).

Song originally was used for both good and evil. Regardless, the reason there are few songs written to instruct people, but numerous poems written about love, is because this is the intrinsic nature of song.

There is nothing that stirs the feelings of the heart as strongly as the feelings of love experienced between a man and a woman. All people without exception desire the realization of this experience, so it is only natural that there should be many love poems. There are few wise people in this world, however, who seek only for the good, strictly governing themselves, putting rules above all else, so there are few poems on the subject. Also, there are few people seeking only evil, meaning there are few poems on that subject.

It is common sense that there are many poems composed about the emotions felt at a certain moment, irrespective of good and evil, doctrine or precepts, because poetry is composed according to the natural feelings of the average person. The feelings of the average person in society are such that they seek pleasure, loathe distress, while everyone enjoys pleasure, and is saddened by sorrow. People simply compose poetry like this according to their natural feelings. If one composes a poem with a wicked heart, he will create a wicked poem. If one composes a poem with the feelings of romantic love, she will compose a romantic poem. If one composes a poem with the feelings of virtue, then he will compose a virtuous poem. Therefore, there is no other reason for saying that song cannot be placed in one limited definition.

If one wishes to express true feelings, then that person should compose poetry with true feelings. If one wishes to express falsehood, then compose a poem with pretended feelings. If one wishes to compose a poem with flowery words, then compose the poem as one pleases, with flowery words. Let each poet do as he pleases. Thus, this is how one obtains the true feelings of a person.

Question: If poetry is something broadly composed as one feels, then why set up so many poetic restrictions, and add so many bothersome rules? If things are as you have just stated, then one should not mind using vulgar diction, or worry about how many syllables in each stanza. He would compose poetry anyway he wanted.

Answer: This question, on the surface, sounds reasonable, but if one were to compose poetry without considering the number of syllables, the product would not be considered poetic. It would simply be ordinary speech. Having an agreeable meter makes it poetry. Even if one uses vulgar words, and ignores the rules, if the words have a meter that is ordered [in the proper syllables], then it is poetry. If a frog in the water sings with a well-ordered rhythm that has meter, then it is nothing other than poetry. This means that all living creatures have their own song. The fowl and beasts, if their cry is well-ordered with rhythm, then it is song. All words uttered that have a well-ordered meter are all considered song.

In spite of this fact, it may appear to some that it is not the original intent of poetry to have various set rules, making things formal so the poet cannot compose as his heart dictates. But constructing a pattern enabling the poet to compose a skilled poem is also the true intention of poetry. Is it not the true sensation of all poets to carefully choose words, and compose a skilled poem? It is the pinnacle of poetry for the poet to earnestly rack his brains in choosing the most appropriate words to compose a good poem. If the person is not worried about good or bad poems, then we need not have this discussion, and the person does not need to bother with learning poetry.

Now, there are times when one wants to produce a good poem, so he carefully selects the words and then he composes it without listening to the feelings in his heart. But even in ordinary speech, there are times when we do not say exactly what we are feeling in our hearts. How much more it is with poetry. We strive to produce a poem with a fine meter, and it is only natural that we become somewhat separated from the true feelings in our heart. This distancing of oneself from one's feelings is also the true form of poetry. For example, one tries to compose a poem of good will, even though he feels ill will in his heart. Thus, the poem he composes has betrayed the feelings in his heart, but there is no falsehood in the desire to compose a good poem. Therefore, the composition of this poem has accurately reflected the feelings of the heart.

And even in the case when one views the cherry blossoms and has not felt much emotion, the poet writes about how moved he was by the sight of the blossoms, following the conventional practice of composing a poem. It is a lie that he was moved by the sight of the blossoms, but there is no deception in the desire to compose a poem about being moved by the sight. This is what is meant by saying that poetry originates from the true feelings of the heart. If we cannot say that having a desire to compose a good poem is the true feeling of poetic composition, then what is it?

While wanting to compose a good poem a person may say that if one contrives to use skilled diction he will lose the true feelings of the heart, so he neglects poetry with these feelings, but this goes against the desire to compose good poetry, and ends up creating a lie. But if one composes poetry just as one feels, without trying to use skilled diction, because he does not want to lose his true feelings, this is also the true feelings of the heart. This I will not deny.

Now there are many restrictions regarding poetic composition, and other rules about the selection of words, which is like getting lumber from a tree. Let us say that using the entire tree is like the natural state of a poem being composed. It definitely is a tree from roots to the top, but when you cut the top and root off, and peel off the bark, the tree gets smaller. By working the wood, shaving it with a plane, getting rid of the knots, you create an unblemished finish, but the tree has become even smaller. If we want to use the wood for mundane purposes, then we do not care about the grain, or mind having knots, or leaving the [unshapely] tip of the tree; we can use the tree in its larger size, but you can only obtain something crude from the tree in its natural form. Analogous to this, to compose good poetry, one must carefully select words from a limited pool of vocabulary and arrange these properly. If you do not mind poor poetry, it is your choice then to use a broad range of vocabulary.

People who do not understand this principle say that *waka* has too many rules, or it is not suited to compose poetry on mundane subjects, but this thinking is mistaken. Because the Way of poetry is to seek for greater elegance within that which is elegant, rules come about naturally, and the amount of poetry remains small. If we call something poetry that is written about average events in the world, composed with monotonous vocabulary, it would not qualify as *good* poetry.

Question: I now understand that all poetry comes from the feelings of the heart. But in recent years more bothersome rules have been added, and various regulations about composition have been established, so one cannot compose poetry according to the feelings of his heart. As one contrives his poetic diction, and uses ornate phrases, he finds he has veered from his true feelings, and poetry becomes nothing but a sport. Even if you insist that the true form of poetry is imbedded in that somewhere, it seems that poetry has meandered from its original purpose and goes against the wishes of the *kami*. What do you think?

Answer: As I have already stated, this question sounds reasonable. It is easy to convince people that poetry helps government, brings order to the household, and governs the individual because it is not sport. These ideas are based on the assumption that the original purpose of poetry was to express the true feelings of the person and please the *kami* and Buddha. Most people easily accept and believe this definition of poetry, but when one really thinks about it, poetry is certainly not that sort of thing. One simply follows his heart and composes poetry. This is the original form. Composing a poem based on false feelings, and avoiding pretentious diction suits human emotion. If the poet is embarrassed because of the wicked intentions in his heart, and hides these feelings with words, or uses flowery diction, then natural human emotion spontaneously springs forth.

Question: But if you have no shame for the wickedness in your heart and only desire to hide this wickedness by composing good poetry, does this not go against the definition of "true heart"?

Answer: If it is not the true heart that desires to compose good poetry, then what is it?

Question: You earlier said that poets seek greater elegance within that which is elegant, but then why place restrictions on what anciently were some of the most elegant words in poetry? For example, phrases like *kinofu fa usuki* "yesterday [the color of the leaves] was faint" and *uturu mo kumoru* "[the hazy moon that should] shine is cloudy."

Answer: Phrases like *kinofu fa usuki* and *uturu mo kumoru* are truly elegant; however, if poets in the present use these phrases in their own poetry, this flies in the face of what is elegant, because the poet is *stealing* the words from ancient poets.

Question: It likely is bad to use these words, knowing they were invented by ancient poets. But if the words naturally come from your heart, would this not be elegant?

Answer: If these words naturally came to you in composition, then it would be elegant. But if someone else judges that you had stolen these words from an ancient poet, the poem would lose its elegance. If we were to permit this kind of behavior, then everyone would feign that the words had occurred to him on the spot, and this would break the restrictions, and everyone would start composing poems like:

fonobono to	I think of that small boat
akasi no ura no	disappearing behind an islet
asagiri ni	in the morning mist
sima ga kureyuku	of the faint light of dawn
fune wo si zo omofu	of the bay of Akashi.

[KKS 409]

Question: This explanation sounds somewhat reasonable, but I am still not convinced. If one composed a poem from the spontaneous feelings of his heart, I would not worry about the criticism of others who might accuse me of plagiarism. Is it not trivial to worry about the intentions of others?

Answer: If you say you do not mind the intentions of others, this would mean you could compose poetry as you wish, without regard to the rules or regulations, and there would be no one who could challenge this. But if a person composes poetry, ignoring the intentions of others, breaking the rules, then naturally he will not feel right, and cannot adequately express his feelings. Suppose a poet does not break the rules, and composes a poem with the feelings of his heart; later he learns a certain phrase that he had used happened to be from an ancient poet. Then he would no longer consider the phrase to be his own, but he would change the wording in that poem—this is the natural emotion of poetic composition. Even if you naturally think up some pleasing phrase on your own, but some ancient poet has already used it, then using this phrase is the same as plagiarism.

The true form of poetry is to compose a poem as one feels; yet as time has marched on, the dishonesty in people's hearts has multiplied, and in the present people are no longer naïve, but it is still imperative that one compose poetry with artful phrases. If one wants to produce good poetry, then it is important to obey the rules, and carefully select one's vocabulary.

In spite of this, we cannot claim that the present age is a period of poetic decline. It is the hearts of the people that have declined. Since the divine age, the Way of poetry has had no episodes of rise and decline. It has only mirrored the hearts of various periods of the people. If a person desires to preserve the original form of poetry, then he will compose poetry as his heart dictates. Surely this is true poetry, and it reflects the true heart. …

Question: If you set aside the feelings of a true heart, no matter how flowery the diction used, the poem one composes will not move the spirits or *kami*, regardless of how good the poem is.

Answer: What sways heaven and earth moves the spirits, and *kami* is the depth of the emotion and the final product of poetic composition. No matter how profound the emotion, only declaring, "Oh, how sad, how terribly sad!" will not move the spirits and *kami*. What moves them is profound emotion and beautiful words springing spontaneously from this emotion, but if one of the two is missing, then the poem fails to inspire. When the emotion is deep, and the words are beautiful, the listener is spontaneously impressed, heaven and earth are swayed, and the spirits and *kami* are moved. Consider the poem of Ono no Komachi:

kotofari ya	Is it reasonable?
fi no moto naraba	If this is the origin of the sun
teri mo seme	that also shines on us—
sari tote mo mata	even if it is true,

ame ga sita to fa	then we are under the heavens/rain.[2]

Because our land is called 日本 "the land where the sun originates," it is natural that the sun should shine down on it. While this poem means that we are blessed because we are below the heavens, I doubt she meant that we can command the rain to fall. And she likely did not believe, as children do, that *ame* "heaven" is the same as *ame* "rain,"[3] but Komachi constructed her poem so it appeared that she believed the two were one and the same. Reading this poem, one feels that rain actually did fall. And we even find the following in the poem by Nōin:

ama no kafa	The river of heaven—
nafasiromidu ni	dam up the irrigation water
seki kudase	of the newly planted rice paddies.
amakudarimasu	If you are the *kami* of heaven,
kami naraba kami	rain the water down on us, *kami*.

[*Kin'yō wakashū* 625]

The poet knows there is no actual water in the Milky Way [literally "the river of heaven"], and yet he composed a poem saying, "Give us the water in the river of heaven," which is a fabrication of his feelings, but the record states that the poem moved heaven and it rained. Both poems were not composed from the actual feelings of the poet, but the desire to pray for rain was deep and poignant, and that is clear because the heavens were moved [and rain fell]. . . .

Generally poets like Tō no Tsuneyori, Sōgi [1421–1502], and [Hosokawa] Yūsai spread various strange theories, and established numerous bothersome rules so they could create this Way [of secret traditions] and poetry began its downhill slide. But it is greatly to be lamented that in the present almost everyone believes these traditions deeply without realizing the folly, because they have nothing to do with the true intention of poetry. And perhaps because these people were acting self-importantly, they say that even the famous poems from ancient poets have an ulterior meaning, and this cannot be understood easily, but So-and-So is the recipient of the

2. This is one of the "seven Komachi" poems, poems attributed to Ono no Komachi but that have disputed origins.

3. It is interesting that both *ame* "heaven" and *ame* "rain" not only have the same phonological structure, they have the same pitch accent so the poet is making a skillful play on words.

true meaning, having heard it from someone else. And there are many people who believe this when they hear it. Until the era of Priest Ton'a [1289–1372] the world of poetry was tranquil and worthy, but when a person named Tō no Tsuneyori began spreading spurious ideas, the world of poetry took a turn for the worse.

Secret traditions are absolutely useless in the composition of poetry. The names of these people [Tō, Sōgi, Yūsai] are well known in the world of poetry, but considering that they have not left any especially good poetry, you will then realize that these traditions are worthless. It would seem that their whole lives were spent in propagating secret traditions and strange ideas. I intend to expound in detail in a future work on the fact that there were no secret traditions during the era of *Kokinshū.*

The first person to realize and teach that the secret traditions were really nothing was Priest Keichū of Naniwa. He was well trained in poetry and researched all the ancient documents, breaking the blind traditions of middle antiquity, correcting the mistakes of several centuries. He left many commentaries on poetic works from *Man'yōshū* on and rescued many people from their mistaken ideas. Keichū wrote many works, but most have not been published, and it is regrettable that many people do not know about this scholar. The people who have been fortunate to read his works realize the error of their ways. Thanks to the intervention of this poetic scholar Keichū, there are now people who do not give ear to the secret traditions. He was of a different breed than the other poetic scholars. Of the many theories of his, there are one or two mistakes among ten correct ones, and of him we say, "Sometimes even great men make mistakes." We should not criticize Keichū. The one thing I regret is that he was not a gifted poet, probably because he concentrated on the study of poetics, and placed too much value on the ancient form of poetry; due to this fervor, he was not able to compose good poetry. In all his compositions he modeled his poetry on poems from *Man'yōshū* or earlier, and he took the stand that by the period of *Kokinshū*, poetry was somewhat corrupted, and I believe this attitude adversely affected his own poetry.

The master of the golden gate [Fujiwara Teika] followed the ancient form of poetry, which generally meant the poetry in the first three imperial anthologies [*Kokinshū, Gosenshū, Shūishū*]. In reality no poetry surpasses that recorded in these three anthologies. For the study of poetics, *Man'yōshū* is the foremost, but for the purpose of poetic composition *Man'yōshū* is a poor model in comparison with these three imperial anthologies. It is a grave error to imitate the poetry of *Man'yōshū*, but if the present-day poet uses the poetry in these three anthologies as his model, he will produce good poetry. Gradually his poetry will gain poetic strength, and his poetic flower will bloom spontaneously, and he will eventually produce both flower and fruit. The reason the poetry in *Shin Kokinshū* is so superior is because its poetry was composed with the ancient style of the earlier three anthologies in mind.

Some say the poetry in *Shin Kokinshū* is all flower and no fruit, its poetic style poor, but this is a terrible mistake, spoken by those who cannot judge a good poem from a bad one. The good poems in *Shin Kokinshū* have both flower and fruit. But when poets have composed poetry modeled after *Shin Kokinshū*, they have tended to compose verse in which the flower is obvious, and there is little fruit, and that is why people have shied away from using *Shin Kokinshū* as a poetic model. The reason some ridicule *Shin Kokinshū* poetry is because these ignorant people do not understand poetics. Only when people study the first three anthologies will they come to understand why *Shin Kokinshū* is so superior. One must discern this fact. … *Man'yōshū* is an extremely old work, and most of its poems cannot be used as models for poetic composition. Even if something appears in *Man'yōshū*, if it is rarely used today, it is better if the poet avoids using it in his poetry. In some cases, however, *Man'yōshū* is the best evidence for some poetic diction. Thus, the best path to learning for the student of poetry is first to master the three anthologies, and then as necessity dictates, refer to *Man'yōshū* next.

Question: There have been countless poems composed through the centuries, and I think that everything that can be said with poetic elegance and charm in a poem has already been said, and a new, pleasing poem can no longer be composed. Poetic diction is very limited, so the ancients have composed all the good poems that can be composed, meaning that the only thing poets now can do is to imitate the remnants of the ancients, gradually changing the poetic diction. This means that you cannot compose your own poem, and poetic composition has become meaningless. What do you think?

Answer: This is a naive question that shows you have no understanding of poetry. All poetry follows the professed rules of relying on archaic diction, the poet carefully selecting each word and [now] everyone uses this acceptable diction. Working diligently within this confined diction is the work of the poet. Even if you can find proper words that have not been used before, even beautiful words, still it is almost impossible to use these in poetry. Thus, the most important point is to try to use the ancient words in a new way. So while you use the ancient diction, you alter one or two words, and change a particle here or there. …

When a beginner wants to compose poetry, if he focuses too much on trying to avoid the repetition of words or worries too much about diction, then he becomes discouraged and unsure, and thinks that poetry is beyond him. This attitude is wrong. In the beginning, regardless of the circumstances, the budding poet sets aside what he does not know, relying only on his innate talents, composing as his feelings dictate. After attaining this level [of being able to compose poetry], then the poet should consider avoiding the repetition of words and other rules, and have others read his compositions. If your verse includes violations you had not noticed, or other mistakes, then you edit it. Doing this, you learn that certain words should not be used, or a specific word should not follow another. With this, you learn how to compose poetry on your own, and finally can compose on any topic. You will also gradually be able to judge between good and bad poetry. It should also be noted that it is a waste of time to employ *tricks* in one's poetry when the poet has not even tried his hand at poetry. …

Question: I have heard the story before how poetry can make it rain or move the spirits and the *kami*, but these things are strange, and I do not think that these events are actually possible. In reality in our day I have never heard of anything like that happening. It is natural to assume that if something does not exist in the present that it did not exist in the past. I think these are made-up stories; what do you think?

Answer: Saying that because something does not exist in the present that it also did not exist in the past is nothing but conjecture. How can one judge the past by the yardstick of the present? The only evidence we have of the past is in written records. Because these things are written in these works, it is clear that means that they existed in the past. It is silly to say you should believe everything in these works, but if you do not believe any of these things, then all events from the past become suspicious, and we lose all clues to understanding the past. Also, claiming that all spiritual and supernatural events are fabrications, thus denying their existence, is the viewpoint of those damned Confucian scholars who have no power of discernment. It is terribly narrow-minded.

The insects of summer do not know about the existence of ice in the winter, which is difficult to explain from the knowledge of a laborer; there are strange things in our world that are difficult to comprehend. These things are also expounded in the doctrines of Buddhism. Confucius also said, "[I] do not talk about extraordinary things, strength, chaos, and spirits," this means he did not try to understand things beyond mortal comprehension. How much more is it a waste of time to try to understand the ordinary blessed things bestowed upon our land from the *kami* and spirits. Those who doubt this should carefully read the divine age section of *Nihon shoki*.

Question: In the present I do not hear anything about the virtue of poetry. While it may have moved the spirits and *kami* in the ancient period, it appears that it does not even move people in the present. Poets only argue about the superiority or inferiority of the finished poem, but we do not hear stories when someone composed a poem that was full of emotion and its diction was mysterious, and something happened when someone heard it. Does this not mean that [the influence of] poetry has declined?

Answer: It is not because poetry has declined. It is due to the state of present society that has caused this to happen. Human emotions have become coarse, filled with deceit. But even now, if one were to hear a superior poem, even the base woodcutter with unrefined emotions is moved and feels sadness or other emotions. This is the natural state of the human heart.

Question: I have heard the following from a high-ranking gentleman, "Poetry is a custom of our land, but the diction is the same as that used by women and children, and if you listen to them, you see that the import of these poems is pointless and suspicious. It is not something men engage in; as there are many poems on the topic on love one can see the act of poetry as little more than an amorous affair. If they have no interest in love, then they write on pointless topics like blossoms, birds, the wind, and the moon, composing poems about things that have no real importance. It has no use in today's world, being worthless. Not only that, it degrades the human heart, and is nothing but a method to lead people into lust. One should never compose poetry." What do you think?

Answer: I will answer that the mistaken conception that poetry helps govern the nation and restrain the body is very old, so the opinion [noted above] will appear once in a while. If one wants to help with government or discipline the individual, there are countless other methods in the present instead of poetry. Why should anyone rely on the roundabout method of poetry? Poetry from its beginnings has not had this type of purpose. Its only purpose is to structure the verbal pattern of the feelings of the heart. Also, among the human emotions, love is a very deep sentiment, so it is only natural that love poems have been popular from ancient times. There are also likely some unjust and lustful poems, but that is not the sin of poetry, but the sin of the person who composed the poem. Poetry follows the feelings of the person composing it, and undergoes a thousand different forms. This is the vast and boundless virtue of poetry. ...

Question: From ancient times, there have been innumerable poems on love composed by black-robed monks who have left the world. Why are they able to compose these poems without hesitation? Buddhism counts lust as its number one sin and deeply condemns it, but people actually praise love poems composed by monks. For example, monks like Bishop Henjō are well known in the world of Japanese poetics. How can people praise these poets who appear to have lost their way in Buddhism? Should they not be despised instead?

Answer: What in the world are you talking about? As I have already explained, poetry is composed according to the feelings of the poet, and arranged in a structured verbal pattern. Poetry comes from the intents of the heart, regardless of whether these are good or evil. Is it not proper that a heart focused on love will compose a poem on that topic? If the poem is composed properly, then there is no need to withhold praise. If the poem is superior, then there is no need to question whether the poet is a monk or not.

We can argue another time about the personality and behavior of the poet as well as whether the individual is good or evil, beautiful or ugly, but we should not say these things from the standpoint of the poem. The only thing we should argue about in the Way of poetry is whether the poem is good or not. There is no need to say that he should not compose a poem on love because he is a monk. By the way, do you delude yourself into thinking that all those who have left the world have the heart of Buddha or a Bodhisattva? If a Buddhist monk has the slightest taint of lust, then he should be censured, as there is a great difference between them and the common man; truly lust is strictly forbidden by Buddhism, and there is nothing worse than this as it is a connection to transmigration and obsession. It is thus natural to expect monks to despise lust and work diligently to avoid it, but monks are the same as ordinary people, and there is no way that they have a different nature than regular people, so they have the same human emotions as us.

As everyone desires music and love, there is no reason for monks to hate these. Naturally while the thoughts of their hearts are the same as regular people, having left the world it is proper that they suppress these feelings; however, someone who censures monks for having thoughts of lust in their hearts does not understand human emotions, because while Buddha strictly admonished against this sin, it is difficult for people to avoid. One will understand how difficult it is to avoid by looking at how strict the commandment is. How important that a monk be prudent, avoid lust, and not get involved in love, but because of all this effort, thoughts of lust still well up in their hearts and naturally these thoughts become repressed. (The only things that do not have hearts are trees and rocks.) So why not let them give vent to these feelings in poetry? Is that not the sympathetic thing to do?

In the end it is inevitable that superior love poems would come from monks than from regular people. However, in the present among monks who compose poetry, most hesitate to write poems on love. But that is not confined to just poems on love; this is not true just of poetry. Monks in the present put on airs that they have absolutely no interest in love. This is proof that the hearts of both monks and regular people in our present society are full of deceit, and their way of thinking is mistaken. Just because they say that they are monks, why should they not have thoughts of passion in their hearts? Be that as it may, recall that anciently people were honest and unsophisticated, and there were few ancient examples of deception or putting on airs.

Once an aged monk came to see a woman called Kyōgoku no Miyasudokoro (and he was touched by the beauty of this woman), so he took her hand and composed the poem, *yuragu tama no wo* "the sound of the rustling bells on a string."[4] This ancient story is profound and kind, but now if a monk composes a poem on love, people will treat him with contempt, call him a lecherous priest, and shun him. And even among the monks, there are many that pretend to be very proper and chaste, and rather than staying away from lust, they are seeking for it in their hearts, and their behavior is more lewd than the average person. This kind of deceit is beyond loathing.

Question: The desire for love is a very deeply rooted emotion, and at the beginning of the three hundred poems in the *Odes* there is a song known as "getting along" [関雎]. *Liji* also notes that love is the great desire of humanity. Naturally this is as it should be. But this is limited to marital relations as husband and wife are intimate with each other, and it is natural that they should have a deep bond with each other. But if one were to have thoughts for a daughter whose parents had not given their permission to see and he tried to tempt her, or if one were to have improper relations with someone else's woman, this is not love. Anciently there were many examples of such lasciviousness in our country. Works such as *Ise monogatari* and *Genji monogatari* are filled with stories like this. So why consider poetry to be an exception and praise these [wicked] situations?

---

4. This originally was MYS 4493, a poem written about the bells on a string attached to a ceremonial broom, which sounded when the person simply touched the broom. This poem later takes on a life of its own, where a story has it that an old monk from Shiga Temple went to see Miyasudokoro, and just touching her hand caused his heart to make a sound, like the bells noted above.

Answer: The answer to this question is the same as my response to the question regarding Buddhist priests and love. Truly unrighteous love is extremely aberrant and should be censured. Thus in the teachings of the sages they have expounded on the doctrine of morality at great length so that no one may misunderstand, and no matter how foolish a person may be, he knows clearly what is unrighteous behavior. This is common knowledge in society and a religious commandment.

However, this knowledge and commandment is irrelevant in the sphere of poetry. Everyone understands that within human emotion there are things you may do and things you should not do. Especially in relation to illicit relations with another person's wife, even a playful child knows that this is wrong. On the other hand, it is the way of love that while we know in our heart that certain emotions lead to actions we should not engage in, there are some emotions that move us because these are so strong and deep that we cannot suppress them. And while we know these actions are wrong there are times when people commit unrighteous actions. So there is a difference between being able to suppress these desires and check oneself, and being unable to do this, letting oneself be swept away by the emotion.

Of course being able to suppress these feelings is better, but when you try to suppress impossible to endure feelings it appears on your face and leads you to commit acts that are not good. This reflects the deep feelings and inner workings of the heart, and poetry is created from these deep emotions. And this is why Genji and Sagoromo [of *Sagoromo monogatari*] act the way they do.

So people read and enjoy poetry, and enjoy tales such as *Ise monogatari* and *Genji monogatari*, keeping in mind that these were written based on emotions that everyone in the world experiences. Since people are not sages, they will do things that are bad and regrettable and encounter these thoughts in their hearts. We do good and bad things, and these come from our thoughts and then these thoughts become actions. Since poetry comes from human emotions, it is reasonable that there will also be poetry that is not virtuous.

At any rate, among the poems that capture deep human emotion, there have been many outstanding poems from ancient times. When reading the ancient poems, one should keep this in mind. A person has feelings for someone else's wife, and he is just a common person, not a sage or a wise man, so how could he suppress these feelings? It has been a truth from the ancient past that humans struggle to conquer their feelings. It is truly the problem of the human heart whether a person can suppress those feelings. But this debate has absolutely nothing to do with the Way of poetry, because poetry is only concerned with admiring superior poetic composition. I have already given a detailed exposition in relation to whether it is proper to call poetry the "great Way of our land," and the fact that people label other ideologies [such as Confucianism or Buddhism] as "the great Way." Aside from what has been said above, there is one more thing I would like to say. For example, Confucian scholars label their teachings "the great Way" based on the instructions of the sages, and claim that other Ways are heresy or "minor Ways." Buddhist scholars make their traditions "the great Way" and denigrate all other teachings in society as "minor Ways" or "deviating Ways." Each group labels their own thinking as "the great Way," and demotes everyone else to something minor, actions that are seen in a variety of situations.

If one wants to compose a good poem, then the first principle is to carefully select the vocabulary. It is important to select elegant words and put these together in an elegant fashion. The reason for this is because poetry is the Way of language. It is the Way of being able to string together the feelings in one's heart gracefully. Simply scribbling down the feelings in one's heart as they are does not constitute poetry. Even if one forms these feelings into the structure of a poem, it becomes an inconsequential, pathetic poem. So you see that carefully selecting your words is of critical importance. If the words chosen are elegant, then even if the emotions are a bit shallow, these feelings are pulled along by the elegance of the vocabulary, and one's heart then becomes moved more deeply. On the other hand, no matter how profound the emotion if the vocabulary is common, then the resulting poem sounds superficial. ...

Question: It is true that *waka* is a wonderful thing, but when compared to the poetry and prose of foreign countries, it only represents the [immature] feelings of women and children, being something frivolous, insincere, silly, and awkward. It is not something that a man would engage in, it lacking even a single upright, clear-cut application, lacking any logical use. So in what way can you claim that it is a superior endeavor?

Answer: I have already explained this in detail previously. Perhaps this viewpoint generally originates from the idea that *waka* is used to govern the state or the individual. Or perhaps it is said in relation to someone who has no feelings, who is like a tree or a stone. Regardless, it is a silly idea. As a person born into this world, as a human being born into this divine country, there is not a single person who does not have human emotions. But in recent years this kind of opinion is frequently expounded because it is based on Chinese literary culture in most cases, and naturally if you look through Chinese works you will see that these are filled with debate and arguments. Even in ordinary poetry and rhapsodies, as these were originally written with Chinese characters, these are not peaceful like our poetry, but somehow have harshness to them, giving the reader a cut-and-dried impression. The feeling of an intense profound emotion is superficial [in these forms of poetry], and if we use this as our standard, then naturally their poetry when compared with *waka* is as different as ice and charcoal.

As people have generally used China as their model, composing only poetry and prose in Chinese, they naturally end up with the human emotions of the Chinese people as if they were able to become Chinese. Of course people should notice that if they were Chinese, both poetry and prose would display natural, deeply embedded human feelings, but in general Japanese people do not notice this. The reason that Japanese people believe that Chinese poetry and prose are inferior to Japanese poetry in the way that it portrays profound emotions is due to a poor understanding of circumstances in other countries. If a person were truly able to become a Chinese person with those attending emotions, then surely that person would say he is able to comprehend the profound emotions of their literature. But when these people look at *waka* from this half-Chinese, half-Japanese emotional standpoint, they feel that *waka* is sloppy and superficial compared to Chinese literature.

These things are all related to customs connected to Chinese literacy. Even in relation to people who should not be influenced by these customs, somehow this foreign masculinity and its cut-and-dry attitude appeals to their emotions, and they come to think that way. This also matches the nature of warriors of recent ages who put emphasis on energy. And there are people completely unrelated to these conditions who criticize poetry for no good reason; these people likely belong to the camp of people lacking any feelings, callous like a tree or a stone. …

Question: *Waka* and Chinese poetry have different geographical origins, and their structure and poetic diction also differ greatly, but they are the same in being composed from raw human emotions as well as undergoing change over time; so in this instance there is no difference. If this is the case, rather than deciding to compose insincere and frivolous *waka*, one should choose to compose Chinese poetry; it is better to compose Chinese poetry that has masculine and clearly demarcated features, allowing one to learn Chinese characters and open the door to many opportunities for something productive. What do you think?

Answer: It is right to allow people to do what they like, and others should not dictate what people do. If one thinks Chinese poetry is superior, then let that person compose Chinese poetry. If a person thinks *waka* is fascinating, then let that person compose *waka*. And if a person is ignorant of both Chinese poetry and *waka*, but finds *haikai* to be closely related in emotion [to these other forms], then let that person compose *haikai*. Furthermore, if a person finds Chinese poetry, *waka*, linked verse, and *haikai* to be unprofitable, then let that person search for something they enjoy doing. It does not, however, mean that if an individual does not have at least this understanding, then it will become an obstacle to the person as he goes through life, so let people do what they enjoy doing. Also, the Way of ethics, one's sense of duty, and the regimen of one's daily life should not be ignored for even one day, meaning that you cannot argue about Chinese poetry and *waka* or other arts in the same vein.

So if one were to ask if there is no difference between Chinese poetry and *waka* compared with other arts, [the answer is] that it is not true. There is a difference. Things that are living that are endowed with emotions will express those emotions, so poetic composition is indispensable. No matter how vulgar a person may be, he should be able to compose a poem worthy of his status. For example, even a child who knows nothing of the world can raise his voice and enjoy singing, which shows clearly that humans are born with an indispensable ability to compose poetry.

At any rate, anything that has innate emotions always has a connection to poetic composition, so an adult who has the ability to discern but does not know how to compose poetry is indeed pitiful, is he not? Thus, Chinese poetry and *waka* are things that cannot be debated in the same spirit as other arts. It is not an overstatement to declare that these are critical to everyday life. I have said things in relation to everyday people, but if we are to speak of people in high authority, or those who govern others, it is even truer. How can these people get along without knowing how to compose poetry? One can glean clues from Chinese poetry and *waka* in relation to discerning the wise and foolish among his retainers, and in learning about local customs, or the intricate affairs of the local populace, and the rise and fall of the times. In consideration of these things, Chinese poetry and *waka* can be of great assistance to rulers. Is it now clear why one cannot debate about Chinese poetry and *waka* in the same vein as other arts?

Next, if one were to ask me which is superior, which is the most excellent between Chinese poetry and *waka*, as I have said before, people should pursue that which they enjoy, and refrain from dictating what a person must do. But if someone were to press me for an answer, I likely would offer the following response. First, Chinese poetry is a product of China, and no matter how accomplished one is, in the end, it is foreign, and since it is written in a language that is not our own, the student has only a superficial knowledge of the poem, gaining hints from the Chinese characters. This superficial knowledge becomes more sharpened with the passing of time, and one gets a better grasp of the depth of meaning by reading other Chinese works, so poets of Chinese poetry in the present are more accurate in their compositions than those in the past. However, that does not change the fact that basically it still is a foreign medium, so naturally it will never reach the level of a Japanese tradition.

This is especially true because poetry is a linguistic endeavor, and Chinese characters have phonological characteristics such as open and closed syllables and the four tones. These differences are naturally apparent to the speakers in China, but for people in our country, no matter how long one studies these it is like a person trying to relieve an itch on his foot by scratching through the top of the shoe. …

Compared to Chinese poetry, *waka* is a tradition dating back to the creation of our land in the divine age, and since it is composed based on the natural characteristics and phonology of our language, according to the natural emotions of our people, clearly there is nothing annoying about composing *waka*. But as time has marched on, both the vocabulary and human nature changed, so that even now the poetic diction of *waka*, in other words, the natural words of our language, have become difficult to understand. These words have become like foreign words, difficult for people to appreciate. But as these are the natural words of our language, when you learn these ancient poems and infuse your heart with these, when you experience a change you find that the elegant vocabulary of the ancient poems has become part of you, and there is nothing difficult about them. This then is natural; there is nothing foreign about these elegant words and the emotions of the ancient people. [At this point] you notice a great difference between our poetry and the itchy foot inside the shoe [Chinese poetry]. If you continue down this same path to elegance, you will find that your heart naturally gravitates toward the poetry of our country and away from the roundabout and convoluted poetry of China. These are my own thoughts on the matter, but as all individuals have their own ideas, it is best if everyone does what they enjoy.

Question: If we are to make ancient poetry our model, replicating poetry composed earnestly from the true feelings of the ancient poets, then why discard the ancient poems found in *Nihon shoki*, *Man'yōshū*, and other works, and select poems from *Kokinshū*, where these poems contain some embellishment and playful design?

Answer: As the poetry found in *Nihon shoki* and *Man'yōshū* is very primitive, we find many poems that are clumsy, provincial, and unappealing. Poetry in the three imperial anthologies has a wonderful balance of flower and fruit, and that is why these poems are generally used as a poetic compass, square, level, and line. Even among the poetry in *Man'yōshū*, poets like Hitomaro, Akahito, and others have superior poems that have all been based on the ancient standard, which is why you find many of the poems quoted in later anthologies, including *Shin Kokinshū*. This idea of a proper standard applies to a variety of things, not just poetry.

For example, Confucius said, "When nature and culture are in balance, you get a gentleman."[5] The phrase "nature and culture are in balance" does not refer to things as they are, failing to appraise the beauty or repulsiveness of something; not only does the substance need to be solid, but this phrase refers to the balance between the substance and the surface, where repulsiveness is withdrawn and beauty is added. So, as poetry is something that should impress the listener, influence heaven and earth, and move the spirits and *kami*, is it thus not natural that we should seek after good poetry as much as possible, beautiful poetry if at all possible?

Question: There is a trend that states that poetry is the great Way of our land. What do you think?

Answer: That is incorrect. Confucian scholars call the path of the sages "the great Way." Buddhist scholars call the doctrine of Buddha "the great Way." Laozi and Zhuangzi claimed that the "great Way" was to place the standard of virtue in a natural state. In each case these people claim that their thinking is some great Way. If someone were to ask what is the great Way of our country, that would be traditional Shintō. "Traditional Shintō" is the Way that was established from the beginning of the creation of our land in the divine age. It is completely different from what people affiliated with Shintō call Shintō today. ...

Question: What do you think about the idea that on the surface *waka* is Shintō, but buried deep within is a Buddhist sentiment?

Answer: This is also mistaken. Poetry has nothing to do with either Shintō or Buddhism. As *waka* is a natural form born in our country, it is not completely unconnected with traditional Shintō, but it is a grave mistake to see the surface of *waka* related to Shintō. Later people are the ones who forced a foreign association on our culture, connecting it with doctrines like Confucianism, Buddhism, and the teachings of Laozi, but originally there was no connection. These people tried to gain a deeper understanding of poetry, but the result is shallow understanding. They tried to broaden their learning, but the result is narrow learning. ...

5. Found in the "Yongye" chapter, *The Analects*. Translation from Nylan (2014:16).

Question: I find it strange when you say that anciently the feelings of the Japanese were sincere and they did not engage in deception, and even in *waka* they composed poetry according to their raw emotions without adding any clever devices.[6] I think that anciently people did engage in deception, and their poetry also included poems that were not written simply according to raw emotion, but included clever devices. What do you say?

Answer: You are correct. Simply because these people lived in the ancient past does not mean that they were all honest, and there were no people who were deceitful to some extent. Even among the ancient people there were many who were full of wickedness, lies, and deception. Even in the present we find that there are some people who are quite sincere and simple, so one cannot make blanket statements about people. However, if you compare the overall characteristics of the ancient past with the present, anyone will notice the change.

One can make the same claim about *waka*. Even among the ancient poems in *Nihon shoki* and *Man'yōshū* there are poems that do not fit the classification of having been composed using the raw emotions of the poet, because some definitely include clever devices. First, arranging one's words into five stanzas totaling thirty-one syllables is a type of clever device. If one were to simply lay out his feelings as he wrote without putting it into some type of framework, it would not be a poem. So if the poet fits his words into a structure and puts those words together in a poetic fashion, he is already using a clever device. One should not interpret a clever device to be a form of deception, however. Even in cases where the poet writes his honest feelings, when he frames these words in a literary structure, at that point these honest feelings are then communicated well and can move the listener. These feelings cannot move the listener if the words are simply lined up without any elegance, as a lack of structure prevents the sincere feelings from being transmitted to the listener.

As an example, when you hear someone crying, if they are just weeping, then their sadness is shallow. And yet when one's sorrow is deep, the person raises his voice in grief, and his words naturally have a kind of literary structure, which profoundly moves the heart of the listener. In gen-

6. In Japanese this is 巧み, various clever ways to express one's feelings. Norinaga goes on to make a distinction by saying that even the 5-stanza, 31-syllable structure of *waka* is in its own right a device, so he is not saying that all these are necessarily bad. He later mentions that these devices used for their own sake are fictions, and this pulls the poet away from expressing his true feelings.

eral when a person is overcome with strong sadness his voice of grief spontaneously takes on a crude type of literary structure, which does not rise to the level of a clever device, but it is not completely natural either. And yet as this literary effect attends the voice of grief, the person's sorrow is transmitted to others in the vicinity and has a profound effect on those around.

On the surface this kind of experience seems to be of little consequence, but such is not the case. For example, in China when a group of people is in mourning, there are regulations governing the manner of performing the act of mourning, and that may appear to be something trivial, but it is based on the profound wisdom of the sages who understand the workings of the human heart.

Waka is much the same, where one arranges his true feelings according to a literary structure; this is poetry. As long as we can label it poetry, then we cannot claim it has no clever devices. This is true of the earliest poetry, and compared with the poetry in *Man'yōshū* this is even more accurate. And while we admit this, the clever devices of later periods are of a vastly different nature. …

Question: It is a long accepted opinion within the circles of *waka* and Chinese poetry that these forms of poetry can be used to assist in government. Upon what do you base your assertion that poetry is not composed to assist in the government?

Answer: Your question is quite logical. This question arises from people not being able to distinguish between the effect of poetry and its essential form. The essential form of *waka* originally was not to aid in governing, but to give voice to the feelings in one's heart, arranged in a literary format. The assistance to government through poetry comes through the effect of poems written for that specific purpose.

However, people utilize poetry that was not specifically written to aid government for that purpose because originally poetry is composed by all people, regardless of their standing in society, from rulers and ministers down to the common people, based on every individual's thoughts, so those in authority can look at the poetry of those under them and clearly see the intents of their hearts. For those in authority it is imperative that they know the inner workings of the minds of the masses, but it can be difficult to know the thoughts of people when the nobility live far away from the main population, so they use poetry written by the populace to gain an understanding of the feelings of the people. In reality there is nothing more useful to know the thoughts of people than to examine the poetry they have composed. Based on this thinking people claim that poetry helps govern the land, and that is why Confucius counted *The Odes* as one of the six classics. And that is why Ki no Tsurayuki said what he did in the preface to *Kokinshū*.[7] As *Kokinshū* and other poetic anthologies were compiled by imperial command, Tsurayuki first needed to justify the existence of poetry as something the state could use. You see this clearly in the words of Tsuryaki's preface, that even though anciently poetry could be leveraged politically, in the present he claims that it is only useful for love and amusement, so he is lamenting that poetry is being misused.

At any rate, the effect of poetry is to aid in governing all under heaven, but it also has an effect on love and amusement. Among these effects, the greatest and best influence is to be of some aid to those in power to govern, but its effect on love and amusement is a minor and evil use. However, the existence of a greater or minor influence, or good and evil usage, comes about because of how the poetry is leveraged, and this has no relation to the original intent of poetry. And that is why Tsurayuki wrote what he did, that in his day poets tended to use poetry for love, which was a minor, unproductive pastime, and he lamented that the poets did not seem to realize that there was a greater use for poetry in being able to aid those in power. It is a narrow-minded individual who interprets Tsurayuki's statement to mean that poetry is generally to be composed for political purposes and should not be written about love. It is in the leveraging of poetry that we get a greater or minor influence, or a good and evil usage. …

Question: You are probably correct that the secret transmissions of *Kokinshū* (*kokin denju*) have no value, but what do you mean that these are actually detrimental?

Answer: The secret transmissions of *Kokinshū* have been a great hindrance to the Way of poetry, having been a great disaster. I say this because in recent generations the importance of your poetic master and the secret traditions he possesses has eclipsed the importance of the skill in composing superior poetry. Because of this it has become more difficult for poetic masters to come from common people interested in poetry, which has closed other avenues in *waka*. People claim that they have received secret traditions about *Kokinshū*, but these are as superficial as dew on the grass, and yet these have been a great hindrance to poetry. Now it would be

---

7. From context it appears that Norinaga has reference to the following paragraph in the preface, "Because people nowadays value outward show and turn their minds toward frivolity, poems are mere empty verses and trivial words. … In the beginning it was entirely different. … We may suppose that the Emperor understood which man was wise and which foolish when he perused their sentiments" (McCullough 1985:5).

difficult to rid oneself of a tradition that came from long ago, but there were no secret traditions about *Kokinshū* until the era of Priest Ton'a [1289–1372]. But after this we have the example of Tō no Tsuneyori who manufactured these "secret traditions," and deceived Sanjōnishi Sanetaka [1455–1537] into believing that these traditions were true, and Sanekata accepted them. That is the beginning of this madness. ...

Question: How do you know that the secret transmissions of *Kokinshū* were fabricated?

Answer: If a person has a little intelligence and is discerning, s/he will be able to see this without any assistance from someone else, however, because everyone in society believes that these secret transmissions are authentic and they pay respect to these, questions like yours arise, so let me outline it for you in detail.

First, should poetry have something like secret transmissions to begin with? It is important that people consider this fact. What kind of secret transmission would there be for something that originates in the hearts of people? A poem that cannot be understood without reliance on some secret transmission is useless; it cannot be called a poem. For example, in these secret transmissions there is mention of the *yobukotori*;[8] do these people want us to believe that the poet of that poem is the only one who knows which bird he has reference to as he composed a poem about it? There are already many poems written about *yobukotori* in *Man'yōshū*, and likewise there are many poems written about this bird in anthologies after *Kokinshū*. These poets knew exactly which bird they were composing about, and they composed poems about these birds because you can find them everywhere. It is silly that something like this be included in the secret transmissions, since poems before and after *Kokinshū* wrote about this bird. It is said that these secrets were transmitted from Tsurayuki down to Fujiwara Mototoshi [1060–1142] through their respective daughters and that is why this information was not available to people in society, but this is a wholly invented story. If there was no one before Mototoshi to receive these secret traditions, then why are there so many poems written about *yobukotori* after *Kokinshū*? Besides, it is suspicious that while there were four compilers of *Kokinshū*, why would only Tsurayuki be privy to these secrets and the other three compilers be ignorant? Also, if Tsurayuki was the only one to know about these traditions, then where did his reputation

8. The name of the bird, "the bird that calls children," is likely a euphemism, but this name obscures the actual bird. Most scholars believe it refers to the cuckoo or the bush warbler. Both have distinctive calls.

for these things come from, if they were secret? There is no mention of these secret transmissions until the age of Ton'a. …

Question: Keichū said that there were many mistakes in the poetry of Minister Teika and he could not accept these. In spite of this, why do you revere Minister Teika as a poetic master?

Answer: First, Keichū pondered on the original form of poetry and through his investigation he broke down the blind theories of recent generations; he put his heart and soul into saving *waka* from the pitiful state that it had fallen into, so he did not have the energy to argue about the style of poetry. He only completed his work in bringing to light how poetry ought to be. I have inherited his work, and so I have pondered on the changes poetry has undergone over time, and I have come to the realization that poetry reached its most beautiful, its most perfect form in *Shin Kokinshū*.

Question: So if you revere Minister Teika as a poetic master, then why do you follow Keichū's theories and not those of the Nijō tradition?

Answer: What you currently call the tradition of the Nijō family is based very loosely on the teachings of Minister Teika, but in essence this tradition actually goes against what Minister Teika taught. I have already explained this in detail, and noted why I do not follow the Nijō tradition. It is because of the work of Keichū that I was able to see that the teachings of the Nijō tradition and those of Minister Teika are at odds, and that is why I follow the teachings of Keichū. …

In general, people all have their own opinions, but there are some who do not feel that the present poetry of the poetic masters is superior; however, they feel that if they do not become students of these poetic masters then no matter how skillful the poems they produce they will not receive recognition. Thus, in order to receive recognition they swallow their pride and join the schools of these poetic masters.

[MNZ 1976, 2:1–79]

☙

MAN'YŌSHŪ KOGI
KOGAKU[1]

Kamochi Masazumi | 1858

[This is the title of one section of Chapter 3 of *Man'yōshū kogi sōron*, which is the introductory part of Kamochi's seminal work, *Man'yōshū kogi*. This work was published in 1891, roughly thirty-three years after his death in 1858. Masazumi follows the tradition of Mabuchi, seeing poetry as more than just an emotional or scholary endeavor: it was the portal through which the people of Japan could gain access to the ancient Way. His title "Kogaku" means "Ancient Studies."]

A person once asked something like the following, "In the sixteenth year of Emperor Ōjin, Wani was sent from Paekche to our court and introduced *kanji*. From the time people began to learn how to read, [these literate] people gradually mixed in foreign customs with those of our own country. Some two hundred fifty years later Buddhism was introduced from Paekche, and then Shōtoku Taishi and Soga no Umako held discussions together, and after they had obtained a deep faith in the religion, Buddhism gradually began to spread. Coming down to the reigns of Emperors Kōtoku and Tenchi, the entire society had become adorned with foreign customs, and even the organization of the government began to use foreign systems in all cases. Poets of the Fujiwara and Nara periods had become more skilled in composing poetry than they had in the past, and famous poets began to appear, but we hear almost nothing about people who remained true to the imperial way of the *kami*, able to avoid the influence of Confucianism or Buddhism.

"On the surface people adorned their words with Confucian ideology, but in the background they were actually clothed in Buddhist theology; this state became increasingly frequent. We see these events in our ancient histories, where nothing is hidden. Because of this, would it be proper to claim that poets in the Fujiwara and Nara eras became more adept at poetic composition because they had studied foreign teachings for several centuries?

1. I have taken the current translation from leaves 83–89.

"It is natural that poets would yearn to compose poetry in imitation of the poetic style of the Fujiwara and Nara eras. This period was the pinnacle of foreign learning, and as these poets came from that time frame, they would have been educated in the customs of that time, so it likely was difficult for them to divorce themselves from this foreign heart. If these people were able to make a clean break from the heart of Confucianism and Buddhism and endeavor to elucidate the legitimacy of the Way of the imperial *kami*, then poets of this time naturally would have yearned for and studied the older style of poetry before the advent of foreign teachings. However, in relation to poetry, until the period under consideration poets generally called their poetry 'the old style,' and in many cases they were apt to claim their poetry was built around the ideal of the Way of the imperial *kami*."

In response to why this is, I answered that I have thoroughly read and digested *Man'yōshū* and I always state that I want to elucidate the Way of the imperial *kami* first, and second I want people to yearn for the elegance in the *kotodama* of the ancient words.[2] Let me explain in detail why I think this is outstanding.

Although it is reasonable that Japanese should revere and admire the Way of the imperial *kami* as supreme, remembering to do this day and night, even people by the time of the Nara era had lost sight of the distinctiveness of our country compared to foreign lands, and they even called foreign lands in general "great China." This was not done to be fawning of the Chinese, but was a natural result of people drowning in foreign ways unawares. Because of this, during the Nara era the hearts and actions of people generally were stained with a foreign influence. In the present aside from this idea that everything is in imitation of foreign things, aside from the style of poetry, there is also the theory that in those days [the Nara era] people did not yearn much to adhere to the Way of the imperial *kami*; however, that is the conclusion of those who view these things, and if we care-

2. *Kotodama* 言霊 is literally the spirit within words or utterances. The *Encyclopedia of Shintō* (1999:384) states, "*Kotodama* refers to the spiritual power that is contained within words, but also refers to the conception that spiritual power can be manifested through the intonation of words. This is explained as *an* aspect of animism, or alternatively is explained from the perspective of its function as influencing a person's mind. There is also the view that this way of thinking is one of the special characteristics that define Japanese culture. Especially in the world of *waka* poetry (thirty-one syllable poems in five lines of five, seven, five, seven, seven) it is traditional to think that words "move heaven and earth." *Kotodama* was also *an* important concept among National Learning (*kokugaku*) and Shintō scholars. However, some have put forth the view that originally only spells and incantations were seen as having the force of divine power, and that historically *kotodama* belief arose during the period when the *Man'yōshū* was compiled."

fully sift through the details, then there is no problem, if people selected the good and rid themselves of the evil. If we believe all the written accounts, did not even the Chinese say that you should probably not write anything? In spite of society being bathed in foreign teachings to this extent, as expected, the customs of the divine age can still be found accurately contained in the rituals of the *kami* and in the words of poetry. It is with awe and trembling that I say this, but when Amaterasu Ōmikami, the divine ancestor, took the imperial mirror in her hand she declared those words to the Imperial Grandson, "This land of gem-like rice ears of eternal, five hundred autumns, even fifteen hundred autumns of the land of Toyo Ashihara is a land that should be governed by my children. Thus, you will descend from heaven and rule over that land. Surely we will watch over the prosperity of the high throne of the imperial inheritance."[3] Thus the imperial line was given a weighty responsibility, and our country was established as a land to govern eternally the other countries to the edges of the world, and [the emperor] as a visible *kami* pacified our land and the four quarters of the ocean and has ruled in peace. At the court of the emperor, the Way was fully prepared from long ago, and though time passed and there were great changes in the world, be it changes from Chinese influence, or Buddhist influence, the Way of the imperial *kami*, the imperial throne and imperial history, has not changed for one thousand reigns or ten thousand years. In the divine age and in the present it is the same light of imperial rule that shines from heaven to earth throughout the country. How awe-inspiring that the divine rituals or the words of poetry within the Way of the *kami* have not changed. There are no mistakes. And because these have remained to the present we say "the solemn land of the imperial *kami*" or "the land where the *kotodama* of words prospers."

Now, through the prosperity of the *kotodama* of words we can appreciate this Way of the imperial *kami* which produces blessings. As this is the case, it is impossible to appreciate this Way unless it is through the thriving *kotodama* of words. *Man'yōshū* is our greatest resource for people to comprehend the reason for the prosperity of the *kotodama* of words. Those people whose hearts follow the learning of China and neglect the way of the sages are vastly different in thinking than those who devalue the learning of poetry. One famous example of people in the Nara era diving head first into this foreign Way is Yamanoe no Okura who wrote the following in Chinese, "There is not a day that I fail to revere the three treasures of Buddhism" and "Confucius said, 'It is the form of man that we re-

3. This is not an actual quote from *Kojiki* or *Nihon shoki*, but is a reworking by Kamochi.

ceive from heaven and do nothing to change it.'"[4] Considering that Okura wrote these things, we see that he was tarnished with foreign ideas to the bottom of his heart, and you can visualize the paths that he believed in, so the poetry that he composed should contain images like bhūta-tathatā,[5] *yin-yang*, and the five virtues.[6] However, on the other hand, surprisingly we find,

kamiyo yori	The tradition from
ifitutekuraku	the divine age
soramitu	that has been orally handed down
yamato no kuni fa	through narrative
sumegami no	and in proclamation is:
itukusiki kuni	that the land of Yamato,
kotodama no	a sky-filling land,
sakifafu kuni to	is the solemn land of the *kami*,
kataritugi	a land thriving through
ifitugafikeri	the *kotodama* of words.
ima no yo no	All people in the present
fito mo kotogoto	see evidence of this,
manomafe ni	hear evidence of this,
mitari siritari	and acknowledge this fact.[7]

Is it not noble that Okura said these things? If these words of Yamanoe Okura were like those of Shintō scholars in later eras, saying things such as we should avoid the Way of foreign countries, analogous to words spoken by followers of the Way of the *kami* then one could state that he is putting on airs and talking about events from the divine age; however, because he had such a deep belief in foreign philosophies like Confucianism and Buddhism, for one man to compose such a poem, I do not think we can level harsh criticism at him. This state is truly one transmitted down to society from the divine age and a variety of the ancient traditions still existed at that time. In that era of Okura's, the heart of the average person still esteemed the ancient vocabulary from the divine age

4. Found in MYS 896. The quote from Confucius appears to be a reworking (or an abbreviation) of a line from *Chunqiu fanlu*, "Man receives life from heaven and he has a disposition for good and evil. He is able to nourish [the body] but cannot change it."

5. This has reference to the nature of Buddha being unchanging through time.

6. The five virtues refer to humanness, righteousness, proper behavior, knowledge, and trust.

7. Quoted from the beginning lines of MYS 894, a poem by Okura.

and we may know that this was a natural circumstance, because he says "all people in the present see evidence of this;" obviously this is something delightful and dear.

From an early period, either during the reign of Emperor Kōtoku or perhaps Tenchi, the workings of society and literature already had begun to change into a foreign style, but Okura's poem provides evidence that in the poetic vocabulary the ancient lexicon still existed. This is not a poem that teaches or sermonizes a principle, and this is a point that people should respect and not hastily overlook.

Again, this same poet [Okura] composed a poem based on emotions that were in commotion:

ame fe yukaba	If you go to heaven
na ga mani mani	you may do as you please.
tuti naraba	If you remain on earth
ofokimi imasu	then there is a great ruler.
kono terasu	Below the sun and the moon
fituki no sita fa	which sheds light here
amakumo no	to the end of where
mukabusu kifami	the clouds of the sky touch;
taniguku no	to the ends of the place
sawataru kifami	where the toads dwell—
kikosiwosu	this is the superior land
kuni no mafora zo	that our sovereign rules over.
kanikaku ni	Certainly it is not a place
fosiki mani mani	where one can do this or that
sika ni fa arazi ka	as his heart desires.[8]

This is a very noble poem. Here the poet forgets about his father and mother, his spouse and children, and the poem has at its core teachings about the vanity of the hearts of people in this world, so it does not completely concern the role of obligation between sovereign and subject; however, on the lexical surface is it not natural to see the main point as the responsibility between sovereign and subject? Truly, as communicated through this poem the land below the sun and moon that shine in the firmament continues "to the ends of where the clouds of the sky are, to the ends of the place to the ends of the place where the toad dwells." How I tremble to speak these words, but this land is governed by the august exis-

8. Quoted from the last third of MYS 800.

tence, the emperor, so there is nowhere below the heavens where someone can just wander off and hide, doing as they please. If one were to journey to heaven then one could do as they wish, but as that is currently an impossible wish, one should compose themselves, and return to reality. This poem displays respect to the imperial court of our ruler, and shows that his actions do not go against, do not defy, the imperial will in the least, but demonstrate that the poet is obedient; it displays a deep, heartfelt reverence. While he loves his father and mother, his spouse and children, he encourages people to put their hearts into the work in society.

Even a poet who yearned so deeply for foreign ideas as found in Confucianism and Buddhism is able to compose a poem speaking to the upbringing from his father and mother; we know this because Ōtomo Yakamochi composed this verse:

ame tuti no	From the beginning
fazime no toki yu	of heaven and earth
utusomi no	it was decided that
yasotomo no wo fa	the many government officials
ofokimi ni	in this visible world
maturofu mono to	would be employed
sadamareru	as servants of the Great Lord.[9]

This demonstrates that at that time the courtiers did not mention how well the emperor governed, and for even a short period of time, people could not spend even one day below the sun and moon that shine in the sky without being of service to the sovereign. Thus, from the beginning of the creation of heaven and earth, to the very borders of the land the distinction between sovereign and subject was firmly established, a principle that never varied, never changed, and all the officials, from Omi and Muraji down to the farmers under heaven in the four quarters and eight directions, all these people never doubted these things in the least. If a crisis occurred, then people made up their minds what to do, as recorded in the ancient vernacular,

umi yukaba	We will promise to die
miduku kabane	by the side of our Great Lord!
yama yukaba	Even if we travel by sea
kusa musu kabane	and our corpses are soaked in sea water

9. A quote from the beginning stanzas of MYS 4214.

ofokimi no	or even if we travel over mountains
fe ni koso siname	and our corpses are overgrown with weeds.[10]

Regardless that the emperor was not the center of all communication, the poet ended up composing a poem with the sovereign as the main subject.

Nevertheless, in that land of China there are stories of subjects who remonstrated with the sovereign three times, and if the sovereign would not give ear then the subject would leave [the sovereign's service]. Or when a son argued with his father three times and the father would not give ear, then the son would cry and sob, demanding that his father comply. It is good for a child to follow his father, but does our country not have a vastly different standard when we consider that in China a subject would take leave of his lord and depart? Among all the many differences between our land and those across the sea, China is a land where it has historically been a difficult task to make a clean distinction between sovereign and subject, so should we consider it servile if a subject were to argue with his lord three or four times, and the lord still did not give ear, so he was obedient out of obligation? It may be true in China, but how unseemly if in our own country one were to remonstrate with the sovereign three times and he still would not give heed, or if one were to retreat from the sovereign's presence because he could not bear to be obedient! Going back to the verse "if one were to go toward heaven," or "as we exist here below the sun and moon," and this is the land "our sovereign rules over," the subject would be obedient out of obligation. Everyone agrees that since the creation of heaven and earth [we would follow the emperor], even if society yearns for foreign customs that much, there were no people in the ancient period who would have confused the great responsibility between the sovereign and the subject. This is because this circumstance does not agree with the ancient customs of our land, and by this single example the reader may understand that anciently the Japanese did not accept evil customs as these.

In the "Quli" section of *Liji* it says, "According to the rules of propriety for a minister, he should not remonstrate with his ruler openly. If he has thrice remonstrated and is still not listened to, he should leave [his service]. In the service of his parents by a son, if he has thrice remonstrated and is still not listened to, he should follow [his remonstrance] with loud crying and tears."[11]

10. Partial quote of MYS 4094.

11. James Legge translation (1967, 2:114).

In *Shiji* it says, "The Viscount of Wei said, "Father and son have [a relationship of] flesh and bone, and subject and lord are connected by righteousness. For this reason, when a father has a fault, if the son tries three times to admonish him and he does not listen, then he will follow him and wail for it; if a minister dissuades his lord three times and he does not listen, then he can, according to the principle, leave him."[12]

In *The Analects* we find, "A great minister is a minister who serves his lord by following the Way, and who resigns as soon as the two are no longer reconcilable."[13] Commentary from Zhu Xi says, "The meaning of 'if he cannot do so, retires' means that if the minister's opinion does not agree with that of his ruler, he retires [or removes himself] from the presence of the prince."

Someone asked, "It is the rule in China that if a person admonishes his lord three times and the lord does not give ear, he retires, or if a son admonishes his father three times and he does not give ear he follows while wailing. However, anciently in that country several ministers admonished their ruler, King Zhou of Yin, who then had the minister Jizi imprisoned, and had Bigan killed, and Huizi left the court. Anyone who studies Chinese literature knows about these three.[14] If like Huizi a person who has a relationship with his father like flesh and bone he would have no other choice than to follow his father even if he resisted admonishing him. As sovereign and subject are bound by righteousness, if one remonstrated with his master three times and he did not listen to him, then you say it is logical that he would leave his presence. If it is reasonable that one should then leave his master's service, then someone like Bigan should have left the presence of his king when the king would not listen to his advice, and if he could not bear to make the king's fault public, then people would decide that there was no righteous bond between the servant unless he fought with the king and paid for it with his life. Someone who has already been put to death has no value to the state, and we should likely label the king as an infamous ruler because of his mistaken actions in putting to death a loyal minister who admonished him. If one were to claim that a subject who fought with his ruler and died in battle followed the path of a righteous servant, then you would have to say that the person who retires from court lacks this righteousness. In spite of this, Confucius labeled these

12. Slightly modified version of Nienhauser (2006, 5:270).

13. Nylan (2014:32).

14. They are often referred to as "the three benevolent ones" (三仁), a title attributed to Confucius.

three as 'the three virtuous men of Yin.' So what do you think is the reasoning behind each one fulfilling the rationality of his own station?"

To this I responded that in reality to die because one had admonished his ruler suited the principle of righteousness, but to retire from his presence does not. That is not all: Huizi later served King Wen of Zhou and was restored to his former status. When we observe these facts from the point of view of our Way, it is truly a filthy trend. However, even Confucius often returned to his lord and served him, but was he not the kind of person who especially abandoned Duke Ding of Lu, and even left the native land of his father and mother? So *The Analects* says, "A great minister, is one who serves his prince according to what is right, and when he finds he cannot do so, retires," but overlooks the mistaken actions of a person. Even for myself, how could I censure someone like Huizi as evil who left the service of his lord, though the person had decided on his own, in his heart, to take such action, and then did? Thus, even in China from ancient times someone like Confucius would retire from his lord's service without admonishing him for his faults, or when he should retire would not. And like the example of Bigan who suffered death because he admonished his ruler, it seems that people anciently were said to have had their suspicions in regards to those who labeled these actions as suiting the Way of righteousness. In the end, even if the actions were not the same, regardless of their seriousness or the circumstances, this trend [toward inconsistency] is the same. Zhou should have left the presence of the king out of respect for the rituals performed for his ancestors. Bigan served as lessor tutor, so he *knew* that his admonition would fall on deaf ears, and he paid with his life for forcing his advice on the king. People in later eras describe things in a good light by switching the positions of these individuals so that their actions are actually the same. It is important to realize that this demonstrates that in China there was no [consistent] standard for righteousness.

Nevertheless, later when circumstances had changed and society had transformed and in a world that had fallen into chaos people forgot that these foreign customs imported into our land were unsuitable for our culture, being unseemly, evil, and filthy. The reason that events occur when a foolish, shameless servant does not consider how his action will affect him is because the world had changed greatly for the worse; it is truly a miserable, deplorable situation. But how awe-inspiring that the truth of the Way of the imperial *kami* came down from heaven along with the three regalia, where the court of the emperor of the sun-lineage wavers not, and we stand on the cusp of being able to return almost completely to the time when the court was at its pinnacle in the ancient period. We live in this glorious age of greatness and how noble that the Way of the imperial *kami* is being rediscovered.

Now, people can get a glimpse of this Way of the imperial *kami* through the thriving *kotodama* of words. Much of the influence of the *kotodama* of words is preserved in the ancient lexicon that was used by people until the [late] Nara period, and that is why people should treasure, read, and enjoy the poetry in this anthology [*Man'yōshū*]. As mentioned above, the reader can peruse and enjoy the anthology by remembering that while we say that society was influenced by foreign culture from an early period, in reality actual change was not that serious, as we still do not find the slightest hint of error between the sovereign and the subject, so the reader should think deeply on this fact and not flippantly overlook it. When the reader examines the poetry with feelings that are not swayed by foreign influence, he finds that the poetry is not there to teach or argue any principle, but there are many things one can learn about the Way. Even when one reads the stanza "the great lord is a *kami*," which idea appears here and there many times, you will see that the emperor is a revered *kami* who is separate from humans. Examples include "our great lord, a distant *kami*," "or 'our great lord, a visible *kami*," or "our great lord, a *kami*," or "the divine actions of the emperor." And there are usages such as *kamunagara* "following the will of the *kami*." The ruler of China is simply a human, but because he was extremely virtuous, he was looked upon as someone like the son of heaven, and it is quite regrettable and frightening when people even temporarily argue that the Chinese sovereign is like the sun.

mononofu no	The men of
omi no wotoko fa	the Mononobe who
ofokimi no	are servants to the crown
make no mani mani	should follow their great lord
kiku to ifu mono so	and be obedient to his commands.
	[MYS 369]

And considering there are many examples of "in awe of the great lord" we understand the ancient custom of offering great reverence to the court of the emperor.

amagumo no	People who are called
mukabusu kuni no	the warriors of the far-off
mononofu	land where the clouds
ifaruru fito fa	stretch to the very horizon

sumeroki no	offer their service
kami no mikado ni	by standing on the outer
to no fe ni	side of the palace gates
tatisamurafi	of our imperial *kami*;
uti no fe ni	they serve him also
tukafematurite	on the inner side of the gates.
tamakadura	And like the long strands of vine
iya tofonagaku	they tell stories
oya no na mo	to their mother and fathers,
tugiyuku mono to	their wives and children,
omotiti ni	how they have inherited
tuma ni kodomo ni	the names of their ancestors
katarafite	who served for so long,
tatinisi fi yori	and from the day they left home.[15]

Not only does this poem display reverence to the emperor, but that author, Yakamochi, also composed the lines, "their posterity will not let their ancestors' name die out"[16] or "it must never happen that the name of our ancestors will die out, even temporarily."[17] The reader should consider that anciently these people, through the generations, attached importance to the ancestor of the family. Also, Emperor Kōken composed:

soramitu no	The land of Yamato
yamato no kuni fa	which fills the sky,
midu no ufe fa	as if the land
tuti yuku gotoku	were gliding on the water—
fune no ufe fa	as if the land
toko ni woru goto	were sitting on the deck of a ship—
ofokami no	it is the land
ifaferu kuni so	protected by the great *kami*.[18]

From this poem it is clear that the people still had plenty of reverence in their general faith in the ancient customs of the indigenous religion. However, from the era of Emperor Tenchi a variety of bothersome events took place in society and those at court faced incidents where they found they could not keep from speaking their minds, but as the poem says,

15. The first third of MYS 443.
16. From MYS 4094.
17. From MYS 4465.
18. From the opening lines of MYS 4264.

asifara no	The land of precious
midufo no kuni fa	rice ears on the plain of reeds,
kamunagara	according to the divine will
kotoagesenu kuni	is a land where we do not speak our minds.
sikaredomo	In spite of that
kotoage zo a ga suru	I will speak my mind.[19]

Thus, any chance of speaking freely was cut off in advance. Again, another poem notes,

sikisima no	The land of Yamato
yamato no kuni fa	of Shikishima,
kotodama no	is a land assisted
tasukuru kuni zo	by the *kotodama* of words.
masakiku ari koso	Please stay safe.

[MYS 3254]

From examples such as these we see that ancient customs have been transmitted down to the Nara era, and the reader should also consider the condition reflected here as coming from a poet either from the Afumi Court [662–70] or the Fujiwara Court [694–710].

Needless to say there is evidence here and there in our written records that when crises arose, for the court and for the state, society had a custom dating back many generations of praying to Buddha and Bodhisattvas, seeking for fortune and trying to avoid misfortune, as people felt these entities were far superior to our *kami*. We also can discern from the example of writing by Yamanoe no Okura that this was also the tendency in *Man'yōshū*, but as far as the vocabulary of the poetry in *Man'yōshū* is concerned, there is very little evidence of this tendency. There are many examples here and there in the anthology of people who generally display a deep belief in the *kami* of heaven and earth by praying to them; for example, when someone set off on a journey, or when there was a problem between a husband and a wife. And when a person suffered physical illness and was in distress, they could call a doctor and then take medicine and while this practice is in no way exceptional at the time they never composed poetry about this, only writing that they had prayed to the *kami* of heaven and earth, demonstrating that regardless of whether the event was serious or trivial, the ancient custom as handed down to these people was to rely on the *kami* and believe in them—this is apparent because this evidence has been preserved in the vocabulary of poetry.

---

19. From the first half of MYS 3253.

Actions such as praying to Buddha and discussing affairs with Buddhist priests, or calling a doctor and relying on him to cure a disease were not originally the custom in the ancient past of Japan, but society changed to where these practices began to become customary. And that is why I have claimed that the ancient customs continued to be preserved in various traditional rituals and the lexicon of poetry, as we find no poems composed on topics where the ancient custom of relying on the divine essence of the *kami* had disappeared and society had become unseemly. Even in the present, there are many cases in the farthest reaches of the provinces where if a person becomes ill, they first pray to the *kami*, even before taking their medicine, and of course this is a relic of the ancient custom, and it is wretched for learned people to think that these relics are silly or insipid.

Now in other areas, one would expect poets to have composed poetry infused with ideas such as *yin* and *yang* or the Chinese hexagrams 乾 "heaven" and 坤 "earth," but there is not a single poem that exhibits this tendency; there are a few examples of "as I have relied on heaven and earth (天地)," one example being from Kakinomoto Hitomaro in a *chōka* written on the topic of "the *kami* of the mountains and rivers." The envoy poem after this *chōka* was written in the same spirit, but especially abbreviates the character 神 "spirit," only mentioning that he, the poet, serves the mountains and rivers, and so you may know that Hitomaro's poem has shortened the older phrase of "*kami* of heaven and earth" down to just "heaven and earth." That the ancient lexicon exemplifies this is also found in commentaries on the poetry. Based on this evidence you may know that "heaven and earth" mentioned in these poems is not the same concept as that of the Chinese.

Occasionally there are poems where people believe that the poet had composed on a topic such as "the mansion of heaven" or "rebirth" or "purifying the original nature," principles found in Buddhist texts, and while we cannot say there are absolutely no examples of these, they are rare, perhaps ten among a thousand, or one among a hundred. As we believe these were written in a playful tone, there is no harm in setting these aside, as the poets were not obligated to compose such poems. Also, some of these examples were composed simply because of their rhythm, and no harm is done even if we ignore the intention behind the poem.

Aside from these examples there are a number of poems written about the tradition of the Chinese man named Yuan Gu[20] or the natural principles of Zhuangzi, but as these poems are also playfully written these should

20. A legendary figure who was able to save his grandfather's life when his father wanted to abandon the old man in the hills because he had become feeble. Yuan Gu reasoned with

be treated as those mentioned above. Concerning the poetry by Kakinomoto Hitomaro and Yamabe no Akahito and others, they say absolutely nothing bothersome about Chinese events, even superficially, so is it not noble that they all touch on events solely from the extremely ancient divine age?

Now, people early on began to argue that "Emperors Yao and Shun received the throne of the son of heaven because of their noble virtue and King Tang drove out [King Jie], while King Wu attacked [King Zhou], and our Way is as different as heaven and earth." A thoughtful person would not mistake the difference here, and I think there is nothing more to add; however, let me say just one more thing. The ordinary Confucian scholars in the world consider that Yao and Shun abdicated the throne to supremely virtuous people, but early on even in China clever people were saying that Yao's virtue had weakened, so Shun had him arrested, imprisoned his son, and took the throne for himself. People have also said that the [recorded] actions of Shun and King Yu are mirror images of the actions of Wang Mang and Cao Cao from a later era, so there is no change. On the other hand, Shun was indeed ruined by the people at that time, but if tradition is true about the descendant of Emperor Huang in the eighth generation, he was clearly a member of the royal lineage. Therefore, as the average person accepts, even if he did receive the right to throne because [Yao] abdicated it, or even if he did steal the authority to rule all under heaven like Wang Mang and Cao Cao, if he was a member of the royal lineage then the key is that he was beyond censure in these actions. Thus it is proper to say that these people truly possessed a matchless kind of virtue, as all the people in the realm down many generations later did not abandon nor forget this tradition. Having said that, the Chinese have a saying, "What kind of person was Shun? What kind of person am I?"[21] Or "Shun was just a man; I am just a man."[22] Thus, regardless of a person's lineage or surname, the standard of viewing someone as a sage or as a regular person is based on the difference of one's level of virtue; it is natural that people admire someone with talent and virtue. But it must be noted that this disregard for one's lineage or surname is certainly something unreliable yet typical of a foreign culture, and it is a regrettable point [concerning China]. Thus, the reason that some people in later years who were counted as less than dirt

---

his father that when he became old and feeble, he, Yuan Gu, would do the same thing to him.

21. Quoted from Mencius, part one of the "Teng Wen Gong" chapter.

22. Quoted from Mencius, part two of the "Li Lou" chapter.

or mud, base and contemptuous, and could not overturn the country was because they would have no way to govern, but would have continued to be insignificant people standing in a corner. This all originates from the fact that lineage and name had nothing to do with who could ascend the throne in China, as they say, "Shun was just a man; I am just a man." They claim that the only criterion was that a person have great virtue or great influence, causing people to revere, fear, and bow down before him. It was a situation that could not be helped. In this way, we see that in foreign countries the order of sovereign and subject, upper and lower classes, was thrown into confusion many centuries earlier, and there are indications of the origins of this.

How wondrous and awe-inspiring that our emperor is an actual *kami*, as we say, a visible *kami*, a distant *kami*, so he is distantly and greatly removed from humans, of a superior quality, and our ruling family has ruled in an unbroken line for a thousand reigns and ten thousand years. The reason that his influence is venerable and he has a wondrous, mystical aura is due to none other than his being a princely descendant of the great sun *kami* in heaven. One cannot argue in any way that he is similar to the base kings of foreign countries.

Now, examples such as King Tang attacking Jie and taking the country, or King Wu striking Zhou and obtaining the realm do not constitute the throne being given to another worthy person; however, it is true that the individual had an exceptional virtue, a heavenly mandate, and he worked for the good of the people in the realm, so the people in the land all praised the work of these men, and even in later generations these traditions were handed down as rare examples of exceptional leaders, which is true based on the customs of that country. Looking at it from the perspective of our land, however, it is truly a deplorable chain of events. Nothing further need be said about events in later eras. And from that we can claim that since these situations surround the rulers of that country, if a mountain man who yesterday was deficient in various areas, but at least had virtue, today he suddenly could be set up as a high authority in the land and take the reins of government. There are more than a few extreme examples of high fortune, but in our country from the earliest days the distinction between sovereign and subject, upper and lower classes, was strictly observed, and all these people down to the eighty serving groups such as the Omi and Muraji valued lineage and title and transmitted the doings of their ancestors, and like the founding *kami* of families these were all treated as if from the same generation. And compared with those who serve the emperor's court, just like in the divine age, it is not too much of stretch to declare that those high officials in foreign countries are in the same class as insects and birds.

Furthermore, in China the ruler who governed called his land "the middle country," and he labeled himself "the son of heaven." All other events followed this example and everything became that much clearer: it was unseemly that he boasted of himself, displayed his authority, and acted arrogant. It is suspicious that the ruler would act humbly by calling himself "the unworthy one" or "the unfruitful one," but even those who call themselves "the son of heaven" originally included men who were just average folk who forcefully took the government, and lost their virtue, even for a short time, and they were constantly worrying about things, thinking that if they could not keep the people of the realm enamored with their policies then suddenly another aveage individual would appear and take the land from them. They were keenly aware of trivial things, so they flattered people by pretending to be humble, rather than show what was truly in their hearts. Following this, even those officials in high places were not promoted according to lineage or name, but anyone who had talent and virtue, even if they were an unexpectedly disreputable person, was able to make a name for themselves in society. This caused envy from those above, and resentment from those below. Not long after this occurred, the person would shortly be removed, and with great fear in their hearts they would believe that their very life was in danger. Because of this, people acted humble in all cases, saying things to try to get on a person's good side. Over time this naturally became a customary thing. Yet this is simply a matter of logic, and we imagine that this is what likely happened in China, so how awe-inspiring that when our own emperor performs rituals before the great *kami* who is his ancestor he acts in the most solemn and dignified manner, but he does not adulate in front of other people, and no matter which country he is in contact with, he will not be swayed by flattery.

However, in *Nihon shoki* and other records there are a number of examples where the emperor acts humbly, such as, "Me? I am incompetent. How could I promote the virtuous work?"[23] But this is simply an artifact of the text, and as the text is written in classical Chinese, this was written in imitation of that, but in reality the emperor never said such a thing, and you may know this by looking at the words in the imperial poems found in *Man'yōshū*. Even Emperor Shōmu who was such a firm believer in foreign ways composed a poem at a banquet when about to dispatch an envoy:

23. A line from the record of Kenzō in *Nihon shoki*. The speaker is Kenzō, being self-deprecating, trying to get his brother to ascend the throne first.

tamudakite	I will make myself comfortable
ware fa imasamu	with my arms folded.
sumera ware	As your emperor
udu no mite moti	I will use my august hands
kaki nade so	to stroke their hair and reward
negitamafu	my ministers for their hard work.[24]

We see other examples of this in many instances written before the poem above was composed. As Shōmu's poem demonstrates the imperial authority to his ministers and those below him, and the usage of the phrase *udu no mite* "august hands" was not said of himself, but is a common phrase used by rulers from the divine age down through successive reigns of emperors, and that is why he said it. Is it not truly a splendid fact that while the ruler of China acts humble, calling himself "the worthless one," in contrast our ruler makes it clear that there is a difference between him and his followers as absolute as coal and snow? If one were to claim that our court generally imitated China in all respects, then analogous to the lines in *Nihon shoki*, our emperor would himself act deferentially and address people in that attitude, but we know such is not the case because in the lexicon of poetry we find practices that date back to the divine age that do not include any influence from the foreign heart. And the reason that we do not see people from the imperial family down to ministers and courtiers acting and saying things deferentially all the time in imitation of China is because while these people studied about China they made an effort not to imitate this characteristic, as it was radically different from our customs. However, they agreed that it was simply a superficial form of flattery for the ruler to take a deferential attitude when speaking, while not doing so would be considered rude, and they did not notice that this subtle change was taking place, being an influence from the foreign heart.

[Kamochi 1891, Sōron part 3, pp. 83–89]

ଓ

24. Partial quote of MYS 973.

This page is intentionally left blank.

Part Two
Views on Literature

SHIKA SHICHIRON

Andō Tameakira | 1703

[This treatise is sometimes called *Genji shichiron* or *Genji monogatari-kō*, based on the fact that the essay is constructed around "seven treatises" concerning the *Tale of Genji*. Instead of being a commentary on parts of the tale, Tameakira wrote about seven issues that he felt impeded a proper understanding of the tale. Being in the employment of Tokugawa Mitsukuni gave Tameakira access to a large amount of material, such as earlier diaries, that provided data so he could debunk previous mistaken theories about the authorship, make-up, and details found within the tale. His work appears to have greatly influenced Motoori Norinaga, who later also argues for the reassessment of the tale. This essay is an attempt to demonstrate that the tale could only have been written by Murasaki, because she had the talent and the circumstantial experience allowing her to write about a world and its interactions few openly talked about.]

(1) ENDOWED WITH SUPERIOR TALENT AND WISDOM

In general, being endowed with superior talent and wisdom is something difficult to expect even from one talented gentleman. How much more so is it a rare occurrence for such a woman to appear in either Japan or China. In this case people from long ago who have discussed *Genji monogatari* have only labeled Murasaki Shikibu as a gifted woman, and having failed to mention her practical wisdom they cannot elucidate the true meaning of the tale. This is also a defective and troublesome treatment of Murasaki. I have carefully read both the tale and Murasaki's diary, weighing the quality of her writing, pondering on the facts surrounding her life, and I have found that she is without peer in Japan, an intelligent woman with superior talent and wisdom.

If I were to add one or two things in relation to the tale, Lady Murasaki is depicted as refined and benevolent, a woman of good judgment and caution. Lady Akashi is portrayed as proud and yet humble; Hanachirusato, as a woman without jealousy; the Fujitsubo empress as pious, someone who regretted her transgression and quickly took Buddhist vows. Her Highness Asagao deeply valued her reputation, while Lady Tamakazura is able to avoid the proposals of men with her skillful words, and Lady Agemaki is true to the dying words of her royal father. The tale records these feminine virtues, especially in [the "Broom Tree" chapter] where women are categorized; we find that frivolous women are rejected and integrity is praised. While we can label these recurrent admonitions as based on the disposition of Murasaki, she represents these as morals found in all ancient tales. Murasaki does not try to act self-righteous, so the reader thinks these events are simply hearsay. As an example, it is like someone in the audience not realizing the singing and dancing of the wooden puppet is due to the skill of the puppetmaster. A reading of Murasaki's diary demonstrates these general principles.

"It is very easy to criticize others but far more difficult to put one's own principles into practice, and it is when one forgets this truth, lauds oneself to the skies, treats everyone else as worthless and generally despises others that one's own character is clearly revealed."[1]

Considering this counsel, one should give ear to what she says, that there is a despicable human tendency to treat others as wrong and yourself as right. The diary goes on, "People who think so much of themselves that they will, at the drop of a hat, compose lame verses that only just hang together, or produce the most pretentious compositions imaginable, are quite odious and rather pathetic."[2]

She also writes, "Others are born pessimists, amused by nothing, the kind who search through old books looking for old things, carry out penances, intone sutras without end, and clack their beads, all of which makes one feel uncomfortable. So I hesitate to do even those things I should be able to do quite freely, only too aware of my own servants' prying eyes. I have many things I would like to say, but always think the better of it, because there would be no point in explaining to people who would never understand. I cannot be bothered to discuss matters in front of those women who continually carp and are so full of themselves: it would only cause trouble. It is so rare to find someone of true understanding; for the most part they judge purely by their own standards and ignore everyone else.

"So all they see of me is a façade. There are times when I am forced to sit with them and on such occasions I simply ignore their petty criticism, not because I am particularly shy but because I consider it pointless. As a result, they do not look upon me as a dullard.

"'Well, we never expected this!' they all say. 'No one liked her. They all said she was pretentious, awkward, difficult to approach, prickly, too fond of her tales, haughty, prone to versifying, disdainful, cantankerous and

1. Bowring (1996:53).

2. I have altered Bowring's translation slightly to account for a minor misunderstanding in the original, as quoted by Tameakira; cf. Bowring (1996:54).

scornful; but when you meet her, she is strangely meek, a completely different person altogether!' How embarrassing! Do they really look upon me as such a dull thing, I wonder? But I am what I am."[3]

The conjecture from people who had never met Murasaki before makes one believe she is quite romantic, a studied person who composes poetry and is judgmental of others. Others who have already made her acquaintance find her to be unexpectedly meek and in all things prone to vulgarity. The tale should be judged based on this personality.

The diary goes on, "Her Majesty has also remarked more than once that she had thought I was not the kind of person with whom she could ever relax, but that I have not become closer to her than any of the others. I am so perverse and standoffish. If only I can avoid putting off those for whom I have a geniuine regard."[4]

Since Murasaki had a meek and calm personality the empress also grew quite close to her. She was incensed by people who pretended to be of high birth and gentle.

The diary continues, "To be pleasant, gentle, calm, and self-possessed: this is the basis of good taste and charm in a woman."[5]

People should digest this part of the diary well. Virtue is the base of the tree, and talent is the tip of the branches.

The diary notes, "'But then I gradually realized that people were saying 'It's bad enough when a man flaunts his Chinese learning; she will come to no good,' and since then I have avoided writing the simplest character. My handwriting is appalling. And as for those 'classics' or whatever they are that I used to read, I gave them up entirely. Yet still I kept on hearing these remarks; so in the end, worried what people would think if they heard such rumors, I pretended to be incapable of reading even the inscriptions on the screens."[6]

Both men and women should consider this concern regarding behavior.

Again, "Why should self-satisfied smugness be seen as a sign of wisdom? And there again why should one continually interfere with other people's lives? To be able to adapt to a situation to the correct degree and then to act accordingly seems to be extremely difficult for most people."[7]

Is it not a good idea when people have so much empathy that they are frequently referred to as "too kind" and react embarrassed by it? Naturally

3. Ibid., p. 56.
4. Ibid.
5. Ibid.
6. Ibid., p. 58.
7. Ibid., p. 52.

one should abhor making light of this situation. These scenes demonstrate to both men and women the natural limits of behavior, and the reader should apply themselves to these instructions. . . .

(2) SEVEN REASONS MURASAKI IS A WORTHY AUTHOR

Reason one is that Murasaki's father, Tametoki,[8] was a student of Sugawara Fumitoki,[9] and he was a literary student of renown who also composed poetry and compiled anthologies. Reason two was her good fortune to have an older brother, Nobunori,[10] who was a poet with some of his poetry included in *Gosenshū* and other anthologies. We see that as his studies progressed, he would forget what he had read, but Murasaki perceived things to an incredible extent, demonstrating that she was a brilliant child who was a prodigy.

The third reason is that while she was an intelligent child she grew into a woman able to obtain scholarly knowledge when that was difficult for a woman, and when we consider what places of learning then were like we see that she read Japanese and Chinese works over a long period of time and studied a variety of arts, starting with music. As it says in *Senzaishū*, "I had served at the palace of Princess Shōshi, but as soon as I returned [from visiting] my native area I received a letter from another lady attendant, saying that [the Princess] wanted me to come back so she could learn to play the thirteen-string *koto*; I sent a messenger with my reply."[11]

tuyu sigeki	The dew is thick—
yomogi ga moto no	like the sound of the crickets
musi no ne wo	in the overgrown foliage
oforoke nite ya	has someone rashly mentioned
fito no tadunen	that I am playing my *koto*?

The fourth reason is that she was a lady attendant in the forbidden precincts, in the empress's palace, and in the palace of the regent, and from

8. Fujiwara Tametoki (949–1029) was the son of Fujiwara no Masatada. Tametoki was a minor courtier, only reaching the fifth rank during his lifetime. He appears to have been a gifted poet, writing poetry in both Japanese and Chinese.

9. Sugawara Fumitoki (899–981) was a grandson of Sugawara Michizane. He was a skilled politician and rose to become minister of the right.

10. Nobunori (d. 1011). went with his father when Tametoki was sent to Echigo as Governor, and died in Echigo.

11. Headnote to poem 977.

[evidence at] the New Year's banquet to the New Year's Eve rituals she was clearly learned in the regular and temporary public events of each year, as well as poetry contests, picture contests, scent contests, and kickball.

The fifth reason is that the era of her life was not that far in the past, nor was it a time of decline. She was born in the middle of our history when literary talents were important to society.

The sixth reason is that she was able to travel and see many famous places and historical sights, like Suma, Akashi, Sumiyoshi, Naniwa, Hatsuse, Mount Ishi, Uji, Ōharano, Sugano, Nishikawa, Eguchi, the plains of Kamizaki, the depths of Ono, the valley of Kurama, Mount Hie, and Hato Peak. These places all enhanced her talent. …

The seventh reason is that there are some places and some word usages [in the tale] that a man could not write in such detail, but as a woman Murasaki was able to write things that other people would not have considered. Among women, those of high nobility do not comprehend what women of lower status do, and it is even more pronounced that women of low station have no idea what women above them do or think. Murasaki just happens to have been born into a family of middle status, and there is nothing she did not know about both worlds.

Because Murasaki was blessed with all these experiences, she was able to complete this tale without the divine aid of Ishiyama Temple. It is a silly tradition of later ages that claims that Murasaki was the incarnation of the Bodhisattva Kannon, conjured up because people have no idea who she is. It is exceedingly rare for someone to have all seven of these experiences, which explains why there was no such tale before or after Murasaki.

(3) A TIMELINE FOR COMPOSITION

Murasaki's diary states (in the eleventh month of Kankō 5 [1008]), "Major Councillor Kintō poked his head in. 'Excuse me,' he said, 'would our Little Murasaki be in attendance by any chance?' 'I cannot see the likes of Genji here, so how could she be present,' I replied."[12] Considering this account Murasaki should have started the tale before this year and it was read promptly by those in the palace, even among the men; Kintō called her "Little Murasaki."

The diary goes on, "(In the first month of Kankō 6 [1009]) His Majesty was listening to someone reading *The Tale of Genji* aloud. …"[13] Consider-

12. Bowring (1996:31).

13. Ibid. (1996:57).

ing that this event was recorded after the fact it is difficult to determine in what year these events actually happened.

The diary goes on, "(In the same year) His Excellency happened to see that Her Majesty had *The Tale of Genji* with her."[14] Now *Kakaishō*[15] claims that the tale was written at the beginning of the Kankō era [1004–11], which may be based on this line in the diary. Regardless perhaps it was composed between the end of the Chōhō era [999–1003] and the beginning of the Kankō when Murasaki had returned home after being widowed. In Kankō 5 [1008] Minister Michinaga was forty-three years of age and made sexual advances to Murasaki and in the sixth year he knocked on her door outside the covered bridgeway, frustrated [by her rejection]. She should not have been that old at this time. By her own admission she writes that she was past her prime, so we cannot assume she was young. Consider this with the line in *Eiga monogatari* [in the "Tenjō hanami" chapter],[16] where it says that Empress Takeko was thirty-one years of age[17] and was past her prime.

In both Japan and China people who are wise and discerning have this talent in whatever they do, so it is not unexpected that she should have been able to write this tale without much effort. People in later eras were not as sharp as Murasaki, so they found the tale to be mysterious and amazing, advancing insipid assertions, such as claiming Murasaki must have had divine assistance [to write the tale] from the Bodhisattva Kannon, or she received assistance from her father, Tametoki, or Minister Michinaga touched up the writing. None of these people *know* Murasaki. Considering the writings [that makes these assertions], I must say these are all crude works. …

(4) UNPARALLELED LITERARY QUALITY

The poetry and prose of this tale has outgrown the older style of *Man'yōshū*, *Kokinshū*, *Ise monogatari*, and *Taketori monogatari*. The tale is generally unassuming and easy to understand, and no one who reads it will tire of it.

14. Bowring (1996:61).

15. A commentary on the *Tale of Genji*, in twenty *maki*, written by Yotsutsuji Yoshinari (1326–1402), completed within a five-year window, between 1362 and 1367. It was one of the first commentaries to produce a comprehensive clarification of the entire tale.

16. The standard text of *Eiga monogatari* consists of thirty chapters, but there is a variant textual tradition where Chapters 31–40 exist. Andō has reference to this tradition. See McCullough and McCullough (1980, 1:xi).

17. Some texts have "thirty-one or two."

The tale is unparalleled among the literature of our country. The entire work displays the elegance of wealth and contentment, and while it is written in the language of the nobility, there are stories of those who leave the world and go into the mountains, stories of people related to markets, wells, and rice paddies. There are also examples in each volume of the tale depicting poverty, pain, romance, and scenery. You feel as if you had actually visited these places, with the characters standing before your eyes, the feelings and scenery are modeled so well. The story is a narrative, and it naturally follows in a chronological order; it includes a variety of narrative types, such as editorials, records, discussions, and documents. The categorization of women found in the "Broom Tree" chapter is especially wonderful. Once I was re-reading this section and noticed that after an introduction, it contains refutations, debate, persuasion, and arm-twisting.[18] These descriptions cover a wide area, ranging from rough to delicate, elegant to vulgar, and straightforward to complex. The sentences are undulating, unpredicatable, interconnected, and gripping. It naturally is arranged according to Chinese grammar, and its literary construction is broad and profound. It is liberal in its euphemisms, and smooth in its style. …

(5) THE AUTHOR'S INTENTION

This tale generally describes human emotions and the state of society, demonstrating the elegance and organization of the upper, middle, and lower classes, depiciting things through romantic encounters, avoiding words of praise or censure, allowing the reader to determine the good or evil of the events. The overarching purpose of the work is to provide moral instructions to women in a figurative way, but there are many areas that naturally teach men. To give one or two examples, the Kiritsubo emperor values love, and when his affection for an intimate[19] became excessive, and his behavior was about to excite the censure of people around him, he still paid no heed. And it is shameful for the imperial virtue to treat her so lavishly, setting a bad precedent for society. He causes anxiety to people in the upper eschelons of society on down to everyone else under heaven. Is not this an allegorical way to admonish emperors in later eras?

And then considering that the emperor treated Lord Genji as his trea-

18. This is a difficult line: 論破あり、論承あり、論腹あり、論尾あり. One manuscript has a marginal note suggesting that 論承 should be 論義 "debate." I have followed this note.

19. I have followed Tyler's translation of 更衣 (2001, 1:3).

sured son after Genji had finished his rites of coming-of-age, everything the emperor did was to demonstrate that Genji was superior to the crown prince, and he even goes so far to suggest Genji might be heir to the throne someday. Does this not show that his perceptiveness was pitifully lacking?

Because of her obstinate and prickly manners, Empress Kōkiden treats the grieving emperor [after Genji's mother's death] as nothing of importance. Where is the virtue one would expect from an empress or princess? Women, from an empress on down, who read this part of the tale should be compelled to reflect on their own behavior and sensitivity, so they may avoid the pitiful label of "evil empress."

Next the categorization of women in the "Broom Tree" chapter forms one kind of lesson for women to avoid being trammeled by love affairs, so every woman worthy of being called such should peruse this. And there are lessons in proper behavior to be found in the "Cicada Shell" chapter, in how Nokiba no Ogi[20] plays *go*, leaves her robes loosely tied in the bedchamber, or oversleeps. And the woman of the cicada shell [Utsusemi] is a wonderful example of chastity, keeping herself aloof and uninterested in Genji's advances. This is Murasaki's intention.

Next, there are many who criticize Yūgao [the twilight beauty] for being obsessed with *amour* because of the memorable poem she wrote on one of her favorite fans. Thus, because she was excessively sweet and yielding, hardly given to deep reflection,[21] she dies having fallen into calamity. Women who hear about this should ponder on what happens when you have a love affair with a person who is unfaithful.

Genji's frivolity from his untethered emotions causes Yūgao's death, and his lack of caution causes him to fall from his horse.[22] Genji's lack of emotional stability should admonish the behavior of male nobility. And Koremitsu's immorality, as he accompanied Genji on his adventures, is not a minor thing. People who serve our imperial family should consider these things and learn from them. ...

(6) THE CORE OF THE TALE 一部大事

There are some who say that the events surrounding Empreor Reizei are fiction and there is no use engaging in deep discussion on it. There are

20. Tyler sticks to the titles in the text, calling her "the lady from the west wing" (2001, 1:48).

21. Ibid., p. 62.

22. A variant text has "causes him to fall from his horse at the river bank."

others who claim the events in the tale are sensitive and recklessly try keep these secret, and there are others who declare that the events are inappropriate and the tale should not be read at all. One is forced to conclude that none of these people understand the intention of Murasaki. I will provide some interpretations and wait for other learned men to criticize me.

In the "Broom Tree" chapter it says, "Genji was not free to live at home for His Majesty summoned him too often. In his heart he saw only Fujitsubo's peerless beauty. Ah, he thought, she is the kind of woman I want to marry; there is no one like her!"[23]

In this way Murasaki predicts that later the story will turn into one of adultery. In the "Young Murasaki" chapter we find that Fujitsubo is pregnant, and the birth of the child appears in "Beneath the Autumn Leaves" chapter. In the "Heart to Heart" chapter the boy is made heir to the throne, and in "The Pilgrimage to Sumiyoshi" chapter he ascends the throne, where he is now known as Emperor Reizei. Later in the "'Wisps of Cloud" chapter a prelate attending the emperor during night attendance announces for the first time that the emperor is actually the son of Genji. As there was no one he could question about the matter, the prelate decided to investigate old precedents himself.

It also says, "He plunged into his studies more ardently than ever in order to peruse all sorts of works. These taught him that while in Cathay there had been many such irregularities, some open and some concealed, no example of the kind was to be found in Japan. And even if something like that happened, how, if it was kept well hidden, could knowledge of it have been passed on?"[24]

In the second half of the "Spring Shoots" chapter, Genji learns of Intendant of the Right Gate Watch Kashiwagi's secret affair with Onna San no Miya, and relates the following ideas:

"In early times as well there were those who might violate an emperor's wife, but that was different. No wonder liaisons like that may occur, when there are so many people in palace service waiting on the sovereign. What with one thing and another it must happen quite often. Even a consort or an intimate may err for this reason or that. They are no all as serious as they might be, and strange things happen, but as long as no obvious lapse comes to light the man can carry on as before. ... When a woman wearies of giving her service meekly and all too respectably, even to the emperor himself, she may yield after all to urgent pleas. ... He (Genji) realized bitterly

23. Tyler (2001, 1:17)

24. Ibid., p. 357.

that despite his fury, he could not afford to show it, and he thought of his father, His Late Eminence. Did *he* really know all the time and just pretended not to? *That*, yes, that *was* a fearful and heinous crime!"[25]

Considering how Murasaki has constructed these events, whether it be an ancient or a recent occurrence, she appears to have written this according to what she had seen and heard. She wrote this with conscientious reflection, and the intention is not trivial. The reader should not overlook this fact. In *Ise monogatari* there is the case of the Nijō Empress (who had relations with Narihira); in *Gosenshū* there is Kyōgoku Miyasudokoro (who had an affair with Prince Motoyoshi); in *Eiga monogatari* there is Lady Kazan (who lost her heart to Lord Sanesuke; Lady Reikeiden and Lady Shōkōden both had relations with Minister Yorisada).[26] These women had an irresolute disposition, blown about by their personal desires. However it is fortunate to report that we do not observe any effects of "the corruption" (物のまぎれ).[27] ...

In later eras among women who were consorts and intimates there may have been some who had an irresolute disposition, and we cannot say that some have not had their blood intermingled in the imperial line, but Murasaki foresaw this and left moral instructions. Even though she was a woman, the beauty of her character and the power of her scholarship harmonize together, and we can say that her perceptive foresight naturally was equal to any Confucian scholar. And the import for demonstrating the punishment of heaven toward Kaoru is the same as found in the work of Luo Dajing.[28]

This entire event is at the core of the tale, and when discussing the tale, people must understand this point. Some people say, "Does it not go against the original intention of Murasaki for people to take a simple and trifiling story and debate about it within a tightly defined system of logic?" I answer that the categorization of women says, "[W]hy should anyone, just because she is a woman, be completely ignorant of what matters in this world, public or private? A woman with any mind at all is bound to retain many

---

25. Tyler (2001, 2:660–61).

26. The *Nihon shisō taikei* text lacks the name Minister Yorisada. I have added it based on a variant text found in *Kokubun chūshaku zensho* (Motoori et al. 1910:14).

27. I have used the translation of this term from Caddeau (2006:57). This term has two meanings: (i) confusion from competing events, (ii) doing things in secret. Andō seems to be combining these two meanings into his label.

28. Luo Dajing (1195–1252) wrote a work known as *Helin yulu* (鶴林玉露 "Crane Forest Jade Dew") around 1250. This work is a mixture of poetic critique, essays, and public discourse about commoners of his day.

things, even if she does not actually study."[29] What an incredibly wonderful line.

If there was a possibility of the blood of the Ariwara or Fujiwara being intermingled in even one generation of the imperial family it would be a misfortune for our country, like that faced by Lu Zhonglian, who disappeared via the eastern sea.[30] In spite of this, the birth of the Reizei emperor through the affair of Genji with Fujitsubo truly should have never happened, and while Genji's crime is great, it did not result in the contamination of the imperial line. Both men are truly sons and grandsons of Emperor Kiritsubo, descendants through the lineage of Emperor Jinmu. They are worthy of worship at the altar of the imperial ancestors at the Ise Shrine, and everyone under heaven is bound to acknowledge their right to rule. Even with that, is it not a casual way for Murasaki to write, where the heir of Reizei is cast aside, and the rule of the country returned to the rightful heir, that of Suzaku? So in the end, which is the more severe consequence, and which is the more tolerable? Having a one-time muddle in morality or a long-term corruption of the imperial line? While this is a difficult decision to make, from the view of those being governed, we should rejoice in the imperial line not taking unexpected turns, and the throne pretending to be unaware of Genji's sin. ...

(7) CORRECTING THE ERRORS IN RECEIVED THEORIES

Uji Dainagon monogatari[31] notes that Murasaki composed the tale when her father, Tametoki, was governor of Echizen. He supposedly related very detailed experiences to his daughter. People in the palace of the empress heard about the tale and summoned the daughter. She told them about how she composed the tale. It is also said that the tale was composed after she was summoned to the palace of the empress. Which account is true?

Mumyōshō[32] states, "Someone related the story that Ōsaiin [Princess Senshi/Nobuko] asked Jōtōmonin [Empress Shōshi/Akiko], 'Do you have

29. Tyler (2001, 1:35).

30. 東海をふむ "disappear via the eastern sea," is a euphemism for committing suicide.

31. A collection of stories that has not survived to the present. It is said to have been the work of Minamoto Takakuni (1004–77), because his name was Uji Dainagon, the Major Councilor of Uji. If this is true, then the work would have been completed during the later years of the Heian era.

32. More commonly known as *Mumyō zōshi* "untitled miscellaneous work." It is one of Japan's earliest texts on literary criticism, completed around 1202 by an unknown hand. It

a tale I can read to relieve boredom?' With this the Empress summoned Murasaki Shikibu and said, 'What shall we give her?' Murasaki replied, 'Too bad we do not have anything unique. We should give her something new to read.' The Empress commanded, 'Then compose something.' Because of this Murasaki wrote the *Tale of Genji*. Is this not a wonderful event? On the other hand [there is the account that] Murasaki wrote the tale at her husband's home before she was summoned to serve at the palace. When she was summoned to serve at the palace [the Empress] named her after a character in the tale." Which account is true?

From long ago people have shared a variety of baseless stories, made off the cuff, about how the tale came to be. No wonder there are commentaries speculating about which are true. I have sifted through these trying to determine the truth, but I have found these are all fictitious. First, the idea that the outline of the story was created by Tametoki and he had his daughter fill in the details demonstrates that these people do not know how literature is interlinked. This account is something that completely worthless people spread. Reading through the story chapter after chapter one finds that there are many events no man would have dreamed up. Overall the story is thoroughly feminine and if the flow of the words were not all from the same brush one would have noticed a change. No one who reads the entire tale through will be deceived by this theory. As I wrote previously, if people consider the superior talent and wisdom and the seven reasons Murasaki is a worthy author it is clear she was able to effortlessly write this tale without any help from her father. Besides, we cannot know if Tametoki died early, even in the Chōhō and Kankō eras.[33] And as for her diary, it was composed without any help from her father, written completely by herself, but her style in the diary is no less impressive than the tale. Anyone who has read her diary will realize how incorrect this theory is. …

Kakaishō notes, "In Anna 2 [969] Nishimiya, minister of the left,[34] was banished and demoted to the post of governor of Dazaifu, and Fujiwara Shikibu [Murasaki] was familiar with this event since she was a little child.

---

was later titled such because the title page of the manuscript has not survived the process of textual transmission.

33. This line is difficult to reconcile with Tameakira's vast knowledge of the historical records, unless this is more like a rhetorical statement.

34. Minamoto Takaakira (914–83). He was a son of Emperor Daigo and his mother was Minamoto Shūshi. He was a talented and learned prince and had great influence at court. Because of his Minamoto name, his status, and his banishment to Kyūshū, many have theorized that he was the individual Murasaki modeled Genji after.

During the period that she was in mourning and sadness [because of the loss of her husband], Ōsaiin asked Empress Jōtōmonin if she had an interesting tale she could read. She was already well aware of tales like *Utsuho* and *Taketori*, and this is the reason for the composition of a new tale. Since she received the command to compile a tale, she spent the night awake at Ishiyama Temple praying, and on the fifteenth night of the eighth month, the moon was reflecting off the surface of the lake. This light infused her soul throughout and the elegant scenes of the story appeared before her in the air. Wanting to write this down before she forgot it, she took the paper placed before the Buddhist statue for patrons to copy down the *Mahāprajñāpāramitā sūtra*, and began writing the two chapters of Suma and Akashi. Perhaps this is the reason that the "Suma" chapter says, "that tonight was the fifteenth of the month."[35] It is said that in order to pay penance to break the barrier of sin, she produced six hundred volumes of the entire *Mahāprajñāpāramitā sūtra*."

Kakaishō is the work of a fine gentleman, so it is distressing that he would record paragraph after paragraph of senseless dribble. Because of his exalted status, people will read his words and trust his account, and whatever I write will be treated as sloppy work, even if one idea out of a hundred is correct; however, if you do not say what you are thinking then the feeling of dissatisfaction swells up inside of you, so I will leave it up to my brush.

Murasaki would have been too young to have any knowledge of the banishment of Prince Nishimiya to base her story of Genji influence at court on his life. One can even say that it is even possible that she was not even born yet.[36] From Anna 2 of Emperor Reizei's reign till Kankō 1 [1004] is a period of thirty-six years. Considering the account in her diary, even if she were alive in the Anna era, she would have still been in diapers. Saying that she was familiar with the events surrounding Prince Nishimiya is unquestionably nonsense from someone who does not understand the chronology. ... And claiming that she wanted to write down the scenes of the tale that floated before her before she forgot them, and thus composed the Suma and Akashi chapters—how can someone in a later period know what was going on in the mind of Murasaki? It makes me laugh. One should consider that the tale was written in order, starting with the "Kiritsubo" chapter.

When I was younger I believed what I read in *Kakaishō*, and I wanted

---

35. Tyler (2001, 1:246).

36. It is clear that Tametoki took the child to Echizen when he was sent as governor in 996, an event too far removed to believe that Murasaki was even alive when Takaakira was banished.

to see the manuscript written on paper used to copy *Mahāprajñāpāramitā sūtra*, so I went to Ishiyama to see a monk I knew there. I asked him about this and he quickly informed me that it was untrue. So in what era and by whose authority did one space at the temple become known as "Genji's room," with a portrait of Murasaki hung there, provided with a desk and an inkstone?

* * * *

In *Hōbutsushū*[37] in the section admonishing people against the sin of lying, it says that because of the sin of Murasaki using falsehoods to create the *Tale of Genji*, she fell into hell and is suffering there. People therefore should immediately destroy their copies and make a copy of a sūtra in one day [to avoid the same fate]. A person said that he had this revelation in a dream, so he called together his poetic associates, and they all made copies of a sūtra in one day.

This is a fantasy born of an outlandish concept so there is no need to expend any energy refuting it, but in the Buddhist section of poetry in *Shinchokusen wakashū* there is a poem written on behalf of Murasaki, "Having copied the 'Company of those wishing to be Buddha' sūtra, I presented this poem as a metaphor for medicinal herbs, Dainagon Muneie:

nori no ame ni	I have become
ware mo ya nuremu	soaked by the rain of dharma.
mutumasiki	I pray for benevolence
waka murasaki no	that comes from having a connection
kusa no yukari ni	with the grass of young Murasaki."[38]

This is recorded as a poem composed and submitted after the poet had performed copying a sūtra in one day. Perhaps a confession was composed at the same time. It is very regretful that there are people who believe that a pointless dream will eventually become an actual reality, and that Murasaki is condemned for committing the crime of lying, though her tale is one of instruction or admonition. It comes from people with shallow thinking being led astray.

There are a variety of evidence and silly theories in various commen-

37. A collection of tales and folklore related to Buddhism. Compiled by Taira Yasuyori, the collection was completed no later than 1181. The text has suffered through poor textual transmission.

38. *Shinchokusen wakashū*, No. 602.

taries, but I have only given one or two examples. In tales like *Uji Dainagon monogatari* there are old accounts, but these contain deceptive traditions, so how much more difficult to accept are later theories. Naturally if one considers the scenes within the tale juxtaposed against the information from Murasaki's diary and reflects on the truth of things, we can minimize the errors in people's thinking.

[NST 39:424–40]

☙

BUN'IKŌ

Kamo no Mabuchi | ca. 1764

[This is a short essay where Mabuchi instructs the reader that while poetry is something that comes from within the individual, literature *"bun"* occurs from without. He discusses the state of ancient literature before the defilement of foreign cultures caused a change. He lists four different traits that ancient literature demonstrated: masculinity, meekness, (the elegance in) festivals, and (the power of) auspicious words for the completion of a new dwelling.]

PREFACE[1]

At present we [Mabuchi's students] are busy publishing this and that of our master's works. People pose various questions to me concerning my master's philosophy; needless to say, in reply, I try to show scholars of antiquity this work, *Bun'ikō*. From among the many of our master's rough draft manuscripts, we have made one selection. This work is not complete, but it is a shame to publish just one manuscript [*Kaikō*], so we add this volume to where *Kaikō* left off.

Tenth month of Kansei 12 [1800]
Arakida Hisaoyu

BUN'IKŌ

People who lived in the divine age put their uncontrollable feelings within their hearts into expression through song. This is known as *uta*. When the eye witnessed something or the ear heard something, and the ancient Japanese could not keep his feelings to himself, he would thus string words together and vocalize these. These words are called words of praise. Later ages labeled this "literature."

Therefore, song occurs from within a person, and literature occurs from without.[2] At certain times people in society mention these two, po-

1. My translation is based on the popular manuscript.

2. That is, poetry occurs from emotions generated within, while literature is a representation of things occurring outside (or around) the person.

etry and literature, for poetry soothes one's heart and comforts one's mind, praising the works of the *kami* of heaven and earth, and becoming the vehicle for the imperial edicts. Because of this, there is nothing in the world that is lacking. Thus, ancient everyday speech was proper, so people composed poetry and literature with everyday words. From among these everyday usages, when the distinction of poetry and literature had evolved, the Japanese began to naturally add ornamental words, and these literary pursuits became beautiful.

It is human nature to compose poetry extolling the beautiful color or fragrance of plants and trees and avoid poorly rhyming sounds like those produced from birds and insects. Any word that was pleasant or stirring was considered fitting for expression. Therefore, the act of expressing oneself is a fearful exercise.[3]

The *kami* of heaven adore beautifully spoken words of praise. Because the eternally brilliant,[4] highly revered emperor also calms violent men through the lofty, splendid words of imperial edicts, what person who was born in the imperial country does not feel joy from these edicts?

And in middle antiquity, central like one of three branches, our country imported written works from foreign countries. With Japan's narrow view of the world, many of these works were easily taken in and accepted, and the common man lost the ability to comprehend the Way of our Imperial ruler, which conforms to heaven and earth. Because people did not study these ancient Japanese works, the Japanese forgot their own customs, and now there is not one person who writes in the ancient tradition. People rarely write in the ancient tradition, but they compose prose in imitation of these foreign works, or worse, they mix in Chinese characters, producing works that are neither truly Japanese nor Chinese, being incomplete representations of each.

Then there have been people who have felt that this situation was unsatisfactory, but [their solution was to] use Japanese words in a literary style where this style is strictly forbidden, or they use phrases unaware of male and female literary nuances. Also, they put sentences together without any thought for the content or purpose of the work. Some people did not differentiate between ancient and later era word usages, but just strung them

---

3. This idea is grounded in the belief in *kotodama*. See note 2, p. 140. The idea that a word became an active entity once vocalized is quite old in Japan. Thus, praise had a wondrous effect, or a terrible result when used as a curse.

4. One of the idiosyncrasies of Mabuchi's writing is an attempt to bring back the ancient custom of using epithets before certain nouns. The use of these make his writing a bit difficult to interpret, but I have tried to keep the flavor of the original by giving rough translations of these epithets. Here the epithet is *fisakata no*, meaning "far off, or eternal."

together within the text. We live in an era where these types of individuals are reappearing. Our master, Kada no Azumamaro of the jeweled capital, went through the various works of the emperor, and has studied them in minute detail, going back a myriad generations. Priest Keichū of Naniwa, the land that shines brightly, started studying the confusion of speech and the ancient words, and came to an understanding of the meaning of literature.[5] There are many elegant words contained within Keichū's works.

I am not very deft, but from a very young age have been fond of this type of research. Little by little, I continually studied, unaware of the passing of the sun and moon; during the summer when the farmers plow the ground, rich in coarse metals, I would ponder the ancient works in my heart while drenched in sweat. During winter nights when storms would blow down from the mountains, where people's legs cramp, my body would nearly freeze solid; during this time I would work at expounding the old works. And now that I have reached fifty years of age, half of a hundred ripples, I finally can understand much of the old words and old meanings. Therefore, I write these things down at the request of those disciples of mine who call me Agatai.

Of those characteristics seen in *Kojiki*, *Nihongi*, the liturgies, the imperial edicts, and *Fudoki*,[6] I will concentrate on meekness, masculinity, joy, delight, sadness, irritation, worshipping of the *kami*, celebrating friendship, celebrating the court, house-warming celebration, the style of the *kami*,[7] court poetic style, provincial poetic style, and the style of travel memoirs;[8] I have selected various aspects that have piqued my interest, expressions that are old and strong, full of fragrance, elegance, and emotion; I will expound upon the meaning of each in some small way, making mention that those words include a rhythm seen within stories and tales, introductions to poems, traveling diaries, and prefaces to poetic anthologies from later generations. When people from later eras read these ancient works, trying to comprehend the text using their contemporary emotions, they think that the ancients could not express themselves sufficiently; how-

5. This is essentially the meaning of the title of this short essay, *bun'ikō*—an examination into the meaning of literature.

6. Topographical works ordered by Emperor Genmei in 713. Each province was ordered to record its topographical information as well as local legends, customs, and locally produced items.

7. The word here is *kamiburi*, which on the surface means "the manner of the *kami*," but it is not clear if that is what Mabuchi intended. Considering the importance of the *kami* in ancient Japan, he may be suggesting the habits of the *kami*.

8. *Michiyukiburi* refers to Kikōbun, often translated as "travel diaries" or "travel memories."

ever, that is an unsophisticated way to approach these texts. There are people who ponder much, blessed with the gift of perception, who fail to find pleasure in those things of the ancient past.

The beauty of literature from later ages cannot compare with the beauty of the past. One can know that the beauty of literature from middle antiquity cannot compare with the finely woven pieces of ancient literature when he gets down and looks at crosswork with his own eyes. Those who engage the literature are those who know its beauty. In this way if one knows about the ancient past, his heart will be changed by the earnestness of things and the elegance of events [portrayed in the ancient literature]. If the student's heart becomes more earnest and elegant, will he not return to an ancient time of peace and fulfillment? Because we cannot discern between the past and now, we are gratified there are many people who yearn for the ancient customs.

There are some people who say that in the divine age there was no such thing as beautiful literature, because it finally appeared in later eras; however, since these people have not seen or know anything about the ancient literature, they express their opinions based on nothing other than their own imagination. Therefore, from the various items that I have been able to find, I will now mention one or two here—those beautiful things from the ancient literature.

Praise be to Emperor Kamu Yamato Iware Hiko,[9] who ruled the country from the Kashiwara Palace, for he is the sole person to put the sturdy pillars of his palace upon the rocks, and lift his rafters high to the High Plain of Heaven, called the first emperor to rule the land, who strengthened the base of those palace pillars, and built lofty the ridges of the palace roof. There is not a single person from middle antiquity whose writings can compare with the elegance of this emperor who generously expanded the empire.[10] There were many parts of this event that were widely known, but the knowledge of Emperor Jinmu has slowly shrunk. Is it not wondrous that he was called the first emperor who ruled the country?

Also, in the prayer for a bountiful harvest, the ancestral *kami* placed their trust in the emperor, and in the prayer for the harvest of rice, foam drips down from the elbows, and mud comes up to the thighs. When the farmers plant rice, the rice paddies of the people overflow with water, and the farmers go down into the mud and proceed to perform their difficult

9. Emperor Jinmu, claimed by both *Kojiki* and *Nihon shoki* to be Japan's first ruler.

10. This is a bold claim, considering that there is very little literature or poetry attributed to Jinmu. There are eleven unique poems attributed to him (seven in *Kojiki* and four in *Nihon shoki*).

task. Are these prayers pointing out all these events? And the country ruled over by the emperor is as wide as the clouds in the heavens, and yet these words make allusion to minute things so close together there is not even room for an inch or a tenth of an inch. These words mention the heavenly clouds coming down and spreading over the vast sky, as far as the bullfrog can cross, as far as the oceans stretch, as far as a ship can traverse. If one reads and knows about these boundless characteristics of ancient literature, how can he resist being consumed by the thoughts of the ancient past?

Masculinity

Brave Susanoo ...[11] when he soared up to heaven, his ascension caused the mountains and the rivers to shake and shudder, and because the entire land quaked, Amaterasu Ōmikami[12] was surprised to hear of his coming and said, "Surely the coming of my younger brother is not with pure intentions. He has come to rob me of my kingdom." So she let down her hair and tied it up into knots behind both her ears,[13] and in both her left and right hands she wrapped large precious jewels strung upon a string. On her back she put a large quiver, and on her right wrist she put a ringing wrist protection pad, and waving the tip of her bow she stamped upon the hard ground in her garden until she had sunken up to her thighs and had turned the ground into powder snow. With this show of vicious masculine nature, she waited to ask Susanoo the reason for his coming here. ...

Meekness

Susanoo replied, "My intentions are pure, and I have given birth to the Tawayame daughters, thus it is fair to say I have won."[14] With this, he broke down the dividing walls of Amaterasu's rice paddies, filled up her irrigation ditches, and urinated and defecated inside her palace where she was to

11. There are a number of ellipses in this section and these are all in the original.

12. The sun goddess; she is Susanoo's older sister. He has returned to heaven to confront her. His ferocity is demonstrated by the effect he has on the surrounding environment.

13. Symbolic of the style of men.

14. Amaterasu tested Susanoo's intentions by making a vow with him, which functioned as a form of divination. Children were born through the vow. Amaterasu said that if the children Susanoo fathered were female, then his intentions were good. If his children were male, then his intentions were evil. The Tawayame daughters were Tagirihime, Tagitsuhime, and Itsukishima Hime, and these were born from grinding up Susanoo's sword. The result of this divinatory act proved that his intentions were pure, which meant that he was right—thus he won.

hold the festival for the first fruits.[15] But though Susanoo committed these crimes against her, Amaterasu Ōmikami did not censure him. She said, "This excretion is surely something that my brother has vomited up from being drunk. As for the breaking down of the divisions of the paddies and filling up of the irrigation ditches, my younger brother surely must be vexed because of the land. This is why my younger brother does these things." Though she said this and tried to make things right, Susanoo did not cease his evil works, but committed worse ones.

The reader should ponder deeply upon these examples of masculinity and meekness. Though she is the great sun goddess, when the necessity arises, Amaterasu becomes brave and ferocious, ruling with strict authority. Nonetheless, she usually possesses a meek nature, generally ruling over heaven, looking down on the good on earth, inquiring repeatedly about certain events. How awe-inspiring is the essence of the Way of the *kami*, teaching us how to rule over the country and over our own homes.

Festivals

The great *kami* Ōkuninushi … had already ceded the central land of Ashihara [Japan] according to the reason of the heavenly decree. "And if you will make stout the pillars upon the rocks of the place where I [Ōkuninushi] will dwell, and raise the rafters high to the High Plain of Heaven, and establish the dwelling of the son of the heavenly *kami* who resides in the illuminous heavens, then I will hide within the far-off world that is distant, down the road of many curves and bends, and I will serve the ruler.[16] And as for my one hundred and eighty children, if Yafe Koto Shironushi will be their leader and their rear protector, then there shall not be one who will be disobedient." Having said this, a heavenly residence was constructed on a small beach in the village of Tagishi in the province of Izumo, and Kushi Yadama, a descendant of the Mito *kami*, was set up as the chef. When the time to present the festival banquet came, the people offered prayers, and Kushi Yadama turned into a cormorant and dove into the ocean, scooping clay from the bottom of the ocean in his mouth, and making eighty vessels from the clay. He then cut the stalks of seaweed, and having made a fire flint out of a board, took the stalks of laver and a wooden

15. This reaction can be interpreted in a number of ways. The basic idea is that Susanoo is gloating over his victory, going on a victory rampage, if you will.

16. The original has *momotarazu yasokumade ni*, literally meaning the "many curves and bends in the road less than one hundred." It is believed this is a euphemistic way to say "land of the dead." However, it is also possible that it is a euphemistic way to show that the land of Izumo is far from the center of Yamato.

pestle and drilled until it produced fire. With this he said, "I will stoke this fire I have started until the dense smoke reaches the innermost areas of the shining residence of the ancestor *kami*, Kami Musubi in the High Plain of Heaven, and until I have melted together the rocks beneath the surface of the earth below. I will offer up dishes of the large-mouthed perch on bending bamboo the fishermen caught in their long ropes made of tapa and boisterously brought ashore. ..."

Liturgy for a Newly Built Dwelling

Prince Woke[17] stood and adjusted his clothes and gave the following auspicious words for the newly built edifice:

> The base and pillars of this newly built edifice will appease the owner's heart. The raised roof-beams will prosper the heart of the head of the household. The strong rafters placed here will set the heart of the patriarch in order. The tight crosspieces will bring peace to his heart. The cords which have been tightly tied around the beams will lengthen the days of the owner. The thatch of the roof represents the master's treasures.
>
> Izumo is a land rich in fertile fields. Out of the long, slender ears of rice, *sake* is made in shallow jars. Oh, how to drink that *sake*, my friends! Taking the horn from a buck of this mountainside, I perform the buck dance. This sweet handmade *sake* cannot be bought for any price at the market of Yega. And with the clapping of hands, I partake of this *sake*! My eternal friends!

The ancient Japanese wrote many old works like these, and the significance of their elegant words is extraordinary. I have only given a partial sampling from among these works.[18]

Kamo no Mabuchi
[NST 39:240–47]

---

17. Later known as Emperor Kenzō. He and his older brother, Prince Oke, were hidden in the provinces after Yūryaku killed their father. Woke offers celebratory words for the house-warming party. It is here that he also announces that he and his brother are of the royal lineage.

18. This line likely was added by a student of Mabuchi's at a later date. There is also a "draft version" of *Bun'ikō* in possession of Mukyūkai (Yamamoto 1942.1:579–90). The most pronounced difference between this draft and the popular version is that there are no titles for the categorization of the characteristics of the ancient people. The "draft version" ends with the following, "There are many examples within these two works [*Kojiki* and *Nihon shoki*], but I have only given one or two examples. The reader will know the distinction among the number of styles within the various examples as I have divided these into specific sections. It is true that I have divided these according to differences in time" (ibid., p. 590).

ISONOKAMI SASAMEGOTO

Motoori Norinaga | 1763

[Written several years after *Ashiwake obune*, *Isonokami sasamegoto* further delineates Norinaga's ideas about poetry and literature. In this essay he introduces his theory that *mono no aware* underpins poetry and literature, and the best literature is that which depicts the true state of human emotions. He criticizes scholars who see morality or ethics as the driving force in literature, and thus censured works like *Genji monogatari*. The draft was completed around 1763, but was not published until after his death. I have only translated a portion of Chapter 1. He begins by defining "poetry" as a song that must have two components: true emotion and artfully arranged words. By doing this, the person unlocks emotions within his/her heart, known as *mono no aware*. Literature is important, because it depicts two types of people: those who understand *mono no aware* and those who do not.]

A person once asked me, "Exactly what is poetry?" I answered that in a broad sense, it begins with verse in thirty-one syllables, and everything like *kagura*,[1] *saibara*,[2] linked verse, *imayō*,[3] *fuzoku*,[4] narrated drama like *Heike monogatari* and *sarugaku*, contemporary songs like satirical poetry, *haikai*, ballads, puppet songs, and the popular songs children recite all belong to the category called poetry. Anything with expressions that are artful and beautiful can be classified as poetry. Within this broad classification, there is a difference between ancient and contemporary, elegant and base, but each one is still considered poetry. Therefore, the songs of comfort composed by the uneducated women of the provinces are also classified as poetry. In other words, this is true poetry.

The so-called thirty-one-syllable verse is the poetry of the ancient Japanese. Ballads and popular songs are the poetry of contemporary Japanese. They are both poetry, and the reason the style varies [as much as it does] is because of changes over time.

---

1. *The Encyclopedia of Shintō* states, "*Kagura* is a sacred artistic rite performed when making an offering to the kami. Usually performed annually or even less frequently, the *kami* is invited (*kanjō*) to occupy the sacred area and is worshiped with performances of music, song and dance" (Inoue et al. 1999:283).

2. *Saibara* is a form of song performed among the nobility, which appears to have begun as folk music in the Nara period.

3. *Imayō* is a four-stanza form of poetry popular during the Heian period.

4. Like *saibara*, *fuzoku* are songs from the provinces that were eventually incorporated into songs sung by the nobility at court.

Ancient poetry excelled in elegant words and refined meaning. Contemporary ballads and popular songs employ vulgar words and tasteless meaning, which destroys the beauty; this is the difference. Thus, the distinction between ancient and contemporary, and elegant and base is pronounced, and it may appear that they are not even the same thing; however, it cannot be said that any one of these forms does not belong to the classification of poetry. Therefore, songs made up by children are also considered to be poetry.

Uta has continued unbroken, handed down from the divine age till the present, and naturally it has never lost its original appellation of "song." The state of poetry, its word usage and meaning, has changed from era to era, but its nature and spirit have not changed from the poetry of the divine age down to the popular ballads of today. I will explain this in greater detail later.

Not only human beings, but beasts and fowl are all endowed with emotions and lift up their voices to sing. The preface to *Kokinshū* says, "The song of the warbler among the blossoms, the voice of the frog dwelling in the water—these teach us that every living creature sings."[5] With their carefully arranged voices, and their natural artifact,[6] birds and insects, also, produce poetry. The thirty-one-syllable song of the warbler and the frog are recorded in the preface of *Kokinshū*, and these were produced by poets fond of such things. Why can creatures create human poetry? A warbler produces warbler songs; a frog produces frog songs; the various songs of the living creatures become their "poetry." Thus, every creature existing in this world possesses its own form of song.

A certain tradition says, "Poetry was prepared for every creature based upon the principle of the way things should be from the creation of heaven and earth, even to the sound of the wind or the echo of water; everything that produces sound produces song."[7] This tradition appears to have taken deep consideration for the nature of things, addressing the broad issue of the meaning of poetry; on the other hand, though, this is a shallow theory. Poetry is a properly arranged text, so simply any sound produced by birds and insects cannot be called poetry. Only a voice that produces its words with an artful technique is labeled song. Also, among the words of human beings, that which is being sung with an artful technique is called poetry.

---

5. Quoted from McCullough (1985:3).

6. Norinaga uses the character 文 to describe the beautiful nature of animal cries and songs.

7. It is unclear what tradition Norinaga is quoting.

All other vocalized words are not labeled verse. Lifeless objects do not produce poetry. Thus, in the preface to *Kokinshū* it mentions "living creatures," but it does not say "everything." In the Chinese preface it says, "All things produce poetry," but *things* refers to living creatures.

Therefore, the idea that "everything that produces sound produces poetry" is false. All living things have emotions, and produce sound of themselves; sounds composed with artful technique from emotions are poetry. Lifeless things cannot produce sound in and of themselves. Rather, they produce sound from outside stimuli. Because song is something produced though emotion, it is not reasonable to expect lifeless objects to produce song. Thus, the beautiful sounds produced by the various musical instruments are not called song in and of themselves. The reason for this is because the sound was not produced through the emotions of the instrument.

Therefore, how can the sound of the wind and the echo of water be classified as poetry? Even if it had an artful technique, we could still not consider it poetry because the object in question does not have emotion. Furthermore, it is reasonable to say that anything lacking a beautifully arranged text is not poetry.

The question was asked, "What constitutes 'beautifully arranged words forming a text?'"

I answered that when one sings, the proper number of words is used, and the sound is flowing and inviting. "Having beauty" means that the words are carefully chosen, arranged without confusion. Generally, arranging the words in five or seven syllables is the proper standard for differentiating ancient and contemporary or elegant and base. Thus, ancient poetry and contemporary ballads both employ five and seven syllables; this is the natural beauty of poetry.

The phrase "in the ancient era, the number of syllables was unregulated" is incorrect.[8] Even in poetry from the divine age, there is no difference in the five- and seven-syllable structure.[9] Among these poems, there are many whose five syllables are produced as four or three, and whose seven syllables are written as six or eight, but the deficient rhythm was made up for by lengthening the syllables and the extra syllables were

8. This is seen twice in the preface to *Kokinshū* (my rendition is slightly modified from McCullough 1985:4). Modern research has shown us that *Kokinshū* is correct while Norinaga is not.

9. Norinaga's proof for his assertion comes from Susanoo's *yakumo tatsu* (NS 1) poem seen in the divine age. It is a perfectly constructed thirty-one-syllable poem. Nevertheless, the ordered structure of this poem argues for a later date of composition.

worked in by shortening the rhythm when the poem was sung. With this, the poetry was sung as five and seven syllables, and the three, four, six, and eight syllables were sung as five and seven. If one were to ask how we know this, we know this by looking at contemporary children's popular songs. When one hears songs sung by rice pounders and lumberjacks, you notice that they all consist of five and seven syllables. The additional or deficient syllables are made to fit the rhythm by lengthening or shortening the sound within the rhythm, making it conform to the five- and seven-syllable structure. When you listen to the song, it is composed of five and seven syllables. This is the natural form of the poetry, and there is no difference between the divine age and the present.

However, an annotational note in the preface to *Kokinshū* says in relation to the song of Shitateru Hime, "Those songs are irregular; they do not resemble waka."[10] The reason for this note is because the author did not understand the logic I have explained above, but only looked at how the song was recorded in *Nihongi*, and recorded this opinion as it was understood from a later generation's point of view. All songs from the divine age consists of properly arranged, beautiful lines. None violates the five–seven-syllable structure. These words in the song from Shitateru Hime are especially well arranged, and it sounds beautiful. If it is true that originally the syllables were not set, the rhythm when sung would have been choppy and chaotic, grating on the ears of the listener. The currently popular ballads would be the same, also. This fact is easy for people to comprehend.

Songs of antiquity were sung as the poet composed, and the poet regulated the rhythm as he sang; therefore, when sung, the fact that there were three, four, six, or eight syllables in the song became irrelevant. So, there are places in the song where it was permissible to have syllables exceed or fall short of the established norm, and there are other places where it was not permissible to exceed or fall short of that norm. When one sang the song, he knew where such spots were. I will explain in greater detail later about the proper arrangement of the five and seven syllables.

"Properly arranged beautiful words" means exactly what I have just explained above. And we know that the voices of living creatures follow the same principle. The five- and seven-syllable principle is the proper arrangement of human words. Birds and insects, also, have their various places where their songs are properly arranged and that is the song of each creature. ...

Again the question was asked, "When did these songs come about?" I

10. McCullough (1985:8).

replied that the line in *Kokinshū* preface that says, "Our poetry appeared at the dawn of creation"[11] is expounded upon in *Yozaishō*,[12] which says, "The divine age section of *Nihon shoki* states, 'In the beginning when heaven and earth were organized, the islands of the rivers and ocean floated upon the water, like a fish swimming on the surface of the ocean.' The *Kokinshū* preface does not have reference to this time. *Kogo shūi* records, 'Another tradition says that when heaven and earth were divided, two *kami*, Izanagi and Izanami, were betrothed, and gave birth to the land of Ōyashima, the mountains, rivers, trees, and plant life.' This is what the preface had reference to."

Another tradition says that the principle of song existed with the division of heaven and earth, expounding the *yin* and *yang* and the principle of the five natural elements, saying, "These came into existence after the division of heaven and earth." This tradition is trying to rationalize the relationship of song and *yin* and *yang*, but this is a mistaken conception. This shows that these people do not understand that Izanagi and Izanami appeared when heaven and earth were divided.[13] Because of the text quoted from *Kogo shūi* in *Yozaishō*, we know that the time of Izanagi and Izanami is also the time when heaven and earth were divided.

The statement that poetry has its origins at this time comes from the fact that Izanagi and Izanami together produced words of praise when they came down from heaven to the island of Onogoro, were betrothed, and went around the pillar of heaven. Those words are recorded thus in *Kojiki*,

> Izanagi first said, "How delightful! A beautiful maiden."
> After that, Izanami, his wife, said, "How delightful! A handsome man."

This is the beginning of song. The meaning of these words is recorded [thus] in the divine age section of *Nihon shoki*.[14] *Kojiki* recorded it in the ancient fashion with phonograms. *Nihon shoki* recorded it in Chinese and gave the significance of these words. The character 妍 (*ana ni*—"how de-

---

11. Ibid., p. 3.

12. More properly called *Kokin Yozaishō*, an annotative work on *Kokinshū*, completed by Keichū around 1691.

13. The Fuji *chōka* by Akahito (MYS 317) says, "At the time that heaven and earth were divided. … " Also, a Hitomaro *chōka* (MYS 167) says, "At the time when heaven and earth were first divided … Amaterasu Hirume ruled over heaven." Another poem (MYS 2089) has the line, "When heaven and earth were first divided, they faced the river of heaven."

14. A Chinese explanation is given, but in translation it is exactly the same, so I have not felt the need to provide it.

lightful") is defined in *Kangxi zidian* as "beautiful," or "delightful." Thus, these are words celebrating their feelings about being able to obtain good spouses.

If we expound further, *Kogo shūi* explains the word *ana* thus, "In ancient Japanese, anything extremely impressive was called *ana*." (This is also seen in *Kujiki*, but because it is a forgery, I will not quote from it.) In *Man'yōshū*, *ana* is written as 痛. It is the same *ana* as *ana koishi* "how I long for you", and *ana tauto* "how noble." The words *ana*, *aya* and *aa* are all from the same root. ...[15]

Now, these words of praise are not labeled as song in either *Kojiki* or *Nihongi*. *Nihongi* records all its poetry in phonograms, and these words of praise are written like the rest of the record in Chinese.[16] So it is clear that we are not talking about song here. However, these words are arranged in sequences of five syllables, and the diction is not composed of ordinary words. Therefore, these are labeled as words of "praise" or "reaction," and this is because they are not everyday words. Thus, it has already been shown in *Yozaishō* that this is the origin of song. The beginnings of things do not necessarily exist in perfectly established forms like the state in later eras.

Again, the question was asked, "Why were these words of praise quoted from *Kojiki* and not from *Nihongi*?"[17]

I answered that *Nihongi* is ornamented with Chinese written with the intention of creating beautiful literature, but the effect of the ancient Japanese words was ignored. There are many cases where the sentences themselves were the main object. *Kojiki* was written with the intent of preserving ancient words, irrespective of the sentences. In spite of this, people in later eras held interest in whether the sentences were correct or not, and they thought nothing of the individual words of old. Because of this, *Nihongi* generally holds people's esteem, but no one knows about *Kojiki*. Through this neglect, the ancient words disappeared day by day. People do not understand that words are the fundamental element, and the orthography is secondary. It is a sad state. Looking at the characters 憙哉 ... we know

---

15. I have elected to skip the rest of Norinaga's linguistic elucidation of the Chinese text of *Nihon shoki*, because it has little value from a literary or poetic standpoint.

16. This is not an accurate statement, as the Saimei song (NS 122) contains the nonphonogrammatic graphs 甲子, making the song difficult to decipher. See Bentley (2013:100–4).

17. *Nihon shoki* was held in higher status until Norinaga's day. It is written in tight, clean Chinese, while *Kojiki* is written in a labyrinthine script mixing Japanese phonograms with Chinese. This person basically is asking, "Why did you quote from an inferior, unknown work when you could have quoted from the standard text of *Nihongi*?"

what it means, but we have no clue how to read it in Japanese. Thus, to the sides of the characters people have interpolated readings, but because this was done by someone at a later date, the readings are often in doubt.

Thus, how will we confirm the original reading of 憙哉? *Nihongi* contains the annotational note, 少男、此云烏等孤 "'Young man' this is read *wotoko*," and the Jinmu section has 可美少男 so this should be read as *umasi*; however, the reading of 憙哉 is uncertain. If we stretch things, and compare *Kojiki*'s text with the variant commentary of *Nihongi*, we could read these characters as *ananiyasi*, or perhaps *ananiweya*. The reason for this is because 妍哉 was later transcribed as 美哉. Also, 可愛 was read as *e*. Since 可美 was later written as 善, perhaps this passage in *Nihongi* should be read *ananiweya, e wotoko wo*. Perhaps the character 遇 was placed in this sentence because the meaning "meet" is inferred, and thus would not represent any ancient word. If we follow the present manuscript [of *Nihon shoki*], then the reading of *anauresiya, umasi wotoko ni afinu* does not sound like words of praise.

At any rate, because this is all speculative, our only recourse is to use the accurate usages of ancient vocabulary in *Kojiki* as the key to unlock the secret to the later *Nihongi*'s Chinese usages. In all things, we should view *Kojiki* as the critical text, and use *Nihongi* as a commentary. Especially from a philological point of view, since we treat the ancient words as the most important part, there is no other work able to surpass *Kojiki*, and for those who wish to research into ancient Japanese lexicography, this work is indispensable.

Again, I was asked, "Exactly in what way did poetry begin?" I answered that the beginnings of poetry are not exactly seen in either *Kojiki* or *Nihongi*, but both works record the Yakumo poem produced by Susanoo as the first poem. *Kojiki* says, "When they constructed the Suga Palace, clouds arose from that place and climbed into the sky. At that time, he composed a song:

yakumo tatu	Endowed with power,
idumo yafegaki	this double Izumo fence—
tuma gomi ni	to conceal ourselves,
yafegaki tukuru	I have built this double fence.
sono yafegaki wo	Yes, within this double fence.[18]

18. My translation of this poem has little to do with how Norinaga understands it. His interpretation is given below the poem.

This is that poem. *Nihongi* has *tuma gomi ni* as *tuma gome ni*—a difference of one character.

Now, there have been many forced theories introduced from ancient times onward to explain the meaning of this poem. Because these commentators are all ignorant of ancient things, we cannot accept any of them. One certainly must not be misled by heretical ideas. *Yozaishō* says,

> The meaning of *yakumo* comes from *ya* being used adjectivally, meaning "many"; thus, "many piled clouds." Words like *yafezakura* or *yafeyamabuki* use it, but though it is not necessarily always employed, there are many instances where this idea of "many layered" is used. *Yakumo tatu* is normally an epithet for the word *idumo*. The place name of Izumo is believed to have its origins in this poem, so *yakumo tatu* was as yet not used as an epithet, and so in this poem it has a concrete meaning. Thus we know that "many piled" has been added to the word *idumo*, meaning "clouds issue forth."

Personally, I believe that the stanza *yakumo tatu* was composed when Susanoo saw the clouds climb up into the sky; thus, it means, "more and more clouds appear." The word *idumo* is seen in *Izumo fudoki*, where it says that the name of the province came from this poem written by Susanoo.[19] Thus, it should not be read here as a place name, but only as "clouds issuing forth." The idea that *yakumo tatu* is an epithet of the place name of Izumo is incorrect. One should not be confused with the epithetical usages in *yafo tadewo fodumi* [MYS 3842] and *masoga yo soga* [NS 103]. *Yafegaki* means a multilevel fence. It does not mean "the true fence of the Suga Palace." The clouds are simply compared metaphorically to the fence. The reason that it does not say *yakumo tati* is because the poem is describing what the poet saw as he looked around. *Idumo yafegaki* is an allusion to the clouds being like a fence, meaning "the clouds like a fence that issue forth." *Tuma gomi ni yafegaki tukuru* means "I will now construct a fence within which to hide away my wife."

There should be people who think it strange that the fence was con-

19. In reality, *Fudoki* says, "The reason it was called Izumo is because the *kami* Yatu Kami Omituno commanded saying, '*Yakumo tatu*.' And that is why it is called Yakumo Tatsu Izumo." Under the heading of Mori Village it says, "The Great *kami*, Ōnamochi, pacified Yakuti, and when he was returning he came to Mount Nagae and proclaimed, 'I will hand over to the Imperial grandson the country that I have created and have ruled over so that he may govern it in safety. But people will worship my spirit within the enclosure of the blue mountains in this, the land of Izumo of many folds of clouds.'" There is no mention of the poem or Susanoo. It is clear, though, that some tradition influenced both the *Fudoki* and the poem.

structed out of clouds, but the fence was not actually built. Susanoo saw the rising clouds, and metaphorically stated that he built a multilevel fence. Because clouds and mists rise up and block objects, they were also used in later ages metaphorically as hedges. Even in China, we see these usages such as "The heavenly clouds were as a fence, already rising up."[20] It is a mistake to make this fence the wall to the Suga Palace. They are merely clouds. The repetition of the fence, *sono yafegaki wo* is often seen in ancient poetry. Ancient songs are analogous to contemporary children's songs where people sing to themselves, and repeat one of the lines. The technique is natural in ancient song, as it was in China. The *wo* at the end is the same form of ending when Izanagi and Izanami produced their words of praise.[21]

Because this occurred during the construction of the Suga Palace, Susanoo made a metaphorical poem when he saw the clouds rise up into the sky. All of these poems were written about the clouds. . . .[22]

The question was asked, "Should we then say that the thirty-one-syllable-style poem originated with the Yakumo poem, and the longer *chōka* originated with Shitateru Hime?"

I answered that the classification of poetry into *chōka*, *tanka*, *konponka*,[23] and *sedōka* was done at a later age; in the divine age no such classification existed, and so without relation to the length of the poem, the Yakumo poem is the first poem of the tradition. Anciently, poetry was composed along the rhythm of five and seven syllables irrespective of length, the poet writing the feelings of his heart as long as he felt necessary, and there was no distinction between *chōka* and *tanka*. That is the logic behind saying that there was no separate beginning to *chōka*.

If we are forced to use the later classification and point out the origins of *tanka* and *chōka*, then thirty-one-syllable poetry had its origins with the Yakumo poem, and *chōka* originated with the poetic exchange between Yachihoko and Numakawa Hime. *Sedōka* and *konponka* are not seen in the divine age. Even when we come to the age of Emperor Jinmu, though we have poems with three and seven stanzas, there is nothing which can truly be labeled *sedōka* or *konponka*. Even after Jinmu's time, there are poems

20. This appears to have been quoted from *Tongqiao taifu* (third century?).

21. Norinaga states the following in *Kojiki-den* about this final *wo*, "The final *wo* is just a particle, and is like an emphatic *yo*" (MNZ 1976, 9:412).

22. If we translate the *Yakumo tatu* poem according to Norinaga's interpretation it becomes: Many clouds rise up— / those clouds like a fence / into which I will hide my bride. / I will build that fence / out of those multilayered clouds.

23. *Konpon* is an unknown style mentioned in the Mana preface of *Kokinshū*. Later, in *Tamakatsuma*, Norinaga mentions that he believes this form to be related to *sedōka* (Bentley 2013:371).

with six stanzas, but these are still slightly different, too. A poem which is truly composed in the *sedōka* style of 5-7-7-5-7-7 is seen in the Yūryaku section of *Nihongi*:

atarasiki	Such a pitiful waste!
winabe no takumi	That inking string used by
kakesi suminafa	the Inabe carpenter.
si ga nakeba	If he is no longer here,
tare ka kakemu yo	what skilled person will remain
atara suminafa	to use the inking string?

[NS 80]

The first *konponka* is seen in *Kojiki*, and it is a song by Emperor Nintoku:

medori no	Princess Medori,
wa ga ofokimi no	my great lady—
orosu fata	for whom do you weave
ta ga tanero kamo	this fabric to make robes?

[KJK 66]

However, the rhythm of these poems naturally came together this way, and it was not intentional. Because there are songs before this one where one or two syllables are deficient, or where the arrangement of five and seven syllables is different, it cannot necessarily be said that this is the beginning of *sedōka* nor *konponka*; however, I have mentioned these two poems because the form meets the standards of *sedōka* and *konponka*, criteria established in a later era. Because ancient poetry started with a core of three stanzas without set rules for the number of stanzas, there was no conscious distinction between *chōka* and *tanka*.

The question was raised, "How about the section in the *Kokinshū* preface which says 'When the human era began, Susanoo introduced the thirty-one-syllable poem?'[24] Is it claiming the age of humanity began with the era of the five generations of earthly *kami*?"

I replied, quoting from *Yozaishō*, "After the beginning of the age of human beings, poetry was composed using the thirty-one-syllable poem composed by Susanoo as a model." We can grasp the answer to this question from this statement. However, what about the idea that people composed poetry in imitation of this poem of *kami*? Later generations gener-

24. McCullough (1985:3).

ally composed much poetry that was thirty-one syllables not based upon Susanoo's poem. It means that with the conception of the age of humanity, most of the thirty-one-syllable poetry produced had its inception with the poem of Susanoo. It does not mean that they imitated the poem, but the poetry naturally followed the form of the original poem, as it was well arranged; as it had a beautiful ring to it, this form [thirty-one syllables] of poetry naturally became the major type for poetic composition. This is the natural course of events.

Aside from the Yakumo poem of Susanoo, there are other thirty-one-syllable poems recorded in the divine age, such as the poem produced by Ninigi:

okitu mo fa	It comes to the shore
fe ni fa yoredomo	the seaweed in the offing,
sanedoko mo	but my wife comes not—
atafanu kamo yo	refusing to give me a bed.
famatutidori yo	Ah! The plovers on the beach!

[NS 4]

And the poem by Toyotama Hime:

akatama fa	Though the red jewels
wo safe fikaredo	glow even to the string,
siratama no	the white jewels that
kimi ga yosofisi	my beloved adorns himself with
tafutoku arikeri	are even more noble.

[KJK 7]

To this Hiko Hohodemi replied:

okitu dori	Birds in the offing,
kamo duku sima ni	on the island where the wild geese gather,
wa ga winesi	I shall not forget
imo wa wasurezi	the night we spent together
yo no kotogoto ni	as long as I live.

[KJK 8]

The poems above are from *Kojiki*. The versions in *Nihongi* are somewhat different. When we enter the age of human beings, we have the following song from Emperor Jinmu:

asifara no	We slept together
sikesiki[25] **oya ni**	in the little, unkempt hut
suga tatami	on the moor of reeds
iya saya sikite	where we slowly spread out
wa ga futari nesi	those rustling mats of sedge.

[KJK 19]

At the same time, Isukeyori Hime sang:

sawigafa yo	From the Sai River
kumotati watari	clouds arise and spread forth;
unebi yama	on Mount Unebi
konofa sayaginu	the leaves of the trees begin to rustle.
kaze fukamu to su	Surely a storm is brewing.

[KJK 20]

She also sang:

unebi yama	Clouds rise up above
firu fa kumo towi	Mount Unebi in the day.
yufu sareba	When the night comes,
kaze fukamu to zo	surely a storm is brewing
konofa sayageru	and the leaves will rustle.

[KJK 21]

These are the first thirty-one-syllable poems written when the age of humanity began.

The question was raised, "Is it true that linked verse began in Japan with Yamato Takeru asking:

nifibari	How many nights
tukufa wo sugite	have we slept since we passed
iku yo ka neturu	Tsukuba and Niibari?

[KJK 25]

and one of his torch-bearing servants replied:

---

25. Norinaga's text has this as *sigekoki,* which he interprets as "ugly." This is due to a variant character in the text. The word should be *sikesiki* "dirty, unkempt." The next problem is the meaning in context. Some take it as "damp," others as "dirty, ruined, or hidden." I have chosen "unkempt," but the other interpretations may be just as worthy. Norinaga's idea of "ugly" is unsupportable, however.

kaga nabete	Combining the days,
yo ni fa kokonoyo	we have slept nine nights
fi ni fa towoka wo	and have spent ten days."

[KJK 26]

I responded that since this is recorded in *Nihongi* as, "At this time there was an old man in charge of lighting the torches who added the following song to the end of the Prince's song: … ," it may sound as if it is what later eras called linked verse, but in reality, he did not "finish the song"; he merely presented the prince with a three-stanza reply to the question. And though this is the first instance of a three-stanza poem in *Nihongi*, there was also one in *Kojiki* in which Emperor Jinmu composed:

katugatu mo	Though she is lacking,
iya sakidateru	I shall take the maid in front
e wo si makamu	and make her my bride.

[KJK 16][26]

The reply to this poem was the poem written at the same time by Isuke-yori Hime:

ametutu	Why do you have
tidori masitodo	tattooed eyes like
nado sakeru tome	the wagtail, the plover, and the bunting?

[KJK 17]

To this, Ōkume replied:

wotome ni	It is to meet
tada ni afamu to	this beautiful maiden firsthand
wa ga sakeru tome	that I have tattooed eyes.

[KJK 18]

Because these occur early in the record, we cannot say that they started with Yamato Takeru's poem. As I mentioned earlier, if people refer only to *Nihongi*, then they end up asking questions like this about Yamato Takeru's poem. The inquirer is completely unaware of what *Kojiki* says.

26. This is believed to have been said in jest. Jinmu looked at the seven maidens in front of him, and teases one in the front, "What the heck! I'll take this little thing in front."

Nevertheless, these two poems are believed to be the beginning of linked verse because of the clause "added to the end of the song." If it must be mentioned, this type of usage is also seen in *Kojiki.* But Ōkume's poem has no such usage; it only says, "He replied by singing. . . ." So it could be said that *this* was the beginning of linked verse, but because all these poems are of the same structure we should not claim that one poem was placed before the other in a linked fashion. The reader must not be confused by the word "added." Just because both *Kojiki* and *Nihongi* use the words "added to the end" in reference to this torch-bearer's poem, it does not necessarily mean that at the time of composition the torch-bearer was under the impression that his reply—which ends up explaining place names to a later audience—was being linked to Prince Yamato Takeru's poem.

As time went on, three-stanza poems disappeared, and society began to produce poems with five or six stanzas, and the reason that we no longer see three-stanza poems is because they were looked upon as half of a six-stanza poem, so the later compilers of these historical records believed the second three-stanza set to be a continuation of the previous poem.

fasikeyasi	How nostalgic!
wagife no kata yo	Clouds have arisen up
kumowi tatikumo	over the land of my home.
	[KJK 32]

This poem is recorded as *kata uta* "part of a poem," and this is based on the classification of later eras.[27]

Now, three-stanza poems are also seen in *Nihongi*, like this children's poem from the reign of Emperor Saimei:

tukusiki	My beautiful,
a ga wakaki ko wo	young child—
okite ka yukamu	Must I leave you and continue?
	[NS 121]

Other than these, there are also many other ancient three-stanza poems in existence. If people wish to see these exchange poems as linked verse, then the set of verse from the age of Emperor Jinmu is the beginning. How-

27. Modern scholarship sees this as a function of the musical quality of these songs, and not a fact that a predetermined number of syllables are left hanging (Kōnoshi and Yamaguchi 2007:234, n7).

ever, because these are merely the upper and lower sections of *sedōka*, it is not the thirty-one-syllable form of linked verse.

In Book 8 of *Manyōshū*, there is a thirty-one-syllable poem that resembles linked verse: The headnote reads [MYS 1635]:

> An exchange poem where the nun asked Ōtomo Yakamochi for a reply, and he added the ending stanzas to the first section written by the nun.

safogafa no	Irrigating the newly planted paddy
midu wo sekiagete	with water from
ufesi ta wo	the dammed up Saho River—
	(The nun's poem)
kareru wasaifi fa	is the early rice cut and boiled
fitori naru besi	for you alone?
	(Yakamochi's addition)

Regardless, though, this is merely one poem composed by two people. The following is in *Shūishū* [SS 1184],

> It was the night when one of the women servants in the palace was supposed to secretly meet a man; he arrived late, and when the call of two in the morning was heard, she produced the following:

fito gokoro	At this hour of two,
usimitu[28] *ima fa*	I now understand how
tayomazi yo	you would feel bitter.
(Yoshimune no Munesada)	
yume ni miyu ya to	I thought that perhaps I
ne[29] *zo suginikeru*	would see you in my dreams.

In *Ise Monogatari*, when Narihira no Ason[30] went hunting in Ise, he met Princess Saigū in the morning:

> The woman handed him the parting cup; upon the saucer was her parting poem. He took it and read:

kati fito no	Though he crosses this shallow river—
wataredo nurenu	shallow like our relationship—
e ni si areba	the wayfarer's hem does not even get wet.

28. This is a play on words with the time of two in the morning (*usimitu*) and bitter (*usi mitu*).

29. This is a play on words for "to sleep through" (*ne zo sugu*) and "past one in the morning" (*ne* [hour of the rat—one a.m.] *zo sugu*).

30. Ariwara no Narihira (825–80). In *Sandai jitsuroku*, in Narihira's obituary it says, "Narihira was very handsome. He was free and unrestrained, doing as he pleased. In general he was lacking in talent and learning, but wrote excellent *waka*" (Kuroita 1982:475).

There was no end to the poem. Upon the saucer of the parting cup, he wrote a concluding couplet with charcoal from the torchlight:

mata afu saka no	I shall cross the Meeting Barrier
seki fa koyenamu	to come see you again."

This is the true form of later linked verse. The classification of "linked verse" is first seen in the poetic collection called *Kin'yōshū*. The technique here of composing the concluding stanzas first and then adding the beginning stanzas is also seen in *Shūishū*.[31]

Again the question was advanced, "Now that you have answered my question about the origin of poetry, in what way does poetry come into existence?" I answered by saying that poetry comes into existence by knowing *mono no aware*.[32]

"So exactly what do you mean by 'knowing *mono no aware*?'"

I replied by quoting from the *Kokinshū* preface, "Japanese poetry has the human heart as the seed and myriads of words as leaves."[33] This idea of "heart" is knowing *mono no aware*. Then the preface says, "It [poetry] comes into being when men use the seen and the heard to give voice to feelings aroused by innumerable events in their lives."[34] The phrase "give voice to feelings" also refers to knowing *mono no aware*. The "human heart" mentioned above is a fundamental principle, and here it discusses concrete examples.[35] In the Mana preface of the same poetic collection, the clause "their [human] thoughts are easily swayed, their moods alternate between sorrow and happiness"[36] also points to knowing *mono no aware*.

The reason that it is called "knowing *mono no aware*" is because every creature is bound by emotion as long as it breathes. The creature is endowed with emotions, so it feels something when coming in contact with something else. Therefore, as long as the creature breathes, it has song.

---

31. There are six poems in *Shūishū*, SS1179–1184, which are considered *renga* or "linked verse."

32. Norinaga then explains in great detail exactly what this is. I have settled on the rendition of "knowing the profundity of emotion."

33. Quoted from McCullough (1985:3). Norinaga appears to have used a variant text. He has *fitotu kokoro wo tane to site*, but the current text has *fito no kokoro wo tane*, "took the hearts of men as seeds, and produced a myriad leaves."

34. Ibid.

35. I have followed the orthodox reading of *fito no kokoro* "the human heart," instead of *fitotu no kokoro* "one heart." Keichū's *Kokin yōzaishō* also notes that the feelings mentioned here reside in the human heart, and as Norinaga was familiar with Keichū's work, I believe that he interpreted this line as "human heart."

36. McCullough (1985:256).

Among these creatures, human beings are especially superior to other living things, and because their hearts are sensitive, their thoughts are frequently profound. Not only that, but of all creatures, human beings experience a wide range of complex encounters, providing greater bonds with a variety of things that give rise to a multiplicity of thoughts. And that is why there is the reasoning that humans cannot survive without song.

When asked why human thought is complex and profound, it is because of the knowledge of *mono no aware*. Due to the complex nature of human experience and the bonds between human beings, the human heart is in constant motion, refusing to remain still.[37] "Motion" refers to times when we feel happy, and at other times we feel sad, sometimes angry, other times pleased, engaged and involved, at times frightened and worried, at times tender, at times bitter, at times in love, and at times disgusted. The human heart experiences many emotions, and thus is moved by knowing *mono no aware*.

The idea of being moved by this knowledge means, for example, that when one encounters something delightful, he feels happy. He is happy because he is able to differentiate between happiness and sadness. When a person encounters sorrow, the reason he feels sad is because he can distinguish sadness from another emotion. Therefore, this ability to distinguish happiness and sorrow when one comes in contact with something is the essence of knowing *mono no aware*. When one's mind does not know these sentiments, there are no feelings of happiness nor sorrow—there is no emotion. When there is no emotion, there is no poetry.

In spite of this, all creatures, as far as they have been endowed with intelligence, have the ability to discern differences. So these creatures feel joy as well as sorrow, and have song. Among these creatures that have the ability to differentiate, there are variations in ability, some shallow, some deep; the ability of animals to feel emotion is shallow. When their ability is compared with human ability, it appears as if they have no feeling at all. People are superior in nature, able to distinguish better, and know what *mono no aware* is. Among people, however, there are those who have limited ability, and those who are very sensitive. When we compare people with limited ability to very sensitive people, it appears as if the people with limited ability lack any sense of *mono no aware*. There is a great difference between the two, because there are many people who really know little

37. Ultimately, these ideas were influenced by early Chinese thought. As a reference, the "great preface" to the *Book of Odes* says, "When emotion moves within the heart it is expressed in words. When words are insufficient, they are expressed as sighs and groans. When sighs and groans are insufficient, they are expressed as song."

about *mono no aware*. This does not mean that they know *nothing* about it; it is just a way of showing the difference in depth of emotion. Poetry springs forth from those deep fountains of knowledge of *mono no aware.*

Simply stated, that is what knowing *mono no aware* means. If one were to request a more detailed explanation, then I would have to say that knowing *mono no aware* is "being moved by some stimulus." "Being moved" commonly is connected with positive events, but this is not always true. The Chinese character 感 "to feel" is defined in *Kangxi Zidian* as meaning "to move about" in a footnote. Words and phrases like 感傷 "sentimental" and 感慨 "deep sorrow" are also listed, showing that the sentiment of sadness or adversity also means to "be moved." However, in our country, the verb "to be moved" has only been viewed as meaning delight or satisfaction. It is proper for one to use the character 感 to represent the word *mezuru* "to wonder at," but it is improper to read the character 感 as *mezuru*. The reason for this is because the feelings of wonder or amazement are part of being moved, and so the character may be employed to represent that word. But being moved does not necessarily equate with "being amazed," and so reading the character 感 as *mezuru* does not do justice to the broader meaning. In all things, having one's heart stimulated by emotion refers to both happy and sad events, and all these feelings point to "being moved." This is called knowing *mono no aware*. This idea of knowing *mono no aware* is given considerable treatment in my work *Shibun yōryō*.

Now, the word *afare* is something felt deep within the heart. This word, too, came to mean specifically "sorrow" in later ages, and even if the character 哀 "sorrow" is written to represent *afare*, sorrow is merely one dimension of *afare*, and people cannot cram *afare* into the narrow confines of the character 哀.[38] *Man'yōshū* represents *afare* with characters such as 痾怜. Again, this is merely one aspect of the word, and cannot satisfy the full meaning of *afare*. *Afare* is a word showing one has been deeply impressed, and regardless of one's social status, that stimulus moves the person's heart in relation to almost anything. *Afare* belongs to the same class of words as *ana* and *aya*. The record of Emperor Ninken in *Nihongi* says, "Ah! My husband!" And the record of Emperor Kōgyoku has "*Aya*!" Based on examples like these, we know that these are related words. Also, in Chinese, many words like 嗚呼, 于嗟, or 猗 are read *aa*, another word for profound emotion.

The record in *Kogo shūi* says, "… the sky cleared and brightened, and

38. This is true even in relation to Western scholars who have tended to translate *aware* as "pathos."

the myriad beings were able to see each other. Everyone's face was illuminated. The *kami* put out their hands and began to sing and dance. They all declared together: '*Afare*! *Ana omosiro*! *Ana tanosi*! *Ana sayake*. …'"[39] There are some points in the text that are suspicious, but these are believed to be ancient words. This is the point where Amaterasu Ōmikami (the sun goddess) comes forth out of the Ame no Iwaya cave. Now notice that the note, "*Afare* means 'aa, the sky is cleared'" is a later interpolation and should not be trusted.[40] Scholars are often led astray by this passage, and believe that the meaning of *afare* is "the sky clears." That is why I have discussed it here. In the text, every word with *afare* or *ana* attached is one of profound emotion.

There is the following poem from Prince Yamato Takeru:

wofari ni	Here stands a pine
tada ni mukaferu	facing straight in
fitotu matu afare	the direction of Owari;
fitotu matu	yes, one single pine
fito ni ariseba	if this tree were a man,
kinu kisemasi wo	I would dress you in your garments.
tati fakemasi wo	I would gird you with a sword.
	[NS 27]

yatume sasu	The sheath of the sword
idumo takeru	girt about the waist of
fakeru tati	Izumo Takeru
tudura safa maki	has many beautiful decorations,
sami nasi ni afare	but, strangely, it has no blade!
	[KJK 23]

Other than these, there are other songs using the stanzas "ah, I miss my spouse," and "Oh! Kagehime." Even in the poem from Shōtoku Taishi, we see the usage:

ifi ni wete	Starving for want of food,
koyaseru	how pitiful is that farmer
sono tabito afare	who has fallen.
	[NS 104]

39. Literally, "The heavens are clear! How striking! How pleasant! How refreshing!" Here, *afare* is believed to have come from *aa fare* "ah, it has cleared up." See Bentley (2002:73) for the full text.

40. All texts have this note, so if this is an interpolation, it is an extremely old one.

These poems may sound like verses of grief, and that may appear to be the meaning of *afare*, but that is a later interpretation. The ancient meaning was not that. All these usages of *afare* are words of profound emotion, and the meaning is the same as if we had used *faya*, "Oh, Kagehime!" or "Oh, that farmer!" We know this from such usages like Prince Yamato Takeru's "Ah, my spouse!" And the usage in the Emperor Ingyō record where Mount Unebi and Miminashi are described by a man from Silla with the words, "Ah Unebi! Ah Mimi!"

Now, the verb *afaremu* "to have compassion" is the essence of feeling *afare*. It is comparative to sorrow being called *kanasimu*. Thus, *afaremu* points to something that deeply impresses the heart, feeling moved by this or that. It is not limited to love.

Nonetheless, the word usage changes from generation to generation, and many times the connotation slowly drifts away from the original meaning; the profound word *afare*, also, was used in various ways in later eras, and its significance has gradually changed. In *Man'yōshū*, there is the poem from Ōtomo Sakanoue Iratsume:

fayakafa no	Lost in thought,
se ni woru tori no	how I long for my daughter—
yosi wo nami	like those birds on
omofite arisi	the swift river current with
wa ga ko fa mo afare	nowhere to find comfort.

[MYS 761]

This usage of *afare* is the same as that seen in *Kojiki* and *Nihongi*. Here are two anonymous poems from *Man'yōshū*:

nago no umi wo	In the morning
asa kogikureba	rowing across the sea of Nago,
watanaka ni	I spotted a deer
kako zo nakunaru	in the water yelping.
afare sono kako	Ah, that pitiful sailor!

[MYS 1417][41]

kakikirasi	On an evening when
ame no furu yo wo	it was overcast and raining,

41. This is a play on the word *kako* "deer" and *kako* "sailor." It would appear that the poet saw a deer struggling to swim across the offing, and was reminded of a sailor who had drowned.

fototogisu
nakite yuku nari
afare sono tori

the cuckoo cried out,
flying off into the darkness.
Ah, that insightful bird!

[MYS 1756]

Here, *afare* has the same meaning, though the usage is slightly different. Both examples above use the characters 𪫧怜 to represent *afare*. These same two characters are read as *waya* in the Ninken record of *Nihongi*; thus we know that *afare* is being used in the same way.

In Book 18 of *Man'yōshū*, Yakamochi wrote a *chōka* when he heard the cry of the cuckoo:

utinageki
afare no tori to
ifanu toki nasi

I let out a sigh,
there will never be a time when
I do not say, "what a lovely bird."

[MYS 4089]

The usage of this poem somewhat resembles the usage of later eras. It is different from the other poems quoted above. The usage in the ancient poems, "How profound! That lone pine tree," "How I feel for that farmer," or "Ah, that poor bird." These come as a result of some object stimulating a person's heart. It resembles a person sighing, "*Sore afare*." The passage *afare sono tori* is the same as saying "Ah, [how I feel for] that bird," and this is the identical type of usage. However, the usage above of "that poor bird" is slightly different, and points to the object of emotion, saying "Ah, that bird."[42]

After the *Man'yōshū* era, the following poems are seen in *Kokinshū*:

arenikeri
afare ikuyo no
yado nare ya
sumikemu fito no
otodure mo senu

Dilapidated!
Ah, but how many years has
the house been like this?
Not a trace of a visit
from those who lived here before.

[KKS 984]

afare mukasibe
ariki tefu

Ah! How grateful I
feel when I think of

42. Most of the poems Norinaga has quoted have used *afare* in reference to the beholder. This last poem has the object of the sentence, the bird, as the reference of *afare*, not Yakamochi.

fitomaro koso fa	him who lived in the past—
uresikere	that Hitomaro!

[KKS 1003]

In *Shūishū* there is a poem from Fujiwara Nagayoshi:

adumadi no	As I step between
nodi no yukima wo	the patches of snow on
wakete kite	the eastern road,
afaremi ya kono	how profound a feeling,
fana wo miru kana	seeing this little flower.

[SS 1094]

These passages of *afare* are absolute examples of intense emotion, and this one level of usage continued on into later generations. The common term *appare* "well done!" comes from making *afare* a double consonant. Also in *Kokinshū* there is the poem:

toritomuru	Since no one can
mono no si araneba	stop the flow of time,
tosituki wo	the months and years
afare ana u to	have been spent in a state
sugusituru kana	of profound feeling and gloom.

[KKS 897]

Part of a *chōka* says:

sumizome no	When the evening comes,
yufube ni nareba	evening black as ink,
fitori wite	I go off by myself.
afare afare to	"Wo is me," I sigh until
nageki amari	I am beset with mourning.

[KKS 1001]

This is also a usage of profound emotion. There is also a line in *Kagerō nikki* that says, "I thought how moving and impressing this barrier on the road was, and when I gazed at where we were headed. ..." This passage shows an inner feeling of emotion.

Again, there are [four] poems found in *Kokinshū*:

afare tefu *koto o amata ni* *yaraji to ya* *faru ni okurete* *fitori sakuramu*	Shall we not divide some of the admiration for this cherry tree that bloomed though spring is past for the surrounding cherry trees? [KKS 136][43]
afare tefu *koto dani naku fa* *nani wo ka fa* *kofi no midare no* *tukane wo ni semu*	Without the use of the profound word "*afare*," with what should we use as a rein to control a heart ravaged by love? [KKS 509]
afare tefu *koto koso utate* *yo no naka wo* *omofifanarenu* *fodasi narikeri*	How vexing it is! This bond that ties one to a detestable world from which no one can escape. This bond called "*afare*!" [KKS 939]
afare tefu *koto no fa goto ni* *oku tuyu fa* *mukasi wo kofuru* *namida narikeri*	Each drop of dew that forms upon the leaves, those leaves of emotion, is nothing but a tear shed because of a love long gone. [KKS 940]

From *Gosenshū* the following are worthy of note:

tiru koto no *uki mo wasurete* *afare tefu* *koto wo sakura ni* *yadosituru kana*	Having forgotten the sorrow when the blossoms scatter on the wind— Alas! Emotion has found a home in the cherry. [GSS 133]
afare tefu *koto ni nagusamu*	In this world where one is comforted by a sigh,

43. I have translated this poem according to Norinaga's interpretation.

yo no naka wo why is it that I
nado ka kanasi to spend my entire life saying,
ifite suguramu "Alas! How lamentable?"

[GSS 1192]

kiku fito mo This parting of death
afare tefu naru that you have heard has caused you
wakare ni fa to feel profound grief,
itodo namida zo but it has caused me to shed
tukisezarikeru tears till there are none left.

[GSS 1395]

The usage of *afare* in these poems means the emotion; it does not mean "the feeling of *afare*." We know this from the *Kokinshū* usage of "those leaves of emotion." Now, this usage of "*afare*" means the expression of profound emotion because some stimulus has moved the poet's heart. Like the poem above, "blooming though spring has past," a person has seen that cherry tree, the sight deeply impressing him, and nothing but the words of "*afare*" will do; this person only wants himself to say those words of feeling. And that is how the poem should be read: "Is this tree blooming so late just so that I may experience this feeling?" It may be understood that the rest was modelled after this. …[44]

We have thus seen that the various usages of the word *afare* have changed, but the basic meaning of all of these is the same: a person's heart is deeply moved and impressed by things seen, heard, and acted upon. *Afare* cannot be interpreted by the common word "sorrow." Everything that is emotional, joy, pleasure, interest, sorrow, and love is denoted as *afare*. There are even many usages of *afare* interpreted as humorous or funny. In the pages of stories, there are passages connected with the clause "ah, how funny," or "ah, how joyous."

In *Ise monogatari* it says, "From the province where he was banished, this man came every night playing his flute in a very fine manner. His voice was peculiar, and he sang with great emotion."[45] This man's fine flute and his elegant voice were what provoked emotion. In *Kagerō nikki* it says, "I am always of a dissatisfied air, but there is no end to my remembrances of joyous feelings." This usage of *afare* comes from a feeling of satisfaction.

44. Norinaga goes to great lengths to prove his thesis by quoting a large amount of poetry. I have only translated a representative portion.

45. This is from the beginning of *dan* 65.

However, in other literary texts like *Genji monogatari*, the words *wokasiki* "funny, humorous" and *afare naru* are often used as opposite words. This is the difference of looking at the whole, or looking at the individual parts. If you look at it as a whole then *wokasiki* is included within *afare* as has been stated above. If you look at the individual parts, then the feelings of humor or joy that move the heart to emotion are shallow feelings. Emotions that move the heart, like sadness or love, are deep.

Therefore, those deeper emotions are separately called *afare*, because they move the heart. The common custom of calling sorrow or pathos *afare* comes from this division. For example, the cherry blossom is called just *fana* "blossom" from among all the different types of flowers, like a word in opposition to the plum blossom. That is why the "Spring Shoots" chapter of *Genji monogatari* notes, "How I would like to see the plum blossoms against the background of the cherry in full bloom." It is the same as the division in music notes where we say there are twelve *ritsu*, but when these twelve are separated, we find that there are six *ritsu* opposite to six *ryo*.[46] Thus, the idea of saying that *afare* is one of the feelings of emotion is a product of a later era. The original essence of *afare* came from all the emotions that move the human heart.

Now, the difference between knowing and not knowing *mono no aware* is like seeing beautiful blossoms, or facing the clear moon and being moved to emotion—this equals "knowing *aware*." It is the ability of one's heart to discern the significance in emotion of the moon and blossoms. The person who cannot discern the sensitivity of the situation is not touched, no matter how beautiful the blossoms, nor how clear the moon. This is a person who does not know *mono no aware*.

But this sensibility is not just concerned with the moon or blossoms; if we can discern the significance and the essence of all things in the world we come in contact, then we are filled with joy when interacting with joyous things; we are pleased with humorous things; we are saddened by sorrowful events, or we are moved by affectionate occasions.

A person who thinks nothing of the sight, feeling no emotion, does not know *mono no aware*. We say that a person has a heart if he is sensitive to *afare*, and is heartless if he is insensitive. Priest Saigyō[47] composed:

46. Chinese and Japanese traditional court music divided an octave into twelve steps. In Japan the first step corresponds to D. The final, or twelfth step, is C#, which completes the octave. Over time, the odd-numbered steps became labeled *ritsu*, and the even numbered steps were called *ryo*.

47. Priest Saigyō (1118–90) was originally known as Satō Norikyo, and was one of the poets of the *Shin Kokinshū*.

kokoro naki	Even a person
mi ni mo afare fa	like me who is insensitive,
sirarekeri	feels strong emotions
sigi tatu safa no	on an autumn evening—
aki no yufugure	snipe rising above the marsh.
	[SKKS 362]

The first stanza tells us all we need to know. *Ise monogatari* states, "Once there was a man and he tried to woo a woman, and the days and months passed. As the woman's heart was not made of stone or wood she began to feel affection for him, perhaps she began to feel pity for him."[48]

Kagerō nikki states, "I am insensitive beyond hope and yet feel these emotions. How much greater must be the emotion of others who cry because they are moved." From these quotes, one gets a feeling for the meaning of knowing *mono no aware*. Again, this is all explained in detail in *Shibun Yōryō*. ...

The question was raised, "I understand that poetry comes from knowing *mono no aware*. For what reason is one unable to endure the emotions of his heart and must produce poetry?"

I answered by saying that composing poetry is the act when one cannot endure *mono no aware*. "Unable to endure *mono no aware*" means that first, though the individual has interacted with something emotional, if he does not feel that emotion, he does not have a reaction. Without the reaction, there can be no poetic composition. For example, though thunder roars fearfully overhead, a deaf person cannot hear it, and so he is not aware of its existence.[49] Because he is not aware of the existence of the thunder, there is no reaction of fear. Thus, a person who knows *mono no aware* and interacts with something emotional may try to suppress the feelings, but this is difficult to achieve. A person who has good hearing may try to suppress the fear of the thunder, but all along he is thinking how terrible the noise really is!

Thus, when nothing can be done but allow yourself to feel deep emotion, the person tries to keep the feelings tied to his thoughts, but he or she cannot suppress the emotions at this level. This is the meaning of not being able to endure *mono no aware*. And when one cannot endure these feel-

48. From *dan* 96.

49. This is one of the strange but fortuitous phenomena of language. *Afare* (modern *aware*) and the English word "(be) aware" can be closely connected here in Norinaga's discussion: knowing *aware* means being aware of the sensibility of emotion.

ings, the thoughts naturally increase and then issue forth as words. Being unable to suppress these feelings, the words that slip out are always stretched out into beautiful form. This is poetry. The usages of "sigh" or "recite" are also used at this time when one cannot endure his inner emotions. (This will be dealt with later.)

In this way, when these words have a literary quality, and the syllables are verbally lengthened, those feelings that have built up, becoming entangled in one's chest, are now given vent; after this, the person feels refreshed. One does not try to say anything special, but the words just naturally flow out. When you cannot endure the feelings inside, you try not to say anything, but things of significance are naturally articulated. It is just like the Tsurayuki poem that we read above, "One cannot remain quiet when the emotions burst forth." Thus, when a person cannot suppress these emotions, poetry is always produced naturally.

The question was advanced, "I agree that one's thoughts become poetry when one cannot endure these feelings. But while everday speech should be sufficient to accomplish [venting one's feelings], I struggle to understand the concept of lengthening the syllables with one's voice and using words with artistic technique. How do you respond to this?"

I replied that in this era, this sort of doubt is reasonable. In relation to everything, one must explore the origin of things, and ponder upon these. If one only pays attention to peripheral detail, then many doubts arise; the student should look deeper into the matter.

First, I have already explained the origin of poetry. Poetry cannot be expressed with everyday words, nor is it consciously lengthening the syllables out loud, using words with artistic technique. Words expressed when one cannot suppress the inner feelings naturally have a literary quality, and the words themselves naturally become drawn out. If these words were to be expressed in everyday speech, then that would mean that the individual was experiencing shallow feelings. Only when those emotions are deeply felt can there be spontaneity, artistic technique, and a lengthening of the syllables. When one is feeling deep emotions, the use of everyday words does not satisfy him. There is nothing better than a word that is drawn out and uttered with artistic technique. With ordinary words, deep emotions are not set free no matter how much you draw them out when you say them.

Nevertheless, when a person uses appropriately artistic techniques and draws words out in song, the deep emotions of the heart are unshackled, set free through the literary quality of the words and one's voice. Thus, an immeasurably deep sense of emotion lays hidden within fine literary words drawn out. The listener also only experiences a shallow reaction if everyday words of speech are employed, no matter how moving the content. However, there is nothing deeper than the emotions felt by the listener when the words are literary, each syllable drawn out when sung. All these phenomena form the natural power of poetry. Even the violent spirits and *kami* feel profound emotion from poetry. ...

Now, as I have explained above, when a person cannot suppress these deep emotions, and when he cannot release these feelings, unable to express himself in words, he borrows the sound of the wind or of insects, sounds familiar to his ears, or the beauty of the blossom or the sight of snow. Using these natural phenomena, he composes poetry. The preface to *Kokinshū* had reference to this when it said, "Poetry is what a person sees or hears." Saying things as they are does not release the emotions. Profound emotion that is difficult to express is easier to relate when used metaphorically through things seen or heard. An example of metaphorical usage is seen in a poem composed by Emperor Jinmu:

midumidusi	You, the intrepid
kume no kora ga	sons of the Kume—
kakimoto ni	Japanese pepper is growing
uwesi fazikami	under the fence of our land.
kuti fibiku	As I will not forget
ware fa wasurezu	the sharp taste of that pepper,
utitesiyamamu	we shall utterly smite them.[50]

This was sung when the emperor attacked Nagasune Hiko. Before this battle, there was a battle on a hill named Kusawe. At that time, the emperor's older brother, Itsuse, had been killed by a stray arrow. The emperor deeply hated Nagasune Hiko for this, and the fact that he could not forget this incident is metaphorically alluded to by the lingering pungent aftertaste of the Japanese pepper. Later, in *Kokinshū* there is the following poem:

oto ni nomi	You are but a rumor—
kiku no siratuyu	my love for you makes me feel
yoru fa okite	like the dew of night
firu fa omofi ni	upon the chrysanthemum,
afezu kenu besi	vanishing before the sun.

[KKS 470]

50. It would appear that Norinaga meant to quote the poem from *Kojiki* (KJK 12), but in reality he has quoted the poem from *Nihon shoki* (NS 14). These two versions are identical, aside from the sixth stanza, which is *ware fa wasurezi*.

These metaphorical usages were used anciently and now, and there are so many of them that they are innumerable. …

Now, these allusions appear to be making deliberate use of natural objects, but when one looks deeper into the essence of this usage, he finds that this is not so. When a person is filled with profound thoughts, the things he sees and hears are all used as a pretext as the things about which he is deeply pondering. Since these things are thought to be profound, poetry is composed using the objects metaphorically; this is a spontaneous action, and the poet did not compose the poem simply to use natural objects as poetic devices.

Poetry is produced when a person cannot suppress his inner feelings, but it naturally is not used only to put one's heart at ease. When a person is feeling very deep emotions, it is not enough to just compose a poem. As regrets linger when produced alone, one needs to let someone else hear the poem in order to feel consolation. When someone else hears the poem and feels emotion, it greatly enhances the effect of putting one's mind to rest. Again, this is the natural course of things.

For example, if there is a person presently who is in anguish, and cannot suppress these strong feelings, he cannot put his mind at ease by simply giving a detailed account of things to himself. When he tells someone else, he is able to find some relief. But when the listener understands and sympathizes with the agonizing person, then the agonizing person is able to bring relief to his heart. Thus, all these acts of feeling deep emotion in one's heart naturally lead to the act of composing poetry meant for someone else to hear. When a person sees or hears something rare, something terrible, something humorous, these cause emotion to well up in the heart, then that person desires to tell someone else, finding he is unable to keep it locked up in his heart. Though a person may tell someone something in this manner, it has no outward value in and of itself; however, it is natural for a person to find it impossible to keep these things to himself. Poetry is based upon the same principle, and the very act of telling a person something is the essence of poetic verse. Poetry is not something trifling.

People who do not understand this principle say that poetry is just an expression of a person's candid thoughts, whether good or bad; true poetry has no bearing on what people hear. Though this idea may at first blush seem to make sense, it shows that these people do not understand the true nature of poetry. In the very first question of the *Gumon Kenchū*,[51] though

---

51. Written in 1363 by the priest Ton'a in response to poetical questions asked by Nijō Yoshizane. It consists of twenty-nine questions and answers, from the essence of *waka* to issues with *ji-amari* and poems written on famous places.

it deals with peripheral affairs, it says that it is crucial in poetry that a person hears something and feels emotion, the issuing words being arranged with an artistic technique. Also, having the words themselves emphasized is the true nature of poetry/song and has been so since the divine age. Because the hearer feels emotion, his own heart is put at ease. If the listener does not feel any emotion from the poem, then the heart of the composer of the poem is only consoled to a small degree. Again, this is natural. It is necessary that people take these principles and apply them to their daily lives so they will become convinced of these things.

There is no profit in telling another person your insuppressible feelings if the listener is not going to feel any emotion. When the listener reacts to our expressed feelings, our hearts are comforted. Therefore, the vital point of poetry is that a person hears the poem and feels emotion because of it.

And that is why the poetry from the divine age is not composed candidly. The words are arranged with artistic technique, the poem sung in an emotional manner. When the poet refers to his "wife," he says "like tender grass." When he wants to say "night," he actually says "like black beads." Do these phrases not have a literary quality, the words being appropriately ornate? …

This is the difference between everyday speech and poetic verse. We understand the meaning and the details about what is being said, but this lacks a profundity of emotion that can only be conveyed through poetry. To the question of why profound emotion is not released unless cut loose through poetry, I reply that this is due to the literary quality of the words. Through these carefully arranged poetic structures, unparalleled emotions appear.

Poetry is not a device, like everyday speech, where the significance of an event is described in detail. Also, there is no deep significance attached to the poem. Poetry is a simple device that allows the person to say, "How profound [this experience]." It is the literary quality of the poetic structures that unleashes a bottomless amount of emotion. …

A certain person asked, "What about the label *yamato uta* versus *waka*?" I responded that the label *yamato uta* is not an ancient usage. The Chinese representation of 倭歌 came first, and later the reading of *yamato uta* was attached.

The follow up question was, "Then let me ask about the characters 倭歌." I answered that the term 倭歌 is not an ancient label, as it does not appear in either *Kojiki* or *Nihon shoki*. We only find the character 歌 *uta*. The term 倭歌 was created generally during the era when people composed poetry in imitation of Chinese literary works. China also has poetry

[歌] and because that was confusing, people invented the term 倭歌 to make a distinction regarding our form of poetry. Thus two different interpretations are possible. The first is that the various kingdoms in China had categories of poetry like "the poetry of Qi" or "the poetry of Chu," so based on this kind of categorization, people invented the term "poetry of Yamato." The other possibility is the term was created to make a distinction with Chinese poetry. In all aspects there are many examples of a binary distinction, with 和 "Japan" and 漢 "China" or *kara* and *yamato*, so I think the second choice is the more appropriate. At any rate, the two appear to be about the same, but I have listed both choices because they have subtle differences. …

The question was asked, "What about the difference between Chinese poetry and *uta*?"

I answered that I do not know much about Chinese poetry, but if you look through even a few areas in ancient Chinese works, it sounds like the basics of Chinese poetry are the same as *uta*. If you look through the poems in the Odes section of the *Book of Odes*, the words themselves are Chinese, but the feelings in the poems are every bit the same as poetry in our land. This is as one would expect, because the direction the human heart takes is always the same. Thus, as time passes, the hearts of people and the customs of the land change in various ways, so in later eras we find a great difference between our land and China, and the purpose of Chinese poetry and our poetry is vastly different. …

Another question was, "So what is the reason that everything that is reasonable and decent comes from the superficial line of fabrication, and if you want to compose poetry based on the truth of human emotion it should be trivial?"

I responded that in general no matter how wise people become, if you peer deep into their hearts, they are no different than women and children. In all aspects, there are many things that are trivial and feminine, and this is the same in China. Perhaps because China is not a divine land, so perhaps this caused many evil people from ancient times to commit countless acts of ruthlessness. This injured many people and threw the country into chaos, and resulted in long periods of unrest. To pacify and govern the land, the rulers worried and pondered, searching for a way to make things better. Naturally wise and intelligent people came to the fore, and they began to ponder and think about even minute things that did not require much thought and they added forced definitions about logic that one cannot see. And they divided even menial things into good and evil, establishing debate about such things as a worthy pursuit, and the customs of that land naturally evolved in such a way that everyone over there strives to appear as if they have wisdom. Thus, they became ashamed of true feelings that are trivial and feminine and do not even represent these in their speech. How much more in their written works it is that they write only things that are decent and reasonable, and if they have any feelings that are frivolous, they pretend not to notice it. And while it is reasonable to govern people, and train and teach them in this way, this only leads to pretentious emotions that do not reflect the true heart of humanity. ...

The question was posed, "When we observe the circumstances of lamentation of parents who have had a precious child proceed them in death, we find that the father is composed, his emotions tightly controlled, his appearance well arranged, but in general the mother is gloomy, weeping, and distraught, continually grumbling about things, buried in sorrow. Is this not the trivial, feminine actions of women and children?"

I replied that he was absolutely correct. We tend to view the emotionally composed, well-arranged appearance of the father as truly masculine, but he does this because he fears the eyes of society, afraid of social opinion; thus, he suppresses the sorrow in his heart, creating a superficial appearance by forcing his emotions to remain hidden. Now the mother does not worry about how others view her, and her crumbling into tears truly appears to people to be a feminine, indecent thing to do, but this is true emotions unadorned.

Thus, while on the surface there appears to be a difference between the one who controls his emotions and endures the anguish and the other who cannot endure the pain, there is no difference deep within the heart of the profound sorrow felt by both father and mother, so one should not judge that either parent is wise or foolish; however, when it comes to composing poetry, it springs from emotions that are not shut up within the heart, and like the Viscount of Ji, some endure their sorrow. And yet there are those who find this impossible to do, and unlike women they may try to create an appearance of composure, but as they suppress their emotions the sadness only increases within their breast till it becomes unbearable. It is times like this when they compose a poem and the pressure of their sorrow is released. This is because poetry must be composed from the stance of femininity. If one tries to compose a poem with a masculine air how can he dispel the sorrow that makes him want to cry?

[MNZ 1976, 2:85–165]

ᘓ

TAMA NO OGUSHI

Motoori Norinaga | 1796

[Norinaga extends his thesis about *mono no aware* and applies it directly to *Genji monogatari*. This work appears to be based on the lectures Norinaga had given through the years on the tale, something he began not long after he established his medical practice in Matsusaka. This translation focuses on the sections dealing specifically with *mono no aware*. His theory of "literature" appeals to evidence from within the tale itself, rather on didactic elements argued by scholars and religious individuals.]

WHAT IS A TALE?

During middle antiquity there was a genre called *monogatari* "tale." In present society *monogatari* is defined as stories, or narratives from the ancient past. In *Nihongi* the character 談 "discussion" is glossed as *monogatari*.[1] In the "Picture Contest" chapter in *Genji monogatari*, we see the first instance where *monogatari* is used in the title of a book, "*The Old Bamboo Cutter*, the ancestor of all tales was pitted against the 'Toshikage' chapter of *The Hollow Tree*."[2] Perhaps *Taketori monogatari* "Tale of the Bamboo Cutter" is thus the first tale of our literature. It is impossible to know when *Taketori monogatari* was written, or who the author was, but it is not that ancient of a tale, having been written after the Engi period [901–23].[3] There also appear to be other tales that existed prior to *Genji monogatari*, and we know the titles of a variety of these, but most manuscripts have not survived down to the present. There are also a variety of works from the same

1. There are thirteen examples of the character 談 in *Nihon shoki*. Five are found in the name of a powerful Ōtomo scion, named Katari Muraji. Two other examples appear in the Yūryaku chapter and are glossed as *monogatari* as Norinaga mentions. These two Chinese examples can be rendered in English as "chat" or "talk."

2. Translated by Tyler (2001:325).

3. Modern scholarship agrees the tale was originally Chinese in origin, and was translated into Japanese. Vovin (2005:265) notes that the Old Japanese nominalizer *-aku* appears frequently in *Taketori monogatari*, but only once in the narrative section of *Ise monogatari*, and not in other tales later in the Heian era. This attests to the work having been translated during the Nara era, or at least before 850 CE.

era as *Genji monogatari* or somewhat later, and many of these still exist. In the "Keburi no nochi" chapter of *Eiga monogatari* "Tale of Flowering Fortunes," it records, "He wanted to have a tale contest [in contrast to a picture contest], so he wrote a new tale and divided the people into left and right, and had them judge his work against twenty some other tales, and it was a very interesting time."

Now, the literary style of these various tales subtly changed over time, but these all share the same format of telling stories from previous eras, basing their stories on actual facts with added fictional details, changing the names of the historical characters to hide their identity, or simply making up some stories out of whole cloth. It is very rare that a tale will tell a historical story without embellishment. In general, tales are works of fiction. Next is the intention of writing a tale and why anyone would read these. These tales describe various things that exist in society, the good, the evil, the rare, the strange, the interesting, and the sad. They include pictures depicting scenes in the story, available for people to amuse themselves and kill time when they are bored. These also lend comfort when people are depressed, and as these are accurate depictions of the feelings of people within society, one can understand the profundity of human emotions through these tales. Thus, as all of these tales are stories based on depictions of relations between men and women, emulating the same logic as the successive anthologies that have large sections on love, these tales show the depth of human emotion, and love is the superior topic. I will next describe these things in greater detail.

THE AUTHOR OF *THE TALE OF GENJI*

It is well known in society that Murasaki Shikibu is the author of this tale, and this fact also appears in her own diary, *Murasaki Shikibu nikki*, so this is beyond question, but in reality there are a number of theories on the subject. First, *Kachō yōsei*[4] quotes from *Uji Dainagon monogatari* where it notes that [an outline of] Genji was written by Tametoki[5] when he was governor of Echizen, and he had his daughter, Shikibu, fill in the details.

---

4. This is a commentary on *The Tale of Genji*, put together by Ichijō Kaneyoshi, finished around the year 1472.

5. This points to Fujiwara Tametoki (949?–1029?). He was sent to Echizen as governor in 996. When Emperor Kazan came to the throne in 984, Tametoki was made a minor official in the Ministry of Ceremonies (*shikibu*), and received the nickname of Shikibu. Thus his daughter was called Murasaki Shikibu, which is likely a pen name.

However, we cannot trust this theory. *Kachō yōsei* says nothing of the sort, but wonders what the truth is. Also, in *Kakaishō* it says that Grand Chancellor Michinaga added a colophon to the manuscript of *Genji*, claiming that an old nun had added parts to the original manuscript. This is also a mistaken theory, but these things are argued in great detail in a treatise by Andō Tameakira titled *Shika shichiron* 紫家七論. Aside from these, there are a variety of other theories, but these are all fabrications of later people, and none can be accepted as truth, aside from the fact that the author was indeed Murasaki Shikibu. There is also the theory that Murasaki was not the author of the last ten chapters of the tale, but this is also erroneous, because it is clear that the same person wrote the entire work. Also, the theory that the "Vanished into the Clouds" chapter contained nothing more than the chapter heading, with no actual text, created this way because that is how Murasaki wanted it, and the current chapter with text is a later addition by some unknown hand is a theory not even worth discussing.[6] Also, at the end of the "Floating Bridge of Dreams" chapter is a section titled "Yamaji no tsuyu" that has been appended. But this has been taken from the fabricated chapter "Vanished in the Clouds" and stuck here in the handwriting of a later person in poor imitation of Murasaki. …

THE ORIGIN OF THE STORY

The events surrounding the creation of this tale are not entirely clear. It is said that when Murasaki was in service to Lady Shōshi, Lady Daisei'in asked her if there were no rare tales in existence, [and as there were not] Murasaki wrote her tale to fulfill this desire and presented it to her. This account is difficult to accept, as *Shika shichiron* argues in detail. Also the theory that Murasaki was familiar with the story of Minamoto Takaakira [914–83] when she was a child does not hold water because the chronology does not match. The idea that she was sequestered away at Ishiyama Temple or that she wrote her tale on the back of paper from the *Mahāprajñāpāramitā sutra* are both wild theories. And the story that Minister Yukinari made a

6. It is the part about someone having added text that Norinaga finds specious and does not want to discuss. The chapter *kumo kakure* means "hidden in the clouds." Norinaga himself later argues, "This chapter has only the chapter heading and no text, because Murasaki wanted to alert the reader to the fact that Genji had passed away [gone into hiding]. She did not write about this, leaving it out, illustrating that she put much deep thought into this" (MNZ 4:468).

fair copy of the work is a fabrication based on the fact that he was a well-known writer.[7] And there is the unbelievable story that when Murasaki was sequestered at Ishiyama Temple, on the fifteenth day of the eighth month, the reflection of the moon on the lake was bright and clear, causing scenes for the story to come to her mind, triggering the inspiration to write the Suma and Akashi chapters first, and that is why there is the line in the Suma chapter, "Genji remembered when a brilliant moon rose that tonight was the fifteenth the month."[8] If one wanted to use the line "that tonight was the fifteenth" as proof, then in the "The Warbler's First Song" chapter would they claim that a line like "today was the day of the rat" was also proof that that chapter was written on the day of the rat in the first month? These are very childish arguments. Presently at Ishiyama Temple there is a room called the "Genji Room," with a portrait of Murasaki, and a desk and ink stone, and these were all fabricated by people who enjoy the fable mentioned above. And people may well believe the idea that Genji was created in imitation of Minister Minamoto Takaakira, but this is all very ridiculous, especially when they claim that Murasaki based the story of the character Murasaki on herself. Why are people drawn to such things they know so little about?

THE DATING OF COMPOSITION

According to *Kakaishō* this tale came about in the beginning years of the Kankō era [1004–12] and by the end of the Kōwa era [1099–1104] the manuscript was in circulation, and the various commentaries adhere to this theory. But considering the information in *Murasaki Shikibu nikki*, it seems very likely that the manuscript was completed in the early years of the Kankō era. *Shika shichiron* has detailed arguments regarding the various theories, and it concludes that the inception of the manuscript is likely between the end of the Chōhō era [999–1003] and the beginning of the Kankō. In spite of this, someone in the "Ura ura no wakare" chapter of *Eiga monogatari* is quoted as saying, "He seemed just such a man as Prince Genji, the Shining One, must have been."[9] This quote occurs in the fourth month of Chōtoku 2 [996], making it appear that the tale was in circulation

7. Fujiwara Yukinari (972–1027) wrote a work on customs and regulations. He also has a number of poems in *Goshūishū*.

8. From Tyler (2001:246)

9. From McCullough and McCullough (1980:191).

before this period. That means that it is a mistake for people to say that it is erroneous to claim the manuscript came about in the beginning of Kankō. This argument would be true if *Eiga monogatari* was a product of Chōtoku 2, which it is not, and since it is a product of a period after the Kankō era, there is no basis to this argument [about *Genji* originating from the Chōtoku era]. Now what about the idea that the manuscript was in circulation by the Kōwa era? Is it not clear from *Murasaki Shikibu nikki* that the manuscript was already in circulation when Murasaki was serving at the palace? And what about the theory that the manuscript was in great demand after the period of Ministers Shunzei [1114–1204] and Teika [1162–1241]? These ideas are careless, based on the words of a judgment by Shunzei in the *Roppyakuban Uta-awase* and words of praise from Teika. This theory is nothing more than conjecture.

THE TITLE OF THIS TALE

In general most tales take their title from the name of the hero. This tale is no different, and as Lord Hikaru Genji is the focus of the tale, it was titled the *Tale of Genji*. The reason that the epithet *hikaru* "shining" is attached to Genji's name is seen in "The Paulownia Pavilion" chapter, "Genji's looks had an indescribably fresh sweetness, one beyond even Her Highness's celebrated and to, His Majesty, peerless beauty, and this moved people to call him the Shining Lord."[10] Also, there is the line, "They say that the nickname, the Shining Lord, was given him in praise by the man from Koma."[11] It is improper to see these as two competing theories, but rather the significance is that society in general called him the Shining One, a name that originally was bestowed on him by the man from Koma. There are a number of cases in the chapters of the tale where the word *hikaru* is used in praise of his appearance. In the "Beneath the Autumn Leaves" chapter we find, "... (Genji's) face glowed with a still-greater beauty."[12] Also in the same chapter, "His new son ... shone with a light equal to Genji's."[13] In the "Heart-to-Heart" chapter there is, "... but the brightness of that single light seemed to eclipse them all."[14] There are many such examples in the tale. ...

10. Tyler (2001:15).

11. Ibid., p. 18.

12. Ibid., p. 135. More literally, "His countenance was more intense than before, being more radiant than usual."

13. Ibid., p. 142.

14. Ibid., p. 168.

Now, Genji is actually the surname of this prince. We find in "The Paulownia Pavilion" chapter that at his coming of age ceremony he was made a commoner and granted the name of Genji. Examples of the designation Shining Lord continue in the "The Broom-Tree," "Young Murasaki," "Tendril Wreath," "Red Plum Blossoms," and "Bamboo River" chapters, so there are people who claim that the title should be "The Tale of the Shining Lord Genji," but there is no reason to go that far. Is it not also true that in her own diary Murasaki calls the work, *The Tale of Genji*?

THE SOURCES FOR THE TALE

The various commentaries debate about the sources for this tale, arguing, for example, that Hikaru Genji was based on the life of Minister Takaakira. However, the various characters in the tale were not necessarily based on actual individuals. The majority are simply fictional, but among a number of the characters there are a few factual details that Murasaki manipulated in some small measure. But there are no characters based on any actual individuals. Even in relation to the single character of Genji you can find a characteristic here and there for him from a number of people in the ancient past, in both Japan and China. There was no single method that the author used to create her characters. In the end, the basis for this tale comes from within the mind of the author, and we cannot necessarily deconstruct the tale in minute detail to uncover sources. These things are really of little importance, but from long ago commentaries have argued along these lines, so I thought it prudent to say just a few words about this. ...

MISCELLANEOUS THINGS

Society refers to the tale as "Genji in sixty chapters," and there is a theory that this usage is based on the sixty chapters of Tendai doctrine, but this is incorrect. This tale has only fifty-four chapters, so there is no reason to call it sixty chapters, and people are simply forcing this number here to make the strained connection with Tendai doctrine. Even if the tale did consist of sixty chapters, there is no connection whatsoever with Tendai. And the theory that the various chapters of the tale follow the practice found in *Shiji*, being "Basic Annals," "Hereditary Houses," and "Biographies," is off the mark. These superficial characteristics are found in a variety of manuscripts, usually added later during textual transmission, and these come about naturally, but claiming that the text is thus based on this or that is illogical.

The theory about intersecting genealogies and chronologies in the chapters[15] is not very useful, but as it has preoccupied the minds of various people in the past, it is worthwhile to say something here about it to clear up any misunderstandings. The reader should commit the genealogy of the characters to memory. If the reader does not know the genealogy, then there will be a lot of confusion as you read. It will also be difficult to follow minute details within the story. Conventional genealogies often have many gaps and lost names, which causes confusion. Later commentaries have tried to correct the gaps in the genealogies from the past, but these are still not complete, so I have felt the need to create a completely new genealogy based on my own investigation of the text; unfortunately I have not had sufficient time to complete this task.

The ages of the characters, as well as the chronology of the various chapters, is something where we must fix the mistakes of the past; regardless that it is a work of fiction, there is consistency throughout the tale in regard to the flow of time. There have been various arguments about this, and there is a work on the chronology of the tale from Ichijō Kaneyoshi, but it has many errors throughout. Until the time of *Uji Dainagon monogatari*, a variety of commentaries compared the works and corrected a number of errors that had crept into the work, but there are still a variety of points that are not resolved satisfactorily, and I will have more to say on this later. …

POETRY QUOTED IN THE TALE

There are quotes from ancient poems woven into the prose in the tale, usually just a quote of one stanza that prompts the meaning of the original poem, or the quote is used to introduce the intention of the following stanza, which is not quoted. This device is called *inka* "poetic allusion." These poems are for the most part quoted in *Kakaishō*. The rare poem that is omitted in *Kakaishō* is noted in *Kachō yōsei*. All quotes from later com-

15. Norinaga calls this theory 縦横の并 "chapters that parallel other chapters," which through the years has meant a number of things (cf. Takeda 1954:70–78; Maruyama 1985). Based on what Norinaga vaguely says about this, it would appear that he interprets the theory as arguing that certain chapters of the tale are interrelated synchronically and diachronically to other chapters.

mentaries have used these two commentaries as their sources. Now, among a few of the poems listed in *Kakaishō*, there are some that are not allusions, and there are a substantial number where the diction is different from the original poem. There are also examples where the first half and the last half of the poem do not match, while other examples are actually not old poems, and some are false poems that do not make any sense, which is terribly reckless. As Keichū also points out, it appears that the author accidentally wrote down poems he had remembered incorrectly. But it is inexcusable that later commentaries would continue to quote mistaken citations from *Kakaishō* without any investigation. One should read this work with that point in mind. Also, in *Kakaishō* and later commentaries there are sometimes poems marked "unknown allusion," meaning it is unclear where the original poem came from, so there is still work to be done to elucidate these. ...

OVERVIEW

There have been a variety of theories about the object of this tale from times past, but none of these theories considers the essential quality of "a tale," discussing issues solely on the gist of Confucian and Buddhist thinking that is common in society. This does not suit the intent of the author. And while there are points in Confucian and Buddhist works that naturally resemble the main points, or match with things in the tale, one must not force the conclusion that the tale is like [Confucian or Buddhist works]. The overall gist of the tale is nothing like this, but as I mentioned earlier, tales have their own distinct character. This *Tale of Genji* has a more profound object than other tales from the past, and I will argue in greater detail about this point later.

When addressing the question of the object of tales in general, and what frame of mind the reader should have when reading, people should realize that answers to these questions appear here and there in the *Tale of Genji* itself. I will select a few quotes from the tale, and add my own thoughts in an attempt to help the reader connect the dots. The "A Waste of Weeds" chapter states,

> Little amusements like old poems and tales are what help to pass the time in a house like that, and to take one's mind off life.[16]

16. Tyler (2001:303).

"A house like that" refers to the house within which Suetsumuhana felt discouragement and loneliness. We read stories for comfort because the description in the tale mirrors how we feel, and we realize there are other people in the world experiencing grief like us. This realization brings us comfort.

The "Picture Contest" chapter notes,

> He removed the record of his travels from its box. … It would have drawn willing tears from anyone in the least familiar with life's sorrows, even if the viewer was only barely acquainted with the circumstances. …[17]

The "record of his travels" refers to the journal Genji kept when he was in that humble dwelling in Suma. "Barely acquainted" refers to the sentiment of a person reading the passage as if he or she were a person who knew nothing of Genji's banishment, but now only saw his journal, and then at that moment realized what he had been through.

The "Butterflies" chapter says, "… the more her reading of old tales taught her what people are like what the ways of the world are. …"[18]

Because all tales are descriptions of things in the world—the types of people, and their hearts—by reading these stories one obtains a knowledge of the condition of the world and the hearts of people. Readers who are reading a tale should keep this point in mind.

In the "Fireflies" chapter we find,

> The long rains were worse this year than most, and to get through the endless wet the ladies amused themselves day and night with illustrated tales.

Also,

> "What a beautifully done picture!" she said, examining one from *The Tale of Kumano.* The little girl, napping there so sweetly (in the picture), reminded her of herself all those years ago.[19]

The lady here is Lady Murasaki, and the line "reminded her of herself all those years ago" refers to when Murasaki was still docile.

In the "Handsome Pillar" chapter it says,

---

17. Ibid., p. 324.
18. Ibid., p. 449.
19. Ibid., pp. 460, 462.

> In the old tales, too, there are fathers who mean well as any and who still turn out to be callous after all, as they change with the times and follow shifting favor.[20]

By reading the tale one can understand the conditions of the world. In part two of the "Spring Shoots" chapter it says,

> As usual on the nights when he was away, the lady in his wing sat up late and had her women read her tales. These old stories are all about what happens in life, she thought, and they are full of women involved with fickle, wanton, or treacherous men, and so on, but each one seems to find her own in the end. How strange it is, the insecure life I have led![21]

Everything from "these old stories" refers to the inner thoughts of Lady Murasaki when she hears details in the tales being read to her. …

The following appears in the "Evening Mist" chapter, "In the old tales, yes, daughter might sometimes hide from her mother things that outsiders knew, but … ."[22] And in the "Maiden of the Bridge" chapter we find, "When he heard young gentlewomen read old tales with scenes like this, he always assumed disappointedly that nothing of the kind could actually happen, but there were after all such corners in real life! He was already losing his heart to them."[23]

In the "Trefoil Knots" chapter we find,

> and if in times yet to come people still talk about all this, I do not doubt they will cite the story, like those in old tales, as a model of how ridiculous someone can be.[24]

The same chapter also earlier includes the line, "… and the memory reminded her how well an old poem may speak for oneself."[25]

This instance of *furukoto* "old words" refers to "old poem," and old tales have the same effect on the heart.

In the "Ivy" chapter Murasaki writes,

---

20. Ibid., p. 533.
21. Ibid., p. 647.
22. Ibid., p. 726.
23. Ibid., p. 837.
24. Ibid., p. 886.
25. Ibid., p. 871.

> Why, she had always wondered, reading an old tale or listening to talk about somebody else, why does the path of love upset people so? But now that these difficulties touched *her*, she knew quite clearly that they were no joke.[26]

This scene is where Uji no Naka no Kimi learns something true about her own experience by reading about the same experience in an old tale. "This path of love" refers to the woman worrying about the two-faced tendency of men.

The same chapter also has the line,

> Yes, crowded, brilliant scenes are well worth seeing, which is doubtless why tales always feature them, but unfortunately it seems to have been impossible to note everything.[27]

And in the "Mayfly" chapter it records,

> [S]he remembered strange things just like that turning up in old tales.[28]

In the same chapter,

> The Commander added some even nicer ones and sent them on to Her Highness the First Princess. He must have seen himself particularly in a love one of Tōgimi, the Serikawa Commander's son, setting out all forlorn in the autumn twilight for love of *his* first princess. The poor gentleman, if only his had been as kind![29]

These words represent the feelings of Kaoru toward the first princess.

In the "Writing Practice" chapter it says, "It sounds like an old romance, doesn't it!"[30] And in the "Floating Bridge of Dreams" chapter we find, "I was reminded in my astonishment of that old tale about someone coming back to life after being put in the soul sanctuary."[31]

In general this is the attitude people took when they read tales. Enjoying tales means to put yourself [and your circumstances] in the shoes of those characters, have empathy for the profound feelings they had, and by juxtaposing these circumstances with those events in the past you learn the

26. Tyler (2001:942).
27. Ibid., p. 944.
28. Ibid., p. 1049.
29. Ibid., p.1067.
30. Ibid., p.1089.
31. Ibid., p.1114.

profound feelings that they had felt, and you receive solace. Thus we have looked through the various chapters of the tale to see with what disposition these characters read the old tales, so people who are about to read *The Tale of Genji* will have the same disposition. It is very different from the attitude one has when reading Confucian or Buddhist works.

Murasaki Shikibu's main object for writing this tale is clearly articulated in the "Fireflies" chapter, which is not openly stated, hidden in the words of Lord Genji, who expressed his feelings on these when he spoke to Lady Tamakazura about those old tales. But the commentaries [on this chapter] contain many errors, and as they have not been able to catch the intentions of the author, let us quote from the text [of "Fireflies"], and I will expound on the meaning, clarifying the author's intentions. This will then become a guide to readers of the tale.

"Fireflies" says, "Among her assemblage of tales she found accounts, whether fact or fiction, of many extraordinary fates, but none, alas, of any like her own."[32]

This shows a rush of emotion by Lady Tamakazura as she reads these old tales.

> The trials faced by the young lady in *Sumiyoshi* were remarkable ... and her narrow escape from the Director of Reckoning certainly had a good deal in common with the terrors of that Audit Commissioner.[33]

Here Tamakazura is comparing her own experience [in Tsukushi] with the lady in *The Tale of Sumiyoshi.*

> Finding her enthralled by works like these, which lay scattered about everywhere. ...[34]

The subject here is Genji. "Works like these" refers to the old tales she had been reading.

> Oh, no, this will never do! Women are obviously born to be duped without a murmur of protest.[35]

From here we have the words of Genji to Lady Tamakazura. His words mean that these tales are full of lies, rambling silliness, quite hard to bear to

32. Tyler (2001:460).
33. Ibid.
34. Ibid., p. 461.
35. Ibid.

read, and so women who become so engrossed in these tales seem to have been born to be deceived by people. Now Genji said this slightly in jest by speaking ill of old tales. By this the author is saying that when you read *this tale* [of Genji], you will speak ill of the tale in the beginning, but as you read you will praise the characters or denigrate them, but in the end you will find that you feel that tales are necessary for people in society.

> "There is hardly a word of truth in all this, as you know perfectly well, but there you are caught up in fables, taking them quite seriously and writing away without a thought for your tangled hair in this stifling warm rain!" He laughed but then went on. ...[36]

The reader will realize that Genji is playing with her, because he has said these words with a laugh. The words "but then went on" shifts the focus. So this means that *The Tale of Genji* is an invention of fiction, critical of people who get lost in reading these things.

> "Without stories like these about the old days, though, how would we ever pass the time when there is nothing else to do?"[37]

So in the beginning he was only joking when he made fun of these tales, but he shifts, now claiming that without these old tales how would we receive any consolation. The use of *geni* here shows the connection between those who love to read these tales and Lord Genji, and is a veiled criticism to Genji's earlier reaction.

> "Besides, among these lies there certainly are some plausibly touching scenes, convincingly told; and yes, we know they are fictions, but even so we are moved and half drawn for no real reason to the pretty, suffering heroine."[38]

Here he is saying that while we know that tales in general are fictitious there are some events in the story that seem true, and these things move us, even while we know they are not true. "Half drawn" refers to the fact that while we are moved by the event, there is still something that makes us hold back from completely believing it. This is seen in the preface to

36. Tyler (2001:461).
37. Ibid.
38. Ibid.

Kokinshū, where it states, "to fall in love with a woman in a picture."[39] ... The phrase "some plausibly touching scenes" should be seen as the main object of *The Tale of Genji*. The tale has as one of its main purposes to help readers understand the profound emotions in people. I will expound on this in greater detail later, but you now realize that seeing the tale as a work "encouraging good and criticizing evil," especially romantic relations, is a mistake, a fact clear from the words above. Reading a tale will stir the emotions of the reader, so how can this tale be an admonition against lust? ...

> We may disbelieve the blatantly impossible but still be amazed by magnificently contrived wonders, and although these pall on quiet, second hearing, some are still fascinating.[40]

This is another aspect of old tales. Above we saw "some plausibly touching scenes," which demonstrates an example of reading an event and feeling emotion about it, but this line above refers to reading something and being amazed by it, a feeling that moves from "amazed" to "fascinating." The juxtaposition of "reading" and "listening" shows that the emotion one feels is the same, whether you have read the event yourself in the tale, or listened as someone else read the event. An event that is too extraordinary or exaggerated will feel distasteful when one has had time to quietly think about it, but it is still interesting. So *The Tale of Genji* separates these into two different categories, and outlines each one. One category is "plausibly touching scenes." Here the heart of the reader is moved and the reader learns about profound emotion. "Being moved" refers to feeling profound emotion because of the events one reads. "Blatantly impossible" is the other category. The former category is the essence of the story, while this second category contains things only written for our entertainment. That is why Murasaki wrote, "these pall on quiet, second hearing." Events found in the tale that are exaggerated and leave one in awe are very rare. Events one keenly feels, causing us to feel profound emotion, are more abundant. In our present society, however, people seem to think it is joyous when an event is strange with some rare thing occurring, and they think it interesting when gentle feelings of emotion appear, but you can say that these are foolish people who do not know the hearts of people.

39. McCullough (1985:7).
40. Tyler (2001:461).

> "Lately, when my little girl has someone read to her and I stand there listening. . . ."[41]

The scene depicts picture stories as first and foremost trivial things that young women amuse themselves in reading, objects that men usually have no interest in, and yet it states that Lord Genji stops and listens to one of the women read the story to his little girl. Thus, in reality men also enjoyed reading these stories, and any man would have used examples from these old stories as precedent in his own life, exactly as numerous scenes in *Genji* depict. The author is being a bit self-deprecating here.

> I think to myself what good talkers there are in the world, and how this story, too, must come straight from someone's persuasively glib imagination—but perhaps not.[42]

While one knows that it is a falsehood, he thinks it is real and his heart is moved. While one thinks such things should not exist, he suddenly feels how interesting it is. One wonders why there are people in the world who are good at weaving lies. The quip "but perhaps not" shows that while one may believe what he has heard, he is not completely persuaded, which appears to be an underlying criticism of the reader. The answer to this criticism appears in the next section, quoted below.

> "Yes, of course, for various reasons someone accustomed to telling lies will no doubt take tales that way, but it seems impossible to me that they should be anything other than simply true." She pushed her inkstone away.[43]

These are the words of Lady Tamakazura. Someone who is used to telling lies will naturally doubt what others say, based on the habits of his own heart, guessing that this too is a lie. Commentaries that claim this refers to Lord Genji are wrong. If these words were said to Genji, then a higher level of honorifics, like *samo kumitamafuran* should have appeared, but Murasaki simply used *faberan*, so this charge is being leveled against people in general. The phrase "simply true" was said in a pouting, cross attitude. The line "pushed her inkstone away" is in reaction to Genji's earlier comment, "writing away without a thought for your tangled hair." This action depicts her pouting attitude.

---

41. Ibid.
42. Ibid.
43. Ibid.

> "I have been very rude to speak so ill to you of tales! They record what has gone ever since the Divine age. *The Chronicles of Japan* and son give only a part of the story. It is tales that contain the truly rewarding particulars!" He laughed.[44]

From this point on we again have the words of Lord Genji, and these words are in reaction to Lady Tamakazura pouting, and her quip, "I think all these stories are true." He plays with her by agreeing, saying, "You are exactly correct." We know this because of the words, "he laughed." From the point of view of the author, who sets up the scene this way to avoid future criticism from society that would claim that the author wanted to praise tales, and paint her own tale in a good light, and took the self-conceited tact of making her own work, *The Tale of Genji*, sound logical and detailed, superior to *The Chronicles of Japan* [*Nihon shoki*] and other records.

> Not that all tales accurately describe any particular person; rather, the telling being when all those things the teller longs to have pass on to future generations—whatever there is about the way people live their lives, for better or worse, that is a sight to see or a wonder to hear—overflow the teller's heart.[45]

The transition from "he laughed" to this next line may seem defective, but perhaps some words between these two sentences have been dropped from the manuscript. Regardless of whether that is true or not, perhaps if Genji had said something like, "I am joking, but in reality … ," then this would flow better. So now we see that Genji's earlier words when he spoke ill of tales was without substance. He simply made fun of Lady Tamakazura when he came upon her and saw her absorbed in her tales, reading and copying the manuscripts, and decided to take a stance opposite from her. But from this point on he changes his attitude with, "not all tales … ." This section starts the real debate about tales. So there are a variety of tales, and in general these are fiction, which shows the underlying object of Murasaki Shikibu as she writes this tale, writing about things that may have actually existed.

The words "for better or worse" in the text are critical for the reader to understand. Later we have the words "good or bad" that have the same purpose, and I will give a detailed analysis of this a little later. The phrase "is a sight to see or a wonder to hear" refers to the fact that regardless of one

44. Ibid.
45. Tyler (2001:461).

seeing an event or hearing about it, people simply cannot get it out of their mind. No matter what the emotion that wells up inside the human heart—be it something joyous, interesting, strange, funny, scary, improper, painful, or sad—people have the need to relate this to other people verbally, or write the experience down, and thus release these pent-up emotions. And when people see or hear about these experiences they are also moved to emotion and the human heart is refreshed.

In the "Paulownia Pavilion" chapter it says, "I would so like to talk to you longer, to lift a little of the unbearable darkness from my heart."[46] Or in the "Bracken Shoots" chapter is the scene,

> [H]is lordship the Counselor went to call on his Highness of War, since he could not unburden himself of his despair to anyone else ... and he so skillfully offered now words of consolation and now appeals to deep feelings that his charm swept the Counselor on little by little to tell him all of the pent-up sorrows in his heart; and he felt better for having done so.[47]

In the "Ivy" chapter Murasaki writes,

> "After the pleasure of hearing about the other day," she replied very circumspectly, "I thought how much I would regret it if as usual I kept my feelings to myself and never even tried to tell you how grateful I am."[48]

In the "Writing Practice" chapter we find,

> She had never been good at telling other people her feelings, and since in any case she now had no one close to talk to, she could only sit before her inkstone and bravely set down her emotions, when they overflowed, as writing practice.[49]

These examples make my point clear. The chapter title "writing practice" means that one must find a way to write down the feelings that bubble up inside of one's heart. Now regardless of the event, this sentiment that someone cannot just leave earnest emotions in their hearts is the same as those in our present society who have no depth to their feelings, but when they see or hear something that is very rare or strange, if it has nothing directly to do with them, they cannot just think in their hearts, "What a

46. Ibid., p. 9.
47. Ibid., p. 918–19.
48. Ibid., p. 946–47.
49. Ibid., p. 1100.

rare event," or "What a strange sight." No, they feel that they must tell the first person they meet. So even if one relates an experience to another person, there is no real advantage for either you or the other person, but it is the natural way of the heart when sharing something it refreshes your feelings. And that is why we compose poetry.

There is an underlying purpose implied in the author's words. The line "how this story, too, must come straight from someone's persuasively glib imagination" was uttered as a criticism of the tale, but the lines after this line are written in response to this criticism, and Murasaki Shikibu makes her intention clear for writing *The Tale of Genji*. So while the tale is a complete work of fiction, it is not a groundless piece of triviality, nor is it a story recording true events with the actual names of individuals. All events [in the tale] are common in society, whether these be good or evil; there were a lifetime of events she had seen and heard that filled her heart and she had a desire to write certain events for later generations, and thus she framed them in the setting of a tale. The reader should appreciate that while the story is fiction the events themselves are not.

Now, it is not necessarily true that all the events in the tale are things that Murasaki Shikibu had witnessed, or experiences from her generation, or names of famous people that she had changed to hide their identity. She created characters, events, and conversations based on common events in the world, and events that she had seen or heard, events that left such a deep impression on her that she could not help but express these on paper.

> [Back to the quote from "Fireflies"]: To put someone in a good light brings out the good only. ...[50]

The intention here is that because the tale is a work of fiction, when one wants to speak well of an individual we make a record, selecting and compiling all the good things that they have done in their life. Murasaki is indirectly praising Lord Genji. The character of Lord Genji is based on a collection of ideal traits of a person in society, needless to say by using his actions and his emotions, his physical features, his status in society, and his advancement at court. This deepens the description of the profundity of emotion and provides a stronger impression on the mind of the reader.

> And to please other people. ...[51]

50. Tyler (2001:461).
51. Ibid.

Comparing this with the next sentence we see that this section is now in opposition to that written above and the author should say "in relation to those who are evil," but she does not, which shows how interesting the ideas of Murasaki are. Here she means that as it is not pleasant to make public the bad aspects of a person, she has no intention of speaking evil of the person, but will allow society to determine whether the actions of a certain person are evil. So the usage of "to please other people" means that she does not want to say bad things, but she is following what people say.

A good example appears in the "Beneath the Autumn Leaves" chapter, where Murasaki writes, "... he changed his mind and humored her by engaging in a bantering exchange. ..."[52]

> She collected examples of rare or bad things and wrote these down. ...

Examples of "bad things" do not fit the definition as found in Confucian or Buddhist writings in relation to evil works. I will address these things later, but I think she had Lady Suetsuhana or Lady Konoe in mind. In all other cases, the definition of "evil things" should be considered the same way. It is not the author's intention to bring personal defects to light and slander the person, but she does this to hold the interest of the reader, which explains why she sometimes depicts evil actions that surprise the reader. One may know the intentions of the author through the use of phrases like "to please people" or "extraordinary things." The two categories I mentioned earlier, with "plausibly touching scenes" and "blatantly impossible," match the two aspects of good and evil, and the previously mentioned case is the attitude of the reader, while here we have the attitude of the author. One thus will know that if we compare this with the previous sentence, putting "a person in a good light" is what moves the heart of the reader because it is a plausibly touching scene. Also, it is not the intention of the tale to take the defects of individual characters and portray these as exceptional and strange, but is simply something interesting. One may know the truth of this statement by what I said earlier with the quote: "Be amazed by magnificently contrived wonders, and although these pall on quiet, second hearing, some are still fascinating."

> but none of this, good or bad, is removed from life as we know it.[53]

52. Ibid., p. 147.
53. Ibid., p. 461.

So whether good or bad all these depictions are found in this world, common events.

> Tales are not told the same way in the other realm. ...[54]

"The other realm" refers to a foreign kingdom. The word *zae* refers to scholarship, and in every tale scholarship is referred to as *zae*. ...[55]

> even in our own (country) the old and new ways are of course not the same.[56]

Manuscripts that read "because events in our ..." are in error. So not only are works in China [a foreign kingdom] different, but even works in our own imperial land different from the ancient and the present in how they were written. The ending verb *naru besi* apparently refers to the difference in time.[57] The works from the ancient past appear to refer to works like *The Chronicles of Japan* noted above, which were written in classical Chinese, and are vastly different in purpose than tales. Works in the present refers to tales. Compared with *The Chronicles of Japan*, tales, even old tales, are a product closer in time than the ancient records, so that *The Tale of Genji* should be counted among tales.

> although one may distinguish between the deep and the shallow. ...[58]

Here we are comparing two different types of books. "Deep works" refers to the type of books that are written in Chinese and are difficult for women to comprehend, such as the works of foreign lands, *The Chronicles of Japan* and others. "Shallow works" refers to tales, which are written in the vernacular in *kana* script without any editing. Because the author did not write just "deep and shallow," but included the nominalizer *koto* here, we should understand that she is pointing to the style of writing.

---

54. Ibid.

55. Norinaga appears to have relied on a variant manuscript from what is currently used, but as Tyler notes, "The original for this whole sentence is confusing and suspect, and it varies especially widely in different manuscripts" (2001:461, n21). Our current manuscript has さへ or *safe* here and not *zae* as Norinaga has it.

56. Tyler (2001:461).

57. Norinaga's manuscript has *kafaru naru besi*, but this appears to have been an eye-skip on the part of the copyist (scribe), because the proper reading is *kafaru besi*.

58. Ibid.

> it is wrong always to dismiss what one finds in tales as false.[59]

"It is wrong" could be said in the contemporary vernacular as "contrary to our knowledge." From the beginning of the sentence, "Not that all tales accurately describe any particular person" continuing to this point constitutes the response to the charge that tales are nothing but fiction, so this is how Murasaki wraps up the argument. The next segment of this section is where Murasaki provides proof to show generally that tales are indispensable to us.

> There is talk of "expedient means" also in the teaching that the Buddha in his great goodness left us. ...[60]

"Great goodness" in the vernacular equals "righteous and correct." In the correct teachings of the Buddha there should be no fabrications, but there is *hauben* [Modern Japanese *hōben*] "expedient means" even in his methodology, so how much more true is it among the common people who say things that are not true, claiming these to be *hauben*. And while we claim these are similar, the usage of fiction and "expedient means" are different. Fiction belongs to falsehood and it is evil to speak them. *Hauben* are words spoken for the benefit of the hearer. The implied meaning is that while tales were criticized earlier as being fiction, here we have the author's response, that tales should not be swept away as just fiction, but because these tales demonstrate all the good and evil in people, it teaches people about the profundity of emotion, meaning that *The Tale of Genji* is analogous to the teachings of the Buddha.

> and many passages of scriptures are all too likely to seem inconsistent and so as to raise doubts in the minds of those who lack understanding.[61]

This means that the ignorant people who do not understand the purpose of "expedient means" in Buddhist doctrine will likely doubt what is being argued here and there in relation to the methodology of Buddhism. Her implied intention is to be self-deprecating toward tales. The method of *hauben* is found in many passages of scripture.

> but in the end they have only a single message. ...[62]

---

59. Ibid.
60. Ibid.
61. Ibid.
62. Ibid.

Hauben appears to be different than direct teaching, but the end result is the same message.

> the gap between enlightenment and the passions is, after all, no wider than the gap that in tales sets off the good from the bad.[63]

"A single message" refers to the enlightened and those with passions. There are a variety of expedient means in Buddhism, and there are differences among all these here and there, but the conclusion is the same as direct teaching. And while there will be differences when teaching about the contrast of the enlightened with those with passions, in the end both settle on the same message. The phrase "the good and the bad" is an analogy for the tale and the use of *kono* "this" points to this tale [*Genji*]. "Good and bad" refer to characters within the tale. The concluding verb *kafarikeru* is written in reference to the gap between the good and the bad, and the meaning is that this is analogous to the gap between enlightenment and the passions in Buddhist doctrine. A person thus asks, "If the conclusion of tales is to demonstrate the good and evil of people, then is the purpose not the same as Chinese works and Confucian and Buddhist scriptures that teaches people to 'encourage the good and punish the evil'? If so, then why do you claim that tales have a different purpose than Confucian and Buddhist works?" My reply is that as I have already discussed the concept of good and evil in the tale is often different in substance from that in Confucian and Buddhist doctrine, so the meaning of these is vastly different. This is where the intention of the author is.

> "To put it nicely, there is nothing that does not have its own value." He mounted a very fine defense of tales.[64]

"To put it nicely" refers to the tendency in people to think that tales are trivial and good for nothing, but if you examine with a fair eye and think logically, this tendency is not necessarily correct. The phrase "a very fine defense" does not refer to vain consolation, but refers to something that must be done. In spite of the fact that women and children amuse themselves with tales and seek superficial consolation from them, in this passage Lord Genji has argued how people must read these. To discuss the object of the author, the sentence "he mounted a very fine defense" is the

---

63. Ibid.
64. Ibid.

concern from Murasaki Shikibu. As noted in the previous section, the descriptions in *The Tale of Genji* appear to argue that the tale has value, but in reality she creates this scene so that the reader gets the impression that it is all just a silly deception. This is self-deprecating, and at this point she sets her brush aside. The reader should really digest these sentences.

To recap, these paragraphs in the "Fireflies" chapter suggest the underlying reason for why the tale was written. The author did not announce the general intention of the tale at the beginning or at the end, so how wonderful that she decided to slip it into a humble section within the tale.

In the past earlier commentaries have only given a cursory treatment of this section of the tale, just touching the surface, their comments filled with errors, and the commentators have not brought to light the intention of the author. Some commentaries have spilled a lot of ink on the analogy to Buddhist scripture, but not a single commentary has hit the nail on the head regarding Murasaki's true intention as I have explained above. Now if the real purpose of this section is not sufficiently clear then the overall purpose of *The Tale of Genji* will not be apparent. …

MONO NO AWARE

What does it mean to understand *mono no aware*? The word *aware* originally meant the sound of the sigh one lets escape when he sees, hears, or touches something that stirs his heart. The words we use in the present like *aa* or *fare* represent this. For example, if one sees the moon or cherry blossoms and is moved to emotion, he will say something like "What a fine moon!" The word *aware* is a fusion of these two words, *aa* and *fare.*[65] In Chinese texts the compound 嗚呼 "Ah! Alas!" is glossed as *aa*, which is the same word. In the ancient language we have words like *ana* "how" or *aya* "oh," which contain the same *a* as above. …

In later eras the word *aware* was written with the character 哀 "sorrow" and it appears that there is a tendency to see *aware* as only referring to sadness. But the word is not limited in meaning to just sorrow; whether the feeling is one of joy, amusement, enjoyment, or fascination, these all refer to *aware* if the thought of heaving a sigh of emotion is present. That is why this is used in phrases, like "movingly interesting" or "movingly joyful."

65. This is a common view of the etymology of this word. *Kogo shūi* believed *apare* (the earlier form of *aware* < *afare* < *apare*) meant "the sky has cleared," based on *fare* "clear sky." The actual etymology is unknown.

This is added because the feeling is added to the action. In many cases, *aware* is used in opposition to feelings of fascination or joy, because these generally have a shallow emotional output, while sorrow, gloom, and love are all feelings from something unexpected, creating an especially deep emotional impression, and this deeper emotional state is often referred to as *aware*. That is why in the vernacular we often refer to sorrow as *aware*. For example, in the "Spring Shoots" chapter in relation to plum blossoms it says, "I should like to put them besides cherry blossoms at their best."[66] Plum blossoms are still blossoms, but the word "blossom" is used especially to refer to cherry blossoms.

It would appear that in general people consider the effect of being moved by something to always refer to a positive action, but it is not limited to this. In dictionaries it says that the character 感 "emotion" means 動 "action," referring to the movement of the heart [emotions]. Whether it be something good or bad, if the heart is stirred to emotion, and you think "*aafare*," then the person has felt something, and that is why the character 感 is often used to represent the word *aware*. In Chinese there is the phrase "move ghosts and spirits," and the Mana preface to *Kokinshū* has this phrase. The Kana preface says, "... stirs emotions in the invisible spirits and gods ... ,"[67] demonstrating that *aware* refers to people being stirred to emotion. ...

Mono no aware is the same, *mono* referring to a thing as the stimulus, a tale being the thing that is related, so that something one goes to see is *monomi* "sightseeing" or *monoimi* "abstinence," a prefix attached when one is speaking in a broad sense. So we call the reaction *mono no aware* when any stimulus stirs the human heart, and the individual knows that it should stir the human heart. We also say "You do not know *mono no aware*" when a person experiences something that should stir the human heart, but there is no emotional response. We also use the same phrase on those who are heartless. An enlightened person cannot help but be moved when a situation arises where the heart is stirred. A person who is not moved in that case is dull of understanding, lacking the proper feelings that would allow him to feel emotion. In *Gosenshū* it says, "In some place, in front of a bamboo screen, some women heard Tsurayuki telling stories about the poems written by this and that person, when from behind the screen the Lady and her women were heard to say, 'What a strange old man who knows so much about *aware*.' Hearing this Tsurayuki composed,

66. Tyler (2001:595).
67. McCullough (1985:3).

afare tefu	There is no effect
koto ni sirusi fa	simply because one has uttered
nakeredomo	the word *aware*,
ifade fa e koso	but one cannot simply get by
aranu mono nare	without saying '*Aware*!'"

[GSS 1271]

This poems means that while there is no actual value in sighing *aafare*, when our emotions are stirred by something and we cannot suppress these, then we have no other choice but to utter this sigh. A person who understands *mono no aware* will react in just such a manner.

As I have noted above, there are a variety of things that will stimulate a person's emotions. *The Tale of Genji* as a work of fiction has described virtually every situation that humans especially will face that stir our emotions and cause us to feel the profundity of emotions. First Murasaki writes about situations that run the gamut from public to private, from interesting and auspicious to wondrous, describing wonderful scenes that deal with flowers, birds, the moon, and snow throughout the seasons of spring summer, fall, and winter. All these scenes depict situations that stir the emotions of the heart and cause one to think "*aware*," and there are times when we think about things that really stir our hearts such as the scenery of the sky, or the color of foliage. Let me give a number of examples from the tale. In the "Paulowania Pavilion" chapter it says,

> The sound of the wind and the calling of crickets only deepened his melancholy. ...[68]

In the "Broom Tree" chapter it says,

> To one viewer the vacant sky intimated romance, while to the other it suggested aloof indifference.[69]

In the "Heart-to-Heart" chapter we find,

> he lay alone and sleepless into a foggy dawn ... a letter arrived. ... The sad news I hear, that a life can pass so soon. ... My heart is so full, you know, beneath this sky.

68. Tyler (2001:11).
69. Ibid., p. 41.

In the same chapter,

> The wild wind blew, the rain poured down … that Her Highness of the bluebells would understand how sad this day had been, and although it was dark by now, he sent her a note.[70]

In the "Wind in the Pines" chapter we read,

> It was autumn, and all things seemed to weigh upon his heart. …[71]

The following appears in the "Bluebell" chapter,

> To the rustling of the leaves Her Highness pondered absorbing passages from her past, and she remembered how thoroughly amusing he had been at times, and at others how profoundly moving.[72]

In the "Mayfly" chapter it reads,

> When something is seriously troubling *me*, even something far short of this, the mere cry of a bird passing overhead can overwhelm me.[73]

Now I cite passages where people are moved by the beauty of someone's countenance. In the "Paulownia Pavilion" chapter it says,

> for the sight of him would have brought smiles to the fiercest warrior, even an enemy one.[74]

In the "Broom Tree" chapter it says,

> He spoke so gently that she could not very well cry out rudely, "There is a man here!" because not even a demonlike *kami* would have wished to resist him.[75]

In the "Twilight Beauty" chapter we find,

> It was therefore all but impossible for a cultivated woman like Chūjō, one who had had occasion to receive poems from him and to bask in the warmth of his beauty, not to be drawn to him.[76]

---

70. Ibid., pp. 179, 182.
71. Ibid., p. 335.
72. Ibid., p. 367.
73. Ibid., p. 1053.
74. Ibid., p. 12.
75. Ibid., p. 39.
76. Ibid., p. 60.

In the "Beneath the Autumn Leaves" chapter it states,

> for no doubt she could not banish that beauty and that dazzling grace from her mind.

The chapter goes on to state,

> "Blue Sea Waves" shone forth with an awesome beauty ... In the waning light ... while Genji in his glory ... Among the undiscerning multitude sheltered beneath the trees, hidden among the rocks, or buried under fallen leaves on the mountainside, those with eyes to see shed tears.[77]

In the "Suma" chapter we find,

> The renewed beauty and grace of his sorrowing form, seen by the light of the sinking moon, would have moved a wolf or tiger to weep.[78]

In the "Evening Mist" chapter it states,

> Handsome as he is, he seems lately to have acquired a new dignity and presence. Who could blame him for occasionally indulging himself a little? With that bright aura of youth and beauty, the very gods would forgive him.[79]

In the "A Drifting Boat" chapter it says,

> She could not have ignored anyone so beautiful, even if he had been her worst enemy in demon form.[80]

As you can see, someone whose heart is not moved by the beauty of a countenance is lower than a tiger or a wolf. It also appears very often throughout the chapters where people's hearts are moved by the status of an individual. In spite of that, it does not mean that these people flatter those with power and wealth in an attempt to get close to them, but they find they cannot help but feel something because of the status the person holds. They feel a connection and must be moved.

---

77. Ibid., pp. 136, 137.
78. Ibid., p. 232.
79. Ibid., p. 746.
80. Ibid., p. 1041.

An example where someone's emotions are stirred because of Genji's status appears in the "Broom Tree" chapter,

> Despite her [Utsusemi] resolve, she suffered acutely to think that he must find her adamant rejection outrageously impertinent.[81]

In the "Suma" chapter we find,

> when there reached them from afar, down the wind, the notes of a *kin*; and such were the place, the man, and the poignancy of the music that all those alive to finer feelings wept.[82]

In this scene everyone weeps because a number of emotions sensitive people should feel have been stirred together, and the phrase "those alive to finer feelings" refers to the fact that when such situations arise, a person who has no such sensitivity will not feel anything, meaning they do not understand the profundity of human emotion. It is important for the reader to consider this in light of what I quoted earlier, with the line "having some knowledge of the essence of things."

Now, the next quote from the "Paulownia Pavilion" chapter demonstrates how not understanding the profundity of human emotion is evil.

> The sound of the wind and the calling of crickets only deepened his melancholy, and meanwhile he heard the Kokiden Consort, who had not come for so long now to wait on him after dark, making the best of a beautiful moon by playing music far into the night. He did not like it and wished it would stop. Those gentlewomen and privy gentlemen who knew his mood found that it grated upon their ears.[83]

This is a depiction of someone who does not understand the profundity of emotions. At the time when the emperor felt sadness because of the sound of the wind and the calling of the crickets, would someone with a sensitive heart look up at the moon and find it beautiful? Would that person have played music? As I pointed out earlier, even in relation to the moon, it changes according to the viewer, becoming elegant or terrifying, but here the usage of "making the best of a beautiful moon" refers to the feelings of Empress Kokiden. The phrase "he wished it would stop" shows that she is

81. Ibid., p. 44. Norinaga interprets Utsusemi's reaction to Genji to mean that juxtaposing her status with his causes her to suffer acutely. Thus, she is reacting to his status.

82. Tyler (2001:246).

83. Ibid., p. 11.

not thinking about how it is affecting the emperor. The phrase "who knew his mood" refers to the state of sadness of the emperor.

In the "Green Branch" chapter we find,

> The Empress Mother, with her sharp temper, had restrained herself while His Late Eminence lived, but now she seemed bent on revenge for every grudge she nursed against him.[84]

Also we have, "The older she grew, the more ill-tempered she became, until even His Eminence found her company unbearable."[85]

Both quotes deal with the Empress Kokiden. In the same "Green Branch" chapter is a description of the "incident" between Lord Genji and Lady Oborozukiyo, and there is the additional part about where both the empress mother and her father the minister are described in severe terms; her father the minister is called "very short tempered" and ill-natured.

> A man of his standing should have seen her embarrassment and restrained himself in consideration of her acute discomfort, even if she was his own daughter, but no, he was too hotheaded and irascible for that. ... Ever a willful man, incapable of discretion, her father had gained nothing from the passing years but testiness of age. ...[86]

In the "Handsome Pillar" chapter it says, "She had an evil temper, that woman."[87] Or in the second part of the "Spring Shoots" chapter, "His Highness of Ceremonial's wife, remained angrily unforgiving."[88] These depictions are about Murasaki's stepmother.

Now it is clear from the above examples that the context of the tale is such that those who do not think well of Lord Genji, treating him poorly, are considered evil people who do not know the profundity of emotion, because aside from his immortal actions, the tale does not describe him in a poor light. The main reason for this is because Lord Genji is depicted as a good person who knows the profundity of emotion. If we follow the standard criticism in society, arguing from the philosophy of the Way of Con-

84. Ibid., p. 200.

85. Ibid., p. 401. Norinaga has constructed this quote with 又 so that it makes it sound as if this is also quoted from the "Green Branch" chapter, but this quote actually comes from the "Maidens" chapter.

86. Ibid., p. 218.

87. Ibid., p. 535.

88. Ibid., p. 630.

fucianism, then we should say that the middle princess of the Fujitsubo Palace [Fujitsubo] is worse than Empress Kokiden. In spite of this the tale depicts her as someone who is superior, a good example in society. Empress Kokiden and others who have not committed any transgressions, on the other hand, are depicted as especially evil people because the purpose of the tale is to spotlight characters that know the profundity of emotions and hold that up as a good standard. Regarding the "incident" between Yūgiri and Kumoi no Kari, the tale depicts the behavior of Kumoi no Kari's father, the minister, as heartless, where he forbids and remonstrates her behavior, and yet the tale does not mention that the relation between Yūgiri and Kumoi no Kari is immoral. From the common point of view of society should not the remonstration of her father the minister be seen as reasonable, and Lord Yūgiri and Kumoi no Kari be found guilty?

By reading through the various chapters in the tale, the reader will naturally come to a realization of characters who know the profundity of emotion and those who do not, and the difference between good and evil. The tale does not make mention that this is good or that is evil, but through the illustration of good and evil makes the distinction clear to the reader.

The tale also depicts Buddhist monks as people who do not understand the profundity of emotion. In the "Oak Tree" chapter it says,

> "Please still have pity on me!" [Genji said]. "I hear that someone like me, now, knows little of human feelings. What can I possibly say, then, since I have never known them anyway?" [replied the third princess].[89]

This scene occurs after the third princess has left the world, and in reply to Genji's entreating that she still have pity on him; the Princess replies, "I have heard that all who leave the world [and take Buddhist vows] do not know the profundity of human emotion, and I originally did not understand human emotion before I left the world, I am therefore a person of no worth, so I do not know how to respond to your request." This scene shows that there was a tradition that monks did not understand the profundity of human emotion.

So why is there a tradition that monks did not understand the profundity of human emotion? In reality the Way of Buddhism causes people to shake off the bonds of affection completely between one's father, mother, wife, and son, and quietly change themselves, forsaking their houses and

89. Tyler (2001:686). I have added referents to this quote to help the reader follow the passage.

wealth. They live a solitary life in the woods of the mountains, and divorce themselves from the taste of fish and meat, music and women, going against all that is important to human emotion. Since someone who took Buddhist vows could not pursue their studies if they had a sensitive heart and understood the profundity of human emotions, it is clear the Way of Buddhism has forced them to be insensitive; they become people who do not understand the profundity of human emotions. And even when those in Buddhism try to lead others to their doctrine they do not succeed with those who know the profundity of human emotion in the world and have sensitive hearts. Outwardly they seem to lack an understanding of the profundity of human emotion, but as they teach the importance of pitying those who are wandering lost in the darkness of a long night, to see it from their point of view, they have a very profound understanding of human emotions. The teachings of Confucianism have the same purpose.

In the "Beneath the Oak" chapter it says, "… they bitterly condemned the Adept's excessively ascetic zeal."[90]

This scene is right after the eighth prince had passed away, and even though his daughters were consumed with sorrow the Adept disregarded the feelings that exist between a parent and child, telling them based on the doctrine of Buddhism that they needed to cut all emotional ties to their father. The daughters were aggravated with the Adept's heartless response as it was so insensitive. This scene demonstrates in a general way that Buddhist monks have no conception of human emotion. And there are even monks who have become enlightened who are ignorant of the events in the world, so it is conceivable that monks in general know nothing of the profundity of human emotion. …

[MNZ 1976, 4:173–210]

ന്ദ

90. Ibid., p. 856.

Part Three
Views on Scholarship

"PETITION TO ESTABLISH A SCHOOL"

Kada no Azumamaro | ca. 1728

[While few modern scholars believe this to be the actual work of Azumamaro, many do at least admit that it represents his basic thoughts. The petition was apparently written near the end of his life, as Azumamaro wanted a school from which to broaden his teachings. The petition, written in classical Chinese, quotes from a variety of Chinese sources, because literary Chinese was the official language of the shogun's court. A deeper desire for the establishment of a school, likely, was to let the public know that there was a place they could come to study things that were uniquely Japanese.]

Respectfully begging your honorable favor, I humbly submit this request to establish a school for Kokugaku.

With trembling in my heart, I reverently submit my offer. Pondering upon the past in awe, we see that the divine lord, Tokugawa Ieyasu, came from Mikawa, and after he had united the country, he ruled the land in tranquility. As the wind drives the grass hither and thither, where is there a person who stands in defiance of Lord Ieyasu? He initiated a reformation in the country, and for the first time established Kōbun no Kan.[1] This established school has flourished and prospered, and there remains nothing to add to it.

Wise shoguns have come to power successively, and our literary culture has only brightened. The splendor of military skill has continued to improve until it is now complete. How can the frugality that the Kamakura rulers were fond of surpass the appearance of talented samurai of our day? How can we mention in the same breath the literary arts supported by the Muromachi rulers compared to the literary achievements of our period? As is fitting for this era of peace, heaven has sent us a magnanimous and benevolent lord endowed with heaven-sent virtues. Our lord rules without stern force, leading us by example. Among the commoners, he surrounds

1. Also known as Shōheikō or Shōheizaka Gakumonjo. It was a school of learning originally established in 1630 when Tokugawa Iemitsu granted land in Ueno to Hayashi Razan, allowing him to open a private school. In 1690 Tokugawa Tsunayoshi had the school removed to Kanda, and the school was expanded. It then became known as Shōheikō.

himself with wise men, like the Yao Dynasty in China, when the government put out a drum for petitions against the government. In the same vein, there are none who have complained against our ruler. There are many honest servants in the government, reminiscent of the Zhou Dynasty when one hundred officials remonstrated with the king.

Our ruler pays respect to the emperor above him, conducting affairs in all honesty. Below, the feudal lords pay obeisance, sending tribute of locally produced articles. The system of the government is well in order, and when our ruler has leisure, he turns to the study of ancient learning. When education in the world is lacking, he researches deeply into the worthy methods of government from our ancient sovereigns. He purchases rare manuscripts at high prices.[2] Famous and talented men willingly offer him their allegiance. These talented men search for valuable works hidden away. Gifted men in the provinces come to see him and partake of his virtue.

When I had occasion to travel to Edo, I was fortunate to have you grant me, a person full of fear, lacking any scholarly merit, permission to organize and collate the books in the library. You lavished such favor on me that I almost forgot what a common citizen I am. There is much we can learn from the words of lamentation of Sima Qian,[3] "For whom do you do this? To whom will these things be spoken? There is no one." Also, there is deep meaning in the words of Mencius of Zou, who said, "A man may have wisdom and discernment, but that is not like waiting for the right season."[4]

Now at this time, under the glory of the Bakufu, if I have received the grace of the shogun in establishing a school of national learning, I wish to voice my heartfelt desires. Nevertheless, I have pondered in my heart why I have as yet been unable to fulfill this desire. If I do not fail in my progress, though I am a lame turtle, I could still travel a thousand leagues.[5]

The progress of learning is the same. I still have not reached the ripe age of sixty years, so how do we know that what is beautiful today will not be ugly tomorrow? How do we know that those who come after us will not be wiser? A fool who tries his hand at everything is like a mantis rearing his front legs in an attempt to confront an oncoming carriage. An unlearned man spouting off at the mouth resembles the fool from Sung, deceived into

---

2. Literally for one thousand pieces of gold.

3. Sima Qian (?145–86 BCE) compiled the Chinese historical work *Shiji* "Records of the Grand Historian," making him the standard of Chinese historiography. The quote here is found in the biography of Sima Qian in *Han shu*.

4. Slightly altered version of Legge (1970:183).

5. Apparently an allusion to a line in *Huainanzi*, "Thus, if it strides forth without resting, even a lame turtle can go a thousand *li*" (Major 2010:707).

thinking the yellow rocks dug from Mount Yan were jewels.[6] With these thoughts, I have not been able to accomplish anything though I have a strong desire, so I hung my head and returned to my hometown down that long road. Without warning, I became ill. The fiery horse sadly is now ill in the stable.[7] This is terribly unexpected, having heaven bestow an illness on me, thrusting me into the dark cage of the bird who never comes out.[8] I am like Master Chen Zhong living in Wu Ling [unable to speak],[9] and like Bian Huo, who had both legs severed when he got to the bottom of the mountain,[10] I am not able to use my legs. My regret will know no end if I become disabled. At this time of misfortune, I narrow my eyebrows and sob alone.

It is our fate that heaven may spare or destroy Japanese literature. It is not the season of destruction. Thus, I must seize the opportunity to say what I feel. Confucian learning has appeared everywhere, and the influence of Buddhism grows daily. The Confucian ethic of benevolence and righteousness is taught in every house, and even servants and horse breeders compose Chinese poetry. Each household recites the sutras, and even porters and household servants talk about the transience of life. Ki no Tsurayuki once lamented the state of society saying, "When the behavior of the people changes, our way of poetry begins to decline."[11] And Miyoshi Kiyoyuki[12] remarked dejectedly, "Subjects drowning in Buddhism fight over land, throwing away their money in support of temples." My own private opinion is that we can view this state of affairs as the symbol of long-lasting peace, but for our country, this state is disheartening.

With the passing of each year, the decline of the teachings from the divine past grows more intense. The lack of attention to our national traditions has reduced those works to a fraction of what they were before. If we lose the books on the regulations and codes, who will be able to revive the

---

6. This story appears in Volume 51 of the thousand-volume Song-era work, *Taiping yulan*, compiled between the years 977 and 983.

7. This is a reference to a line in Volume 21 of *Weishu*, in the "Biography of Liu Shao."

8. Apparently a reference to a line at the beginning of Volume 37 of *Baopuzi*, compiled between 317 and 318 CE.

9. A reference to the line in *Mencius*, "Kuang Zhang said to Mencius, 'Is not Chen Zhong a man of true self-denying purity? He was living in Wu Ling, and for three days was without food, till he could neither hear nor see'" (Legge 1970:284).

10. A reference to a story in Volume 805 of *Taiping yulan*.

11. This may have reference to the line in the *Kana* preface, "Because people nowadays value outward show and turn their minds toward frivolity, poems are mere empty verse and trivial words" (McCullough 1985:5).

12. Miyoshi Kiyoyuki (847–919) was a poet of Chinese poetry and served as a professor in the imperial university. He is also well known as a poetic scholar.

study of ancient things? If our society abandons the Way of poetry, how will true elegance rise up? All the teachers of Shintō adhere to Chinese ideas like *yin* and *yang* and the five principles. Those who expound on Japanese poetry interpret verse according to the four doctrines of Tendai teachings. If these people are not praising the dribble of Confucian scholars of the Tang and Song, then they flounder in the secret philosophies of the Diamond Realm and the Womb Realm traditions.[13] These people are like a man who tries to drill a hole with a chisel in imaginary space, debating meaningless things in great detail. If these people are not following unfounded theories, then they elaborate upon personal ideas that have no reasonable foundation. They proclaim these to be secret teachings or orally transmitted knowledge, but why should the wise men of the past have secret teachings or deep mysteries? The majority of these secret traditions are recent fabrications.

Since my youth, I have struggled to rid myself of such foreign ideas, sacrificing sleep and nourishment. For this purpose I have studied and pondered, believing that it is imperative to revive the old Way. If I do not now arouse my senses, and expound correct principles against those that are incorrect, then later people will have ears that do not hear and hearts that are confused, wandering lost among a confusion of orthodox and perverted ideas. I would like to go forward, but I am old and sickly; however, if I were to retire from this work, then our literature would drift off into oblivion. My heart hesitates and I lack resolve. In this state of confusion, I am unsure of what to do.

I respectfully address you. If you would see fit to bestow on me a pitiful parcel of land in Kyōto, or Fushimi, or even in Higashiyama, I desire to establish a school dedicated to the learning of our indigenous traditions. I have a library of private books collected since my youth, plus many important works. I also have many old works and records that I have collected in my old age. I desire to place these all in the school for later research. There are many people in the distant provinces with no material for this work, or financially weak people who wish to pursue these studies but do not know how. If these people had borrowed and read my books, they would know about the weakening of the ceremonies of the court from reading one book alone, as if a hundred princes had deftly poured light *sake* from a great height.[14] A discerning person who understands the workings of so-

13. A Buddhist practice where ascetics go into the mountains. The Kumano area was designated the Womb Realm, while Yoshino was designated the Diamond Realm.

14. In this last clause, written 百王之澆醨此知, I have interpreted 澆醨 literally as referring to light *sake* poured ceremonially from a high spot, which requires great skill.

ciety from a thousand years ago can spare the people from many trials. Through this, if a gifted samurai appears, then perhaps the deftly poured wine of Prince Toneri[15] would not rot on the ground. If a talented poet who produces golden gems of poetry arises, then the poetic Way taught by Hitomaro will rise up again. If the Six National Histories[16] are well known, then how would government officials not be enabled to better educate the people with a small amount of effort? If society employed the regulations of the three imperial reigns,[17] then the country would be at a greater advantage.

Man'yōshū is a poetic anthology of the east [Japan], and when a person studies its contents, then others will not chastise him as lacking in aesthetics. *Kokinshū* is a carefully compiled anthology of poetry. If people do not know this work, they will be castigated as people who should not speak.

Originally, the first school in Japan was established in the reign of the Ōmi court.[18] Added emphasis was given to literary studies in the reign of Emperor Saga. The Sugawara and Ōe families established schools afterwards. The Minamoto, Fujiwara, Tachibana, and Wake families followed suit, establishing schools of their own. There also was a school set up in the Dazaifu. And then there was an Ashikaga and Kanazawa school. Nonetheless, these schools taught the three histories of China with the nine classics, instructing the offspring of the imperial family to make sacrificial offerings in the Chinese tradition.[19] These schools ground their studies in the Four Ways and the Six Accomplishments.[20] How lamentable. The ancient Confucian scholars were intellectually empty, lacking an iota of information about

15. Prince Toneri (676–735) was the son of Tenmu, and later fathered Emperor Junnin. *Shoku Nihongi* records that Prince Toneri was the head of the compilation of *Nihon shoki*, but as the work has no preface or document of presentation, little is known of his actual work, though scholars believe most of the work of compilation was done before he came on the scene. *Shoku Nihongi* notes in a terse statement dated the twenty-first day of the fifth month of 720, "Before this, Prince Toneri of the first princely rank received the imperial command and compiled *Nihongi*. At this time he presented it to the throne, consisting of thirty volumes and one volume of genealogy."

16. The six imperially ordered histories are: *Nihon shoki* (720), *Shoku Nihongi* (797), *Nihon kōki* (840), *Shoku Nihon kōki* (869), *Nihon Montoku Tennō jitsuroku* (879), and *Nihon sandai jitsuroku* (901).

17. Separately known as Kōnin, Teikan, and Engi regulations.

18. Pointing to an origin during the reign of Tenchi [r. 668–72); however, *Nihon shoki* does not mention this event. Perhaps Azumamaro is connecting the dots with the assumed creation of the Ōmi codes, which may have included an imperial university, as the Taihō and Yōrō codes did.

19. The three histories are the Chinese historical records *Shiji*, *Hanshu*, and *Hou Hanshu*. The nine classics are *Book of Odes*, *Shangshu*, *Zhouli*, *Liji*, *Zhouyi*, *Annals of Spring and Autumn*, *Yili*, *Kaojing*, and *The Analects*.

20. The Four Ways refers to courses originally taught at the imperial university: histor-

our indigenous traditions. What is worse, there was not a single scholar in later eras who bemoaned the continuing destruction of Japanese learning. Therefore, foreign learning prospered, invading our country to the core, infiltrating the gossip of commoners. Our Japanese Way has splintered, and erroneous theories and heretical ideas have sprung up through the cracks.

If you would grant your sympathy on my pitiful lamentations, permitting me to establish this school, allowing me to correct the ideas of men in society, turning this decline around, then will this not surely be the great success in governing the country? And if we can easily combine our resources and study the ancient past, then this will result in prosperity that will know no decline. I am nothing but a fool, lacking knowledge. If there is one area, however, in which I have great confidence, it is the interpretation of words. Most people know about the many corrupted readings in our ancient national works.[21] These works are still extant, but as few people have engaged in textual criticism, we do not hear of people well versed in these ancient works. The commentaries as well as the learned scholars of our day are inadequate. It has been several hundred years since anyone expounded upon national learning. During this interval, there have only been three or four people who engaged in textual or lexical studies. Even our gifted masters argued over strange or trite problems, explaining why there is not a single theory worthy of note. Without elucidating the old lexicon, the meaning of old words will not be clear. Without the clear meaning of the old lexicon, it is impossible to revive the study of ancient learning.

The transmitted details of the courtly ceremonies of former kings are vanishing, and even the theories of the ancient scholars are on their way to oblivion.[22] This is because we do not teach people about linguistics. This is the reason I have spent the energies of my life studying the ancient lexicon.

I respectfully believe that whether this petition to establishment this school is accepted or rejected will determine whether our national literature survives or perishes. I humbly beg your attention on this matter, and ask you to grant my request. I, Azumamaro, do humbly present this petition with awe and reverence.

[NST 39:330–36]

---

ical records, Confucianism, legal codes, and literature. The Six Accomplishments are proper behavior, music, archery, horsemanship, literature, and mathematics.

21. Azumamaro is mainly thinking of the state of *Man'yōshū*, and how the majority of people cannot appreciate it because they do not understand the text.

22. A good example is the court-sponsored lectures on *Nihon shoki*, known as *Shiki*. Only fragments remain of these valuable lessons.

NIIMANABI

Kamo no Mabuchi | 1765

[Mabuchi sees the composition of poetry as a fundamental characteristic of Japan. He argues that studying the poetry of *Man'yōshū* helps the student learn that the ancient Japanese had a masculine character that was later weakened by continental influence. He outlines this decline, and proposes the solution to return to the state of the ancient past, which will remedy the situation. Thus, the Japanese people will be able to return to a natural state, one suitable to nature, as he believed the ancient Japanese had been before foreign influences shattered that ideal.]

Ancient poetry is mainly concerned with melody. This is because ancient poetry was originally sung vocally. Generally speaking, the melody of poetry was tranquil, clear, pure, and slightly melancholy; a variety of human emotions produced numerous melodies, but the common factor among all these was that the poetry was lofty and straightforward. A sense of elegance exists within this loftiness, while a feeling of masculinity underlies its straightforwardness. The reason for stating this is because heaven and earth—which are the father and mother of everything—are divided into spring, summer, autumn, and winter. Everything the earth has created is divided into these four seasons; one can divide things into these four classifications, and the melody of the singer is the same. Also, each season does not have completely peculiar traits, spring overlapping with summer and autumn overlapping with winter. Resembling the actual state of the seasons, there are melodies borrowed from two different variations. Though there are many varieties, each variety has its own excelling rhythmical song.

Therefore, to come to an understanding of the ancient state of life, when one experiences the structure of ancient poetry, we come to see that the ancient capital in the province of Yamato was masculine in nature, and women followed the style of men. Thus, the poetry in *Man'yōshū* is for the most part masculine in nature. The next era, when the capital was in the province of Yamashiro, was feminine in nature, and men followed the style of women. That is why most of the poetry in *Kokinshū* is written in a feminine style. And when one debates about the six styles in *Kokinshū*, people judge the peaceful and refreshing style as superior. The reason the *Kokinshū* preface says that the provincial style is strong and masculine[1] is because poets in the present place and time think that the current style is ideal, and they do not even attempt a broad study of the poetic styles of the ancients. Now, though there are changes in everything like the four seasons, *Kokinshū*, following the mood of its preface, places value only on spring with its elegance, and discards summer and winter; it values the feminine element while avoiding the masculine. Now, in the era when successive rulers made Yamato their capital, the emperor ruled the country. The emperor showed courageous authority on the surface, but underneath he was generous and gentle. Because of this, imperial reigns rolled on, and the prosperity of the state increased, the common man generally respected and honored his rulers, being straightforward and sincere, which disposition [of the common man] continued for generations. After the court removed the capital to the province of Yamashiro, the authority of the august emperor gradually declined, and the commoner was flattered by the change, and their disposition worsened. Why do people think this occurred? The reason is because the people in the capital located in Yamashiro did not accept the tradition of the masculine disposition common in the Yamato era, but acquired an affinity for feminine things. Add to this the popularity of Chinese learning, and the common people lost their respect for their rulers, and an increasingly wicked disposition only worsened.

Therefore, everything in the world is lacking, because we have lost the true variation of the four seasons, the elegance of spring, the strength of summer, the ephemeral flight of autumn, and the dreariness of winter. Since the appearance of *Kokinshū*, people think that meekness has become the essence of poetry. It is a terrible mistake to believe that a poem with masculine strength is crude. One should always read *Man'yōshū* poetry to comprehend what it means to be masculine and strong. If you produce poetry that you feel resembles that of *Man'yōshū*, after many years surely this masculine melody will become etched in your heart.

The student should want to compose poetry like that in *Man'yōshū*, but few of the *maki* in the anthology contain carefully selected poems. Many of the *maki* are based on private collections, so there are some poor poems and poor poetic expressions. Therefore if one wishes to use *Man'yōshū* as his model, he should select fine poems with good poetic expressions. It is difficult to select fine poems, but one should select poems based on what I have said above about melody. Also, there are some poems where the first

1. Society generally looked down on this idea of strong and masculine traits hinted at by the *Kokinshū* compilers.

half is well done, but the concluding stanza is poor. One should learn from the beginning and discard the ending.

The Kamakura minister of the right[2] was very adept at this type of selection, so you should look through his work and study those poems. While I recommend this practice, the student should still read *Kokinshū*. This anthology is mainly composed of feminine poetry, but among the anonymous poetry, there are some from the Nara era, and there are some that have had their words exchanged with more contemporary ones. Even after the beginning of the Heian period, the first three emperors after the capital was removed still adhered to the ancient traditions, composing their poetry in that style. Thus, many of the anonymous poems in *Kokinshū* are very well done. Among poems composed at a later date, there are some that engage in minute variation of rhetoric and expression. The student should avoid these poems. Though these are all collections of poems, when one wishes to study the past, why do not people choose poems from among these collections? He should be careful.

After the student has come to this understanding,[3] he should read *Gosenshū*, *Shūishū*, *Kokin rokujō*, and the ancient tales. Then he should start back into the ancient past and read *Kojiki* and *Nihon shoki*. If the student has thoroughly studied the imperial edicts in *Shoku Nihongi*, and the liturgy in the *Engi shiki*, he will be able to compose not only poetry, but prose in the ancient tradition.

POETRY BY WOMEN

When women composed poetry, in fact, when women performed any thing in ancient times, they acted in a masculine manner. Thus, women's poetry in *Man'yōshū* is no different than that composed by the men. Well-composed poems naturally are gentle and this reflects the state of things. (This includes the masculine air of Ōtomo Sakanoe Iratsume[4] and the elegant style of Ishikawa Iratsume.[5])

---

2. Referring to Minamoto Sanetomo (1192–1219). He was the third Shōgun of the Kamakura Bakufu. He also compiled *Kinkai wakashū*, a collection of his private poetry. Sanetomo received a copy of *Man'yōshū* from Fujiwara Teika and appears to have been influenced by its poetry.

3. That he should not take the ancient standard uncritically as his own, but should be particular in every case.

4. Her dates are unknown. Ōtomo Sakanoe Iratsume was born to Saho Dainagon and was the younger sister of Tabito and aunt to Yakamochi.

5. From what we know about the *Man'yōshū* text, it becomes clear there was more than

This state occurs because the male is born through the violent nature of *kami*, while the female is born through the tender nature of *kami*.[6] This being the case, women of our country differ from women in other countries, for their lofty, straightforward feelings appear in *Man'yōshū*, but when they compose elegant poetry like that in *Kokinshū*, we should appraise such poetry as superb. The image of women originated from the foundation of our present capital [Kyōto].

Thus, there are poets who only rely on *Kokinshū* as their poetic model, but among these poems are many that are constricted. It has been the practice of people in later eras to do as they please in experimenting within this confined poetic sphere, and they have forgotten about the lofty, straightforward spirit of Yamato. The student should ponder upon this reciprocal relation, which resulted in the gradual decline of poetic quality, resulting in regrettable, lamentable practices. There are thousands of people who only imitate the poetry in *Kokinshū*.[7] If even one person did not produce poetry resembling that in *Kokinshū*, there would be no value in studying the later anthologies.

If students study poetry from the beginning and work forward chronologically there would be no problem. This mainly concerns poetry composed by women. I now address the female practices in the ancient imperial court. (With reverence we address her name) Izanami created our country and all other things in it along with the male *kami* [Izanagi]. Later they quarreled, and Izanami called the army of Yomi to arms and faced the male *kami* and severed their bond. Amaterasu Ōmikami also had problems [with her brother], and she put a quiver on her back and took a bow in her hand. She showed a masculine and intrepid air. Thus, she pacified the evil *kami*, and after having subdued him, she rectified all evil with her eyes and mouth. After this, she established the eternal state of imperial rule.

Kono Hana Sakuya Hime who was betrothed to the heavenly grandchild [Ninigi] set fire to her birthing hut and brought all secrets to light.[8]

---

one female poet named Ishikawa Iratsume. *Nihon kodai jinmei jiten* lists seven different people with the same name (Takeuchi et al. 1962, 1:164–65).

6. The myths contained in *Nihon shoki* show there were two types of *kami*: one was violent (*araburu*) and the other was gentle (*nikoyaka*).

7. Some texts have 幾十人 "twenty or thirty people." 幾千人 "Several thousands" is likely the original (cf., Yamamoto 1942, 2:938, note 26).

8. The myths record that Ninigi had mocked Kono Hana Sakuya Hime for getting pregnant so easily, so she set fire to her hut, a direct attempt at suicide with her sons, but this only proved that her children were the divine offspring of Ninigi. This is the "secret" she brought to light.

Emperor Suinin's empress did not come out of the burning castle of rice stalks, but let justice take its due course.[9] Emperor Okinaga Tarashi Hime [Jingū] subdued the three Han [in Korea], while Emperor Hirono [Jitō, r. 687–96] rendered assistance to the imperial army and acted meritoriously.[10] Tachibana Hime dove into the ocean as a proxy for Prince Yamato Takeru, while Princess Yamabe was punished along with her husband.

And during times of tranquility, Empress Hatahi used words of peace to soothe the anger of the savage Emperor [Nintoku], and Emperor Kōgyoku [r. 642–45) herself prayed and caused rain to fall. And while these events continued without fail, women desired to retain this influence. Concerning the commoner, a husband went at the head of his army of men, and the wife went at the head of her army of women and they both went to fight the enemy. Women even ruled their lands and did not participate in the crimes of others, and in other ways established the order of things. There are countless examples where women were honest. Even in later eras, there are more than just a few examples where a woman became the head of a household, and went out to avenge the death of her husband, though she was nothing more than a provincial maiden. Therefore, how could this spirit of Yamato weaken in women? One should never forget that a woman truly can become a person of military strategy.

In the ancient past of the imperial court, women were revered as the foundation of everything. Beginning with raising children, women were superior even to valiant fathers. Nevertheless, during times of tranquility, they generally concerned themselves with comforting others; however, following the example of the mother and father being heaven and earth, at times these women can be violent, but the words they speak are comforting.

These events are all true, but in later eras people made the mistake of thinking this meek trait was something to be used skillfully; furthermore, later people forgot the fundamental spirit of Yamato, because a once solemn trait had become twisted. Who would fail to obtain the true form of the ancients if he studied the poetry in *Man'yōshū*, came to an understanding of this essence, and then researched into *Kokinshū*? Ancient poetry is the true essence of the myriad people. When the student comprehends the meaning of this true essence, then what is beyond his grasp?

9. Her brother had rebelled against the court, and she decided to die with her brother to atone for the crime.

10. Meaning she fought alongside her husband, Emperor Tenmu, during the Jinshin Revolt.

There is a path of learning and people always want to study its precepts, but as time passes, it becomes a short path to foolishness. People compose poetry in their spare time and this is the honest, true essence that lacks training. This indeed is the awe-inspiring Way of our divine rulers.

PEOPLE IN LATER ERAS

People in later eras read *Man'yōshū*, and in spite of their faulty comprehension of the text, they attached interpretations that we now know do no justice to the original. Whether it be in Japan or China, everything is thought to have been better in the ancient past and ancient things appear to be more valuable. Where is there a place that abandons the past and people in later generations teach social customs? These [teachers] are people who know nothing, but put on airs to deceive the ignorant. A person may learn about various eras in the ancient past through reading histories, but even in these histories ancient events fail to be included, or are transmitted incorrectly, or are added later by someone, or are interpolations from Chinese literature. This obscures the ancient lexicon, making some things in the histories unacceptable.

When a poet correctly employs the vocabulary from ancient poetry, he finds that Akahito[11] and Hitomaro who lived a thousand years ago appear before his eyes and it is the same as if he were listening to the poem in the present. Ancient poetry brings antiquity to the immediate realm of understanding. First, poetry composed by ancient poets was produced according to natural events, and the poet did not hide his true feelings, so ancient poetry becomes a window to the soul of these people. By composing such poetry repeatedly, the student comes to an understanding of what constitutes the heart of the ancients.

Furthermore, in histories where the lexicon is recorded in a Chinese style there are many places where different meanings are possible, so a change in meaning within a poem with its restricted vocabulary robs the poem of its essence. Questioning this and pondering that, and then composing poetry allows the student to ascertain the ancient lexicon. Therefore, ancient poetry is a good vehicle to help the student understand the ancient lexicon. Though much occurs under the heavens, nothing actually

---

11. Some manuscripts have [Takechi] Kurohito. I have followed the manuscript with Akahito, because Akahito and Hitomaro are often grouped together. Mabuchi also groups them in his essay, "Man'yō kaitsūshaku to shakurei."

exists except essence and [verbal] expressions. When a student has understood the significance of these two, he will be able to comprehend the ancient meanings, after thoroughly researching into the ancient people and reading the ancient histories without falling into textual pitfalls.

Also, because later people indulged in the mistaken perception that *Man'yōshū* is poetry, and all poetry is an effort in playful experimentation, they could not comprehend the ancient poetry, nor did they know what was in the ancient works. They were coerced into reading Chinese works, and many people expounded upon the divine age with sophistry. Acting thus, the explication from these people equals a false logic and nothing these people say fits with the ancient Way of our imperial court.

First, the student must study ancient poetry and compose poetry in the ancient style. Then he must study ancient literature and produce prose in the ancient style. After this, he must peruse *Kojiki* and then *Nihon shoki*, and all histories after *Shoku Nihongi*. He then should read the regulations of the codes, the ceremonial rituals, and the various records (up to *Saigūki*, *Kitayamashō* and *Gōke shidai*). He should study works written in *kana* script, picking up ancient events and ancient words, pondering things like the ancient harp, flute, robes, and utensils. All other items can be researched from the ancient histories. When one has thoroughly studied the ancient era of the imperial court, then he can begin his study on the divine age. It is then that he is united with heaven and earth, governed by the ancient reigns, comprehending the ancient Way of the divine sovereigns.

THE ANCIENT LEXICON

It is imperative that the student ponders and elucidates the ancient lexicon, but elucidating the ancient vocabulary is difficult. First, the student must understand well the fifty sounds of the language. These disappeared in later eras and no one now is aware of them, so the student should peruse my work, *Goikō*,[12] and think about the division of words and their use. There are people who expound upon the fifty sounds of Japanese from the perspective of other countries' phonology, like *Xi tan* [Sanskrit] or *Yun jing* [Chinese rhyme book], but none of these works will lead to an understanding of our country. The student must realize how different the lexicon in our country is by composing poetry in the ancient style.

12. Some believe this to be a later interpolation, as *Niimanabi* is dated 1765, but *Goikō* was completed in 1769; however, it seems probable that *Goikō* (and other works) existed in some draft form years earlier.

Also, the student must consider the ancient phonetic script [*man'yōgana*]. Phonetic script is the basis for the ancient lexicon and through these phonetic graphemes one can elucidate the meaning of the words, but generally one needs to remember the phonetic principles exactly. This phonetic script starts with *Kojiki*, *Nihon shoki*, *Man'yōshū*, and other ancient records and continues unchanged until *Wamyōshō*.[13] When one reads these works, he will understand the principles.

After this period, mistakes appear in *Shūishū*. From this period on, the scholarship of the imperial court lost its plenary state. All attempts in later eras to use foreign phonology to expound upon the phonology of the imperial court are groundless.

THE CODES

The student should also study the administrative and penal codes. The imperial court created the codes based on the laws and penal codes of China, then adapted them to the customs of our country; though it can be said these codes do not reflect the general sentiment of the country, we understand that the Taihō codes were prepared according to the Ōmi codes,[14] and these have been the ways of society for a long time. Without a knowledge of the codes, there is no way to comprehend what happened in middle antiquity. The codes are strict and minutely detailed, constructed around the customs of China, something that appears good on the surface, but these are really evil underneath. Because of this, the authority of the crown later was usurped. Those who yearn for the ancient eras will not think it proper to study the codes, but if the student is to study later era historical records, he cannot proceed without first studying the codes.

THE TEN POETIC STYLES

Among the ten poetic styles established in later eras, the "clever and energetic" style (*kiryō*) is found in *Kokinshū*:

13. Mabuchi is correct that the essential system of *man'yōgana* continued until *Wamyōshō*, but the traditional system was in decay. With the collapse of the *kō-otsu* system of Old Japanese vowels, distinctions made in earlier works became confused. By the early tenth-century when *Wamyōshō* came about, the *kō-otsu* system had collapsed, and none of these earlier vocalic distinctions are preserved.

14. *Nihon shoki* records that the court of Tenji promulgated the Ōmi codes in 668, making them the first attempt to construct the government around the emperor, imitating a system in China; however, there are some scholars who doubt the veracity of the account in *Shoki*, as nothing concrete has survived other than the title.

mume no fana	We cannot even tell
sore tomo miyezu	what are plum blossoms
fisakata no	and what are not—
amagiru yuki no	Snowflakes have hidden them
nabete furereba	as a fog covers the sky.

[KKS 334]

This poem demonstrates the survival of the tradition of older poetry.[15] The poem was written by a person from the Nara era, and it has inherited the essence and melody of Hitomaro's poetry. This poem is not trying to delineate detailed emotions, but exhibits a lofty melody even as it displays a soaring, broad talent. There are many poems in *Kokinshū* about plum blossoms that sound interesting, but they conceal constricted emotions. The student should ponder this fact and grasp the loftiness of the hearts of people from the Nara era. And you should also consider the poetry by the Kamakura minister.

The power in Hitomaro's poetry is like a flying dragon, while his literary expressions are like the rushing of the tide. His melody resembles the twanging of the true bow of Sotsu Hiko of Katsuragi.[16] The vocabulary of Akahito includes "Like Yoshino River, clearly, my heart is like the base of Fuji." His poetry is unparalleled in its loftiness. Hitomaro is as different as heaven and earth from Akahito, but both poets composed splendid poetry in the ancient past. There were other poets before Hitomaro who had superb poetry, but since their names were not recorded in the anthologies, I will not elaborate upon them here.

THE POETRY OF THE KAMAKURA MINISTER

The poetry composed by the Kamakura minister is the best among poets who appeared after the capital was established in the present city [Kyōto]. His poetic style reflects that of antiquity, and though he sometimes employs vocabulary from the era of *Kokinshū*, it does not resemble "Kokin poetry." We thus know that the essence of the poem and its melody are splendid and lofty. He composed such poems as:

---

15. A note after the poem in *Kokinshū* says, "Some say this poem was composed by Kakinomoto Hitomaro." This, however, is nothing but a legend.

16. Sotsu Hiko is a legendary figure, the son of the famed Takeshi Uchi. Sotsu Hiko is famed for his military adventures in Korea. This has reference to MYS 2639.

fakonedi wo	When I passed over
ware koekureba	the road of Hakone …
	[KKWS 593]

mononofu no	The warrior mends
yanami tukurofu	the shafts of his arrows.
	[KKWS 348]

He has composed so many wonderful poems that I will not say more. A person listens tranquilly to such poems like:

kono nenuru	On this sleepless dawn,
asake no kaze ni	wisps of scented beauty
kaforu nari	waft on the morning breeze.
kiba no ume no	The plum tree by my eaves
faru no fatu fana	has started to blossom.
	[KKWS 35]

tamamo karu	The fence by the well,
wi de no sigarami	as if harvesting gemweed,
faru kakete	lets spring pass to summer.
saku ya kafabe no	The yellow rose is in bloom,
yamabuki no fana	the one by the river bank.
	[KKWS 115]

These show an older, original state of poetry. The poet uses everyday mundane occurrences in his poetry, but observes the loftiness of the rhythm in the final stanzas. And observe the beginning of a poem titled "Dreary Rain on Plum Blossoms":

wa ga yado no	The plum tree by my house
ume no fana sakeri	is now in full bloom.
farusame fa	Spring rains, I beg of you
itaku na furi so	not to fall on my blossoms,
tiramaku mo wosi	and scatter their beauty.
	[KKWS 36]

Considering when he composed this poem, poets at court in that era all had constricted emotions and used skill and logic in their verse. And the reader gets a natural impression that the Kamakura minister looked down on the poetry at that time and wanted to show others the merits of the ancient style. Poets who did not have this masculine nature found it hard to go against, or distance themselves from the skillful poetry of poets before them. The student should ponder the reason for this, because the feelings of the ancients could not stretch that far. There are everyday deeds in this life, and there is no distinction between elite or common in the Way of scholarship.

Poets examined the good from good poets in the past and waited to call such things good [in their era], but since there were no such people in later eras, there were no people who made the ancient poets their friends. Remember that a fence sitter will never praise something that is indeed good.

KOKINSHŪ

Kokinshū is mainly a collection of feminine poetic styles, but there indeed are many ancient poems included, and as I have stated already, the anthology does include some emotionally lofty and masculine poems. All poems the student selects should have such a lofty essence. One should not argue about *Gosenshū* being inferior compared to *Kokinshū* on the same day. Even when the *Gosenshū* compiler has included ancient poems, there are many mistakes. And what person compiled *Shūishū*? The compiler has especially erred when quoting *Man'yōshū* poetry, and it is difficult to count all the mistakes where the poetry of ancient poets has been misquoted.

Nevertheless, these two anthologies appearing after the Engi era [901–23] when the capital was moved to its present location do contain good poems, and the student should spend some time looking at them. And though *Kokin rokujō* has misquoted many *Man'yōshū* poems, there are some gentle poems.[17] The topics in *Kokin rokujō* are indeed pleasant. The topic of "Thought (*omofu*)" in the miscellaneous section where the poetry uses the word *omofu* is interesting. Later era people read the topics in Chinese, making the poetry stuffy and trifling. The same poem if written in *kana* script spontaneously becomes productive and elegant.

The words in the headnote of a poem are well thought out in *Kokinshū*, and the words of the headnote and the poem itself complement each other, making comprehension easier. The standard for the language of a headnote should be to use interesting but short phrases and keep the message lucid. Writing the same idea in a headnote [as in the poem] makes it long and

17. A careful inspection of *Man'yō* poems quoted in *Kokin waka rokujō* clearly demonstrates that there is more going on in *Rokujō* than a simple misquoting of poetry.

tedious. The student should divide the poem into upper and lower groups, and avoid including ideas found in the poem in the headnote. Ponder upon the flow of the words, because this is one form of text.

There are two kinds of texts: one includes many ideas compressed into one expression, and the other has little to say, so it employs beautiful language to give it substance. The text that compressed and used beautiful language displays the elegance of the ancient era, but by middle antiquity this trait had declined. Down to the present era, we find that everything is mistaken. The student should learn how to compose concise sentences with beautiful language. The language in a headnote should not be ornate but as concise as possible, while remaining true to its role as an explanatory statement. A look inside the anthologies shows how difficult this task is, for there are few headnotes that flawlessly achieve their goal.

CHŌKA

The student should continue to study a large amount of *chōka* [long poetry]. There are many in *Kojiki* and *Nihongi*, but the poetic work that deals with various styles of long poetry is *Man'yōshū*. The student should look through the various styles and learn each. We laud *tanka* [short poetry] for its lofty essence and rich melody, so you cannot compose *tanka* unless you are careful with the words you use. Among the various styles of *chōka*, worthy ones are powerful, antique, and elegant. On this traditional poetry has imitated this old style, and the trend in *tanka* to write with provincial air comes from this *chōka* tradition, giving us poetry that sometimes is old and interesting.

In the ancient era, when a person was filled with thoughts he composed *chōka*. The poet also composed many *tanka* in a burst and this act soothed his heart. Later generations tried to compress complex emotions into a single poem, but like a hunter who crams too many provisions into a small sack, the poem exhibits a vulgar character and the melody is not worthy of being called poetry.

THE PREFATORY ODE STYLE

The student should also study the prefatory ode [*jokotoba*] style. It was the intent of the ancients that various ideas be expressed in the beginning as a foundation, and only one idea be used at the end as a concluding thought.

The stanzas of *sedōka* comprise a 5-7-7 syllabic structure in the beginning, and end with another 5-7-7 pattern. You may know this is true because *Man'yōshū* contains over one hundred poems composed in this style. The concept of this kind of poetry now found in *Kokinshū* as a model is a corruption. There is a poem comprising the stanzas *wotikata fito ni / mono mawosu / ware* "I address a question / to the person from far away / I" as the foundation and ending with *sono soko ni. ...* "close to you" [KKS 1007].

Also, the next poem has the same problem, using *miredo akanu / fana* (no matter how often I view them, I never tire / of the blossoms) as the foundation and *mafinasi ni. ...* "I have no way to repay the flowers" as the conclusion [KKS 1008].

LITERARY TEXTS

Literary texts have two styles, a masculine and a feminine. First, masculine texts are serious, court works and the student must study these to excel. Reading *Kojiki*, *Nihongi*, *Man'yōshū*, the imperial edicts, the liturgies, and other ancient records is no different than what I have said about composing poetry. Among these works, *Kojiki* is a truly Japanese record.[18] *Nihon shoki* also contains the original Japanese traditions. Many of the ancient records compiled in the Nara era are translations in classical Chinese and the ancient reading has been lost. Only about a third of the original remains. Later scribes wrote the reading in interlinear script, but these are not the original readings.

For example, "became possessed and spoke divine words" is read *kamugakari*.[19] Also, "oh, how to drink that sweet *sake*" is read *umara ni wo yarafuru kawa*.[20] The student should understand that neither of these is the

18. It seems that Mabuchi says this in comparison with *Nihon shoki*, which is written completely in Chinese. Sadly, this distinction of Mabuchi, and inherited by Norinaga, is somewhat misleading, because *Kojiki* is actually written in a hybrid form of Chinese with a large amount of phonetic script.

19. In the first book of *Nihon shoki*, Ame no Uzume dances before the cave, where the sun goddess had hidden herself. The text has, "Ceremonial fires were lit, a tub was inverted, and Ame no Uzume became possessed and spoke divine words" (cf. Ienaga et al. 1967, 1:112).

20. These are ceremonial words seen in the opening story of Kenzō; cf. Ienaga et al. 1967, 1:512. Mabuchi has the reading as *umara ni woyarafuru kaneya*. Textual criticism has shown that Mabuchi's *ne* is an abbreviated character for *wa* (cf. Ienaga et al. 1967, 1:651, n. 5). The *ya* is a ghost character used as a copula.

ancient [original] reading.[21] The ancient imperial edicts and liturgies are genuine, archaic texts. Once the student has acquired knowledge of the literary qualities of these texts, then he should use them in all writing.

The student should also use the *chōka* style found in *Man'yōshū*, comprehending the ancient lexicon, experimenting with poetry like that of Hitomaro. The style in this poetry where words are strung together is no different from that in a literary text. Descending through time, we find there are ancient textual fragments contained in *kana* works like *Ise monogatari*, so the student should select his models from a wide range of texts. However, if you select your words recklessly, you will confuse ancient words with those of a newer era [like Heian], and this produces worthless sentences. The production of ancient sentences depends on the interpretation of selected words, but you can review this after you have made your selection. And you will find remnants of ancient words in the speech of people from the provinces. If you are careful in your selection, your sentences will have ancient words as its core.

There are writers who use the vocabulary of *Genji monogatari*, but this is a feminine text, being a tale. It is not suitable to include this style within the ancient, serious works. The student should seriously consider this distinction. The preface to *Kokinshū* is a construct, failing to find the original, ancient meaning of poetry composed at our imperial court. The author describes the essence of Japanese poetry using the style of Tang poetics, borrowing the poetic theory of Chinese verse.

Poetry composed with a model that is based on verse written with a feminine air will result in a poem with some pleasant phrases, but many mistakes. Therefore, you will find this is not the ancient state of poetry. And though the same person [who wrote the *Kokinshū* preface] wrote *Tosa nikki*, this text is superior to his preface. He wrote in a powerful manner, writing down things just as they occurred.

Now you know there are various styles in the writing of literary texts. If the student carefully examines texts from *Kojiki* till the liturgies, he will come to a natural understanding. Feminine literature is an improvement on the ancient style, for some have taken the ancient texts, and imitated them in a feminine air. If a woman enters into this study and imitates *Genji monogatari*, she will naturally be able to compose in that style; however,

---

21. Most scholars now believe these interlinear readings to be exceptionally old. Linguistic work has shown that most, if not all, of these readings are indeed authentic, though the Chinese characters selected to represent the Old Japanese syllables are quite innovative in *Nihon shoki*.

the student should not think this alone is sufficient. The student should search further into the past. If you learn the finer points of these styles, in the end you will compose proper prose. If people from far-off provinces join in this study and want to know more, the finer details cannot be fully explained. When a student reads the ancient corpus with the attitude of wanting to learn about the ancient Way, and composes poetry and prose with this same attitude, and receives answers to his questions, there will not be a single student who fails to reach a clear understanding.

There are commentaries dealing with all the ancient works. If the student understands these and puts forth the effort himself, then he will naturally come to an understanding. Nevertheless, the commentaries about the various schools of thought in the present era are based on a specific tradition, so you must be honest with yourself, realizing that you cannot get there alone without asking questions. It is easier to reach an understanding of these works by suppressing your emotions.

Written by Kamo no Mabuchi on the sixteenth day of the seventh month of Meiwa 2 [1765].

[NST 39:358–68]

ᘓ

NIIMANABI IKEN

Kagawa Kageki | 1811

[Kageki wrote a rebuttal to Mabuchi's *Niimanabi*, writing his own *iken* "objections." Much like Norinaga valued *Shin Kokinshū* over *Man'yōshū*, Kageki argues that *Kokinshū* and its display of sincerity was a better model for students to use than *Man'yōshū*, which Mabuchi had argued for. Kageki is aligned, however, with Mabuchi and Norinaga in arguing for an authentic emotion from the poet, and not one written from a poet who puts on airs.]

The work *Niimanabi* [by Mabuchi] states, "Ancient poetry mainly concerned itself with melody. This is because ancient poetry was originally sung vocally."

I, Kageki, believe there is no special reason for poetic melody being set other than it originating from *magokoro* [the true heart]. Poetry produced from *magokoro* was just a form of the universal melody of heaven and earth. And as the wind produces sound by striking objects, there is nothing that cannot be sung with an orderly melody if sung with sincerity. The same can be said for clouds and water. When clouds appear in the sky, they climb upward like waves, or they hang downward like drooping blossoms, or they spread outward like the scarf of a woman, or pile upward like a mountain peak. When water runs downward, the surface becomes rough, producing patterns; when the water comes to a deep spot, the water turns a deep blue; when it freezes over it appears like a mirror; when the water is violent and sprays upward, the surging energy produces white jewels. Thus, clouds and water are able to change a thousand ways, forming hundreds of variations, but none of them take shape because of any volition of the object. The clouds are blown about by the wind, and the rivers bend and shift due to the nature of the land. Poetic expression is much the same. A song produced in a short breath we label *tanka*, while a long-winded song is *chōka*; the variations come from the different ways we are impressed from visual and auditory stimuli. This great variation in expression is due to the various ways in which human emotions come into contact with objects. And just like a song naturally possesses its own melody, if a person has to work at a poem, adding various ornamentation, and yet cannot acquire a high degree of artistic melody, then it is because the person's heart lacks mental sincerity and genuine beauty. And that is why ancient poetry had a natural beauty to its melody. It is a great mistake to think that the poet consciously arrived at this melody. It may appear to the reader that there is only a subtle difference between the author of *Niimanabi* and myself, but because of an intrinsic difference, there is no way of getting around the tremendous problem this difference brings up. Also, the idea that ancient poetry was "sung vocally" means that the poet lengthened the words, drawing them out, and creating a melody, thus differing from the contemporary idea of singing to a tune. The original meaning of *utafu* is most likely to expel one's breath in a long, strong fashion through puckered lips. And the word *utafe* "to bring forth a lawsuit" used in relation to governmental officials shows that one is giving voice to depressing feelings within one's heart. Here *utafe* means to heave a deep sigh.[1] And the practice of calling the cry of a chicken *utafu* is also because the animal's voice is long and drawn out. When something occurs in society, we call the act of causing an uproar *yo ni utafaru*. This is likely a fragment of this original ancient word. Therefore, when one wishes to sing, he expels the pent-up feelings in his heart by drawing out his voice, so it is only natural that we call this action *utafu*.

Because we have become accustomed to labeling "singing" something consciously produced from middle antiquity on, we naturally think of something with a melody attached. But this is thinking about the word backwards, looking at original meaning and derivation in the wrong order. If we look at singing as something done with a melody, that is only one form that appeared later. We cannot call this the original meaning of *utafu*. Even in ancient times, not all poems had beautiful rhythms, notwithstanding they originated from sincere feelings stimulated by some sensation. Because of this, the current usage of *yomu* "produce poetry" is an accurate representation of the ancient word *utafu*. Naturally, ancient usages of *yomu* contained the same meaning.

Thus, because of these reasons, it is a mistake to believe *Niimanabi* in thinking that anciently all verse (*uta*) was sung vocally.

> *Niimanabi* says, "Generally speaking, the melody of poetry was tranquil, clear, pure, and slightly melancholy; a variety of human emotions produced numerous melodies, but the common factor among all these was that the poetry was lofty and straightforward. A sense of elegance exists within this loftiness, while a feeling of masculinity underlies its straightforwardness."

---

1. Kageki is proposing a common etymological source with *utafu* "to sing" and *utafe* "to sue." Nevertheless, the evolution for the verb "to sue" is *urutafu* > *uttafu* > *utafu*, making Kageki's theory implausible.

My rebuttal. I believe that the variations mentioned in the line, "generally speaking, the melody of poetry was tranquil, clear" represents the changes in the four seasons of heaven and earth, a product of the natural rhythm of the life of nature. The author's statement concerning a sense of loftiness and straightforwardness being intertwined into these representations means that the mental state of people anciently was unornamented and sincere. I will attach my own opinions later.

> *Niimanabi* continues, "The reason for stating this is because heaven and earth—which are the father and mother of everything—are divided into spring, summer, autumn, and winter. Everything the earth has created is divided into these four seasons; one can divide things into these four classifications, and the melody of the singer is the same. Also, each season does not have completely peculiar traits, spring overlapping with summer and autumn overlapping with winter. Resembling the actual state of the seasons, there are melodies borrowed from two different variations. Though there are many varieties, each variety has its own excelling rhythmical song."

My rebuttal. I believe that when we look at this theory of poetic melody based upon the movement of nature, changing like the four seasons, it appears as if the author has understood what I said above. Nevertheless, this is because he is only superficially following logic, and no doubt has never had any real experience with what he is telling us. This is because there are inconsistencies in his overall theory. Though the argument is of high quality, it is only a theory that is not based upon personal experience. He is trying to grasp voices or shadows.

This kind of ambiguous exposition is very confusing to new students. How can an enigmatic work like this serve as a manual to new students?[2] Because of this anxiety, we must add a few clarifying opinions.

> *Niimanabi* states, "Therefore, to come to an understanding of the ancient state of life, when one experiences the structure of ancient poetry, we come to see that the ancient capital in the province of Yamato was masculine in nature, and women followed the style of men. Thus, the poetry in *Man'yōshū* is for the most part masculine in nature. The next era, when the capital was in the province of Yamashiro was feminine in nature, and men followed the style of women. That is why most of the poetry in *Kokinshū* is written in a feminine style."

---

2. As Kageki criticizes, the title *niimanabi* means "those who are studying for the first time," or a manual for new students.

My rebuttal. I think that we cannot say that this theory about a masculine capital in Yamato and a feminine capital in Yamashiro was shocking when Mabuchi announced it, but that on the surface it really appears to be so—society was persuaded by his theory. However, if this was actually true, then logically it follows that the province of Yamato should still be masculine, and anciently Yamashiro out of necessity would originally have been feminine. So why is it that anciently both Yamato and Yamashiro were masculine and later both provinces became feminine? It is very curious. The next problem is in seeing strong and firm as masculine and elegant and innocent as feminine. This is because the era of *Man'yōshū* was simple and unornamented while the era of *Kokinshū* was elegant and innocent. The reason for this is in the transition of time. It is not something we can expound upon from the point of view of the peculiarities of one province. The trend toward a refreshing style was a natural movement, leading the hearts of men in the direction of elegance. We may label this as the courtly style. Also, the trend toward a masculine style is naturally due to the unornamented, simple nature of people at the time, and we may label it the provincial style. And this is the true state of men's hearts in every era in that a natural melody is found without any conscious involvement. Therefore, if this represents the true state of the people's minds, then a style without ornamentation cannot be selected over a style with ornamentation. Each era has its own characteristics in style, and within a masculine-dominated era, poetry produced by women will still be feminine in nature, and within an elegantly dominated era, poetry produced by men will be masculine in nature; the two forms of poetry will not be the same. Therefore, when arguing about the poetic styles in *Kokinshū*, it is very misleading to argue by comparing men and women. This type of argument should be avoided. I will deal with this problem a little later.

> *Niimanabi* says, "And when debating about the six styles in *Kokinshū*, I judge the peaceful and refreshing style as superior."

My rebuttal. This statement comes from the *Kokinshū* preface where it says, "Archbishop Henjō masters style but is deficient on substance."[3] The preface, however, was debating the six poetic masters, and degraded this poem for being short on substance but praised it for being full of poetic

3. Compare McCullough (1985:7). Henjō (816–90) is a well-known poet who took Buddhist vows after the passing of Emperor Ninmyō [r. 833–50). He was a grandson of Emperor Kanmu. He is well known for having exchanged poetry with Ono no Komachi. He is known as one of the six poetic sages.

expression. It does not necessarily mean that Henjō became the model for others to follow. Therefore, Tsurayuki, is not saying that the other five poetic masters were criticized for their style. Thus, the other five poetic masters had their own style. And there is a reason the preface noted Henjō for being superior in poetic expression. The reader may find the answer in reading his poetry. There is a clean feeling in Henjō's style, but it is not tranquil or refreshing. We cannot say confidently that the theory about ancient poetry being masculine with later poetry feminine is correct. On the other hand, we also cannot state strongly that this theory is mistaken.[4] So the theory in *Niimanabi* is short on evidence, and I have addressed the issues accordingly.

> *Niimanabi* states, "The reason the *Kokinshū* preface says that the provincial style is strong and masculine is …"

My rebuttal. This view from *Niimanabi* hints at such lines in the *Kokinshū* preface like, "Fun'ya Yasuhide's language is skillful, but his style is inappropriate to his content. His poems are like peddlers tricked out in fancy costumes" or "The style of Ōtomo no Kuronushi's poems is crude."[5] First, it is a terrible mistake to misinterpret the *Kokinshū* preface as stating that Fun'ya's style was vulgar. The preface is stating that Fun'ya's poetical tone is excessive and not fitting for the subject he composed on; it does not mean that the poem itself is vulgar. Mabuchi based his interpretation in *Niimanabi* upon the simile about the peddler, and the old theory as stated in the Mana preface that Fun'ya's style is *almost* vulgar. Therefore, the Kana preface meant that only Kuronushi's poetry was vulgar. Now, Kuronushi's poetry resembles Henjō's in that his verse lacks substance, though these poetic expressions of the two poets are far from related. Kuronushi's poetry truly has a vulgar ring to it. *Niimanabi*'s criticism that this kind of poetry is strong and firm is not completely off the mark, but it is absurd to add Yasuhide's skillful verse to this classification. *Niimanabi*'s theory is not saying that the poem fits with the poetic substance, or that there is any consciousness of poetic style; however, Mabuchi criticized these poems according to precedence from poetic criticism in ages past. In the ancient past[6] everything was simple and sincere, and when those poets in the thriving Heian

4. Kageki's main complaint is that Mabuchi is making over-generalizations in his division of poetic styles, erasing any and all individuality in the poetry.

5. Both quotes are from McCullough (1985:7).

6. Pointing to Mabuchi's favorite topic, the Nara era or the era of *Man'yōshū*.

era looked back upon this earlier era, they found many customs, acts, and ideas the ancient people engaged in that appeared vulgar to them, whether it be imperial excursions or the building of imperial palaces. Thus, it is only reasonable to assume that these people would view poetry from that same era in a similar light. And definitely there is a certain vulgarity in the poetic language of these ancient poems, but we have no evidence to claim that the emotional substance of these poems is vulgar. The criticism that these poems are vulgar is the product of a later era, based upon the standards of later-era poetics. The poets did not view this ancient poetry as vulgar when they wrote it. And though the poetry of the poetic masters of the ancient era sometimes stumbles into vulgarity, this is because the style of that era was simple and straightforward. The reason that poets considered Kuronushi's poetry to be crass though he wrote it in a period of prosperity is because his style is not suitable to the style of his day compared with other poets of ancient times.

Thus, Kuronushi's vulgarity is very different from the vulgarity of more ancient poets. Recite poems from both periods and the reader will see why. For example, vulgarity from the ancient past is like saying that winter is cold, an actual, simple feeling, showing how sincere and straightforward the poet is. Vulgarity in Kuronushi's poetry is in that he would say that summer is cold, a base expression unworthy of the poetic style of his day. The expression of "cold" is common between both, but the reader is conscious of the difference between the substances of both poems.

> *Niimanabi* says, "Poets in the present place and time think that the current style is ideal, and they do not even attempt a broad study of the poetic styles of the ancients."

My rebuttal. How can one deny his own present tradition and pick some earlier tradition as his model? Also, the author mentions "a broad study of the poetic styles of the ancients," but the *Kokinshū* preface argues about the far-off era of the *kami* as, "The syllables in each poem were irregular, the poetry simple in so much that it must have been difficult to understand what the poet meant." And the preface describes past eras closer to their own as the era when "Kakimoto no Hitomaro was a poetic sage." We also see, "There was another man, Yamabe no Akahito, who was also an extraordinary poet."[7] The preface also adds, "Other superior poets also became famous in each of the reigns that followed one another like the

7. Compare McCullough (1985:6).

spaces between joints of black bamboo."[8] Is this not what the author of *Niimanabi* is pointing to? And we can tell that Hitomaro and Akahito were highly revered because Tsurayuki praised them as "poetic sages."

> *Niimanabi* states, "Now, though there are changes in everything like the four seasons, *Kokinshū*, following the mood of its preface, places value only on spring with its elegance, and discards summer and winter; it values the feminine element while avoiding the masculine."

My rebuttal. It is natural that poetic substance and emotion should differ from poet to poet. But that is not why the preface criticizes the differences in the six poetic masters starting with Hitomaro and Akahito; is not the preface pointing out the strengths and weaknesses of each poet? And within the actual text of *Kokinshū* itself, do we not see such diversified styles as *haikai*, and ancient songs like folk songs?[9] Not only that, but there are also many poems from the Nara era itself. *Kokinshū* is not an anthology selected from only elegant poems. The style of *Kokinshū* differs from *Man'yōshū* because of the difference in the style of the era, and this has nothing to do with the intentions of the compilers. Also, the reason this author [Mabuchi] thinks the compilers did not pick anything but pure and refined poetry is because he does not really understand *Kokinshū*, taking Henjō as the basis for his argument. Being particular to strong and firm poetry is equal to revering masculine over feminine, and treasuring only the raw and cold feelings of winter, discarding spring and autumn. There is an inconsistency here, because the author is actually advocating a balance between the poetry like the four seasons.

> *Niimanabi* says, "Now, in the era when successive rulers made Yamato their capital, the emperor ruled the country. The emperor showed courageous authority on the surface, but underneath was generous and gentle. Because of this, Imperial reigns rolled on, and the prosperity of the state increased, the common man generally respected and honored his rulers, being straightforward and sincere, which disposition [of the common man] continued for generations. After the court removed the capital to the province of Yamashiro, the authority of the august emperor gradually declined, and the commoner was flattered by the change, and their disposition worsened. Why do people think this occurred? The reason is because the people in the capital located in Yamashiro did not accept the tradition of the masculine disposition common in the Yamato era, but acquired an

8. Ibid.
9. Seen at the beginning of Book 20 of *Kokinshū*.

> affinity for feminine things. Add to this the popularity of Chinese learning, and the common people lost their respect for their rulers, and an increasingly wicked disposition only worsened.
>
> "Therefore, everything in the world is lacking, because we have lost the true variation of the four seasons, the elegance of spring, the strength of summer, the ephemeral flight of autumn, and the dreariness of winter."

My rebuttal. The main problem brought up in this paragraph of *Niimanabi* generally has to do with the government of the emperor, so I will withhold my criticism for a moment. Naturally, I have no knowledge concerning political matters, but intend to give criticism only in relation to problems with poetics. Relative to poetry or even politics, however, the fundamental principle has not changed in the past or the present. This position of mine still allows for a person to say that later periods were more superior in poetical composition than the ancient past, and when comparing the past with later eras, the great amount of weaknesses in later poetry is also apparent; this is the norm for the transition of time. A person who gazes at something from a far distance realizes that some things have not changed from the past while others have become superior to the past. A person who gazes at an object from a close distance easily overlooks those aspects that have not changed since the ancient past, only taking issue with those parts that are not as superior as those in the past.

> *Niimanabi* goes on to say, "Since the appearance of *Kokinshū*, people think that meekness has become the essence of poetry. It is a terrible mistake to believe that a poem with masculine strength is crude."

My rebuttal. This idea of "masculine strength" apparently refers to poetry that is strong and simple. It is natural and logically sound to say that something simple and unornamented is *crude*. Why should that be a mistake? Arguing from the point of view that men are simple and sincere and women are gentle and meek, thus, men are honorable and women are base is a confusing way to argue and only misleads the new student. Therefore, to use well-known antonyms like firm and supple, or covert and overt leaves the argument ambiguous, so we conclude that the author is forced to contrast men and women. Nonetheless, I will move away from the man-woman motif and give another example to clarify what the author of *Niimanabi* is trying to say.

We may feel that the figure of a high court noble standing with his formal robes is weak and crude, while the same person arrayed in his suit of armor with sword and spear appears strong and respectable. Yet, that kind of concrete logic does not exist.

> *Niimanabi* states, "One should always read *Man'yōshū* to comprehend what it means to be masculine and strong. If you produce poetry that you feel resembles that of *Man'yōshū*, after many years surely this masculine melody will become etched in your heart."

My rebuttal. This is an extremely mistaken concept. Poetry is a melody naturally springing forth from within the emotions of a person. Since there is no room for the poet to introduce intellect into this natural melody, he cannot produce poetry in an intellectual manner. If one has composed poetry in imitation of another poet, then he has done nothing but produce a fraud. Even if one tries to compose poetry in imitation of an ancient poem, the product will still not resemble the ancient poem. It is reckless to compose a poem in imitation of an old one, and then believe that the copy resembles the original. First off, poetic melody originates from within the action of life of the universe and while it undergoes change, it becomes each poetic style of that era. There, also, is a form of melody inherent in each individual person. Each person has certain poetic characteristics, much like the variation in each person's face. Though we may say that each person's poetic melody is somewhat different, a poet cannot pull himself away from his generation's poetical style. If we make an allegory of this situation in relation to textiles, then each person's individual poetic traits are like the warp on a loom, and the thoughts and feelings at the time are the woof. The poet weaves his poetry according to the natural melody within all of us. At times one will weave a high grade of cloth, and at others a poor grade. And though there are variations, these all belong to that era's poetic style; even if one weaves a superior quality of brocade, or a coarsely woven cloth, they are all woven according to the style of that period. Therefore, poetic style is a private affair that cannot be altered. Even if a poet were able to imitate ancient poetry ingeniously, it is something that cannot be done.[10] Thus, mixing poetic composition with the Chinese ideal of producing verses to assist in governing a troubled country in transition is a very mistaken notion. If a country has a style like a so-called feminine disposition, then the delicate poetry produced would surely be a product of the true melody of the universe. In this state, demanding that a person compose in a masculine tone or wishing to imitate poetry in *Man'yōshū* is to teach something contradictory to truth, muddying up the true feelings from which sincere poetry emanates. How terrifying that thought is! If one

10. Thus, like a loom, one can vary the woof, but the warp is already set on the machine, unchangeable. Kageki is saying that Mabuchi's idea of changing one's entire poetic structure is impossible, and it is absurd to try.

had followed those instructions and had composed that sort of poetry for many years, he would unknowingly enter into a distant world of emptiness, losing his true soul, transformed into the insane poetry he had produced. He would feel as though he were listening to some foreign tongue.

Poetry is feeling an emotion immediately upon composing the poem. It is not tilting one's head while pondering, nor searching for an expression. Therefore, a teacher should not mislead the listener. Contemporary poetry should be composed in current language using the style of the present. But since there is an inherent difference between poets, some poetry is naturally going to resemble the Man'yō style, Kokin style, or any number of other styles; however, the poet is not able to step outside his modern poetical style, so the poems he produces will vary from the styles in the age of *Man'yōshū* and *Kokinshū*, being naturally a part of the modern style. The characteristics of the present poetic style will be made clear when the next era comes and those future poets look back on our era.

> *Niimanabi* records, "The student should want to compose poetry like that in *Man'yōshū*, but few of the *maki* in the anthology contain carefully selected poems. Many of the *maki* are based on private collections, so there are some poor poems and poor poetic expressions. Therefore, if one wishes to use *Man'yōshū* as his model, he should select fine poems with good poetic expressions. It is difficult to select fine poems, but one should select poems based on what I have said above about melody. Also, there are some poems where the first half is well done, but the concluding stanza is poor. One should learn from the beginning and discard the ending. The Kamakura minister of the right was very adept at this type of selection, so you should look though his work and study those poems."

My rebuttal. As I have said above, poetry is only a vehicle for the expression of a person's emotions. Thus, poems a student may use as his model do not exist. Also, the Kamakura minister of the right's poetic collection is absolutely unnecessary reading for anyone interested in poetic composition. Also, his poems do not demand the attention one would wish a student to imitate. The reason for respecting and reading old poetry is because the expressions have sprung up from sincere emotions, and since a certain period's human and social state are also clearly visible from the poetry, one need not be taught about the warmth or peaceful nature of humans; it is not difficult to learn these things from reading the poetry. When a person produces poetry himself, he is able to compose the poetry without any pretense, like the poets of old. On the other hand, people like the Kamakura minister of the right stole the melody of a poem from another work, robbing an old poem of a stanza. Upon seeing the new poem, one person will honor it as verse resembling those from the era of the Fujiwara or Heijō Palace, while another will despise it as a fraudulent representation of human emotion. It is fine for the one person to despise the poem, but the person who reveres the poem will have many evils awaiting him. This is something that a person must be aware. If one thinks like those in contemporary schools of thought who imitate Chinese poetry like the ancient Japanese who discarded their own tradition, then we have surely committed a great error.

> *Niimanabi* further states, "While I recommend this practice, the student should still read *Kokinshū*. This anthology is mainly composed of feminine poetry, but among the anonymous poetry, there are some from the Nara era, and there are some that have had their words exchanged with more contemporary ones. Even after the beginning of the Heian period, the first three emperors after the capital was removed still adhered to the ancient traditions, composing their poetry in that style. Thus, many of the anonymous poems in *Kokinshū* are very well done. Among poems composed at a later date, there are some that engage in minute variation of rhetoric and expression. The student should avoid these poems. Though these are all collections of poems, when one wishes to study the past, why do not people choose poems from among these collections?"

My rebuttal. The reason that *Kokinshū* poetry is concerned with minute expressions of human emotions is because that was one of the characteristics of the time, so it naturally turned out that way. This type of minutely emotional poetry is very much different from the poetry composed by those scholars of poetics[11] who try to construct the melody of their poetry consciously. These old complicated poems are natural and their complexity is proper [as that was the characteristic of the times]. It is not the same if a trained poet composes a complex poem using simple emotions. Poetry contained in *Kokinshū*—be it minute or complicated—was written from *magokoro* and accurately reflects that disposition. And as I have said above, a person definitely should not imitate ancient poetry nor the customs and ways of the ancient people. And one should not encourage a person to imitate or discard certain poems from among the poetic anthologies. One should study and enjoy the overall characteristics of *Kokinshū*. There is nothing as foul as discarding one's true emotions, and composing poetry in imitation of some ancient poetical style.

---

11. People such as Mabuchi.

> *Niimanabi* goes on, "After the student has come to this understanding, he should read *Gosenshū*, *Shūishū*, *Kokin rokujō* and the ancient tales. Then he should start back into the ancient past and read *Kojiki* and *Nihon shoki*. If the student has thoroughly studied the imperial edicts in *Shoku Nihongi*, and the liturgy in the *Engi shiki*, he will be able to compose not only poetry, but prose in the ancient tradition."

My rebuttal. It is natural that a person who wishes to engage in scholarship should read the works the author listed above. Nevertheless, as I have already stated, as far as the composition of poetry is concerned, reading these works is fruitless. Prose mainly concerns itself with the transmission of ideas, while the main concern of poetry is expression of deep emotions. To give an example, prose is the blossom and poetry is the fragrance. One can explain the shape of the blossom, but he cannot explain the fragrance. The student must keep in mind that this is the major difference between the two. Also, prose has a style varying from era to era, and this will naturally be clear to the student if he will read these works starting with the imperial edicts, religious liturgy, prose accompanying certain poems in the successive poetic anthologies, later tales, diaries, and traveling diaries.

After the student has come to the understanding that ancient culture was built on the characteristics of a certain old period, then that person should try to reconstruct and study that ancient culture with the understanding that the present culture is a representation of all that exists in the present. The main object of ancient prose and contemporary prose, however, is merely to illuminate clearly an idea, so there would be nothing but contradictions if one were to ask someone in the present to compose prose in the ancient tradition by collecting ancient words that he does not understand. There is probably no one who understands this. Therefore, one must not even think of discarding contemporary prose and composing in the ancient fashion. There is no precedent for this,[12] and there is no good reason for starting now. But prose is different from poetry in that the student may add intellectual creations to the expressions of one's heart. Regardless of the content that one is writing, or the subject he is addressing, prose is the natural result when a person sits down to write. The student should learn about styles in prose, and while he studies, he must be careful. Even if one tries to abandon the present style and write in an early tradition, it is impossible, and I have given sufficient warning in my explanation

12. There is a precedent for this, and Sorai, Mabuchi, and later Norinaga all engaged in it to some extent.

about poetry. One should consider these words of advice in reference to what I have said above.

I had intended to quote the rest of *Niimanabi* and criticize it, but the remaining sections deal with trifling problems, and so I will not address them. Surely, the student will be able to comprehend the rest of the work by reading just the first section, which I have explained above.

[Hashimoto et al. 1975:585–604]

☙

GOIKŌ

Kamo no Mabuchi | ca. 1764

[Mabuchi divides this grammatically oriented essay into three sections: overview, verbal conjugations, and etymology. He compares Japanese to the languages of China and India and concludes that the language of Japan is superior, because it has as few as fifty sounds, compared to the complex languages of China and India; this demonstrates, he asserts, that the hearts of the people anciently were straightforward and simple, and so their language reflected the state of their hearts. Thus the ancient people had less to say than people in other countries.]

PREFACE

Yes, there are bad people in the world, and Mr. So-and-So writes something or Mr. Such and Such proposes a certain theory, damaging the reputation of a good person. There are many scholars who deceive and spread falsehoods, so why not have the reader judge the merits and demerits of the theory contained in this work, *Goikō*, on his own? The words of our elderly master, Mabuchi, are very clear. This late great man was my teacher, and this work is one of the Five Treatises. For years his disciples have transmitted his work in the form of a handwritten manuscript, but a bookseller in Kyōto named Nishimura something or other was able to obtain the manuscript from the Kamo family, and recently brought this work out in printed form. He asked me to write a few lines for a small preface to add to the work. The worthy words of my master are as follows.

Motoori Norinaga

GOIKŌ

1

This land of the rising sun is a country of people who created words using only fifty sounds. The ancients transmitted everything orally using these sounds. The land far from the sun [in other words, China] is a country of signs representing all their words through the use of characters. The land where the sun sets [in other words India[1]] is a country representing the

1. The court of Emperor Suiko sent a famous letter to the emperor of China in 607,

pronunciation of its language with fifty characters. Therefore, those who doubt that Japan was the only country not to have employed characters are scholarly puerile. The reason [for their doubts] is because of their affinity for the Chinese and their ingenuity, creating many homonyms in their language, making it impossible to tell what a word means without seeing the character. Nevertheless, it is terribly disgusting to create characters for the multitude of sounds in a language. The people in India take pleasure in pondering things in minute detail, and there are many phrases and sounds. Perhaps that is the reason they used characters, also. But with just fifty characters representing fifty sounds, India is able to express anything. They have thought deeply and in detail about this principle. In this land of the rising sun, too, since the hearts of the Japanese are sincere, there have been few tasks, and thus, few words. With few tasks and few words, the ancients avoided confusion, there never being a time when people forgot things. Thus, Japan only has fifty sounds that naturally came into existence when the *kami* formed heaven and earth. Why would someone bring man-made characters to our country? Nevertheless, the people who claim that Japan has fifty organized sounds because this was originally based upon the system in India are insipid. Was it that the ancient people in Japan did not say anything? Our father and mother of heaven and earth taught us the art of speaking. Therefore, it appears that these fifty sounds came into existence without our knowledge. Those scholars who believe the Japanese phonetic system came from India have not considered the state in the ancient period. They create this problem because these scholars do not know anything about their own country's ancient past, spending all their time studying foreign countries.

The practice of learning from India started in the reign of the Owarida Palace,[2] and later the commoner followed the court in learning about this country. Before that time, scholars introduced Chinese learning to our court during the reign of the Karushima Palace.[3] This occurred at the height of divine liturgies or ancient songs vocalized by the ancient Japanese. Setting aside the fifty sounds of Japanese,[4] the hearts of men changed, and their words became empty expressions, and this laid the foundation

which started off with the words, "The Child of Heaven of the country where the sun rises addresses the Child of Heaven in the land where the sun sets." It is unclear why Mabuchi felt the sun set in India.

2. Suiko (r. 593–628).

3. Emperor Ōjin, who tradition states reigned around the fifth century.

4. Meaning the Japanese ignored their own tradition, and spent their time writing Chinese.

for later developments. I will outline the events of the ancient past for those who do not know them.

When I question these scholars about the lack of evidence showing that the ancient Japanese went to India, and transmitted the Indian sounds and characters to Japan, they only say that the Japanese method of arranging sounds in a phonetic series[5] and the linear similarity of sounds[6] resemble India. The key to telling if the Japanese imported their phonetic system from India in the ancient past is to be found in the linear sounds. First, there are the cardinal sounds. Second, there are immovable words [nouns]; third are moving words [adjectives, verbs]; fourth, commands, and fifth are helping words [advice].[7] Only when you classify the linguistic types can you make the words clear. Therefore, our divine ancestors taught these words to their posterity when the *kami* separated and formed heaven and earth. The reader may know that this is a model of words that foreign countries do not possess. Therefore, no matter which Japanese sound you scrutinize, these words were not invented by Japanese in middle antiquity.[8] This is evident since the Japanese lexicon in that awe-inspiring period of the "divine age," and the endless reigns of the grandchild of heaven did not change. Thus, the spiritually powerful words that brought blessings upon the land were established in the ancient times.[9]

2

China and India merely speak using sounds, but this country puts the words first and the sounds second.[10] I will explain what that entails; in

5. Such as the *a*-series (*a-i-u-e-o*) or the *ka*-series (*ka-ki-ku-ke-ko*).

6. By linear is meant all the sounds that have the same vowel, like, *a*, *ka*, *sa*, and *ta*.

7. Mabuchi takes each of the five vowels, and assigns a function based on his observation of its function. Many nouns or infinitives of verbs end in *i*. Verbs end in *u*, while imperatives end in *e*. Advice is given in the form of *o* (or *yo*).

8. Most likely this refers to the early Heian era, when the importation of things Chinese was at its height, as this is when Mabuchi felt that the Japanese lost their native sensibility.

9. One of the first and most provocative examples of *kotodama* in Japan is seen in *Man'yōshū*, MYS 2506:

kotodama no	Dusk divination
yaso no timata ni	was performed at the point where
yufuke tofu	many roads converge—
ura masa ni noru	a metaphysical place.
imo wa afiyoramu	My love's probable coming has been foretold.

10. Mabuchi adds the following note, "The word 音 'sound' in our country does not mean the pronunciation of a Chinese character. It has to do with the fact that there are three types of tones in Japanese, level tone, rising tone, and a falling tone." This is an attempt to describe pitch accent in Japanese.

Japan, when a child is born, he can articulate the sound *aa* from birth, and before much time has passed, that child can recognize words. By the time he or she reaches two years of age, it appears that the child can speak. The child learns the words in the region where he lives, and in the end he has picked up that region's accent. Thus, the sound comes after the word. This has been the symbol of this country's language. Nevertheless, people in the present have learned and memorized Chinese pronunciation in a haphazard fashion;[11] since these people interpret the words and the sounds in such a manner, the result is incomprehensible. Even from the distant past, when the Japanese imported Chinese characters and employed them in writing, they did not alter the original Chinese pronunciation. Words in *Kojiki* were written phonetically, like *ubitini* (rising tone) *no kami*, then *imasubidini* (falling tone) *no kami*. In the first example, the tone rises, and in the next, the tone falls, but there is no difference in the character *ni* [to which the accent rises or falls]. And in the word *ana niyasie* (rising tone) *otoko wo*, the reader normally lowers the *o* of *otoko*, but in this case it is raised; however, the writer has not altered the character. And though there are many differences in pronunciation due to euphony, we know from the annotative notes in *Nihon shoki* that the characters employed to represent the original sound have not been altered.

For example, the place name *kamo* is a level tone and so is *yama* "mountain." Nevertheless, when "mountain" is attached, *kamo yama*, the reader says this with a rising tone, but the characters for *kamo* have not changed. Also, "eastern poetry" in *Man'yōshū* is recorded in the pronunciation of the eastern dialect, but the characters employed are all the same as those used in the poetry of the court. In foreign countries, the individual sound of a character is different from the sound produced when grouping that character with another; however, since the character does not change to reflect the variation in pronunciation, I need not state how many people make mistakes in their composition. There is no character variation in *Kojiki*, *Nihon shoki*, *Man'yōshū*, or other records up to the time of *Shinsen Jikyō* and *Wamyōshō*. After the time of *Wamyōshō*, writers made mistakes in character usage, resulting in confusion; since there is not one scholar who goes back and checks the usage in the ancient records, no one corrects character usage.

Also, there are usages differing from those used in the most ancient

---

11. Mabuchi is talking about how Sino-Japanese pronunciation has changed (or his idea of corruption). Earlier texts preserve older variations of Sino-Japanese, like *daugu* "tool," which by Mabuchi's day was pronounced as *dōgu*.

records when characters were imported. There are many cases where the original usage was later altered. In China, the pronunciation of characters is different from work to work and difficult to organize, so it is wise to leave the pronunciation of the characters as they were when the characters were first introduced into Japan. Thus, 670 years—a total of forty-six imperial reigns—have passed from the time when Japanese imported Chinese during the reign of the Karushima Palace until the Shōhei [931–37] era when *Wamyōshō* was compiled.[12] During that time, the state of society changed somewhat, but the same pronunciation and script from the prosperous ancient past remained in use. In later eras a profuse amount of information vanished, and people came along who used Japanese unaware of the ancient meaning or ancient lexicon. Surely scholars can only comprehend the original meanings through a study of the ancient period, ancient records, and ancient remains.

3

The pronunciation of sounds is as I have discussed above. In this country, Japanese expressed the thoughts of their hearts verbally. The act of dividing words into individual sounds is not something man-made, but a natural phenomenon based upon the natural Japanese sounds. Therefore, the pronunciation in the Kinai area is correct and clear, but there are many deficiencies with the language in the surrounding provinces. Even when a person who uses the proper pronunciation converses with a person employing incorrect pronunciation, they can still communicate with each other, though the phonetic quality of the words varies. It is only when the words themselves are incorrect that communication becomes impossible. Thus, the words should come first, with the sound subordinate. Though the standard states that proper pronunciation is worthy, it has no intrinsic value because the people in the provinces cannot pronounce words properly. Because the commoner is known as the treasure of the sovereign, served by the same, we should not despise the provinces simply because their pronunciation differs from that in the capital.

Therefore, I feel there is no need to touch upon pronunciation any further. Nonetheless, the ancient records originated in the capital in Yamato, so there are many places where we cannot analyze pronunciation without knowing the pronunciation of the capital [as a standard]. For example, though awe fills our breasts when we speak of them, princes Oke and

12. The preface to *Wamyōshō* notes that the work was begun in 934, but most scholars believe the work was not completed till around 938.

Woke[13] were brothers, residing in the same palace. Thus, if *o* and *wo* had the same sound, how confusing that would have been [because their names would have sounded the same]. But there was no confusion, the distinction being clear, because this is how people addressed the two princes.

Therefore, among the fifty sounds of Japanese, the pronunciation and meaning of *wo* and *o*,[14] *e* and *we*, and *i* and *wi* were clearly different. If this had not been the case, ancient Japanese would not have functioned as a language, recording sounds that resemble each other next to one another in the ancient records. I have given the method for classifying these groups in charts at the end of this essay.[15] Also, in making a distinction between these two princes' names, *o* has a level tone, being an abbreviated form of *ofo* "great," and *ke* is a shortened form of *wake*.[16] Thus, he would have been known as Ofowake. *Wo* has a falling tone, and it means small or lesser, so his name would have been Owake. Thus, the elder brother was known as Ofowake "the greater," and the younger brother was known as Owake "the lesser." And yet, the actions of the person known as Myōgi of Yoshino[17] who destroyed Japanese script are a private affair of a man who knew nothing about the ancient past. Be aware, and do not become confused by Myōgi's theories about ancient words; ground your knowledge in the original phonetic usage. If you esteem these ancient words, you will obtain unexpected enjoyment from them. Blindly pondering the ancient lexicon is an act of a different variety.

4

A person once said to me, "This sounds as if you are rejoicing over the eras before Chinese was imported, putting the words of our land first. However, do you not wonder how the ancients would have transmitted the

---

13. They were the sons of Prince Ichinobe Oshihawake. Prince Oke was later named Ninken (r. 488–98) and Woke became Kenzō (r. 499–506).

14. It is not till the work of Motoori Norinaga that *wo* and *o* are reversed, with *o* belonging to the *a-i-u* series, and *wo* belonging to the *wa*-series.

15. I have abbreviated these from the translation.

16. There is debate over the etymology of this title that is often attached to the names of royalty. It is possible that it is a title imported from Paekche, an ancient kingdom on the Korean peninsula.

17. Though the characters are different (traditionally written 明魏 but Mabuchi has this as 明義), this is believed to refer to Fujiwara Nagachika, who was born in Yoshino (d. 1429). He wrote a work called *Yamato Katakana Hansetsu Gige*. Some doubt the authorship of this work. What appears to have upset Mabuchi is that Myōgi states in this work that Sino-Japanese usages are superior to the use of *katakana*, which should be treated as subordinate.

traditions of Japan for so long if our court had not borrowed [Chinese] characters?"[18] I replied that this is like wishing to scoop up water at the muddied end of the river, hating the upper stream where the water is clear. As I have said early on, the original hearts of the Japanese were sincere, so there were few tasks and few words; there was no confusion in speech, and people did not forget what they had once heard. If there was no confusion in communication, and nothing was forgotten in that era, then the ancients should have transmitted their traditions for a long time. Since the hearts of the people were straightforward, there were few edicts from the emperor. And when the court gave an imperial edict, it spread throughout the land like the wind, penetrating the hearts of the people like water. Since this was the case, heaven caused the population to increase, and there were no mistakes in the orally transmitted traditions. The pure people protected the traditions for many generations, nothing varying. What need did the ancient Japanese have for characters? What are you arguing for? The hearts of foreigners hide their many evils, and this differs from the many wonderful things they say with words. Thus, when Chinese practices came to Japan, the ancient Japanese took interest in them because of their rarity; the Japanese let their guard down because they were accustomed to the generous practices of the *kami*. The customs of the Chinese show that they were fond of logic and skillfully debating the meaning of everything in minute circles. This is the epicenter of this problem. We have now paid the price for having bound ourselves to an unpropitious foreign country.[19]

[NST 39:394–400]

☙

18. Mabuchi adds the following note, "The Chinese have a book known as *Zi hui* that lists thirty-three thousand characters currently in use. Indian Sanskrit employs over forty characters and has recorded the five thousand works of Buddha. Is it better to have many characters or few? It is best to rule the country with few actions. However, things can be transmitted without using India's forty-plus characters, and the divinely inherited throne of Japan that has lasted for a myriad generations is indeed more superior. It is lamentable that there is no one who studies the ancient meaning of Japanese, as modern scholars ignore the superiority of Japan, chaotically trusting in foreign countries."

19. Mabuchi then diagrams the fifty sounds of Japanese, giving a detailed discussion of each sound and its usage and meaning. This entire section has been abbreviated since it is of little interest to anyone but a linguist.

ASHI KARI YOSHI[1]

Ueda Akinari and Motoori Norinaga | 1787

[This Q and A essay is a record of correspondence between Ueda Akinari and Motoori Norinaga, as recorded by Norinaga. In letters to Norinaga, Akinari pushed back against what he considered to be rules and ideas about Japanese culture and language he did not believe. The topics of discussion range from the phonology of Old Japanese to Norinaga's stance taken in his work *Kenkyōjin* (1785). The correspondence dates between the years 1786 and 1787. This is sometimes called *Kagaika*, using the Sino-Japanese readings of the characters 呵刈葭, as Norinaga sometimes calls it in his own letters. I have left the title in its Japanese form.]

PART ONE

Article One

Akinari: abbreviated.[2]

Norinaga: Is not this exchange with the question from Tayasu Chūnagon and the answer from Katō Umaki[3] all a fabrication created by someone else? There are many suspicious points to this. Please check into the matter.

Akinari: I previously borrowed *Kana Montō* from Master Umaki when I met him, copied the text, and have it stored away. Tayasu Chūnagon told me that his question originated from seeing a story found in Master Umaki's preface attached at the beginning of Katori Nahiko's[4] *Kogentei*. This certainly is not the fraudulent work of some other person. Master Umaki would not recklessly use Tayasu Chūnagon's name without permission, and I certainly would not misrepresent my master in using his name. Are

1. The ground-breaking Norinaga scholar Muraoka Tsunetsugu read the title as *Ashi kari yoshi*, but it is also clear from a letter sent by Norinaga to one of his students, Ozasa Minu (dated second day of the fourth month of 1790), that Norinaga himself vacillated between a Japanese pronunciation of the title and one based on the Sino-Japanese reading of the characters, *kagaika* (see MNZ 1976, 8:48).

2. Since Norinaga recorded this exchange, only things that he felt were important have been recorded. Here Norinaga left the text out, apparently feeling that the context was obvious at the time.

3. Katō Umaki (1721–77) wrote a work called *Kana Montō* in which he answers questions by Munetake regarding *kana* usage.

4. Katori Nahiko (1723–82) was a student of Mabuchi.

you using a euphemistic phraseology to suggest that this work is nothing more than shallow scholarship consisting of questions and answers? I would appreciate a frank response.

Norinaga: There is no euphemistic usage with my question about the work being a possible fraud. I only asked because I truly had my doubts about the work. However, if you borrowed the work directly from Umaki and copied it down yourself, then it could not be a fraud. I have nothing further to say on the subject.

Article Two

Akinari: The statement that ancient Japanese had no mora-final /*n*/ is nothing but a spurious private opinion of yours. And yet you have taught us to read the word "divine wind" as *kamukaze*.

Norinaga: What do you mean by "nothing but a spurious private opinion?" Is not the act of arbitrarily following your own will, making a statement without any proof grounded in ancient textual examples or making logical sense a spurious private opinion itself? I have already said in a former statement there is a mountain of clear textual evidence showing mora-final /*n*/ did not exist anciently.[5] It is a grave mistake to stick to examples from later ages when the pronunciation of /*mu*/ had already changed [to /*n*/] due to euphonic influence, and believe that the past was exactly the same. That does not mean there are no contemporary examples that are not applicable to the ancient past, but each example is independent. If you were to prove from recent examples that /*n*/ existed anciently, then you would say something like the phrase "just one" (*tatta fitotu*) was read as *tada fitotu* in the ancient texts, and certainly the ancients said *tatta fitotu* in colloquial usage, but that thinking would lead to the bizarre logic of saying that since there was no way to represent double consonants in *man'yōgana*, the double consonant was abbreviated and written as *tada fitotu*; however, when the text was vocalized, the reader said *tatta fitotu*.

In the same light, the words *yukamu* "will go" and *kaferamu* "will return" would presently be read as *yuko* and *kafero*. So are you proclaiming that the basis for your argument is that these ancient textual examples of *yukamu* and *kaferamu* should be read as *yuko* and *kafero*? Nonetheless, when we read a work, even in the present we still have the practice of pronouncing the words as *tada fitotu*, *yukan*, and *kaferan*, and since we are accustomed to this type of reading, does that not imply that everyone is

5. Norinaga is pointing to the fact that anciently there was only the pronunciation /*mu*/, and this later evolved into /*n*/.

conscious of the fact that the readings of *tatta fitotu*, *yuko*, and *kafero* are colloquial? Because of this, take one step further back into time and think about this principle.

The usages in middle antiquity of *yukan* and *kaferan* are corruptions, and you will see that the true pronunciation was *yukamu* and *kaferamu*. Now, for example, when you read a work and see the word "divine wind" written as *kamukaze*, you read it that way; however, when you separate yourself from the text, it is hard to say that word unless you say *kankaze* or *kamikaze*. The reason you think *kamukaze* is strange is because you have become accustomed to the later, corrupted reading. Having become accustomed to something for a long time means that we believe it to be suitable; even when something is good, since we are not accustomed to it, we think it to be unsuitable, so I believe that if the ancients heard the later usage of *kankaze*, it would grate on their ears. …

Akinari: In Western countries that specialize in phonology, they say *suran* and do not have a specific character for the final sound, not because /*n*/ is a syllable, but because it is a rhyme.[6] Therefore, you say in our country there is no single use of a word with mora-final /*n*/. Even in words in our country there are cases where a sound assimilates to the previous sound according to sandhi and naturally becomes /*n*/. So I believe that poets selected the closest character and wrote *mu* 牟, *ni* 爾, and *mo* 毛 for this /*n*/, and when they read the poetry out loud they pronounce it as /*n*/.

Norinaga: It is true that even in Western countries /n/ is not a syllable, but is a rhyme. However, in the phonology of the language of our country, we speak directly, so there are no rhymes. (Lengthening out our syllables is a different issue.)

Now, following the principle of sandhi where some sounds naturally become /*n*/, this is a phenomenon found after middle antiquity, and it is a form of assimilation through euphony, but it does not represent the original "correct" form of these words. There is no difference then and now in the natural sounds of our language, if people in the present have the sound /*n*/, then likely the ancients also had the sound /*n*/. However, as this is an incorrect sound, the ancients would not have used it in their language.

Speaking of natural sounds, as half-muddied stops such as /*pa pi pu pe po*/ are still found in the language of present speakers, then you may know that the ancients also had these sounds. Nonetheless, these are extremely

---

6. This is based on Chinese observations of their own phonology. Here Akinari is juxtaposing 音 "syllable" and 韻 "rhyme." A syllable was considered to have a consonant, a vowel, and a coda. Akinari appears to equate *n* with a rhyme, because it is voiced.

inaccurate sounds, so is it not true that even in middle antiquity these were almost never used in the vocabulary of the language? Based on this you make a judgment about the sound /*n*/. Even if the natural sound is found in the language of the individual, there is a distinction between those that are used in the language and those that are not. If you want to use as proof that naturally occurring sounds were used in the ancient past also, then the half-muddied stops /*pa pi pu pe po*/ should also have been used in the ancient lexicon, but as there is not a single example [in the ancient texts], how do we account for this?

Article Three

Akinari: In ancient times, there was the sound /*n*/, and as proof, you, yourself, stated there is a Chinese rhyme that represents the sound /*n*/.[7] There are many examples in *Man'yōshū* where this character has been borrowed, representing the sound /*n*/. Examples such as *miten*, *tugeken*, *yukuran*, *wakarenan*, *midarekon kamo*, and *kofiyakuran san*; these are all clear examples of employing Chinese to represent the sound /*n*/. Since ancient Japanese had no set character for /*n*/, they used such characters like /*mu*/. Sandhi from the proceeding syllable affects the pronunciation, and people wrote the morpheme to represent the sound emitted from the opening of the mouth, whether it be /*mu*/ or /*n*/. The sound /*mu*/ just does not represent all the minute differences when people open their mouths.

Norinaga: The examples you noted (*ten*, *ken*, *ran*, *nan*) were clearly pronounced in ancient times as *temu*, *kemu*, *ramu*, and *namu*. The reason the poets used such characters as *ten* (点), *ken* (兼), *ran* (覧), *nan* (南) here is because the Chinese pronunciation of the final /*n*/ closely resembled Japanese /*mu*/.

An abundance of examples of borrowed Chinese characters exists in *Man'yōshū* and other works; thus, think about the example of writing the place name *kaminami* as 甘 (*kami*) and 南 (*nami*). If this character were used to represent /*n*/, and it is proof that this is consistently so, then would not the place name become *kaminan*? And concerning your example of *wakarenamu*, some people write *namu* with the character 嘗 "lick." Even today, we read this as *namu* and not as *nan*. Also in *Wamyōshō*, we see the

7. Akinari has reference to *Kanji san'onkō*, where Norinaga wrote, "Chinese especially has many of these *n* rhymes. It is clear that this sound is incorrect because when they [the Chinese] pronounce these sounds, they use not only their voice, but mix in the sound from their nasal cavity to say it. Anciently in our imperial land there was not a single person who used the sound *n*" (MNZ, 1976, 5:384).

ancient place name of Taniha written as 丹波; there is not a single example of *Tanba*.[8] These examples will surely open your eyes to the fact that the ancient Japanese used these characters because their Chinese reading of /*n*/ was close to /*mu*/. ...

Now, as a set structure [i.e., *kakari musubi*], when a sentence has *koso* the final verb ends in the fourth position [i.e., *izenkei* or the evidential], and when the sentence contains *zo* the final verb ends in the third position [i.e., *rentaikei*] or the adnominal. As an example, verbs like *mimu* "see" or *kikoyu* "hear" change to *mime* and *kikoyure* when the sentence contains *koso*. This is because *mu* and *me* are sounds in the same phonological line, and the third and fourth sounds alternate. But if you say *min* or *kikan*, you find that /*n*/ is not a sound of the same phonological line as *me*. It goes without saying this is different from the example above. Also, people become confused because in the present they are accustomed to not being able actively to use certain words because of the type of Chinese character that is used to represent that sound, due to the fact that they do not consider what the correct form of the word was in the ancient past. I argue this point in detail later.

Article Four

Akinari: The pronunciation of the name 三郎 as *samurou* comes from the reading of the Chinese characters, but that is an example of sandhi in our language; it is an example of the interchangeable nature of the pronunciation of /*mu*/ and /*n*/. The character for /*mu*/ was simply borrowed for a time, but that does not mean that it was always pronounced as /*mu*/. The Tang era emperor Xuan Zong is recorded as 李三郎 "the third son of Empress Yang," and Confucian scholars read this as *risanrou*, not as *risamurou*. And his nickname of 源三郎 is read as *gensanrou*, but where is there a person who calls him *gensamurou*? And the pronunciation of the title for the three recitations dealing with old ladies in Noh 三老女 is *sanroudiyo*. These are all examples of natural sandhi. And the ancient Golden Light Army is called *konmyougun*, not *komumyougumu*. Even your name of Shunamu[9] employs sandhi, but if it were read as Shumuamu it would not sound proper.

Norinaga: This is evidence I should have mentioned earlier, but it makes me smile to think that you have supplied my counterargument in

8. It was later called Tanba. Norinaga is trying to show that such an evolution (*tanifa* > *tanba*) was a later phenomenon.

9. Shun'an was Norinaga's scholarly name.

your own letter. If you will calm down and think about this one more time, you will realize what you have done, and then turn bright red with embarrassment.

In other words, the root of this argument is that you have criticized *kamu* as something hard to pronounce within a word like *kamikaze*. My reply is that we are accustomed to pronouncing this with /*n*/; everything that we are accustomed to is easy to say and pleasant to hear, but what we are not accustomed to is saying things that are difficult and grate on our ears. One of those examples is this name that we still read as *samurou*, and it is not in the least offensive to our ears. That is because we are accustomed to daily usage of this name. And that is where this argument should have started. And then you have supplied the counterargument, saying in one instance the character 三 "three" can be read *san*, while at other times it can be read as *samu* or *sabu*. However, do not all of these examples depict the ordinary pronunciation to which we are accustomed, showing that none of these are hard to pronounce or offensive to our ears?

Among these three examples, the example of *sabu* should be more offensive to our ears than *samu*, but the reason that it is not is because we have grown accustomed to the sound. Because of this, I am the one who should have brought the subject up first. ...

Article Five

Akinari: Among the things that you have said, you imply that since the sounds of metal, stone, stringed instruments, grass, trees, fowl, and beasts are natural sounds, and not the sounds of humans, they are not proper sounds. The pronunciation of the Chinese is much the same, so do you mean that it is also improper? If the sound from stringed instruments is erroneous, then humans should not sing words accompanied by these sounds. Also, why could the sound of plants appease the *kami*? Did not people in ancient times lift up their voices to the sound of stringed instruments and produce songs? And when Amaterasu Ōmikami hid herself in the Iwato cave, if the sound that Ame no Uzume produced when she pounded her feet on the empty tub did not harmonize with the pleasant voices of the *kami* making merry at the time, then would not the sun goddess have hidden deeper within the cave?

If the sounds of men and other things did not suit each other, but were unpleasant to hear, then why do we have such events as the one I mentioned above in the first place? Also, it is said that the wind is the great breath of Shinato, but if he were to expel his breath, would you say that it is incorrect for him to lengthen out the sound and say, "Oh?" Also, when sound comes in contact with something, a harmonizing resonance is produced.

And do you imply that in the beginning when our country was first created that the sound of water dripping (*koworo koworo*[10]) is also improper? Though it is said that the sound of stringed or bamboo instruments and that of plants and trees soothes the hearts of *kami* and men alike, one single man proclaiming his insipid personal opinion that these sounds are improper will not convince anyone.

It is also a private and self-centered idea to say that the languages of foreign countries are like the sounds of wings and fur. And as you argued about the Chinese custom of folding the fabric of a robe right side first, left side second as proper, and left side first, right side second as barbaric, what should we think about this logical conclusion that since the sounds of all foreign countries are lengthened out, and only the sounds of our imperial land are simple and do not assimilate?

Your idea that the sounds that are simple and do not assimilate is the true state of language, while sounds that are lengthened out are not correct was simply concocted in your own heart. In every country, the sounds that naturally come out of people's mouths should not be judged as correct or incorrect. The theory that ours are noble, and theirs are base is not the thinking of the heart of the straightforward spirit of our imperial land. Surely the ancients [of our land] made more mistakes in their language than the tiny *sasa* chestnutlike mistakes [you mention], did they not?

Norinaga: In what way have you misinterpreted my words to criticize me? What you have said is far off the mark. And when did I ever say that the sounds of *anything* were incorrect? All I said was that as humans it was incorrect for the sounds we produce to be closely related to the sounds that other things produced. For men have human sounds, and all creations each have a sound they produce, so the correctness or incorrectness of those sounds depends on an independent standard. But as a human, if it is not mistaken to imitate the sounds of other things, then what is it? And the other way around, it would be improper for an object to produce a sound close to the sounds that humans produced.

For example, if one were to play the *koto*, and if it produced a noise that sounded just like that of a human, who would say that that was a proper sound? And it is not merely a matter of the sound being improper, it would

10. Found in *Kojiki* when the procreator *kami*, Izanagi and Izanami, first created the land of Japan. See Philippi (1967:49), where he has "churning-churning sound." Heldt (2014:8) renders this as "its brine sloshed and swished about as they churned it."

be an apparition. Also, if the sound a human made was similar to that of a *koto*, it is the same problem. We should consider that it is improper for human sounds to be closely related to the sounds made by all creation. …

Also, you have retorted that it is incorrect to lengthen one's syllables, but this is far from the meaning of what I said. Since producing poetry is the act of drawing out the syllables, why would I have said something to the effect that this practice is incorrect? What I said was that it is impossible to slow down or shorten the pronunciation of foreign languages. If you abbreviated the pronunciation, the end would be choked, and it would not be smooth. Also, if you said things slowly, then the words would be drawn out, and that would be incorrect.[11]

As an example, the sound *ah* 阿 would become a choked form of あっ if shortened, while it would become a long form of *aah* if said slowly, making it impossible to say *ah* correctly. That is why I said it was incorrect. You criticize me without pondering on what I had said, saying, "So there! All the words of foreign lands are long, are they not?" But this is completely different from what I had said. It is not my opinion that all vowels in foreign tongues are long. Foreign languages also have shortened vowels. Chinese has the entering tone.

Now, concerning my opinion that Japanese is the only language with simple sounds and correct pronunciation differing from foreign tongues, you have taken examples from foreigners who wear their clothes on the left side, changed my words of "differing from foreign tongues" to "incorrect" and criticized me. This attitude of yours betrays a certain discrimination. In all countries things that are proper are correct, and those that differ from this standard are judged incorrect. You cannot accurately judge by ignoring half of the equation. For example, no matter which country you go to, the head, hands, and feet all resemble each other. But on the island of "long arms" or the island of "long feet," the inhabitants have exceptionally long limbs, so they would judge long limbs are correct, and the other countries as incorrect [because those limbs are short]. Is this not the standard to judge against?

Furthermore, it is correct that our pronunciation should differ from other languages. Nevertheless, since this is the point you wish to take issue with, I will set it aside for a moment. It is indeed awe-inspiring, but our imperial family has descended in unbroken succession, and this is a great difference with other foreign countries, because our sovereign has not changed easily. Is this not proper? If you label everything else that differed

11. Norinaga appears to be talking mainly about Chinese, where the semantics of words is dependent on the rise or drop of the tone on the vowel.

improper, would you label our ruling family improper, too? It is an unheard of mistake to think that everything in Japan is wonderful and everything foreign is bad. This is not the heart of our country, which is fair and just. Everything respectful should be treated such, while all base items should remain such. This is fair and just. This is because our country has been like a father, like a ruler, while foreign countries are like children, like servants. Why should there be any argument about respecting your sovereign and father, and looking down on servants and children?

You were born in this wondrous land, enjoying its blessings, and yet you do not even know how to honor your land. What kind of wicked heart would possess a man to criticize people for honoring their country?

Article Six

Akinari: Do you also claim that the half-muddied sound in Japanese is incorrect?[12] I will reluctantly follow what you assert, /*n*/ is to be read just as the character represents—thus, as /*mu*/—and leave it at that. But I cannot accept your definition of the half-muddied sound. When all words are pronounced, if there was no sandhi, then the sound would never come together smoothly. The w-sound is situated between voiced and voiceless phonemes, and truly should be labeled a harmonizing sound.[13] Based on what evidence does your theory make a distinction between the words *afa* (阿波) and *awa* (安和)?

It appears that there are various theories about this, and since there was a distinction between /*o*/ and /*wo*/, there are two different characters used (於 for *o* and 袁 for *wo*), so people's mouths could clearly pronounce this difference, and their ears could clearly hear the difference. So why should there be any difficulty in pronouncing *fa* versus *wa*? When you try to force your biased opinions on people, you end up with this type of self-contradictory argument. If I were allowed to voice my personal opinion, I would declare that it must be said that these two syllables are closely related sounds. For the present, you will no doubt say that people of ancient times were able to deftly make a distinction in pronunciation between the aphonic *fa* and *wa*, and this is because you say there is a difference between /*o*/ and /*wo*/. Next ...[14]

12. Akinari uses the word 半濁 *handaku*, which generally refers to –p– in Japanese, but it is clear from his examples that he is referring to *ha, hi, hu, he, ho* when pronounced as *wa, wi, u, we, wo*.

13. I interpret this to mean that Akinari is arguing that –w– is neither a voiceless or voiced phoneme, but is rather a glide.

14. Norinaga cut Akinari's letter off here, but from simple context, it appears that the letter continues with the next entry in article seven.

Norinaga: First, the definition of the distinction half-muddied [*handa-kuon*] is as follows: the pronunciation of *pa, pi, pu, pe, po* is made as if it were voiceless, by puckering your lips together. Furthermore, I have already stated in *Kanji san'onkō*[15] that this set of syllables is voiceless, even if one asserts that it is the result of sandhi.[16] This would even be true if the phenomenon was not due to sandhi. Therefore, the ancient language of the imperial country did not have a single example of any p-sounds at the beginning of words, even if you assert that sandhi was present. My usage of "half-muddied" refers to all of these. However, some of our elder Japanese linguistic scholars call the phenomenon where *fa, fi, fu, fe, fo* are euphonically changed through sandhi to *wa, wi, u, we, wo* "half-muddied." The examples that you have brought up fall under this category.

In reality, this phenomenon [labeled by other Japanese scholars] should not be referred to as "half-muddied." To do so would mean that all examples of *wa, wi, u, we, wo* that are not euphonically altered must be referred to in the same manner. However, this series is one of the ten series within the fifty sounds of Japanese, being voiceless, and there is no reason to refer to it as voiced. Perhaps these linguistic scholars have adopted this usage because of examples seen in foreign languages, but they cannot label this phenomenon in the imperial country as such.

Now, these examples of "half-muddied" that I have given above refer to extremely corrupt sounds. The sounds *wa, wi, u, we, wo* are not corrupt, but it is incorrect to say that these sounds originated from a euphonic change from the sounds *fa, fi, fu, fe, fo* in ancient Japanese. You, the refuter, have taken two differing categories and conflated these into one, saying that what I meant by "half-muddied" includes the sounds *wa, wi, u, we, wo*, but this is a misunderstanding. Your refutation that if the pronunciation for */o/* and */wo/* can be distinguished in speech and hearing, then why cannot *fa* and *wa* be distinguished is based on a mistaken premise, because you believe that the ancient sandhi for the *fa* series of Japanese sounds was always pronounced as the *wa* series. In all ancient Japanese words, there never were any words where a *fa* phonogram was pronounced as *wa*, but was always pronounced as *fa*, so why should there have been a need for the existence of what you term as "half-muddied"? (I have elected to follow your definition for the moment, but I do not want you to misunderstand.) …

15. Written by Norinaga in 1784. He researched the differences between Japanese and Chinese, and examined the differences between the three strata of Sino-Japanese: *Go-on*, *Kan-on*, and *Tō-on*. This quote is from MNZ 1976, 5:383.

16. Norinaga's usage here of *incorrect* means that the sound did not exist originally in ancient Japanese, and so its modern presence means there has been a move away from the original, correct state of Japanese.

Let me add a remark about /o/ and /wo/. These two sounds became utterly confused in later eras so it is difficult to distinguish the pronunciation now, but we must recognize the fact that two different characters exist to write these syllables. If, as you state, "half-muddied" did exist in ancient Japan, then there should be traces of the distinction in writing. However, no such orthographic distinction exists. This also tells us that it did not exist in ancient Japan.

Article Seven

Akinari: The names of fishes like *efi* "a ray" and *ebi* "shrimp" are both written as 衣比 (*efi*) in ancient script, and trees and shrubs like *itifi* "yew tree" and *itibi* "Indian mallow" are written as 伊知比 *itifi*. If one does not carefully use the distinction of voiceless, voiced, and "half-muddied" between these types of words, then the listener will not be able to tell which word you are using. If one were to pronounce the word exactly as it was written, then certainly the word would not fulfill its purpose.

Also, what would you say if I said the reason we make an orthographic distinction between words that are the same in poetry, like *afa* "sparse" and *awa* "millet," *fafe* "lengthen" and *fae* "prosper," *tafe* "endure" and *tae* "vanish" has nothing to do with how we pronounce the words, but these are written to produce a distinction in semantics? When Chinese characters came to our country from the east, perhaps people quickly came to be vexed by the convenience of the writing, and set up this kind of system.

Over time in China, society combined two characters to help people distinguish between objects and ideas. As an example, people added the character 日 "day" to the character 莫 "nothing" to create 暮 "sun goes down" [or the sun disappears], or added 馬 to the same graph to create 驀 "dash off." We find many of these kinds of characters. One could say "the sun goes down and the way is far," but it was the thinking of later people to be able to say the same thing with only one character. In response to Tayasu Chūnagon's question I replied that people say that it is deliberately done this way, and you will figure that out if you examine the language, and this is the kind of thing my master was talking about.

I do not understand what you are implying when you say that in the Eastern songs in *Man'yōshū*, you understand the sounds, but you cannot understand the meaning of the poem. Are you suggesting that when the poet wrote *amosisi* that courtiers at court at the time did not understand that this mean mother and father?[17] Likely the listener would hear *faru*

17. 阿母志志 *amosisi* "father and mother" appears in MYS 4376. It is believed that *amo*

famo and interpret this as *faru kana* "oh spring."[18] It is difficult for the person to figure out that the poem means "oh that needle." Is this not the meaning that when you understand the poem, you see that this word has this meaning, and that word has that meaning? Even if you find this line of reasoning to be incorrect, it is because with my lack of learning I am not able to investigate thoroughly, and it is easy to correct your ideas when someone else has instructed you. But even if you realized that you had written and published some worthless theory that is incorrect, it would be almost impossible to publish a correction.

Norinaga: There was a distinction between voiceless and voiced sounds in the ancient past, and since it is clearly differentiated in *kana* script, there is no chance of confusion between the words *efi* and *ebi*.[19] And "yew tree" is written *itifi* while "Indian mallow" is written as *itigo*, and there should not be any confusion. It is because of your carelessness that you have compared these two sets of words. These words have nothing to do with the argument at hand. And it will be the same thing even if you dig up different words.

In short, your point of argument is that without a clear distinction between voiceless, voiced, and "half-muddied" syllables one cannot distinguish the meaning of words. This is a grave mistake. First, in relation to voiced versus voiceless syllables, there is a clear distinction in *kana* usage, so there should be no problem. And I have already stated that your idea of "half-muddied" syllables occurring through euphony did not exist in ancient Japanese. What kind of inconvenience would there be in the language if the phenomenon of "half-muddied" did not exist? And have not you yourself asserted that the meaning of one word can be discerned through context [semantics]? If you assert that the meaning of a word cannot be distinguished without this added sound, then how will we make a distinction between "chopsticks" (*fasi*), "bridge" (*fasi*), and "edge" (*fasi*)? These three words can be distinguished by pitch accent,[20] but since the pitch ac-

---

is a variant of *omo* "mother." *Sisi* is believed to be *titi* "father," where *ti* has lost its place of articulation (*ti* > *si*).

18. No such example appears in *Man'yōshū*. Perhaps Akinari is thinking of an example like that in MYS 4420, where we find the stanza 波流母志 *faru mosi* "holding the needle." Here *fari* "needle" exhibits a backing of the high vowel to *ru*, and again *moti* exhibits a loss of articulation.

19. As Norinaga states, in contemporary Japanese the first is written *ei*, while the latter is *ebi*; there is no confusion in the present. *Kojiki* is highly consistent in making a distinction between voiced and voiceless syllables.

20. In modern Japanese *fasi* "chopsticks" belongs to the pitch accent class 2.4 (LH), "bridge" is 2.2 (HL), and "edge" is 2.1 (HH).

cent of "deity" (*kami*), "hair" (*kami*), and "paper" (*kami*) is exactly the same, no distinction exists.[21] But even so, in reality, there is no confusion, is there? In spite of this, saying that "sparse" was written *afa* and "millet" was written as *awa* in order to make a distinction between the two words is truly preposterous.

If, for the sake of argument, we attempt to differentiate *kafa* as "river" and *kawa* as "skin [bark]," while *nawo* is "straight" and *nafo* is "furthermore," we have merely engaged in a meaningless exercise that deals solely with the /*fa*/ and /*wa*/ set of words. If there actually was a semantic method of differentiating homophones, then it should appear in all ten phonetic groups. There should be examples of differentiation related to "heaven" and "rain" (both *ame*), "cloud" and "spider" (*kumo*), "frost" and "downward" (*simo*), "stand" and "vanish" (*tatu*), "forehead" and "rice bran" (*nuka*), "bush clover" and "shin" (*fagi*), "pine tree" and "wait" (*matu*), "protect" and "leak" (*moru*), "darkness" and "cease" (*yami*), or "I" and "ring" (*wa*). Without examples in each of the ten groups, what use is semantic differentiation as a principle?

Article Eight

Akinari: Master Norinaga's argument about *kana* drew the conclusion that all usages of the character 婆 /*ba*/ were voiced. Regardless, there are examples when it is pronounced as /*wa*/. For example, in *Kojiki* we see *arikayowase*, *kake wa naku* and *munamiru toki wa*.[22] In *Nihon shoki* we also find examples of *kuwasime wo* and *naniwa fe mukite*. ... If these were all voiced, then the meaning would not make any sense. These are concrete examples proving that "half-muddied" syllables did exist in ancient Japanese. In all *kana* usages, voiceless syllables could be used to represent "half-mudded" and voiced ones. And in rare cases voiced syllables could be used to represent voiceless syllables. If one wished to look for examples of confusion in the voicing of *kana* within the old records, there would be no end.[23]

---

21. This may have been true in Norinaga's dialect, but in other dialects a distinction in pitch accent is preserved: historically "paper" belongs to accent class 2.2 (HL), but "hair" and *kami* are both 2.3 (LL).

22. Akinari is mistaken here, and seems to be relying on his current speech to read the text, where the focus particle *fa* is pronounced as *wa*. In spite of this, I have transcribed these poetic stanzas as an underlined *wa* to highlight what he is saying.

23. While Akinari is incorrect with his data and *wa*, he is correct in pointing out that there is a polyphonic principle going on, where a voiced phonogram could represent a voiceless syllable, and vice versa.

To the master's dogmatic ears the sound of these "half-muddied" syllables may sound indistinct, but to my trained ears, these syllables sound like a soft sound located between voiceless and voiced. In the long run, written works are just that and the eye may be able to re-create things for a thousand years, but the ears are not that delicate. Theories are generally established upon texts, so can it be said that the natural sound conforming to the character is incorrect when we do not even know if the pronunciation of each Chinese character clearly reflects the ancient Japanese sounds?[24]

There is a reason why scholars of Siddham characters do not label the sound /*n*/ that exists between /*u*/ and /*mu*/ as incorrect. Having thought upon this issue, the sound of words should be established as they were actually said along with *kotodama*. Should it not be said that labels establishing the sounds of words according to the way in which they were articulated is a self-serving hypothesis of Chinese-infested linguists? There is nothing detailed in the theories of the scholars of Siddham characters. And even if you attempt to argue about Chinese or Japanese phonology from the point of view of Siddham, nothing of value is gained; truly, it is only natural that nothing of value has been obtained from this methodology.

The reason that we do not see /*n*/ in the ancient records is because there was no character with which to represent such a sound. Writers borrowed characters like /*mu*/, /*ni*/, and /*mo*/ that were closely related to /*n*/ to represent this sound, but because this usage was terribly bothersome, in the Heian era, someone invented a character that would accurately represent the sound /*n*/.[25] This does not mean that a completely new character was created, but in *hiragana* the character に became ん (/*n*/), and in *katakana* ニ became ン. Through this, one may realize this character was created by bringing the last stroke [of /*ni*/] up sharply, and that is the origin of the sound. In Sanskrit this is called an anomaly (変躰), and perhaps /*n*/ was modeled after that. As I have observed in general, there is nothing to the idea that everything was wonderful in the ancient past, and everything created in later eras is evil. There are both good and bad in what has been supplemented in later eras, and one cannot indiscriminately select just one

24. Akinari has a good point here, as a perfect one-to-one match was impossible between Chinese and Japanese. What further complicates this is Old Japanese actually did not have voiced phonemes in the true sense, but had prenasalized phonemes. This is evident from examples like *yama no kafa* > *yamagafa*, where *no* devoices to *n*, and this prenasalizes the following *k*: *nk* > ^{n}g > *g*.

25. It is odd and a bit surprising that Akinari does not seem to realize that the *kana* for *n* ん is a cursive form of 无 *mu*.

side. Therefore, if linguists select evidence from texts on the one hand, should they not also study about how the sounds were employed in actual speech? One should not become obsessed with just characters, and teach others the pronunciation of bothersome foreign dialects.

Norinaga: Among the poetry in *Kojiki* there are over 160 examples of the sound *fa* later employed as *wa* and labeled as "half-muddied." Of these 160 examples, roughly 140 are all written with the voiceless character 波 *fa*, and there are only fourteen examples where the voiced character 婆 *ba* is used. And of these fourteen examples, six or seven are written as 波 *fa* in other manuscripts, which leaves only seven or eight as voiced. This is the result of my collating three or four old manuscripts of *Kojiki*. Thus, when I finish collating the other three or four manuscripts, surely there will be other examples where *ba* was written as *fa*, and then it will become clear that the usage of *ba* was primarily scribal error from a later era. The characters *fa* and *ba* are easily confused, and there are many other examples of this. For example, even if it is not scribal error, if you take the remaining seven or eight examples of *ba*, and say they are definitely examples of *handaku* usages, then how would you explain the remaining 140 or so examples that are written *fa*?

If there was such a thing as "half-muddied" characters, and there existed a graphic method for distinguishing between the two, then all 160 of these examples should have been written as *ba*. Not only that, but there is an example in *Kojiki* where a wild cherry tree is called 婆婆迦 **babaka**. Because this is not sandhi, it should not be read as *wawaka*. The word **tofore** "passing through" is written 杼富礼, and the first syllable should be read as a voiceless *to*, and this is not an example of "half-muddied." As I said above, since *babaka* never should be interpreted as "half-muddied," it must be scribal error for *fafaka*.[26] If it is not scribal error, then it must an exception like *tofore*,[27] and we see that there are rare cases where the voiceless *fa* is represented with *ba* and the reason is as I have said above—they should be viewed as either scribal errors or exceptions.

There are many examples of what I have called exceptions in *Nihon shoki* and *Man'yōshū*. Overall, among the usages that make clear distinctions between the usage of voiceless and voiced characters, there are many

26. Here Norinaga's keen textual insight is clear. Three manuscripts of *Kojiki* do have the word *babaka* (cf. Onoda 1977:125–28). Norinaga may have been the first to notice that Old Japanese free morphemes never begin with a voiced phoneme.

27. Norinaga uses the character 変, which means different or changed. His own explanation of this usage is given below.

examples here and there where a voiced character has been employed with a voiceless syllable. However, that does not mean there was no distinction between voiceless and voiced syllables. An exception is where there is a difference in one character within a work that makes a clear distinction between voiceless and voiced syllables. Using this idea of exceptions as the basis for your argument, it cannot be said that there was no distinction between voiceless and voiced syllables. …

An example of this would be, cherry blossoms always bloom in the spring, but sometimes there occurs a phenomenon known as reblooming when the flower blooms in the autumn. This is an exceptional phenomenon that is not normal. The usage of *ba* you have used as evidence for *handaku* is like a person viewing this reblooming and stating that cherry blossoms bloom in the autumn. Even if there was such a phenomenon as *handaku* in the *fa* series of Japanese sounds, represented by a voiced character, then this should not stop with just *ba*. There should be *handaku* sounds for *fi*, *fu*, *fe*, and *fo*, but there is not a single example in the ancient records. Is it not silly to assert that among the five sounds in the *fa* series, only *fa* exhibits the traits of *handaku*? In *Kojiki* there is one example of **tufi ni** "at last" written as 都毘爾, but this is just one exception from among many examples.

Now, you stated that the eyes of a scholar may be able to re-create sounds for a thousand years by reading through written works, but the ears are not that delicate. Truly, the ears of men cannot return a thousand years into the past and distinguish the pronunciation of the ancients, but fortunately, we have phonetic script, so we can reascertain the pronunciation with our eyes. Needless to say that what we can obtain through our eyes surpass what we obtain with our ears; however, since there is no reason for our ears to pick up the ancient pronunciation, we have no other means for knowing about the ancient sounds than through the phonetic script. In relation to this *kana* script, we cannot argue about how the characters were pronounced in China. It is about the same as saying that listening to the foreign sounds and repeating them is much better [than reading the script]. I have already addressed this topic in detail in *Kanji san'onkō*, so you cannot argue about how the characters sounded in China.[28]

In spite of this, you doubt the phonology of *kana*, and only trust what

28. It has only been in the last fifty years that through the painstaking work of Li (1971), Tōdō (1978), Pulleyblank (1962, 1992), Coblin (1994), Miyake (2003), Schuessler (2007), Baxter and Sagart (2014), and other linguists that we have been able to get a better picture of the phonology of earlier states of Chinese pronunciation.

your own mouth can produce and upon this standard try to determine the ancient phonology of Japanese, but this is extremely self-serving. What the human mouth can produce changes according to the time and environment, so it is difficult to make this your standard. If you were to use the phonology in the present as your standard, then as I mentioned previously, you should be able to state that *nengoro* would be the correct form (and not *nemukoro*). The word *tanba* would be correct (and not *tanifa*). The word *dannai* would be correct and not *daizi nai*. And the words *sonna* and *konna* would be correct, instead of *sono you na* and *kono you na*.

However, as you well know, these are all the results of euphony that have caused contraction, so why do you believe that words like *kankaze* where there is an intervocalic *-n-* are the correct forms? The word *kankaze* is in the same group as *nengoro*, and yet you do not realize this is a contraction through euphony. You are too focused on what your own mouth is able to pronounce, and judge the appropriateness based on this, but you are obsessed with this futile practice, and are blinded by the fact that these forms are simply later corruptions. It is analogous to someone anciently pronouncing the word as *kamukaze* representing a person arrayed properly in robes and cap sitting down, and later eras pronouncing the word as *kankaze* as someone lying down, dressed in everyday clothing. The person lying down in everyday clothes is at ease and comfortable, but why would anyone label this as correct? ...

Article Nine

Akinari: According to the opinions of some, the next sound after *a-i-u-e* is /*o*/ and not /*wo*/. Also, the next sound after *wa-wi-u-we* is /*wo*/ and not /*o*/. ...[29] So how are we to understand words like *inu* and *wenu,* which are valid?[30] Furthermore, "big" is always written /*o*/ while "small" is always written /*wo*/, so if one were to change the order of these two, the meaning would be backwards, because /*o*/ has a deeper, significance than the trivial /*wo*/. ...

29. The "opinions of some" refers directly to Norinaga. Mabuchi had helped solidify the idea that the *a* series of Japanese was *a-i-u-e-wo* and the *wa* series was *wa-wi-u-we-o*, but Norinaga argued this was mistaken, and he flipped the order of *wo* and *o*. The following abbreviation is Norinaga's.

30. The usage of *valid* here refers to the phenomenon of phonetic transformation within the same series of sounds without a change in lexical meaning. For example *i* becoming an *e* without the meaning of either word changing. However, the *i* of *inu* "dog" and the *we* of *wenu* "dog" do not belong to the same series.

Norinaga: A man named Tanaka Michimaro[31] from Nagoya in the province of Owari heard my theory about switching the order of /o/ and /wo/, and immediately realized the incorrectness of the older theory. Though there are valid exceptions like *inu*/*wenu* and *wotikoti*/*atikoti*, he realized that these examples did not hamper the theory, and came right away and became my student. Michimaro understands perfectly that these examples do not hamper the theory. On the other hand, you still persist in holding to this old theory; perhaps the reason you still have doubts is because you are truly senseless.

Your confusion stems from the *a*, *ya*, and *wa* series having interrelated sounds, so there is no reason why a resemblance is impossible. If you are going to stick to the old theory and doubt the proper placement of /o/ and /wo/, then should you not also doubt the placement of *a* and *wa* because of words like *ware* and *are* [both "I"] or *wakatu* and *akatu* [both "to divide"]? There are still many other examples about validity of words common in the *a*, *ya*, and *wa* series. Therefore, *inu* and *wenu* belong to the same group as words like *ware* and *are*, and there is no problem with this.

Also, it is a mistake to bring up the idea of significant and trivial just because "big" is /o/ and "small" is /wo/. The weight of the semantics of words and the depth of their phonetic value are all different problems, and have no relevance here. Therefore, even if "big" is significant and "small" is trivial, that has absolutely nothing to do with the pronunciation of the word. For example *ifa* "boulder" is a very heavy object, but the sound of *i* is very light. *Wata* "cotton" is very light, but the sound for *wa* is heavy. Also, with the case above of *ware* and *are*, there is a difference in the weight of the phonetic value, but there is no such difference in the meaning. From these examples, it is clear there is no relevance between the phonetic value of a word and its meaning. So from these examples you can see that there is no relation between the weight of the semantics and its phonology. I have already clearly argued in *Jion kanazukai*[32] that *o* belongs to the *a*-series because it is light, and *wo* belongs to the *wa*-series because it is heavy.

Now, there is one more thing I would like to say. Many of my colleagues believe that *otagi* and *atago* have the same meaning, but this is not an accurate theory. There is no example of an Otagi District being called Atago

31. Tanaka Michimaro (1730–84) was a student of *Man'yōshū* who entered Mabuchi's school to study. After Mabuchi died, Michimaro entered Norinaga's school and became his student.

32. Written in 1775, and published the following year. It deals with the proper spelling of words in *man'yōgana*. Regarding the issue of where *o* versus *wo* belong, see MNZ 1976, 5:331–34.

District, and there is no example of Mount Atago being called Mount Otagi; thus, one cannot accept this as an example of linguistic similarity. The only similarity is in the Chinese characters employed. There are many examples like this in the employment of characters with place names. I have simply offered advice on this.

Akinari: I think that the explanation that you have offered in relation to ancient Japanese and the series *a-i-u-e-wo* is persuasive. Some people have asked me concerning *inu/wenu* and *wotikoti/atikoti*, and since I had my own ideas, I answered their queries with the ideas that I have given you already. However, in relation to altering the position of /*o*/ and /*wo*/, there has been much meritorious work done by you and Fujitani Nariakira[33] As I see it, it is logical that some words in Japanese perform interserial transference while others do not. Thus, I do not agree with what the man from Owari states in there being no harm. And yet, I do not think that there is any great danger either in overlooking things in a general way. Also, I have seen many instances of what you mentioned in Otagi and Atago; it is exactly as you explained.

Norinaga: I haven't the faintest idea about what you mean when you bring up what the man from Owari said.

Article Ten

Akinari: Regarding the question in [Tayasu Chūnagon's] letter, he says that he humbly accepts your answers, as the examples about "big" being *ofo* and "small" being *wo* are based on secure textual evidence. However, he cannot accept the idea of light and heavy, as /*o*/ is simply an abbreviation. Words become deeper or lighter through sandhi, so the depth or lightness of one word resembles the use of characters in Chinese, and has nothing to do with *kotodama* in our august language.

Norinaga: Saying that a word increases in depth of its own is like saying that when there is a word like *yamagafa* "mountain river" or *tanigafa* "valley river," "mountain" or "valley" are light, while river is "heavy." But when you have *kafabune* "river boat" or *kafayanagi* "river willow," then "boat" and "willow" are heavy, while "river" is now light. Is this what you are referring to? If this is what you mean, then I understand what you wish to say. However, this is not sandhi; it is more properly called accent shift in word compounds. Is not what you have called sandhi, like that above? The argument here is not very clear.

33. Fujitani Nariakira (1738–79) was a scholar of the Kokugaku movement, but was mainly interested in linguistics. Norinaga mentions him in *Tamakatsuma* (cf. Bentley 2013:223–24).

Article Eleven

Akinari: What about *afa* "sparse" and *awa* "millet"...?

Norinaga: This type of word in ancient times was pronounced as *afa*, and was not articulated *awa* as we do now. The reason there is no current distinction between these two words is due to a corruption in the pronunciation. Since we in the present have become accustomed to this pronunciation, we must not use this as a springboard from which to theorize about the past. If "sparse" had anciently been pronounced as *awa*, then during the time when there was no script, there would have been no distinction between "sparse" and "millet," so when writing finally entered Japan, what evidence would people have used to make a distinction between *fa* and *wa*? The evidence for a set, distinct pronunciation in phonetic script comes from there originally having been a difference in the spoken word. If there had been no distinction in verbal usage, then why would anyone have invented such a bothersome system for writing words down?

Article Twelve

Akinari: In the phrase *mina sokofu omi no wotome*,[34] this is one long phrase from the beginning, and perhaps continued on to the word *uwo* "fish," because the poets did not make a distinction between the /*o*/ in *omi* and the /*wo*/ in *uwo*.

Norinaga: According to this theory, there is confusion between /*o*/ and /*wo*/ without making a clear distinction. In the ancient texts there are examples where /*a*/ and /*wa*/ are interchangeable, but there are no examples for /*o*/ and /*wo*/.

Akinari: If you lengthen out the *fu* of *mina soko fu*, then the vowel *u* is produced, so the listener can then hear the /*o*/ of *omi*, and the /*wo*/ of *uwo*, right?

Norinaga: This theory truly is close to what I think. However, Mr. Ueda seems to still hold to the old theory of which series /*o*/ and /*wo*/ belong, and according to the old theory /*o*/ is the same vowel in *uwo*, so your theory about the lengthening of *fu* is pointless. My own idea is based on the fact that all poetry in the ancient past was sung out loud, so when people lengthened out *fu*, it became *fuu*, and if you lengthened it further, you got

34. This refers to poem NS 44. The interpretation of the epithet *mina soko fu* is "glide along the bottom of the ocean," so it is unclear why this should attach to the noun *omi* "servant." One theory is that *omi* was an earlier form of *umi* "ocean." In NS 97 is a stanza *mina sitafu uwo*, which appears to be closely related to the epithet above. Hence the question insinuates that the epithet connects to the next syllable, here *wo*.

fuuu. When the singer continued to /*o*/, it then became *fuuwo*. The vowel / *wo*/ contains the vocalic element *u*, and so becomes *uwo*. …

Akinari: We still have some questions about the epithet *mina sosogu*. In Master Mabuchi's *Kanjikō* there is no explanation of *mina sosogu*. Tayasu Chūnagon's question understands the explanation [as you have put it forth]. He can accept your theory as one possibility. I say that as colleagues there are probably other theories.

Article Thirteen

Akinari: A colleague of mine named Imamichi[35] spent some time in Ōsaka. One night, as we talked about various things, Imamichi said, "You surely stumped Norinaga, the master, for a while when you brought up the example of *tatta* in relation to your debate about /*n*/. The sound of /*n*/ is produced by sandhi when expelling the breath. Sounds like *tu* are produce by *sandhi* when one inhales his breath. So there is an obvious difference in the pronunciation. While I have pondered the various examples in the ancient works, I believe there existed an aesthetic difference between inhaled and exhaled sounds. In poetry, a poet would not use inhaled sounds for even a moment. There is also a mixture of medium in the place names of districts and villages.

Nevertheless, in works written before *Man'yōshū*, there are no examples of this vulgar usage, so we know that this standard came about after the period of *Wamyōshō*. … If you can theorize by properly using the standard in existence, there is no danger of confusion." This was the opinion of Imamichi.

Norinaga: When I explained the sound /*n*/ earlier, I brought up the word *tatta* as an example of slang, showing how certain sounds had changed in the present. There is absolutely no need to bring up exhaled and inhaled sounds. Furthermore, it is a mistake to judge aestheticism using exhalation and inhalation. Are not the ten sounds *u-ku-su-tu* and so on examples of back vowels?[36] If exhaled sounds are labeled vulgar, then why are these not avoided in poetry? I believe what Tonami alludes to is nothing more than double consonants and nothing so broad as *u-ku-su-tu* sounds. Therefore, your colleague has said something amiss by stating that some form of aesthetic distinction can be made by inhaling or exhaling. …

---

35. His full name was Tonami Imamichi, and he was a friend of Akinari's. Very little is known about him. He wrote a work called *Kōon yōjikō* "A Treatise on Characters Used to Represent Guttural Sounds."

36. Meaning, when these vowels are articulated, the sound comes out from the back of the mouth.

Article Fourteen

Akinari: Let me again say (this is Imamichi's theory) that you said that if there existed any examples of /*n*/ in the historical corpus, they were all read as /*mu*/. But can we not say surely there is no evidence for the reading of /*mu*/? As I have stated earlier, the eyes can pick up many things, but the ears are not as sensitive. It is reasonable to say there is no other method but to test our mouths and ears. You probably sit and read ancient texts, your eyes skimming over each character, and you recite each sound, believing this to have been the sound from the ancient past. There is no easier method than this. This is the gist of what Imamichi has said. Language is a field where people write down things in order to convey the meaning, employing lifeless characters to convey the sound of living speech. Since we call the ancient past myriad of years before, a myriad of miles behind us, we in the present can still read the characters and pronounce the sounds, listening with our ears and understanding what is said. This is only logical. Thus, in order to extract living words from these lifeless characters, we must have a definite methodology. That methodology is none other than the proper employment of the rhythm of sound. In order to do this, we must know how sounds are created. The origins of human sound are the throat, tongue, teeth and lips. … It is true in India and China that the sound /*n*/ is not firmly established. It is just as well that we discern these foreign sounds with the same reasoning.

Norinaga: What exactly do you mean by asking me, "Surely there is no evidence that they said /*mu*/?" Are not the phonetic characters 牟 and 无 indisputable evidence for the sound /*mu*/? How can you say there is no evidence? There is no other method for discerning the pronunciation of ancient words without relying on *kana*. The method of using the principle of the way things should being and establishing sounds using your own mouth and ears is based on Zhu Xi Confucianism. This method is as different from the design of the study of our ancient country as heaven and earth are separated. Exactly what is the standard you base your observation of how things should be? Is it not based upon the fickle hearts of man?

There is no way to escape scholarly bias when establishing things based on one's feelings. Also, Tonami's allegory about characters being lifeless and words having life is terribly mistaken. The reason is that living means to act, but words do not work by phonetics. Phonetics is a lifeless sphere. *Kana* is also lifeless, because it is nothing more than signs to represent certain sounds. Nonetheless, this lifeless phonetic sign attached to this dead phonetic character is able to perform a living function. Therefore, the animated function of pronunciation is irrelevant to the phonetic symbol. If a dead phonetic symbol were to actually have some form of life, then the word itself would not link properly within a sentence. Therefore, phonetic signs are lifeless, so their linking within a sentence causes the meaning to come to life. On the contrary, if there were some independent germ of life in the sign, then this would prevent the free interaction of the word.

For example, there are many phonetic usages in *Nihon shoki* that employ one character to represent two or three sounds, which is extremely confusing. This is an example of phonetic usage and differs from the phonetic sign having life; however, I would like you to understand there are times when the phonetic symbol can cause the word to change and be incorrect. ...

Article Fifteen

Akinari: Let me again say (this is Imamichi's theory) that your theory about *mina soko fu* is logical and should be followed. This should also be noted with your meritorious theory about altering the position of */o/* and */wo/*. I would be delighted if you would allow me to have one or two more examples. Right now I cannot think of any more. However, I do not agree with the way you explained that Japanese has never used contracted sounds.

Norinaga: It is somewhat careless to think that all of these things fall under the classification of contracted sounds. Contracted sounds refer to things like *kya*, *sha*, *shu*, *kyu*, and *kuwa*. In ancient Japanese, there was not a single one of these. What I theorized in relation to *mina soko fu omi* was that the *fu* was lengthened and */u/* and */o/* contracted together,[37] forming *sokou*. Generally, there are many instances where a word is lengthened or contracted, so one cannot label all of these as contracted sounds. I stated that contraction occurs with the *ya* and *wa* series in order to explain the origin of this phenomenon; I did not mean that the *ya* and *wa* series immediately contracted. Both of these series and their original essences are pure sounds. Therefore, these sounds were originally part of the fifty Japanese sounds and were employed anciently. To give an example, in ancient Japanese, the word *waga-ife* "my house" became *wagife* because *gai* was shortened to *gi*. Thus, the */gi/* originated from a contraction of the sounds *-a* and *-i*, but it cannot be said that *gi* itself is a contracted sound. And if one researches into the origins of the *gi* of this *wagife*, he will find that it is a contracted form of *gai*, but not all instances of *gai* can be labeled as con-

37. Called monophthongization, see Unger (1993).

tractions. The reason for this is because the root for this comes from two different words; *ga* comes from *waga* "my" and *i* comes from *ife* "house." With that, I think that you can understand how *mina soko fu omi* is contracted.

First month of Tenmei 7 [1787]
[MNZ 1976, 8:377–99]

ര

UIYAMABUMI

Motoori Norinaga | 1798

[According to Norinaga's account, after he finished *Kojiki-den*, his students pressed him to write down advice for them to follow as they continued to learn about the Way. It is a rather short outline of things to do, and what texts to concentrate, with endnotes added to expound upon the twenty-eight main principles in the essay. I have included the notes in a reduced font. Norinaga divides the core of his methodology into four areas: Japanese religion, the principles of the Japanese court, history, and poetry. He also stresses reading the early Japanese records to help one see how the student can rid himself of Chinese influence.]

There are not one, but many schools of learning in society.[1] Learning refers to the study of the imperial court. Ever since ancient times, "scholarship" has only referred to Chinese learning. To differentiate between Chinese and Japanese studies, terms like *wagaku* or *kokugaku* have been employed, but these usages are particularly dreadful. Because this is the study of our own country, scholarship centered on Japan should be labeled just as "scholarship." To make a distinction between the studying of China, the label "Chinese learning" (*kangaku*) should be used. If one is talking about Chinese studies, and there is confusion concerning Japanese studies, too, then it would be proper to use the title of Japanese court studies; at any rate, the usage of *wagaku* or *kokugaku* gives one the impression that we treat Japanese studies as something foreign. From the point of view of China, Korea, or Holland, our scholarship is foreign, but there is no reason for us to label Japanese things thus. Everything about China is foreign, and all things from that country are foreign, so we should say "So-and-So from China" or "Such and such of Tang China" when talking about things. Because things related to our imperial country are domestic, there is no need to use the prefix "Japanese." From the time of the distant past there has been a general trend to make Chinese studies the focal point, and in all things Japanese have treated China as if it were their native country. Treating Japan as a foreign land is a misconception and a grave mistake. I bring this up first because it has to do with part of making sure one's Yamato spirit is firmly grounded. By "many schools" I mean that we should first start with learning about the Way, which is mainly seen in the records of the divine age.[2] This type of study is known as *shingaku* "the study of the *kami*," and a

1. Norinaga interpolates more than twenty-five notes in this short treatise. I have put his notes in the text, in a reduced font.

2. Norinaga writes divine age as 神代紀, giving one the impression that he meant it from

person engaged in this study is known as a follower of the Way of the *Kami*, and these people generally have studied ancient governmental posts, ceremonies, and the legal codes. In addition, there is research centered on ancient rites and practices, dress and accessories. This is called the study of ancient court precedent. And anciently, there was the nebulous study not connected to any one school of learning that researches into the old records starting with the six national histories continuing down to records in later eras. There are perhaps several divisions within this school of learning. And then there is also the study of poetics. Among this group, there are two branches, one that deals with the composition of poetry and the other that is centered on the study of ancient anthologies and ancient tales.

That is an overview and people follow the course of study that interests them. The student's method of study varies from the designs of the teacher and the intentions of the student. Among the people who wish to enter the Way of learning, there are some who have a predetermined school they want to join, and they desire to discover the proper method on their own. Then there are those students who have no predetermined course they wish to follow, and have not pondered any research method, but inquire of those with knowledge, asking things like which course of study should be pursued, what is the best way for a beginner to study, and from which works should one start reading. This last situation is common in society, and this is how things should be. It is preferable for a new student to enter the path of scholarship by correctly selecting his course of study, acquiring the proper research methodology, preserving an attitude that allows one to avoid the pitfalls of mistaken theories, and pondering the method of being able to quickly achieve results and increase one's merits. And in the same light, it is only natural that even though one pours his heart into the work, there will be some advantages and disadvantages depending upon the chosen course of study and the selected methodology.

The nature of scholarship is such that there are a variety of fields, so it is difficult for another person to tell a student which course of study he should pursue. On the whole, it is best to allow a student to pursue the path he has chosen. No matter how green the beginning student is, he surely is not like an ignorant child, and if the person really wishes to pursue the path of scholarship, then he will certainly have an idea of what he wishes to do. As

---

the point of view of *Nihon shoki*, especially since *Shoki* contains a more eclectic telling of the early mythology, but it seems more sensible—as Norinaga never put *Nihon shoki* above *Kojiki* after he seriously started his annotation of *Kojiki-den*—that Norinaga meant the mythology as found in both records.

there are things that the student is interested in and others that he is not, the student will have some natural abilities and some weaknesses, so no matter how much a student tries, if he is only engaged in things he has no interest in, or exerts himself in areas where his weaknesses are, there rarely is progress. And regardless of the path of scholarship that is being pursued, it is easy to teach a student using logic as the standard, but is that an effective way to teach? It may actually end up being ineffective, will it not? Because it is difficult to judge whether or not what is taught is good; even these things should not be forced upon the student, but should be left to his interests and desires.

In the long run, it is critical to one's learning that the student works tirelessly and carefully over a long period of time, regardless of what method one pursues; a student should not be obsessed with methodology. No matter how wonderful a person's method of study is, if he is negligent in his research, he will be ineffective. Also, there will be great differences in the effectiveness of students depending upon their abilities, but since talent is something innate, nothing further can be done. However, it is usually the case that if a student works hard without wasting time, even if he lacks some ability, he will be effective to an extent. Even students in the twilight years of their life can be unexpectedly effective in research if they apply themselves. Sometimes people who have very little free time surprisingly achieve greater results than those blessed with a great amount of time. Thus, a student should not become discouraged and terminate his pursuit of scholarship simply because he lacks ability, is gaining in years, or is not blessed with sufficient time. Keep in mind that one can achieve results if he applies himself. Becoming discouraged is the one thing that must be avoided above all when pursuing learning.

As I have mentioned above, it is difficult to say that someone should study this or that, and it is problematic to say that a student should employ this or that method. There actually is no difficulty when the student has yet to decide on a method of study, so the act of learning should be left to the desire of the individual student. However, if I leave the discussion at that, then the beginner will have nothing to rely on, may become disgusted, and I fear that this will lead to neglect. Thinking thus, I, Norinaga, have found myself with no other choice but to write down suggestions that I feel are necessary. Nevertheless, when it comes to teaching, what one man thinks is satisfactory another may feel is poor, so I in no way force my ideas upon others. I only write these ideas down for those who are inclined to give ear to my words.

First, among the various schools of learning each and every one is honorable and inescapable in its import for research. This refers to the diverse types of schools mentioned in the beginning, and each school must be well understood. Among these, the codes were established by carefully blending the ancient imperial system with the Tang system. However, the simplistic Japanese system was influenced by the cumbersome Chinese system, so the ancient system of the imperial country was altered in many areas; when the student studies the codes he must be mindful of these alterations. And in this field, unless one has a detailed grasp of Chinese records [in relation to administrative codes], one's research will make little headway; to make any headway [in studying the codes] it is necessary for the student to put great energy in studying these Chinese records, and his own study into Japanese will require more diligence to accomplish. The student should keep this in mind.

There are many aspects of governmental posts and ceremonies that also are based on Chinese models, so unlike the codes, it is not necessary for the student to put much effort into studying Chinese records. It is sufficient to elucidate governmental posts according to the Code on Government Posts. Most modern scholars base their work on Kitabatake Chikafusa's *Shokugenshō*, but this work is a description of the later state of government posts. Because everything naturally changes through the course of time, even the various aspects of our imperial court have been transformed through successive reigns, so the student first must elucidate the original state of each aspect of government. There are a number of works from later eras written on the topic of governmental posts.

In relation to the various ceremonies, the works *Jōgan gishiki* and *Kōnin no Dairishiki* are old. There is also *Gōke shidai* [by Ōe Masafusa], which is generally used as a reference work, but there are a number of areas where its descriptions are somewhat different from the ancient ceremonies. Students should compare this with *Jōgan gishiki* and other works. There is also a fine work published by the Mito Fief, called *Reigi ruiten* [compiled by Tokugawa Mitsukuni], but as it consists of several hundred volumes, it is not easy for the student to digest.

Also, in relation to the dress at court, and household effects, present scholars engage in detailed research into treatises on these works written in middle antiquity, and very few study these things from the ancient past. There are many later era works, but the student must start by studying the ancient records. Among these ancient records, there are works like *Engi shiki*, as well as *Saigūki* and *Hokuzanshō*. These last two works are not only concerned with dress at court and household effects, but also cover the myriad aspects at court, including the codes, governmental posts, and ceremonies. These works definitely must be read by students.

In relation to the various fields of scholarship mentioned above, the student should have reference to the various accounts recorded in the six national histories. The student should also refer to later-era works written by the various houses that exist here and there. I will address the study of poetry later in this essay.

Anciently there were a variety of versions of the study of the four fields and as these are all based on Chinese scholarship, there is no need to argue about that here. The label "four fields" refers to history and literature, Chinese classics, law, and mathematics. Among these the field of law deals with the codes, and as I have already explained above, the study of that anciently was closer to the original state, and so it is of a different type of study than that which people attempt in the present from books. Regarding foreign scholarship, there are many varieties among Confucian and Buddhist studies. As these are all foreign to Japan, there is no need to address them here. I believe that rather than have the student spend energy studying foreign ideas, he would be better off putting his effort into the study of Japanese things. He should set aside any evaluation about which is superior and which is inferior—is it not regrettable that people spend their time studying foreign ideas and are ignorant of things within their own country? so preferably, each should be studied; however, one person cannot elucidate the mysteries of each field during his lifetime, so a student must decide upon his main field of focus, and study it thoroughly. The student must aim his ambition high and wide from the beginning. When beginning any study, the student should be ambitious, and aim high and wide, being resolved to search and study, not quitting until he has elucidated the mysteries of his field. If one's resolve is weak, then the student does not make progress in his studies, but becomes weary and idles away his time. With this, he then should apply himself to other fields of study as much as his ability allows. Now, the chief area that one should focus on is the study of the Way. I do not necessarily need to give details about why one should apply himself to study a specific field, but if I were to give a few points, first, the student—as a human being—must comprehend the Way of humanity. Those who have no desire to pursue the Way of scholarship are irrelevant to the subject at hand; even if a student has but a small desire to learn, all the same, he must apply himself fully to studying the Way. However, it is not the true object of scholarship to devote the bulk of one's time to the study of trivial issues. Now, concerning studying the Way, it is a superior Way spanning the space between heaven and earth—how fortunate you are to have been born in this country where the true Way has been transmitted to us; thus, it goes without saying that you should be engaged in studying this honorable Way. This is the Way of Amaterasu Ōmikami, the Way through which the emperor governs the nation, the true Way that has spread across the four seas to the myriad nations in the world, but it has only been transmitted in this, the Imperial land. And in response to what kind of Way is it, the Way is described in the various events found in the divine age recorded in the two records, *Kojiki* and *Nihon shoki*. The Way is found in the record of events in the divine age as contained in these two works. However, unlike Confucianism or Buddhism, this Way is not something that can be taught by saying, "This is so, and that is such." Thus, if one reads *Kojiki* and *Nihon shoki* the same way he would read a Confucian or Buddhist work, he will find it difficult to comprehend the Way, and like a [bridge] with no railing, even a learned person who has studied things from the past will find that he has nothing to grasp, he has comprehended nothing. Or there are people who, not understanding these texts, expound the Way from the point of view of Buddhism or Confucianism. Originally, most of these older theories were based on Buddhism, but in the past 150 or 160 years, scholars have begun to realize this error, and have labeled theories based on Buddhism incorrect, and most of these older theories have been swept aside; however, many of our colleagues are still trapped by Confucian thinking, and all recent Shintō scholars belong to this group. Among this group are different schools of thought that vary slightly, but they are basically the same: their treatment of the divine age section in *Nihon shoki* and other ancient works are judged upon the Chinese system of divination, *yin* and *yang*, the eight hexagrams of divination, or the principle of the five elements. None of these do any justice to the ancient mind, being Shintō learning in name only, operating under the guise of Confucian learning. When Confucian scholars hear theories from these Shintō scholars, it is only natural that they laugh with contempt, declaring that the Shintō movement is a recent phenomenon. While these Shintō scholars realize that past Buddhism theories are incorrect, it is hilarious that they do not realize that basing their interpretations upon Confucianism is precisely the same mistake. If I were to inform these Shintō scholars of this fact, no doubt they would say that since Shintō and Confucianism are the same in essence, that is why they interpret passages thus; therefore, it is not the same as forcing a Buddhist idea upon the subject. However, their thinking is due to their lack of understanding the spirit of this Way. If they respond in this manner, then those who interpret these works from the point of view of Buddhism would be able to state that since Shintō and Buddhism are the same in essence, there is no problem. Both sides—Buddhist and Confucian—are gradually becoming lost in the mist, and that is why they think the way that they do. The true Way of Shintō is completely different from Confucianism and Buddhism, and there is not a single place where they agree.

As all recent Shintō scholars are in this state, they resemble the Zhu Xi school, putting their soul wholeheartedly into the study of one single train of thought without a glance to the right or left. However, they are shackled by the chains of Chinese logic, not inquiring into the hearts of the ancients; these areas resemble the Confucian way of thinking, and the more these scholars search for the Way, the farther they become separated from it. Also those scholars who have established their theories based upon Buddhism imitate Buddhist ceremonies, but the ancient ceremonies of our imperial land were nothing like these. There are recent Shintō scholars infected with Confucian ideas who create ceremonies they label as Shintō and unveil these for people, performing ceremonies like burial, mourning, and festivals that are different from those [traditional] ceremonies performed in society. Many of these things are creations based on Confucianism, and none have any ancient precedence.

In the past, Chinese things were more popular than Japanese, and many aspects of the ancient system were altered according to the Chinese system, so that the ancient, original form of Japanese ceremonies has been lost. Also, there are many Japanese things that have not been handed down to the present, so it is difficult to know any details, and this is deplorable. Once in a while, it appears that an ancient ritual has been partly preserved in the provinces, but it is truly rare that a ceremony has been transmitted down to the present without having been fused together with some Buddhism tradition.

The Way is performed by those above, and then handed down to those below; it is not established in private. Therefore, present Shintō scholars who perform ceremonies that differ from society are private in nature, regardless that some aspect in the ceremony matches something in ancient ritual. The Way is the great, just, public path of the country governed by the emperor, and it is truly wretched and lamentable when these scholars claim that Shintō is a tiny private affair interpreted in a narrow sense, performed like a shamanistic ritual, or some strange operation. The mentality of the ancient Way was for the common people to observe all laws that come from above, whether good or evil. This is how I interpret the ancient Way, and in my household, all hereditary festivals, alms given to Buddha on the altar, and ceremonies performed by monks are all conducted in the manner that my parents conducted them, nothing differing from that in society, and I do nothing but endeavor to be dutiful. A scholar should simply attempt to seek after the Way and elucidate it; it is not good for it to become a private affair. However, as far as one has energy, a scholar should research and uncover the ancient Way, then teach the basic points to others, writing these things down in a book. It may take five hundred or even one thousand years, but we must wait until the time is right when those above will adopt these ideas, perform them, and promulgate these to the common man below. This is my desire.

The student should read through the ancient sections of these two works over and over. Also, beginning students should read my *Kamiyo Masagoto* twenty or thirty times, It may appear egoistic for me to proclaim that you should read my works before reading the other many commentaries written on the sacred scripture of Shintō, but there is a good reason behind this. There are many commentaries, and if you first look through *Shaku Nihongi*, you will see that there is no attempt to illustrate the Way in its pages, and while it quotes from *Shiki* [private minutes of lectures], these theories are insufficient and childish. Commentaries after this are based on the thinking of Buddhism and Confucianism, being removed from the ancient heart, and in the end these commentaries do a great deal of damage to the Way. Thus, at present there is not a single work that one should read to support the Way. In spite of this, no matter how much effort the beginning student expends in trying to understand the text of these two works [*Kojiki* and *Nihon shoki*], it will likely not be an easy task to comprehend the import of the Way. It is here that our master, Agatai no Ushi, realized that scholars in society had fallen under the evil influence of the Chinese heart, and he generously taught how to avoid this, forcefully proclaiming the merits of the ancient Way; however, he put most of his energy in *Man'yōshū* and did not have time to focus on the Way itself. And while there are places where he touches upon the Way, these are not far-reaching ideas, as he lacked sufficient time to study the Way. Even in the study of the Way, there are many incomplete areas within the theories of the Way from our master. There are no other works in society than mine for the student to read in order to quickly comprehend the overall meaning of the Way. Thus, below I have without hesitation listed my *Kojiki-den* along with the ancient works.

Having said this, there will likely be an individual who will interpret what I have said as big talk from an arrogant person. But if I were to worry about the criticism I may receive, and not impart my opinions about the Way, in the end I have not been true and faithful to the beginning student, so what kind of criticism would I then receive? so that their mouths will become accustomed to the ancient lexicon. I also recommend that as soon as a student embarks on his studies, he should read *Naobi no Mitama*, *Tamaboko Hyakushu*, *Tamakushige*, *Kuzubana,* and other works of mine along with *Kojiki* and *Nihon shoki*. If you do this, you will realize that the Way is fully explained in the events recorded in these two ancient works, and be persuaded as to what generally constitutes the Way. If one reads the works I mentioned above early on, you will fortify the foundation of your Yamato spirit, and it will protect you from the pitfalls of the Chinese Heart. First, it is important that a student embarking on the journey of studying the Way wash himself clean of the Chinese Heart and the Confucian Heart (漢意儒意), and endeavor to solidify his Yamato spirit. In all things, I do not ask a person to rid himself of these things without a good reason, not simply because I dislike them. There is a serious reason. When asked why the Way is as yet not elucidated and why people make such terrible mistakes in interpreting the Way, it is because these people are led astray by the Chinese Heart, obstructed by it. This is a chronic disease that contaminated the hearts of Japanese over a thousand years ago, so it is difficult to cure. Recently, I hear of people who have come to the realization that it is not wise to combine Confucian ideas when elucidating the Way, but it is exactly these kinds of people who have not come completely clean from the disease, for their theories have fallen into the trap of the Chinese heart. Because of this, the most important, critical point in coming to an understanding of the Way is to completely rid oneself of the Chinese Heart. If one does not come completely clean, it is difficult to obtain the Way.

As a beginning student, purging yourself of the Chinese Heart, and firmly grounding your Yamato spirit is like a soldier going into battle who first carefully checks his armor and then girds himself with it. If you read the sacred works without having yourself prepared, it is like going into battle without your helmet or armor on; you will surely succumb to the blows of the enemy, and fall victim to the Chinese Heart.

Now, of these two ancient works mentioned above, the student should read *Kojiki* first in order to gain an understanding of the Way. First, the Shintō classics have been known as the tripartite scripture since ancient times, consisting of *Kujiki*, *Kojiki*, and *Nihon shoki*. Among these, scholars have mainly concentrated their studies on *Nihon shoki*, and next they studied *Kujiki*, supposedly compiled by Prince Shōtoku. *Kojiki* was not held in high esteem and no one has studied it deeply. However, in recent years, it has become clear that *Kujiki* is not an authentic work, but was compiled by someone later, and people rarely study it now. On the other hand, there are many people who have found that *Kojiki* is a valuable work, and this is all due to the teachings of my teacher, Master Agatai, who opened the way.

Truly, *Kojiki* has no embellishment from classical Chinese woven into its text; the legends have been recorded in their ancient, genuine state in a splendid manner. In comprehending the state of affairs of antiquity, not only is there no comparable work, but it includes more detail regarding the divine age than *Nihon shoki*, so this work should be esteemed and studied by the students of ancient learning above all other works. Therefore, I have dedicated my physical and mental energy to this work for the last several decades of my life, and have compiled a work in forty-four volumes on *Kojiki* as a study guide for the students of ancient learning.

This *Kojiki* is a record that contains the myths in their genuine state, so why is it written in classical Chinese? The answer to this question is because there was no record written in *kana* script until the Nara era, so all records were composed in classical Chinese. Writing and literature were originally imported from China, so the method of composition would naturally have been in imitation of Chinese, and though the words were different between our two countries, *katakana* nor *hiragana* did not exist yet, so in the beginning, everything was written just as the Chinese did. *Kana* script appeared after the *i-ro-ha* system, which appeared after the capital was removed to Heian-kyō. Therefore, it was the standard practice in ancient times for all records to be written in classical Chinese, and is not the type of phenomenon seen in later eras when people enjoyed writing in Chinese.

Song [or poetry] has a melodic interaction with each word in a line, and a change in even one character alters the meaning, so in the ancient records, song was written using phonetic script. The liturgies of Shintō and the Imperial edicts also are delicately arranged utterances, and so these were recorded in a different manner due to the difficulty of transposing these into purely classical Chinese.

However, as time passed, *katakana* and *hiragana* appeared, allowing people to write Japanese words in a natural script as they desired, so people did not need to write in classical Chinese like the ancient past. It is sheer foolishness to discard those things that are good and correct, and preserve those things that are mistaken and inconvenient. It is a grave mistake for people who do not understand what has been explained above to think it proper to compose things in classical Chinese even now because all the ancient records were originally written in Chinese. In later eras, we have the custom of recording family histories, everyday writings, and letters in classical Chinese, saying that this is masculine writing, or the male style of writing, and the *i-ro-ha* syllabary and *kana* script is feminine writing. This designation is due to men naturally adhering to the ancient custom, and women writing in the *i-ro-ha* style out of convenience. Reading *Nihon shoki* requires great care. *Nihon shoki* is our imperial court's official history, and everything in the successive imperial reigns has been based upon the record in this work, and successive generations of scholars have centered their studies on it. *Kojiki*'s writing style is truly grand, but the record of the successive emperors from Emperor Jinmu onward is scarce, shallow, and ambiguous. *Nihon* shoki's record is unparalleled in depth and detail, and is a valuable record. Without this record, we would not know many things in detail about the ancient past. But while this is true, one should not read the record without first being aware of Chinese ideas, due to the great amount of embellishment from classical Chinese. However, theological scholars in society have read the record without the slightest knowledge of these things, taking the record at face value, and have found joy in and praised the embellished areas of the text. Since these scholars put their hearts and souls in the work, their interpretations follow Chinese logic, and their ideas are far off the mark regarding the ancient Japanese meaning. I have dealt with many of these things in the first chapter of *Kojiki-den*. In another work, *Shindaiki no Uzu no Yamakage*, I have given my theories, also. The student is advised to refer to this work. Comprehending the work based solely on the text leads to a greatly altered form of the ancient meaning, and this leads the reader into the trap of the Chinese Heart. Next, the student should read *Kogo shūi*. This work was written somewhat later, but there are many places in *Kogo shūi* that supplement the text in *Kojiki* and *Nihon shoki*. It should be read early on. Next, the student should read *Man'yōshū*. It is an anthology of poetry, but it is a very important work in elucidating the Way. One should be careful when studying this work. I will explain why later. I have mentioned above most of the works the student should study when he wants to study the Way; however a student cannot ignore the records that were compiled after *Nihon shoki*, consisting of *Shoku Nihongi*, then *Nihon kōki*, then *Shoku Nihon kōki*, then *Montoku Jitsuroku* and *Sandai Jitsuroku*. Together, these works make up *Rikkokushi*, all official histories of the court. Of these six, *Nihon kōki* has for some unknown reason been lost and is no longer extant. The work that currently bears the same title in twenty volumes is not the complete work. However, recently, a man named Kamo no Sukeyuki went through *Ruijū Kokushi* primarily, adding information from other old reliable works, and compiled *Nihon Isshi* in forty volumes. This work suffices as a replacement for the lost *Nihon kōki*. *Ruijū Kokushi* is a work that has taken the information recorded in the six national histories and arranged these by category; it was compiled by Minister Sugawara.

Now, there is no official history after *Sandai Jitsuroku*. The only way to know about events after the reign of Emperor Uda is to go through various secondary records. Among these secondary records, there are many that resemble the national histories. Of late, there is a fine record compiled in Mito titled *Dai Nihonshi*, dealing with events from Emperor Jinmu down to the ascension of Emperor Go-Kameyama. These must be read in order. Also, these successive histories contain *senmyō* "imperial edicts," containing the ancient meaning and lexicon, so these should be read with care. Regardless that the imperial edicts recorded in *Nihon shoki* are all written in classical Chinese, those recorded in *Shoku Nihongi* and later are recorded using ancient words. To distinguish this style of writing the edicts from those written in classical Chinese, they are called *senmyō* "imperial edicts." As *Shoku Nihongi* is concerned with ancient times, there are many ancient words in the edicts. With each successive history, the number of ancient words used in the edicts decreases, and the use of classical Chinese increases. Not only the imperial edicts, but there are many records—no matter what they may be—where words dealing with our ancient customs are recorded without the influence by Chinese thought, so the student should pay special attention when he does research, for these words will assist you in knowing more about antiquity. Next the works that students of ancient learning should read include Ancient learning refers to the study of researching into the origin of all things as they are written in ancient records, and elucidating the ancient past in detail, ignoring theories from later ages. This study has its origin in the recent past. The priest Keichū was only concerned with poetic works, but he is the pioneer of our field. He should be called the father of our scholarship. Kada no Azumamaro, known as Master Hakura, appeared on the scene some time later, and established our discipline, concentrating on all ancient works, not just poetic ones.

And my teacher, Kamo no Mabuchi, inherited the teachings of Master Hakura, moving to Edo in the east, and he advanced this study in the prime of his life, and due to this, our discipline has generally spread throughout society. It was my master who thought deeply on the events of antiquity up to the Nara era, and conducted detailed research. Thanks to the merit of his teachings this knowledge is now within our grasp. *Engi shiki,*[3] *Shōjiroku,*[4] *Wamyōshō, Jōgan gishiki, Izumo fudoki,*[5] *Shaku Nihongi,*[6] This record [*Shaku Nihongi*] is from a later era, and every theory contained inside is juvenile, but there are truly rare and valuable records quoted inside that no

3. A compilation of court ceremony compiled during the Engi era (901–22). It is valuable for what it tells us about the Heian court.

4. The full title is *Shinsen Shōjiroku*. Compiled in 815 under the direction of Prince Manta. Its purpose was to legitimize those families at court that could prove they descended from *kami* or emperors.

5. The only ancient topographical record which Norinaga considered to be authentic. Others, like Bungo, Hitachi, Harima, and Hizen are still extant, but incomplete. However, Norinaga considered them compilations from later eras.

6. A compilation of question and answer sessions on the meaning of various aspects of

longer survive. None of the topographical works of the various provinces are in existence any more, aside from the quotes seen in *Shaku Nihongi* and Senkaku's *Man'yōshū chūshaku*, and these quotes are valuable for the study of ancient learning. *Shaku Nihongi* also quotes many of the ancient *Shiki* discussions on *Nihon shoki* that no longer survive. The *Shiki* theories are all naive, but because they are ancient, there are some areas that students should study. Of the works I have listed, starting with the six national histories, all contain many mistaken or omitted characters in the printed editions and the hand-copied manuscripts, so when one is able to obtain an old manuscript, much correction must be done. However, it is difficult to come by old manuscripts, so the student should seek after the revised manuscripts of his elders, and made gradual corrections. Incidentally, it may be said that there are many people today who value and enjoy things from antiquity, and sometimes one comes across a rare old work that has been hidden for ages. Along with this, many fraudulent works are also appearing, and though a specialist may be able to discern the fraud from the authentic, it often happens that a beginning student cannot discern the truth, and is deceived. The student should be aware. Therefore, it is best that a beginning student not focus on trying to procure rare old works. the statute section of the codes, *Seikyūki*, *Hokuzanshō*, and my *Kojiki-den* Listing a work that I wrote myself with these other valuable ancient works is conceited, and I would gladly refrain from doing so, but as I have stated above, there is no other commentary on ancient works that elucidates the ancient past from the point of view of ancient learning. Thus, it is satisfactory to read my work along with *Kojiki* and *Nihon shoki*, but I have listed it here because the work has many volumes. should be read by students of ancient learning. However, because it is no simple task for a beginning student to read through these many records, it would be wise to set aside the large works of many volumes and focus on reading the shorter works first. Among these works, the *norito* "liturgy" volume and the *Jinmyōchō* "register of the *kami*" volumes of *Engi shiki* should be read as early as possible.

It is not necessary to read all the works mentioned above in the order stated. Read this or that as you desire, not worrying about the order. And no matter which work you read, the beginning student will only understand a fraction of the meaning of every sentence. A student who tries to absorb difficult-to-comprehend sentences one by one from the beginning will become bogged down, and make little progress. Thus, it is better to skip the areas one does not understand for the time being and continue through the work he is reading. And it is really dreadful to try comprehending sections of works that scholars in general do not understand. Apply yourself to those sections that you do understand well, and relish

---

the *Nihon shoki* text held at court through the Heian era. It is valuable for its information, quoting many no longer extant works.

them deeply. If you pass lightly over these passages because you think that you understand them well, then you will overlook the finer details, and miss the subtle meaning. With this, you will embrace many mistaken ideas, and will forever be unable to realize that what you believe is incorrect. First, read through a work quickly, move on to another, and after reading several books, return to the former work, and after having read the same work several times, you will find that the sections you did not understand in the beginning are now becoming clearer to you. While you are reading these books, you will be inspired that there are other books you should read, and in what manner you ought to study them, so there is no need here to give detailed advice. I suddenly thought of something on this subject, so I composed a poem, and write it down here.

toru tebi mo	What shall be done with
ima wa nani semu	the lantern in your hands?
yo wa akete	Day dawn is breaking—
hogara hogara to	the shadows are vanishing
michi mieyuku o	from the path you see before you.

It is fine to allow the student to pursue his course as he sees fit, if the student wishes to read ancient as well as later works as far as he has strength, and it is also proper if he sees fit to narrow the field from which he selects his reading material. It is fine to be learned and read widely, but because these types of people have the tendency to be negligent in reading necessary works, I cannot say that reading widely is always good. It is perhaps better to put the same amount of energy into reading those works that are critical. For the most part, there is a reward in paying attention to reading this and that, but there are also times when it is damaging. The student must consider ways to deal with this problem.

The student also must pay close attention to the fifty sounds of the Japanese syllabary and *kana* usage. This concerns the so-called phenomenon of contraction, and looking at a sound chart, where consonants are arranged at the top and vowels down the side. We find that there is evolution from one vowel or consonant to another in a different phonetic series, epenthesis, or elision, which is very important in interpreting the ancient lexicon. The student must pay careful attention from the beginning. By "Japanese syllabary" I am referring to that used in ancient times. The one currently used in poetics originated during the Heian era and is not suitable for the ancient lexicon. The student need not be particular about etymology. Etymology here implies researching into the original meaning of words, and then expounding upon that meaning. For example, minutely interpreting the meaning of works like *ame* "heaven" or *tsuchi* "earth" to find out what they really mean. This is one of the things scholars would first like to know, but the student need not pay such deep attention to detail. For the most part, it is difficult to get a good etymology [or words] as the entire process is difficult. There is little loss in not knowing the etymology of a word, and little to be gained from knowing it.

Thus, instead of focusing on what the original etymology was, it is better to consider how the ancient people used a specific word—it is critical to know that certain words were used in a certain semantic way. Without knowing how specific words were used, the student cannot understand part of what he is reading. Also, when you write something, you will make mistakes when using certain words [from the ancient lexicon]. Scholars engaged presently in the study of the ancient Way tend to apply themselves to etymology and neglect the actual meaning of words as they were originally used. Thus, they misunderstand what they read in the ancient works, and the poetry they compose, along with what they write, contains errors in their diction and usage. They make so many ridiculous mistakes! Also, it is good to read Chinese works while you do your research. There is great reward in reading Chinese works. If your Japanese spirit is firmly grounded and unmovable, you will not be led astray, even if you were to read Chinese works day and night. However, people in society today find it hard to firmly ground their Yamato spirit, and when they read Chinese works, they are led astray by the skillfully worded passages, and have a tendency to shy away [from truth]. "Skillfully worded passages" does not insinuate that those paragraphs are beautiful. What I mean is that the words are employed in a creative fashion, making it easy for the reader to become trapped and led astray.

Because Chinese works are generally written skillfully, and are based on a tradition of effective argument through logic, a reader is readily convinced of their truth. Even when one considers lay matters, an intelligent person who has a gifted tongue can persuade another person easily, and so the student should remember that Chinese works are much the same.

All old works are written in classical Chinese, using Chinese script. Especially, from the time of emperors Kōtoku and Tenchi onward, many things were established according to the Chinese system, so there are many places in the records you cannot comprehend without some knowledge of Chinese. But when you read these Chinese works, if your Yamato spirit is not sufficiently grounded, you will be misled by the style of the Chinese words. It is critical to remember this.

Now, as you gradually make progress in your studies, and gain a general knowledge about your field, it is worthy to prepare your mind to produce a commentary on an ancient work, any work. When a person reads through a work, there is a limit as to how much he can learn if he has read the work casually. However, if you read with the intention of adding annotation and pay special attention, you will be able to read thoroughly, no matter what work it may be, and gain a treasure of information in other areas. Therefore, even though your commentary may not actually materialize, this kind of research has great benefits in all areas of scholarship. And this goes not only for commentaries, but you should pay attention when writing in general. Producing a commentary on something does much to further scholarship. Now, as I have stated above, after having read *Kojiki* and *Nihon shoki*, you must carefully study *Man'yōshū*. Even though this work is a poetic collection, it is listed after *Kojiki* and *Nihon shoki*, and it may seem difficult to fathom why this work is so valuable in comprehending the Way, but most of the teachings of my master rest upon this work. According to his theory, if one wishes to come to an understanding of the ancient Way, one must first learn ancient poetry, composing in the ancient tradition. Then the student must learn ancient prose, composing it in the ancient style. The student must understand the ancient lexicon well, and read *Kojiki* and *Nihon shoki* thoroughly. My master always taught that without knowledge of the ancient lexicon, a student could not comprehend the ancient heart, and without knowledge of the ancient heart, a student could not come to an understanding of the ancient Way. This may sound like beating around the bush, but this is certainly not the case. Let me explain these points in detail. The words, actions, and thoughts of humans resemble each other for the most part. For example, an intelligent person's words and actions are usually intelligent, while a foolish fellow's words and actions are accordingly foolish. Also, if one is a man, his thoughts, words, and actions are masculine, while the thoughts, words, and actions of a woman are feminine.

It follows that the differences in historical eras also differ likewise; the thoughts, words, and actions of the people of the ancient past were after the ancient manner, while people in middle antiquity act in a manner after that period; people in recent eras act in a contemporary manner—the words, actions, and thoughts of these people resemble each other within their respective historical eras. However, if one—in the present—is to research into the words, actions, and thoughts of people in the ancient past, you will find that their words are recorded in poetry, and their actions are written down in historical works. Because historical works are recorded through words, only words come forth, but one can know the thoughts of the ancients through their poetry. Since words, actions, and thoughts are closely interrelated, from a later perspective, the only way to understand the thoughts of the ancients, and comprehend their actions is to look into the ancient lexicon and ancient song. The ancient Way is found within the events recorded in the divine age sections of *Kojiki* and *Nihon shoki*, and when a student has deeply studied the ancient lexicon and ancient song, and reads these two works, the significance of the ancient Way will naturally become clear. Thus, in the past I have demonstrated this to my beginning students, instructing them that they should peruse my *Kamiyo no Masagoto*, so that they will become accustomed to the usage of the ancient lexicon.

Kojiki has recorded the ancient traditions in their pure form, but because it is also written in classical Chinese, it does not approach the value of *Man'yōshū* in order to properly understand the ancient lexicon. Also, the value of *Nihon shoki* is diminished because it is full of Chinese embellishment. Now, since the songs recorded in *Kojiki* and *Nihon shoki* are ancient, these are prized treasures that further an understanding of the ancient lexicon and the ancient meaning. However there are relatively few songs included in these two works, so it is insufficient when trying to do in-depth research. *Man'yōshū* contains a great number of poems, and has been transmitted down to the present with little loss in relation to ancient words, and that is why my master advised me to study *Man'yōshū* first.

In all respects, the [true] Way of Shintō differs from the Ways of Buddhism and Confucianism, and there is not even a hint of the bothersome debate about good and evil. This Way simply abounds in generosity and elegance, and the beauty of poetry suits this Way well. When reading *Man'yōshū*, the reader should be aware that the present text is full of incorrect characters, and there are many places where the reading of the text is unacceptable. It is also good to study and produce ancient poetry yourself. There is a difference in depth of feeling in contrast to something that one experiences for himself and something that someone else has experienced. No matter how deep the experience may be of someone else, it will not be as deep as something experienced by you. It is the same with poetry. Even though ancient poetry may be profound in emotion, it will not draw out deep emotions from you, because it is another's experience; however, when you compose your own poetry, you pay attention as it is your own experience and come to understand the profound meaning of the poem. And that is why my teacher, Master Mabuchi, taught me to compose ancient poetry and prose on my own.

Concerning prose, there are literary sections of ancient prose still available in the eighth volume of *Engi shiki,* where the liturgies are recorded, and the successive imperial edicts written in pure ancient Japanese in *Shoku Nihongi*. Occasionally there are sections in *Kojiki* and *Nihon shoki* written with ancient Japanese words. There are also instances where ancient prose is mixed in the texts of other ancient works. It is well to use this and that as a model. *Man'yōshū* is poetic in nature, and while there is a difference between poetic and prosaic usage, if one is careful in selecting his words based on the standard of diction, many poetic usages can also be employed in prose. *Man'yōshū* is a work that must be learned well even for practicing the composition of ancient prose.

There is much that can be said concerning the method for practicing the composition of prose, comprehension, ancient style, contemporary style, and the techniques of various periods, but it is difficult to explain these all here. One may comprehend the method in the same manner as he has understood poetry. There are various aesthetic levels of prose, and with each level there are many differences in word usage and literary style, so one must have a good command of these. "Various aesthetic levels" refers to prefaces, treatises, records, correspondence, and so forth.

If we were to mention people in later eras who had a good habit of producing poetry in the *Man'yō* tradition, I know of no one other than the Kamakura minister of the right [Minamoto Sanetomo]. And yet after my master started composing poetry in the *Man'yō* style, many people have followed his teachings, but their aims are not necessarily to elucidate the ancient Way; they merely produce poetry because they get pleasure from such composition, much like the poets who compose in the contemporary style. And there is no difference in their desire to produce skilled verse. Let me now focus my discussion on poetry and its comprehension, leaving aside the view that poetry can be a vehicle to understand the Way.

It is said that poetry is a verbal expression of what is felt in one's heart, but poetry is the tradition of using elegant expression and avoiding colloquial usages, employing a beautiful melody in the stanzas. It has been this way since the divine age. Simply saying what you feel without any concern for the melody of the stanzas is everyday speech and not poetry. There is a difference between good poetry and bad poetry in relation to the elegance in word use in each stanza, but the ancients simply produced poetry within the confines of a set syllable count; they did not attempt poetry like later eras, where the poet pondered a theme, assumed a posture, and skillfully composed a verse. But within the poetry the ancients produced there naturally was superior and poor verse. Superior verse was sung in society and handed down, and these types of poems are recorded in *Kojiki* and *Nihon shoki*. Thus, the student may know that the poetry contained in these two works is the finest in antiquity. In *Kojiki* the events surrounding the composition are often recorded because a poem was so well written.

In this way, there has been superior and poor poetry since the ancient past, and superior poetry was the type that echoed in the hearts of men and moved the *kami* to emotion. Poor poetry was the type that failed to move human or *kami*. When Amaterasu was hiding in the Ama no Iwato cave in the divine age, she was moved by the words of the liturgy recited by Ame no Koyane. The splendidness of this event can be seen in the divine age section of *Nihon shoki*. The student can see parallels here in relation to poetry.

Thus, as time passed, people tried to produce poetry on themes, which occurred because of the natural emotional pull where a poet could not restrain his feelings. Most of the poetry contained in *Man'yōshū* was composed upon themes, and there are few poems that were composed spontaneously. If this was the case in the era of *Man'yōshū*, why should a person be chastised in a later era or even in the present for wanting to compose superior poetry? Since this is the natural force within us, people who want to compose ancient poetry must carefully select their vocabulary, and produce poetry in an elegant and skillful manner. Everyone should produce poetry, but it is especially vital that a scholar compose poetry. Without composing poetry, it is difficult to comprehend the subtle things of the ancient ages, and savor the elegance of the past. Among the poems of *Man'yōshū*, one should imitate poems that are simple, lofty, and elevating. *Man'yōshū* is not an anthology compiled just from superior poems, but contains verse selected regardless of its quality. So though the poetry is ancient, there are many inferior poems. If a student wishes to rely upon *Man'yōshū*, then he must discern the superior from the poor. If one looks at the ancient poetry composed by recent scholars, they use the vile method of purposely including strange words from *Man'yōshū* to give the poem an archaic feeling, and amaze the listener. It is a great bother and quite unattractive to go to such lengths to make one's poetry or prose appear ancient. One should only take as his model poetry in *Man'yōshū* that is flowing and well organized; avoid those poems that use strange words.

Now there are different levels in ancient poetry and ancient prose, some being extremely old while others are not. Thus, the words and usages of the poem must agree with the entire style of the poem, but many of the ancient poems produced presently have no unity in word usage. In a poem or a paragraph of prose, one finds a very old usage and then in the next line there is a thoughtlessly included contemporary usage, so the style is incoherent.

Generally, those who follow the ancient poetic tradition are so caught up in detesting the excessive restrictions of later-style poetry that they try to avoid any and all restrictions, resulting in their poetry being utter confusion. And while there were no written regulations in the *Man'yō* era, there was a natural set of rules, so the poet did not simply do as he pleased. It is a misinterpretation to think that the ancient poetic style is not controlled by regulations.

In the present era, one cannot label poetry as "the ancient style" simply because he tries to imitate that style, if the poetry does not conform to the standards of the ancient poetic style. People today arrogantly claim that their poetry is in the ancient style, but they do not understand the rules of that style, believing in something that does not exist. Composing poetry in the *Man'yō* style is a recent phenomenon, and since there are no books that illustrate the ancient regulations of that tradition, there are many who recklessly compose their poetry. The student should compose *chōka* "long poems," also. The ancient style of *chōka* poems is especially excellent. Not all *chōka* in *Kokinshū* are good; some of these are terrible. After the capital was removed to Heian-kyō, the composition of *chōka* gradually became uncommon, and the style deteriorated. In later eras, there are no examples of *chōka*, but *Man'yō* poetry came back in vogue, and recently many people are composing these; among these, a few are so well done that there would be no shame in including these in the anthology, itself. This is proof of the celebrated eminence of the present imperial reign. When one tries to communicate the various events that occur in the present, it is difficult to express them in the contemporary poetic style, but there are many times when the ancient *chōka* style is suitable. In this respect, every student should learn to produce poetry in the *chōka* style.

Concerning poetry, there are various styles, the ancient style, middle antiquity style, each different according to varying eras, but it goes without saying that the student of ancient learning must make it his main goal to master the ancient style; the student should also compose poetry in the later style, and not just ignore it. Those students who compose poetry in the *Man'yō* tradition generally criticize later styles of poetry as being poor, but this does not mean that they have based their judgment on a firm knowledge of the superiority or inferiority of later poetry. They merely cling to one branch of logic, unsparingly supposing that anything ancient is good and everything from later eras is bad. And forcing the superiority and inferiority of poetry into the mold of peace and war, prosperity and decline within history is a one-sided way to argue, and far from reality. And like poetry from antiquity, if a poet always composed a poem when he was stimulated by some emotion, then perhaps this form of argument could be employed. However, since poetry from later eras was all composed upon preselected themes, if a poet learned a poor style of poetic composition during an era of peace, then he would still produce poor poetry. And if a poet learned a skillful style during a time of unrest, then why would his poetry be poor? It is not important to make the distinction between masculine and feminine styles of poetry. Also, I have dealt with the idea of strong and weak poetic styles in another work [see *Isonokami Sasamegoto*].

The debate about the superiority and inferiority of poetic styles from the ancient past and later eras is extremely important, and since the debate cannot be resolved easily, it is unfathomable how scholars in ancient learning can look superficially at the matter, and carelessly hand down a decision.

One reason that scholars who follow the ancient style of poetry think that later verse is unworthy is because poetry is a medium to express emotions felt in the heart. Emotionless poetry of later eras composed upon a predetermined subject contains no personal emotion from the poet, and is thus lacking in feeling and substance, having originated in a forced environment. This criticism states that this kind of poetry is deceptive, which goes against the true meaning of poetry. On the surface this argument appears to be logical, but these people do comprehend the minute details of poetry. As I have stated above, poetry is not something immediately produced when a person has felt something in his heart, but it is the Way where the words are given elegance, and the melody is tightened. Poetry has been like this since the divine age, and superior poetry caused man and *kami* alike to feel emotion. Even poetry included in *Man'yōshū* was composed with a definite purpose—to compose a good poem—and these were embellished; these were not necessarily composed only from simple emotion. The student may realize this from the use of epithets and prefatory stanzas in poetry composed in the ancient past. Epithets and prologues to poetry are not things a poet feels in his heart. This is the artful use of words, and does it not show that poetry was also constructed?

Originally, poetry was composed when someone felt something and expressed this to another person, the listener moved by the emotion of the poem, his heart uplifted. Thus, the original meaning of poetry must also consider the feelings of the listener. However, as times changed, there was a natural tendency to make one's poetry more refined, and reach for higher plateaus of skill. Some poetry in later eras was composed from actual emotions, but that does not even constitute one-hundredth of all poetry composed, poetry now having become a device of fiction. And while this is true, the act of producing poetry changed from era to era, composed from the thoughts of the human heart. Though poetry became an act of creation, there were no poems that failed to reflect human emotions, and all poetry fits into the elegant style of ancient poetry. However, if a scholar outright rejects later poetry and concentrates only on the changes from era to era, then he has not fathomed the fact that some things have remained unchanged. It is good to realize that later poetry has specific aspects that are exactly the same as ancient poetry.

Additionally, having a student produce poetry in the *Man'yō* style does not correspond to real emotion, but is a fictitious act of imitation. If a person right now wishes to express the feelings within his heart, he should use a poetic style that is current, and should not imitate the ancients. Since imitating *Man'yō* poetry is a fictional act, why should it be bad to determine a subject to which poetry would be composed? In order to produce good poetry, a person must practice composing many poems. In order to produce many poems, a person needs a theme to use. This is a natural chain of events.

It goes without saying that there is some terrible poetry composed in later eras. However, if one intended to select just poor poetry and criticize it, then there would also be poor poetry selected from the ancient times. It is not good to discriminate against later poetry. Considering poetry composed in later eras, there are some remarkably beautiful poems that express feelings that certainly could not have been expressed in the ancient style. In almost everything, there are areas where later eras are superior to the ancient past, so you cannot say that later eras are uniformly poor. And if one intends to compare ancient and later era poetry, there are strengths and weaknesses, and I have composed poetry for the last twenty or thirty years, pondering this very subject. Obviously there is an abundance of fine, elegant poetry in *Man'yōshū*; however, when people take this style and try to imitate it, there is a tendency for failure, as it takes generation after generation for a poetic style to cultivate elegance. People in the present generation who engage in poetry in the ancient style compose poetry in an indiscriminate manner when they are beginners, but when they discover some discretion, there are many instances when it is difficult to compose in the *Man'yō* style, so they gradually come to interweave their thoughts and words into a later poetic style, slowly approaching recent poetic styles. Sometimes they produce poetry in the ancient style, not always relying on a later style, nor in the *Kokin* style; there are many times when a person produces in an impulsive style. This is because the ancient style was unsuitable for a specific emotion.

If a person states that the poet must also produce in the later style, when we look at the poetry in *Man'yōshū*, we notice that many of the excellent serene poems are basically the same; the essence of the poems resembles one another, and the meaning is normally standardized, some having the last two stanzas set. Those few poems composed upon a rare topic are for the most part sordid, and their poetic style is poor. However, if during the more than one thousand years that have passed since the *Man'yō* era, everyone who produced poetry attempted to preserve the *Man'yō* style and always composed excellent poetry, then there would be nothing but imitation of *Man'yōshū* poems, nothing new being composed; there would be no value in producing poetry on any new topic. Thus, as generations change, when a poet desires to compose poetry on a theme that the ancients did not employ, then the poetic style is obliged to change with the times. Versification is a tradition in which poetic skill must gradually be sharpened and deepened. If a poet composes poetry in the same way that many of the ancients did, even if the poem produced is superior, humans and *kami* alike will not feel any emotion from the poem. And if a poet attempts to compose poetry in a rare form within the *Man'yō* tradition, then the result will be am unsuitable and loathsome poem. Since some of the poems in *Man'yōshū* fall into this snare, we must be especially careful in the present. …

When the beginning student attempts to follow my teachings and compose poetry in both the ancient and contemporary styles, he will wonder whether he should start with ancient or later poetry, but in all things the student should make the trunk of his learning firm, and then branch out. But there are times when one can start with the branches and work back toward the trunk of learning, so I believe that it is best to master the style of later poetry and then proceed back to the ancient style. There are one or two reasons behind this thought: first, when one first composes poetry in the later style, he comes to know the rules and minute details of verse, and this enables the poet to have discipline when composing ancient poetry, allowing him to avoid composing outrageous verse. Also, since the ancient days are far in the past, no matter how well a poet may have learned poetry, he is still a product of the present, and it is very difficult for him to mirror the feelings of the ancients. Thus, it is easy to include later or newer vocabulary in the poetry composed, even though you think you used the ancient style. In spite of the fact that there must be a distinction between ancient and later in poetry and in prose, people of the present cannot avoid mixing ancient with new in their poetry and prose to some extent; however, if the person has a good grasp of the later style, then there will be fewer mistakes after the person has acquired the ability to distinguish later style from others. Since most people do not have the ability to distinguish styles, they fall into the snare of the later style. It is ridiculous that those scholars who follow the ancient style and detest the later style do not realize that their poetry is an amalgamation of old and new. There are other advantages for learning the style of later poetry, even for a person who composes in the ancient tradition. When one clearly sees the difference between ancient and later traditions, there will be no harm in producing verse in the later style, and one should not feel the need to detest later poetry. What one should detest is the mixing of poetic styles. This is not only true of poetry, but all scholarship connected with the pursuit of the ancient Way; if one does not know the difference between old and new, then he will become ensnared unknowingly thinking of later eras and the Chinese Heart. The key point of ancient learning is being able to distinguish between ancient, later, and Chinese thought.

There are good and bad styles among the later era poetic traditions, so the student must be careful in his selection. Just as there are beautiful and unattractive colors among dyed robes, there are good and bad styles among the later poetic traditions that have changed from era to era. Among these styles, *Kokinshū* is first worthy of note because of its antiquity and the care taken in compilation; it is truly a fine work containing few poor poems. As my master always pointed out, many of the anonymous poems in *Kokinshū* are splendid. Many of these are especially superb old poems. This work appears between the style of antiquity and later eras, and many of the old poems in this anthology are similar to poems in *Man'yōshū*; these poems should be used as models for beginning students as they are splendid. However, the poems composed from the reign of emperors Kōkō and Uda onward are very different from those in *Man'yōshū*, being closer to the style of later eras, so I have decided to label *Kokinshū* as a fine piece representing the later era. This work should be studied from morning till dusk, and special care should be placed on the poems composed after the capital was removed to Heian.

Next, the manner of compilation of *Gosenshū* and *Shūishū* is wild and chaotic, and there are many poems that are unbelievably poor. In spite of this, there are many poems that are good, with even a few wonderful poems mixed in. Looking at the successive anthologies after *Goshūishū*, we see a continuation of the rise and fall of superior and inferior compilations, but it would be laborious to expound upon all the details, so I will give but a brief overview.

During this period, *Shin Kokinshū* appeared. At that time, the verse of skilled poets was unparalleled in meaning, vocabulary, and the manner of interweaving images. Among the poetry of this anthology are superb, well-composed poems, interesting beyond description, carrying meaning to a profound depth—a splendid illustration of later ages. When examining poetry from high antiquity till the present, one may insist that the poetic apex in poetry is *Kokinshū*, but when this anthology is compared with *Shin Kokinshū*, one realizes that there are failings in *Kokinshū*, so it surely would not be a mistake to call *Shin Kokinshū* the apex of Japanese poetry. Nevertheless, our colleagues in ancient learning engage in absurd and reckless speculation when they denigrate *Shin Kokinshū* as a poor literary work. Certainly the only reason these scholars do not recognize the splendid poetry of *Shin Kokinshū* is due to the fact that they do not comprehend the elegance of emotion. And yet, the poets of this era attained such a height of skill and profundity that there is a tendency to become conventional, and there are many forced poems, some being hard to comprehend because they were so poorly composed. But even so, it is the characteristic of *Shin Kokinshū* poetry that though some of the poems are forced, their diction is so beautiful and refined, composed with such sonorous vocabulary that it is difficult to discard them. However, this is a peculiar refined skill that poets of that day possessed, and it is not something that later poets can normally hope to imitate. If one were to force himself to imitate this style, his poetry would become an indescribable joke. A poet whose verse is still undeveloped should not attempt poetry in the style of *Shin Kokin*. Yet, if you have a thorough knowledge of poetry, then my advice should not obstruct you in your pursuit. Why should one not have the desire to produce poetry like the *Shin Kokin* poets after he has established his poetic groundwork? …

This practice of esteeming dogma is not particular to just Shintō scholars and poets, but has been practiced by many fields of learning and art since middle antiquity; it is truly a very inane practice. No matter how wonderful the tradition may be, if the teachings are inadequate or the skill is inferior, then the dogma cannot be used. There are fields in the arts where the tradition must be esteemed because of the acquired skill, but when it comes to scholarship and poetry, the superiority or inferiority of the field is not defined by the tradition. The student can comprehend this by looking through the various poetic anthologies. Poetry from a broad range of poets is contained in the collections, regardless of the poet's background or tradition. Did not noble Teika teach that there is no master in Japanese poetry?

There are many rules and regulations set down by the poets of the past that people should observe, but there are many others that are foolish and one should not feel obliged to adhere to. In spite of this, in recent years, poetry has degenerated simply because poets continue to adhere to these many silly regulations. One must select the good rules from the poor in this Way of poetry. There is no need to follow a regulation simply because it is a regulation. It is also inane to blindly revere the poetry of ancient poets as the unattainable poetic pinnacle without investigating whether such poetry is superior or inferior. No matter how superior a past poet, there is much that is inferior in ancient poetry; no matter how revered a poetic sage, it does not mean that all of his poetry is superior. For example, the student should closely examine the poetry of Hitomaro and Tsurayuki to see if it is superior or inferior. And even if you cannot completely attain the heights they did, it is wise to critique their poetry. There is nothing better in learning about poetry than discerning the superior and inferior. There is much advantage to this routine. However, if you take the attitude of contemporary poets that superior poetry is unattainable and do not turn the discerning eye to see whether poetry is really fine or poor, then you will not be able to judge whether your own poetry is improving. Is it not worthless to go throughout life living in the shadow of the poetic masters? You should thus remember that if you acquire the vapid, erroneous poetic method of contemporary poets, you will go throughout life unable to compose good poetry.

As I mentioned in the beginning, the study of poetry is not just about composing verse but is also the scholarship of commenting on those things written down in poetic works. Society labels people engaged in this field as poetic scholars. Poetics is concerned with the composition of poetry, but for the moment let us divide this into two branches. Anciently, the monk Kenshō was a scholar of poetics, and while there are many facets of his thinking that will not hold water, he wrote many things that can be quoted simply because he lived so long ago. When we come to the theories of people who have lived in the last three hundred years, there are many who adhere to the silly traditions of the contemporary poets; whatever they say is puerile; there is nothing worthy of note. But in recent years, the monk Keichū appeared, and the study of poetics made great leaps, and his methodology of using poetic works has improved scholarship.

Among these two branches, one of poetic composition and the other of concentrating on poetics, scholars who have chosen the path of poetics starting with Kenshō tend to excel in poetic scholarship, but fail in poetic production. And a poet who is gifted usually is not engaged in poetics. Is this predicament due to the poet being devoted to poetry or indifferent to it? Regardless, it is a mistake to declare that all those who are engaged in poetics produce poor poetry. If a person has a keen understanding about the differences of these two branches, then why should poetics become an obstacle to producing poetry? If it does become an obstacle and the scholar cannot produce good poetry, then it is due to his not knowing the distinction between the two. So the student may study something about poetics, but in the end he should concentrate on the composition of poetry. The student cannot sufficiently study poetics without having widely read Buddhist and Chinese works, so there have been many instances where the student spends too much time concentrating on meaningless works. And it is well for the student to always read tales like *Ise monogatari* and *Genji monogatari* and others. I will leave this aside, because I have dealt with this subject in detail in my *Genji monogatari Tama no Ogushi*. Producing poetry on your own, regularly reading the tales, and coming to an understanding of the elegance of the ancients will not only be of great value to the person studying poetics, but will be invaluable to the student who is pursuing the Way. No one can make progress in their studies without a knowledge of the significance of elegance. If one does not know about elegance, then one also does not understand *mono no aware*, and that person is without feeling. When one knows about elegance, then he composes poetry and carefully peruses tales. Knowing the elegance of the ancient human emotions and having knowledge of the elegance of the ancient past is a step toward knowing about the ancient Way. However, when we examine the state of scholars of contemporary learning, we find that as has been mentioned above, those who concentrate on the Way are mainly concerned with Chinese-tainted debate and logic, believing that poetic composition is fruitless; they do not attempt to open and read poetic anthologies, and since they do not know the meaning of the elegance of the ancients—they do not even see it in their dreams—they cannot comprehend the principal areas of the ancient Way. In this state, what they label as Shintō is for the most part a construct of foreign ideas, and in no way can it be said that they are studying a Way. Those scholars who produce poetry, compose prose, and delight in doing those things the ancients did are generally enthralled by the superficial refinement, having neglected the Way, and have little interest in learning about it. These people imitate ancient customs, delighting in ancient fashion or accessories, and their entertainment in reading old works is nothing more than a mere trifling sprinkled with superficial elegance.

No matter who a person may be, he must have some knowledge of the Way of humanity. And no matter what course of study you may pursue, a person who reads books should not thoughtlessly waste away his life neglecting the Way, ignorant of the praiseworthy blessings of the *kami*. If a person wishes to experience antiquity and esteems it, then he should first set his heart on the fundamental Way, and elucidate and comprehend it. One does not really delight in antiquity if he puts the Way on a shelf and trifles with peripheral matters. In a state like this, it is a waste of time to compose poetry. People who follow what I have said and wish to study should comprehend the meaning of the things I have said above, and ponder these. One must not think that he can neglectfully trifle with the Way.

In relation to writing this work, my students have requested that I write down advice, but for years I have had no time, and have turned a deaf ear to their requests. However, I have finished *Kojiki-den*, and can no longer ignore their request, so with brush in hand I have written this work. I wrote my ideas down on the spur of the moment, and there are many things that I perhaps have left out. However, perchance this will be of some small benefit to the beginning student.

ikanaramu	Will it be helpful
ufiyamabumi no	this handbook that was meant
asagoromo	to be a white robe
asaki susono no	for the student standing at
sirube bakarimo	the base of his first mountain?

Motoori Norinaga
Completed on the evening of the twenty-first day
of the tenth month of Kansei 10 [1798]
[MNZ 1976, 1:3–30]

☙

This page is intentionally left blank.

Part Four
Views on Japan/Religion

KOKUIKŌ[1]

Kamo no Mabuchi | 1765

[Mabuchi wrote this essay based on what may have been an imaginary conversation with someone representing Confucian learning, though it is clear that he had *Bendōsho*, written by Dazai Shundai (1735), in mind, as his questions parallel those in the earlier work.[2] Mabuchi appealed to what he thought Japanese culture should be based on his concept, through his reading of ancient texts—mainly *Man'yōshū*—of what the ancient culture had been. He sees the ancient, pristine culture of Japan as being in harmony with Nature and heaven, but with the introduction of Chinese culture a fundamental change occurred. His claim is based on what he sees as a lack of spontaneity in later culture, where ancient culture was replete with natural phenomena. He asserts that through careful study of the past, it was possible to change this condition back to what it had been.]

A person once said, "I have no interest in something frivolous like poetry, but I do have great interest in the Chinese system of ruling the country."

Hearing this, I just smiled, not responding to what he had said. Later, when I met the same man again, he said to me, "Why were you simply smiling at me last time, even though I was discussing the reasoning of various things?"

I replied, "Were you referring to Confucianism, which came from China? Confucianism is a man-made idea that is trivial when compared to the heart of heaven and earth."

Hearing this, the man became very angry, "How can you call this great Way trivial?"

I then said, "So, I would like to know if a country has ever been governed effectively by Confucianism?"

Having asked this, he answered me that the reigns of the Yao, Shun, Xia, Yin, and Zhou dynasties are examples of China being effectively governed. To this I replied, "And there have not been any after that?" He answered that there have been none since. I again asked, "How many reigns does China's tradition claim that it has had?" He replied that from the Yao

1. One manuscript has 国乃許々呂 *kuni no kokoro* "the heart of the state." Most other manuscripts have 国意考 "thoughts on the meaning of the state." I have followed the latter, since it is most commonly known by this title.

2. See Flueckiger (2008:213).

Dynasty down to the present there have been numerous reigns (for thousands of years). I further inquired, "If it is true that the state was governed effectively from the reigns of the Yao down to the Zhou, then what happened afterward? In other words, you are saying that a tradition that has existed for thousands of years only governed the very ancient times well? However, these are just tales from antiquity. You see, the world cannot be governed simply by Confucian logic."

After I said this, this man became all the more flustered, and explained all the events in ancient history. I retorted, "You are biased towards Confucianism. Do you believe that Yao conceded the throne to that despicable Shun? You make it sound as if this event was for the welfare of the country, but in this, the imperial country, we call this 'ablutions to invite good events'[3] and is viewed as very worthy. Therefore, in China there appeared vile men who refused to concede the throne, stole control of the government, and assassinated the ruler. This is 'ablutions to rid one of evil.'[4] Thus, when something good is abundant, it turns out to be abundant in evil. Also, a man known as Mencius said, 'People who lived in the Yao and Shun eras were all virtuous because of the influence of the virtuous ruler, so some of them were given land and made feudal lords.'[5]

Taking this into consideration, was the father of Emperor Shun called an obstinate man[6] because he pretended not to see the virtue in his son [and tried to kill him]? Shun's father was one of the people of the Yao era, so how could he have been given territory and made a feudal lord? After Shun came Emperor Yu. And was not Yu's father an evil man, and banished to a far-off province? He was a person from the reign of Shun, and though he was the father of Yu, was he someone to whom territory could have been [rightly] given? Now, if these facts are secure, then Mencius is what is now called "a wise man whose wisdom resides in his tongue."

I do not know how long the Yin era continued, but the founding emperor is said to have been a good man who received the throne from Yu. If this was so, then would not the successors have been good people, too? And at the end of the Yin era there appeared the evil King Zhou who was

3. Mabuchi's use of よしきらひもの is not clear. It appears to be based on a phrase found in *Nihon shoki*, 吉棄物 "ablutions to invite good events."

4. Based on the phrase in *Nihon shoki*, 凶棄物, "ablutions performed to pay for sins that have been committed."

5. It is unclear where Mabuchi's quote is from, as there is no recorded account of Mencius ever saying this.

6. *Shiji* says that Shun's father was blind. The record says that Shun's father was obstinate and his mother mean (cf. Nienhauser 1994:11).

without parallel. Thus, if a ruler abdicated the throne to another good person, did this only continue for one or two reigns? This is not an acceptable accomplishment.

Now, King Wen of the Zhou era, as even common people know, was careless and became a prisoner. Because of the evil of King Zhou, the feudal lords gave their allegiance to King Wen. During the reign of King Wu, they put King Zhou to death, and this is known as the battle inspired by the heavenly mandate, but the brothers Bai Yi and Shu Zhai admonished Wu not to kill King Zhou, and a man named Confucius said that these two brothers were just men. If this is true, then what can be said about King Wu? If he was truly a just man, then he should have been made emperor after Zhou. At the end of the era, he should have abdicated the throne in favor of the sons of Zhou, but Wu had Zhou's posterity, namely Ji Zi, banished to Han on the Korean Peninsula, and abdicated the throne in favor of his own grandson.

King Gong[7] of the Zhou era took control of the government, and destroyed over forty of the feudal lords. This is seen in the record left by Mencius. Now, were all forty or so of these feudal lords evil? It should be remembered that it is clear that King Gong was forced to destroy them because they were a threat to him. This is what the ruler did, but can this be labeled virtuous? The prosperity of this dynasty is said to have lasted eight hundred years, but should it not be said that the ruler governed the state in peace for two reigns, or a little over forty years? Finally, there was great civil unrest, and the state gradually fell into decline. During this forty-some odd years of rule, the virtuous King Gong was betrayed by his younger brother and forced to flee for his life. We say that society tends to fall into chaos, but the evil acts committed between these two brothers are of the vilest kind.

Accepting this as fact, then the state was not even governed peacefully for the first forty years. After this period, during the reign of Emperor Wen of the Han Dynasty, the state appears to have been ruled in peace for a while. Afterward foul men appear on the scene, assassinated the ruler, and set themselves up as emperors. The citizens then all bowed their heads and paid obeisance. And this is not all; they label the countries along their borders as barbarians and despise them, but when a new emperor comes from one of these barbaric countries and takes the throne, the citizens bow themselves to the earth and pledge their allegiance. Is it not senseless to have despised these people as barbarians when they later revered them as their rulers? The word 'barbarian' never should be used on an entire group.

7. He was a son of King Wen, and younger brother to King Wu.

And thus, even though the Chinese have been plagued by confusion, never having seen a peaceful era, they claim to have the Way of Confucianism, which expounds the principles for governing the nation. Having heard some of what these Confucian scholars believe, it appears as if there is no room for argument; however, as Confucianism debates things superficially, it is very easy to convince people. What these Confucian advocates concentrate on is revering the government of the state, and the transmission of that government.

The logic of Confucianism is like the people who live in the same nation having something in common while they are all different on an individual level,[8] so the country appears to follow Confucianism when in reality the rulers do not; thus, we know that Confucianism does not affect the heart of the people. Nevertheless, Confucianism was transmitted to our country, and it is all lies, stating that Tang China was governed effectively according to this doctrine. How I wish I could send all those people shackled by Confucianism to China so that they could see the actual state of that country. Those people would return to their native land feeling like Urashima Tarō.[9]

This land of ours was governed according to the mind and will of heaven and earth, and there was no such trivial doctrine like Confucianism. After Confucianism was introduced to our country, it quickly spread throughout due to the naive mind of the ancient Japanese who believed this doctrine. From antiquity Japan had gradually prospered through the many successive reigns of the emperors, but after this Confucian Way came to Japan, there was a great revolt [known as the Jinshin Disturbance of 672] during the reign of Emperor Tenmu. In the Nara era Japan adopted Chinese robes, crowns, and other accessories, and everything gained a superficial elegance, and evil grew thick in the hearts of many people. Confucianism generally turned the hearts of men into pretentious vessels of wisdom, and led the people to revere the emperor to excess, causing the citizens to feel like vassals.

After this things deteriorated to where people had no trepidation in banishing the emperor to an island.[10] These events have their origin in the

---

8. There is a small note written in the margins of this sentence that reads, "This sentence is hard to decipher."

9. A very old story, much like Rip Van Winkle, where Urashima rescues a turtle and is allowed to visit the palace of the sea emperor. He visits for three days, and when he returns to his home, he finds he has been gone for three hundred years. Everything has changed.

10. The Buddhist Priest Dōkyō was able to gain power and eventually had Emperor Junnin banished to Awaji Island in 764. There is also the case where Go-Daigo was banished to Oki Island in 1332 as a result of the Genkō Incident.

importation of Chinese thinking to Japan. Some people think that Buddhism is evil, but it causes the mind to grow moronic, and the state cannot prosper under the ruler unless the common people are foolish. Therefore, Buddhism is not as great a threat to the state.

In the same manner that a path naturally appears when people live in far-off mountains or fields [and travel back and forth], the Way in the divine age spontaneously came about, and the prosperity of this Way that existed in Japan caused the rulers of Japan to prosper. As I have said over and over, this Confucian Way not only plunged China into turmoil, but has brought about the same results in Japan, also. Nonetheless, there are many who do not understand this state of affairs, simply clinging to the superficial aspects of Confucianism, revering it as an instrument to govern the state.

Poetry is the expressions of the human heart. Poetry may appear to be of no use to society, but when one comes to a full understanding of poetry, one naturally comes to an understanding of human emotions. When one understands human emotions then he sees the origins of chaos in society. Even Confucius did not abandon *The Odes*, but put it foremost among Chinese writings. The idea that existence must be connected with principle is the same as saying that it is dead. Things that operate together with heaven and earth are alive, endowed with a natural law and order. I do not mean to imply that it is bad to have a general knowledge about a variety of things, but it is human tendency to become obsessed with the pursuit of knowledge. It is best to rid oneself of knowledge.[11] Even when poetry is composed on subjects that are evil and corrupting,[12] the act does not throw the human heart into turmoil, but softens it and gives insights into myriad things. I have already addressed the merits of poetic composition.[13]

When it comes to governing the people in a country, it simply is not possible to manage affairs during a crisis, though one may say that he has a knowledge of things in China. During these trying times, someone will naturally appear on the scene who will proclaim words that are wise and reasonable. For example, medical doctors study Chinese medical books, but there are very few times when this knowledge helps them cure disease. However, [Japanese] medicine that naturally has been handed down for

11. It appears that Mabuchi is not counseling against knowing things, because he saw the study that he advocated as something centered on *knowing* the ancient lexicon. What Mabuchi is advising against is using knowledge as a chain with which to trammel others.

12. Such as writing poetry about meeting one's lover.

13. See *Kaikō*.

years without any discussion of origins or principles will always cure the disease. It is best when a person spontaneously realizes these things after reflective thought, but does not become obsessed with them. How I would like to take a person and have him realize what is good in the Japanese Way.[14] Students of Confucianism know nothing about government, and this can be seen in the chaos and turmoil that besets China whenever the Confucian people have control of the government.

A person once said, "Anciently in this country, a man could marry a relative just like the fowls and beasts do. When the Way of China was imported into Japan, this act was condemned. Everything has become better thanks to Confucianism." Hearing this, I burst into laughter. A person standing to my side asked why, so I said, "China had a regulation that stated that you could not marry someone with the same family name as you, and since some people committed acts of incest with their mothers, these regulations existed in name only, and tongue cannot tell how much evil there was in China. Do you not see things like this? They thought that the rulers had only said that it is better not to marry people with the same family name, but it is insipid to think that the people in society only paid lip service to the regulation. And are such things to be said in secret? In the ancient past of the imperial country, one could not marry brothers or sisters of the same mother, but they could marry brothers and sisters of the same father but different mothers. Laws and regulations that spring up in a certain area are best for those people, and rules from the outside should not be introduced.

As I have already said, in one imperial reign there was prosperity year after year, and after the introduction of Confucianism there was civil unrest for a while, and things turned out as they are now. Is it proper for a school of thought to set down bothersome rules such as one cannot marry a person with the same family name, and at the same time usurp the throne reign after reign, being conquered by the surrounding lands which they despised? And it goes without saying that a fool who still does not realize that a nation cannot be governed by a detailed set of rules should remember the proverb "a paradise on hearsay, a hell at sight."

There is also the habit of the Chinese saying that men are better than fowls and beasts, giving praise to humans and despising everything that is different. They label the countries in the four directions as barbaric and detest them, and I have given my opinion concerning their usage of "bar-

14. Manuscripts do not seem to agree here, but from context, there should be *wa ga* before *nari yosi*, or *nari* is a mistake for *wa ga*.

barian." Is not everything that lives and breathes under heaven on earth creatures? And does that therefore mean that among these creatures only man is so worthy of praise, so superior? In China they praise the essence of man as being the most exalted of all things in the universe. However, I believe that man should be labeled as the vilest of creatures. The reason for this is because as the heaven and earth, sun and moon have remained unchanged, there is not a fowl of the air, beast of the field, fish of the sea, nor plant and tree of the earth that has changed from its ancient, original state. But even though the outward appearance of man has not changed, there is not a person who has the same heart as the ancients. This is because man has that impulsive desire to know and wishes to use that knowledge for himself. Afterward wicked intentions appear between men, and in the end, the world is thrown into chaos. Even during times of peaceful rule, men were engaged in deception among themselves. If only one or two men had knowledge, then it would be acceptable, but when everyone claims to be learned, there is incessant contention among the people, and in the long run, their knowledge is worthless. Seeing things from the point of view of the fowls and beasts, they would counsel, "It is man who is evil. Do not emulate him." Therefore, man perhaps originated from one set of relatives.[15] But using another, foreign standard goes against the laws of heaven and earth. As we can see, how many times is the regulation against marrying relatives broken!

The man then said, "But there was no written script in Japan. We employed Chinese characters, and from this we came to understand myriads of things."[16]

I replied that first, it was not necessary to rehearse the facts that China was a troubled, evil, and chaotic country. If one were to give a small piece of evidence, the pictographic characters of which you speak provide a perfect example.[17] If we examine just the commonly used characters that were

15. A reference to Izanagi and Izanami, or a related genesis legend. The key point he is making is that humans came from one set of parents, and then their numbers increased.

16. During Mabuchi's day and for almost a century into the future there were two camps. Those who followed Imibe Hironari, who in *Kogo shūi* said, "In ancient times, when Japan had no written script, everyone, noble and base, old and young, performed every duty by word of mouth, forgetting nothing" (Bentley 2001:67). The other camp followed a group of Shintō scholars who claimed that Japan anciently had an indigenous script called *jindai moji* "divine age script." Mabuchi gives some vague support to the second group. Later, Hirata Atsutane would argue strongly for a script predating *kanji*, but this was debunked later. It is clear that some of these scripts were imitations of *hangul*.

17. There is confusion in the texts. Some believe that 絵 *e* "picture" is a mistake for 給 *notamafu* "to say." I have followed *notamafu* as it makes the sentence run smoother.

defined by a person called Tanjō [Dansheng],[18] there are thirty-eight thousand. For example, just in relation to the word "flower," there are more than ten different characters that can be used to represent 咲 "bloom," 散 "blossoms scatter," 蘂 "stamen," 樹 "tree," and 茎 "stalk." Also, there are separate characters for country names, and there are characters that have no other function but to represent the name of each plant and tree. Thus, how can someone remember so many characters, even for the person who diligently applies himself to the task? Some characters are written incorrectly, while others evolve from generation to generation; it would be fruitless and troublesome to try and debate the subject further. On the other hand, in India, the five thousand volumes of Buddha's sacred writings are written using just fifty letters. When a person knows just fifty letters, he knows all the words whether they be ancient or contemporary, and can pass them on. But the matter does not end with characters, for the fifty articulated Japanese sounds are the sounds of heaven and earth, and words conceived from among these sounds are natural. In this way, whatever shape or nature of the ancient script the Japanese may have had, it has deteriorated, because of the transmission of Chinese characters, and now only the ancient words remain, Japanese having been overcome. These Japanese words are not the same as the fifty articulated Indian sounds, but the way every word is articulated within the fifty Japanese sounds are, for good or evil, easily used without the employment or bother of characters; using the same example above concerning flowers, in Japanese we have the words *saku* "to bloom," *tiru* "to scatter," *tubomu* "a blossom closes," *uturofu* "to fade," *sibe* "stamen," and *kuki* "stalk." And I understand that there are only twenty-five letters in the Dutch alphabet. In India[19] they use fifty characters, and the state of characters is much the same generally throughout the world; China is the only country that invented such an irritating system of writing, and could not rule the country in peace; it is all very annoying.

The Japanese have been using Chinese characters, but anciently only the phonetic value of the character was employed as pronunciation markers within words.[20] After a while, the meaning of characters was gradually intermixed in sentences, but generally only the Japanese meaning, which

18. The text has 丹生, but another manuscript has 誕生. The *Nihon shisō taikei* manuscript has ○○てふ人 (1972:380), perhaps showing that the characters were lost, or were later interpolated.

19. There is confusion here, one manuscript has 此国 "this country," with the interlinear note of 天竺 "India." Another manuscript has 北国 "northern country." Since Mabuchi is talking about *other* countries, I have followed the idea of India.

20. Mabuchi appears to be addressing the issue of *man'yōgana*, where in many cases the

was clearly reflected in Chinese characters, was employed, there being no change in the essence of the sentence.[21]

Thus, the words were the masters, and the characters were the slaves, and the Japanese were able to use the characters freely. But through the use of Chinese script [the phonetic tradition died], and the characters became the masters. It would be horrifying if the evil custom of a slave of China becoming the ruler of the country were to spread, and nothing more need be said about those people who do not understand this principle, but esteem Chinese characters highly.

Another person then said, "The barbarians act this way, and it is only the Chinese who have an elegant manner of writing, and that is why there are so many characters in Chinese." I looked up to the sky and laughed. I replied that this so-called elegance is based upon the principle [of being able to rule one's own country]. Elegance that clings to reducing life to a system of principles only leads to chaos, but just as there are beautiful patterns in the many things between heaven and earth, poetry can soften the heart and bring comfort.

Furthermore, anciently in China, they also did not originally have characters, but a rope was tied to remind the person of something. After that, did not the Chinese take the shapes of everything, trees, grass, birds, and beasts and make them into characters? Perhaps even the fifty letters of India were originally pictures of objects. No matter what it is, characters are something common between people and should not be labeled "elegant" simply because the number of those objects is large. And the act from later eras of writing originally round glyphs in a square fashion and claiming this to be a different style of calligraphy is utterly hilarious.[22] If these characters were to vanish, and we were to obtain genuine characters

---

phonetic value of the character was used, ignoring the semantics. However, his description shows he did not fully understand how the system functioned.

21. An example would be 日 "sun," where both languages have a common bond, since the sun is universal. Mabuchi adds the following note, "In Book 1 of *Man'yōshū* is the following poem composed by the captain of the army in reply to another poem (MYS 6):

yamagosi no	The wind blows
kaze wo toki zimi	continuously over the mountains;
nuru yo otizu	it is for my wife
ife naru imo wo	who remains at home
kakete sinofitu	that I yearn night after night.

It is easy to get examples from the four thousand poems contained in *Man'yōshū*, and it would be well for the reader to check for himself. I have quoted this poem because it came to mind first. The characters in this poem have mainly used the Japanese meaning of the Chinese characters."

22. Mabuchi seems to be talking about various styles of writing in China, seal script

from heaven, then certainly the ruler could govern the country in peace, and we could end all confrontation.

Now, as I have been arguing about the meaning and the words of ancient poetry, people think this only concerns the words in poetry; however, as I have stated before, the heart of the ancients is in their feelings [the meaning behind the words]. One can know the hearts of the ancients through ancient poetry, and through the method of deduction of this knowledge, one can know the ancient state of society. After one has knowledge of the ancient state of society, then he can reach back into time and ponder the divine age. However, in later eras there have been many scholars who speak about events [found in] the books of the divine age,[23] but when one listens to what they have to say, their theories draw on a multitude of foreign ideas. These scholars put a high value on the meaning [of the words], talking about the divine age as if it were right before their very eyes. They create theories in detail as if these things had been established before in the hearts of men. But how did these scholars come to this knowledge? One is impressed by their desire to know about the ancient past, but when you hear or read the works of these scholars, you come to the realization that these scholars know absolutely nothing about the ancient past.[24] Nevertheless, how can one know about the divine age when each era grows farther away in time, and these pretentious scholars have no knowledge about the period of these ancient people? Japanese scholars peeked inside Chinese works, and noticed the later era of the Song Dynasty. During this time terribly restrictive Confucian thinking was growing more restrained, and these scholars were envious of the Zhu Xi school of thought, and they quietly placed the divine age in a Chinese context. Because of this, people who do not read these works believe that the teachings of these scholars are the truth; however, a person who knows some-

---

versus standardized characters. Seal script was more rounded than the later, standardized version which had sharper corners.

23. *Kamiyo no maki no koto wo.* Literally "the things about the books of the divine age." This seems to have reference to the first two volumes of *Nihon shoki*; however, it also is apparent that Mabuchi is drawing attention to commentaries written by people like Fujiwara Teika (*Nihon shoki Sanso*) and Imibe Masamichi (*Shindai maki kuketsu*), who studied mainly the two books of *Shoki*. The first two books of *Nihon shoki* took on a life of their own among Shintō scholars, who often copied these two as a work separate from the rest of *Nihon shoki*.

24. This sentence is difficult to decipher. The verb is *sirifaberazaru*. The subject of this verb is believed to be those Shintō scholars who follow the commentaries on the divine age, but know nothing about the ancient past. If this is the case—and that is the only logical subject—the usage of *faberi* here is unnecessary. It might be a later edition or a result of scribal error.

thing about Japanese and Chinese works will realize that their interpretation of the divine age has been tainted by Zhu Xi philosophy, and will roll with laughter.

Now, what kind of things occurred in the ancient past of China? Surely there was no complicated rhetoric. As this Chinese philosophy was created later by men, will the reader also think that it is proper to create the same sort of thing in Japan? Things that are put together by the will of men are often problematic. Examining the principles that were created by wise men, we notice that they did not suit the will of heaven and thus were never put into practice. Therefore, the words of Laozi, to act in compliance with the nature of heaven and earth, suits the governing of everything under heaven. When one reads the words of Laozi, you realize that the hearts of the Chinese originally were sincere. They were sincere like the poetry of the ancient Japanese mentioned above. In the ancient past there were few words for the Japanese, and the actions of people were simple. When life is simple and the hearts of men are sincere, some incomprehensible doctrine is useless. Even without doctrine, if the hearts of men are sincere, things get accomplished. And because the hearts of men are diverse, there are still evil men who commit evil acts, but as these originate from *magokoro* ["the true heart"], they cannot be hidden. If they cannot be hidden, then great scandals do not occur. The uproar lasts but a moment and then fades. Now, that does not mean that the teachings of great men did not exist in ancient Japan, but the ancients were satisfied with a few, unpretentious teachings. Now as China is an evil-hearted country, their deep and profound teachings appear reasonable on the surface, but great evils have occurred, and the country has been thrown into confusion. Since our country was originally inhabited by sincere people who observed a few simple teachings, they were more apt to be obedient to the natural order of heaven and earth, and there was no need for other teachings.

However, the Way of China came into Japan, and the hearts of the Japanese were corrupted, and though the teachings now resemble those in China, one forgets in the evening what he had heard in the morning. This was not the ancient state of Japanese affairs. They followed the natural way of heaven and earth, and the ruler was the sun and moon. The commoners were the stars.[25] The stars were obedient to the sun and the moon, just as it is today, so the stars could never cloak the sun and moon. Now, just as the sun, moon, and stars in the firmament have been transmitted down to the present in their ancient form, our emperor—the sun

25. While this is an analogy, it is a clear reference to the sun goddess and the moon *kami* (Tsukuyomi), both offspring of Izanagi and Izanami.

and moon, and the subjects, the stars—have come down to the present without change, and the country has been governed in peace. However, vile individuals appeared on the scene, having read and learned from Chinese records how the Chinese became rulers, and being naturally infected with this knowledge, and as the throne declines, so do the subjects.[26] I must address the books of the divine age as we discuss the ancient state of the spirit. In order to infer about this ancient state of Japan, we must know about the heart and words of the ancients through their poetry, and then we must read through those ancient Japanese records I have mentioned above.

A person said, "Because the ancient Japanese had no idea of humaneness, righteousness, proper conduct, and knowledge, there were no such words for these." It is a very juvenile way of thinking to despise the ancient Japanese in this manner. In the first place, the Chinese set up these five principles of behavior,[27] and anything that deviated from this system was labeled as evil. These five principles of behavior exist in the country naturally just as the four seasons. Is there anyone who would believe there is someone without these principles? But as the seasons progress, spring becomes tranquil, and then summer gradually becomes hot; in the same vein, the natural order of heaven and earth is that these things occur in perfect harmony, and yet, if things occurred exactly as the Chinese teach, as soon as spring had come it would be warm, and by the time summer had arrived it would instantly be hot. The Chinese way of thinking goes against the natural order of heaven and earth, and their principles are impulsive and incomprehensible. When a person hears a small bit of Chinese rhetoric, he may find it easy to listen to, the logic reasonable, but things do not work this way. This is because Chinese thinking goes against the natural order of the changing of the four seasons on the earth. Why should people who are simply creatures and obediently follow the natural order of heaven and earth put into practice inferior doctrines? Among those people in Japan, there exists a set of standards; just as there exists the distinction among the four seasons, there are naturally behaviors like love, anger, reason, and understanding.[28] As long as the four seasons exist, these things will exist, also. To state that humans naturally need things labeled humaneness, righteous-

26. This sentence appears to have been truncated in the text. A small addition has been written to the side, and I have added that to my translation.

27. Known as the "five virtues" or the "five constants." The fifth virtue, 信 "trust or honesty" has been dropped from the quote above.

28. The *Nihon shisō taikei* (1973:384) edition only lists four corresponding Japanese principles, but a draft of Mabuchi's work has five, the fifth being ゐや "good behavior" or "etiquette" (Yamamoto 1942:1146).

ness, proper conduct, and knowledge other than their naturally inherited traits is to make things constricted and difficult. It is better to leave people just as their hearts are—natural as heaven and earth—without attaching such traits. Do these scholars not know about how our country was ruled according to the will of heaven and earth, and accomplished these things? Nothing further should be said about those asinine people who are accustomed to looking at themselves in their present state, but I think I will address the subject somewhat more for those youth who still do not understand this.

Since Chinese learning was first created based upon the hearts of men, it is easy to become convinced due to their squarelike principles constructed on formality. The ancient Way [of Japan] was round [smooth] and peaceful when followed in its natural state, and neither the tongue nor the heart could sufficiently describe it; thus, people in later ages found it difficult to comprehend. Now, people will say that the ancient Way has vanished, but as long as heaven and earth do not expire the ancient Way will not vanish. The Way of Japan for a time has been overshadowed by the easy-to-comprehend Way of China. When one remembers how long heaven and earth have lasted, five hundred or one thousand years is but an instant. The Way of our country is not the same as those philosophies that are narrow, difficult, and revered as something transmitted by people. Our Way follows the natural order of heaven and earth, and like the sun and moon, everything within this Way is round.[29] And to use the dew that sits on top of the blade of grass as an example, when that dewdrop sits on an uneven leaf, it follows the shape of the leaf and adopts the same shape. However, when the dewdrop is on a flat surface, it returns to its round shape. In the same light, everything returns to its original shape: round. And when someone rules the country, when he imitates this smooth principle, the country is certainly ruled in peace. And one may know from looking at the reigns in China that ruling with a four-cornered doctrine will only lead to chaos. And it is the natural will of heaven and earth that Japan return to the ancient, natural Way, and when heaven and earth sees fit, they will certainly set Japan back to her natural shape. To use a vile, narrow, and corrupt human heart imprudently to rule over a country leads to nothing but confusion.[30]

---

29. Mabuchi felt that the natural shape to describe Japan was a circle; this contrasted with a square, which Mabuchi felt demonstrated a formulaic rhetoric or logic, the things Chinese took interest in, square like *kanji*.

30. The "Agatai-shū Genroku" manuscript has one page of text added here, but it is

Chinese demonstrate that those above shine the light of authority and dignity down upon those below, but regardless of this authority, even though it is good for rulers to be plain or simple, putting on airs of authority is the root of contention. The supernal way to show authority is the Way of the military. One must act in this manner without forgetting these principles. Especially, one should examine how our imperial land has been built upon the military.[31] Also, when those below see how simple and plain the rulers are, it causes a feeling of respect within them, and every man in his own way emulates those above, and in all things, the country becomes plain and simple. When the people have become unsophisticated, then there are few cravings. With such selfish desires suppressed, peace is brought to the heart. If the hearts of the people are at peace, then society is tranquil. The reason that putting on airs of authority is evil can be found first in opulence, starting with the palace and court dress, the ladies of the court arrayed in flowery robes, and the courtiers adorned in beautifully designed robes. It is true that the commoner sees these and is filled with respect. However, a person who would show heart-felt respect does not need to have his authority on display. And yet, among these people, especially men, there are those who have great desires to do the will of heaven and earth, and they start to think that this is the true meaning for their existence, to be like those in authority who put on airs of prestige. Then these people believe that since life is no longer than one hundred years,[32] and the thought occurs to them that it is fate, they lead a rebellion to overthrow the throne. Also, since these people do not have the military might to overthrow the throne, they hold back their plans, and tolerate the current sovereign; just how deep does the envy of these people run? Some people are conceited, saying, "See! Here am I, a powerful individual! No matter where you may be, let us revolt!" These people wait for such an opportunity, thinking in their hearts to launch a sweet victory; every man has at least some of these ambitious feelings in his heart.

But if things in that country followed the Way heaven and earth had designed, handed down in the ancient tradition, then the palace would

---

merely a rehashing of what has been given above about circular versus square. I have ignored it.

31. Mabuchi appears to be juxtaposing the *samurai* with the warlords of China.

32. Here the text is confused. Three readings are present, *ito sebaki* "very narrow," *iku tose kuru* "after many years," and *momo tose kuru* "after one hundred years." *Iku tose* appears to be a scribal corruption of *ito* "many" and *sebaki* "narrow." The problem is which is the original, the first or the third. I have elected to translate the third choice, as *ito sebaki* sounds very awkward in the present context.

have a wooden roof, walls of earth, the people inside wearing clothing of tree bark and hemp, and the hilts of their swords wrapped with vine; if the emperor himself had taken the bow and arrow in his hands and went out hunting, then why should it be any different today? The hearts of men are drawn to beauty, and they revere things that are noble, but from the time that the Japanese envied Chinese things, wishing to imitate them, only the palace and the court robes have become splendid. Those courtiers paid so much esteem to those above that their hearts became irrational and effeminate. These people became so intelligent that they pushed those people in power aside, and even in politics, the commoner has been able to do as he pleases. These usurpers of power then gave themselves titles they did not deserve, and even if they did not go as far as to defame those to whom the real authority resided like the Chinese, while rightful heirs were alive [and could have ruled the country], it was as if they did not exist. If this was the case, when one thinks that these commoners are in power, one finds that only the names of the retainers have been recorded, and the ancients have been ignored by the commoners of later eras. This state of affairs comes from the error of imitating foreign ways, forgetting the Way of our own country.

A person asked, "If that is so, were there no evil people in the past? Was there no internal strife, either?" I replied that this question comes from not knowing the true meaning of being sincere. If a person's heart is completely sincere, then there is simplicity in everything he undertakes to do. If there is simplicity, then there is no need for deep pondering. There have been times, rare, I will admit, when there has been a person who was sincere but committed evil and wished to overthrow the throne; however, because these desires originate from a straightforward heart, that person could not hide his feelings [for rebellion], and as there was no way to conceal his thoughts, people were able to suppress him. In this way, there was no great revolt. Even when a person is sincere, there is a certain amount of evil in the heart, like naive, sincere men in the country who test each other's strength by fighting; these situations are easy to quell.

It is foolish to view man among all creatures that live in this world as the only creature who is noble. From the point of view of heaven and earth, which are the parents of all creations, men, beasts, fowl, and insects are the same. Among these creations, nothing is wiser than man. A person may think that this wisdom is good, and if there were only one or two wise people in the world, it would be for the benefit of society; however, when everyone thinks that they are wise, then they try to build themselves up as more knowledgeable than other people, and that is why great evil sometimes occurs. In the era of spontaneity and simplicity there was no profound thinking; people only reacted to what they saw before their very eyes, so wisdom was limited. Thus, there were small incidents, but no severe crises. As an example, it is like a village with many dogs, and when a dog from another village tried to enter, the dogs in the village prevented this; also, among the dogs there are fights about food or mates, but the affair always ends with one simple explosion of anger, and there is no bearing of grudges. In China, it is said to be good for those in power to have knowledge and perform things that the commoner does not know,[33] and this makes everything dark and vague. For example, the Chinese rulers Yao or Shun are recorded as being splendid individuals like Amitabha or Buddha, and later rulers such as Xia, Yin, and Zhou are listed as evidence of this. Yao, Shun, Xia, Yin, and Zhou were in fact very evil men, not worthy figures as portrayed in the legends, and so their evil acts were later concealed because they could not be used as evidence for moral teaching; it is these actions that have caused ambiguity in China, leading many to confusion. These things have been passed on, but in the later ages of Japan, these things were discussed and pondered, but as I think about it now, the commoners of Japan were not convinced. In relation to the events of ancient Japan there is not the slightest shade of deception, but people discussed things as they saw them; we should tell people that there was not a whole lot going on in the world in the ancient days—and this is true—in these later eras we must teach that anciently this was the proper way for people to live.

When a person has a smattering of knowledge, he says that he will teach others, and spread the Way to govern the country and save the commoners. But even the teachings of Confucius, which form the basis for their knowledge, have never been put into practice, even in China, so why should such doctrine be of any value to Japan? The reason that people think these teachings should be followed and obeyed is because they do not truly understand the natural heart of heaven and earth. Dogs and birds, which have no teachings, have a part of this natural heart, and they react to the change in the four seasons without mishap. People in Japan believe that the Chinese law of not marrying a relative is good, and think that the ancient Japanese were just like beasts because they married brothers and sisters, but when did the mind of heaven ever say that men were different from beasts? Every

33. A reference to a supposed saying from Confucius found in the "Taibo" section of *The Analects*, "The Master said, 'You can make the people follow the Way, you cannot make them understand it'" (Nylan 2014:22).

creature that lives and breathes is the same. It is the humans who wish to establish a set of systems and laws for a while, and the reason that these systems and laws are different from country to country and place to place is the same as the reason why plants, trees, fowl, or beasts are different from location to location. Therefore, the good laws and systems that have naturally sprung up in a location are a lot like the teachings of heaven and earth, the parents of all creations. In ancient Japanese history, brother and sister by the same mother were considered siblings, while children of different mothers were not treated as such. Thus, because the hearts of the ancient Japanese were sincere, there was no incest among siblings, but there was much marrying between brother and sister of different mothers. The occasional incestuous relationship was punished harshly. The origin of our human existence is due to a brother and sister marrying each other.[34] However, when the human era began [after the divine age], the law stating that brother and sister of the same mother cannot marry each other naturally arose. Even in China where society tries to create separate categories of men and beasts, stating that relatives cannot marry, one sees instances of sexual relations with sons and mothers. Thinking that these instances have accidentally been recorded in Chinese documents, they were hidden from society so that others would not know what was going on. It is foolish to believe that once a system has been established people in later ages are going to abide by those laws. Take the law that prohibits the marriage to a relative; if there were so many people who obeyed that law, then why did they try killing the emperor? It is the epitome of ignorance to think that a person will adhere to the law of not marrying a relative while he breaks the law about murdering the sovereign or one's father. People should not worry about the small problems of society, for the good actions of the emperors of the successive reigns have been handed down to us. If the people in power transmit things down for posterity, so will the commoner. As the Chinese say, it is better to have a reign last for a thousand years though there a few minor disturbances, than have a reign last a hundred years where not even dust stirs. Since a thousand years, or even ten thousand years is but an instant in relation to the age of the earth, it is better for things to be round, with its good and evil. Chinese square rhetoric is worthless.

It need not be rehashed how corrupt the hearts of the people of Japan have become since Buddhism entered our country, but the true heart of Buddhism should not be like that. The people who lead Buddhism have been enticed by their ambitions, and spread falsehood and foolishness

---

34. According to the mythology, the creators of the Japanese race were Izanagi and Izanami. *Kojiki* calls Izanagi the brother and Izanami his younger sister.

through Buddhism. Furthermore, Buddhism only focuses on the sins of humanity, separating humans from the beasts. All creatures on this earth are the same, so where is it written that Buddha said that fowl and beasts have no sin? Many people think of karma as having to do only with humans. There is so much evidence in the ancient past demonstrating that this idea of karma is a fallacy that it would be a bother to quote it all; however, since people continue to doubt these things even though they hear what I have to say, let us use an example from the present; is there any sin greater than murder? And yet a period in the past was thrown into great turmoil, and during long stretches there was war and great slaughter. During that time, the only people who did not commit murder are those we presently call commoners. Those who killed but few people are what we presently label as *hatamoto* [bannermen]. Feudal lords murdered a few more people than the *hatamoto*. Those who killed more were the provincial lords. The person who killed in limitless numbers is the one who came to power and whose lineage has continued unbroken.[35] Why is there no retribution for this? Thus, one may know that killing a person is just like killing an insect. It is the actions of foxes and badgers to talk about karma and other mysterious things. Everyone in the country has their claim on some gift, but even though the average man can see with his very own eyes these things, only foxes and badgers know the method to deceive men. If there are people in the present who believe that there is some destiny awaiting the posterity of a man who killed many people long ago, badgers will come to the knowledge of that thought, and will have fun deceiving people about fate. In the end, having killed many people is a label of praise to be passed down from one's ancestors to oneself. If from now on, a person is called to participate in a battle, he should try to kill more people than anyone else, increase his treasure, and leave a name for himself.[36] People will speak bravely of you, and badgers will not be able to approach.[37] However, when the nation is peacefully governed, even killing a flea or a mosquito has become meaningless, and people are deceived by Buddhist monks and badgers.

In reference to what I said about valor being the most important thing

---

35. Mabuchi is using this vague description for Tokugawa Ieyasu and his lineage who hold the title of shogun.

36. The following is seen in one manuscript, "Thus, when later people talk about the ancient happenings, they will say of you, 'He slew tens of thousands of people here and there, dropping them into the valley, and sent one thousand bodies afloat down the river.'"

37. The Japanese believed that badgers (*mujina*) had transformational powers, and Mabuchi is saying that if there was such a thing as fate, badgers would prey on that fear of humans, and endeavor to make it appear as if they were bound by karma.

for a warrior in governing the country in peace, a person once said the following to me, "As I look around me and see those who study warfare, they hope for war and desire to become generals, and when they imagine the heroes of war, those in the Way of warfare wish that the world would fall into chaos. No matter how strong a warrior may be, he knows that he will defend his front and kill all enemies who approach. Because of this, warfare is bad for peaceful government." I said that this was not true. This statement demonstrates that people do not understand the hearts of men. You should take a good look at your own heart. Having been born in tranquility, when nothing happens you become disgusted with the status quo. At times like that, will you still feel like you do now? In the ancient past, a person thought of his ancestors who tried to acquire status, but now there is no purpose. So you do all that you can, and your life comes to an end. You have various thoughts in your heart, and you follow the flow of time, for there is nothing else to do. Those who learn the valiant Way of warfare sit around all day in the same manner, and though they wish in their hearts for some chaos in the world, society simply does not fall into confusion. One or two students will do as their hearts desire, but unless you follow society, it is almost impossible to live out the day. There is nothing that can be done, and so the students of warfare put all their ambitions away. That is the way the human heart is, and when someone in power has gallant authority, everyone follows after him for a while, even if they do not really wish to. If so, then is it not good to study the bold Way of warfare, passing it on to one's posterity, hoping that it may be of some help in case of emergency? Some say that such a person is heartless and evil, but those who learn well the Way of warfare are not heartless. Sure, there will always be one who is heartless, but is there not a mountain of people who are heartless and evil without studying warfare? One must avoid generalizations. And because you know nothing about military strategy, in case of war, this heartless warrior will on the other hand be someone you can rely upon. Do you think that the world will always remain as it is, peaceful and tranquil? One never knows the future. The person who believes that everything in the present is wonderful has foolishness as his mistress. It is good to have various characters among one's retainers. If you know that valor is the core of warriors[38] you will have no other choice than to avoid angering those

---

38. The text is corrupt here with *mono no moto* "center of things," but an interlinear note says, "Perhaps this is *mononofu* 'warrior.'" As Mabuchi is talking about warfare, a vague noun like *things* is inappropriate. It seems plausible that the *fu* of *mononofu* has been dropped through scribal error. I have rendered this as "warriors."

warriors hidden here and there, and respect those who only show ferocity on the surface. If the average person is calm on the surface, does he not feel so in his heart, also? Everyone practices some distortion in their minds. When anyone has a little authority over another, the person below will be obedient, but do you think that that lower person does not care about what will happen to him? No, they follow for a while because there is no way out of the situation. Now, for example, even if there is a binding agreement between master and servant, if the master gives a stingy reward, do you think the servant will be grateful? Everyone remembers the bad things in life, forgetting all the good things that have happened so far, so it is silly to think that just because one good thing has occurred, the person will never forget it. One must understand this principle. Also, a person who has even the slightest status and has over one hundred retainers must learn the Way of warfare. This is because though it appears that the person learns the average posture for war, or how to prepare for battle, without such preparations, even a valiant warrior in actual combat will be useless. Even when the commander gives an order, if the soldiers do not follow, then everything is meaningless. If the warriors do not fall in line when the order to take the field is given, then the fear of what to do next will naturally arise. Even if they think that someone will follow, who would quickly fall into line? They have parents, a wife, and children. They do not want to die in battle, so they run and hide. And how could you achieve perfect unity among the soldiers if you have those who have been forced to participate in battle? The leader should pay attention to such detail, and not put on such airs of authority, but strive to keep unity among the officers and the warriors by being friendly to them, treating them like their own children. If you do this, you will have something better than the label of a ruler, you will have a feeling of gratitude that sinks clear to the bone. …[39]

A person asked me, "The effect of poetry mentioned in the preface to *Kokinshū* sounds very reasonable to me, but is there any other meaning to poetry?" I responded that the words in the preface, "It is song that moves heaven and earth without effort, stirs emotions in the invisible spirits and gods, brings harmony to the relations of men and women, and calms the hearts of fierce warriors"[40] refer to the things that are expected and catego-

39. A variant text adds a very long footnote here, addressing the issue of government, starting off by saying, "Whenever a person in later times was given some authority, he put on airs of prestige, trying to show everyone that he had power. Authority in other words is military power."

40. McCullough (1985:3).

rized, so this is the most reasonable explanation. If one were to address things in general, then this has reference to an elegant heart.[41] The heart of man is selfish and self-serving, fighting with others, judging things based on reasoning, but when man has the poetic feelings described above, he experiences a softening of the heart, society becomes peaceful, and the people become tranquil. As an example, it is like the change of the four seasons. It is reasonable that summer is hot, but if it suddenly became hot when summer arrived, then we would not be able to endure it. Also, it is the trait of winter to be cold, but no one could stand winter if it were always bitter cold. However, things are in gradual change and within this world of hot and cold there are variations so that one can endure differences in temperature between morning and evening, day and night. There are times when one feels relieved, allowing us to endure these hot or cold seasons. If there was no such moderation, who could survive in this world? The same thing can be said for Chinese poetry. Nevertheless, Chinese poetry became formulaic in later eras, and the poets wrote poetry without any deep emotions. They wrote poetry to surprise others, or to reap criticism, or please someone. Because these poets did not compose poetry based on their actual feelings, these poems cannot be called actual poems; however, even though present poetry is poor, it still arises from this sense of effect, so there is a sufficient feeling of softening within the poetry. Anyone knows about this sensation, and it is only natural that this exists in the hearts of people beyond any rhetoric. To frame this in a theoretical argument, a powerful man who holds high rank can ignore everyone below him, and perform his duties. However, court rank means that no matter how high a rank, he cannot always treat those below him scornfully, so he mixes in words of kindness. Even if the man is a fierce ruffian, can he always trample the weaklings under his feet? Again, he must make sensitivity his model. Poetry originally was not composed from the feeling of sensitivity, but was a product of expressing the feelings of one's heart in a beautiful, poetic manner, so naturally poetry became a sensitive expression of gentleness.[42]

A person asked me, "What you have said is very reasonable, and your description refers to very ancient poetry. But in the present world, the customs of our country have greatly changed, and since the hearts of men have become corrupt, how can we revert to the past? It is thus best to follow the

41. One manuscript has "a gentle heart." I have followed the critical text.

42. One manuscript adds the following, "Therefore, as poetry is the basis for the heart of man, poetry is an unconscious product. But later generations tried to add skill to the poem, and inserted rhetoric into poetic composition."

present practice and deal with it properly. The things of the ancients are worthless to us in the present." I answered, saying that everyone feels the same, but as I argued about military strategy and the government, we must first lay the foundation. And yet according to the will of the ruler, many tens of thousands of the people's hearts are put in order; however, among the many people it is very difficult for a good ruler to be born. The evil ruler follows his own heart and governs the country, but nothing good comes from it. On a rare occasion, the people wait for a good ruler to come along, but in the end it is all talk. If those in power have an interest in the ancient past, and a person comes to power who wishes that the people in society were sincere, then within ten or twenty years, society will change to one full of sincerity. It is juvenile to believe that any common method will change society. Society can be changed by the will of one man in power. Even in a battle where one's life is on the line, victory is dependent on the will of the commander, and if the commander is determined, then tens of thousands of soldiers will follow suit and put their lives on the line, too. In anything undertaken, it is wise to look back and see if it was done in all sincerity.[43]

[NST 39:374–93]

☙

43. One manuscript lacks this last sentence, but adds a long footnote talking about the Chinese custom of flattery.

SHINTŌ DOKUGO

Ise Sadatake | 1782

[Using textual tools much like Norinaga, Sadatake takes a scalpel to what his generation called "Shintō" and determines that it is not a pure, ancient religion as some Shintō priests pretended. He categorizes Shintō into three groups: remnant Shintō, one based on the *Book of Changes*, and the amalgamated form. He concludes that remnant Shintō, which is preserved in festivals, is close to the original. He also indicates that there are two types of *yuiitsu Shintō*: a new one and an old one. Thus he tries to unravel years of secretion of ideas not original to the ancient, indigenous religion of Japan.]

Shintō is the great Way of our land, and has been highly prized at the imperial court since ancient times. The Statute on Government Personnel [in *Ritsuryō*] begins with the regulations on the indigenous religion, and the first section of *Engi shiki* is devoted to procedures of the same religion. From the divine age the three houses of the Nakatomi, Imibe, and Urabe have had exclusive rights to officiate within the religion. [Later] the house of the Imibe came to an end, but the other two houses are still prosperous in the present. Both houses represent the orthodox brand of the religion that has been handed down since the divine age, and people have given unmatched respect to it. With this prestige these two families competed to have direct control over the shrines in the various provinces, because one or the other has always wanted to conduct research into the shrines. However, the traditions are very profound, and as these Shintō officials could not search and discern the truth, I have nothing further to add about their learning.

There are many people in society who are not Shintō officials but label themselves "Shintō scholars" and trifle with this [the doctrine of Shintō]. When I hear their theories, I do not feel there is any ancient proof there, their theories full of unfounded new ideas. I also am not a Shintō official, but I have had some small experience in reading the ancient texts, and am able to criticize the inaccurate theories of these people. I cannot remain silent while these [unfounded] theories gain currency in society. It may be too late to try saying this or that, and even if I look into the matter there may be no effect; however, I feel that I will become ill if I do not say something, so I have completed the following which are musings to myself.[1]

---

1. This is where the title of the manuscript comes from: *Shintō dokugo* "musings to myself about Shintō."

1

Among the theories of Shintō scholars is the idea of "singular Shintō" (*yuiitsu shintō*). The term does not refer to the fact that the teachings have not been influenced by Buddhist thought. It is with fear and trembling that I say the word *yuiitsu shintō*, but in the divine age Amaterasu Ōmikami taught the people, and established the way for the state, and all under heaven, to be governed, which tradition Saruta Hiko preserved.[2] From the time when the world was first created, a *kami* spontaneously appeared in the essences that filled the void, and tradition records his name as Ame no Minaka Nushi. All things and events in both heaven and earth from ancient times down to the present were created by Ame no Minaka Nushi. Therefore, I and other people belong to this *kami*.

The Way of heaven is therefore the Way of man. Likewise, the Way of man eventually becomes the Way of heaven. In the end it is called "singular Shintō" because heaven and man are the same. And as the Way was established below [heaven] on the principle that heaven and man are the same, this is also called *Rigaku Shintō*. This is the true form of Shintō and that is extremely important. Festivals, ritual prayers, ritual purification, and other rites are also called Shrine Official Shintō or Ritual Shintō, and compared to that mentioned above this is a superficial form of Shintō. This is generally how those scholars explain these differences, but I think this explanation about differences in superficial or profound Shintō are completely ridiculous.

2

I categorize Shintō into three groups: first is Shintō based on the writings of the Chinese work the *Book of Changes*. The second is Shintō mentioned in the ancient period of our country. The third is Shintō that has been altered over time.

Shintō based on the *Book of Changes* is defined according to the line in the "Da Guan [Great Looking Up]" section of the "Tuan Zhuan" chapter of the *Changes*, "Viewing the spiritlike Way of heaven, one finds the four seasons never deviate, and so the sage established his teachings on the basis of

---

2. Sadatake seems to be implying that the Sarume, of whom Saruta Hiko is recorded as being the founder, were in charge of mime and dance. It is possible that they were related to the *kataribe*, and preserved part of the ancient traditions in their performances.

this spiritlike Way, and all under heaven submit to him."[3] Now, regarding why it was called "the spiritlike way of heaven," all things under heaven and on the earth, starting with the sun and moon, the stars and the polar star, day and night, cold and heat, wind and rain, frost and dew, all these naturally grow and produce without any assistance from humans, because these all are products of the *kami*. That is why it is called this. This heavenly Shintō was not confined to China, but is the same in our country, and in all the other countries. Thus, what was known as ancient Shintō in our country was something completely different, and not what is referred to as heavenly Shintō. Regardless that the name between these is the same, the fundamental points are different. It is thus confusing to argue about one or the other when they use the same label.

The second one, ancient Shintō of our land, worships the *kami* of heaven and earth, and has reference to festivals, ritual prayers, and ritual purification as well as officiating in all the rites at the shrines. Anciently the three imperial regalia received from Amaterasu Ōmikami were enshrined in the palace, and the emperor himself worshipped these, and down till the reign of Emperor Sujin he reverently shared space with these regalia in the palace, and then he gave the divine mirror to Princess Toyo Sukiiri, and she searched the various provinces for an appropriate place to enshrine the mirror. At that time a replacement for the divine mirror was cast and placed in the palace, and the emperor worshipped it [like he had with the actual mirror]. This is called Kensho or Naishidokoro.[4]

Now, with the ascension of each successive emperor, the court held the Dajōsai, and they established the yearly "Tasting of the First Fruits" festival. This is a festival where the emperor himself worships the *kami* of heaven and earth. The various provinces also have a predetermined festival that is performed at the various shrines, and the court set up an officiating administrator to take charge within the forbidden precincts of the palace. China also worships the *kami* of heaven and earth, where they pray for consolation for the spirits of their ancestors, but in our country people did not place as much value on the rituals [as China did]. At our imperial court people put the greatest emphasis on the political value of worshipping the *kami* of heaven and earth. And that is why the character 政 "government"

3. The basic translation is from Lynn (1994:260), but I have altered the wording to fit the preconceived notion of Sadatake. Lynn translates 神道 as "numinous Dao."

4. *Kensho* refers to the room where the court placed and worshipped the imperial mirror within the palace. *Naishidokoro* refers to a room where female palace attendants were in charge of the mirror, and by extension, it was the name of the room where the mirror was kept.

is read in Japanese as *maturigoto* "a festival event." Thus, anciently what was called Shintō concerned the conducting of ceremonies such as the worship of the *kami* of heaven and earth, ritual prayers, ritual purification, and other ceremonials.

In the Yōmei record in *Nihon shoki* it says, "The emperor believed in the law of the Buddha, and esteemed the Way of the *kami*." Also in the record of Emperor Kōtoku is says, "He revered the Way of Buddhism, and had contempt for the Way of the *kami*." Here we find the term 神道 "Way of the *kami*." As I mentioned above, it is proper to interpret this as ancient Shintō, with festivals and ancient rituals. As Shintō is mentioned in contrast to Buddhism, Shintō 神道 is written with two characters, like Buddhism 仏法, but it is a misconception to interpret Shintō as something that teaches a Way [道].

There are many places in the text in *Nihon shoki* that have been colored by Chinese philosophies, so as the writer had added the character 法 "law" to Buddha, naturally he added 道 "Way" to the *kami*. However, the meaning of "law" is completely different from the meaning of "Way." Even though the two terms are set in opposition to each other, the reader must not confuse the two terms. In later eras the majority of people had taught that Shintō represents the teachings of the Way of the *kami*, and this is based on a mistaken understanding of the word Shintō as found in *Nihon shoki*. After Shintō became an independent entity in opposition to Buddhism, the ancient meaning of Shintō as a set of rituals performed by officiators at shrines, or a religion of rituals, became a digression among Shintō scholars. [These Shintō scholars] claimed that in later eras Amaterasu Ōmikami gave teachings to people, demonstrating [these teachings] to people who to govern the state, and everything under heaven. They claimed that Saruta Hiko preserved the true tradition, [and their teachings] focus on the two characters 神道, creating a completely new version of Shintō, and that is why we now talk about the Way of Buddhism, the Way of Confucianism, and the Way of the *kami*. These scholars were embarrassed by the fact that China has Confucianism, India has Buddhism, but out country is the only one with no Way. They were envious of Confucianism and Buddhism, so they pretended that Amaterasu Ōmikami had also bestowed teachings that formed a Way, and they created one called Shintō. This is all because they do not comprehend that it is a noble quality of our country to lack a Way.

In general, people living in our country, China, and India all have different traits. The reason is perhaps because of the location of each country in relation to the principles of *yin* and *yang*, or by extension perhaps because of the geographical qualities of each land, or perhaps by extension of that different lands generate different products. Therefore, the trait of the Chinese people generally is toward having too much knowledge and this leads them down an evil path where they have little patience for people. The trait of the people of India generally is a lack of knowledge and this leads them in the direction of greed and they have a deficiency in moderation. The trait of people in our land of Japan generally is clear, transparent, and plain, but we are very intrepid. Based on these differing traits, the customs of each country naturally will be different.

(When Confucianism entered our land, our customs underwent a complete change, then Buddhism entered our country and there was another change. Later the teachings of Laozi and Zhuangzi came to our land and these intermixed with Confucian and Buddhist teachings, and our customs drifted even further away from the ancient state. Also whenever a great military upheaval occurred in later ages, as in the Hogen, Heiji, Juei, Genryaku, Genkō, Kenmu, Ōnin, Eiroku, Tenshō, Bunroku, and Keichō,[5] our customs were altered even more. Now the true state of the customs of our land has become completely hidden. Xie Zhaozhi of the Ming Dynasty wrote in *Wu zazu*,[6] "There are no people more cunning that the Wa knaves." The meaning is that there is no more evil and shrewd people than the Japanese. This criticism may have been true in later eras, but it was not accurate in regards to the ancient Japanese.)

The sages of China established teachings based on the character and customs of the Chinese. Sakamuni of India established his teachings based on the character and customs of India. All teachings of certain philosophies are based on the traits and customs of each individual country, and

---

5. The Hogen Rebellion lasted for three weeks in the summer of 1156. The Heiji Rebellion was fought in the winter of early 1160. The reference to Juei implies the battle between Yoshitsune and the Taira, culminating in the defeat of the Taira in early 1185. Genryaku is a reference to the defeat of the Taira at Dannoura in early 1185. The Genkō War lasted from the summer of 1331 till early 1334. The Kenmu Restoration of 1333 resulted in the creation of a northern and southern court. The Ōnin War lasted for ten years from 1467 till 1477 and destroyed much of Kyōto. The Eiroku era saw upheaval as Oda Nobunaga tried to unify the country from 1560 to 1564. The Tenshō era saw more upheaval from 1576 till the destruction of Odawara Castle in 1590. In Bunroku 1 [1592] Hideyoshi invaded the Korean Peninsula. In Keichō 1 [1596] Hideyoshi invaded the peninsula a second time. With the death of Hideyoshi in 1598 war comes to Japan again, lasting until late 1600 as Tokugawa Ieyasu solidified his control over Japan.

6. Xie Zhaozhi (1567–1624). The title as Sadatake has it is 五雜俎, which means "five various offerings," but the original title was 五雜組 *"five [colors] of woven fabric."* The work was completed in 1608 in sixteen volumes and is a compilation of miscellaneous information, arranged by five categories: heaven, earth, man, things, and events.

that is why they each serve a different purpose. Furthermore, these Ways are set up to prevent evil tendencies in the people of that country. The traits and customs of the people of this land of Japan have no evil tendencies that need to be prevented, so the divine *kami* of our land did not feel the need to establish any specific teachings.

Thus, it is a noble fact that our country did not have a predetermined Way. There is nothing shameful about our country lacking a Way, and there is no need to envy other countries because they have one. While China has the Way established by the sages, there are endless examples through time where the ministers and people murdered the son of heaven and stole the throne. By this we may know that the character and customs of the people of China are evil. And there is no need to debate the fact that the people of India are no different than the birds and insects. … Thus, I believe that the disposition of our land is the best. With no evil disposition, there was no need to establish a Way to teach the people. Again, it is noble that our land does not have a Way to teach the people. People in later eras do not realize this point. There are people who are ashamed of this fact and say, "Because Japan is a barbaric land it did not have a Way" (The term "barbaric" was used by the Chinese to humiliate foreign countries, and there are no examples where any country would use this label on their own land.) Some person created a foolish doctrine by deceptively saying that Shintō was the Way taught by Amaterasu Ōmikami, and then they rashly fashion together teachings that are a mixture of the study of the mind and the study of reason [rational thinking], teaching based on Confucian and Buddhist belief.

If it is true that the great sun goddess did establish this Way it would represent a very important event, so it should have been clearly delineated in *Nihon shoki*, *Kojiki*, *Kogo shūi*, and other national histories (*Kuji hongi* is a forgery and is not included here) and venerable records, but there is no such account. After this there are various records and household accounts regarding this brand of Shintō, but they cannot be trusted. Also, there are no canonical works that contain the teachings supposedly taught by the great sun goddess. In the divine age there was no written script, so by the time the language was written down with the introduction of Chinese characters there should have been an imperial edict issued so these teachings [if they had existed] could be written down as canonical works; they would have been that important. And yet in the successive national histories this fact [about an edict causing] the recording of these teachings in canonical works is not even mentioned. In the teachings of these Shintō scholars they state that the divine age had no written script so everything was transmitted orally, but there is another group who claim there was a kind of written script called *jindai moji* "divine age script," and these records are stored at a certain shrine [but are not available for examination]. There is a great chasm of debate between the group of Shintō scholars who claim there was no written script in the divine age and the group that claim that there was. If there was a written script from the divine age then there should be some evidence of previously written canonical works; why would these teachings have been transmitted primarily through a linguistic medium? If people argue that these teachings were transmitted primarily through a linguistic medium without written works [such as through oral transmission], then there would have been lapses in the memory and the narrative, since the divine age was so far in the past. It is a trivial argument. Why did the person who fabricated this foolish idea that the great sun goddess bestowed her teachings of the Way not also fabricate canonical works containing these things [as proof]?[7] Perhaps he did not have the ability to put the words together [and create the text].

Now there is a document that survives in one volume called "The Statutes on the Native Religion." People claim that it expounds on the teachings of the *kami*, but the contents are primarily Confucian in nature and the words are borrowed from the liturgies and the words of purification. It is not trustworthy. Now, the foolish tradition of Shintō is also labeled Fundamental Principle Shintō [理学神道].[8] What is often called the study of *li* "reason" or the study of *xin* "the mind" started in the Song Dynasty in China. The period of the Zhu Xi school of thought in Song China corresponds to the Hogen-Heiji period in our country. During the time of Amaterasu Ōmikami the learning of China had not yet come to our country. Furthermore, the study of *li* from the Song Dynasty naturally did not exist. I think people will realize that by simply looking at the name of Fundamental Principle Shintō they will realize it is a fabrication.

3

There are two types of *yuiitsu Shintō*, a new one and an old one. On the surface, the old type of *yuiitsu Shintō* does not resemble Buddhism, but if you look deeper you see that it is built around a Buddhist doctrine of logic,

7. To an extent, this did happen. The fabricated work is *Yamato hime seiki*.

8. 理学神道 is translated as "Shintō of the fundamental principle" in the *Encyclopedia of Shintō*. See http://k-amc.kokugakuin.ac.jp/DM/detail.do?class_name=col_eos&data_id=23683.

like the Vajradhātu, the Garbhadhātu, exoteric, and esoteric teachings. As this does not outwardly demonstrate any Buddhist influence it was called *yuiitsu Shintō*. The newer type of *yuiitsu Shintō* is said to be a re-creation built around the study of reason and the mind without any Buddhist influence, and is commonly known as *tenjin yuiitsu Shintō* "singular Shintō of heavenly men" and Fundamental Principle Shintō.

Also there is a type called *Ryōbu shūgō Shintō* "Syncretic Dual Shintō," and it claims to have the doctrine of *honji suijaku.*[9] *Honji suijaku* refers to a certain Shintō *kami* being a Buddhist deity in a previous life. This is a doctrine where they claim that in order to lead the souls of men to Nirvana, a certain Buddhist deity takes the form of a Shintō *kami* and its "traces" hang down [into our world]. In some work we find that within this Syncretic Dual Shintō there are four great teachers: Kōhō, Dengyō, Jikaku, and Chishō,[10] but this is a scheme to take Shintō festivals and ritual prayers and make them the property of Buddhist monks. This idea that Japanese *kami* are actually Buddhist *kami* is nowhere seen in the records of Sakyamuni's teachings. What evidence do they have to make such an irrational claim? It can be said that in the era when these teachings were first proclaimed that the Buddhist monks were lucky that more people were not suspicious about these. In the Buddhist canon the names of Buddha starting with Amida are all allegorical, so even if one has that name, there is no substance. Why would Buddha, a formless being, come to Japan and change into a Japanese *kami*? To me it is evident that this doctrine of *honji suijaku* is nothing but fallacious dogma.

4

There are more than a few Shintō scholars in society who profess that Japan had written script back to the divine age. They claim that some shrine,

---

9. *The Encyclopedia of Shintō* states, "The term *honji suijaku* refers to the idea that the Buddhist *kami* provisionally appear as Shintō *kami* in order to spiritually save sentient beings in Japan. The *kami* are thus the manifestations (*suijaku*; literally, 'traces'; i.e., the form appearing in the world to save sentient beings) of the Buddhist *kami*, and the Buddhist *kami* are the *honji* (literally 'original ground') of the Shintō *kami* (namely, their true form and substance)" (Inoue et al. 1999:404).

10. These can be taken as both the names of monks and principles. Kōhō can represent the famous monk Hungfa or "vast law." Dengyō is the founder of the Tendai school in Japan, but also means to "spread the teachings." Jikaku means "to remember mercy," and Chishō means "the wisdom that gives one an assurance of salvation."

some Shintō household has several bamboo slats with this writing in ink as annotation. They claim these characters are neither Sanskrit nor Chinese in origin, but resemble characters used to make a text by Daoist scholars. They claim that because of the secrecy of this, there are very few people who have actually seen these characters. [But in reality] these characters were concocted by someone who is curious and will not let anyone examine these. He keeps these hidden so he can deceive people.

In both *Nihon shoki* and *Kojiki* there is no record of the *kami* establishing written script, and there is no mention of the various *kami* exchanging any kind of written documents. The beginning of *Kogo shūi* says, "To begin with, I have heard that in ancient times, when Japan had no written script, everyone, noble and base, old and young, performed every duty by word of mouth, forgetting nothing."[11] This provides unambiguous evidence that there was no written script in the divine age. However, there are some scholars who say, "It is written in *Kogo shūi* that anciently there was no written script, but we have bamboo slats with characters written in ink as annotation that have come down to us in the present." With this they try to justify the existence of this fraud and refute the description in *Kogo shūi*, and they are ashamed that our country had no written script, even though China has characters and India has Sanskrit. It is honest to simply say that something did not exist; this is a fact, so why deceive people? Pretending something existed that did not goes against the customs of our country. If these bamboo slats were real, it would be desirable for the person to make a copy of the writing so it could be displayed widely to society, preserving an artifact from the divine age so it would not die out. Again, it is not the ancient custom of our people to begrudge this, and keep the actual form a secret, refusing to show it to people.

There were absolutely no secret objects in ancient Japan, but in later eras the Japanese gradually began to be greedy about things. It is not the custom of the divine period for people to have secrets about this or that in relation to the *kami*. In the majority of cases, when we hear about something that is sacred [and thus is kept secret], upon examining it, we find that there is no reason why it should be treated thus. Also, according to the teachings of some of these Shintō scholars, because there was no written script in the divine age the Way was transmitted primarily through an oral medium. What an obnoxious thing for one group to argue about there being no written script in the past with a group that argues that such a script actually existed.

---

11. Translation from Bentley (2002:67).

5

Shintō scholars are always saying that it is extremely important to preserve the vernacular reading of the [two books] of the divine age *Nihon shoki*, but one cannot achieve this level of ability by the common form of study. People should not believe this statement. Generally in Confucian studies one must read through the six Confucian classics, and in Buddhist studies there is the Buddhist canon. Some time later someone concocted the Way of Shintō, but they apparently did not have the energy to also fabricate a canon to go with this foolish notion. They simply converted the divine age books of *Nihon shoki* into a vernacular rendition and it all follows from this. It is natural that there would be some difficulty when taking the record of the divine age and using that to create teachings for the Way of the *kami*. They claim that there are allegories in the text, explaining things from converting the text into the philosophy of *yin* and *yang* and the five principles, forcing together ideas from the two Ways of Confucianism and Buddhism, adding things from the study of the mind and reason. And as if they were unraveling a puzzle, they explain things according to Buddhist allegories, so can we believe that this is a proper attitude when they force their own ideas into a reckless doctrine?

Nihon shoki is an orthodox history and a record of ancient events, but there is nothing in there that resembles the teachings of a Way. It is proper to record history exactly as it happened, so why should it contain allegories. If it did contain allegories, then it could not be treated as an orthodox history. They interpret "direct" [as in direct history] as "allegory," perverting the interpretation of things; taking extratextual information means that this doctrine is a distortion. Imposing an explanation about the Way according to a text that does not mention the Way is to declare a mysterious event a rational one, which creates difficult problems, such as oral traditions and secret artifacts. Chinese histories from the ancient past are not simply oral traditions from people in later eras that were written down, so there are many places that are suspicious or strange. They have simply recorded things, even if they were suspicious or strange. It is desirable that people treat *Nihon shoki* in the same manner.

6

Shintō scholars also teach about the "three fundamental texts" of Shintō, which are *Sendai kuji hongi*, *Nihon shoki*, and *Kojiki*. *Kuji hongi* is a fraudulent text, claiming to be compiled by both Shōtoku Taishi and Soga no Umako, but the text of *Kuji hongi* records events that happened after the deaths of both individuals. There are many other pieces of evidence demonstrating that it is a fraud, but there is no need to list these.[12] Texts [that *Kuji hongi* has relied on] include the entire *Nihon shoki* and *Kogo shūi* with a few sections from other works included. Even though the work is fraudulent, its conception is very old, so no one knows the reason why it was created, and many people have quoted from its text. When you see that many scholars in later ages have quoted from *Kuji hongi* it is quite ridiculous.

Aside from *Kuji hongi*, there is also a book with the same title in seventy-two volumes. It is also known as *Kuji hongi taiseikyō*.[13] It is the creation in recent years by a Buddhist monk named [Shaku] Chō-on (a person from Hizen Province who served at the Kōsaiji Temple of the Tatebayashi Clan in Ueno Province; he belonged to the Ōbaku school) and a Shintō Priest named Nagano Uneme Such-and-such from the Izawa Shrine in Shima Province, who laid plans together and concocted this work. Later this deception came to light and in Tenwa 1 [1681] both individuals were sentenced to banishment. There are Shintō scholars and other scholars who still quote from this work.

7

Shintō scholars also talk about three divine texts of Shintō: *Tengen jinpen jinmyōkyō*, *Chigen jinzu jinmyōkyō*, and *Jingen jinriki jinmyōkyō*.[14] They

---

12. For a revision of this theory, see Bentley (2006).

13. The *Encyclopedia of Shintō* notes that Chō-on appears to have published this text between the years of 1676 and 1679. They make no mention of Nagano (Inoue et al. 1999:581–82).

14. As The *Encyclopedia of Shintō* explains, these form the three scriptures of esoteric teaching of Yoshida Shintō: "These explain the spiritual force of the three entities (*sansai no reiō*), the three wondrous empowerments (*sanmyō no kaji*), and the three kinds of sacred treasures (*sanshu no reihō*); the practices they presuppose aim at internal purification. Furthermore, Shinto is divided into substance (*tai*), function (*yū*), and appearance (*sō*); from these, the following series of classifications arises: three principles (*sangen*, i.e., the previous three items), nine wondrous altars (*kubu myōdan*, i.e., the combination of the above three with the three elements heaven, man, and earth), and eighteen kinds of Shinto (*jūhachi Shintō*, i.e., a further, more detailed articulation of the previous nine meant to encompass all existing phenomena). These doctrines are all used to explicate Yoshida Shintō's fundamental principle that Shinto permeates the three entities (heaven, earth, and humans)" [Inoue et al. 1999:446].

claim that these originally were transmitted by Ame no Koyane, and later that one of the seven stars of the Big Dipper came down from heaven and converted the traditions [that Ame no Koyane had preserved] to Chinese characters. I have not had occasion to actually view these texts, but these are clearly fraudulent works by simply considering the titles.

The phrases *jinpen*, *jinzu*, and *jinriki* are all Buddhist terms.[15] During the time of Ame no Koyane Buddhism did not exist in Japan, so he would have had no knowledge of Buddhist terminology. Also, the story about one of the seven stars of the Big Dipper falling from heaven sounds a lot like the story told in Daoist circles. Daoism teaches that in heaven there is a Lord Taiyizhen, that the stars of the Big Dipper became a Daoist, or changed into a child and came to earth and so on. The idea that this was then converted into Chinese characters makes it sound as if the conversion was from the divine age script into Chinese. However, I have already noted that there was no writing in the divine age. They then claim this [conversion into Chinese characters] happened later, but they never specify when this occurred. If this was such an important event, then no one will believe them if they cannot say, "On this day in this month of this year of Emperor So-and-So, this event occurred when he came to our land and converted the text." Considering this evidence, I believe that these works are fraudulent. The families with an ancient pedigree like the Nakatomi and Urabe families would not use such works.

8

Shintō scholars list five important works: *Yamato hime seiki* (also known as *Daijingū hongi*),[16] *Hōki hongi*, *Awarawa no mikoto-ki* (also known as *Gochinza shidai-ki*), *Asuka hongi* (also known as *Gochinza hongi*), and *Ōta no mikoto hongi* (also known as *Gochinza denki* or *Saruta hiko no mikoto-ki*). These are labeled sacred records of the Ise Shrine, but these are fraudulent, concocted to look like ancient records. First, in *Yamato hime seiki* we find the line, "They strangled the law of Buddhism and again worshipped the *kami* of heaven and earth." Originally, Princess Yamato was the daughter of the eleventh emperor, Suinin. In the twenty-fifth year of his reign, she was

15. *Jinpen* 神変 means "super transformational power"; *jinzu* 神通 means "superhuman power," and *jinriki* 神力 means "supernatural power."

16. One of the five works of Shintō. A work that details the origins of Yamato Hime and her relation with both the Inner and Outer Shrines of Ise Jingū. Scholars have determined that the work is a later creation from the Kamakura era (cf. Inoue et al. 1999:578–79).

sent to serve at the Great Shrine of Ise, as the shrine was first established in that year on the upper reaches of the Isuzu River in Ise Province. However, Buddhism did not enter our country for another 571 years, in the thirteenth year of the thirtieth emperor, Kinmei. It is impossible that 571 years before this, Princess Yamato was able to imagine that Buddhism would come to our land, and then mention about it strangling the religion. Can we not say that the whole work is a deception based on this one line? Looking through these five works one finds that these are filled with Buddhist terminology. There are also fallacious ideas that contradict records preserved in the national histories and veritable records. …

9

Some Shintō scholars refer to Japan as "the divine land" because they claim that we have "the Way of the *kami*," or because we have the three imperial regalia, or because our emperor is a direct descendant of Amaterasu Ōmikami. But these several theories are difficult to accept. Starting with *Nihon shoki*, and the other orthodox histories and veritable records from the ancient past, our country is never once labeled "the divine land." In later eras a number of works appear that use this term, but these cannot be believed. (In works such as *Shokugenshō* and *Jinnō shōtōki*[17] Japan is called "the divine land," but I do not rely on these records because they were compiled in later eras.) Remember, however, that in the Jingū record of *Nihon shoki* it notes that when the imperial ship arrived in Silla for the conquest the king of Silla was overcome by the brilliant authority of the imperial army and looking at the imperial ship said, "I have heard that in the east there is a divine country, called Yamato. It has a sagacious king who calls himself *sumera mikoto*. Surely it is their divine soldiers who have come. How can we raise troops and fight against them?" So the King had a white flag raised, and surrendered.

Perhaps Shintō scholars have misunderstood this sentence, and think that it means that our land is a "divine land." This quote includes the character 神 "divine" in phrases like "divine land" and "divine soldiers," but this

17. Kitabatake Chikafusa (1293–1354) compiled *Shokugenshō* in 1340 for Emperor Go-Murakami. In it he outlines the rank systems of the court, along with a description of court regulations and ceremonies. *Jinnō shōtōki* was completed by Chikafusa in 1339. He compiled this record to demonstrate that the southern branch of the split court was the legitimate one.

is a usage of respect from the king of Silla, and as I have mentioned above, it does not provide proof for any of the three theories. Just as the Chinese will use a respectful tone when calling their land "the divine region" (In the work *Zhuoshi zaolin*[18] we find this usage of "divine region"), I think some Japanese people call Japan the "divine land" out of respect. It is impossible to argue any of the three theories noted above according to this phrase. The usage of 神 "divine" in this manner of veneration once had the virtue of mystery or wonder.

Shintō scholars often call the Nakatomi Words of Expiation simply the Nakatomi Expiation, dropping the character 詞 "words," but this is improper. The words of expiation conducted by the Nakatomi refers to actual words proclaimed by the Nakatomi when performing the act of purification at court. This comes from the Great Purification, which is performed every year in the sixth and twelfth months of the year, on behalf of the male and female officials at court. Currently this is called the Words of the Great Purification, as these words are spoken by the Nakatomi. These words are found in the "Words of the Liturgies" section of the "Regulations of the Native Religion" in *Engi shiki*. Other cases of purifications are similar to this Great Purification, other than a few changes here and there. Purification cleanses the individual from the filth of transgression. Once purification has been performed the person feels at ease because his body and spirit have been cleansed, and in reality the person is now clean.

Originally, the words of the purification were only pronounced once. Even in cases of the Great Purification held at court, it was performed once. But as time went on, rituals such as one thousand purifications or ten thousand purifications appeared. These originated from Shintō followers becoming envious of Buddhist practices, such as the practice of reading a sutra a thousand or ten thousand times, or the one million Buddhist chants, or the thousand volumes of the Dhāranī, and began to imitate these. As I have noted earlier, the established method is that after one performance of the words of purification, all the filth from transgressions is then cleansed; people do not understand the main purpose of the ritual of purification, falsely believing that the more times you say the words, the greater the effect.

Also, people in later eras who began to call this the "Way of the *kami*" lacked any understanding of the essence of ritual purification, and with an ulterior motive, they interpreted the words of purification as performed by

---

18. Written by Zhuo Mingqing (dates unknown) and Wang Shimao (1536–88) and published in 1581. It is a collection of philosophical writings.

the Nakatomi to be evidence that Amaterasu Ōmikami bestowed teachings for the Way. They took the various prohibitions and recklessly concocted a doctrine based on the philosophy of Buddhism, dogma of reason, and the mind, and created commandments. The words of the Nakatomi purification were uttered to expiate a variety of transgressions and are not found in any written work as commandments. Interpreting these as commandments is not a proper understanding, but an unnecessary extension of the purpose.

In the words of the Great Purification found in *Engi shiki,* there is "the High Plain of Heaven," and in another place are the words of the imperial proclamation of orders. Part of that includes the words, "Give ear all of you to this command, that in this, the Great Purification ritual of the sixth month, the various and sundry transgressions committed by the many officials who serve in the government will be expiated and cleansed." In this quote is the phrase "transgressions committed" (過犯), which means transgressions committed unintentionally. We see the following in a dictionary: "An unintentional error is known as 過. An intentional error is known as 悪." Based on this, one cannot prohibit by commandment an unintentional mistake.

10

There is also something called "the words of the purification of the six senses." This is clearly based on Buddhist doctrine and is a creation of someone in later eras. According to Buddhist doctrine, the six senses are sight, hearing, smell, taste, touch, and mind. Also known as the six *cauras*, while color, sound, scent, flavor, sensation, and truth are the six dusts or the six entries. The six dusts are the filthy clods that defile the six senses, and these six dusts enter the body mainly through the six senses; if one devotes himself to his religious studies, he can prevent these from bothering his mind and entering his heart. That is why we find someone who created the words, "The eyes see a variety of filth, but a variety of filth does not stay in the heart."

Originally the true meaning of Buddhism was to cut ties with father, mother, wife, and children, leave one's home, severing all ties with society, focusing on one's own identity, residing below a tree, or on top of a rock, preventing the six dusts from entering the six senses, ridding one's heart of torment and worry. Buddhism has as an excellent goal of purifying one's heart and making it so it cannot be swayed, as if one had the mind of the dead. In other words, there is no difference with the custom and actions of the beggar in India who has renounced the world. As a member of society who resides in the world, we each have a responsibility we can control, with the emperor above us and everyone below till we come to ourselves. In spite of this, if one were to put into practice this idea of the six senses and the six dusts people would lose all interest in their specific responsibility [to society] and there would be great harm to the function of society. The beggar in India only survives because he is able to beg for food from other people in society. If everyone in the world, irrespective of their station or status, were to renounce the world and become beggars, who would be left to give them food? Therefore, it is natural that we should avoid and shun Buddhist doctrine from Shintō rituals and eschew imposing Buddhist doctrine on the ceremonies of Shintō. In spite of this, Shintō scholars conducting this ritual of purification of the six senses go against the intention of the officiator, and in the end actually end up defiling everyone.

There are more rituals of purification than just this ritual of purification of the six senses I have mentioned, but all these are concoctions of people in later eras. These do not appear in the "Regulations of the Native Religion" in *Engi shiki*, and the words used within these rituals are new, so you may know that these are frauds.

Also, "expiation" means to expiate a transgression, and is performed to cleanse a person of defilement. However, it is a mistake for these Shintō scholars to come before the *kami* and pronounce the words of this purification. What transgression or defilement do the *kami* have? So why should they pronounce these words before the *kami*? Perhaps these people think that they are reciting words to the *kami*, as if a monk were reciting the words of a sutra to Buddha.

11

In the teachings of people connected to Shintō they say, "The clapping of hands in Shintō is known as *kasifa no te* 'the hand of oak leaves' because the shape of hands being clapped resembles the shape of oak leaves." In general people say that there is a deep and mysterious meaning to this, but this is in error. It is an ancient custom of respect in our country to clap one's hands toward someone. Thus, it is simply an extension of this ancient custom when we do this toward the *kami*. Because the custom is to clap eight times, it was called *yafirate* (八ひら手). In the paragraph on the First

Fruits Festival in the "Regulations of the Native Religion" in *Engi shiki* it says, "Those of fifth rank and above rise together and go to the posting-board in the middle courtyard. They kneel and clap their hands four times. Each time there are eight claps."[19] An annotational note here says, "Anciently this was called *yafirate* (八開手)." Also, in the Jitō record of *Nihon shoki* it says, "The queen ascended the throne. The ministers and the hundred officials lined up and everyone bowed and clapped their hands together." Thus, clapping one's hands is not limited to the *kami*.

It is a mistake to call clapping one's hands *kasifate*. It would appear that some Shintō scholars who did not know the reading of the characters took 拍手 "clap hands" found in some ancient documents to be 柏手 "oak hands" and read it *kasifate*, and this custom has spread. However, in later eras as people forgot the meaning of the word *kasifate* they concocted the fallacious theory noted above and then labeled it a secret tradition. The character 拍 belongs to the "hand" radical series, while 柏 "oak tree" belongs to the "tree" radical series. In *Nihon shoki* the characters 拍手 are glossed as *te wo utu* "clap one's hands." Thus, one may know that the reading of *kasifate* is a later creation. In ancient times *kasifa* referred to those who served in the imperial kitchen.

There is also something called *ama no sakate utu*, which is a custom where someone claps their hands when meeting someone for the first time; they clap together at the beginning and at the end of their first meeting. The first clap is called *susumi no rei* "advance salutation" and when the two part, the clap is known as *sirizoku no rei* "retreat salutation." They write *sakate* as 逆手 "backhand," but this error arises from simply attaching a set of characters according to the sound of the word and ignoring the meaning. (A similar example is the name Ama no Sakahoko. The original meaning was "heavenly-wise-halberd," but it is customary to write this as "heavenly-backward-halberd.") The word *sakate* means *sakarite*, and *sakaru* means "to retire [retreat]." Even the example in poetry of calling a land far removed from the imperial capital *amasakaru fina* uses the word *ama* "heaven" as a metaphor for the capital. (The example of *takamahara* "high heavenly plain" is the same meaning.) Also, in *Kojiki*, in the section where Ōkuninushi cedes his right to rule, we see the line, "Yafe Koto Shironushi … immediately he stepped on the side of the boat that had arrived to take him, causing it to capsize, and he clapped his hands backwards,[20] changing

19. Translation from Bock (1972:51).

20. Instead of clapping his hands with the palms together, he claps his hands using the back of his hand.

the boat into a green brushwood fence and hid his form." This signifies that he would not be returning to this land again. (The green brushwood fence blocks the road so no one can travel down it. Consider the character 成 "accomplish" in the sentence.[21])

Some theorize that the backward clapping was used as a curse, and when divers come up out of the ocean they clap their hands, but this theory is too beholden to the meaning of the character 逆 "backward." It is not correct to interpret *ama* "heaven" as ocean. (The example of *ama no sakate* found in *Ise monogatari* refers to a man clapping, signifying that he is leaving, cutting off his relationship with a woman.)

12

Shintō scholars claim that the use of mulberry strips to tuck up the sleeves of officiators is to prevent defilement, but this is also a mistake. It is also incorrect to use rope made of plant fibers in place of mulberry (which is now called cotton, but this is different from the ancient mulberry fibers) to tie up the sleeves. In the section on trees in *Wamyōshō* it says, "Annotational note after '*Bencao* by Tao Hongjing,' another name for mulberry. The tree is *duzhong*, and the Japanese name is *fafimayumi* 'spindle tree.' If you break the branches it is filled with white fiber.'" The characters 緜 and 綿 were originally the same [just inverted]. What is known as *fafimayumi* is also called *turumayumi*, and the blossoms and leaves resemble the spindle tree, but with vines. If you remove the bark there is a thin layer underneath that is white, and if you strip this thin layer you get white fibers. As our ancient customs were very simple, there was no need to be flowery, so the people simply made strings out of these fibers and tied up their hair. The people also used these fibers for all kinds of decorations, and this was called *yufu site*. …

13

Shintō scholars claim, "The reason that we ring bells in front of the *kami* is because in *Kogo shūi* we find that when Amaterasu Ōmikami went into the

---

21. Sadatake is correct that the verb here is 打成 "he clapped and (the magical response of the clap of changing the boat into a fence) was accomplished." However, his quote from *Kojiki* does not contain this character: 天逆手矣於青柴垣打出而隱也. Perhaps this is a copyist's error.

Ama no Iwato, Ame no Uzume danced [in front of the cave]. At this time she held a halberd with bells attached. The character 鐸 refers to bells. Also, when the palace of Amaterasu Ōmikami was established in the province of Ise, it was a divine command that anciently a heavenly backward broad sword and a heavenly backward spear with bells came down from heaven, as seen in *Yamato hime seiki*. That is why we ring bells."

This is a deceptive practice created by people from later eras. In the phrase "a halberd with bells attached," the halberd is the main object, and the bells are simply decorative. Why would anyone ignore the main object and instead use the decorative bells? As mentioned above, *Yamato hime seiki* is a fraudulent untrustworthy work. There is no account in older documents that various objects came down from heaven, and the name "heavenly backward broad sword" is a fabrication not seen in any other record. None of this can be trusted. In the "Regulations of the Native Religion" in *Engi shiki* is a detailed list of objects used in Shintō festivals, such as vessels, utensils, and objects, but there is not one mention of bells. There also are no examples of the emperor ringing bells during the Four Quarters Ritual of the first day of the first month, or the New Harvest Festival in the eleventh month of the Tasting of the First Fruits after an emperor has newly ascended the throne. In *Nihon shoki*, *Kojiki*, *Kogo shūi* or other records there are absolutely no accounts of the various *kami* ringing bells. This practice is done by later-era Shintō officials in imitation of Buddhist monks who ring Buddhist bells or wave staffs with bells on them during their ritual ceremonies.

Within the words that Shintō officials use when they pray is the [Chinese] phrase *mujō reihō shintō kaji.*[22] The words used in the Shintō rituals are all Old Japanese, and there are no examples of Chinese phrases. The liturgies contained in the "Regulations of the Native Religion" in *Engi shiki* demonstrate no examples of phrases like *mujō reihō*, which are Sino-Japanese. The word *kaji* "aid" is a word from Buddhist doctrine. And then there is the word *kajima kajitori,* which Shintō scholars claim dates back to Take Mikazuchi, a transparent lie, where they are trying to persuade people they are not imitating Buddhism, but it clearly is Buddhist in origin.

Shintō officials also make symbolic gestures with their hands during their worship and prayers. One is called *sankō no in* "the symbol of the three lights" and refers to the sign of the sun, moon, and stars. These belong to the same category as Onogorojima sign and Yashirodono sign. There is no evidence in *Nihon shoki*, *Kojiki*, or *Kogo shūi* that the various

22. Meaning "The Supreme Spiritual Jewel, an Aid to Shintō."

kami made symbolic gestures with their hands. If there actually were any signs, the character 印 would not have been pronounced as *win*. I wonder what it would have been called in Old Japanese.[23] The word *on* is a different usage, and there are no examples of this in the ancient documents.

On the day that the emperor ascended the throne, it is said there was an anointing of the head. These Shintō officials claim that at this time they use the bright sign (but through the ages there have been times when they have used this sign and times when they did not), but this is the same as the bright sign of Buddhism. (The Shintō officials purposely do not record the Buddhist name of this sign, because it is terrifying to record secret traditions of the court.) If the *kami* had their own signs, then why would these officials discard those signs, and rely on Buddhist ones? These Shintō signs are Buddhist imitations, based on envy of Buddhist monks.

14

When Shintō officials worship the *kami* they have people write something on a paper offering, but this is inappropriate. These offerings are known as *nusa* or *nigi*, and people in the ancient eras presented these as formal offerings, used as signs of respect. Thus, people in the ancient days took our word *nusa* and matched the Chinese character 幣 or the two graph set of 幣帛, and in China objects sent as presents were known as 幣, while gifts of silk were known as 幣帛. Therefore, our word *nusa* (or *nigi*, or even *mitegura*) has the same meaning and that is why the Chinese character 幣 is used. These offerings were created from the bark of the spindle tree (which is the *fafimayumi* tree mentioned above), pierced with a stick. There are also some examples of people using the skin of flax. In the record of the festivals of the native religion in *Engi shiki* among the list of vessels and items we find several pounds of cotton (or spindle tree) paper, and this cotton paper is made from the thin inner bark of the spindle tree. When the outer, blue bark is used, these are known as "blue offerings." When the inner, white fibers are used these are known as "white offerings." It is the same with flax. In later eras people ripped paper and used these in place of these fiber-made offerings. These offerings in general are presented to the *kami*, and we see in the "Regulations of the Native Religion" examples where the court sends gifts of offerings to the various shrines. And it is customary for average citizens to take their own paper offerings when they

23. In *Nihon shoki* the character 印 is glossed *sirusi* "sign."

visit a shrine to present something to the *kami*. However, it is contrary to the custom when people in the provinces do not bring their own paper offerings, but receive these from the shrine and write something on these. Also, at smaller shrines they set up paper offerings as *shintai*,[24] but as noted above, these offerings should not be worshipped.

In the doctrine of some Shintō officials is the belief that the reason that the mirror is worshipped as a *shintai* is because it is uniform with no corners and no defects. The mirror was created in imitation of the shape of heaven, while the flat surface represents the earth. The light (reflected from it) is bright and clear, with no hint of cloudiness, allowing the light (of heaven) to uniformly shine on the people. When people who worship the *kami* face this divine mirror their form is reflected clearly. This reflects the path of honesty, and the *kami* is thus the body of the person [who is reflected in the mirror]. There is no other *kami*. The *shintai* of the mirror teaches us that rather than pray to the *kami*, one should focus on his own self and preserve the path of honesty.

This doctrine originated from Buddhism, and it is the same as the Buddhist notion of "the merciful light of Amida shines uniformly throughout the ten quarters of the world." The idea that the deity is the person in the mirror is the same as the pure land idea that "My body is the same as Amida." So even if someone sets up a mirror and people worship the mirror unaware of the facts I have mentioned above, the person is just looking at a mirror—there are no teachings or precepts here. It is not part of our ancient customs to teach people in oblique, circuitous ways, using difficult allegories.

Buddhism uses statutes to teach doctrine, and teaches the people through Buddhist statutes starting with doctrine such as the Vajradhātu, the Garbhadhātu, the nine grades of the pure land, the universals, the hells, and so forth. Our land in ancient times absolutely had no such teachings. Making a mirror a *shintai* is a replication of the Yata mirror at Ise Shrine, which was said to be a *shintai*. However, Amaterasu Ōmikami always kept the Yata mirror, so when she presented it to the heavenly grandson, Ninigi, she said that every time he looked at the mirror it was as if he was looking

---

24. The *Encyclopedia of Shintō* states, "A physical object serving as an object of worship at shrines, and in which the spirit of the *kami* is believed to reside. Those used in Shrine Shinto (Jinja Shintō) are frequently called *mitamashiro*. *Shintai* are typically mirrors, swords, and jewels, although ritual wands (*gohei*) and sculptures of *kami* (*shinzō*) are also found, and in some cases natural objects such as stones, mountains, and waterfalls may also serve as *shintai*. The term *shintai* has been used since the mid-Heian period and is found in such works as *Iroha jirui kagami* and *Shaku Nihongi*" (Inoue et al. 1999:195).

at her. The Ise Shrine was established during the era of Emperor Suinin, and the mirror was then worshipped as a *shintai* at that point. Naturally there is an important reason for this, and the various shrines copied this Ise tradition, regardless that the *kami* they worship have no connection with a mirror at all. They should just be honest about this, as it is a grave mistake to create something based on the reasoning of Buddhism.

15

Another brand of Shintō doctrine is the idea of the origin of *sansha takusen* of Shintō.[25] This is erroneous. Can they tell us on what day in what month of what year of what emperor these divine words originated? They were received in what province by what individual? When one asks these questions, naturally you can immediately determine the veracity of all this by their vague answers, since no one knows the date or the place of the origin of these oracles. The trinity (such as the three *kami* of *waka* or the three *kami* of the military) are all based on the model of the three honored ones of Amida. Examples such as the three shrines, Amaterasu Ōmikami, the Great Hachiman Bodhisattva, and the Kasuda Great *Kami* of Light are all from the same category of imitations. …

The doctrine in Shintō about the two ancestral temples, being Ise and Kamo, as well as the altars of soil and grain are all misconceptions. Both the concept of "ancestral temple" and "altars of soil and grain" are Chinese in origin, but in our country these words did not exist anciently. Differences in countries results in differences in customs and ceremonies. While our court did imitate ceremonies from China, there were many customs they did not adopt. Thus, there are many customs from China that do not match the circumstances of our land, though people will try to introduce these. It is worthless to try to introduce something and force it on the people. In the record of Keikō in *Nihon shoki* it says, "Has not heaven sent you to weave the fabric of the work of heaven and preserve the ancestral

25. The *Encyclopedia of Shintō* says, "Oracles (*takusen*) of the three *kami* Tenshō-kōtaijingū (Amaterasu), Hachiman Daibosatsu, and Kasuga Daimyōjin that circulated widely from the middle ages until the early modern period. This term also refers to an object of worship that takes the form of a hanging scroll inscribed with the divine titles (*shingō*) and the oracles of these three *kami*. Their divine titles—Tenshō-kōtaijingū being in the center, Hachiman Daibosatsu on the right and Kasuga Daimyōjin on the left—and respective oracle texts form a trinity that is often accompanied by depictions of the *kami* as well" (Inoue et al. 1999:399).

temple?" This does not mean that the word "ancestral temple" existed in our country at the time, but *Nihon shoki* originally wrote about our country adorning the text using the language from Chinese works, so the characters 宗廟 "ancestral temple" are an embellishment of the [original] description. Across *Nihon shoki* there are a great many examples like this. People do not realize this fact, but are too focused on the text, and they try to force Chinese cultural traits on our country and come up with these far-fetched theories. (Within *Nihon shoki* there are examples where "ancestral temple" and "altars of soil and grain" appear together, but these are simply embellishments of the text.)

In the theories of Shintō scholars they claim that the readings found in *Nihon shoki* were attached by Prince Toneri, but that is not correct. These readings were attached at a later date. We know this because we find inaccurate readings as well as bothersome readings. [For example] the character 徳 "virtue" has the inappropriate reading of *mi-ikiwofi* "august-vigor" attached. It is proper to read the character 勢 "energy, vigor" as *ikiwofi*, but not the character 徳.[26] There is a reading of *kuni-ife* for 宗廟 "ancestral temple," but this is not appropriate. The record also fails to make a distinction between 聖 "a sage" and 仙 "an immortal," reading both characters as *fiziri*.[27] The measurement character 尺 "one foot" is glossed as *saka*, which is a confusing sound change from *shaku*.[28] And reading the character 僧 "monk" as *fousi* is based on the Sino-Japanese reading of 法師 "teacher of the law," and not *sou*, which is the Chinese pronunciation. It is unclear what reading of *fousi* was borrowed to gloss the character 僧. ... My own opinion is that the style of *Nihon shoki* was created by lifting phrases from Chinese works like *Huainanzi*, *Shiji*, *Hanshu*, *Wenxuan*, and other texts and embellishing its original text. Thus, Prince Toneri created a Chinese-

26. Sadatake has failed to notice that the older pronunciation would be *ikifofi*, not *ikiwofi*, which likely is a product of sound change around the tenth century. Prince Toneri (or anyone connected with *Nihon shoki*) would not have made that kind of mistake.

27. It can be argued that during the early Nara era after *Nihon shoki* was completed Japanese culture and the indigenous religion still lacked a sufficiently advanced vocabulary (without using Chinese loans) to make a distinction between a sage and an immortal. *Fiziri* means something akin to a virtuous person. Martin (1987:412) speculates that the etymology is *pi* "sun" *no* "of" and *siri* "know." Thus, someone who knows the sun, or extraordinary things.

28. The lack of sufficient knowledge of linguistics as well as how Chinese has changed over time prevents Sadatake from making a more cogent argument. The character 尺 likely entered Paekche as *tshak*, and when introduced into Japan, the *tsha* was simplified to *sa*. Old Japanese does not allow closed syllables, so an echo vowel was added, creating the earlier form *saka*.

style text so people could read it like they would read a sutra and its commentary. But in order to aid in the reading of words, like 葉木国 as *fako kuni* "land of leaves and trees," or 可美 as *umasi* "excellent," the prince added readings in the text when necessary. ...[29]

In the words of Shintō scholars they say things like "the High Plain of Heaven" is the great sky above, and "the heavenly *kami*" are those *kami* we call *tenjin* that reside above in heaven. This is the truth. "The High Plain of Heaven" originally referred to heaven. And no matter which country, when they refer to the capital where our ruler resides, they call it "the High Plain of Heaven," which is a metaphorical reference to heaven. It is analogous to the usage in later eras when the palace of the emperor was referred to as "above the clouds." In the Upper Katsuragi District of the province of Yamato is Mount Takama and Takama Plain. Both the mountain and the plain are where Amaterasu Ōmikami resided, so this entire area is called Takamahara. The reason for this is that in Toichi District is Mount Kagu (examples of Mount Kaku or Mount Kata are simply changes in the pronunciation.) Because both Takamahara and Mount Kagu are in the same province, during the time when Amaterasu Ōmikami dwelt there, she used products produced on Mount Kagu. Those products are the true *sakaki* tree from Mount Kagu, a Japanese bird cherry tree, a true stag from Mount Kagu, gold and copper from Mount Kagu, as well as a Gardenia tree. (During the period of Emperor Jinmu he went to Mount Kagu and took clay and made flat plates. The various items mentioned above are also found in *Nihon shoki*, *Kojiiki*, and *Kogo shūi*.) Also, when Amaterasu Ōmikami went into the Ama no Iwato cave, one variant tradition in *Nihon shoki* records that, "The myriad *kami* were gathered together at the High Market Place (Taketi) of heaven." It is quite plausible that this refers to Takechi District in Yamato Province. Considering all these facts, it is without a doubt that Takamahara, the capital of Amaterasu Ōmikami, was located in the area of Mount Takama and the Takama Plain in Yamato Province.

In the teachings of the Shintō scholars there is something called the seven generations of heavenly *kami* and the five generations of earthly *kami*. These do not appear in the orthodox histories and veritable records, so we cannot trust later records where these events do appear. We see that Kuni Toko Tachi was spontaneously generated from the essence of heaven.

---

29. Sadatake brings up a good point. The text of *Nihon shoki*, especially the first three books, has many phonetic readings included in the text. Later-era copyists added interlinear readings. These two need to be kept separate when arguing about origins and compilers.

The text then has that in the second generation we have Kuni Satsuchi [continuing] down to Izanagi, who were created from the essence. According to a quote from one of these later works it says that these *kami* were born to a father and mother, but the events of the ancient past are shrouded in mystery and we do not have many details. Thus, the generations after Ōhirume[30] are not the same *kami* and should be made a separate category of *kami*, and record that from Kuni Toko Tachi down to Izanagi and Izanami are the seven generations of heavenly *kami*. The character 神 used here refers to a mystical and mysterious quality. Thus, in *Nihon shoki* it mentions the seven generations of the heavenly period, seven generations of heavenly *kami*, and the five generations of earthly *kami* but makes no other distinction. The idea about the five generations of earthly *kami* does not appear in either *Nihon shoki* or *Kojiki*. (In *Jingi hongen* by Watarai Ieyuki or *Jinnō shōtōki* by Kitabatake Chikafusa at the end of their records they both mention the seven generations of heavenly *kami* and the five generations of earthly *kami*. These later works cannot be trusted.)

It is a grave mistake to interpret "heavenly *kami*" as referring to *kami* that reside in heaven, while "earthly *kami*" refers to *kami* who reside on the earth. Perhaps people interpret "heavenly *kami*" from the view of Buddhism when they talk about 天人 "celestial beings." Even in the ancient past, *kami* then were like humans now; even if they wanted to ascend to heaven they could not. Perhaps 天神 "heavenly *kami*" and 地祇 "earthly *kami*" were misremembered as 天神 "heavenly spirit" and 地神 "earthly spirit." In other words, "heavenly *kami*" refers to the ruler who resides and rules everything under heaven, while 地祇 "earthly *kami*" refers to the offspring of the ruler who are not eligible to rule the country, continuing down to the ministers. Using the difference between heaven and earth, there is a distinction made between the ruler and his subjects. While we say "heaven," it does not refer to the firmament, and saying "earth" does not mean the actual soil and ground. It refers to a difference in status. Also it is a mistake to construe that rulers from the reign of Emperor Jinmu onward are not "*kami*," but should be labeled rulers of the reign of humans. A *kami* is also a human, and there is no difference between the two. From Emperor Jinmu onward we use the title "emperor" out of respect. The era when there was no title of "emperor" is distinguished by the term "the divine period." There is no mention of a "human reign" in any of the ancient records.

Shintō scholars also talk about how the number eight is highly revered in Shintō, found in examples like eight million [*kami*], "eight layers of clouds" (*yakumo*), "the eight-layered fence," eighty strands, eighty indus-

30. *Nihon shoki* notes that this is a variant name of Amaterasu Ōmikami.

trial groups, the *yasaka* jewel [eight feet in length], the eight islands, the eight maidens, the eight hooks, and so on. They claim that if you take the number eighty (八十) and delete the one and the remaining stroke, you get a remainder of eight.[31] It means that there is no beginning and no end, an endless number that cannot be exhausted, revered because of the magical properties of the number. This theory is like those that solve riddles, and there was no such thing in the ancient culture. There is also another theory where the eight hexagrams suit the logic of heaven and earth, so people in Shintō revere the number eight. This theory is based on the philosophy of the "reason" branch of Neo-Confucianism, as the eight hexagrams is a Chinese idea, and it is a mistake to take a Chinese cultural item and infuse it into ancient practices of our country.

Kamo no Mabuchi stated that the character 八 "eight" read *ya* is actually 彌 *ya* "more, increasing," and this is truly a well-thought-out theory. So the word *ya* 彌 was represented by the character 八, so there is no need to be preoccupied with the underlying number "eight." The character 彌 is read *iya* with the first sound elided. *Iya* is a magical word, which means that something becomes greater in number or volume without being exhausted, so in the beginning the character 彌 was used to represent this word, but over time the character 八 replaced it. If you look up 彌 in a dictionary, you will find an annotational note which says, "It means 'great,' 'a side,' 'extremely,' 'long,' 'prosperous,' 'a long time,' and 'full.'" Our word *iya* matched the meaning of the Chinese character 彌, so that is why the ancients used 彌 to represent the word *iya*.

The character 八 "eight" can also represent the character 彌. Examples of this usage include the label "eight maidens" or "a ceremonial table with eight legs." Here the character "eight" is a loan graph and actually represents the meaning of 彌 "increasingly." Using the character "eight" as a concrete number does not happen until later, but in ancient times there was no measurement for length, volume, or weight, so the ancients could not accurately calculate. In the divine age there was no set distinction in size, length, weight, or number of objects, so the magical usage of *iya* was all that was transmitted to later ages.

16

Shintō scholars revere what they call the tripartite scriptures of Shintō, consisting of *Kuji hongi*, *Nihon shoki*, and *Kojiki*. However, as I have al-

31. It is the same silly argument in English that if you take the number 80 and delete the 0 you get the number 8.

ready mentioned above, *Kuji hongi* is a forgery and cannot be trusted. *Nihon shoki* and *Kojiki* are orthodox histories and we should revere these. And while we label these orthodox histories these two works record the ancient successive historical traditions at a much later date; someone from the divine age did not write these. Thus, there will be falsehoods as well as truth in these events. There are a variety of types of ancient traditions, so when Prince Toneri compiled *Nihon shoki* he took special note of areas where many of the old traditions from the various families did not agree, and as it was difficult to determine the truth of each one, he listed each variant tradition with the three words, "Another work says. ..." There is nothing included here from him personally. [If he could not determine the veracity of these,] how can we determine the truth of these in the present?

Shintō scholars in the present take everything in these works as the truth, and interpret things according to their own convenient circumstances, according to some vague idea about Shintō. They treat these things as exceedingly important, calling these secret traditions, or oral transmission. Even though the *kami* smile down upon people who are honest, unpretentious, fair in all things, how can people who have deceitful hearts call themselves followers of Shintō? ...

I wrote these ideas to repudiate the misunderstanding of Shintō scholars who are not hereditary priests and trifle with Shintō. The true traditions of the two families of the Nakatomi and Urabe who have received the correct information from the divine age down are impenetrable to average people like ourselves, so I say nothing further.

This day, the third day of the fourth month of Tenmei 2 [1782]
[Katō 1929:95–138]

ଓ

KOKUGŌKŌ

Motoori Norinaga | 1787

[This is Norinaga's exposition about the six recorded appellations of Japan, and the origin and meaning of each, demonstrating his breadth of knowledge and textual expertise. This type of work has rarely been attempted, and makes this essay worthy of note. He argues that the older term *wa* 倭 originated from China, while *wa* 和 was a Japanese development to soften the semantic sting of the older graph.]

ŌYASHIMA

There were two names for the imperial land [Japan] used in the divine age; one was Ōyashima and the other was the central land of Ashihara. *Kojiki* records the name Ōyashima thus, "Izanagi and Izanami wed and gave birth to the child Afadi Fonosa Wake; then they gave birth to Iyo Futana Sima, then to the three islands of Oki, then to the island of Tukusi, then to the island of Iki, then to Sado Island, then to the island of Ofoyamato Toyo-akitu. Thus, these eight islands first created by the two *kami* were called Ofoyasima [Ōyashima]."[1]

In *Nihon shoki*, this scene about the birth of the land appears, and though the order of birth of the islands is different from tradition to tradition, the number eight remains the same. The record says, "And this is the origin of the name Ofoyasima." Originally, the word *sima* meant a limit around how far one could go, a specified area. *Sima* has the same root as words like *simaru* "to close in," *sizimaru* "to shrink," *semaru* "to get close," and *sebashi* "narrow."[2] These words imply an area with defined limits—not unloosed, wide, and free—pulled closely together. Therefore, the word *sima* originally did not mean just an island in the ocean, but also meant an area enclosed by mountains and valleys inland.[3] We see this meaning from the other name that was given, Akitu Sima. And, as the name Ōyashima implies, it can refer to some place that is large, not necessarily limited only to small locations.

---

1. Compare Kurano and Takeda (1985:55–57).

2. This etymology is flawed, but the extension of the noun to verbs and stative verbs (adjectives) is intriguing, especially since the noun "island" and the other words Norinaga mentioned have a low pitch accent.

3. It is interesting that the word in some languages of the Ryūkyūs means village.

Since the small confines of a piece of land in the middle of the ocean is so stark, people naturally applied the word *sima* specifically to islands. Now, whether a writer represents the word *sima* by the character 嶋 or 洲, the meaning is an island in the ocean. Nevertheless, do not make the mistake of thinking that both characters refer to something originally in the middle of the ocean, nor that the word implies something with small confines. Of all the Chinese characters used to represent Japanese words, some accurately reflect the original Japanese meaning, while others only partially reflect the lexical value of the Japanese words. In later eras, people interpreted the meaning of certain words solely by relying on the character employed, and this resulted in many mistaken explanations related to the etymology.

Now, the *sima* of Ōyashima refers to one territory enclosed by the confines of the ocean; we find an example in *Nihon shoki*, divine age when the three Han [of Korea] are labeled *karakuni no sima*. Also, a poet referred to the Yamato Province in a poem from *Man'yōshū* as *yamatozima*.[4] There are also examples of Ōyashima read as *yamato simane*.[5] These all have the same meaning. Now, the reading of *yasima* "eight islands" means "connected as one territory without being separated by the ocean." Or, one island with many territories and the number of the territories is eight. The character 八 "eight" (represents the sound *ya*), which originally meant "increasingly, very," and at some rather later date, it was interpreted as the actual number eight. It does seem doubtful, however, that a word meaning "increasingly" came to mean a specific number through oral transmission. Nonetheless, the usage of the number eight (*ya*) is seen in *Kojiki*, where the interior district and seven provinces are listed. This does not include any of the other islands, and nothing is added or taken away from this number. Thus, the record in *Kojiki* points to eight actual items, establishing the concrete nature of *ya*.

In the various traditions in *Nihon shoki*, the editors include other islands in the list, resulting in totals that do not equal the number eight, but scholars should address this question based upon the correct record as it stands in *Kojiki*. This name, Ōyashima, is not a reference to foreign countries, but is a word referring alone to the land ruled under heaven. In the poem from Yachihoko, we see the usage of Yashima, and in the words from Yamato Takeru we have, "I am the son of Emperor Ofotarasi Hiko Osirowake who resides in the Makimuku Hishiro Palace and rules over the land of Ōyashima."[6]

---

4. The land of Yamato, also seen in MYS 255.
5. See MYS 366 and 4487.
6. Compare Kurano and Takeda (1985:209).

In the imperial decree from Emperor Kōtoku, there is the usage, "The emperor who rules over the land of Yashima as a visible *kami*." Even in the Statute on Official Correspondence, in the section addressing the style of imperial decrees, there is the usage, "The emperor who rules the land of Ōyashima as a visible *kami* declares the following."

THE CENTRAL LAND OF ASHIHARA[7] [WITH *MIDUFO NO KUNI* ATTACHED]

The term "Central land of Ashihara" was originally used in the divine age by the *kami* who resided in the high plain of heaven, but the people of this land did not refer to their country as such. Now the meaning of this designation originated in the high plain of heaven long ago when the *kami* looked down from heaven and saw a country in the middle of a plain of reeds, surrounded by ocean. Therefore, this name in *Kojiki* and *Nihon shoki* is only used as long as the scene remains in heaven. One should take interest in this and ponder its profundity.

In spite of the ancient corpus calling this "the country among the reeds Japan," and though the usage itself is not uncommon, it only occurred after the august grandchild descended from heaven. This usage was inherited by the grandchild from the time he dwelt in heaven. Now, evidence that reeds actually covered the area like the ocean is seen in *Shoku Nihon kōki*, in celebratory words written in a *chōka* by the bonze of the Kōfuku temple, commemorating the fortieth birthday of Emperor Nimmyō:

fi no moto no	Where the sun rises—
yamato no kuni wo	in the land of Yamato,
kamirogi no	Sukuna bikona,
sukunabikona ga	the heavenly ancestor's son,
asisuge wo	is said to have put
uweofu situtu	this country together by
kunikatame	hardening the land
tukurikemu yori	with sedge that he had planted.[8]

This labor by Sukuna bikona is not seen in any ancient record now, but from the evidence apparent in this poem, surely this tradition relied on some evidence at hand at the time. Therefore, originally the two *kami*

7. *Asifara* means the plain of reeds.

8. Norinaga has abbreviated this rather long poem. I have translated this poem according to Norinaga's own interpretation. See Kuroita (1983:223).

Ōnamuji[9] and Sukuna Bikona planted sedge round about to cement together the country they had created.[10] We may know that this is true from the many poems up till middle antiquity that make mention that many rushes and sedge existed in the waves of the ocean.

There are various theories dealing with the meaning of the appellation "Central land of Ashihara," but none do justice to the ancient meaning. It would be bothersome to list the deficiencies in these poor theories, so I will leave them out.

This land of Japan is also called Toyo Ashihara Mizuho. *Toyo* is an honorific prefix, much like the *ofo* of *ofoyasima* [meaning "great"]. *Toyo* is attached to the entire name of our country, not merely to the word reed (*asi*). *Asifara* has the same meaning as I discussed above. The character 水 "water" is a false substitute character, actually being a word of praise for things that are beautiful, here modifying 穂 "rice ears." … Now, all the events and objects within the imperial country are superior to those of foreign countries, and Japanese rice especially is without peer among the myriad countries of the world, being very exceptional and delightful. This fact is deeply rooted in the divine age, and even now our country is worthy to bear the name *midufo no kuni* "the land of precious rice ears." As the subjects below heaven partake of this delightful rice morning and night, how can they neglect pondering on the wonderful blessings given them from the imperial *kami*? There is nothing more important than a person's life, and it is the energy from rice that sustains this life; thus, is there any treasure more precious in this life than rice? It seems evident that the more superior and delightful Japan's rice becomes, the greater its superiority and worth among other foreign countries grows.

YAMATO [WITH *AKIZUSHIMA, SHIKI SHIMA* ATTACHED]

The word Yamato originally was the name of the province of Yamato located in the Kinai area. Emperor Jinmu build his palace here where he dwelt, and because our emperors located every capital after this time in the province of Yamato, the name naturally came to refer to the entire county under the jurisdiction of the emperor. The name *yamato* is an old word used when Nigi Hayahi[11] descended from heaven, saying, "This is the land

9. Another name for Ōkuninushi.

10. Since it was mainly marsh with reeds, the two *kami* planted sedge to displace the water and give strength to the land, i.e., make it possible to dwell on.

11. Many scholars claim that this is simply an obscure *kami* from some no longer extant

of Yamato seen from the sky."[12] It is an ancient word from the divine age. Also, in the song from Yachihoko [composed] before the descent of Nigi Hayahi, we see the phrase "a lone eulalia tree by itself," but I believe that the word in this poem is not pointing to the name of the province.[13]

Near the end of the Jinmu section of *Nihon shoki*, there is the sentence, "Anciently Izanagi gave the county a name, saying, 'Yamato is a country of calm bays, a country beautifully narrow like a halberd, a superior, country with its center high, surrounded by boulders.'"[14] Therefore, because Emperor Jinmu established his palace in this province, he was given the honorary title of Kamu Yamato Iware Hiko. On the other hand, the theory that the place name Yamato had its origins in the emperor's name is gravely mistaken. Also, another theory states that *yamato* was a generic term for the whole land from the divine age, but after Jinmu unified the country, it became a designation pointing to the capital. And that is why it says in the Jinmu record of *Nihon shoki*, "The imperial carriage toured the area. He climbed up Hohoma Hill in Wakigami, and looked down upon the land, and said, 'How beautiful the country we have obtained! Though it is narrow like the bark of the mulberry tree, it resembles a dragonfly that is licking its tail.' Because of this, the land was called Akizusima. Anciently Izanagi gave the county a name, saying . . . ."[15]

The names Akizushima and Urayasu "land of calm bays" are all honorary names within Japan given by Izanagi. All theories stating that the name Yamato, Toyo Akizushima, and the other names in the divine age were concrete names for the country, and were viewed that way until the time of unification [by Jinmu] are incorrect. First, the name Akizushima is a place name within Yamato Province, and not a name referring to the entire country. This can be seen from the usage of "looked down upon the land." How could the emperor have been able to look down at the very broad land of Japan just from climbing Mount Hooma? And we should

---

tradition. Nevertheless, the record in *Kujiki* states that he was the eldest son of Oshihomimi, the son of the sun goddess. His descent to Yamato thus takes on a special importance.

12. The phrase here is 虚空見日本國, glossed as *sora mitu yamato no kuni*. My translation follows the standard interpretation, which Norinaga seems to believe, but it needs to be mentioned that the grammar does not match, as the adnominal form of "to see" would be *mituru* not *mitu*. I follow Vovin (2011:141–42), where *mitu* is seen as a Korean loan, "below," related to MK *mith*. Thus, this actually means "below heaven."

13. Keichū believed that this *yamato* meant the province of Yamato. Some scholars now take this to mean "widow/widower" and not a specific place name as Norinaga perceptively discerns it (see Kōnoshi and Yamaguchi 2007:90, n1).

14. Compare Ienaga et al. (1967, 1:215).

15. Compare ibid., pp. 214–15.

understand the usage of "it is narrow like the bark of the mulberry tree" as meaning a province that is small. ...

Now, about the name Urayasu. *Shaku Nihongi*[16] makes it clear that Urayasu is one place name, and other theories about it pointing to the entire country are mistaken. Because Yamato is not located next to the ocean, ancient Japanese certainly would not have labeled it a "calm bay." There are people who still doubt this, but the character 浦 "bay" is a substitute character. *Ura* actually means inside, or in the heart, like the words *urasabisi* "lonely" and *uraganasi* "melancholy." A poem in Book 14 of *Man'yōshū* supports this theory. Part of the poem reads:

urayasu ni	There have been no nights
sanuru yo zo naki	when I slept peacefully ...
	[MYS 3504]

Also, the theory from later eras stating that the line in the ancient records that says, "They gave birth to the land Ōyamato Toyo Akizushima ..." does not point to an ancient saying from the divine age. This is clear, because as I have said before, the appellation Akizushima originated in the era of Emperor Jinmu. Now, to address the question about the records that say that from the divine age people used the name Ōyamato and did not use Ōyashima, Ashihara Nakatsu Kuni, let me just say this: These two names are overall designations for the eight territories, and later had reference to the province of Yamato, and did not apply to the other seven areas. Because this title for the individual province is not seen anywhere else, it was called Ōyamato for a time. Yamato is the name of one province, but is also the title for all of Japan. Also, the ancient Japanese came to use the name to show the provincial seat in each territory, a name used in a broad and narrow sense. Place names like Tsukushi and Iyo are used to point to one individual province, but also were used to refer to the islands of Kyūshū and Shikoku. This double usage also applies to Yamato. ... Therefore, the place name Yamato was originally not a general term. There is no doubt that it was first the name of one province, for there are many examples of names starting in a narrow sense and later expanding to a broader meaning. We see in the national histories that names like Dewa and Kaga originally were the names of districts, and later became provincial names. ...

---

16. A collection of lectures held at court in the eighth, ninth, tenth, and eleventh centuries, dealing with *Nihon shoki* text. Questions of meaning, interpretation, and usage were addressed and answered.

In the poem in the Sujin record of *Nihon shoki* it says,

yamato nasu	It is the *sake*
ofomononusi no	of Ōmononushi,
kamisi miki	he who created Yamato.

[NS 15]

Since Ōmononushi established all of Japan, this appellation "Yamato" may sound like a general usage, but it becomes clearer if we were to give a contemporary example. For example, it would be like a title Nippon Ichi no Gō "the strongest man in all of Japan." This usage of *nippon* points to all of Japan, but the meaning naturally points to this title, a person without peer in the whole country. In the same way, anciently when the capital was located in Yamato, this provincial name came to be applied to the whole country, and naturally reflected upon the whole country. Nonetheless, it does not have actual reference to the entire country. Therefore, the meaning of the word points to the nation as a whole, but the basic meaning of the word refers to one province, that of Yamato. …

The word *yamato* has its origin in the village of Yamato in the district of Yamanobe, and this is given detailed treatment in a separate volume to Kamo no Mabuchi's *Man'yōkō*. There are various opinions about Mabuchi's theory. First, this village of Yamato is seen in the *Wamyōshō* as "Ōyamato in the district of Lower Shiki." Nonetheless, *Jinmyōchō*[17] records it as, "The shrine in Ōyamato in the district of Yamanobe that worships Ōkuni Mitama." The district mentioned here is incorrect. Mabuchi picked Lower Shiki District as the correct one from the two, saying the other [Yamanobe] was from a later era. Early on in *Shoku Nihongi* in Tenpyō Hōji 2 [758] we see Ōyamato Kamiyama in the district of Lower Shiki. Therefore, Lower Shiki was the original district, and this was later annexed by Yamanobe District. The shrine in question still exists in Niizumi Village and this is in the Yamanobe District. In all cases, the entries in *Wamyōshō* are from later eras, but the list of place names was put together in the Nara era. Thus, it is better to look at the list in *Wamyōshō*, it being older than *Jinmyōshō*. …

The meaning of the name Yamato, as is seen in one place in *Man'yōkō*, is "the entrance to this province on all four sides is through a mountain pass (*yama-to*)." This explains the etymology in detail, and this theory is plausible.[18] I also have my own theory; first, in the Jinmu record in *Nihon*

17. One section of *Engi shiki*, recording various shrines throughout Japan, which *kami* they worship, and certain other festivals.

18. A clearer understanding of the etymology of Old Japanese words is determined by

shoki, within the 's own words we see, "Now, the old man, Shiotsutsu, told me, 'There is a beautiful land in the east encircled about by green mountains.'" Also Ōanamuji called the land "the country encircled by a jeweled fence." And in a poem from Yamato Takeru in *Kojiki*, we see,

yamato fa	Yamato is
kuni no maforoba	an extraordinary land,
tatanaduku	hidden within
awokaki	the mountains
yama gomoreru	that stand around like green fences.
yamato si urufasi	How beautiful Yamato is.

[KJK 30]

Also the poem by Iwanohime contains the phrase, "Yamato surrounded by mountains." This usage in her poem has reference to the village of Yamato, but the usage of *wodateyama* is an epithet attached to the name of the province of Yamato, meaning that the poet has alluded to the mountains surrounding the area as shields set up by warriors in battle. All these ancient usages point to the idea that this province is surrounded by mountains. It is beyond argument that the *yama* of Yamato points to mountains. There are, however, three theories about what *to* means. First, *to* means "place," and so the interpretation would be "a place in the mountains." . . .[19] The second theory is that *to* is an abbreviated form of *tufo*, and the original would have been *yama-tufo*. *Tu* is just the possessive particle, like *no*, and *fo* is represented by a phonogram, an old word meaning "everything enclosed by something." Thus, this is a place completely enclosed by mountains. A poem by Emperor Ōjin provides more details for this etymology. When he looked out over Kazuno he sang,

tiba no	Gazing out upon
kaduno wo mireba	the greenery of Kazuno,
momotidaru	I can see that
yanifa mo miyu	the plain is filled with houses and land,
kuni no fo mo miyu	and that the land is sublime.

[KJK 41]

knowledge of Old Japanese phonology, which Norinaga's student Ishizuka Tatsumaro began to elucidate. There was a very old theory that *yamato* was from *yama* "mountain" *ato* "footprints." Both Mabuchi's and Norinaga's idea of "gateway to the mountains" is not plausible, as that would be *yamatwo*, whereas the word actually is *yamato*.

19. This is perhaps the most plausible (and simplest) theory.

The area of Kazuno is now the land of the Heian-kyō [modern Kyōto], nestled among the surrounding mountains. It is in the middle of Yamashiro Province, known as the treasure of the land. … The third theory is that *to* is *utu* having dropped the initial *u*, forming *yama-utu*. Therefore, this *utu* is believed to be the same as *utufo* "cave" and *utumuro* "a room with no door," but we should understand it to mean "inside." Anciently there were many examples where *uti* "inside" was often written as *utu*.[20] An example in *Man'yōshū* is found in the word *kakitu* "within the fence,"[21] written as 垣内 as well as 垣都, which is the same as writing it out phonetically as *kakitu*, and this is proof of the reading. The present text reads this as *kakiuti,* which is a poor rendition. Thus "inside" is *utu* where the initial *u*- drops. … The Ōjin poem above used the name Kazuno, but *Wamyōshō* has Kadono [*du* changing to *do*]. Examples seen in *Wamyōshō* where the district of Shiwadu in Sagami Province is recorded as Shiwado, and *Man'yōshū* writes Takamatsu as Takamato, which is closely related to this. …

THE LABEL WA 倭

The character 倭 [Wa] originally was a designation given by China. This label first appears in the Geographical section of *Qian Hanshu* where it says, "The nature of the people of the Eastern Barbarians is one of gentleness and obedience, which is different from the territories in the other three directions. Thus Confucius lamented when people did not follow the Way, built a raft to cross the sea, and wanted to live among the people of the nine barbaric tribes. He must have had a good reason. In the middle of the ocean of Lolang are the people of Wa. They are divided into over one hundred territories, and their [envoys] appear at court according to the seasons." In other records after this all references are to the people of Wa (倭人). There are also cases where this is abbreviated to just Wa. So on what basis did they label our people Wa? There is no solid proof for the reason behind this, but in *Hanshu* they write that the nature of the people was one of gentleness and obedience, and considering that this description is followed by the phrase "there are the people of Wa," [the compiler] Bangu's intention appears to be the same as that found in

20. Norinaga is thinking of examples such as *utunuki* "to hollow out," *utufata* "a type of cloth found at shrines," often written 内幡, and *utufo* "empty inside."

21. MYS 1503.

Shuowen,[22] where it says that the original meaning of the graph 倭 is "having a disposition of obedience." So it sounds as if we should interpret this label to mean that the people of Wa were called such because they were meek and docile. However, this is all conjecture based on the characters. Also, in the old records of our imperial land we find, "The people of this land anciently reached that country [China]. The people of China asked them, 'What is the name of your land?' They pointed to the east and answered saying *wanu kuni* … This is how they said 'Our country (*wanu*).' From that time on our country has been called *wanu*." This theory is found in *Shaku Nihongi* and *Gengenshū*, but this theory is difficult to accept, because the label 倭奴 *wanu* first appears in *Hou Hanshu* and it is located on the southernmost border of the land of Wa. So Chinese works misinterpreted this one place name to be located south within our borders; they describe it as if it was the full name of our imperial land. All works after this make the same mistake and this is a terrible blunder that has been propagated in China as well as in Japan. …

There is also a theory that if you convert *wanu* into the phonetics of Chinese that it becomes *onoko,* which points to Onogoro Island, but this is also mistaken. Onogoro Island was created before Ōyashima, and is actually the name of a small island near Awaji Island. From the divine age there has been a full name for all of this land under heaven. So how could a foreign people bestow a label for our land that they knew from our people who do not say the name? This theory is circulated by recent Shintō scholars who claim that the original name of our imperial land was Onogoro Island. And the theory that claims that *wanu* represents Onogoro, or that Onogoro Island means *wonoko* "the stout man" is especially off the mark. This results in sheer confusion as these people do not comprehend that the sounds *o* and *wo* are different. It is also seen that the reading *yamato* was represented by the graph 倭 in writing at a very early time. *Kojiki* represents all cases of *yamato* with this graph. And even in *Nihon shoki* the compilers represent *yamato* with the characters 日本, but in the divine-age section there is an annotational note added informing the reader that these two characters should be read *yamato*. But when the graph 倭 is used, there was no need to attach a note, demonstrating that this reading was well known throughout society. In all cases, Chinese characters were attached to all the nouns in our country, but these are

22. One of China's first dictionaries. It was compiled during the first decade of 100 CE. It is well known as the first dictionary to arrange characters by radical.

loans from China, demonstrating that the use of 倭 is also borrowed from China. …

THE LABEL WA 和

The character 和 is a later alteration for the name of our imperial land. The reason is that there are no examples in foreign records where this character is used to represent our country's full name. I believe that anciently we used the character 倭, but as this was a label given by a foreign country without any auspicious significance, the court selected a character with the same reading but one with an auspicious meaning and altered the usage. Thus, anciently the character was generally used to represent the name *yamato*, so no matter what the character, the characters were simply representations and there was no thought about whether the characters were auspicious or unfavorable. Our land used the character 倭 as is, but as time passed the court was able to select characters based on the auspiciousness of the meaning. The meaning of this character 和 is "harmonious and obedient," much like the meaning found in the note quoted above from *Hanshu*. Considering this evidence the meaning of 和 is not that far removed from the meaning of 倭. Also, in the words of an edict in the Keitai record of *Shoki* it says, "The land of Yamato is tranquil, and everyone will have a reputation throughout." The character 邕 "enclosed" is interchangeable with 雝 "soft" and in the "Greater Odes" of the *Book of Odes* there is an explanatory note after 雝雝 "harmoniously," saying that this is the harmonious cry of the phoenix, and it is also the pinnacle of harmony.

Furthermore, in the beginning of the constitution by Shōtoku Taishi it says, "Prize harmony. …" Also in China there was a province called "Harmony Province," which originally was the name of the royal capital, so in later eras our imperial land imitated this usage, where people called Yamashiro Province "Harmony Province." The character 雍 is interchangeable with 雝, and there is a note that says, "It is harmony" (和也). Since this is the origin, one might think that anyone could have just selected one of these examples based on the meaning, but the process did not operate that way. If we think about these things we realize that things occur naturally based on their various origins. Also, in the work *Zihuazi*,[23] it mentions 太和国 but this usage is baseless. …

23. Written by Cheng Ben. Norinaga's text must have been corrupt, because the current

NIHON [ALSO CALLED *FI NO MOTO*]

The name Nihon originally was not a character set written for the Japanese word *finomoto* "origin of the sun." It was specially selected to show to ambassadors from foreign countries. We know this because the Imperial Edict section of the Statute on Official Communication contains one line reading, "The imperial edict our emperor who rules over Ōyashima as a visible *kami*."

Ryō no gige gives the following annotation to this sentence: "Word usage employed during major events at the court of the emperor …" and another line adds "The imperial edict of our emperor who rules over Nihon as a visible *kami*" is defined as "word usage employed during major events when addressing envoys from foreign countries."[24] Concerning when the court established this label (*Nihon*), first, this usage is not seen within *Kojiki*. Also, in *Nihon shoki* up to the record of Emperor Kōgyoku, the characters 日本 are consistently read *yamato*, meaning that the compilers altered the reading of *yamato* during compilation. "Yamato" was the current usage at the time seen within the record. This is clear from the record of Emperor Kōtoku's ascension where the text says,

> First year of Taika, seventh month, autumn, tenth day. The countries of Koguryŏ, Paekche, and Silla all sent envoys with tribute. … Kose Tokuda no Omi gave a command to the Koma envoy, saying, "The emperor, a visible *kami* who rules over Yamato, declares. …" An edict was given to the ambassador from Paekche, "The emperor, a visible *kami* who rules over Yamato, declares. …"[25]

This is the first time that the usage of Nihon is newly used to foreign envoys. Therefore, these imperial commands were of a different nature than the other edicts. Also, in the same reign, second year, second month, fifteenth day, *Nihon shoki* records,

> The emperor went to the eastern gate of the palace. He conveyed to Minister of the Right Soga [Soga no Yamada Ishikawa Maro] the following decree, "The emperor Yamato Neko who rules the realm as a visible *kami* declares to the gathered ministers, Omi, Murazi, provincial chieftains, Tomo no Miyatuko, and the various commoners."[26]

---

text has 夫是之謂大。和之，國無待於意而為醫 "And this is called 'great,' and it makes it mild. The country will not wait for his intentions and make him a physician."

24. Compare Inoue et al. (1985:365–66).
25. Ienaga et al. (1967, 2:271–73).
26. Ibid., 2:283.

Though this usage is not addressed to someone from a foreign country, because this edict is the first one to use this form, it shows that the emperor is also using this new title on those people who serve him at court. If this were not so, then saying Yamato and Yamato Neko would be nothing more than a bothersome use of the same words: Yamato Yamato. Therefore, it becomes clear that the usage of this title of Nihon was first established in the reign of Emperor Kōtoku, Taika first year [645]; however, because the scholars of later eras did not think deeply about the structure of these sentences, they could not determine from which reign this usage arose. All of the regnal era names originate from the reign of Emperor Kōtoku.[27] Because there were many other new things determined in this era, it makes more and more sense that this title also was established at this time. ...

The meaning attached to the title Nihon was perhaps the august country created by the great sun goddess who shines down upon the myriad countries. Or it may conform to the meaning of the many Western barbaric countries from which the sun rises. Of these two ideas, the former suits logic very well, but when we ponder upon the actual import of this title when it was established, the basic meaning probably originating from the latter interpretation. This is the same meaning as that used during the reign of Emperor Suiko, when the emperor said [to the emperor of China], "The child of heaven in the land where the sun rises."

The use of the characters 日本 for the word *yamato* originated with *Nihon shoki*. Writing the name of the country with these characters was unprecedented, and would cause a stir among the people in society, so a note in *Nihon shoki* says, "'*Nihon,*' this is read *yamato*. All examples below follow this one."

Kojiki was compiled long after the Taika era, but all the characters, everything, is recorded down precisely as they were taken from the ancient records, and every word read *yamato* is written only with the character 倭, and nowhere do we see the characters 日本. Because *Nihon shoki* is a record decorated with specially selected Chinese characters, the compilers chose this newly created, auspicious title. Nonetheless, many write the name of the province of Yamato with the character 倭, and the greater title of Yamato in reference to all of Japan with Nihon. ...

The title *finomoto* is not seen in any ancient record. And though the word *nihon* does have the same meaning [as *finomoto*], it was established

27. If we take the text of *Nihon shoki* at face value, then it was during the reign of Kōtoku that *nengō* "regnal era names" were introduced in imitation of the Chinese. The first *nengō* was thus Taika. Taika literally means "great change."

for use in international relations, so the word would not have been read *finomoto*. … The reason that many of the 日本之 character sets in *Man'yōshū* have the reading of *finomoto no* is because someone later made the mistake of thinking that this character set was supposed to have been read with five syllables, when in fact these should be read with just four syllables: *yamato no*.

Only the usages in *chōka* in Book 3 of *Man'yōshū* (The Land of Yamato of the Land of the Rising Sun) and Book 19 of *Shoku Nihon kōki* (same wording as above) are read as *finomoto*.[28] These were not used as titles for the nation, but rather were epithets for the preceding word of *yamato*. When I was a young man, I reasoned that reading the characters 日本 as *yamato* was normal, an epithetical example like so many others, reading 春日 as *kasuga* and 飛鳥 as *asuka*. First off, *kasuga* comes from the meaning of the mist from the spring sun (*kasumu*); *asuka* is seen in *Nihon shoki* in the fifteenth year of the reign of Emperor Tenmu, where it says, "The court altered the name of the era to the first year of Akamidori. With this, the palace was known as the Tobutori Kiyomihara Palace."[29] This was done because of the auspicious appearance of a red bird *akamidori*, and so the name of the era was accordingly changed. Also, the court changed the name of the palace to that seen above. The name of the palace, however, is read "Tobutori no Kiyomihara." Since the area is already named Asuka Kiyomihara, it would not have made much sense to make the record say that the name of the palace was changed to Asuka Kiyomihara. Tobutori "flying bird" is the same as "crawling bug"; it merely points to a bird. Now, because the palace is called that, it caps off the place name, becoming Tobutori no Asuka.

Now the reason that *kasuga* is written 春日 and *asuka* is written 飛鳥 is that these were well-known character usages for epithets and over time these characters also came to represent the place names [that were described according to the epithet]. The well-known epithet for Nara, *awo ni yosi,* over time came to refer to Nara and Naniwa, and the reasoning is similar. Therefore, since *farufi* becoming *kasuga*, and *tobutori* becoming *asuka* are not just normal epithetical evolutions from characters used on place names, then it follows that 日本 should not have been written in place of the name of the country, *yamato*. It simply means Yamato, land of the Rising Sun. Therefore, if this epithet had existed from ancient times,

28. The *Man'yōshū* poem is MYS 319. The quote from *Shoku Nihon kōki* is found in a *chōka* in the entry dated 849.3.26.

29. All texts with interlinear readings read 飛鳥浄御原 as *asuka kiyomihara*.

then Emperor Kōtoku also had this name of *nihon* established during his reign. However, since the Mount Fuji poem [in Book 19 of *Shoku Nihon kōki*] is not very old, and is not seen at any time afterward, and in consideration of the meaning of the name of *nihon*, perhaps someone invented this usage at a later date. It is very difficult to distinguish the origins of this word. …

[MNZ 1976, 8:449–70]

ࡈ

NAOBI NO MITAMA
(This section talks about the Way)

Motoori Norinaga | 1771

[This is actually a section in the beginning of *Kojiki-den*, but because it is essential in understanding Norinaga's view of the Way, I have made it a separate piece. He argues that the Japanese received the Way directly from the *kami*, through their emperor, a descendant of Amaterasu. He notes that two other, man-made philosophies, Daoism and schools like Zhu Xi Confucianism, were evil and altered the Japanese, infecting them with the Chinese Heart. To Norinaga the Japanese Way provided a method to overcome defilement, which as seen in *Kojiki*, is provided by the rectifying *kami Naobi no mitama*. Thus, he insists that Japan can link with this rectifying power and correct the defilement from foreign influences, but only if people will accurately identify and then be willing to pray to this *kami*.]

"The great imperial land [of Japan] is the majestic country given its existence by the awe-inspiring ancestor of the gods, Amaterasu Ōmikami."[1]

Among the reasons that this country is superior to the myriad other countries this is the most remarkable. There is not a single country that fails to receive blessings from this great *kami*.

"The great *kami* took in her hand the imperial symbols of the heavenly inheritance,"

The reference here is to the three imperial regalia, symbols of the emperor that have been handed down from generation to generation.

"[A]nd declared 'My son will rule over this land eternally, like a myriad endless autumns,' and then she bestowed the right to rule upon him [Ninigi]."

The immovable and unchangeable nature of the heavenly inherited throne—immovable like heaven and earth—was established very early.

1. From hereon Norinaga consistently calls her 大御神 "the great august *kami*."

"She established the land that the imperial grandchild was to govern, extending to the edge of the land where the clouds trail down, to the end of the crossing of the toads, and there were no violent *kami*, nor disobedient servants in all the land."

Through ten thousand generations where would there be a subject who would rebel against their emperor? How awe-inspiring! During the reigns of the emperors, there have sometimes been disobedient, filthy servants, but the imperial authority as it has been handed down from the divine age has shone forth, instantly cutting down these disobedient servants.

"Until the end of the innumerable reigns, the emperor will remain a descendant of the great august *kami* [Amaterasu]."

The successive emperors *are* sons of Amaterasu Ōmikami. Therefore, they are called the sons of the heavenly *kami*, or the children of the sun.

"The will of the heavenly *kami* is the will of the Sovereign."

Concerning any matter, the sovereign does not follow his own wisdom, but follows the ancient precedence from the divine age in leading the people: if he has doubts about something, then the emperor performs divination and inquires into the will of the heavenly *kami*.

"There is no difference between the present and the divine age."

This is true not only in relation to the imperial dignity, but even the Omi, Muraji and the eighty attending families have continued to respect their family names and titles handed down from father to son, continuing their inherited occupations. Thus there has been no difference between the people and the ancestral *kami*. These attendants have served the *kami* as if they belong to the same generation.

"The emperors ruled the great land in peace and tranquility following in the path of the *kami*."

Consider what *Nihon shoki* records in the book of the Naniwa Nagara Palace Court [Kōtoku] who ruled in Naniwa [Kōtoku], "惟神 (*kamunagara*) refers to following the will of the *kami*. It also means that this is naturally prepared in advance." Following the will of the *kami* means that the great government ruling the land operates mainly as it did in the divine age without putting on airs of sophistry. That being the case, when the emperors ruled generously as in the divine age, the will of the *kami* was naturally fulfilling, with nothing lacking; this is what is meant by having possession of the Way of the *kami*. And though we say that the emperor rules the land of the great eight islands, the governing of the successive emperors is actually the will of the *kami*. Poems in *Man'yōshū* also mention this *kamunagara*, and the meaning is exactly the same.[2] And thus it was truly fitting that the Koreans called Japan the "divine country."[3]

"In ancient reigns there was absolutely no verbal declaration[4] about *the Way*."

Thus we find in the ancient language the phrase, "the precious rice ear reed-plain country, the land following the *kami* lacking verbal declarations."

"It [*michi* 'way'] was simply a word used for a path one travels."

The word *michi*—written as *umasi miti* "suitable route"—means a path (路) through the mountains or fields, with the honorific prefix *mi* added. Thus, anciently, there was no word for *miti* "the Way [for a certain teaching]."

"The idea that a Way teaches the fundamental principle of things or is a collection of various doctrine [moral and philosophical] has its roots in foreign countries."

"Foreign countries" refers to territory not included in the land ruled by Amaterasu Ōmikami. Therefore, they have no established ruler. Vicious *kami*, violent in nature like the flies in spring, turned the hearts of the people to wickedness, and threw the customs of these lands into chaos. Even servants of no status were able to seize the government, if they only

---

2. There are nineteen poems in *Man'yōshū* that use the phrase *kamunagara*. One example is MYS 50: **takasirasamu to / kamunaraga / omofosu nafe ni / ame tuti mo / yorite are koso**, "He tried to make his palace high / and pondering / according to the will of the *kami* / because the *kami* of heaven and earth / abide by (the emperor's) course. …"

3. A reference to words supposedly spoken by the king of Silla as recorded in the record of Jingū, "Filled with trepidation, the king was bewildered and confused. At last he regained his composure and said to the people, 'I have heard that there is a divine country to the east, called Yamato. It has a sagacious king who calls himself *sumera mikoto*. Surely it is their divine soldiers who have come. How can we raise troops and fight against them?'"

4. Norinaga uses the ancient word 言挙 *kotoage*, literally "word raising." This usage is based on the belief in *kotodama*. See note 2, p. 140.

tried. Thus, those in power kept their guard up because they felt they would be overthrown by those below, while subjects planned to overthrow those in power if the chance appeared. The two sides have continued to hate each other, and from ancient times on, these countries have been difficult to rule. In this situation, powerful people appeared, deep in wisdom, loved by the citizens. These men seized the land, and defended themselves against those who might try to seize it back, and for a while they were able to rule the country. After a while, they governed adroitly, and in China these men were known as *sages*, models set up for later generations.

For example, in a generation torn with strife, people grew accustomed to war, and many great generals appeared, forcing order on the land that had been difficult to govern because the customs of the country gradually degenerated. Because these people tried to rule the country forcefully, generation after generation began to ponder upon various philosophies in the world, and attempted to put them into practice, though inconsistently. With the reinforcement of this cycle, wise men appeared on the scene. Nevertheless, it is wrong to believe that these sages are superior entities like our *kami*, having naturally mysterious wisdom and power. People labeled the inventions of these sages as "the Way." Nevertheless, when we examine the substance of this so-called Way of China, we find that it consists of two simple elements: seize the country, and protect it from others. Now, while these people plan to seize the country, they worry about everything; their bodies are tormented, and they give their all to do good, befriending various people. In this way, people view these sages as worthy men. Also, at first glance their self-made Way may appear beautiful and fulfilling overall; however, the sages themselves have violated their own Way, killing their sovereign, and stealing the country. They are all deceivers, and in truth are not virtuous men, but the most evil.

Perhaps because these people created their Way in the beginning with evil hearts they were able to deceive the people. Later generations feigned reverence and obedience on the outside, but since there is not one soul who abides by the Way, it does not profit the country; only the name is handed down, the Way itself remaining unperformed. This Way of the sages is vain, and has become the prattle of successive Confucian scholars who only demean people. In spite of this, Confucian scholars make the blatant mistake of only focusing on the six [Confucian] classics, loudly claiming that China is the only country possessing the correct law. When someone else tries to reform this Way, these sages prove to us that it was not correct to begin with. On the other hand, it is a joke for these scholars to think or claim that this Way is superior; from the historical records it is clear that not a single person could actually put this Way into practice.

Now, their Way is given bothersome titles like benevolence, righteousness, courtesy, humility, filial piety, brotherly love, loyalty, and conviction:

man-made devices to teach people harshly. And though the law of later generations violates the Way of the ideal sovereigns, and though the Confucian scholars speak ill of it, is not the Way of the ideal sovereigns at least the more ancient? Again, these Confucian scholars have fabricated things like divination through which they feign to possess profound doctrine, believing that they have mastered the reasoning of heaven and earth. But this is just another ploy to befriend people so they can rule over them. Now, the reasoning of heaven and earth belongs to the workings of the *kami*, something unfathomable [to humans]. Since these workings are profound, man's limited knowledge cannot comprehend it. How is it that these [human] sages have mastered cosmic knowledge? Thus, it is extremely foolish to believe the words of the sages on all counts, paying gratitude to them. And it is the evil habit of Chinese to imitate the sages in later generations, trying to comprehend all things with one's limited knowledge. People studying about Japan should understand that this is the state of affairs in China—do not be deceived by the opinions of people schooled in Chinese learning.

Because the Chinese put excessive emphasis on minute detail, philosophizing about this or that, false wisdom moves their hearts, resulting in polluting their minds. And with the affairs of the state half aggravated in this way, the country became harder to rule. Therefore, originally the Way of these sages was set up to govern the country, but it ends up throwing the country into confusion.

In all respects, it is more desirable to have some leeway, leaving some areas undefined. Thus, from ancient times, the imperial country had none of these bothersome teachings; the foundation of the country was firmly grounded down to the roots, and the emperor ruled the country peacefully without effort. Imperial rule has continued successively from ancient times. To borrow a phrase from China, this is the unparalleled *Way*, which did exist in Japan, making it unnecessary for the existence of the term "the Way." Think about the difference of debating one's position versus holding one's tongue. Holding one's tongue refers to the distinction of not being like other foreign countries who noisily voice their opinions. As an example, an intellectually gifted person will keep his opinions to himself, but a half-learned person arrogantly gives his opinion on any subject. Because countries like China have very little substance to their Ways, they only talk about there being a Way. Confucian scholars in Japan cannot understand this, and they even mock the imperial country for not having a Way. What these Confucian scholars do not understand is that they argue illogically, saying there is nothing wrong with complete devotion to China. What Japanese scholars fail to comprehend is that they have become so envious of China that they have invented their own Way in imitation of China. This kind of debate is much like monkeys who see humans, and mock them because they do not have fur on their bodies. The humans in turn become embarrassed, and begin to say that they do have fur, too, and search to find any trace of hair. Is it not the action of fools because they do not realize that it is better not to have hair all over one's body?

"In spite of this, after the passage of some time, books entered our country, and as the people began reading and studying them, they started to embrace Chinese customs. There came a time when people intermixed these Chinese practices in all cases with Japanese customs, and in order to differentiate between those ancient customs and practices of our Great Country from the Chinese, people invented the term *kami no michi* [Shintō]. They modeled the term after the foreign practice of 'a Way' with the word *kami* added because it was divine."

I will explain in detail later the reason our divine practices were called *kami no michi.*

"Thus, as each reign came and went, the act of imitating Chinese customs gradually reached its height, and even the bureaucracy of our great government became a model of Chinese."

During the reigns of the Naniwa-Nagara [Kōken] and Afumi-Ōtsu [Tenchi] palaces, the entire workings of the government were modeled after the Chinese. After this, the Japanese only performed the ancient practices in the indigenous religious ceremonies. Thus, even now, the only places where we see true "natural" customs are in religious ceremonies.

"Even the minds of the people changed, becoming like the Chinese heart."

The people do not align their will with the will of the emperor, but boast in their own shrewd knowledge. This is the change to the Chinese heart.

"And because of this change, confusion entered into this country, a country that had been continually tranquil and at peace. Incidents that had occurred in China began to appear in Japan."

These people set aside the very wonderful Way of Japan, and because they imitated the wise and bothersome foreign ideas they had deemed "good," the true and pure mind and actions of the people became completely defiled and deceitful. It became difficult to rule the country unless it was through this [foreign] cruel Way. But when we view later Japanese history, we see that the reason later people felt that a country could not be ruled unless it was by the Way of the sages was because they originally did not grasp the dark reality that by ruling according to the Way of the sages made the act of governing more difficult. Remember that in the ancient days, there was no Way, and yet our country was well governed.

"Every act that occurs in heaven and earth is in harmony with the will of the *kami*."

Everything that happens in this world, be it the changing of the seasons, the falling of the rain, the blowing of the wind, or the good and bad fortune that comes to nations and people, are all the work of *kami*. Now, there are good *kami* and evil *kami*, and they derive their conduct from their nature. It is extremely difficult to analyze this fact based upon the reasoning of the world. But the various Ways of foreign countries dazzle the minds of men of the world, the wise and the foolish alike, and they do not know about these *kami*. Even people who study the learning of the imperial country should discover something regarding these *kami* by reading the ancient works, but they are ignorant, also. Foreign countries claim that good and evil are the result of retribution, as Buddhism states, or the will of heaven, as the Chinese claim. These are all incorrect concepts. There are many scholars who discuss this life according to the various doctrines of Buddhism, and I will not debate that here. The Chinese idea of the will of heaven (天命) dazzles wise men, and since there are few who perceive the erroneous nature of this doctrine, I will endeavor to explain it here to help people understand.

The idea of the will of heaven is something that the sages of ancient days fabricated as an excuse for murdering the ruler and seizing the country without being held guilty. Truly, since heaven and earth have no mind [or will], they have no life. If heaven actually had a mind [or will] endowed with reason, and bestowed the country on good men, allowing it to be properly governed, then why did sages fail to appear at the end of the Zhou era? Even if one were to claim that Zhou Kung or Confucius already established the Way, meaning that the appearance of sages was unnecessary, it still does not convince me. It would make sense if after Confucius, the Chinese universally practiced the Way, governing the country properly; however, after Confucius's day, the Chinese gradually abandoned the Way, with its bothersome mandate, and the country gradually turned into a land of confusion. With that no more sages appeared. No one addressed the problems of the country, and violent rulers took over the government, like the first emperor of Sung. What kind of will of heaven would torment the commoner? This manner of thinking is incomprehensible.

Also, some may use twisted logic to say that because rulers such as the first emperor of Sung did not receive the right to rule from heaven, he could not maintain it for long. But is it logical that the right to rule should be given to a wicked person even for a short time? And if there is the mandate of heaven above the ruler of a country, then there should be good and evil signs above the many common people showing that the good prosper long, and the wicked quickly become perverted. But this is not the case. There are abundant examples in the past and even now of evil attending some good people, and evil people being blessed with good. If these are the workings of the will of heaven, would there be such inconsistencies?

Now, in later generations, people's minds grew sharper, and those desiring to seize power realized that the common man did not believe that the mandate of heaven had allowed them to seize the country, so they made it appear on the surface as if a previous ruler transferred the throne to them. The reader could say that these actions are scandalous, but in reality, the sages of ancient times did the same thing. It is bewildering to try to comprehend why later rulers do not believe in the mandate of heaven in their era, but apply it to rulers in the ancient past. It is ludicrous to say there was a mandate of heaven in ancient times, but there is none now.

A certain person stated that Emperor Shun seized the land of Yao, then Yu seized Shun's land in return, which story is probable. And then there are people like later Wang Mang[5] and Cao Cao[6] who appeared to have the throne transferred to them, but in reality it was seizure. Thus, it is believed that Shun and Yao did the same. People of ancient times were naive and simple, and it is clear that the rulers mocked the people by claiming they had been given the right to rule. During the reigns of Wang Mang and Cao Cao, the people finally wised up and those in power could not fool them, so their evil works came to light. If people such as these [Wang Mang and Cao Cao] had been alive during ancient times, the commoner would no doubt have worshipped them like sages.

"Nothing can be done concerning the violent nature of the *kami* Magatsubi, and this is very lamentable."

All the evil and damaging acts within the world that are without reason and full of wickedness originate from the mind of this *kami* [Magatsubi].

---

5. Wang Mang 王莽 (45 BCE–23 CE) was an official at the end of the Former Han Dynasty. He poisoned Emperor Ping and put himself on the throne. He made drastic changes to the government resulting in economic failures. When a famine hit in 11 CE, rebellions occurred in the provinces, resulting in war that ultimately saw his death.

6. A chancellor during the Eastern Han Dynasty, Cao Cao 曹操 (155–220) generally is viewed as a hero in Chinese history but his methods were ruthless and cruel.

When this *kami* is extremely violent, even Amaterasu Ōmikami and Takagi Ōmikami[7] cannot control him. If they cannot, then how much less can the power of men control him? Good men commit evil, and evil men prosper. These many events that are contrary to logic are the doings of this *kami*. Because foreign countries do not have the true record of the divine age, foreigners cannot understand this *kami*, so they invent ideas like the mandate of heaven. It is insipid to establish everything based upon the principle of the way things should be.

"However, the great radiant light of Amaterasu Ōmikami who resides in the High Plain of Heaven dims not in the slightest, but shines down upon this world. The heavenly imperial symbols have been handed down faithfully, the commands have been given, and the imperial grandson rules the country."

As foreign countries were not governed by a previously chosen ruler, some simple man suddenly became ruler, while some rulers suddenly became common men. And this is the custom from ancient times, to destroy and ruin. Now, the masses label a person who plans to seize the country but fails in the attempt "a rebel," and they hate him, while they call someone who succeeds in seizing the country "a sage" and they revere him. These so-called sages, however, are just rebels who succeeded in their designs.

Nevertheless, our emperor whom we revere with awe in our hearts cannot be compared with these rulers of base countries. The heavenly ancestor *kami* who gave birth to this land [of Japan], and bestowed the right of rule, determined who should rule the land from the time of the creation of heaven and earth. The great *kami* has never commanded the people of this country to ignore the words of the emperor if he be evil, and though we have had good emperors and evil emperors, people cannot overthrow the emperor.[8] The throne has been our ruler, unchangeable, as long as heaven and earth stand, as long as the sun and moon shed forth their light—no matter how many generations pass away.

In ancient Japanese, the emperor was denoted as *a kami*, and since the emperor truly was divine, one must discard debate about good and bad actions, and offer up undivided reverence filled with trepidation. This is the true Way. During the upheavals of middle antiquity, people such as Hōjō Yoshitoki, Hōjō Yasutoki, and Ashikaga Takauji betrayed this Way, rebelled against the court, and tormented the emperor. The heart of Ma-

7. Another name for Takami Musubi.

8. Needless to say, this statement cannot be supported from the Japanese records themselves. For example, according to *Nihon shoki* Ankō was assassinated by Mayuwa out of revenge, and Sushun was assassinated by Soga no Umako out of fear.

gatsubi is mysterious; the people of the world followed these evil men, and prospered for a period of time. There are people in the world who know that the sun goddess shines down upon this land and ought to be revered, but fail to perceive that they should serve the emperor with trepidation, also. The reason there are ignorant people is because they have been led astray by the Chinese heart contained in Chinese works. They also believe in the chaotic customs and ways of China, and therefore cannot comprehend the true Way of this, the imperial country. Therefore, these people do not believe in the sun goddess, Amaterasu Ōmikami, and have forgotten that our emperor who now reigns is a descendant of hers.

"Regarding the lofty throne of the heavenly Inheritance,"

The reason that the ascension of the emperor is called *fitugi* is because the emperor is inheriting (*tugi*) the right to work the will of the sun (*fi*) goddess. The throne is called *taka mikura* not only because the imperial throne is the highest, but because it is where the sun goddess dwells. Remember that in ancient Japanese there were words like *takafikaru* "high-shining," *takahi,* and *fidaka* "sun-high" when referring to the sun. The throne of the sun goddess passes from generation to generation, and since that essence resides within the emperor, it goes without saying that the emperor has the same authority as the sun goddess. And because of this, those who receive the imperial blessings of the sun goddess, serve and revere with awe whoever the emperor may be.

"It is the unchanging throne which is immovable like heaven and earth. The Way [of Japan] is mysterious and profound, surpassing the myriad Ways that exist in foreign countries. Our Way is the proper, lofty, noble symbol."

In countries like China, they have the word "way," but because there is no substance to this Way, originally what was just nonsense gradually grew more chaotic; in the end, a neighboring people completely seized the government. The Chinese called these people barbarians, and despised them as less than humans; however, the momentum of these people was great, and they seized the country. Thus, the people looked up to them as the sons of heaven, though there was no evidence to support this move. Is it not particularly lamentable? How can Confucian scholars still believe that China is a good country? The [Chinese] ruler, with most of the nobles and commoners, has no consistent genealogy. There may have been some distinction in the feudal system that lasted until the Zhou era, but the royal lineage changed, and everything below them changed, too. Therefore, we can state that there never was any distinction. After the Qin era the people gradually abandoned the Way, resulting in more chaos, and even daughters of common men were given royal affection and suddenly made queens. Royal daughters of the king mingled with men of no heritage, feeling no shame. Yesterday's woodcutters of the mountains have suddenly climbed to the high posts of bureaus in the government today. In all aspects, the difference between base and noble was left undetermined, and the Chinese are no different from the birds and beasts.

"If one were to ask what kind of Way this is, he finds that it is not the natural way of heaven and earth."

Mark the difference. Do not think that this Chinese Way is the same as that of Laozi and Zhuangzi of China.

"Our [Japanese] Way is not man-made. This Way has come about through the spirit of the awe-inspiring *kami*, Takami Musubi."

All entities and events have their origins in the spirit of this *kami*.

"The heavenly ancestors, the Great Izanagi and Izanami, created all things."

Every event and every thing in this world was created by these two *kami*.

"Amaterasu Ōmikami received this Way from Izanagi and Izanami, and it has been maintained and transmitted ever since. And that is why we call this the 'Way of the *kami*.'"

This word *shintō* [神道] is first seen in the "Iware Ikegokoro Palace" [Yōmei] chapter of *Nihon shoki*. However, this simply points to the worshipping of the *kami*. Now, in the "Naniwa Nagara Palace" [Kōtoku] chapter of *Nihon shoki*, it says, "*Kamunagara* refers to following the will of the *kami*. It also means this is naturally prepared in advance." This is the first time that the Way of the imperial country is alluded to generally. Now, just because this is the Way, it does not mean there were any special contrivances, as I mentioned above. Therefore, it is the same as saying the Way is to worship and revere the *kami*.

In spite of this, quoting the line in the Chinese classics which says, "The sage established his teachings on the basis of this spiritlike Way (神道)";[9] thus saying that the characters for *Shintō* in *Nihon shoki* had their origin

9. Quoted from the *Book of Changes*, "Viewing the numinous Dao of Heaven, one finds

here shows that the author confused context, not understanding the proper meaning.[10] First, in relation to the *kami*, the origin of this word is not the same in Japan and China. In China, this word [神道] points to the so-called incomprehensible and mysterious idea of heaven–earth and *yin* and *yang*. Thus, it is just empty logic, and certainly there is no such thing. Yet, the *kami* of the imperial country are the ancestors of the current emperor, who is real; he is not the same as empty logic. The Way of the *kami* in the Chinese classics points to an incomprehensible and mysterious Way, while the Way of the imperial country has its beginnings with the imperial ancestral *kami*. There is a great difference between the Japanese and Chinese meaning.

"Now, a person can understand the deep significance of this Way by reading the ancient records, starting with *Kojiki*, but the minds of the learned scholars of the various ages were all cursed by Magatsubi, and Chinese learning led them astray. Their thoughts and ideas were all based on Buddhist and Chinese learning, but one cannot comprehend the true Way through these [foreign teachings]."

Because there was no word for the Way anciently, in the ancient records there is not one single word that even hints at a Way. Thus, starting with Prince Toneri, the various learned scholars at court could not comprehend the meaning of the Way. They only were able to use the bothersome usage of a Way, based on a Chinese idea. These ideas from Chinese works became affixed in their minds, and because they thought that this was the natural Way of heaven and earth, their work proceeded in that direction, regardless of whether it was deliberate or subconscious. And it must be said that Chinese learning seized their hearts because they began to think that this foreign Way should augment our own Way.

Generally, these Chinese ideas—starting with *yin* and *yang* and *qian* and *kun*[11]—are all originally man-made ideas of the sages themselves. When a person hears about these ideas, it sounds as if they are profound, but when one steps away from the fence of their sphere of learning and examines the facts, he realizes how shallow and empty these foreign ideas are. But people of ancient times as well as today are still wandering lost within this fence, and it is regrettable that they cannot escape from it. The ideas of our great country have been handed down since the divine age,

---

that the four seasons never deviate, and so the sage establishes his teachings on the basis of this numinous Dao, and all under heaven submit to him!" (Lynn 1994:260).

10. This is criticism against the Confucian scholar Dazai Shundai, who suggested that *Nihon shoki*'s usage of Shintō was influenced by the Chinese.

11. Representing opposing elements, like heaven and earth, or male and female.

> without the addition of human wisdom, and these ideas may sound shallow and be of no consequence, but in reality the significance of these ideas is without limit, beyond human understanding. Our traditions have a deep, mysterious profundity, and the reason that these ideas cannot be easily understood is because the reader wanders lost within the fence of Chinese learning. If one does not try to distance himself from this fence, even if he were to spend a hundred or even a thousand years in study, it would profit him nothing as far as the Way is concerned, but would only be an act in self-mockery. Since the ancient records are written in classical Chinese, one should know something about China. To know more about Chinese writing, one should read Chinese works, time permitting. If one's Japanese spirit is firmly grounded, and you watch your step, the influence in Chinese works will not sway you.

"Thus, there are many men teaching various doctrines today under the name of Shintō. Varied though they be, these teachers are all envious of the true Way, teaching private interpretations of recent ages."

> These so-called secret theories and the like selected by men and handed down in private are all inventions of later ages. If this doctrine was good, then it would have been proper for these to have spread through society; however, it is the corrupt disposition of men to secretly hide these things, making those ideas one's private estate, so the average man is ignorant of these.

"How reprehensible that the Way of the emperors who rule the nation has been made the private possession of the common man."

> When the common man simply obeys the orders of those above him this suits the Way. For example, even if it is not teaching the people to perform the Way of the *kami*, is it not a private affair of disobedience to one's superiors to teach a person privately about performing the Way of the *kami*?

"All people were created through the spirit of the *kami* Musubi. The things we undertake to do of our own should be that which we know and understand well."

> Every living creature in the world, even birds and insects, know exactly what they should do, and they know this through the spirit of Musubi. Among these living creatures, man has been born the most superior, and as is proper with that knowledge, he has sufficient intellect to know exactly what he should do. Why should there be someone above him forcing him

to do things he ought to do? If you say that without teaching, a man cannot know or do things, then it must be that he is inferior to even the birds and insects. Empty labels like benevolence, righteousness, courtesy, humility, filial piety, brotherly love, loyalty, and conviction, are things that all men should perform, and since we enjoy this knowledge, they need not be taught, but should be practiced because we already have knowledge. This Way of the sages, however, was invented so an unruly country could be forcibly governed, and they exceeded the limit of what men should do, strictly teaching and forcing people to do things. Thus, this moral system is not a true Way. The Chinese raucously preach this system, but in reality there are very few who practice it. It is very different from believing that this is the Way of heavenly principle.

Also, it is hard to comprehend what these people say when they deviate from this Way out of human greed. Exactly where did human greed come from and why does it appear? Since human greed must have its origins in some logical place, then is not human greed part of heavenly principle? And though the Chinese claim that they have the ancient law stating that a person cannot marry someone with the same family name even after one hundred generations, this is not an ancient law, but one that has its origins in the Zhou Dynasty. Because laws like this were strictly enforced, Chinese customs turned evil, and there were many incestuous marriages between parents, children, brothers, and sisters. It was difficult to govern with any standard, so these strict laws ended up bringing the country to shame. In all respects, severe laws exist because there are so many lawbreakers. So they set up regulations for the sake of having regulations, but this is not a true Way, because these do not suit the feelings of the people; there are few people who obey them. In later eras, not to mention the days of the Zhou Dynasty, many of those of the rank of feudal lord were already breaking these laws, and from this we can speculate how later periods in history fared. We even have examples of immoral acts between sisters.

Even so, Confucian scholars in our country have ignored the fact that from ancient times the people have not been able to obey these laws, and they set up a skeleton of the Way, in order to force the people to look down upon the imperial country. And it often happened that these scholars censured ancient Japanese marriages between brothers and sisters as animalistic behavior. Those learned men here in Japan believed that this behavior was foolish and shameful, so they spread nonsensical teachings, and advocated doctrine which still cannot be conclusively demonstrated [as efficacious]. In this way, these Japanese Confucian scholars became obsessed with the wisdom of Chinese sages, believing that their doctrine was reasonable. That is why these Japanese Confucian scholars are disposed to flattery. If they have no intention to flatter people, then the only difference with the Chinese sages would be in knowing no shame.

Anciently in Japan, only marriages between children of the same mother were forbidden, but even the emperor practiced marriages between children of different mothers. This was commonplace in society, even when the capital was removed to Heian. However, the ancient Japanese kept the distinction between nobility and commoner intact, avoiding any confusion. This is the true Way bestowed by the heavenly ancestors. In later ages, laws from China were introduced, and obeyed so even brothers and sisters of different mothers could not marry each other. Thus, now it is an offense to break such a law. Since this law regarding marriage was established in ancient times, there is no reason to debate a foreign system overtaking our own.

"In the great reigns of ancient times, the common man's will was simply the will of the emperor."

The commoner served the emperor as his will dictated, and there was not even the slightest feeling of personal will.

"By fearing and revering the emperor, by hiding in the shadow of the affection of the emperor, you worship the emperor."

As one worships before the great ancestor *kami*, it is common practice to worship the ancestral *kami* from the Omi, Muraji, and eighty Tomonoo down to the commoner. Also, in the same manner that the emperor worships the various *kami* of heaven and earth for the court and the country, all the servants below him worship good *kami* so they might obtain fortune, and worship and pacify evil *kami* to avoid misfortune. With the occasional defilement of the body, the priests perform ritual purification. These are all suitable rites that should be performed. Sayings like "If my heart observes the Way, the *kami* will protect me though I offer no prayers"[12] are just like Buddhist teachings or Confucian beliefs, and should be avoided because they deviate from the Way of the *kami*.

Also, in foreign countries, they value reason above all, even when it comes to worship. There is also something known as polluted worship[13] and other various commandments, but these are all arrogant displays of empty wisdom. *Kami* are different in nature from entities like Buddha, and

---

12. This refers to a poem attributed to Sugawara Michizane.

kokoro dani	If you comply with
makoto no miti ni	the true Way of the *kami*
kanafinaba	even in your heart,
inorazu totemo	they will protect you,
kami ya mamoramu	though you offer no prayers.

13. Praying for something that you should not.

not all are necessarily good. Some are evil and their minds and deeds are dependent on their nature; because of this, people who commit evil sometimes prosper, and good people meet with misfortune. It is commonplace in society. Therefore, one should not think about whether a *kami* suits reason or not. We should only fear their wrath, faithfully worshipping them. Therefore, in worship, it is important that everything be performed to please the *kami*. To do that, everything must be purified so there is no defilement. Also, there should be many beautiful and wonderful items of offering, in as far as possible. Some might play the *koto* or the flute, dance, or perform something interesting and entertaining within the worship. All these things have precedence in the divine age, and this is the ancient Way. It is one of the mistakes of Chinese learning, however, which says that it is the deep feelings of the heart that counts, and not the offerings or method of worship.

Again, in worshipping the *kami*, the avoidance and purification of fire should be solemnly remembered more than anything else, and this is underscored by the example in the record of the divine age, in the section dealing with Yomi. This not only correlates to acts pertaining to the *kami*, it is also true of everyday life. Things pertaining to fire should not be treated lightly. If fire defiles a person, that person becomes dominated by Magatsubi, and due to his violent nature, a myriad of evil events are bound to occur in the world. Thus, for the sake of the world as much as for other people, defilement from all fire should be avoided. In this generation, during the time of Shintō ceremonies at the court or at shrines, this avoidance appears to have been heeded even if only in some small degree, but this is not true of society in general. Because of the continuing expansion of the half-baked thinking of China, people generally think that this avoidance of fire is nonsense. Now, how should we look upon those learned scholars who expound the sacred scriptures of Japan and preach the Chinese heart, but treat the defilement of fire lightly?

"There was nothing else to do but try to do one's best in all endeavors, and pass through this life peacefully and happily."

Other than this, what other doctrine do we need? Children were taught essential things; carpenters were taught the art of building and a variety of other skills, as was done in the ancient days; the method of teaching resembles the doctrine of Confucianism and Buddhism, but if one looks closely, he will discover that they are not the same.

"No matter what the Way may be called, is there any point in studying and performing anything other than the Japanese Way?"

> A person asked if the Way of the *kami* was the same as the doctrine of Laozi and Zhuangzi. Let me answer this by saying that Laozi and Zhuangzi were bothered by the arrogant sophistry of the Chinese scholars. They both honored and praised naturalism, and because of this their thinking appears to resemble our Way. Nonetheless, they were born in a corrupt country, not in the country of the *kami*! Because they became accustomed to the successive theories of the Chinese scholars, what they believed to be naturalism was what the Chinese scholars deemed "natural." They did not know that every action here is the doing of the will of the *kami*, so the basic import of their ideas is different from ours.

"If you still desire to find a Way, rid yourselves of the corrupt thinking of the China heart, and replace that with a pure, natural Japanese way of thinking; having done that, you should peruse the ancient Japanese texts. If you do this, you will find on your own there is no Way that should be followed. Knowing that, you will see that you should accept and practice the Way of the *kami*. Because of this, I have argued thus, and though it is not in the teachings of the Way, I could not remain still, knowing and seeing the works of Magatsubi. Through the spirits of the *kami* Kamu Naobi and Ōnaobi, this evil can be rectified."

> The passages above cannot be said to be my own conclusions. Everything that I have said is taken from ancient texts, and if a person will search for himself, he will have no doubts.

This was written with fear and trembling on the ninth day of the tenth month of Meiwa 8 [1771] in Mitami of Iidaka District, Ise Province by Taira no Asomi Norinaga.

[MNZ 1976, 9:49–63]

☙

KOJIKI-DEN

Motoori Norinaga (1798)

[One of the great achievements of the Kokugaku movement was Norinaga's elucidation of *Kojiki* in *Kojiki-den*. A key element to strengthen the essential foundation for the complete evolution of Kokugaku from a nature-oriented, literary movement into one with an ideological purpose was the exposition of a concrete, Japanese Way. A clearer idea of this Japanese Way came about with the exhaustive annotation of *Kojiki*, a work Norinaga stated held the essence of the ancient Japanese mind. I have included excerpts from *Kojiki-den*, starting with his introduction. The majority of the excerpts deal with the critical areas of Shintō.]

INTRODUCTION[1]

In what era did the recording of events from previous eras start in our history? In the "Richū" chapter of *Nihon shoki* it says, "Fourth year, autumn, eighth month. The court established recorders in the various provinces for the first time." Taking this line into consideration, before the era of *Kojiki* and *Nihon shoki*, the court already employed historians who kept records. Those records are likely documents from each successive era, but we do not know how far into the past these went. Nevertheless, as they should have recorded things around the time of their individual eras, events of the past should have been recorded, even if only fragmentary. Historical records probably started with this era.

Therefore, I believe that when the court compiled *Nihon shoki* there were already many various records in existence. **[**This can also be inferred from the fact that there are so many quotes from variant sources in the divine age section of *Shoki*.**]** In the twenty-eighth year of Emperor Suiko [620], Prince Shōtoku made a compilation with Soga no Umako of *Tennōki*, *Kokki*, and the records of the 180 families of the court, including the Omi, Muraji, Tomo Miyakko, and Kuni Miyakko. This is the first instance of historical writing in Japan. Also, in the tenth year of Emperor Tenmu [681], the emperor issued a decree to twelve men, including Prince Kawashima,

1. Norinaga's original parenthetical material appears in dark brackets **[]**, but I have ignored many of the shorter ones without using ellipses.

to compile a record from *Teiki* and the various accounts of ancient times. Unfortunately these two records have not survived.

During the reign of Emperor Genmei, on the eighth day of the ninth month of Wadō 4 [711], the emperor issued an order to Ō no Yasumaro to compile this work, *Kojiki*. Ō no Yasumaro presented the manuscript to the court in the first month, twenty-eighth day of the following year. This is all seen in the preface.[2] [This fact is missing from *Shoku Nihongi*.] Thus, *Kojiki* is the oldest surviving record Japan possesses. *Nihon shoki* was presented to the court in Yōrō 4 [720] during the reign of Emperor Genshō, a fact recorded in *Shoku Nihongi*, so *Nihon shoki* came about eight years after *Kojiki*.

As a matter of fact, we see from the preface that the compiler left the sentences in *Kojiki* unornamented, endeavoring to preserve the state of ancient Japan by placing emphasis on the ancient vocabulary. Nevertheless, since *Nihon shoki*'s compilation, society has lavished praise and respect on *Shoki*, and there are many people who have not even heard of *Kojiki*. The cause of this is the study of Chinese works, which scholars and courtiers emphasize as important. The ancient Japanese viewed Chinese things as the most superior, obtaining a strong affinity for anything Chinese, so the court rejoiced in compiling *Nihon shoki* in the style of Chinese annals, and treated *Kojiki* as an artless relic that deviated from the true style of national histories.

A person I know took offense at this attitude of mine and told me, "Wasn't *Nihon shoki* compiled a few years after *Kojiki* because there were errors in the latter's text?"

My reply was that what he said was not true. The reason both *Kojiki* and *Nihon shoki* exist is because the court at the time was terribly fond of Chinese learning, and *Kojiki*'s text was so bland that they feared the work would seem unbecoming when compared with the histories from China. Also, the contents were shallow and the court soon tired of reading the work, so they ordered a compilation that relied on a variety of works, adopting a chronological system, imitating Chinese records, even adding segments from Chinese texts. With this, they were able to compile a record that conformed to the style of Chinese record keeping.

For a deeper explanation, I have already mentioned Prince Kawashima's project of compilation of *Teiki* and other records; however, later, in

2. Most scholars now believe that the majority of Ō no Yasumaro's task was to arrange, annotate, and commit to paper the work of Hieda no Are. Yasumaro, thus, is not a compiler in the literal sense, but an editor, putting the finishing touches on the text.

Wadō 7 [714], the court issued an order to Ki Asomi Kiyobito and Miyake Omi Fujimaro to compile a national history. This is seen in *Shoku Nihongi*.

Of these two compilations, Prince Kawashima's work was much like the rough draft of *Kojiki*, having been put together in the reign of Emperor Tenmu. It is difficult to know if *Kojiki*'s text took form before or after Kawashima's. However, if Prince Kawashima's work took form before *Kojiki*, then the sentence in *Kojiki*'s preface, "*Teiki* and *Kuji* who are in possession of the various families deviate from the truth, being full of prevarications" would be false.[3] There is another problem if Prince Kawashima's work took form after *Kojiki*, for the work of *Kojiki* should have been sufficient in doing what the court had commanded Kawashima's to do; however, as seen from *Kojiki*'s preface, "The imperial reign changed and the compilation did not reach fruition," we realize that *Kojiki* and Prince Kawashima's work were compiled for different purposes.[4] The difference is that Prince Kawashima's work concentrated on ornate sentences modeled after the Chinese records, while *Kojiki* placed its emphasis on giving an accurate account of things. This intention is seen in the preface.

By the [early] Nara era, Ō no Yasumaro received the command to continue the work in finishing Emperor Tenmu's wish, and he compiled the text corrected by Hieda no Are. The national history compiled in 714 was no doubt a work following the tradition of Chinese learning. Then, in the Yōrō era [717–24], the court commanded Prince Toneri to compile *Nihon shoki*. Therefore, the continuation of historical compilations resembling the Chinese tradition was based on the court's displeasure with the results of the previous two projects. It appears that these early compilations were destroyed rather early, and we have neither title nor report about these. Now, since *Nihon shoki*'s texts were more magnificent than anything compiled earlier, this became the orthodox history and the court ordered no further compilations. One reason *Kojiki*, compiled before *Shoki*, was not discarded is because it differed so much from the other earlier compilations, it being a true representation of ancient things. Thus, *Nihon shoki* came about not because *Kojiki* contained errors, but because the nature of its text differed from the other works. If there indeed were errors in the text, then the court would have destroyed it early on, like these other two

3. This issue about the veracity or falsehood of *Teiki* needs to be studied. We know that *Teiki* in two volumes was still in the imperial library as late as the Nara era, making some believe that it was not corrupt, like Tenmu had stated. A corrupt work surely would have been burned like those mentioned in *Jinnō shōtōki*.

4. Umezawa (1976:434) later reached the same conclusion, but it was based on a more pragmatic analysis of the texts.

records. You should consider the fact that of these three records, only *Kojiki* has survived.

In relation to this, a person may say that it is simply chance that a manuscript should be transmitted down to the present. A manuscript is not transmitted because its contents are good or bad. In China as well as in Japan, many good ancient works no longer survive, while there are some trivial works that have survived till the present.

To this I would reply that what he says is for the most part correct; however, *Kojiki*'s circumstances are different. The other two chronicles are mentioned in *Nihon shoki* and *Shoku Nihongi*, showing that they were official compilations. Even if these manuscripts had disappeared, there still would have been people who knew something about them, so at least the title would have remained in other works. But the titles of these works are unknown, and by the Nara era, people did not know anything about these compilations, for there are no quotes in *Man'yōshū*, which quotes many old works from these chronicles as evidence. On the other hand, the artless and bland *Kojiki* differs completely from the records modeled after Chinese records; if its text was fraught with problems, surely the Nara court with its reverence for Chinese learning would have suppressed the work. No one would have read it, and surely it would not have survived till the present.

Considering that the text was transmitted for a thousand years, you realize that even after Prince Toneri presented *Nihon shoki* to the court, courtiers and people in later generations read *Kojiki*. Are there not quotes from *Kojiki* here and there in *Man'yōshū*? [I do not fully understand the events surrounding things mentioned above, but I have given the account as I envisioned it after comparing *Kojiki*'s preface and the records concerning these two other chronicles.]

Having explained this, the next question was, "The Tenmu edict to Prince Kawashima to compile a record is seen in *Nihon shoki*, while the 714 edict is seen in *Shoku Nihongi*. Since we do not see anything concerning *Kojiki* in the record that must mean that *Kojiki* was not a large, public project of the court, but was a privately compiled record. Also, there are many places in the chapters dealing with the divine age in *Shoki* where variant records are quoted, and some of these appear to have come from *Kojiki*. This would mean that *Kojiki* was thus one of these 'other, variant records.' *Nihon shoki*, however, was a large-scale project completed under imperial auspices, compiling events from these various records, making sure that nothing was lacking, so it is unfair to compare *Nihon shoki* to *Kojiki*."

I would reply that the theory that *Kojiki* was a variant text, and all of these were compiled together into the *Shoki* text, and the historians made *Nihon shoki*'s text complete is reasonable. In reality, *Shoki*'s text is broad and detailed, being complete with dates given to the month or day. It is a well-prepared historical chronicle, and there are many points where *Kojiki* cannot compare. In spite of this, let me point out the strengths of *Kojiki*. First, in ancient times, there were no historical records, everything transmitted by word of mouth. These oral traditions were not necessarily passed down in the form recorded in *Shoki*, but the true form is preserved in *Kojiki*. *Nihon shoki* is mainly concerned with Chinese philosophy, and its sentences are highly ornate, while *Kojiki* has nothing to do with Chinese learning, but records the ancient traditions in such a way so these will not vanish.

Essence, entity, and expression are interrelated. Ancient essences, entities, and expressions belong to the ancient period, while later essences, entities, and expressions belong to the later period. Chinese essences, entities, and expressions belong to the Chinese sphere. *Nihon shoki* took later era essences and mapped them onto ancient entities. *Shoki* relied on Chinese expressions to describe our country's lexical essences, so there are many instances where the proper relation has broken down. *Kojiki* contains no strict interpretations, but recorded things as they had been handed down from antiquity. Thus, *Kojiki* preserves the interrelationship between essence, entity, and expression, conveying the truth of things from the ancient past. *Kojiki* accomplishes this feat because it concentrates on the ancient lexicon. All essences and entities are expressed with words, so this forms the core of the work. Since *Nihon shoki* concentrates on beautiful Chinese prose, there are many instances where the beauty of ancient Japan has vanished. *Kojiki* preserves the beauty of ancient Japan, because its text is centered on recording the ancient lexicon.

In fact, even if *Kojiki* was just one of the reference materials for *Nihon shoki*, meaning it was not an important, large-scale project, it is still worthy of our respect; how much more so because it was compiled by the strong desire of Emperor Tenmu. Again Emperor Genmei's edict brought about the final compilation, so it is not a work that we can scorn as a private work.

Considering these various facts, the work that deserves our greater respect is, of course, *Kojiki*. In spite of this, Chinese learning grew popular, and the legal system of our country was altered in imitation of China. Works modeled on a Chinese style were eagerly displayed in public, while works that accurately conveyed the ancient past were kept in the dark, treated like illegitimate private compilations. And that is why there is no record of *Kojiki* in *Shoku Nihongi* or other orthodox histories. This trend only increased, resulting in fewer and fewer people reading *Kojiki*; it is very lamentable that the courtiers did not consider *Kojiki* to be an orthodox record, but neglected it altogether.

Since we have no other ancient records in Japan, we have nothing else but Chinese-based records from which to theorize what the ancient Japanese style of historiography was. Scholars have rejoiced over chronicles fashioned after Chinese models. If you do not have an affinity for the vanity so prevalent in Chinese studies, then you have no problem with a record that does not resemble Chinese annals. The widespread practice of basing everything on China, deciding which is good and bad, is sheer nonsense. Nonetheless, my master, Okabe Ushi [Mabuchi], worked with the Edo government in eastern Japan and speaks highly of the study of ancient learning. Through this study he has been able to cleanse the thousand-year-old corruption of Chinese learning. There are now people, few though they be, who are coming to an understanding of this learning. Also, there are people in society who are beginning to appreciate *Kojiki*. As far as this ancient learning is concerned, my master has accomplished a marvelous feat, something unparalleled since the divine age.

I received my master's blessing and have come to some understanding of this ancient spirit, and as time passes I have been able to recognize the defilement of Chinese philosophy and am now cognizant of the pure, sincere spirit from antiquity. Using *Kojiki* as the standard, I have determined it to be the oldest record we possess, being the most superior, *Nihon shoki* next in line. Those people who wish to pursue this ancient path to scholarship should not misinterpret the ancient records, even for a moment (MNZ 1976, 9:3–7). …

ABOUT HEAVEN

The High Plain of Heaven is, in other words, heaven. [Now, the theory that "the High Plain of Heaven" refers to the capital of the emperor is a private interpretation that goes strictly against the ancient traditions. All knowledgeable people in society are drowning in the Chinese heart based on the philosophy of Chinese works, harboring suspicions about the wondrous spirit of the *kami*. How truly foolish not to be able to believe that the High Plain of Heaven exists above the sky!] And so if we only say heaven, then what is the difference between that and the High Plain of Heaven? First, because heaven is the land where the *kami* reside, objects like mountains, rivers, trees, grass, and the heavenly palace, in short, the myriad heavenly things resemble this land where the heavenly grandson rules. And since these articles are all superior, and the objects in the land of the *kami* are just like the myriad objects we now have before us now.

When we say the High Plain of Heaven, we are talking about a specific part of heaven. The reason we use this special name is because heaven itself is *high*, which is slightly different than just saying "high." An epithet for the sun is *takafikaru* "shines high," which has the same meaning as *amaterasu* "shining in heaven"; *takamikura* "the high throne" is also called the throne of heaven. These usages with *taka* "high" have the same significance. Also, *takayuku* and *fayabusa wake* "the swift falcon that flies high" use the word *taka* in place of sky. Even now, we call the sky *amatusora* "the heavenly sky." And so, with the adjective *high* attached, we call the land of the *kami* the High Plain of Heaven ... (MNZ 1976, 9:123–24).

ABOUT DIVINE BIRTH

The verb *naru* has three meanings. One, the appearance of something out of nothingness [such as the birth of man]—the meaning here is when *kami* come into existence; two, when an object *becomes* something else ... ; three, completing the formation (or building) of something. An example is when Princess Toyo Tama Hime turned into a *wani* of eight feet as she was about to give birth. The third is the meaning of completion when something is being created. The text [of *Kojiki*] records that the land had firmly been created. These are the three meanings of *naru*. [In Chinese, the difference in meaning of these three is represented by different characters: 生 "give birth," 成 "become," and 変化 "change," but in the ancient language of the imperial country, there are many examples where these three meanings were subsumed under the same word *naru* ...] (MNZ 1976, 9:124).

ABOUT THE *KAMI*

I have as yet to tease out the meaning of *kami*. [All the old theories attempting an etymology are incorrect.] Everything denoted as *kami* include first off the various *kami* we see in the ancient records, and the spirits residing in the various shrines. And of course, we can call people *kami*. Objects like birds, beasts, trees, plants, the sea, mountains, and almost anything else, anything uncommon in this world, having superior qualities and inspiring reverence can be denoted as *kami*. [The word "superior" does not simply imply noble, good, or meritorious. If attributes such as evil and mysterious are terrifyingly superior, then we can also denote these attributes as related to *kami*. It goes without saying that the unspeakably noble successive emperors are the first *kami* among men. The reason the ancients called the emperor "a distant *kami*" is because he is far-removed from the commoner, requiring our honor and reverence. And thus we see in ancient times as well as in the present there were other people denoted as *kami*. There are minor *kami* in each province, each village, each household, be they discreet and unknown on a national level. Also, most of the *kami* of the divine age were men connected to that era, and because they were all *kami*, the ancients referred to this as *kami no yo* "the divine age." Also, needless to say that thunder (*kaminari*)—which is not human—is a wonderfully mysterious existence, and a terrible *kami*, that is why it is referred to as *narukami* or *kaminari*. …]

And so there are many types of *kami*, some noble and some base, some strong others weak, some good and some evil. Their minds and deeds are as varied as they are, and because of this it is difficult to argue that a *kami* is mainly this or that. [However, it is a grave mistake for people in society to assume that foreign *kami*, such as Bodhisattva of Buddhism and sages, are in the same category as our *kami*, and that they are ranked above our *kami*, based on "the principle of the way things should be." Evil, wicked *kami* engage only in things that go against reason, and if these wicked *kami* try to be good they cannot do things that are reasonable. If they are caused to become angry they become violent. And even though they are wicked *kami*, they are pacified when pleased. …] Furthermore, whether they be good or evil *kami* the greater their place of reverence and superiority the greater their mysterious, mystical, and wondrous nature; their existence is beyond the comprehension of man with his limited insight, and we cannot understand one layer of the thousand layers of their reasoning. We can only pay deference to their dignity and stand in awe and trembling before them … (MNZ 1976, 9:125–26).

ABOUT AME NO MINAKA NUSHI KAMI

Minaka in this name is the same as *manaka* "the middle." The syllables *ma* and *mi* were originally related, and at a somewhat later time separated into two different lexical spheres. *Mi* means "respected or revered," and *ma* means "to praise, to be blunt, or to completely use." There are many ancient remnants of this usage, such as *makumanu* and *mikumanu*. And there are many examples where *ma* should be used, but *mi* has been attached, like *misora*, *miyuki*, *miti*. *Minaka* is an example of this. This does not only have to do with heaven. We also see in the poetry of *Man'yōshū*, *kuni no minaka sato no minaka* "within the middle of the village of the province. …"

The word *nusi* "lord" is the same as 大人 *usi* and is a contraction of *no usi*. [There are examples of writing *usi* as 主人. In *Shoki* we see Prince Hiko Ushi, who was the father of Emperor Keitai. In *Shoku Nihongi* we see the name Abe Asomi Miushi. The current readings have been corrupted.] Therefore, anciently any name with the suffix *usi* always had *no* attached. The suffix *nusi* was attached to nouns without *no*. Examples include Akiguhi no Ushi no Kami, Ohosehi no Mikuma no Ushi, Ohokuni Nushi, Ohomono Nushi, Koto Shiro Nushi, and Futsu Nushi. … Therefore, this *kami* resides in the middle of heaven, and the meaning of his name is the lord of the middle of the world (MNZ 1976, 9:127).

ABOUT TAKAMI MUSUBI KAMI

The *taka* of this name is a beautifying appellation; another name by which he is known is Takagi no Kami "the high-tree *kami*." The *mi* is also ornamental. Kami Musubi is a name paired off with Takami Musubi, and so both these names have *mi* attached. … The word *musubi* is written with borrowed Chinese characters; *musu* means "to give birth to." That is why Japanese call sons and daughters, their offspring, *musuko* "son" and *musume* "daughter." Also, like moss, having a plant reproduce and grow is called *musu*. The *Nihon shoki* compilers wrote 日 *bi* (*fi*) with the character for spirit, and this fits well. Everything that has a mysterious air about it is called *fi*. The sun goddess who resides in the High Plain of Heaven gazes down from her land, and we call her *fi* "sun." This is because there is no such thing on the earth, and she was given this name as she is the most mysterious and superior of all. The *fi* of prince and princess (*fiko/fime*) is a good prefix of praise. And *fi* [here voiced as *bi*] of the *kami* Magatsubi Naobi is of the same type. Therefore, *musubi* means the wondrous and mysterious power of the spirit of the *kami* who produces life. Other than these, we have names like Ho Musubi, Tamatsume Musubi, Iku Musubi, Taru Musubi, and Tsunokori Musubi. These all have the same meaning with *musubi*. Starting with heaven and earth, all things and actions originated with these two *kami*. Thus, though there are many *kami* in the world, the Japanese should revere this *kami* (Takami Musubi). It goes without saying that this *kami* provides the blessing of prosperity, a *kami* worthy of respect and worship of men … (MNZ 1976, 9:128–30).

CONCERNING KUNI NO TOKO TACHI

We can see from the characters (国之常立) that his name means the *kami* who stands eternally in heaven. [All the [traditional] explanations about the two characters of this name, 常立, are unsuitable.] It is not proper to leave out *no* and abbreviate the name to Kuni Toko Tachi. … When we consider the origin of these twelve *kami* from Kuni no Toko Tachi until Izanami, we find that the two *kami* before Kuni no Toko Tachi, Ashikabi-hikoji and Ame no Toko Tachi, were heavenly *kami* born first in heaven like the sprouting reed. The *kami* from Kuni no Toko Tachi on were born from the substance that became the land floating like oil. [The substance that later became heaven had already sprouted, grown, and disappeared. The remaining residue became heaven.] Earth was created through the substance that settled downward, and then there is the substance that was pulled upward, as a variant tradition in *Shoki* notes, "Then there was another object resembling floating oil that had formed in the void. It changed into a *kami* named Kuni no Toko Tachi."

The reason the name Kuni no Toko Tachi exists in contrast to Ame no Toko Tachi is because he was born of the earth (*kuni*). Thus, the clause "when the substance resembling floating oil drifted about" is a phrase connected to the birth of Izanami, and all the *kami* from Kuni no Toko Tachi (until Izanami) are born successively from this substance; this reading is the more natural of the two. Nonetheless, it is still difficult to be so decisive … (MNZ 1976, 9:142–143).

ABOUT IZANAGI AND IZANAMI

The meaning of the names of the *kami* Izanagi and Izanami, according to *Nihon shoki kuketsu*, is "to invite." My master also said that Izanagi is the nobleman of invitation, and Izanami is the lady of invitation. Truly, this is the meaning of these two *kami* who had intercourse and gave birth to the land; they invited each other and came together. This is as it should be. There are examples where the noble man is designated with just the suffix *gi*. We see examples such as in the section of the Great Words of the Aki Palace [Ōjin] we see the words *sazaki agi* "Sazaki, my son … ," and in the song from Prince Oshikuma [in the reign of Chūai] we have the words *iza agi* "Come on, my Lord." These both mean "my lord." Also, the suffix *megi* "lady" coalesces into *mi.*[5] [One theory says that *ki* is an inverted abbreviation of *fiko*, and *mi* is an inverted abbreviation of *fime*. However, while this may happen sometimes, it does not apply here.] As I have thought on this, when these [two *kami*] were about to have intercourse they invited each other with the words *iza na* "I invite you," so these two were named thus. The *na* in both names should be interpreted as "you." [It is much the same type as *iza agi* from above, and in *Man'yōshū* and other works there are examples of *iza kodomo* "come, children." So the suffix *ki* and *mi* have the meaning I mentioned above, and these words become part of their names as a form of praise. One could also claim that these were named thus because they spoke their words together, but that is not the case. And I have also thought that while *iza* is a form of invitation, then *nagi* is "my lord-*i*", and *nami* is *nanimo-i* "my sister-*i*." The final *i* here is a form like the emphatic *yo*. ...]

So I also thought that *gi* is a shortened form of *gii*, where the final *i* is a rhyming sound. The form *nanimo-i* becomes *mi* with the dropping of *ni* and to monophthongization of *moi*. I had thought thusly, but then comparing this with the name *kamurogi* and *kamuromi* I find that my theory does not work in these two examples, so I need to discard it ... (MNZ 1976, 9:151–52).

ABOUT THE SEVEN GENERATIONS OF *KAMI*

The divine age is called such because it is different from the age of men—a usage seen in the preface to *Kokinshū*. Japanese called it the divine age because people of ancient times were all *kami*. Since there is no obvious difference between the era when men were *kami* and the era when men were men, ancient times are broadly termed "the divine age," as seen in some *Man'yōshū* poetry. When we have to make a distinction, however, the time until Ugayafukiaezu[6] constitutes "the divine age," and the time after the reign at the Kashiwara Palace [Jinmu] is the age of men. Since the condi-

5. Based on what we know about Old Japanese phonology, this type of sound change is difficult to accept. However, Unger (2008:50) proposed that an earlier *g lenited to zero in certain environments, triggering other changes, such as monophthongization of dipthongs. The environment Norinaga is explaining likely would not be a candidate for this sound change.

6. This is the father of Emperor Jinmu. His name is sometimes shortened to Fukiaezu.

tion of the world was truly different after the beginning of this reign, how fitting that we call it a new era.[7] In spite of this, the reason that the time until Izanami is called the realm of the *kami* is because the five reigns after her[8] still were called the reign of the *kami*. After the age of men began, then we are able to say that with the seven generations of *kami*, these other five reigns also constituted a part of the divine age. Truly, this seven-generation era was during the beginning of heaven and earth, the state of the *kami*, and the state of this world were as such as there has never been since. ... Of these twelve *kami*, the first two were produced alone, and the last ten were produced in pairs of male and female. We simply call these the era of twelve *kami* because it is difficult to divide them any farther. With the help of later examples of succession, we borrowed the term "seven generations" ... (MNZ 1976, 9:153).

ABOUT THE CREATION OF ONOGORO ISLAND

"Amano ukifasi"
This is a bridge placed between heaven and earth, creating a path that the *kami* can use to move up or down. Because it is placed in the firmament, it was called *ukifasi* "the floating bridge." Even when Ame no Oshihomimi Ninigi was about to descend down to our country he stood on this floating bridge of heaven and looked down. Based on the false wisdom from later people infected with the Chinese heart grounded in Chinese knowledge, people have argued about the nature of this bridge, but their arguments are deficient. *Tango fudoki* says, "Yosa District. In the northeast direction of the area under supervision by the District office is a village called Hayasi. The coastal area of the village has a very large and long cape. It is 1229 *jō* [12, 290 feet] in length, but its width is less than nine *jō* [90 feet] in some places, and in others it is between ten and twenty *jō*. The tip of the coast is called 'the floating bridge of heaven.' The rear part of the cape is called Kushi Beach. The reason for these names is because the great *kami* Izanagi who created the land created a bridge so he could go back and forth to

7. Both *Kojiki* and *Nihon shoki* make a textual distinction between the divine age and the age of men. Book 1 of *Kojiki* contains the myths of the *kami*, and Book 2 starts with Jinmu. Books 1 and 2 of *Nihon shoki* are the myths of the *kami*, and Book 3 is the record of Jinmu.

8. The reign of the *kami* includes the sun goddess, her son, her grandson, Ninigi, his son Hohodemi, and then Ugayafukiaezu.

heaven. Thus it was named 'the bridge of heaven.' However, when the great *kami* was sleeping, the bridge fell down. ..." According to this tradition, this floating bridge was originally constructed by this great *kami*. Now, because this bridge leads up to heaven, it became a ladder that was set upright, but when the *kami* went to sleep, it fell down, and the remains are on the coast of the sea in Tango. This story is the same type as Ame no Kaguyama in Yamato or Mo Yama in Mino.[9] There are many such instances from the divine age. People in later eras whose thinking is based on Confucianism do not find this fact amazing ... (MNZ 1976, 9:161–62).

ONOGORO ISLAND

The island of Onogoro ... appears in *Shiki* where it says, "It is an island that congealed on its own. That is why it is called *onogoro sima* 'the self-congealing island.'" The name of the island is based on the action of the tide being stirred up, dripping off the tip of the halberd and then drying with a crackling noise. [Thus the word *koworo* "drying with a crackling noise" is simplified to *koro*. Now as this island was the first part of the land to be created, the word *tuti* "land, earth" was a creation from mud, and that is how you know the word is a contraction of *tudufidi*.] The prefix *ono* "self" was added because the other islands were all created by the two *kami* [Izanagi and Izanami]. Only this island was different. It formed by itself. That's why later in the text it says, "The only island they did not give birth to was Onogoro ..." (MNZ 1976, 9:164).

CONCERNING DIVINATION

In the section of the imperial reign in the Tamagaki Palace [Suinin] there is the usage of *futomani ni uranafete*. In *Nihon shoki* "great divination" is written as *futomani*, "And Ame no Koyane is the person who originally was granted authority over religious ceremonies. And that is why he per-

9. A tradition found in a fragment of *Iyo fudoki* says a mountain came down from heaven, and on its way down it split in two. One part landed in Yamato and is known as Mount Ame no Kagu. The other part landed in Iyo and is known as Mount Ame. Regarding Mo Yama, *Kojiki* records that at the funeral in heaven of Ama Waka Hiko, people mistook Ajishiki Takahikone for Ama Waka Hiko, which insulted him, and he cut down the mourning hut and it fell to earth and became Mount Mo, "Mount Mourning."

formed divination here." The word *futo* "thick" is like *futonorito* "powerful liturgy" and *futodama* "thick jewels"; it is an honorific prefix. Nevertheless, it is still unclear as to exactly what *mani* points to. [The usage of the character 占 "divination" in *Nihon shoki* was selected to represent the act of divination, but that does not necessarily mean that *mani* means divination. In general the characters used in *Shoki* do not fit the Japanese words but in most cases were selected for their meaning. In Chinese texts the characters 卜 "divination through the cracks in bones and scapula" and 占 "divination" are used in different contexts, but in our country both characters are used for the same word. In spite of this, the theory that there are different meanings for this act [in Japanese] based on the characters is completely wrong.] *Futomani* was one of the methods of ancient divination, and was one of the most important among the various ways to divine. …

The actual phrase 卜相而 "having divined together" should be read as *urafete.* … *urafe* is a shortened form of *uraafe*, and *afe* is an abbreviated form of *afase.* … Now, concerning the method of divination, one should read the section about Ama no Iwatoya (MNZ 1976, 9:180–82).

In *Nihon shoki*, Emperor Sujin section, it says, "The command to perform divine divination was given." The compilers of *Nihon shoki*, however, merely wrote this in imitation of Chinese literature, and in reality, the ancient Japanese performed divination on the shoulder blade of a stag. Since the Urabe family [who were in charge of divination] originated on the island of Iki, they brought divination by tortoise shell over from Korea. And it is seen in *Nihon shoki*, fourteenth year of Emperor Kinmei that Paekche presented divination and the use of the calendar to the Japanese envoys. It is from this time on that the Japanese used the Chinese method of divination. In an interpretation of *Nihon shoki*, however, a work known as *Gui zhao chuan* is quoted saying that divination by tortoise scapula originated in the divine age, and because of this, many scholars believed that divination originated thus. *Nihon shoki* abandoned the ancient method of stag divination, spreading the falsehood that the ancient Japanese employed divination by tortoise scapula from the beginning. The slandering of the ancient records is clear. How lamentable that the Japanese abandoned divination by stag, allowing divination by tortoise scapula to become the general method! In the codes on the ceremonies, the record only mentions divination by tortoise scapula, saying nothing about the older method of using the shoulder blade of a stag (MNZ 1976, 9:359–60).

ABOUT YOMI

Yomi is the place where the dead go. The word *yomi* is seen in *Man'yōshū*, *Genji monogatari*, and *Eiga monogatari*. The word for resurrection or being brought back from the dead (*yomigaeru*) literally means to come back from Yomi. The definition of this word as recorded in *Nihon shoki kuketsu* is "the land seen at night." Though the last character 土 "land" is incorrect, the *yomi* part "seen at night" is indeed proper. Later we see the episode where Izanagi lights a torch, showing that this is a dark place. Also, the name of the moon *kami* [Tsukuyomi] who rules the world of the night has *yomi* attached to his name.

Now we see Izanami's words, "My Lord should rule the upper land, and I will stay and rule the lower." Also, Susanoo later says that he wishes "to go to the nether land below to where my mother has gone." Thus, we see that this place is somewhere below the land where humans reside. Later people who studied everything about the reasoning of life and death from Confucian and Buddhist books that came from abroad gave their own views about Yomi, but each of these is mistaken. These people should come to their senses about these foreign books which contain nothing about the ancient feelings of our people, and realize that Yomi is nothing more than the place where the dead go.

[A person once asked me, "When we die and go to Yomi, will we go with this body, or will only our spirit go?" I replied, "Since we lose this body in death, and it stays in this clearly visible world, only our spirits will go to Yomi." Whether you are rich or poor, good or evil, when people die, everyone goes to Yomi. ...**]**

Izanami lamented to Izanagi, "I have eaten the food of Yomi." This food of Yomi means that she had eaten food prepared in the oven of Yomi. The reason this is foreboding is because fire is the origin of abstinence and purification. The numberless terrible evils originate from pollution by fire, and these evils have their origins in the spirit of Magatsubi who was formed from the pollution of Yomi. When fire defiles a person, countless evils occur because of the violent nature of this *kami*. Those who wish to pursue the Way of Shintō must rid themselves of the meaningless Chinese disposition, and remember what I have said.

Because of the existence of this evil *kami*, those who wish to love and govern the people must first purify themselves and abhor the fires in the country, and follow the will of the *kami*. Now, what I have been saying is that Izanami did not wish to part with her family [Izanagi], desiring to return to this world, but because the cooking fire of Yomi defiled her, it had thus become impossible for her to return. Ponder these words in *Kojiki*, and never take this terrible defilement of fire lightly! (MNZ 1976, 9:237–41)

ABOUT PURIFICATION

In ancient Japanese this is called *farafi* or *farafe*, and later the meanings of these two words were confused, being understood by people as meaning the same thing. Originally, these were different words. *Farafi* meant to perform purification of one's own volition, while *farafe* comes from the abbreviation of "cause to perform purification" (*farafase*). This is for people who have committed crimes or transgressions. In *Shoki* we see that Susanoo was caused to perform ablutions, which is 祓具, read *farafetumono*. ...

Then there is *misogifarafi*. These two characters (禊祓) should be read as a verb [as opposed to a noun]. *Misogi* means to wash one's body. In the text below we see *kazukite sosogitamau*. ... Even now, when people come out of mourning, they go to the ocean or river and cleanse themselves. Also, lustration by bathing in water comes from the original act of *misogi*. *Farafi* means to discard something, which *Nihon shoki* writes as 拂濯 "wash away." The earlier example from *Shoki* with 濯去 is the same thing, as the character 去 has the same meaning as 除 "rid." This word also has a connection with the word *arafi*, "to wash oneself." Now, *misogi* and *farafi* are by this time nominalized forms, but originally the ancient Japanese used them as verbs; *farafi* is original, and *misogi* also is seen in *Man'yōshū* in Book 3: **amanokafara ni / idetatite / misogitemasi wo** "I should have gone out to the plain of the Milky Way and performed ritual purification. ..."[10] We also find in Book 6: **suga no ne torite / sinofu kusa / farafete masi wo** "I should have pulled out the sedge by the roots and presented it as forget-me-nots for my ablutions. ..."[11]

We also find that the verb *farafimisogasimu* "performed their ablutions and then purified themselves in water" is also seen in the Richū section of *Nihon shoki*. Tradition says *misogi* is to be performed only on the shore by water [river or ocean]. The old records all state this, and this is what the Chinese character 禊 means. *Farafi* has a broader meaning, because it can be performed with or without water ... (MNZ 1976, 9:261–64).

10. From MYS 420.

11. From MYS 948.

The imposition of one thousand tables on Susanoo for his evil conduct in the High Plain of Heaven is also called *farafi*. Therefore, there are two general meanings for *farafi*: one is like the ritual purification with water by Izanagi at the Ahagi Plain (*misogi*), and the other is like exacting a fine. The fine levied on a criminal is reparation of property. Thus, though there are two acts performed here with interrelated purposes, they originally were one and the same act. The example in the Richū section of *Nihon shoki* says, "… the emperor had them perform ablutions for evil and ablutions for good. They went to Nagasu Cape and performed their ablutions and then purified themselves in water." This shows that even criminals were caused to perform purification with water. A criminal offense and defilement are the same thing. The reader should remember what the Great Purification says, "Beginning with the eighty Tomonowo of the Tomonowo, the many administrators on this last day of this the sixth month, now have their various offenses that may have been committed hereby expiated, and you all are cleansed. …

"Let the *kami* Seori Hime who resides in the shoals of the fast river take these offences out to sea. … The diviners of the four provinces will take the defilement out to sea via the great river road and purge them in the water." The act of expiation of crimes committed, and the purification of defilement are exactly the same. … Now, whether you have committed a crime, or have become defiled, it is the law of the ancients that purification be performed according to the extent and nature of the crime or pollution. It can be seen from old records that this law was part of the ceremonies carried out by the court until middle antiquity.

Now, we see two meanings concerning the fine levied on Susanoo. One is the imposition of various articles with which to perform the ablution. *Nihon shoki* writes this as *farafetumono* (祓具). Let us think about the character 具. The record goes on to say, "And they took his spittle and made of it white linen offerings. …" These were used in the purification. Also, in the Yūryaku section of *Nihon shoki*, where it talks about the crime of Hatane, it says, "He expiated his crime with eight horses and eight swords." Also, in an official decree from the Council of State in the fifth month of Enryaku 20 [801] we see, "The court establishes the following in levying fines for purification against a criminal. There will be twenty-eight items for a Great Purification … twenty-six items for a Greater Purification … twenty-two items for a Middle Purification … and twenty-two items for a Lesser Purification." These various items were part of the fine imposed for the purification, and the court established these in accordance to the seriousness of the crime.

First, when Izanagi purified himself in the plain of Ahagi, he threw down the various items he was wearing. In the same way, a criminal must throw away [or give away] his possessions because they have become defiled through his unclean actions. Thus, in later ages, the various items used in purification were put in water, and caused to float away.

Concerning the thousand tables (千位) paid by Susanoo, *Shiki*[12] says that it is the name of a table or dais upon which the articles were placed. This means that it is a table where the items for purification are set, just as a throne where one sits is called a *kurawi*. … According to the seriousness of the crime, the items varied in number. This shows that Susanoo's crimes were of a very grave nature, and so an extreme number, one thousand, was imposed. ... (MNZ 1976, 9:383–85)

CONCERNING YASO MAGATSUBI

I will talk about the word *maga* in a moment. … *Yaso* means much evil. The prefix *ofo* means extreme, and while there is no example of Ofomagatsubi in *Nihon shoki*, there is the name Ofoayatsubi. *Aya* and *maga* have the same basic meaning. … Now, all the evil, wicked events in the world have their origins in the spirit of Magatsubi. …

Let us now look at all the *kami* from Magatsubi until Izunome in detail. First, all the evil and damage that exists in the world comes from the pollution in Yomi. Thus, anciently, all the wicked and evil was called *kitanasi* "filthy" and *maga* "twisted." In *Nihon shoki*, when describing a lying heart, a filthy heart, or an evil heart, the usage is always read as *kitanaki kokoro*. The imperial edicts in *Shoku Nihongi* use the words *kitanaku asiki yatuko* and *kitanaki yatuko*. The liturgies use the ancient usage of *magakoto* when talking about evil events. In *Nihon shoki*, in the Keikō account, we see 過害 "wicked injury" glossed as *maga*; *Kojiki* also has "evil" written as *maga*. Death is written as *magare*, because whether the word is *kitanasi* or *maga*, the meaning is the same: evil. Now, *nafosu* means to rectify evil by turning it into good, "be well" known as *naforu*. Thus, we have already seen where Izanagi washes the defilement away through purification, rectifying the evil and making it good. Defilement is evil, and purification through washing turns that evil into good. In spite of the fact that later generations believe *nafosu* is simply to fix or repair something bent or broken, it is a

12. A record or minutes of lectures held at court on the text of *Nihon shoki* that were held several times during the first two centuries of the Heian era. Only fragments of it are still extant, but *Shaku Nihongi* quotes it rather liberally.

mistake to think that purification fixes the flaws in one's heart. Nevertheless, as I noted above, *maga* in ancient times meant everything evil, and *nafosu* meant to turn all forms of evil into good, to use a contemporary word that all would understand. So, anciently, all good things were called *akasi*, or *kiyosi*, or *nafosi* ... (MNZ 1976, 9:272, 276).

CONCERNING AMATERASU ŌMIKAMI

This name *terasu* "shine" does not exactly mean to shine in heaven. The verb *teru* has been elongated into *terasu* according to ancient Japanese grammar.[13] *Amaterasu* means to reside in heaven and shine down. It is the same as *takafikaru* "to shine high above." And the reason that the character 大 "big" is written as 太 "fat" in the Nobuyoshi manuscript of the *Kojiki* is that Nobuyoshi foolishly altered these to appear wise. ... Now, *Nihon shoki* states, "Hereupon they gave birth to the sun goddess, called Ohohirume no Muchi. Another record says, 'Amaterasu Ohomikami.' Another record has, 'Amaterasu Ohohirume.'"

[The editors of *Nihon shoki* should not have recorded these names for the sun goddess [Ameratsu Ōmikami] as "another record says," but as "She is also known as ..."[14] The reason for this is that the record hereafter in *Shoki* continually refers to her as Amaterasu Ōmikami. ...] One record calls her Amaterasu Ohomikami, while another calls her Ohohirume; *Man'yōshū* calls her Amaterasu Hirume. Thus, this great *kami* is the very sun that exists before our eyes and illuminates the world. Therefore, the moon and sun are created for the first time through this act of purification [by Izanagi]. [Before this, there was no moon or sun. Nonetheless, the learned men of the day say that the moon and sun naturally appear when heaven and earth were formed. They also say that these are natural objects different from Amaterasu and Tsukuyomi, but in what record does it say that? These are simply personal theories from people drowning in Chinese reason based on Chinese works, and they turn their backs on these extremely old records. If the moon and sun existed previous to this event [the purification of Izanagi], then what *kami* did Izanagi's act of purification produce? It says the sun [sun goddess], but if these learned men want to

---

13. This is not quite accurate. The verbal suffix *su* is honorific, elevating the plain verb *teru* and making it more fitting for a *kami* like the sun goddess.

14. Norinaga apparently did not comprehend that the *Shoki* compilers had merely noted that the name of the sun goddess was *recorded* differently in other works. There were variant records, and this is the importance of *Shoki*'s word-usage. Norinaga's suggestion would lessen the importance of these data.

twist the record and say that the *kami* created here is not the sun, then how do we deal with the passage in *Nihon shoki* where it mentions that Izanagi gave birth to the sun and moon? These scholars strain at a gnat and swallow a camel in relation to theories recorded in foreign works, but are not these theories heretical, causing men to disbelieve the true, ancient records of this country in which it is clearly stated that the sun and moon were produced here? And as was stated at the beginning of this chapter, it is a mistake to argue theories on the Chinese basis of this so-called *yin* and *yang* principle. ...] (MNZ 1976, 9: 283–84)

CONCERNING THE *KAMI* TSUKUYOMI

This name should be read *tukuyomi*. *Shoki* records, "Next he gave birth to the moon *kami*. Another record states that he is Tsukuyomi (written as 月弓, 月夜見, and 月読). My master explained the meaning of this name thus: *mi* means to carry, to hold, as in the case of the names Watatsu*mi* and Yamatsu*mi*; so it means the moon that carries the night (*tuki-yo-moti*). Since this is the great *kami* who rules the land of night, such a name is only fitting. We see the older reading of *tukuyomi*. Moon-night is read as *tsukuyo*, which is what we see in *Man'yōshū*. The name of Yomi [the land of the dead] is related. I have one idea about the *mi* in this word, which I have made mention of in the section about Ame no Oshiho Mimi.

Now, this great *kami* is also in heaven and is the moon. Moonlight is recorded in *Man'yōshū* as *tukuyomi no fikari*. There is no doubt that this *kami* is male, but you can be sure by what *Man'yōshū* says, "The beautiful man of the moon, the man of the moon, the wonderful, superior man."[15] And even in *Nihon shoki*, where we see the moon *kami* pull out his sword and slay Ukemochi, which demonstrates that Tsukuyomi acts like a man ... (MNZ 1976, 9:284–85).

CONCERNING TAKE SUSANOO

I will discuss the prefix *take* or *faya* later. *Susa* comes from the word *sabi*, which comes from *susabi*. This is abbreviated to *sabi*, the *susa* being shortened to just *sa* ... and it means "to go forward committing violent acts."

15. Norinaga has created his list based on the poetry found in MYS 985, 1372, and 983. It is interesting that he makes such a strong statement about the gender of this *kami*. Hirata Atsutane, who claimed to have inherited the mantle of the Motoori school after Norinaga's death, stated that the Moon *kami* was actually a female.

Nowo means male. Now, let us look at the washing of the eyes and nose.[16] We only see the washing of these two body parts. There is no washing of the mouth or ears. The reason for this is because the eyes became defiled through the pollution Izanagi had *seen*, and the nose had smelled the putrefied state of things [especially Izanami] in Yomi. Thus, because Izanagi did not partake of anything in Yomi, his mouth was free from defilement. And though he heard Izanami's words, and heard the sound of the *kami* of thunder, and had in fact come in contact with their voices, there is no defilement or pollution in sound [in the voice]. Therefore, the true cause of defilement or pollution comes through contact with sight and smell. Now within these two, the defilement beheld through the eyes was light and free of stain, and that is why we had the birth of good *kami* like the moon and sun.[17] The moon *kami* is called a wicked *kami* by Amaterasu in *Nihon shoki*, but this is in relation to only one action. On the whole, the moon *kami* was good. … Because the defilement of the nose—the smell was evil and putrid—was strong almost unto death, Susanoo was born an evil *kami* (MNZ 1976, 9:285–86, 342).

CONCERNING THE THREE PRECIOUS CHILDREN

Regarding the birth of the three precious children, the character 子 "child" is used not only for *kami*, but also for the islands and territory that Izanagi and Izanami gave birth to. … The three precious children are seen in *Shoki* through the words [of Izanagi], "I wish to give birth to precious children to rule the creations below heaven." An annotational note says that the character 珍 is to be read *udu* "precious." Here the three great *kami* are born. In the Jinmu record we also see the character 珍 used in the name Utsu Hiko. … The theory of my master is that *udu* means "noble and dignified."

It goes without saying that the jeweled necklace refers to pearls on a string both the men and women anciently put around their necks, as well as wrapped around their wrists and ankles, as well as jewels used as decoration on people's clothing. In the story of Hoori, we find that he had decorations known as a "jeweled necklace." Also, in *Shoki* we see where Susanoo had a string of five hundred jewels around his neck. …

16. The act that gave birth to the sun goddess and the moon *kami*. Izanagi washed his left then right eye as an act of ritual purification, and the sun and moon *kami* were born in that order. Susanoo was born when Izanagi washed his nose.

17. It should be noted that in *Shoki*, after the moon *kami* slays Ukemochi, the sun goddess declares, "'You are an evil *kami*! You are no longer allowed to dwell here!' And that is why the moon and sun are not seen together." Norinaga's reply to this is below.

The characters 汝命 "you" should be read *nagamikoto*, where the *ga* functions as a possessive. In the edicts in *Shoku Nihongi* we find 汝賀命 *na ga mikoto* in the words "[The emperor] said, 'You should now inherit [the throne] and rule. …'" Also, in *Kojiki*, in a song by Takeshi Uchi we find that he calls Ōsazaki "you, the prince." This kind of usage is very prevalent in *Kojiki*. As I have stated previously, in later eras the personal pronoun *na* was used as a pejorative, but in the ancient era it was a word of respect. And that is why the deferential suffix *mikoto* was also added. …

The High Plain of Heaven, as I have mentioned previously, points to heaven. The sun goddess even now looks down upon us, right before our eyes, and just as the words of Izanagi when he entrusted her with her duty, she was given eternal rule over heaven, and it is clear that she shines down on the oceans and the myriad countries of earth. [In spite of this, the learned men of the day argue that she set up her capital in the province of Yamato, or in Afumi, or in Buzen. These are all wretched theories. These mischievous theories state that because she is the founder of the imperial family, her virtue *was like the sun*, used metaphorically, and that is why she is called the sun goddess, but they do not think that she is actually the sun in the sky. They also believe that "heaven" is simply the great firmament, and since it has no shape or substance like our land and so on, they believe that there is no such existence because it is not rational. Thus, while the records call it the High Plain of Heaven, it is simply a name for her capital, so we should understand that all the events in the record surrounding her actually took place in our land. These are incorrect, dogmatic theories from people drowning in the learning of Chinese works. In general Chinese people are trammeled by conventional wisdom based on what they can see and hear in the present, and they are unable to process information that comes from rationality based on inexplicable and mysterious events. Because of this, people in our country have blindly become accustomed to this reasoning, so these people then take the wondrous events of the divine age and force these into the framework of conventional wisdom, but in the end this is wrong. Among these theories, the one stating that the capital of the sun goddess is in this land or that land is truly far-fetched.

On the whole, if one believes that the sun goddess is an entity different from the orb in the sky and ruled in our land, then how do you interpret the story about her hiding in the heavenly cave? At that time, even if she were in the cave for a small amount of time, but later then passed away, the world from that time onward would have been cast into eternal darkness. But that did not happen, and the world has been illuminated from the ancient past. How do people explain this? If people then claim that she did not pass away, but has been on the earth all these years, then where did she move after we entered the age of humans? Or why did she withdraw from the land she ruled over? This theory is completely incomprehensible. If she had actually ruled over Yamato or Afumi, then naturally her posterity would come forward and claim their right to rule. And what reason would there be for her to abandon her capital and journey to the land in the west?]. … (MNZ 1976, 9:287–90).

CONCERNING THE LAND OF THE NIGHT

First, the phrase 食国 is a general term referring to the land that the descendants of the sun goddess rule over. The verb *wosu* means "to partake of something." **[**Shoki glosses the graph 食 as *miwosisu* and food is glossed as *wosimono*. In the Book 12 of *Man'yōshū* the particle *wosi* is represented with the *kungana* 食.**]** However, when something is internalized, be it seen, heard, understood, or eaten, these all have the same meaning, and the verbs *misu* "see," *kikosu* "hear," *sirasu* "know," and *wosu* "eat" are often used interchangeably, and whether one means the land that the sovereign rules over or the territory that he controls, the verb *sirasu* or *wosu* is used. The verb *kikosimesu* is also used. As one sees something, hears something, understands something, eats something, our lord rules over the land, he controls that territory—he has possession of it, has ownership of it. …

Now, the sun goddess rules the day, and the moon *kami* rules over the night, and they both dwell in the High Plain of Heaven. Some may question why the verb 食国 "govern the land" is used when they do not dwell in this land, but my master's theory states, "The word *kuni* refers to anything that has boundaries. In the dialect of the eastern countries there is the word *kune* 'fence,' and this is the same word. Therefore, when Susanoo journeyed up to heaven Amaterasu Ōmikami said, 'You have come here with the intention of robbing me of my land.' Susanoo was given the command 'to rule over the oceans.' Izanagi later said, 'You will not rule over the land I entrusted to you.' Originally, the posterity of the sun goddess were entrusted to rule over everything under the heavens, be it the heavens, the land, or the oceans. …"

However, the record does not say that the sun goddess rules over the day, but that she rules over the High Plain of Heaven, and the reason that in contrast to the sun goddess, Tsukuyomi was commanded to rule over the night, or the land of the night, is because this is temporally limited in scope. [While there is the contrast of night and day, day is the principal element.] ... (MNZ 1976, 9:292).

ON UNDERSTANDING THE DIVINE AGE

People debate the divine age from the point of view of human experience. [The learned scholars of the world cannot comprehend the mysterious reasoning of the divine age. They simply twist it, arguing from the perspective of all the men in the world, and this because they are drowning in Chinese learning.] I comprehend human experience by using the perspective of the divine age. Let me give a detailed discussion on the significance of this view. The reasoning of the state of the world, of the continual cycle of good and evil from generation to generation, from era to era, comes from the original state of things, great and small, at the beginning of the divine age. The significance of that logic started with the intercourse of the male and female *kami*, resulting in the birth of the various islands, and the many *kami*; thus, with the birth of the three precious children [sun goddess, Tsukuyomi, and Susanoo], Izanagi assigned each a responsibility, giving them charge over some sphere. From the act of intercourse until the birth of the countries and the *kami*, everything that existed was good. [However, we must say that the seed of evil is planted when the female *kami* spoke before the male.] With the birth of the fire *kami*, the great mother *kami* [Izanami] died, thus allowing evil to enter the world for the first time. [Through this evil, it is only reasonable that the people of the world should die. The reason for death, be it sickness or anything else, is because all these things are evil. ...]

And thus, because of this evil, Izanami went to the land of Yomi, which is actually a move from good to evil, and since she has remained in Yomi forever, we see that evil remains in the world, it being the source of the same. [Until Izanami gave birth to the fire god, she was a good *kami* who had given birth to various things [*kami* and islands]. But after, she entered Yomi and stayed there for a long time and became an evil *kami*, and it is here that she tried to kill one thousand people a day. Upon becoming a wicked *kami*, she became the source from which Magatsubi was produced.]

Now as for the male *kami*, he [Izanagi] went after Izanami and entered this land [Yomi], unexpectedly coming in contact with pollution, because the entire world had turned evil. However, Izanagi quickly returned to the visible world, and performed expiation. [He performed this ritual to rectify evil and return to good, to change the evil of the world into good. The Way of humanity is based upon this principle, to perform good.]

The reason that Magatsubi came into existence is due to the filth in Yomi. As Izanagi expiated and cleansed himself from the defilement, he was able to give birth to the three noble children. [However, even among these three, Susanoo was an evil *kami*, and the reason that he was violent and destructive was because though Izanagi was a good *kami* from beginning to end, he came in contact with the evil of Yomi.] Finally, having Amaterasu rule the High Plain of Heaven meant that everything returned to the state of good, and this is how things should be in the world.

Now the reader should diligently ponder these acts, understanding that this is the condition of this world, that evil comes from good, and that this is the principle of common interaction. Also, people should understand that though we have this type of evil in the world, in the end it will not overcome good. [Though Izanami killed one thousand people a day, Izanagi gave birth to fifteen hundred people a day, displacing the force of evil. Because of the violence of Susanoo, Amaterasu hid herself in the Ama no Iwato cave, but she came back out after a while, shining upon this world ever since, and the myriad *kami* banished Susanoo from heaven. This is that principle at work.] The reader also should understand that a person should avoid and abhor evil, instead performing good acts. How mysterious! How wondrous! How profound! How very profound! (MNZ 1976, 9:294–96)

LITURGIES

Book 17 of *Man'yōshū* contains the poem: **nakatomi no / futo noritogoto / ififarafe** "The Nakatomi speak the thick [words of] the liturgy and perform purification. ..."[18] In *Shoki* we see the words "They put Ame no Koyane in charge of the thick words of the liturgies of expiation. 'Thick words of the liturgies' is read *futo norito*." In the liturgy of the Great Purification, we find the following, "Recite the words of the thick liturgy of heaven from the Nakatomi family." This refers to the recitation of the purification liturgy. ... This is the purpose of liturgies. The etymology is *noru* "speak" *toki* "expound" *goto* "words." *Noru* is not necessarily the commands of high-ranking people, but points to saying and asking things of a person. The word *toku* "to explain" is written in *Nihon shoki* with the character 諄

18. In MYS 4031.

"to teach and enlighten," in the compound verb 太諄辭, and the contemporary word *kudoku* "entreat someone" is close in meaning to this. …[19]

"Express words of congratulation." These words are also seen at the end of this book of *Kojiki*.[20] The characters 禱白而 should be read *negimaturite*.[21] The character 禱 is also read *fogi* and *nomi*. When we consider these words from the angle of the ancient vocabulary, *fogu* is a phrase of prayer through praise. *Nomu* is a prayer of supplication. The verb *negu* includes both meanings. Now in regard to what constituted the congratulatory, thick words of this liturgy, *Shoki* mentions, "… Ame no Koyane, the distant ancestor of the Nakatomi, enumerated words of celebration for the *kami*." We also see the phrase "[Imibe Obito] proffered a liturgy full of generous and affectionate words of praise." And other examples aside from in this record of words of congratulation include examples from the various liturgies, and gathering these examples and considering them, these words were used to praise the various objects of offering that Futotama had collected and held [in the branch he had decorated]. Thus, these are said to be divine words of prayer and praise … (MNZ 1976, 9:368–69).

CONCERNING THE NETHER LAND

All examples of land of Tokoyo "nether land " in the ancient period can be grouped into three meanings: one, it points to Tokoyo Naganakidori Tokoyo Omoikane "Eternal-World-Endlessly-Crying-Bird." This is the meaning of *tokoyo*, as mentioned above. Two … our land (Japan) is eternal and unchanging. The meaning of the character 常 is "to be unchanging." Three points to the actual land of Tokoyo. These three all use the same character set (常世), but the three meanings are different and are not interchangeable. Now, as for the meaning of the nether land, it is not the name of a country. It points to an area that is very remote from the imperial land, no matter what direction you travel. The nether land is the name broadly used for this land, a land that is difficult to reach. Thus, the word refers to a remote place. Anciently, all the usages of the nether land had no other

19. Linguistically, there are a few problems with this theory, the greatest being that *norito* is written with a type-one character (*two*) while the *to* of *toku* (found in *kudoku*) is written with a type-two character; therefore, the two words are etymologically unrelated.

20. Those congratulatory words are spoken by Ōkuninushi in the section where he cedes authority over his land to Ninigi.

21. Onoda's textual work on *Kojiki* reconstructs the interlinear gloss as *fokimawosite* (1977:126).

meaning than this. … Because this place, as I have explained above, is a place that must be reached by crossing the distant oceans—regardless of the direction you travel—all the myriad countries other than the imperial country belong to the designation of Tokoyo (MNZ 1976, 10:8–10).

CONCERNING WORSHIP

Of all the usages of *agamimafe* in the ancient lexicon many have to do with "being in the presence of a *kami*." At the end of this [the twelfth book of *Shoki*] section, we see a command from Amaterasu where she says, "Hold ritual services for [my spirit] as if I were here before you." Also she said, "Omoikane will receive my words and will officiate in worship for me." In the second book of *Kojiki*, in the record of the Mizugaki emperor [Sujin] in the dream of the emperor we have the words of the command of Ōmononushi, "If you worship me [as if I were here], then no disease will appear from my divine curse. …"

Also, the meaning of the constant use of the noun *mafe* "before" is a bit difficult to interpret, but having pondered the usages, [I believe that] *mafe* has the same meaning as "throne," and is used in reference to the throne where the *kami* originally sat. So the word originally referred to the august throne of the *kami*, but eventually as it came to refer to the *kami*, the usage of "rule before me" came to mean "rule for me." If you ponder the passages quoted above, you will understand this (MNZ 1976, 10:14).

Shrines to the *kami* of heaven and earth. *Nihon shoki* records this as "shrines to the *kami* of heaven and earth," and as "*kami* of heaven and the state. …" *Ryō no gige* explains, "Heavenly *kami* are the kind that are worshipped at the great shrines of Ise, Yamashiro, Kamo, Sumiyoshi, and Izumo. Earthly *kami* refer to the great ones of Ōmiwa, Ōyamato, Katsuragi, Kamo, and Izumo. The great heavenly *kami* at Izumo refers to Susanoo. …" Heavenly *kami* are those who reside in heaven, or those who descended to earth from heaven. Earthly *kami* are those who reside in Japan (MNZ 1976, 10:27).

THE DIVINE EDICT

In reference to the line "According to the words of Takami Musubi and Amaterasu … ," whenever the *kami* make a declaration, there are instances where these two *kami* are listed together, as above, and there are instances where Amaterasu is listed before Takami Musubi, and there are places where Takami Musubi has been dropped and only Amaterasu is listed as the subject. The reason for this is because Amaterasu is the paramount and Takami Musubi is the subordinate *kami*. The reason I can state that is because Takami Musubi does not rule over the High Plain of Heaven. It was Amaterasu who was given charge of ruling over the High Plain of Heaven by command of the great *kami* Izanagi, and it this divine decree that we are addressing here where she transfers that right to rule to her child and orders him to descend down to the land.

However, Takami Musubi dwelt in the High Plain of Heaven from the beginning when heaven and earth were created. All things and events in the world were utterly given birth through the power and virtue of his binding spirit. And that is why even this decree was given with both *kami* present, and thus he is worshipped as a distant ancestor of the imperial grandchildren (MNZ 1976, 10:44–45).

INHERITING THE HEAVENLY THRONE

In *Man'yōshū* this term 天津日継 "heavenly-sun-inheritance" is read *ama no fitugi*. This is named because it has reference to one who receives the great, divine commission from the great *kami* of the sun in the heavens, and these people undertake the great work of ruling over the land through successive generations. In the record of Tenmu, after the phrase "recited a eulogy about the successive rulers and their ascensions to the throne" the text notes, "Anciently ascension to the throne was called *fitugi*."[22] The princes that have the right to ascend to this position were called *fitugi no miko* "princes of the sun inheritance." Thus, the meaning noted above surely cannot be altered, and anybody would think that this is as it should be, but at the moment I have a different idea about this one section. The character 継 means "to provide," so perhaps it is known as the inheritance of the heavenly realm because the great *kami* of heaven provides and bequeaths things and those in authority receive and accept them. Things that are provided and bequeathed refers to the many offerings presented by the masses under the heavens, so this by extension is "a thing" bestowed by Amaterasu and received by the emperor. Among the various objects that are presented, rice stalks are the chief among these, and the reason for this is seen in

22. Norinaga is incorrect here, as this actually appears in the record of Jitō, and not Tenmu.

Shoki, where Amaterasu "also decreed, 'I will bestow this rice from the sacred paddy of mine in the High Plain of Heaven upon my son ...'" (MNZ 1976, 10:114–15).

CONCERNING A FIRE DRILL

The characters 鑽出火 should be read *fi wo kiri idete* "drill and start a fire." In *Wamyōshō* the character 火鑽 "fire drill" is glossed as *fikiri*, and 燧 "flint" is read as *fiuti*. When starting a fire, there are differences between flints and sparks. In the second book of *Kojiki* in the story of Yamato Takeru there is the line "and using a flint he caused a counterfire." This idea of a flint is common knowledge in the world. In the ancient period fires that were abhorred and purified were all started by using a fire drill. Even up to the present the Great Shrine of Ise uses this type of fire to cook the rice for their offerings ... (MNZ 1976, 10:130).

ABOUT NINIGI[23]

Nigisi is simply a prefix of honor. ... *Amatu fidaka* is seen in the Great Purification, where it says, "*Ofoyamato fidakami no Kuni*." My master says, "The *kami* are praising the land of Yamato, praised for being settled on all fronts. The higher the ordered firmament is, the greater the land. This is the metaphor. As always, the sun resides in the ordered heavens, and thus, the heaven is high (*fidaka*), and this has been the way of saying it from ancient times. ..." The name Fono Ninigi comes from the word for rice ear (*fo*). *Ni* refers to the ripening of the ear. ... *Gi* is an abbreviation of *kafi* (*kai*), which means an abundance of rice ears (MNZ 1976, 10:142–44).

CONCERNING PRINCES

All males are *fiko* and females are *fime*, and these are appellations of praise. The first syllable, *fi*, refers to the mysterious power in all things. When *Shoki* talks about the birth of Amaterasu it says, "The two *kami* were pleased, and said, 'Though our children have been numerous, none have

23. *Kojiki* records his full name as Ame Nigisi Kuninigisi Amatu Fidaka Fiko Fono Ninigi.

been as wonderful or mysterious as this child.'" And in the Seinei record of *Shoki* it notes, "Of all his children [Yūryaku] recognized that this one had an especially wondrous omen." Based on this, *fiko* and *fime* have the meaning of wondrous ... (MNZ 1976, 10:143).

CONCERNING THE IMPERIAL REGALIA[24]

Tamano Oya made the mirror and hung it on the middle branch of the sacred *sakaki* tree, with the jewels hung on the upper branches, as seen in the section on the Ama no Iwato cave story. At that time, the sun goddess had hidden in the cave, and the *kami* used these objects to entice Amaterasu out of the cave. That is why this mirror is also called Okishitama Kagami "the spirit that prays and invites."

Susanoo found the Kusa Nagi sword when he cut open the tail of the eight-headed monster. Because of its mysterious nature, Susanoo presented it to Amaterasu.

The jewels *(tama)* added to the mirror and sword only have relation to the mirror (*okisitama*),[25] and the sword came from a different time.[26] *Nihon shoki* says, "Amaterasu presented the jewels, mirror, and sword, the three imperial regalia, to Amatu Fikofiko Foninigi." Now that we have discussed somewhat concerning these three imperial regalia, let us discuss the principle of order: should it be mirror, sword, jewel, or mirror, jewel, sword? In *Kojiki* as well as in *Nihon shoki*, the jewels are noted first; *Nihon shoki* puts emphasis here by placing the character 及 "and" between the jewel and the mirror. The reason for this is because up to the reign of the Mizugaki Palace [Sujin], the court worshipped the mirror and sword in different places. The objects the emperor possessed were not the original sword and mirror from the ancient days of the divine age; only the jewel was original. That is why the jewel is noted first when Amaterasu gave the three symbols to Ninigi. Therefore, after the reign of Emperor Sujin, it became habitual to mention the jewel first, and that is why it is recorded so in *Kojiki* and *Nihon shoki*, but it was not that way from the divine age. Of course, it is readily apparent when we talk about what Amaterasu gave to Ninigi that the mirror was the first given. Then she gave him the sword, and then the jewel. ... Of these three symbols, the jewel was the least important. Nevertheless,

---

24. Consisting of the mirror, sword, and jewels.
25. Because *tama* can mean either spirit or jewel.
26. Meaning it had no relation to the incident at the cave.

the jewel is the only regalia of the three that the emperor possessed that was original. Now it is the most precious of the imperial regalia (MNZ 1976, 10:155–57).

CONCERNING THE MIRROR BEING THE SPIRIT OF THE SUN GODDESS

As it says in the liturgy for the governors of the Izumo shrine ... "the spirit was caused to ascend upon the mirror," the spirit of the Great heavenly is affixed to the mirror. [The general word *spirit* is used both as an action [verb] and a state [noun]. If we talk about this *kami*, she actually resides in and rules over the High Plain of Heaven. It is the *action* of the spirit of this *kami* that shines down upon the world, and the mirror is the state of this spirit. Now, her spirit has fixed upon the mirror, and it is an object, but the power to act has also been attached to the mirror. The sun goddess, however, has transferred all her energy to act to the mirror, and within the visible body residing in the High Plain of Heaven there is no power. Because the spirits of *kami* are very wondrous and mysterious, though they dwell here on earth, they do not diminish in presence in another sphere; though they do not diminish in presence in another sphere, these spirits are completely endowed with power here. In spite of the body being divided among a myriad places, no matter where it be, the power of that spirit does not decrease.]

However, the spirit of Amaterasu resides completely in this mirror. How noble and how awe-inspiring! Never look upon these things lightly! ... It is clear that this mirror is the most precious of the regalia (MNZ 1976, 10:159).

CONCERNING *YASAKA NO MAGATAMA*

In *Magatama-kō* by Yokoi Chiaki[27] it says, "According to the ideas of my master, *yasaka no magatama* means *ya* 'more' and *saka* is 'true brightness.' *Sa* is interchangeable with *ma* 'true.' Therefore, the name originated from

27. Yokoi Chiaki (1738–1801) was a scholar of Kokugaku from Aichi Prefecture. He joined Norinaga's school in 1785. He used some of his own money to assist in the publication of *Kojiki-den*. He was a prolific writer, but most of his works were lost through fires. The full title of this work is *Yasaka no magatama-kō*, date unknown.

iya saaka no magatama. …" According to this theory, the meaning of *yasaka* is "how bright." I found this theory appealing, and as I have further pondered it, I believe that the word *magatama* "curved jewel" has nothing to do with the shape of the jewel. The characters 勾玉 are loan graphs, and the word *maga* appears in the section under Emperor Tarashi Nakatsu Hiko [Chūai] in *Kojiki* where we have "there are various kinds of treasures that dazzle the eyes." And in the same section in *Shoki* it says, "This land is full of eye-dazzling gold, silver, and brilliant colors." The words *makagayaku* "eye-dazzling" gets shortened to *maga*. The idea of "eye-dazzling" appears in tales, where examples such as "your eyes also sparkle" or in the vulgar language, "astonish someone" or "be gleaming" have much the same meaning. Thus, *yasaka magatama* means "how bright these jewels that dazzle the eyes." This is the name of jewels that are the most superior in the world, glisteningly brilliant, and exquisite. …

In spite of this, from ancient times people who understood the meaning disappeared and they only understood the meaning of the words to be *maga* "curved" *tama* "jewel," which is a mistaken interpretation. In the present there are many examples of curved jewels being excavated from the ground, and as they have a slightly bent shape they interpret these to be *magatama* from the ancient era. And while these are recklessly called 曲玉 "curved jewels," the currently discovered jewels are not that beautiful. People believe that because so many of these curved jewels are being excavated from the ground that there must have been a lot of these anciently, and they do not appreciate these as anything special. What were known as *magatama* anciently were rare in the world, and these were beautiful jewels. They were not common like the things we label as *magatama* in the present. Thus you may know that these anciently were not named thus because of their shape, even if the shape as we find in the present is slightly curved. What wonder is there in the shape being slightly curved? And yet in the Chūai record in *Shoki* we find the following, "Itote, the founder of the rulers of the district of Ito in Tsukushi, heard that the emperor was coming, and uprooted a *sakaki* tree with many branches. He put the tree on the bow of his ship. On the upper branches, he hung *yasaka* jewels. On the middle branch he hung a white copper mirror, and on the lower he hung a large sword. He headed to Hiko Island and presented the tree to the emperor. He said, 'Let these things that I boldly present to you be representative symbols. May your reign be magnificent and auspicious like these curved jewels.'"

As it is said that generally these jewels are curved, and the characters used to represent the word also include 曲 "curved," and as the reading of these characters was attached because they superficially matched, it is difficult to comprehend why some interpret this comment to be that these jewels are "magnificent and auspicious because they are curved." Now, the verb *magaru* certainly refers to the unsatisfactory nature of some object, so why would someone then add 妙 *tafe* "mysterious" to this? Thus, this line in the ancient documents had "mysterious like these *yasaka magatama*." The character 勾 *maga* originally was a loan character, and with that character, the compiler of *Shoki* created the word 曲妙. These characters appear in Chinese texts [such as the *Book of Changes*], "by an ever-varying adaptation he completes [the nature of] all things without exception." Also "the wonder of exhausting intertwined possibilities." With these examples, there is no other explanation than that this sentence [from *Shoki*] is using the Chinese characters stylistically, and the reading of *tafe ni* is based on nothing more than an ancient reading tradition. Therefore, there is no basis for using the graph 曲 "curved" in this sentence. All examples from *Shoki* are tainted with philosophies from Chinese works and in many of these instances the ancient meaning has been lost and that is why one is disappointed [with *Shoki*]. If the reader is not careful, he will certainly become confused ... (MNZ 1976, 10:201–2).

THE THREE SPIRITS OF SARUTABIKO

At this time events caused Sarutabiko's spirit to split into three entities. [There is a theory by a person from Ise that these three spirits of Sarutabiko represent his three wives. His statement that there are many examples where the spirit is compared to a wife is without foundation. It is a deficient and incorrect theory.] In the Jinmyōchō section [of *Engi shiki*] there are three *kami* worshipped at the Azaka Shrine in the Ishi District of Ise Province. The present shrine is known as Azaka Shrine, and has been divided among two villages, Ōasaka and Koasaka Village. Both appear in the same forest, and the names appear in ancient texts, both written with three characters. It is difficult to discern which shrine is the older and original.

Now, the *kami* of this shrine, Azaka, anciently was one who engaged in some violent acts, and in the *Yamato hime no mikoto seiki* it says, "In the eighteenth year [of Suinin], the emperor traveled to Fujikata and resided in the Katahi Palace in Azaka. As time passed, after four years he worshipped the spirits. At this time he resided at Mine in Azaka. However, at this time a sacred and violent *kami* blocked the way so that if one hundred people traveled, fifty would perish. If forty passed through, the *kami* would kill twenty. During this time of sacred violence [a person known as] Ōwakago was presented at the court of Yamato Hime, and he outlined the acts of that *kami*, and she commanded, "You will present to the *kami* a variety of handmade items from me, and this will pacify and calm the *kami*." She sent him back. It was determined that a shrine be built to this *kami* on the peak of Mount Azaka, and people worshipped this *kami*, which pacified and calmed him ..." (MNZ 1976, 10:210–11).

THE CURSE OF THE HOOK

[In the hook story of Hohodemi], the meaning of 淤煩鉤 **obodi** is "great hook." Consider that in one variation of the story in *Nihon shoki*, it says, "The *kami* [of the sea] presented the hook to Hohodemi, with the following instructions, 'When you wish to give this hook back to your older brother, say to the hook, "An honorably plain hook, a hook of chaos, of poverty, of stupidity." After you have said this, throw the hook with your hand behind your back.'"[28] While the second syllable, *bo*, is voiced, the word can also be said with the syllable voiceless. This word appears in various books in *Man'yōshū*, written many times as 鬱 or 悒, read **ofo**. In Book 4 of the anthology there is the stanza **asa wiru kumo no ofosiku** "and like the clouds that hang low in the morning, (I can only see) dimly ..." (MYS 677). It has the meaning of "ambiguous. ..."

According to *Kanjikō* from my master, 須須鉤 **susudi** means "'random,' as can be seen in the words **fuse yataki sususi kisofi** 'as the gentlemen come forward, competing for (her hand), like smoke from the burning of thatch)... '" (MYS 1809). Here is an example of one competing and losing awareness of themselves. *Kojiki*'s example of *susudi* is written as *susu no midi* "hook of chaos." This is also means "unaware. ... "

The word 貧鉤 **maditi** "hook of poverty" is also found in *Nihon shoki*, and this reading is quite ancient. **Madi** is perhaps a contraction of *madusi* "poor." Or perhaps *madusi* comes from an original *madisi*.

The word 宇流鉤 **uruti** appears in *Shoki* as **urukedi** "hook of stupidity."

28. These are words of a curse meant to animate the hook. Here, however, though *Nihon shoki* represents this as 大鉤, this likely is a play on words, as *opo* means "plain, common" as well as "large." The interpretation here should be "a plain, common hook." The word in *Kojiki*, however, is clearly *obo*, which may be "dim, vapid" (cf. Kōnoshi and Yamaguchi 2007:131). It is ironic that Norinaga's own quote from MYS 677 underscores and supports what modern scholars have said.

That is the meaning of this word. In the record of Keikō there is the word **oroke** "lose one's senses," so perhaps these are the same meaning. …

Now, the four hooks noted above should all be read *di* according to the reading gloss found in *Nihon shoki*. I have two thoughts on this. First, the *ti* is the same as *sati* "game," meaning something the hunter obtains. The reason for this is that the lost fishing hook originally had been lucky for Umi Sachibiko to catch fish. The meaning is based on the fact that this hook has been cursed and now it will do the opposite and be unlucky in catching anything. … The second thought is that the character 鉤 "hook" originally was 釣 and a later scribe was trying to be smart and thought that it was a mistaken character and corrected it to 鉤 … (MNZ 1976, 10:260–62).

ABOUT EMPEROR JINMU

The great name Kamu Yamato Iware Hiko was given in praise because Jinmu moved his capital to Yamato, and ruled the Empire. … He is called *kamu* "divine" and *yamato*, and I feel no need to explain why these two names have been added. It is also unclear what the origin of the praiseworthy name of *ifare* is.[29] … The name of this emperor, Jinmu, is a posthumous name modeled after Chinese tradition. *Nihon shoki shiki* tells us, "The scholars said that the posthumous names from Jinmu on were selected and presented by Afumi Mifune." And this is exactly the case. It is also said that these came from the era of Emperor Kanmu. …

Let us ponder the succession of the throne. Ituse was the eldest son of Fukiaezu, and he should have succeeded to the imperial reign. Therefore, Iware Hiko and his two brothers Inafi and Mikeno were employed in the service of Ituse. Ituse died early before the conferment of the reign over the central land took place. Though he died before the imperial work could be finished, and though the records are scant about his reign, we know that the others served him, and so we should think of him as having reigned. If at this time Iware Hiko had already ascended and taken power, since Inahi and Mikeno are his elder brothers, they should have had their names recorded when Jinmu took counsel with his brethren. But this is not so because the record only speaks of Ituse. Therefore, if *Kojiki* recorded the ac-

29. It is clear that it is a place name. Ledyard (1976) discusses the nature of this name and the idea that it can be linked back to the Korean Peninsula.

tual state of affairs, then though the record says, "Ituse took counsel with his younger brother Waka Mikeno (Iware Hiko)," then they should have completed the imperial work, with the empire already under his rule. This would be the first words of his reign, and Ituse would be the first ruler noted. Now, when Ituse passed away, the second brother, Inahi, should have succeeded to the imperial inheritance. But considering the last child, Iware Hiko, inherited the throne, we see that anciently, an heir was established from among the various princes, and it did not necessarily have to have been just one prince who was established. … Thus, among these four brothers, Itsuse and Iware Hiko were established as heirs to the throne (MNZ 1976, 10:294, 318–20).

ABOUT EMPEROR SUJIN

The title *fatukuni sirasisi* "The First to Rule the Land" was attached at a later date. This title was not used during the reign of Emperor Sujin and he was not known as this during his era. In the Emperor Jinmu record of *Nihon shoki* it says, "And that is why we have the old saying that states, 'In Kashiwara of Unebi, the base pillars of the palace were made sturdy, and the roof rafters were raised high to heaven. And the emperor who first ruled the empire. … '" Here, the compiler [of *Nihon shoki*] is praising Emperor Jinmu, and the reason for this is because before Jinmu's time no one subjugated the far-off districts of the country. Jinmu was the first to extend imperial rule, and it was during his reign that the empire was peaceful. Now the usage above of "first" modifies "rule." A person might ask, "What about having it modify 'country'?" In the first place, country means a land under the rule of a sovereign, also called *wosu kuni*. In relation to the entire country, however, when we reach the reign of Emperor Sujin, the usage of "first to rule" means that this was the first time for him to rule over the land. This is what this usage refers to (MNZ 1976, 11:63–64).

ௐ

SANDAIKŌ

Hattori Nakatsune | 1791

[Nakatsune borrowed a draft of Norinaga's *Tenchizu* "Diagram of Heaven and Earth" in 1788. Based on this simple diagram and explanation Nakatsune sketched out a draft of his own interpretation of this realm and other worldly realms, titled *Tenchi shohatsu-kō* "A Treatise on the Beginning of Heaven and Earth" (1789). The title is based on the opening line of *Kojiki*, "When heaven and earth first appeared and there was movement. … " Nakatsune later reworked this into the current text of *Sandaikō*. This work attempts to fashion a coherent theology of life and death based on the creation and evolution of three realms: heaven, earth, and the afterlife.]

In relation to the state of heaven, earth, the imperial land, and the beginning of the formation of these, foreign theories, whether they be Buddhist or Confucian, are all ideas of the disputant's mind, views of the limits of one's understanding, thoughts on how life should be, mere guesses and imaginative fables. Among these, the theories of India are simply like women's fairy tales, and as these are blind speculation, we need not discuss them any further. Also, the theories from China deal with the deep logic of things, but since they represent man-made ideas, we might believe them when we hear them, but upon pondering deeply, you realize that the so-called logic of the universe, *yin* and *yang*, the eight boundaries, and the five principles are titles given by the debaters to objects that never originally existed. This is true of almost everything, and as this logic has come about in the same fashion, the Chinese discussions about heaven, earth, and the myriad creations also follow this development of reason, and as such are all blind traditions. The reason of things has no limit, and since it is not within the sphere of human understanding and discussion, we cannot believe what people say about heaven and earth when they base it on their reasoning. The only things that men can think and know are those things before their very eyes, or what their hearts can feel, or what can be calculated. When we deal with subjects that fall outside this sphere, no matter how much we may contemplate, there is no way to *know*. Thus, will we be able to comprehend the beginning and end of the creation of heaven and earth, the various myriad creations, and man who was created after myriad millennia of years?

Hereupon, the two *kami*, Izanagi and Izanami, created our imperial country, that country in which Amaterasu resides, the country over which the imperial grandson has governed together with heaven and earth from ancient times, a country greater in superiority and excellence than all other nations. Because this country is the father of the four seas, it heals and corrects the hearts of man and, unlike the foreign countries, does not put on airs and expound falsehoods. We know the truth about the beginning of the creation of heaven and earth, and without adding one whit of our own ideas the truth has been handed down from the divine age in its purity. This represents truth without vain deceptions. People say the ideas of China are deeply logical, believed by many to be true, while they say that Japanese ideas are shallow, based on nothing logical. While this may be how one thinks, in reality Chinese ideas are blind tales, and ours are those of the truth. As time has passed, we have shown in detail that these various ways of thinking [by foreigners] are erroneous. These true traditions [of Japan] do not differ in the least. The reason for all this is because lately people have come from countries far in the West who let their hearts float upon the seas, coming continually, and study this great country of ours. The country is round, and the sun and the moon float around in the sky, and this differs greatly from ancient Chinese theories, and so all their logic equals mere guessing—tales no one can believe.

Now the ancient traditions of the imperial country state there was one globe in the sky, and all objects follow after this. Taking all this information together, we can show that even now, there is not one fact amiss. Thus, we see that the ancient traditions are correct. And these people from far-off countries of the West come to our country, study us, and ponder about various things. They reflect on the great sky, and though there are many aspects of the Chinese intellect that surpass us, they are confined to the sphere of [the physical] senses. There are many objects not in the sphere of sense, like the beginning of the sun and moon of the marvelous country that lies beyond human comprehension. If you think about it, these foreign countries all have their own traditions, and these, like India and China, are all later imaginations. The traditions of the imperial country do not belong to this category. First, the imperial land is where *kami* speak, unlike foreign lands that appear intelligent and speak loudly, arguing about everything. . . .

First Diagram: Heaven is like a circle. The circle is only a temporary illusion. In reality it does not exist. All diagrams that follow are thus metaphorical. Within this sphere there were three *kami*: Ame no Minaka Nushi, Takami Musubi, and Kamu Musubi.

Second Diagram: In the midst of this sphere, diagram two, there is one substance resembling floating oil. This substance, which appeared in the sphere of heaven, was given birth to by Takami Musubi and Kamu Musubi. It is the source of creation by these two *kami* down till the tenth diagram, when the act of creation ceases.

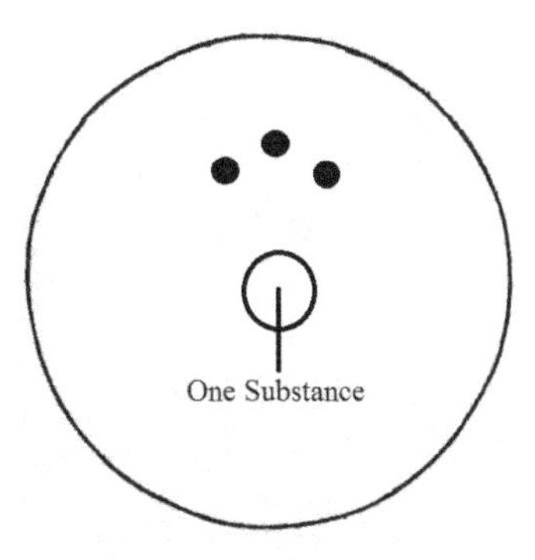

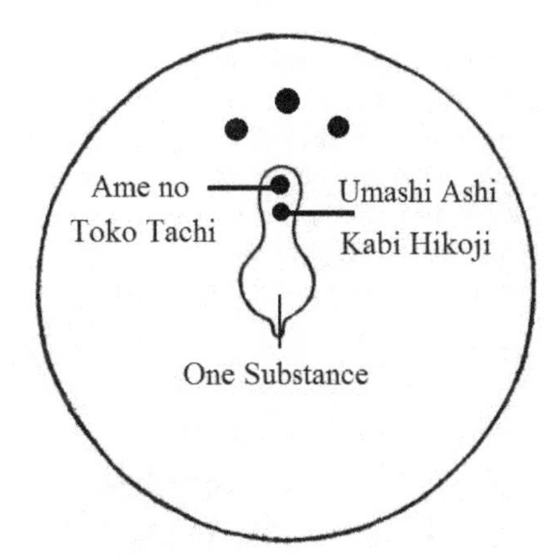

Third Diagram: From this one substance two *kami* appear: Umashi Ashi Kabi Hikoji and Ame no Toko Tachi.

Fourth Diagram: Now this sphere divides into three spheres connected by a small passage. The three spheres are heaven, earth, and Yomi. In heaven there appear the first five *kami*. On the earth, Kuni no Toko Tachi and Toyo Kumono appear. Then, the five paired *kami* groups appear:

(a) Uijini~Suijini
(b) Tsuno Gui~Iku Gui
(c) Ōtonoji~Ōtonoben
(d) Omotaru~Ayakashi Kone, and
(e) Izanagi~Izanami.

In Yomi, there appears the *kami* of Yomi. Hereafter, heaven, earth, and Yomi gradually separate, but not too far, until they completely separate.

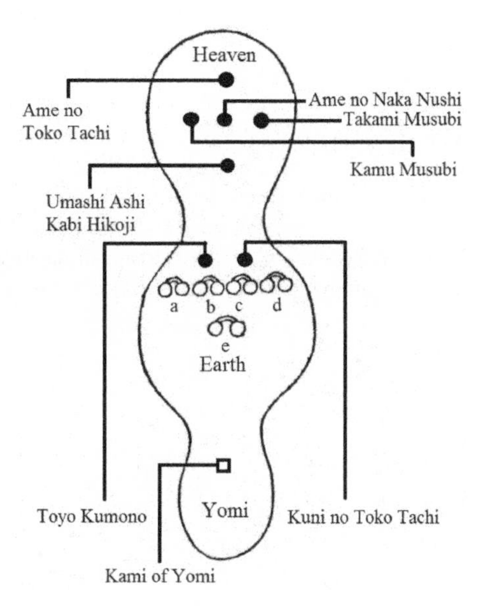

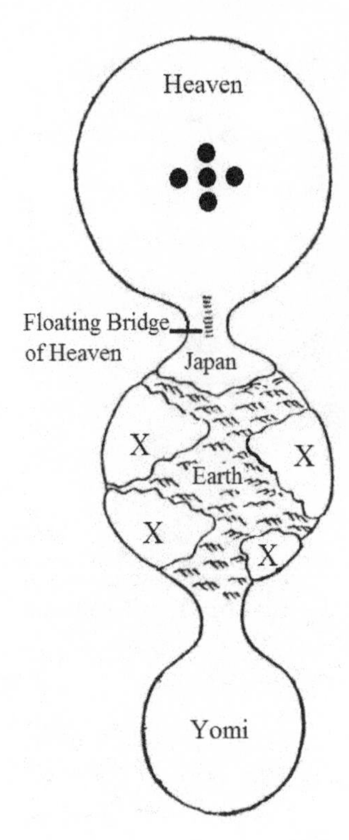

Fifth Diagram: The floating bridge of heaven is located between heaven and the earth. The bridge is the path from heaven to the imperial country, which is located directly below the bridge, with the various foreign countries [represented by X] located to the east and west, farther away from heaven. The two creator *kami* [Izanagi~Izanami] give birth to the imperial country. The beginning of the foreign countries starts with the division hither and thither of the imperial land and surrounding water, with the foam and tide naturally hardening. The foreign countries were created from these large and small pieces of hardened material. Takami Musubi and Kamu Musubi gave birth to these hardened pieces of material, each piece being equal. Izanagi and Izanami did not give birth to the foreign countries. This is the original difference between the noble imperial land and the base lands, the beautiful and the evil.

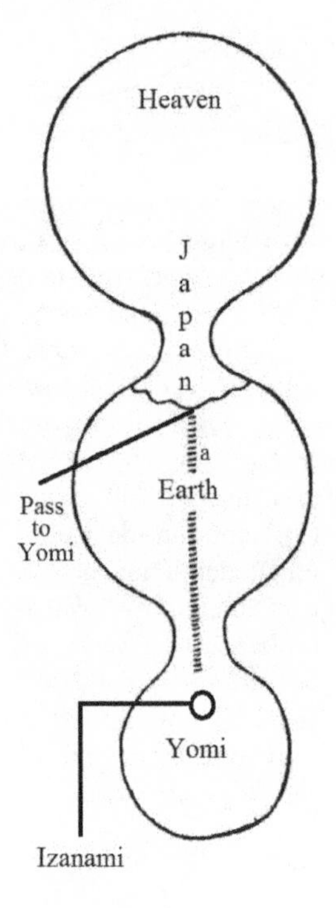

Sixth Diagram: Izanagi took a path (a) straight through the land down to Yomi. This path went through the Ifuya Pass in Izumo. Izanami has now departed to Yomi. Because we have Izanami's words, "I will go and discuss it with the *kami* of Yomi," we know another *kami* already exists in Yomi. I noted this in Diagram Four, but we do not know his name.

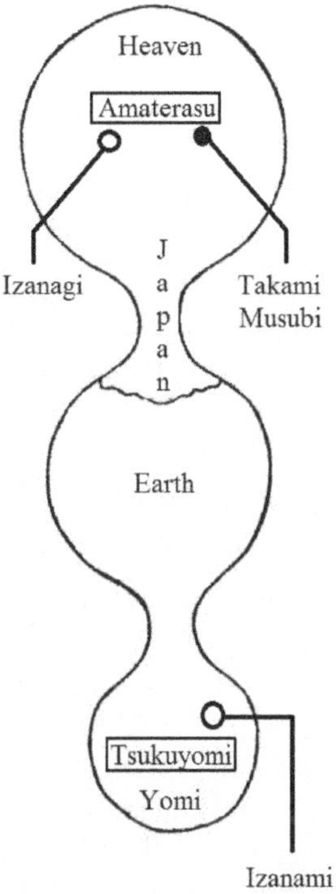

Seventh Diagram: Heaven now becomes the sun, and the country within is called the High Plain of Heaven. Takami Musubi resides there. Izanagi also resides there in the Hinowaka Palace. Amaterasu dwells in the center. Izanami still dwells in the land of Yomi, but the central figure is now the *kami* of the moon, Tsukuyomi, who received the command to rule the land of the night.

The place called heaven is the sky according to the Chinese, lacking form. Some advocate this theory, basing it upon logic, others upon their own imagination. There are other theories about this, but they are basically the same. The ancient traditions of the imperial country, however, make heaven and the sky two different spheres. Heaven originated from something that sprouted up, and that is the proper form of heaven. The High Plain of Heaven is a country. The theories in India are somewhat like those of Japan, stating that heaven has a shape and form, but the rest [of India's tradition] is simply an unbelievable tale, and I say no more. The High Plain of Heaven could be said to be higher than the sky, which anyone would appear to believe, but the ruler of heaven, Amaterasu, is visible in the sky while the land of the High Plain of Heaven is not. Also, Amaterasu revolves around the wondrous land. She also sinks below. But we cannot say that the High Plain of Heaven is above. How do we deal with the sun setting if the High Plain of heaven is remote and undetectable, and Amaterasu is the sun, with her visible light? Also, if the High Plain of Heaven is like heaven in foreign countries, and envelopes the great land on all four sides, then it would not conform to the substance that sprouted up like a small shoot. The heaven of foreign countries is, at any rate, not the High Plain of Heaven mentioned in our ancient records because our heaven does not conform to the sky. Also, it is not located above the sky. The sun *is* the High Plain of Heaven! But the sun is not Amaterasu. Amaterasu resides in the land within the sun, and she is a *kami* who rules over the sun. That is why Emperor Jinmu said in *Kojiki*, "I am the grandchild of the sun. It is not good that I should fight while facing the sun." Through this we then know that the sun and the sun goddess are different entities. The title "sun goddess" (日神) means that she rules the sun, which is to say that she rules over the High Plain of Heaven. And when Susanoo ascended to heaven, the sun goddess arrayed herself in masculine military garb and waited for him. So it is apparent that this *kami* is in the form like man. It is difficult to call her the sun. We say that the Yata mirror[1] is the embodiment of the sun goddess's form,[2] and in reality, though she is in the form of a human, because her radiance is at its apex, and as we see her so far away, she appears to be a circle in the sky. …

I, Nakatsune, believe that the phrase "the country that rules the night" is the land of Yomi. It is also called the nether land or the bottom land, and is located below the other countries. As the diagrams that follow demonstrate, the moon *kami* rules over Yomi; in other words, it is Tsukuyomi, who *is not* the moon, but is a *kami* dwelling within the moon, just as the sun goddess dwells within the sun. As I have stated, "the country that rules the night" does not mean that the moon shines at night. There must be a different sphere. Yomi is the country of the night, and because Tsukuyomi rules over that country, he is so named. The name of the land Yomi and the *yomi* in the name of the moon *kami* are the same word. *Yomi* means that the moon can be seen at night. … One of the names of the sun goddess is Ōhirume, and as long as the sun shines, we say it is daytime (*firu*), and when that light disappears, we call it night (*yoru*). The land of the night is a country where sunlight cannot reach. …

Now, Izanami still dwells in the land of Yomi, but the ruler of Yomi is Tsukuyomi. Some doubt this and ask, "The land of the night is the moon. It cannot be said, however, that the nether land and Yomi are the same thing. The nether land is the place of Susanoo's banishment, and the place to which he went. It is not the land where Tsukuyomi reigns. What do you think about this idea?"

I reply, "There is no need to debate about Yomi and the nether land being the same place. First, Izanami went to Yomi, and Susanoo said that he wished to go to the land where his mother had gone. The reason that the

1. Given to Ninigi by his grandmother, Amaterasu. It is a representation of one of the imperial regalia.

2. The idea that the mirror is the embodiment of the sun goddess extends from the simple fact that the mirror reflects the essence of the sun—light. This is a critical element of natural (original) Shintō.

nether land is the land of the night is first because many people believe that Tsukuyomi and Susanoo are the same *kami*, as our master [Norinaga] expounded in the ninth chapter of *Kojiki-den*. My belief is based on *Nihon shoki* and *Kojiki* passages. … Tsukuyomi and Susanoo are truly one and the same *kami*, with Tsukuyomi being another name for him. …"

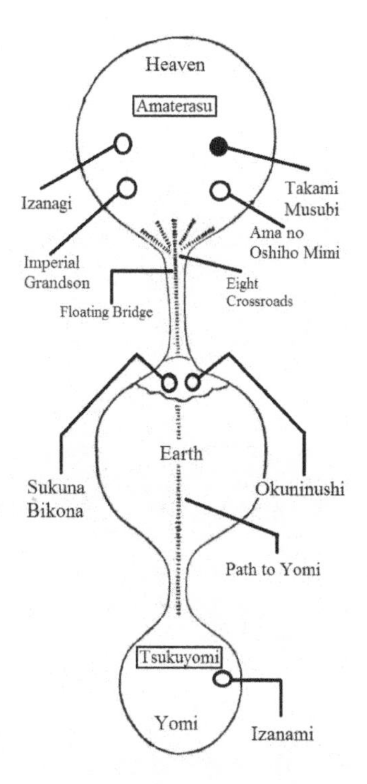

Eighth Diagram: Within the High Plain of Heaven, the imperial Grandson (Ninigi) and Ame Oshiho Mimi appeared. In the imperial land dwells Ōkuninushi, and Sukuna Bikona. The spaces between heaven, the land, and Yomi are gradually growing farther apart, and the passages between these spheres are getting narrower and longer.

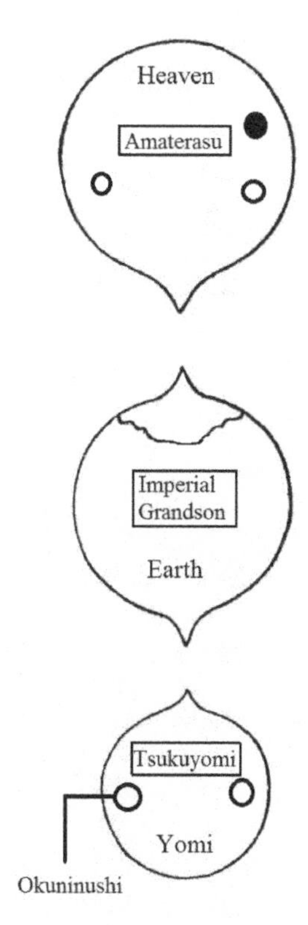

Ninth Diagram: The passageway between the three spheres now vanishes, making it impossible to shuttle between the spheres. As an example, it is like cutting the umbilical cord at birth. …

It is difficult to calculate when the passage between the earth and Yomi separated; however, we can estimate the time by using the period when the passage between the High Plain of Heaven and the earth was severed. As I noted above, Ōkuninushi first appeared, and came and went, hiding himself in the Yaso Kumade,[3] leaving this world forever. Hiding himself in Yomi, he took charge of the hidden, spiritual matters. This appears to be what we now call death, but at that time, the passage between heaven and earth was already severed. It is difficult to learn the minute details. Generally, when people die, and go to Yomi, their body stays in the ground, and only their spirit goes. Nonetheless, if there is no path or passage by which to go, how could they reach Yomi? They could not.

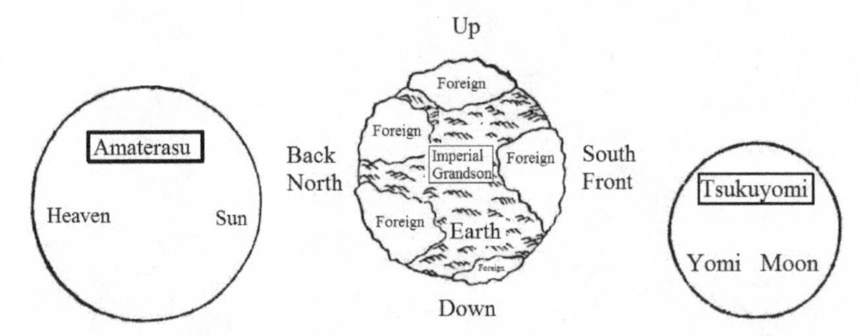

Tenth Diagram: Heaven, earth, and Yomi are now independent spheres. This diagram shows the relationship of both heaven and Yomi. Thus, the layout of this diagram represents noon time on the fifteenth day of the lunar month, viewed from the direction of the west. These diagrams are not drawn to scale. …

Heaven is represented by the sun. Yomi is represented by the moon. As the diagrams represent, in the beginning these three spheres were strung together, like pearls on a string, and heaven was always above the earth, with Yomi always below. These spheres did not move or separate, until the imperial grandson descended from heaven, and then the connection between these spheres was severed. …

In foreign lands these list stars along with the sun and the moon, and treat these as wondrous objects, but in the ancient traditions of the imperial land stars are not mentioned. The only mention is in *Nihon shoki*, where we have the *kami* of the stars, Kagasewo, which is a rare name. There is nothing that is listed as wondrous as the sun and the moon.

NORINAGA'S EPILOGUE TO NAKATSUNE'S *SANDAIKŌ*

Hattori Nakatsune's thoughts on heaven, earth, and Yomi are of profound insight that the people of western countries have not grasped from ancient

3. This name is most likely a euphemistic way of saying within the valleys of the mountains.

times till the present. What exceptional conceptions! What mysterious notions! He has enlightened us on the curious worlds of the High Plain of Heaven and the land of the night. Because of this exposition, the praise and value of the traditions of ancient days is finally on its way to increasing. And the cause of the imperial country is at last gaining respect and honor.

[MNZ 1976, 10:297–316]

☙

KODŌ TAII

Hirata Atsutane | 1811

[This somewhat lengthy work written in colloquial Japanese is a record of lectures Atsutane gave his students. He discusses the characteristics of the ancient Way, and expounds upon how students may come to their own knowledge, mainly by studying *Kojiki* and other ancient texts. In this lecture he gives his version of the ancient mythology, from the creation down through Ninigi descending to Japan to the establishment of Jinmu as the first emperor, demonstrating a trend where he exhibits a lack of concern about blending together the stories in *Kojiki* and *Nihon shoki.*]

PART ONE[1]

The subject that I would like to address presently is that of the significance of the ancient Way.[2] First, the subjects I would like to discuss are (1) the reason that our study is labeled *kogaku* "ancient learning," (2) the origin of our field, (3) give a general summary of the pioneers of this field and a biography of those people who spread the teachings of our field, (4) discuss what [texts] *kogaku* is based on, (5) provide an outline of the "divine age," (6) explain why we should be grateful for the virtue of the *kami*, (7) why our country is the divine land, and (8) the reason why you and I—down to the lowliest man—are undisputedly the progeny of the *kami*. Also, I will give a general breakdown about the beginning of heaven and earth starting with the so-called opening of creation, the prosperity of the unbroken imperial line, why our country is unparalleled among all the nations of the world, why everything we do is superior to the other nations, and why our people naturally possess hearts of integrity (真の心) because they belong to the divine country; it is this heart of integrity that anciently was called *yamatogokoro* or *yamatodamashii.* I will address these topics briefly.

Now, the legends in the divine age and the deeds of these *kami* are very strange and hard to believe for the common mind of people. I will disabuse you of any errors, and within my discussion concerning the things men-

1. I have had reference to Odronic's translation (1967).

2. This is where the title of the work comes from: the ancient way (古道) and general outline (大意).

tioned above, the overall meaning of the true Way naturally will come to light. However, when it comes to an outline of the divine age or the reason for our gratitude to the *kami*, though I should talk for twenty or even thirty days on end without pausing to take a breath, I could not expound upon one ten-thousandth of the boundless, noble, exceptional virtue of the *kami*. Thus, it might sound as if what I will summarize here in this brief period of two or three days is shallow and superficial, but though these things are roughly abbreviated, if I do not address the divine age there will be much that you will not be able to comprehend. Therefore, I will address the "divine age," being obliged to summarize it, addressing the issue as if I were running through the story, as it were. Thus, I will not touch upon the well-known story of [the sun goddess] hiding in the Ama no Iwato cave, nor will I deal with the slaying of the [eight-headed] monster by Susanoo. As regards the minute details of these legends, I will address certain points at a later time by taking the story in its pure form from the legends in the ancient records.

Perhaps there are some who think, "Why does he not give us a detailed exposition now?" There is a reason for this. And that reason is this: the central point of the ancient Way, the so-called great Way under heaven that I will discuss is the Way of man, and since we are all citizens of the imperial country, you all should be able to comprehend the overall gist of these things without studying about it. Therefore, though we expound upon these things, there should not be one person who finds the ideas difficult to accept, regardless that in present society there are a variety of Ways, starting with Confucianism and Buddhism, which are spreading. Various people put their hearts into these various Ways, some into Buddhism, some into Confucianism, others into what is commonly called Shintō, or the Zhu Xi school of thought, or the school of Ishida.[3] And even if a person has not set his heart upon these schools of learning, every person is accustomed to seeing, hearing, and discussing these philosophies mentioned above, being influenced to some extent by these schools' dogma. Thus, if we were to suddenly start expounding about the first principle of the ancient Way, very often what happens is that we are prevented from progressing because of various examples of people in the world being already accustomed to seeing, hearing, and discussing these doctrines. If we try to provide a thor-

3. Called 心学 "studies of the mind," the school was started by Ishida Baigan (1685–1744). He believed that the general principles for learning were a concrete part of the human intellect, stating that no matter how basic one's lifestyle was, a person could be enlightened through learning.

ough understanding, the student cannot comprehend the true meaning. And because they cannot hear the proper words—their minds being accustomed to other doctrines—they misunderstand the principles, and great errors arise. Not only do they make errors, but they fail to believe the points of the principles that we explain, and fail to hearken to our words, only hearing a fragment of what we say; and with that smattering of knowledge, they exaggerate their mistakes, which originated from their unbelief, and journey to other places, treating me with contempt. Looking throughout society we see that there have been many people like this.

Naturally, the things that I will expound here belong to the general outline of the Way, things you are all familiar with, and I cannot expound even one ten-thousandth of the ancient Way. If you have only heard this small one ten-thousandth of the Way once or twice, then there is nothing you can say. For example, suppose there is a large ox here, but a blind person cannot see it. And he tries to figure out the size by only handling the tail without touching the entire animal. He then takes an attitude of belittling the animal, believing the ox is small in size. [In similar fashion] trifling disparagements [about the Way] are worthless. In spite of this, you will come to comprehend these things about the Way when we lecture about them; however, when we speak of that important record [*Kojiki*] wisely put together anciently that chronicles the events from the beginning of creation and transmitted down to the present, we should be filled with trepidation if we were to neglect the will of the *kami* of heaven and earth, and all the visible *kami* (the emperors) from antiquity. Thus, let us first address the true state of things that we are accustomed to hearing and seeing, and the existing fallacies. Remember what you know about Buddhism, Confucianism, as well as the Dharma of the mind and the way to enlightenment,[4] or even vulgar Shintō,[5] and when your resolve is firm, and we lecture deliberately about the mysteries of the ancient Way through the ancient legends, then there will be no doubt about what we say if we convince you based upon [these ancient traditions]. If we do this, then surely there will

4. Atsutane writes 心法悟道, which if translated directly is "the Dharma of the mind, and the way to enlightenment." Odronic (1967:58) interpreted this as a set term.

5. Atsutane and other Kokugaku scholars found Shintō in their time to have become a bewildering amalgamation of Japanese traditions altered by Buddhist and Confucian thought, known by names such as *Yuiitsu Shintō* "only-one Shintō" (Inoue et al. 1999:445), *Ryōbu Shintō* "combinatory Shintō based on the dual fundamental mandalas of Shingon esoteric Buddhism" (ibid., p. 447), *Honjaku engi Shintō* "Shintō of essence and trace" (ibid., p. 11), or *Suika Shintō* "compilation Shintō … the way of preserving the unity of sovereign and subject" (ibid., pp. 437–38).

be no misunderstanding due to insufficient knowledge, or speaking evil of someone because he has only heard part of the story from another person. …

Now, there is something I would like to add. There appears to only be one kind of scholarship in society, but in reality there are many types. Using some granularity, the scholarship of our imperial country can be divided into seven or eight areas. First there is the study of "the Way of the *kami*," and next there is poetics, or what some call the Way of poetry. Then there is the study of the legal codes, and there is the study of literary works like *Ise monogatari* and *Genji monogatari*; then there is the study of history, which researches into the events of the successive imperial reigns. Then there is the study of ancient precedent and ceremony, and there are several competing schools that focus on what is commonly called Shintō. Even within the Way of poetry there are two or three different schools. If one is going to briefly study all the things of the imperial land, there are varying branches within that study. …

And now, as I lecture to you, skipping over things here and there, I will examine things over and over so that I say nothing that goes against the true meaning of the ancient Way, basing my theories on the ancients, and the public lectures and profound theories of the elders of our field of learning. But during this long lecture, there may perhaps be places where I lose some thought, or say something wrong. The reason for this is because I am originally a person of dull wit, and do not know even one ten-thousandth of the things in society, and I am prepared for such things as a misspoken thought. …

The beginning of our scholarship lies in the Great Ruler-Lord Tōshō,[6] and [his son] Yoshinao of Owari[7] inherited his desire to take care of the ancient things of Japan; later Minister Mito Chūnagon Mitsukuni[8] took this learning to greater heights. It is well known by people in society how excellent this Minister Mitsukuni was, and it is this same man who received the title of Mito no Kōmon. He lamented the fact that people of the time were only interested in Chinese study, and there was no one diligently studying the ancient things of our country, so he esteemed the imperial court above all else, and gathered scholars around him who collected an-

---

6. Tokugawa Ieyasu (1542–1616). After his death Emperor Gomizunoo gave Ieyasu the posthumous title of Tōshō Daigonken. Ieyasu was later deified, and worshipped as the Great God Tōshō, and Atsutane has used this form of this title.

7. Tokugawa Yoshinao (1600–50). He was the ninth son of Ieyasu.

8. Tokugawa Mitsukuni (1628–1700). He is known in Japan by his popular appellation Mitō Kōmon.

cient works on all subjects. He sent many people to the shrines and Buddhist establishments in the various provinces, even to the remote places in Japan to collect ancient works, even if these were no more than one or two leaves in length. He then carefully examined these ancient records, and compiled a large record called *Dai Nihonshi* starting with the reign of Emperor Jinmu down to the hundredth sovereign, Emperor Go-Komatsu, totaling a period over two thousand years. He also compiled a work known as *Shintō shūsei* and he compiled a record of ceremonies at court, gleaned from hundreds of old records kept by the nobility at court, and this became a work of over five hundred volumes. To pay for this large work, he set aside 100,000 *koku* of rice out of his yearly revenue of 350,000 *koku*.[9] After several decades of hard labor, the work was accomplished. When he presented the finished product to the court it received unusual praise and was granted the honorary title of *Reigi ruiten*.

* * * *

During the same era, there was a man called Keichū from Naniwa. He became a monk in the Shingon sect of Buddhism for some reason, but he dearly believed the ancient things of our country, and using the ancient vocabulary as it is preserved in old manuscripts, he produced a work called *Waji seiranshō* in which he corrected the usage of the *kana* syllabary that had been muddled since middle antiquity. He also put together other worthy works, and his reputation is indeed great. Keichū's reputation reached Minister Mitsukuni's ears and deeply impressed him, and he sent messengers on many occasions to announce that the minister wanted to officially meet Keichū, but the monk firmly declined, and the meeting never took place. However, Minister Mitsukuni continued to yearn to meet Keichū, so he sent one of his retainers, Andō Tameakira, who also had a deep affection for the learning of the imperial country, and made him a disciple of Keichū's. *Man'yōshū* is a poetic anthology that has been a great help in studying about all ancient Japanese things, not just ancient poetry, but all commentaries on this anthology were inferior, so Mitsukuni asked Keichū to put together a new commentary on it. Keichū humbly accepted the request, and wrote *Man'yōshū daishōki* and presented it to the minister. Our study on *Man'yōshū* starts with this work. Minister Mitsukuni looked

9. One *koku* of rice originally was a measurement that supposedly was enough rice to feed an individual for a year. One *koku* is roughly equivalent to five bushels of rice. Here the values are less important than the fact that Atustane is trying to reinforce in his students' minds that Mitsukuni spent about 30 percent of his allotted yearly income on the study of the ancient Way.

through this work, which was vastly different from other commentaries in that it provided annotation about the ancient vocabulary and ancient meaning of Japanese, and being superbly well done, the minister was very pleased, and sent one thousand pieces of silver, and three thousand rolls of silk to Keichū. It is said that Keichū did not keep the gifts, but gave them all to the poor. And while he was collecting ancient records for his compilation, *Daishōki*, Keichū also put his energies into a commentary on *Kokinshū*, which is titled *Kokin yozaishō*. This commentary is well written and is greatly different from other commentaries on *Kokinshū*. Keichū left this world at the age of sixty-three, on the twenty-fifth day of the first month of Genroku 14 [1701]. There are twenty-five different works written by him, and they come to over 120 volumes.

After Keichū, there appeared a man named Kada no Sukune Azumamaro, commonly known as Hakura Saigū, and he did a great service to the spread of scholarship on our imperial country. In the four quarters of the land his reputation is great, and he obtained permission from the government to build a school of learning in Kyōto. He purchased the land for that school in Higashiyama, but his dream was never realized, and he fell sick and died. His works are said to number around twenty or thirty, coming to several hundred volumes, but for some reason he burned most of these in the latter years of his life, and only five or six works survive, equaling only a few volumes. And yet, it was this person who laid the foundation for the study of our ancient Way.

The next person after Kada is Kamo no Agatai Ushi Mabuchi, who is commonly known as Okabe Eji. Because his house was known as Agatai, he is known as Master Agatai. This master was a disciple of Master Kada, and he received his master's kindness and was supported in his studies. One of Mabuchi's distant ancestors was Kamo Taketsunumi, a descendant of Kamu Mimusubi. He turned into the Yata crow, and this is the *kami* who guided Emperor Jinmu in his quest to unite Japan, so Mabuchi is a descendant of this *kami*. This family has been successive priests at the Kamo Shrine in the village of Okabe within the imperial land of Hamamatsu in Tōtōmi Province. A person known as Masasada, a grandfather of Minister Agatai five generations back obtained great glory in the Battle of Hikumahara[10] and received from Lord Tōshō a sword forged by Rai Kuniyuki[11] and a Ganryū suit of armor with a helmet as gifts.

---

10. This refers to the Battle of Mikatagahara in Tōtōmi Province fought at the end of the twelfth month of Genki 3 [1572]. Here Tokugawa Ieyasu suffered defeat at the hands of Takeda Shingen.

11. Dates unclear. He was a renowned swordsmith of the Kamakura era (1185–1333).

Mabuchi pondered and researched higher and deeper than his master Azumamaro, and taught that unless one rid himself of Chinese and Buddhist thinking he would not be able to obtain true understanding to elucidate the ancient Way. He also kindly taught that composing poetry and interpreting the ancient lexicon were all steps to comprehending the ancient Way of the divine age. After a while he was invited to the residence of Lord Tayasu, and became a teacher of the learning of Japan. There were many excellent scholars among his disciples, people such as Fujiwara Umaki, Katori Nahiko, Katō Chikage, and Murata Harumi, the last two of whom were with us till lately.[12] Our master passed away on the last day of the tenth month of Meiwa 6 [1769] at the age of seventy-three. He left forty-nine works, equaling roughly one hundred volumes.

The next person is our master, Motoori, the man we look up to as our mentor, known as Taira no Asomi Norinaga. He originally was engaged in medicine, and was known as Motoori Shun'an, but was later summoned by the Chūnagon in the province of Kii,[13] and his name was altered to Chūe. Norinaga's ancestor was a descendant of Emperor Kanmu, through Taira no Tatesato, an inspector, a six-generation descendant through Dainagon Yorimori of Ike. Norinaga was from Matsusaka in the province of Ise, and as he called his residence Suzunoya, he is often known as the great master of Suzunoya or the elderly man of Suzunoya. His scholarship knows no parallel in society, and needless to say, if you read through Motoori's works, you will reach the same conclusion. However, in the beginning, Norinaga studied Chinese learning deeply, but then moved on to the study of our imperial country, following in the footsteps of Master Agatai. He received the greatest of his master's affection and achieved great scholarly merit concerning the learning of our Way, which has no equal anciently or present. …

I have in my possession a reply to a letter sent to Norinaga from Murata Hashihiko, a person from Shirako in Ise who wished to become his student. Norinaga replied, "I have not even a dewdrop of information from

---

Kuniyuki never used the character Rai (来) in his name, but he is acknowledged as the founder of the Rai school of swordmaking.

12. Fujiwara Umaki (1721–77), Katori Nahiko (1723–82), Katō Chikage (1735–1808), and Murata Harumi (1746–1811).

13. Tokugawa Harusada (1728–89) had the title of Chūnagon. He was the ninth feudal lord over Kii. It is possible, however, that Atsutane had Harusada's son, Harutomi (1771–1852) in mind, but Harutomi was Dainagon, not Chūnagon. Harutomi's grandmother, Seishin-in (1718–1800), was a student at Mabuchi's school. Motoori Norinaga had occasion to lecture at her residence.

these so-called secretly passed traditions. Every one of these traditions is evil. Since my purpose is to expound the Way widely, I have nothing secret to pass on, even if you are not a student of mine. Because of this, nothing is more joyful or satisfying to me than to hear that you are an earnest seeker after the ancient Way of the imperial court."

Those groups who call themselves poetic or Shintō scholars refer to various secret traditions. For example, poetic scholars clamor about the secret *Kokinshū* traditions, such as *Three Plants Three Birds* tradition,[14] or the *Te-ni-wo-fa* tradition,[15] while Shintō scholars claim to have the *Floating Bridge of Heaven* tradition or the *Tsuchikane* tradition,[16] but as the intentions of these people are corrupt, it is wise for a student who wishes to pursue open scholarship to simply stay away from these strange traditions. As I will hereafter discuss, Master Motoori of Suzunoya passed on without reluctance to his disciples what he had learned, and established the method of learning in a pure and clear form. Because of this, in the beginning he was deeply hated by those groups that cherish these secret traditions. But as time went on, Norinaga's scholarship spread far and wide just like his generosity, and if one examines his student enrollment book, [you find] he had students from all sixty-six provinces in Japan, save two, enrolled in his school. In Kyōwa 1 [1801], Norinaga traveled to Kyōto, and during the time that he stayed in an inn on Fourth Avenue, and distinguished court nobles and other men who were officially engaged in scholarship came to visit and enroll as students. Starting with Lord Nakayama Chūnagon[17] who is well known in society, Tomi no Kōjishin Sanmi, Shibayama Chūnagon, and others came in abundance and joined Norinaga's school. Even the poetic master Hino Ichii Sukeki was interested in Norinaga's work, and sent his grandson, Hino Chūgū Gondaijin, to Master Norinaga to become a student … [HAZ 1.3–12].

* * * *

14. 三木三鳥. One form of the secret tradition of *Kokinshū*. This one refers to secret traditions constructed around three specific plants (*ogatamanoki* "*Michelia compressa*," *kawanagusa* "river weed," and *medonikezuribana* "sericea") and three birds (*inaoosedori* "unknown," *momochidori* "plover" or "bush warbler," and *yobukodori* "cuckoo"). The tradition sprung up because the identification of these six objects became obscure over time.

15. A secret tradition about how the particles *te, ni, wo*, and *fa* were used or should be interpreted in *Kokinshū* poetry for special poetic effect

16. Apparently both titles refer to the same tradition, where Yoshida Shintō has created a tradition constructed around the Chinese ideology of *yin* and *yang* and the five principles.

17. Perhaps this points to Nakayama Tadayori (1778–1825).

From this point the study of the ancient Way has spread throughout society, and people working in this discipline have consistently increased, and while they have low social status, the three great names of this movement are Master Kada no Sukune Hakura Azumamaro, Master Kamo no Agatai Nushi Okabe Mabuchi, and Master Taira no Asomi Motoori Norinaga. They each studied and taught in succession. Their students are numerous and this is how their work has prospered and we all, including myself, have been blessed by their efforts; we can teach about ancient things from the generosity of our hearts. Much of this is generally due to Lord Tōshō, and filled with gratitude and reverence I am left speechless. I have written extensively on this in a different work.[18] Now I have simply run through a very basic outline of a basic description of these events.

In relation to what the source material is that my lectures of the Way are based on, it is the orthodox records of our imperial court that have documented the facts of antiquity. In all reality, we already possess the true Way. However, many scholars believe that if you do not have a record containing the precepts and doctrine [of the Way] then you cannot obtain it. This is a serious misconception, because precepts are much lower in importance than facts. The reason for this is because if you have facts, then you do not need the teachings. Precepts spring up because there are no facts in other "Ways." The words of Laozi of China see right through to the core of this problem, for he said, "When the Great Way has been abandoned there are the teachings of benevolence and integrity."[19]

It is a fact that precepts do not sink into the depths of the hearts of men. For example, to give courage to the heart of a soldier, it is better to let him read an account of actual, honorable events of a brave soldier taking the initiative and fighting intrepidly in a battle instead of having him read a work that says, "When you go out in battle, take the lead and do not get left behind." These actual events sink deep into the heart, and with courage will say, "When the occasion arises, I will do just like So-and-So from the an-

18. Perhaps a reference to *maki* 9 of *Tamadasuki*, where Atsutane provides a more detailed history of Kokugaku, outlining important episodes from the schools of Azumamaro, Mabuchi, and Norinaga. It is here that Atsutane quotes from the "Petition to Establish a School" (supposedly) by Azumamaro.

19. Atsutane appears to interpret this as "teachings" replace the Way. The original text is found in Section 18 of *Dao de jing*. Wagner (2003:176) translates this section as, "Once (a ruler) has abandoned the Great Way, there will be humaneness and justice (guiding his actions)." It is also interesting that in an excavated text, the *Mawangdui*, this is quoted as "Thus, when the Great Way has been abandoned, that is when I believe there will be benevolence and integrity."

cient past!" Having the words to get out ahead of everyone and not get left behind simply does not stir the hearts of men. And in recent times, rather than teaching that one should destroy his master's enemy, it would be better to relate the actual events about Ōishi Kuranosuke and the other forty-seven *samurai* who killed Kira Kōzuke no Suke, the enemy of their master, Asano Takumi no Kami.[20] The facts from this story sink into the soul, causing the hair on one's head to stand and tears to flow ... (HAZ 1.14–15).

* * * *

Now, as I have stated, one cannot savor the true Way through precepts. The singular book that contains the actual events of the ancient, true Way is *Furugotobumi*.[21] This *Furugotobumi* is commonly known as *Kojiki*, and the reason that this work was compiled is because Emperor Tenmu wanted to demonstrate his gratitude for the thirty-nine successive emperors, starting with Emperor Jinmu.

Before *Kojiki* was put together, the imperial court and the various families had their own versions of the legends from the opening of heaven and earth on down, recorded in the ancient language of the divine age. However, within these records, there were errors and misleading parts, so Emperor Tenmu advised the court, "If we do not select the truth from among these misleading traditions at this time, then people in later periods will not be able to discern truth from falsehood." Starting with the court records, the records in possession of the noble families were also brought together, carefully examined, and the accurate, correct accounts were put in order without the slightest inaccuracies.

At the time of compilation, even the voiceless and voiced sounds of the ancient lexicon were strictly researched into, and the text itself was read aloud by the emperor to make sure that there were no mistakes and that nothing was amiss.[22] At that time, there was a twenty-eight-year-old woman known as Hieda no Are[23] who was known for her intelligence and

20. Asano Naganori (1667–1701). This is the famous story of the 47 *rōnin*. Kira Yoshinaka's cruel treatment of Naganori ended in the latter wounding Yoshinaka, which act brought about the suicide of Naganori, leaving his retainers without a master. Forty-seven of these retainers avenged Naganori by cutting off the head of Yoshinaka.

21. Atsutane follows Norinaga in reading of the title *Kojiki* 古事記 as *furu-goto-bumi*, the Japanese rendering.

22. Atsutane is extrapolating some information based on the preface of *Kojiki*.

23. In *Koshi-chō* Atsutane argues that Hieda no Are was a woman, because she was a descendant of Ame no Uzume, another woman. Atsutane is the first person to propose that

wisdom. Anything she read or heard once was inscribed into her memory and she never forgot what met her eyes or ears. The court summoned Hieda and Emperor Tenmu taught her from his own lips the texts that had been carefully examined and selected, from the beginning of heaven and earth down to the events of his own father, Emperor Jomei, and had Hieda repeat those words until she had them memorized.

Originally, our country was known in the ancient language as "the land blessed by the spirit of the word."[24] The *kami* who protects and blesses the Way of our language dwelt here, and since the exact essence of the true Way resides in the vocabulary of our imperial country, these words have been esteemed so that they would not be altered nor lost. Thus, after having Hieda read through the text, memorizing the voiceless and voiced syllables along with the pitch accent of separate words (上下までを), the emperor had the wonderful idea of causing the work of Hieda to be written down.

During this time, the imperial reigns changed, and Emperor Jitō ascended the throne. After her appeared Emperor Monmu. But during the reigns of these two emperors, the work that Are had memorized was not written down for some unknown reason. Next appeared Emperor Genmei, and during her reign Are was now over fifty years of age.

Nevertheless, on the eighteenth day of the ninth month of Wadō 4 [711], an imperial command was given to a man named Ō no Asomi Yasumaro to write down what Are had memorized. Yasumaro finished his work on the twenty-eighth day of the first month of the following year, and presented the text to the throne. And that is basically what is written in the preface to *Kojiki*. It is now 1101 years from Wadō 5 [712] down to this year, Bunka 10 [1813]. Due to the profound idea of Emperor Tenmu, the true and accurate legends of antiquity were selected by the emperor himself, and the ancient vocabulary was read aloud; thus, this record [*Kojiki*] is peerless in the world, a work that is highly esteemed. If the imperial command had not been accepted in the reign of Emperor Genmei, and the text had not been committed to paper, then these exalted and appreciative words would have departed from the world with the passing of the woman Are. But how fortunate that these words were written down in the Wadō era and have been transmitted to us in the present, and we should be

---

Are was really a woman and not a man as had been supposed. Naturally there is no solid proof either way.

24. Two places of note make mention of this: MYS 894 where it says "The country which has been called 'The Land blessed by the spirit of the word.'" The other is in *Shoku Nihon kōki*, 849 CE, third month, where it says, "Our land of Yamato, the place where the sun originates, has been called the land blessed by the spirit of the word for generations."

grateful that we are able to cast our eyes upon them even now. And anyone who has a great or small desire to pursue the Way should feel gratitude in his heart for these two emperors, Tenmu and Genmei, and never forget the dedication of Hieda no Are and Ō no Asomi Yasumaro.

This *Kojiki* starts with the events of the *kami* when heaven and earth were created and includes other events surrounding the myriad things in the universe, and the true essence of the Way permeates throughout. And that is why our master Motoori composed the following poem:

kamituyo no	When one examines
katati yoku miyo	the configuration of
isonokami	the "divine age,"
furugotobumi fa	it is reflected in that translucent mirror,
masomi no kagami	the record of ancient matters.

The first two stanzas mean that one should examine the state of the divine age carefully, and if one truly wishes to know about the divine age, and reads through *Kojiki*, then the true meaning of the ancient Way will be apparent, like looking into a mirror that is not darkened. My lecture will center on the facts in *Kojiki*, expounding clearly upon the ancient Way, and since I will talk about the *kami*, anyone can comprehend the profound foresight of these two emperors, Tenmu and Genmei. I am a person of low social status, but what I will speak to you are facts about the *kami*, the thoughts of the ancient emperors who we revere with awe, words that we should not take lightly—words of the august traditions, recorded from the august lips of the emperor.

There are many people in society who study Shintō, and they have revered and studied the first two books of the divine age of *Nihon shoki*[25] from the beginning, printing the two books of the divine age separately. These crude Shintō scholars then added bothersome and confusing commentary and annotation to the text. They believe that in order to know about the events of the opening of heaven and earth and the conception of the *kami*, that *Nihon shoki* is the only record available, but this is a misconception.

The reason for this chain of events is explained in the beginning of Master Norinaga's *Kojiki-den*, but let me give a brief overview of his ideas.

25. Atsutane goes on later to claim that the original and true title is *Nihongi*; however, he uses *Nihon shoki* here as well as in a few other places. I have standardized the title to *Nihon shoki*.

First, this record called *Nihon shoki* was compiled and presented to court in the fifth month of Yōrō 4 [720], during the reign of Emperor Genshō, who was the forty-fourth sovereign. This was eight years after *Kojiki* was presented to the court in the first month of Wadō 5. This work was compiled by imperial command at the hands of Prince Toneri. The reason that the court ordered the compilation of *Nihon shoki* even though *Kojiki* had already been abridged at an earlier date is, as I have stated above, because *Kojiki* was the wondrous idea of Emperor Tenmu, and Yasumaro kept that purpose in mind as he recorded Are's words. He recorded the essence of the events of antiquity just as they were, without embellishment, so the resulting record did not resemble the national histories of China. At the time, Chinese learning was in vogue at court, and the courtiers were dissatisfied with the plain, unembellished, unattractive, and shallow text of *Kojiki*. Thus, the courtiers widened the scope, adding a chronology, adorning the text with Chinese phrases, taking whole Chinese passages out of Chinese histories, and the record they put together resembled the Chinese national histories.

Nihon shoki was compiled for this general reason, and as it is Chinese in style it has lost a great amount of the facts of the ancient Way. In the first place, the meaning, substance, and words should be in harmony; thus, an ancient meaning, substance, and words had the characteristics of the ancient era, while the meaning, substance, and words of later eras had characteristics of the later period. In China meaning, substance, and words had Chinese characteristics. However, *Nihon shoki* represents ancient events (substance) via latter-era ideas (meaning), recording the entire story in classical Chinese (word), and so these three essences do not harmonize. That is why there are so many places where the facts of the ancient Way have been lost. *Kojiki* does not add an iota of sophistry, but records events as they have been transmitted from the ancient past, so the meaning, substance, and word are in harmony. These are the facts from antiquity, and that is why the first principle employed when *Kojiki* was compiled was recording the events in the ancient language. Because the meaning and substance are both transmitted via the word, the "word" employed within a record becomes the most important characteristic. …

* * * *

Now, when we compare these two accounts, the Chinese version [in *Nihon shoki*] sounds more reasonable, and people believe this to be the case, while the version that represents the ancient traditions sounds simple and shallow, so anyone would be entrapped by Chinese accounts. The learned men of history, starting with Prince Toneri, the compiler of *Nihon shoki*, up to the present have all been led astray. Therefore, they interpreted the true essence of the Way through a Chinese lens, and produced bothersome, dismal commentaries, clamoring that this was a secret tradition, or that was orally transmitted knowledge, but all of these are nothing but frivolous foolishness.

Also, *Nihon shoki* says, "These *kami* were formed in the path of *yang*, and because they did not have any contact with the *yin* elements, they were undefiled male *kami*." Then it says, "Hereupon, they came into contact with the *yin* (female) elements and were made male and female *kami*." These passages reflect the thinking of the compilers who took sentences from the *Shiyi*, a commentary of the *Book of Changes* and spliced them into the text. Also, it is not proper to call Izanagi the "yang" *kami* and Izanami the "yin" *kami*. Things were written this way because society was pleased with Chinese culture from top to bottom, but this culture has turned out to be the great deceiver of later ages. Scholars of later eras also enjoyed Chinese learning, for the same reason, and with their puerile intelligence they believe Izanagi and Izanami are tentative appellations attached to beings that are anything but *kami*; they view these two *kami* as re-creations of the Chinese *yin* and *yang* elements. These scholars teach about these *kami* basing their thought on the divination work *Zhouyi*, and refer to the five-element *yin-yang* divination, making all the events in the divine age mere fabrications; the ancient legends are thus overpowered by Chinese learning, and the facts in these legends have been buried and are no longer visible ... [HAZ 1.16–20].

* * * *

Hereupon, Master Motoori realized the worthlessness of learning obtained through Chinese works, and expounded to the world that there is no better vehicle than *Kojiki* for clearly seeing the actual state of the ancient, serious Way, which was reflected unmistakably in the mirror. And he put together the valuable forty-four volume *Kojiki-den,* which is unparalleled in its scope. In order to appreciate the esteemed value of *Kojiki*, the student must know about the many tainted areas of *Nihon shoki*. Without curing oneself of the bewildering disease of Chinese learning, the worthy sections of *Kojiki* will not be obvious, and one cannot know the true ancient learning without knowing the worthy areas of *Kojiki*. Master Motoori thought about it, and demonstrated that *Kojiki* was the most superior historical record, and made *Nihon shoki* secondary. He munificently taught us how we can avoid being deceived, even those who aspire to study our imperial land.

Now the title *Nihongi* is often written as *Nihon shoki*, but this is layman usage, and the true title is Nihongi, without *sho*. But even the title *Nihongi* is difficult to fathom, as the title is in imitation of Chinese histories like *Hanshu* and *Tangshu*, putting the name of Japan first. Because the name of China changed with each era, if the era name was not attached, it would be unclear which history the work referred to; in this respect, the ruler of our country has never changed, enduring for many generations, so there is no reason to add the name of Japan to the title and call it Nihon *shoki*. Adding the name of the country to the title is the attitude one takes when talking about the records from other foreign countries ... [HAZ 1.21–22].

* * * *

Everyone in society calls Japan the land of the *kami*, and that we are the offspring of the *kami*, and this is certainly true. Through the special blessings of the *kami* of heaven, our country was created, and the myriad foreign countries are unworthy of comparison with Japan. Japan is a very fortunate country, and is surely the land of the *kami*, and we are all the offspring of the *kami*, even down to the basest of men and women. But there are many people who do not know the basis for Japan being a divine country and its people being the descendants of the *kami*. What a terrible shame to be born in the divine country, and then need someone to tell them that they are the offspring of the *kami*. And these people do not know about the divinity of Japan, nor the divinity of the Japanese, nor do they have any interest in knowing about these things; there is nothing that can be done about people living their life in an insipid manner. But those of you who have come here to hear the generous words of the *kami* demonstrate that you have the desire to know. Even if you are of menial birth, if you have the desire to know about the true Way, then I hope you will investigate one fact that I will present.

Even the Chinese mentioned this fact. In *Liji* it says, "In this way the superior men of antiquity panegyrized the excellent qualities of their ancestors, and clearly exhibited them to future generations ... if they did not take knowledge of the good qualities which [their ancestors] possess, that showed their want of intelligence ... , which a superior man should have been ashamed."[26] The meaning of this is that a person who walks down the true Way should collect the virtuous deeds of his ancestors, and transmit them for future generations. But if one does not know that his ancestors did worthy acts, then he is called "lacking intelligence," and he is blind to the way of reason. Also if one knows about the good deeds of his ancestors,

26. Translation from Legge (1967, 2:253).

but does not make the attempt to transmit them clearly for his own posterity, then he is unrighteous, and in a word he is unfaithful and unfilial to his ancestors. And this is shameful for the person who is pursuing the true Way.

Now if a Chinese individual says things like this, how regrettable that we, who are fortunate enough to have been born in the divine country as offspring of the *kami*, do not even know the truth about our existence. Japan is vastly different, more venerated, and far more superior than all the nations in the world, more excellent than China, India, Russia, Holland, Siam, or Cambodia. It is not for self-adoration that the people of this country are called the citizens of the divine land. The beginning of this usage is seen when all the nations of the world were created by the *kami* in the "divine age," and these *kami* were all born in this, the imperial land. This country is the birthplace of the *kami*, and that is the reason that it is known as the divine land; this is a universally acknowledged fact and requires no further discussion; however, even in countries where they lack knowledge about our ancient traditions, they recognize Japan as the divine country from which naturally emanates the light of authority.

The contemporary [unified country of] Korea originally was divided into three countries known as the three Han: Silla, Koguryŏ, and Paekche. During that era, those people heard that there was a mysterious and blessed country, and since this country was located to the east of Korea, those people said that in the east there is a divine land known as the land where the sun rises, and they trembled with awe. Those words have gradually spread over the entire earth and whether they know it or not, this country has been known as the divine land. Even the Chinese used this appellation, and one can know that this land is surely the land of the *kami* when he studies the divine age.

First off, this world is vast and wide, and naturally there are many countries. Some people say that it sounds self-conceited to state that among all these countries that only Japan is the divine land, but as I have stated above, this is a universally accepted fact, and I will now give evidence to show that without a doubt Japan is the land of the gods.

Now, according to the divine oral tradition about the beginning of the world, there was no sun or moon in the beginning of the heaven and the earth; there only was a great expanse. This great expanse was very wide without end, and it was so great that words cannot describe it. Within this great, boundless expanse there appeared a *kami* known as Ame no Minaka Nushi, then two other *kami* appeared, Takami Musubi and Kamu Musubi, who were very venerable and miraculous. Because of the mysterious and superior virtue of these two imperial-bearing-spiritual *kami*, within this boundless expanse there appeared an object that could not be described, and it floated in the expanse like a cloud floating about in the sky with nowhere to go. Now, from this object there appeared something like a reed that fluttered as it climbed upward. This was a shoot from the reed, and that is why it was described in this manner. …

Now, after this reed had climbed upward, a *kami* was created, named Umashima Ashikabi Hikoji. The reed floated upward and became heaven. The next *kami* who was born high up in the expanse was called Ame no Toko Tachi. Now there was something which dripped down from the root of the reed, and there appeared Kuni no Toko Tachi. The *kami* who was born next clinging to Kuni no Toko Tachi was named Toyo Kumunu. The object that had dripped down from the root of the reed was later severed and became the moon.

Now, at this time there was nothing upward and nothing below, and the first two *kami* who established the foundation for these things are known as Uihijini, a male, and Suhijini, a female. After this came the pairs Ōtonoji and Ōtonoben, then Omodaru and Kashikone, then the pair that is well known in the world, Izanagi and Izanami … [HAZ 1.22–25].

* * * *

Now, at this time, the sun goddess and the moon *kami* appeared to men, and they instructed them with the words that Takami Musubi is "our honorable parent," but at this time this usage meant something like "ancestor." Now, to explain the fact that while the sun goddess and moon *kami* are the offspring of Izanagi and Izanami, they are also called the children of Takami Musubi, if one were to trace back the lineages of all the *kami* that had been born, they would all come back to Takami Musubi and Kamu Musubi, for there was nothing that did not receive its existence through the procreation of these two spirits. And that is why the sun goddess and moon *kami* refer to him as "our parent."

Now in the record of the "divine age," it says that the procreative spirit had fifteen hundred children. The text writes "fifteen hundred," but it is not restricted to that number. This is the ancient form for writing a limitless number, and it is also written as eight million, and it is in reality a fine expression because all of the myriad *kami* could be considered offspring of this *kami*. And this means that all *kami* and all men were born through the mysterious power of the divine virtue of this *kami*.

Shūishū, the third imperial commissioned anthology, contains this poem:

kimi mireba	When I look at you,
musubu no kami zo	I think that perhaps
uramesiki	the Musubi *kami*
turenaki fito wo	are vexed for having
nani tukurikemu	created a heartless man.

[SS 1265]

The meaning of this poem is, "You are pitiful. Every time I look at you, I think that the Musubi *kami* must be irritated, feeling keenly, 'Why did I create such a cruel soul?'" This was originally a love poem, but at the time, people in society still remembered the divine virtue of this *kami*, and that is why there is a poem like this. In this way, there is an actual, ancient event recorded from the divine age under the name of Kamu Musubi, and it is obvious from this poem that everything exists due to the mysterious spirit of this *kami*. And from the words of the sun goddess and moon *kami* who said, "These are the distinguished acts of our parent, Takami Musubi, who created the heavens and the earth," one can sense appreciative virtue for this *kami*, and realize that he is the true leader of this world which is enveloped by the heavens.

And though the things described above make perfect sense, those scholars who are ruining Chinese learning and the Indian schools, and even those groups that have no learning, but were born with fatuous knowledge doubt these things not even knowing they were given their very existence by the spirit of this *kami*. They find it hard to believe that this legend is typical of Japan, and that these events actually occurred. I have more to say to these groups. Human beings were created in all the foreign countries, not just our imperial land, and though these people were evil, they coalesced into nations, and were able to make merchandise—all of these events were generated through the spirit of this *kami*, and as evidence there are legends in each land. First, the old myth in China calls Kamu Musubi the ruler of the upper sphere, or the ruler of heaven, or even calling him the sovereign of heaven (上帝・天帝). This *kami* went up to heaven and became the master of the world; the human race was born through his spirit, and this old tradition states that even the essence of the true heart, benevolence, integrity, courtesy, and wisdom, were prepared by this *kami*. This is from a work of the Han era, and one may find even older examples if he sifts through words like *Shijing* (Book of Odes), *Shujing* (Book of Documents), and *Lunyu* (The Analects). However, since Chinese learning is flawed in its understanding, there are places where the story has been strangely perverted through allegories. But I have discussed these things in a general way in *Shinki shinron,* which I wrote some years ago … [HAZ 1.26–27].

* * * *

And now we see that there are numerous *kami* in the world, but [the two] Musubi *kami* are the creative fountain, and they should be revered especially. Needless to say, we should be grateful for the divine virtue of their spirit, and it is this *kami* that should be worshipped and venerated the highest. Because of this, in the reign of Emperor Jinmu, the emperor himself went up into the mountains of Tomi, built an altar, and worshipped the eight protective *kami* of the court. He worshipped these two procreative *kami* first, then he worshipped Tama Tsume Musubi, then Iku Musubi, then Taru Musubi, and then he paid tribute to the other *kami* Ōmiya no Hime, Miketsu, and Koto Shironushi; eight *kami* in all. These are the eight *kami* that the Shintō priests of the court worship. Among these *kami*, Tama Tsume Musubi, Iku Musubi, and Taru Musubi are the ones who control life, which fact should receive special attention. Now, the people of this country who are the offspring of the *kami* born in Japan through the procreative power of the spirit of this *kami* should worship him above the others because of his virtue. Even in other countries like China, the southern barbarians, and Columbo do not realize how important this *kami* is, nor do they attempt to venerate Kamu Musubi, and this is the grossest of mistakes, a terrible waste, and something more terrifying than anything.

Nonetheless, since the common man, speaking generally, is not engaged in the study of ancient things, I do not fault them; it is the scholars who until this day have been blinded by the meaningless dribble of China and the empty wisdom of Buddhism [I fault]. They have failed to notice the virtue of the procreative *kami*, not understanding them, failing to expound upon these things to those in society. And even if we were to say nothing further about these foolish scholars, people in society still say things like, "It is the Way of heaven," or "We were born this way due to the Way of heaven." In reality, these people know nothing about the Way of heaven, but are only speaking utter foolishness. But in ancient times, the Japanese understood well the virtue of these procreative *kami*, and the poem in *Shūishū* [quoted above] can basically be taken to mean the way of heaven: When I look at you / I think that perhaps / the Musubi *kami* / are vexed for having / created a heartless man. There are those who say, "Well, I suppose we must," and revere and worship this procreative *kami* without knowing why. If they knew why they should worship this *kami*, then it would be well to remember his name and worship him. It may appear somewhat tedious why, but when you consider that this procreative *kami* created the heaven and earth, governing everything, gave birth to the various *kami* through his virtuous power, is limitless in power in heaven and earth, and existed before anything else was created, regardless of what may happen to heaven and earth, it is this *kami* who bestows boundless fortune and blessings. Since every one of us, Shaka and Confucius, cats and ladles, everything received its existence through the mysterious power of the spirit of the creative *kami*, should we not follow in the path of truth and remember to acknowledge this great central *kami*?

As in China, even people of countries whose ancient traditions are incorrect produce great men like Confucius who say things such as, "If you are punished by heaven, there is nothing left to pray about."[27] The meaning of this is if you are censured by the heavenly ruler, in other words the heavenly *kami*, then there is nowhere else to go to pray for forgiveness. The reason for this is because the heavenly *kami* is the governing entity over all the other various *kami*, and if you are punished by this the highest of powers, then there is nothing which can be done. The interpretation of these words by Confucius is dealt with in detail in my work, *Kishin shinron*. As I have repeatedly stated, the virtue of this procreative *kami* should not be forgotten day and night; it is well that you check yourself so that you remember to do these things … [HAZ 1.28–29].

* * * *

By the way, when one searches after ancient meaning of meanings of all usages of the word *kami* in the imperial vocabulary, we find from the ancient corpus that these all refer to the spirits of *kami*, starting with the various *kami* of heaven and earth, and all the other spirits that descend down to the shrines. Also, it is needless to state that anything that is exceptional, possessing a special virtue and inspiring awe and respect, like humans, birds, beasts, trees and shrubbery, mountains and seas, and anything else, can be referred to as *kami* according to the ancient meaning. What I mean by *special* are virtues like respect, goodness, and courage, and it does not refer only to superior traits, but can also refer to evil or strange characteristics; anything that is awe-inspiring and deserving of respect can be labeled as *kami*[28] … [HAZ 1.31].

---

27. Atsutane has given what must have been a vulgar version of this saying. The original appears in the "Bayi" Section of *The Analects*, and actually says, "If you offend Heaven, prayer is useless" (Nylan 2014:8).

28. I have abbreviated the rest of this, as it is basically a long quote from Norinaga's definition of kami, found in *Kojiki-den*. See pp. 423–24 in this volume.

PART TWO

As I lectured to you the other day, from the beginning when the world sprang forth from the existence that was floating in the great expanse, the heavens were created from the one bud that put forth its head and grew upward. And from the bottom of the object that forms the foundation of the heavens another thing sprang forth and from it the *kami* Kuni no Toko Tachi and Toyo Kumunu were created. We call the thing that sprang forth from below "the underworld" or "the solid land underneath," but later on it separated from the heavens and is now what we see before us as the moon. By the way, the heavens were created from pure and bright matter that grew upward, and Amaterasu later was given dominion over this realm; that light shines everywhere and gradually increases in brilliance. In relation to the oral tradition that Amaterasu ruled over the High Plain of Heaven, some Shintō scholars have said that heaven is really the capital, and the idea that she rose to heaven refers to her having ascended the imperial throne. These scholars say impertinent things, but it is only idle talk. These scholars twist the tradition of the heavenly *kami* and the truth handed down from the thoughts of the ancient emperors about her, and it is no small crime to err when talking about the sun goddess. Also, Tsukuyomi was given the command to "rule over the country of the night," and Izanagi accomplished the command that he himself received from Takami Musubi, so he returned to heaven and made his report to the ancestral *kami*. And from that time forth, he has long dwelt in the Hinowaka Palace in heaven.

There is an ancient legend in China that resembles the tradition of the *kami* of the sun and moon having been born from the eyes of Izanagi. That legend says that in the beginning of the creation of heaven and earth, there appeared a person named Pan Ku, and his left eye became the sun while his right eye became the moon. This legend is believed to be the Japanese tradition transmitted to China in a degenerated form. But there are scholars who argue the following:

> I have been listening to your lecture on the "Divine age," and you have quoted things that greatly resemble traditions in foreign countries. Thus, having a commonality of traditions in other countries does not necessarily mean that the traditions from the divine age are correct. The reason for this is that if a group of foreigners were gathered in one place, and shared their ancient traditions with each other, they would argue that "my own tradition is correct," "my country's tradition is the original," "my country is where the sun goddess was born." If such were the case who would be able to judge the truth and reach a decision? It is impossible to

> expect that there would be individuals from the beginning when heaven and earth were created still alive, and by saying that foreign ideas are all incorrect and that everything from the divine age is infallible, I get the feeling that we are pursuing the idea that everything in one's own country is noble. And the fact that there is confusion here and there proves that it is difficult to decide which is "correct" and which is "incorrect." Thus, it is better not to believe the whole story of the divine age.

To outsiders it may seem distressing to have been criticized thusly, but I was not distressed in the least. Rather that is where the virtue of scholarship shows through, for I replied in this manner:

> First, as far as the confusion is concerned, when one looks at it with the eyes of scholarship, he can immediately discern truth from falsehood. To give a familiar example of what I mean, the *hyakunin isshu* [one hundred poems from one hundred poets] that Lord Teika compiled in the mountain villa of Mount Ogura should have originally been written on a square piece of colored paper, one poem per sheet. However, whether it is the poem of Sugawara[29] or Semimaru,[30] we find that ten different men have possession of that one piece of paper. And these men engaged in debating that their piece of paper was the original. This debate appears extremely confusing, but a person trained in differentiating between ancient strokes of a brush could discern the original poem in every case, locating the original from among the ten. In exactly the same way, one can discern the truth; it may appear wise to discard everything by saying that it is a fraud, but this is not wise because the person does not have the intellect to discern the truth. Therefore, it is exactly the same when you say that you do not believe the traditions from the divine age because they resemble the legends of foreign countries, and the truth cannot be comprehended. Let me give another familiar example of discerning the truth. People who engage in selling rice can tell by looking at a handful of mixed rice what is excellent rice from Mino, or rice from Sendai or Kyūshū, even if the mixture is from five or ten provinces. To an unlearned man this may sound unbelievable, but when one watches the seller examine rice, he realizes that each strain of rice has a different shape, and the difference is so distinct that there is no confusion. This leaves the unlearned man speechless. Scholarship is much the same; by looking through the traditions with precise eyes that have been trained justly in scholarship, eyes that are able to survey the ancient and present, there is no difficulty in discerning the truth when taking the truth and the ancient state into consideration. The truth of the ancient traditions from the divine age when considered with the facts we now have does not shift one iota, even though one may say that the legends resemble that in other countries.

Now, to answer the question about why I quote foreign legends that tend to be incorrect, it gives us a baseline. In order to enlighten the im-

---

29. Sugawara Michizane (845–903). His poem is no. 24 in the sequence.

30. Semimaru's dates are unknown, but it is believed he lived in the latter half of the ninth century.

penitent souls who doubt the truth of the ancient traditions, when you quote to them the foreign legends that resemble ours, even if they are incorrect, then we can take these things together and realize the fact that all the countries in the world have fragments of the ancient traditions of Japan in one aspect or another. After they have come to this realization and compare this and that, there are often people who are freed from the disbelief that our tradition is true among all of the legends of the countries. Quoting foreign legends that resemble our tradition aids in this realization and after the person has obtained this enlightenment, then any further quoting of foreign legends becomes meaningless.

Here is a teaching from Buddhist scripture. A person wishing to show where the moon is lifts his finger into the air and says, "There! There it is." But after the person finds the moon himself, the finger is no longer needed and the other person puts it down. Referring to foreign legends is the same, and it is fine to think of me doing this to enable a student to locate the ancient legends of the imperial country. Now, even if I could summarize even a hundredth of the story about the two *kami* Izanagi and Izanami receiving the command from the heavenly *kami* in the beginning and descending down to Onogoro Island and giving birth to the islands of the land of Ōyashima, those who cannot comprehend these things no doubt think that these events concern a few years. However, the life of the *kami* is eternally long and incomprehensible. Many years passed but even at this stage in the tradition, the imperial land was still not finished. But various *kami* had been created and their descendants began to increase; among these, the descendants of Susanoo had strong power and there was an excellent *kami* named Ōnamuji. He had eighty brothers, and in the beginning Ōnamuji suffered great trials at the hands of his brothers; however, due to the intervention of Susanoo, who resided in the land of Yomi, these brothers were brought into submission and Ōnamuji ruled over this country. We also know that he ruled over this land because he is also known as Ōkuninushi. He had many children, the eldest being Koto Shironushi, and he is one of the eight protective *kami* of the court worshipped by the Shintō officials. Also, another child named Ajisuki Takahikone is the *kami* of Takakamo. And Take Minakata is the one who went to Suwa in the province of Shinano; these *kami* are very powerful. This Ōkuninushi has many names, and one of them, Ōnamochi evolved into Ōnamuji. This Ōnamuji came upon a large, divine halberd. He combined his strength with a *kami* named Sukuna Bikona, and they established and strengthened the country. That is, they put the finishing touches on the important work that Izanagi and Izanami had begun. These two *kami* also established the Way of medicine and medicinal herbs; I will say more about this in my discussion on medicine.

Hereupon, Amaterasu did exactly as Izanagi had stated, and became the ruler of the High Plain of Heaven. She bestows blessings on every corner of this world—not to mention the High Plain of Heaven—with Takami Musubi and Kamu Musubi. And she spoke those divine words to her son, Masaka Akatsu Kachihayahi Ame no Oshihomimi, saying, "My son will govern the central land of Reeds." This Ame no Oshihomimi is the product of Amaterasu and Susanoo, appearing through the vow the latter two *kami* made with (the power of) the jewel and the sword. The secret tradition of the jewel and the sword that followers of Shintō noisily talk about refers to this. This *kami* (Ame no Oshihomimi) married Tamayorihime, the daughter of Yorozuhata Toyoakitsu Shihime, who was the daughter of Takami Musubi. The child born from these two is Ame Nigishi Kuni Nigishi Amatsuhidaka Hikoho Ninigi. Because of this genealogy, Ninigi is the actual descendant of the sun goddess, while being a great grandson to Takami Musubi. That is why we refer to Ninigi as the imperial grandchild. He is also known as the Heavenly grandchild ... [HAZ 1.34–37].

The *kami* that accompanied the imperial grandchild were Ama Koyane and Ama Futotama. Ame no Koyane is enshrined in Hiraoka in Kawachi Province and is the ancestor of the Nakatomi~Fujiwara families. Ame no Futotama is the ancestor of the Imibe family. There were five *kami* who accompanied Ninigi including these two. Other than these five, there was another *kami* set up to protect Ninigi with his spiritual power, and his name is Ame no Tejikarao. He is enshrined in Shinano. There is also Toyo Ukebime who made sure that all the food prepared for the people from the imperial grandchild down to the lowest person was safe. She is enshrined in the outer shrine at Ise. Also, there is Ama Iwatowake, who was in charge of making sure that all manner of evil did not enter the imperial camp from the four quarters. And there is Ama Omoikane, whose spirit was blessed with a discerning power, able to comprehend marvelous things. Here we see that many eminent *kami* were prepared to accompany the imperial grandchild. From here the group crossed the floating bridge of heaven. As it says in the Great Purification liturgy, "He divided the many layers of clouds," meaning that Ninigi divided asunder the many layers of thick clouds, with the rock quiver on his back, given to him by his father Ama no Oshimimi. Girded with the great sword, he held the heavenly bow made from the wax tree and carried arrows made from deer bones.[31] With these protective *kami* surrounding Ninigi, he descended down to Japan, landing

31. The arrows are known as *makagoya*. *Ma* is an honorific, while *kago* refers to deer. We know from *Weizhi* that the ancient Japanese made their arrowheads out of deer bones.

on Mount Takachiho in the land of Hyūga. The first person Ninigi met was a local *kami* named Saruta Hiko. When Ninigi descended down from heaven, the sky darkened, making it impossible to distinguish the shape of objects. Ninigi plucked rice ears and scattered the chaff in all directions, upon which the sky brightened. This area is now called Kirishima or Mount Kirishima. To the west of this mountain is Soo District in Ōsumi Province. To the east is Morokata District in Hyūga. There are many strange aspects about this mountain. Even now, people find rice growing there that began growing with the divine command, and sometimes thick fog envelops the peak. When this occurs, the people grab rice ears and thrash them about like their elders taught them, following the ancient traditions. Once they have done this, the fog dissipates, and a person can safely climb the mountain.

Nevertheless, the floating bridge of heaven that legend says the heavenly grandchild rode when he descended is a vehicle used to cross the interval between heaven and earth. Since it floats, it is called "a floating bridge." Resembling boats on this earth, it is also known as the heavenly rock boat. This is the same floating bridge of heaven upon which in the beginning the records said that Izanagi and Izanami stood, and searched for a country with the spear in the mud. Now the riding of this floating bridge implies that Ninigi descended from a high place, and we believe that the ladders located in the various provinces are remnants of this vehicle created by the *kami*.

First, in *Harima Fudoki* it says that in the village of Masuki in the district of Kako there was a ladder.[32] Also, in *Tango Fudoki* it says that there was a ladder by the ocean in Hayaishi Village in Yosa District.[33] This ladder was very large, measuring 2,229 *tsue* in length and the width was nine or ten *tsue*. It also says that the widest spot was some twenty *tsue*.[34] People in

---

32. The beginning of *Harima fudoki* has been lost. Atsutane appears to have either misremembered this passage, or simply garbled it. The entry for Yake Village actually says, "There is a mountain within the limits of the village, called Mount Masukata. It was constructed of stone vessels and wooden tubs. There is also a stone bridge. An old tradition says that in the ancient past the bridge reached heaven and people in groups of eighty ascended and descended the bridge. Thus it is called the Eighty Bridge."

33. *Shaku Nihongi* records, "Yosa District. Northeast of the Miyake District is the village of Hayashi. By the ocean in this village is a long and large cape. The tip of the cape is known as the Heavenly Ladder, while the rear is called Kushi Beach. The reason for the first name is because when Izanagi, who created the country, traveled down from heaven, he set up a heavenly ladder."

34. One *tsue* is about three meters (9.5 feet). There is some confusion in the *Shaku Nihongi* text concerning the first figure. The text reads "20 (twenty) 229. Perhaps this is 1000."

the country know about this place, and many go to see this ladder. Many of my friends have gone to see this ladder, but all were afraid. Even those who tend to be proud were sufficiently humbled at the sight. This floating bridge was originally created for Izanagi and Izanami to traverse space, and later other *kami* used it to descend down to earth.

On the other hand, when Amaterasu climbed up to heaven, the record says that she used the Heavenly Ladder. This is likely a different object. But remember that at this time it was said that the distance between heaven and earth was not that great, so I believe that it was fairly simple to ascend to heaven. At this point in the story, however, the heavenly grandchild, Ninigi, is riding in the floating bridge and descending to earth. And as the record says, "He divided the many layers of clouds," so we believe that the distance between heaven and earth was great. Now, after he descended from heaven, the distance back to heaven grew greater and greater, and so the *kami* abandoned the floating bridge as a means of travel back to heaven. The ladder also fell back to earth, and the remains are in Harima and Tango.

In this way, the sun rose into heaven and its position became fixed in the sky. It never moves to any other place. It only rotates to the right. This is the state of the heavenly globe. And the great land makes the heavenly globe her focal point, revolving to the right in one large circle. This represents one year. But within this revolution there is rotation. When the earth faces the sun it is day, and when it faces away, it is night. This rotation is called one day. With more than 360 of these revolutions, the earth revolves completely around the heavenly sun, and this is one year. Now, the land of Yomi cut away from the earth when it began its revolution and became the moon. It revolves around the earth going from a fully visible state to invisible one, and in 29½ days it returns to its original state. This is known as one month. That is an overview of the current state of the sun, earth, and moon … HAZ 1.39–41].

* * * *

Our honorable country is the root of heaven and earth, and the student may understand that in relation to everything our country is superior to all the other countries according to what I have said above. And because of what I have said, the various foreign countries have fragments of our old myths remaining because these were not properly transmitted as in Japan.

The Taiei manuscript says 1,229. Hirata has read the text as 2,229. NKBT *Fudoki* has 1,229. Also Atsutane has accidentally or deliberately misread the grammar of the text. The figures for length and width are for the cape, *not* the ladder.

An example of this is news of an event that happened in the capital being orally transmitted to people in the provinces. Naturally the information people receive in the provinces will not be as accurate as that transmitted to people living in the capital. And the fact that our myths were transmitted to foreign countries in distorted fragments is much like the analogy of news being transmitted to the provinces. These foreigners now start claiming these fragments are really their country's tradition. After many years have passed, the people forget where the story originated, and transmit the story as if these events had occurred in their own land. If the student ponders carefully this principle, then it becomes crystal clear that the heavenly child [emperor] should reign over the myriad countries of the four seas. Though he deserves reverence, he deserves more than the average reverence of people in the world. And yet, the scholars of the world are only interested in the learning of foreign countries, drowning in such scholarship, ignorant of any respect for Japan. Once in a while there are scholars who hear the truth about Japan, and cannot believe it, so they turn around and attempt to refute it. This is a mistake in the extreme.

Also, there are scholars who are partial to anything connected to foreign learning and often declare that our country is a tiny state, a late bloomer. These scholars repeatedly mention that our country is small, but what they forget to mention is that the respect or vulgarity, the good or evil of everything has no relation to size. A gigantic rock does not compare to a tiny gem. And large animals like bulls, horses, and elephants cannot compare to the smaller humans. No matter how big a country is, an inferior country is still inferior. And even if it is narrow and small, a superior country is indeed superior. When you look at a recent map of the world you see countries like Russia and America. There are many other large countries like this, and in some of these there are lands where grass does not grow, where people do not exist. So are these examples of superior countries? We need not use foreign examples, for there are plenty of examples of things that are superior, average, and inferior in Japan alone. This quality is not determined by the size of the object. We decide upon the quality of the country by the type of merchandise produced there along with the climate.

Concerning the claim that our country is a late bloomer,[35] these scholars criticize Japan by saying that it is slow in acquiring wisdom. In reality, we

35. Atsutane is referring to the fact brought up by some that because Japan follows a policy of national isolation, it lags behind the West in technology, medicine, and other areas of development.

lack prudence. In other words, since Japan is the progenitor of the various countries, being the core country, the essence of our land is thick. So the Japanese seem to be slow in excelling in wisdom and talent. A good example is a person like Minister of the Right Oda Nobunaga.[36] Nobunaga was a lazy dolt until the age of twenty. Everyone called him stupid. And Ōishi Yoshio[37] was a superior person whose fame will last forever like heaven and earth, but even he was labeled a fool until he was twenty years of age. Many of Japan's great men have been of this disposition. Even in the animal world, birds and beasts can peck at rice and insects from the moment of birth, while they can have intercourse after only two or three months pass, and can do other base things. From that perspective, humans cannot become quick experts at anything. But that is why human beings are worthier than animals. The student may make a connection between foreigners who quickly become experts in sophistry, while many Japanese preserve the innocent state from the divine age and are not cunning.

In a Chinese work titled *Laozi* it says, "Great men are created slowly."[38] The meaning of this phrase is the same as what I said above about great men and superior wisdom taking time to create. Though he was a foreigner, Laozi described this state accurately. I just remembered this, but as I have said, Japan is the root of heaven and earth. To be allegorical, Japan is the calyx of fruit. Fruit like melons and peaches grow in size as the meat of the fruit expands away from the calyx. When the fruit ripens, however, it ripens from the surface backwards, the calyx being the last part to ripen. This is because the calyx is the core of the fruit, and its essence is the thickest. Whether it be the ripening of fruit, or the birth of humans, the matter is the same. There is no difference from this and the creation of heaven and earth.

Now, though I have explained this principle in detail, there will be people slow of understanding who will not be able to comprehend my words. These people are absent-minded and dull-witted, but as time goes on, they will gradually perceive what I am saying. When they consider this and that, they will understand. When this happens, they will not be satisfied with the tedious words of Atsutane, and try to commit these words to paper, but as the Chinese say, the pen does not do justice to the tongue. So

36. Oda Nobunaga (1534–82) began a course to unify Japan, but his life was cut short by a retainer who assassinated him. The movement to unify Japan was only later completed by Tokugawa Ieyasu.

37. Ōishi Yoshio (1659–1703) was the leader of the famous forty-seven *rōnin*. See note 20 this chapter.

38. Found in section 41 of *Dao de jing*.

they will attempt to express these words, but the expressions are insufficient to convey the thoughts. Therefore, like a person who does not know the hand movements or the steps to a dance, they shuffle about in a comfortable fashion. So something like my speech can be endured even if you doze off once in a while. …

[As I noted earlier] Ninigi first descended from heaven onto the top of a peak in Takachiho in the province of Hyūga in Tsukushi. He then went in search of a proper place for his capital, and ruled the country from Takejima in Nagaya on Kasaya Cape in Ata. Thus, the earthly *kami* revered the imperial grandson as the son of the heavenly *kami*, and served him. And that is why the successive emperors are called the son of the heavenly *kami*. The usage of the characters 天子 "son of heaven" is Chinese in origin, and is a proper appellation for the son of the heavenly *kami*; the only person who should be labeled "the son of heaven" is our emperor. I expound upon the reason that "son of heaven" does not apply to the ruler in China in *Saiseki gairon.*[39]

Now, Ninigi built his palace in Takejima on Kasaya Cape and governed the land. Here he wed Konohana Sakuyahime, the daughter of Ōyamatsumi. They gave birth to Amatsu Hidaka Hiko Hohodemi. This Hiko Hohodemi went to the palace of the sea *kami*, married Toyo Tamahime, the daughter of the sea *kami*, and they gave birth to Hiko Nagisatake Fukiaezu. Fukiaezu also married a daughter of the sea *kami*, known as Tamayori Hime, and they gave birth to Kamu Yamato Iware Hiko. During the reign of this individual, the capital was moved from Kasaya Cape to Yamato. During this time, he put to death Nagasune Hiko and other bandits, and the "he" we are talking about is the well-known Emperor Jinmu. However, the name Jinmu is not his real name. His actual name was seen above, Kamu Yamato Iware Hiko, and the name Emperor Jinmu was bestowed upon him in the Chinese fashion over one thousand years later.

Now, there is something that must be said here. The theories of scholars in society as well as the average man all say that there are seven generations of heavenly *kami*, five generations of earthly *kami*, and twenty or thirty reigns of earthly rulers. What kind of fool started this? It is very incorrect and does not apply here. *Kojiki* and *Nihon shoki* do say that from Kuni Toko Tachi to Izanagi and Izanami consists of seven generations, but the words "heavenly *kami*" are nowhere to be found. This is only proper. These seven generations of *kami* from Kuni Toko Tachi to Izanagi and Izanami

39. Completed in 1811, *Saiseki gairen* is also known as *Judō taii.*

deal with *kami* born from this country [Japan], and there is no reason to call them "heavenly *kami*."

The *kami* who appeared when heaven and earth were first created are Ame Minakanushi, Takami Musubi, Kamu Musubi, then Umashi Ashikabi Hikoji, and Ame Toko Tachi. *Kojiki* calls these five generations of *kami* "heavenly *kami*"; therefore, it is clear that the seven *kami* (from Kuni Toko Tachi to Izanagi and Izanami) were not labeled "heavenly *kami*." In spite of this, there is also no record that labels these *kami* "earthly *kami*." The usage of "earthly *kami*" is used after Ninigi to make a distinction between the *kami* in heaven.

It is also a serious mistake to call the five generations from Amaterasu to Fukiaezu "earthly *kami*." The reason is that Amaterasu was born in this country, but rules over heaven according to the will of her father, Izanagi. Thus, there is no doubt that she is a heavenly *kami*, the one ruling over the sun we worship before our very eyes. The sun goddess's son, Oshiho Mimi and his son, Ninigi, were both born in heaven, so they are also heavenly *kami*. Because of this, Ninigi descended from heaven and ruled over this country. His descendants after his son Hohodemi are called children of the heavenly land. Nevertheless, Hohodemi and Fukiaezu were born in this country, and are not labeled heavenly *kami*. Again, though, there is no record where they are called earthly *kami*. They were born on the earth, but they come from the lineage of heavenly *kami*, so they are known as imperial grandchildren, or as the Chinese tradition states, heavenly grandchildren ... [HAZ 1.42–46].

* * * *

Kamu Yamato Iware Hiko, also known as Emperor Jinmu, ruled the country from Kashiwara in Yamato. The imperial line has continued in an unbroken succession from this emperor until the present, being one hundred and twenty generations.[40] There is no other nation on earth that can compare with this, nor is there any other nation that is so blessed. This is the original purpose of the Way, and it differs entirely from the thinking of the Chinese. Japan is a country born from the profound thoughts of these special *kami* who created heaven and earth, the foundation supported by Ōanamuji and Sukuna Bikona, descendants of these *kami* who were blessed with an especially strong authority. The existence of the myriad countries of the four seas, as well as the fowl, beasts, shrubbery, and trees originate

40. During Atsutane's day this would have been Emperor Ninkō (r. 1817–46), who was the 120th sovereign according to the traditional genealogy.

entirely from this country, the original essence being that of the bud that sprouted and grew upward to become the heavenly shining globe. This land is also the birthplace of the sun goddess, who rules over the sun, bestowing blessings on the entire world within the sphere of existence. And Ninigi is the great grandson of Takami Musubi, the grandson of Amaterasu, given special affection by these two *kami*, and he is particularly noble among all the *kami* in heaven. A number of *kami* who had won the confidence of these two great *kami* were selected to accompany Ninigi [when he descended], and he received from Amaterasu as imperial proof the three regalia, which were particularly revered. The sun goddess herself used these sacred words, "The land of Ashihara Mizuho will be ruled by successive generations of my descendants, a land that will stand forever."[41] According to the divine command, our rulers have governed this land every day since the reign of Ninigi. And in relation to the descendants of the *kami* who accompanied Ninigi to earth, they continue in an unbroken line, their descendants spreading throughout Japan. Some of the imperial descendants were granted surnames such as Taira and Minamoto, and their descendants have entered the ranks of the imperial subjects, and have increased in number. We together now are their progeny. …

Through the facts found in these ancient records, I have made things clear; we can say that our country is the divine land, and that we are descendants of the *kami*. For you people who are too busy with the affairs of daily life and cannot elucidate the records by yourselves, you have come to hear and remember this speech, and now surely are able to step forward and repeat these things with vigor. If you cannot, when a person censures you by saying, "How can you say that only your country is a divine country, and only your people are descendants of the *kami*?" I am afraid you will be shocked. But when you are censured like this, if you can answer as I have told you, then you will not be ashamed of the words that even the Chinese whom we despise use. That is, "We are collecting and clarifying for later generations the splendid works of our ancestors. Not knowing that our ancestors have performed noble works is to say that certain facts are un-

41. Atsutane is taking some liberties with the story. *Kojiki* says, "They gave a command to Ninigi, saying, 'The land of Toyo Ashihara Mizuho is a land we entrust to you to govern. Therefore, descend down there according to our will'" (Kōnoshi et al. 2007:115). *Nihon shoki* records, "Amaterasu said, 'The land of Toyo Asihara Nakatu is the place over which my son should rule'" (Kojima et al. 2002, 1:123). A different variation says, "Amaterasu gave a command to Ninigi, saying, 'The land of Asihara Nakatu is the land over which my descendants should rule. You, imperial grandson, go and rule. Now off with you. May the prosperity of your reign know no bounds, like heaven and earth'" (Kojima et al. 2002, 1:130).

known to you; thus, this casts a shadow over reason. Knowing about these ancient works and not passing them onto posterity is corrupt, showing you are unfaithful and unfilial to your ancestors."

Therefore, we are the posterity of the *kami* as the record points out, and this country is the divine country. The many foreign countries that span the edge of heaven and earth, lacking nothing, enjoy satisfaction and beauty, and it is wonderful that the five grains are the first link to life in the myriad countries. Since people eat rice till they are full—the five grains exist thanks to Tamayori Hime, the *kami* of the Outer Shrine in Ise who was born in this land full of the wonders of nature; thus, we call the people born in Japan "the seeds." All foreigners, though they are not the same age, are powerful and of great intelligence. But when a person uses this knowledge of the ancient traditions properly and expounds upon things truthfully, people blinded by foreign learning and people who think they are wise end up saying that no matter what Hirata says about Japan, he is just biased. So though you try and tell these types of people about the facts about Japan, they refute this and that, quoting astronomy, geography, and foreign theories. These people say that the idea that Japan is superior to all other foreign countries is mere public opinion lodged between heaven and earth. I will address this issue at our next meeting. ... [HAZ 1:49–51]

* * * *

The earth is perfectly round, like a device used by fortune-tellers. People construct a globe with the outlines of countries attached to the outside. Like the device used in fortune-telling, there are many rings revolving around the inner sphere, just like an astrolabe. The round sphere where the various countries are attached is the earth. Because it is round, we also call it 地球 "the globe." The character 球 is "ball" [so ball of land]. The outer surface of this round earth is land and sea. To give an example, depressed places became oceans and rivers because water gathered there. Elevated places became the countries. Extremely high places became mountains. If you think of this example, you will not go wrong. A proverb says the earth is six parts water, three parts mountain, and one part plain. So sixty percent of the surroundings consist of ocean, thirty percent being mountains, and the remaining ten percent flat land. There is also the saying that the earth is half water and half land.

Now, we can divide this great land mass into five spheres. The first is Asia, the second Europe, the third Africa,[42] the fourth South America, and

42. Atsutane's text has アメリカ *amerika* "America," but this clearly is a mistake for ア

the fifth North America. These are called the five great continents. Our imperial country, China, Mongolia, and India belong to the first large group, Asia. So there are still four other spheres like this one stretching from Japan to Mongolia and India. And even if you put all the land together, there still is an even greater area of ocean. So is not the land terribly large? Something this large floats in the firmament without falling, but since it does not move up and down, how did anyone find out about all this? People from Europe, a place in the second continent I mentioned above, have traveled freely all over the globe in ships, visiting all the countries. There is a small place in Europe called Holland, and they have traveled freely all over the globe. To do this they had to be skilled in astronomy and geography, so they made these subjects foremost in studying. These people are possessed of a patient nature, and they think things through. Through their thinking, they have manufactured various measuring devices, like the telescope and sun reflector[43] to view the sun, moon, and stars, surveying devices to measure the size and distance of things on land. In making these devices, some took five years, others ten, some a whole lifetime. When ideas were greater than the lifetime of man, these men wrote down their ideas, leaving the finishing of ideas to their posterity. Generation after generation of posterity and students continued to work on these problems, trying to develop the device in question. But I will refrain from mentioning things related to countries that do arbitrary things, like China, where they engage in slippery subjects built on conjecture. Therefore, when there are things that man cannot comprehend, no matter how much he studies, this is called *Gotto*,[44] where the Dutch say it is incomprehensible, the work of the heavenly deity. …

So this globe is round and floats in space. Proof of this can be seen by a boat that sails east later appears in the west. We confirm this theory with this as proof. Now if the earth is round, it would appear to be difficult to fix top and bottom, but if you look at the sky you will see the North Pole and South Pole, locations that are immovable. … When these astronomical theories came to our country, a man from Nagasaki called Nishikawa Kyūrinsai[45] made these things public. He lived during the Genroku era. It is well known that nothing was known of astronomy or geography or for-

---

フリカ *afurika* "Africa," because North and South America appear next in the line. I have translated it thus.

43. Written 遮日鏡, glossed as *zongarasu*. This is from Dutch *zonneglas* "sun glass." Apparently this was a device like a helioscope (cf. Odronic 1967:184).

44. Atsutane writes this as 造物主 "the creator," but glosses this as *gotto*. This likely is a German version of the word ("Got" or "Gott"), as Dutch has "God" back to Old Dutch.

45. Nishikawa Kyūrinsai (1648–1724). More commonly known as Nishikawa Joken. He

eign countries before this time, and theories that did exist were fanciful, as described by Nishikawa in *Tenkei wakumon*[46] and *Kaitsūshōkō*.[47] These works introduced us to foreign customs, spreading this knowledge far and wide. Nishikawa has many other works. From his time on, people know about foreign countries. He was a gifted man with a strong Japanese spirit, and through his study of Western astronomy, geography, and Chinese learning, he was able to publish a work called *Nihon Suidokō* "The Topography of Japan"[48]... [HAZ 1.52–54].

* * * *

Among the works that have reached our country from the far west is one called *Beschreibung von Japan*. In our language the title means *A Description of Japan*, and it was written by a man named Engelbert Kaempfer.[49] This man wished to know about various countries, and traveled around without any specific destination in mind. He desired to investigate our country, and became an official called *Kafitan* on a Dutch ship.[50] During the Shōtoku period (1711–15), Kaempfer came to this country, and visited Kyōto as well as Edo.[51] He published a topographical work on various countries in the world, which has become famous. He worked hard to leave his name to posterity, and created a very detailed work. From the point of view of Japan, Holland is indeed a distant land, and I do not intend to play favorites with Japan over other nations, but Kaempfer visited the

---

was a man from Nagasaki who originally studied Neo-Confucianism, but after having contacts with the Dutch, he started seeking information from them.

46. A description of Chinese and Western astronomy, written by Nishikawa in 1720.

47. Written by Nishikawa in 1695. The work was expanded in 1708. It describes various aspects of foreign countries, such as the geographical location, notes on the people and population, including topographical information. This work introduced to Japanese the existence of North and South America.

48. Written in 1720.

49. Engelbert Kaempfer (1651–1716) was a German scholar who made a long voyage to Asia, eventually arriving in Japan. He wrote exactly what he saw and titled his work *Heutiges Japan* "Japan Today." Nevertheless, the work was only published some eighty years after Kaempfer wrote it. At that time, the title had become *Geschichte und Beschreibung von Japan* "A History and Description of Japan." Atsutane's quotation of the title appears to be an abbreviation. See Bodart-Bailey (1999) for a translation of this work.

50. No doubt the word *kafitan* is simply a Japanese rendering of the German *Kapitän* "captain." Of course, Kaempfer was never the captain of a ship. He was sent as a physician to Dejima.

51. In reality, Kaempfer set foot on Japanese soil on September 25, 1690. He spent two years in Japan and left on October 31, 1692.

world over, and he could not find another country as fine as ours, and he wrote it as he saw it ...[52] [HAZ 1.54, 56].

* * * * [53]

There is any number of teachings in the world. Having heard them, most are Confucian, and these scholars teach in a clever, narrow-minded manner. And there are scholars who follow Daoism who deal with strengthening the mind and enlightenment, things which smell of Buddhism and hell. They display a lack of human feeling, trying to establish a doctrine that is weak in the knees. When a person gets a whiff of these doctrines, they appear to make perfect sense, but upon pondering the ideas, you find that they go against the true Way. If this is true, then some ask if the Way is difficult to pursue, but in reality it is actually simple, not difficult to attain like *shinpō* "law of mind" or "the way to enlightenment." There is no obstacle to the Great Way, a way of peace where one can walk triumphantly; everyone is already walking down this path without knowing it ... [HAZ 1.65].

An ancient poet once wrote:

mononofu no	The sword girt about
torifaku tati no	the waist of the soldier;
tuka no ma mo	I will not forget
wasurezi to omofu	the sensation of the hilt,
yamato tamasifi	nor my Japanese spirit.[54]

The meaning of this poem is that like the soldier who always wears his sword about his waist, his feelings are under control. The use of *tuka no ma*

52. Beatrice Bodart-Bailey gives the following passage from Kaempfer, "The citizens surpass all others in manners, the arts, virtue, and all kinds of polite behavior, and they prosper as regards internal trade, fertility of soil, good health, strength of spirit, the necessities of life, and the peace of their land" (1988:7).

53. Hirata Atsutane goes to great lengths to deal with Kaempfer, especially since the German sided with the Japanese when it came to their closed-country policy. Atsutane's reasoning simply was, "When a country is strong, her people are strong like ours, have an abundance of goods on hand, and there is no necessity to have trade with foreign countries. And that is why our country is closed and we do not engage in trade." This quote is representative of five pages of text that I have abbreviated.

54. I have not been able to find any poem such as this quoted. The stanza *yamato tamasifi* is actually a product of the language after the Warring States period. Also, the epithet *mononofu no* attaches to either the toponym Uji or the number eighty *yaso*. This leads me to believe the poem is a later product. It is possible that Atsutane has fabricated this poem by splicing stanzas from two older poems together.

is a pun on hilt and "not for a moment," the poet will not forget his Japanese spirit even for a moment.

Our master, Norinaga, wrote another poem:

sikisima no	If asked what is
yamato kokoro wo	the heart of natural poetry,
fito tofaba	it is the scent
asafi ni niofu	of mountain cherry blossoms
yama sakurabana	lingering in the morning sun.[55]

First, *sikisima* refers to our country, but anciently it was an epithet for the place name of Yamato, as it is here. The meaning of this verse is, "If a person were to ask me how my heart was, wishing to know what the Japanese spirit is, I would say it is like beautiful cherry blossoms in bloom on a mountain in spring. The morning sun climbs into the sky above the blossoms, the petals dancing in the sunlight. My heart is just like this."

There is nothing more beautiful, more enjoyable, and more charming among all the sights than this. It may be tedious to repeat, but everyone born in this country possesses this beautiful, enjoyable disposition deep in their souls; many Japanese, however, have shifted their hearts to foreign learning, these feelings covered with a cloud. I urge you all to polish this heart and restore it to its original beauty. When you have not sufficiently polished your Japanese spirit, then we find that many misunderstandings occur in various respects. The words of the Chinese, "After you lay the foundation, then the Way appears naturally," is applicable here. . . .[56]

There is an abundance of scholars in this present age, but most have bad habits and are good-for-nothing. There is a well-known phrase, "People despise what they always see, but adore what they have never heard before." There are many people like this. In other words, they blindly follow something said by a foreigner or people from the past, but take no heed of something a Japanese or a living person has said. And even when these people believe that I have said something worthy, they do not change their prejudices. They part the hair and look for small scars, obsessed with the spirit of failure, looking for the smallest failing. And there are even people now

55. Norinaga composed this poem to praise the day when he made a portrait of himself in honor of his sixty-first year. Norinaga appears to be saying, "I see your outward appearance, but what is your heart like?" The poem is thus a response to this question. Cf. MNZ 1976, 15:462.

56. Found in the "Xue er" section of *The Analects*, "Once the root is secured, the Way unfolds" (Nylan 2014:3).

and then who do not even realize that they are going directly against the spirit of scholarship.

This was a bad habit of the ancient Chinese, and there are three or four places in *The Analects* of Confucius where he chastises the people for this. Nevertheless, there is nothing we can do about these people who are overlooking the good; however, people who wish to pursue scholarship should be very careful not to forget this. If people pay attention to you, then do not hesitate to correct your mistakes, making a clean break from this bad habit of not being able to make quick alterations in one's thinking. Remember the words of our old master: Pick the new bud without breaking the old one from last year. How we all wish to travel together down the path of learning.

The true way of humanity means that you do not keep everything to yourself, but let others hear about your learning. The Chinese say, "If you hear about the Way in the morning, then you may die in the evening [without regrets]."[57] If you hear the truth in the morning, then you are so happy that you do not mind if you leave this world in the evening. Even the Chinese know this, so if they understood how indebted they are to this country, then they would not be able to restrain themselves from telling others.

Thus, though I am lacking, I strive to inform others about this Way, encouraging them to follow it. This is the virtue of the heavenly and earthly *kami*. I have no desire to forget the generous blessings of the awe-inspiring emperor and the shogun. This is how I show my gratitude for my parents who raised me from a child, and I believe that is the way of humanity. I entreat all of you to strive to follow this way, for it is best to continue making progress [HAZ 1.66–68] … .

ꝏ

57. Found in the "Li ren" section of the *Analects*, "In the morning hear the Way; in the evening die content" (Nylan 2014:10).

TAMA NO MIHASHIRA

Hirata Atsutane | 1812

[Atsutane was greatly influenced by "Sandaikō," found in *Kojiki-den*, and reuses those diagrams to tweak the theory of Norinaga and Nakatsune, thus creating his own theology. While he accepted the overall framework, he pushed back against the idea of Yomi as the afterlife as framed by Norinaga and Nakatsune. Instead of seeing the dead spirits journeying to a separate realm, Atsutane argued that the spirits remained here on earth, though in a different dimension. Thus, those dead spirits were still near and could offer assistance and protection to the living.]

PART ONE

The pillar I thrust into the ground here is what supports the [true] Yamato Heart (*yamato gokoro*) of the students who study ancient learning. And this pillar is thrust down and erected upon the deep bedrock at the bottom of the earth. If this foundation is not built upon an unmoveable rock, then all our words, all our works, whether they are words or works—will be without support—having no pillar. If there are no pillars, then the beams and crossbeams, doors and windows creak, the anchor ropes loosen, the roof thatch becomes disturbed, and noises in the night along with a multitude of other disasters occur. But that is not all. A person's spirit does not know which way to go, and that person begins to follow theories that have come bounding over the seas from foreign countries, and we find it difficult to watch people blindly following these theories. Because we strongly desire to make the pillar of one's heart thick and sturdy, planted upon a large rock so that one will not be swayed by foreign ideas, we have obtained the power from the *kami* Yabune,[1] and this is the pillar we wish to set erect. This pillar [figuratively] opens and elucidates the true Way for each spirit after death, causing each to be at ease, making it such that the Japanese soul is not swayed by other forces.

makibasira	A pillar of black pine—
futoki kokoro wo	it is said he will protect
tifafemu to	your stout heart,

1. The *kami* who protects a person's roof. The name of this entity appears in the Ōtonosai liturgy.

sosoru kokoro fa	combining protection and comfort
sizume kanetu mo	in the heart that progresses.

The first thing that a student of ancient learning must do is make his Yamato spirit unshakeable. My master, Motoori, generously taught me that if a person is not firmly grounded, he will not be able to comprehend the Way.[2] These teachings are like an immoveable, solemn pillar erected upon bedrock. Nevertheless, when one desires to make his Yamato spirit firm and unshakeable, the most important point is to know where one's spirit goes and resides after death. Now, in order to know where the spirit goes to settles down, I will teach you about the origin of the three places of heaven, earth, and the afterworld.[3] I will explain about the conditions of heaven, earth, and the afterworld in detail, and then you will for the first time know sufficiently about the merits of the *kami* of these three places, how superior Japan is, it being the origin of all the various countries and everything which is in them, and how truly venerable is our emperor, who is the ruler of all nations. The student will first comprehend these things when he realizes where the spirit goes. (The reader should look at the following illustrations.)

Now, in order to know about the state of heaven, earth, and the afterworld, our elder scholar, Hattori Nakatsune, has written about them in his work *Sandaikō* ...[4][NST 50.12–13].

* * * *

Now, the countries had all been created, but before time had passed a mist clung to part of an area that was still fresh, and this is as it should be. That is the place where the wind *kami* was born.

> The ancient tradition states, "Hereupon, Izanami gave birth to her adorable, last son, Ho Musubi, and then hid her form, proclaiming to Izanagi, 'Do not look upon me for seven nights and seven days.' But before the seven-day period had expired, Izanagi looked in upon the mysterious place where Izanami had hidden herself. Izanami had given birth to the fire *kami*, scorched her pubic area, and she lay ill on the ground.[5] When the

2. It must be noted that Atsutane never met Norinaga face to face, Norinaga leaving this world right after Atsutane joined his school.

3. Jpn. *yomi*. Often written in Chinese as 黄泉 "yellow spring." Here Atsutane writes it just as 泉 "spring" or "fountain."

4. Atustane then quotes a large chunk of *Sandaikō*. I have abbreviated this section because a large portion of *Sandaikō* is included in this anthology. See pp. 453–61.

5. This is quoted from the "Chinkasai" liturgy.

flames were hot and scorched her, Izanami vomited, and the *kami* created from this were named Kanayama Hiko and Kanayama Hime. Izanami said, 'My beloved husband, I told you not to look at me, but you have gazed upon me.' Then she said, 'My beloved will rule the upper land, and I will rule the lower.' With this she arrived at the pass of Yomi, and thought to herself, 'I have born and forsaken an evil child in the land where my beloved rules.' So she returned to the upper land, and gave birth to another child. Thus, the *kami* formed from her defecation was called Haniyasu Hiko and then Haniyasu Hime. These are the *kami* of the earth. From her urine was formed the *kami* Mitsuho Hime, and this is the *kami* of water. And she gave birth to heavenly arrowroot and river seaweed. And she instructed them that if this evil child should ever become violent, that they could appease him through the water *kami*, gourds, the *kami* of the earth, and the river seaweed. The child born to the fire *kami* (also known as Hi no Kagutsuchi, and so forth) who wed Haniyama Hime was called Waku Musubi. This child's daughter is known as Toyoukebime (also called Ukemochi or Ugetsuhime). Having given birth to the fire *kami*, Izanami at last left the world."

The reason that Izanami hid herself in a rock when she gave birth to the fire *kami* was because she knew in advance how terrible the birth would be, and she did not want her husband to see it. … Now, at this time, neither the fire *kami* nor Ōhirume [Amaterasu] had been created yet, but since we see the usage of seven nights and seven days, at this point in time there was a clear division between days and nights. Thus, taking this fact into consideration, we should believe that the object that sprouted, climbed upward, and became heaven was of a clear and luminous nature, and that heaven and earth have already been separated. That is to say, heaven is the sun, and was separated from the earth early on, floating upward to its present position; also, since the earth was a floating object from the beginning, after it had been separated from heaven [the sun], it continues to float as before, and when it floats toward the sun, we have daytime, and when it floats away from the sun, it becomes night. And that is why such a usage [as days and nights] came about. If at this time heaven and earth were as yet unseparated, then there should have been nothing like night. (I have confidence in the validity of this theory. If my master had used this theory, then there would have been no necessity for him to have used the analogy in *Kuzuhana* of rats and weasels being able to see in the dark.)

The meaning of "give birth to fire" [pointing to Ho Musubi] refers to this being the first time that fire had come into existence via Izanami, as I have mentioned above; fire did not exist before this time. It is likely that the *kami* who creates fire came into existence when fire did. Or, perhaps the noun "fire" represents the fire *kami*, Ho Musubi, and his body is fire. (To the sciolistic Chinese and Japanese scholars: you must not rely on later learning and doubt these things. Because this is the *kami* Ho Musubi, this state of affairs is quite possible.) And because it is the place where this *kami* was born, it is called *hodo*. (Mabuchi's theory that *hodo* means the enclosed place is repugnant, and should be labeled as a layman's view.[6]) Again, taking this into consideration, when a woman's menstrual period starts, they say *fi ni naru* "becomes fire," and when the period ends, they say *fi no tomaru* "fire stops," and it perhaps relates to Izanami's birth to the fire *kami*. (In a later section the reader will find the passage where Izanagi slays the fire *kami* with a sword. The passage then says, "The blood from the fire *kami* spurted out violently, covering rocks, trees, and plants. And this is the reason why grass, trees, and, sand naturally contain fire." Even taking this passage into consideration, the fire that Izanami gave birth to was blood, and we then realize that blood is in reality fire.) Also, the usage of seven days and seven nights is different from the general usage of the word many (be it five hundred or eight hundred) in that it represents a set number of days. If this is the case, then perhaps this number of days is representing the length of the female menstruation period. (I thought of some other things, but I have already mentioned these in *Koshi-den*) … [NST 50.36–38].

The usage of "upper land" refers to the land of Japan, while "lower" refers to the land of Yomi, which exists below. The reason that Izanami went to this other world is because she had been severely burned giving birth to the fire *kami*, and in order to avoid the shame of being seen by her husband in that condition, she demanded that he not look upon her. However, he did look at her, bringing her to shame, and she was vexed and did not wish to dwell in the same land as him, so she decided to go to the lower land. … Izanami went as far as the pass of Yomi, leaving the fire *kami* in the upper land, and thought about the disasters that this *kami* would cause. Izanami felt grief about the situation, and turned around and returned to give birth to the *kami* of earth and water to quench the violence of the fire *kami*. (The reason that dirt and water are used to prevent fire now comes from this historic event.) Guessing the mind of Izanami at the time, it appears that

6. *Poto* is the Old Japanese word for vulva. Atsutane writes this word as 火処 "fire-place," glossed as *hodo*, but his reading of *hodo* is incorrect. It is true that this *ho* is homophonic with *ho* "fire," but that simply lends itself to the dramatic nature of this story. It is not proof of an etymology connecting the word to "fire."

she returned to the upper land because she treasured the world that she had created through the command of the heavenly *kami*. The defecation from Izanami represents "clay" and her urine represents "water." And from these two elements were born the *kami* of water and earth. And one may know the bounds they operate within by what has been said above about the fire *kami* and Kanayama Hiko. Therefore, water and clay were first formed at this time. (A person once asked, "I believe that fire did not exist before this period because there is no mentioning of fire, but it seems that water and clay were already in existence at the time. As explained in diagram number five, 'this was created from the hardening of the foam and tide,' so if *tide* does not refer to water, then what does it point to? Also, if you say that clay was first created at this stage, then it does not agree with the place earlier where Ujihini [*hiji* being 'mud'] appeared. If mud is not clay, then what is it?" I replied that this question has confused "tide" with "water," and "mud," "clay," and "earth." Tide and water appear to be related, but their essence is completely different. In order words, there is water mixed in with the flow of the tide of the ocean, but what is commonly called *brine* is the true essence of the tide. You will understand this better if you compare brine with water. Again, mud and clay may appear to be the same substance, but they are different in that clay has the dense adhesiveness to make pottery jugs, but mud is coarse with no adhesiveness. Taking both in one's hands, it is easy to feel the difference. "Earth" is an umbrella term for clay, mud, sand, and when used in a general sense it can refer to the entire land. …)

Now, before Izanami went to the land of Yomi, Izanagi and Izanami had only given birth to four *kami*—wind, fire, water, and earth *kami*. Other than these four, there were no other *kami* created through the will of these two creative powers. This is truly awe-inspiring, something mysterious and wondrous. The student should study deeply the power of each of the spirits of these four creative *kami*. Is there even one thing among all the creations in heaven and earth that does not fall within the sphere of one of these four *kami*? Also, is there anything that cannot be comprehended by the logic of the creative spiritual power of these four *kami*? However, since these are the doings of *kami*, one may sometimes think this way, but when the student ponders the origin of these things, he realizes that Izanagi and Izanami esteemed the command from the heavenly *kami* to create a world, and gave birth to the land as they had been instructed. After this, they gave birth to these *kami*, and it is difficult to express in language the mystery of this event, it being very reverent and awe-inspiring. One should take the time to think deeply about these things. (People in Western countries have researched deeply into the myriad things in our world, and what they have discovered is that everything can be broken down into the four elements of wind, fire, water, or earth; these elements are very important. This is a very reasonable way of thinking. But as Westerners do not have the correct, ancient legends, they do not know about the origins of these four elements; we cannot say that it is sufficient for them to simply discover the elements and use logic to understand them.)

The sentence "and at last she left the world" refers to the fact that Izanami left for the lower land, as mentioned previously, but she returned when halfway there, and gave birth to the *kami* of water and earth. And yet, she was still ashamed of having been looked upon, and this sentence means that she left her husband and went back down to the lower land. (The adverbial "at last" should not be treated lightly.) The usage of "went to the lower land" refers to her going in her present state, and does not mean that she died and only her spirit went.

> The ancient tradition states, "Hereupon, Izanagi said, 'My beloved wife! Must I trade you for one child?' …[7] Izanagi drew his large sword and cut Kagutsuchi into three pieces. Hereupon, the blood dripping from the blade of the sword became the boulder cluster in the plain of the heavenly Yasu River. This is the ancestor of Futsunushi. … The blood from the fire *kami* spurt out violently, covering rocks, trees, and plants. And this is the reason why grass, trees, and sand naturally contain fire in them. … Now, the *kami* created from one of the sections that had been severed as Kagutsuchi was being killed was called Ikatsuchi; the next *kami* formed from the next section severed was called Ōyamatsumi; the last *kami* formed from the last section was called Taka Okami."

The blood from the blade of the sword used to decapitate Ho Musubi violently spurted up to heaven and first became the boulder cluster there. Also, the blood from the sword guard, the tip, and the hilt splashed upward to the boulder cluster and turned into many *kami*. From its conception, fire has had the energy of shooting upward, and there is proud significance in the fact that fire still reacts in this manner. And it is because of this tradition noted above that when one looks upward at the sun [it appears] that fire is burning at its peak. Because there is fire, from our vantage point here on earth, the sun appears as a big fire. The object that sprouted and rose upward becoming heaven not only contained a clear and luminous essence from the beginning, but when fire drew near, heaven grew brighter, later

7. The ellipses are in the original.

becoming the land governed by the sun goddess. The light shined forth and gradually increased in radiance. (Foreigners do not know about the origin of this tradition, and say that the sun merely appears as an accumulation of fire when gazed at from our land, or they say that it is only the essence of fire;[8] they say things like this because the ancient legends of the divine age have not been transmitted in their countries.) Now, since the sun appears as if it were fire when looked upon from our country, it was probably from that that the sun was called *fi*[9] in the divine age … [NST 50.38–42].

Now, I would like to briefly address the merit and virtue of the *kami* of heaven and earth, which brings fortune to our land. First, the two procreative *kami* dwelt in the great expanse early on, creating one entity that later divided to become heaven and earth. When the land was still unsteady, *kami* were produced in succession from Uhijini down to Izanagi and Izanami. The spear was given to Izanagi and Izanami, and they formed our country by hardening the land; these two *kami* fulfilled the heavenly command with trepidation; every aspect of their work was related to the forming of our land. (This work began when they thrust the spear into the ground on the isle of Onogoro, making it the pillar of the land. And the beginning and end of the exchange of wedding vows itself, too, was a step toward giving birth to the country, and this is also clear from their words uttered at the time. Also, the birth of the wind *kami* was part of their work in that they wished to disperse the fog from the land. And even when Izanami gave birth to the fire *kami*, she gave birth to something that had to exist in the land, and because she treasured the land that she had given birth to, she also created the *kami* of the earth and water to quench the violent nature of the fire *kami*. …)

Now, since these various *kami* were born through the will of Izanagi and Izanami, who treasured this land—some being created according to this act and others being created according to that act—there is not a single aspect about these traditions that is amiss; the reader will realize this because these *kami* are even now continually bringing fortune to this land

8. This appears to be criticism aimed at China. *Lun heng* says, "The fiery essence of the sun regularly produces poison" (Forke 1962, 1:298). *Huainanzi* also records, "The hot *qi* (essences) of accumulated yang produced fire; the essence of fiery *qi* became the sun" (Major 2010:115).

9. In modern Japanese *fi* can mean both "fire" and "sun." However, linguistically there is a problem with Atsutane's reasoning. In ancient *man'yōgana* script, sun (日) was written with a type-one character (such as 比, Middle Chinese *pji*), while fire (火) was written with a type-two character (such as 肥, Middle Chinese *buj*). These are two unrelated words. The pitch accent for these two words is also different: "sun" is H(L) and "fire" is L(H).

because of the merit of these creative *kami*. For example, the rays of the sun beating down upon a rice seed, heating it up and causing it to sprout and bear fruit, are the same as the fire *kami* wedding Haniyama Hime and giving birth to Waka Musubi. These things all come about due to the spirit of the fire, earth, and water *kami*. If the sun should shine violently down upon the earth, then there would be an outbreak of evil insects, and the rice stalks would wither, baked by the violent rays of the sun. Then the water in the mountains would rise up into the sky as a mist, and fall as rain upon the earth; this is the blessing of the earth and water *kami*. ... Thus, when the fire and water *kami* quarrel, the thunder *kami* groan, and the water *kami* (Okami) even causes a cold autumn rain to fall. (The following poem is seen in *Man'yōshū*:

wa ga woka no	You commanded the water *kami*
okami ni ifite	of the hill where I dwell
furasimesi	to make it snow,
yuki no kudakesi	and perhaps he caused to scatter
soko ni tirikemu	some delicate snow where you are)
	[MYS 104].

Since even humans are overcome with dread, how the more so that insects should hide deep in their holes, and some even die. When there is an overabundance of fog and rain, the wind blows both away; with the passing of the wind, the rain and wind let up, and we see that the various *kami* work together to send blessings down upon our land. If the reader were to research the reason for this state of affairs, he would come to find that these *kami* are all the offspring born through the will of the two creative *kami* (Izanagi and Izanami) who diligently obeyed the great command from the heavenly *kami* to form and strengthen this land ... [NST 50.44–45].

The ancient legend states, "Izanagi wished to see his wife, Izanami, again, so he set off for the land of Yomi. Thus, when Izanami came out of the (Yomi) palace door to greet Izanagi, he said to her, 'My beloved wife, please come back with me for the land we created together is not complete.' Hereupon, Izanami replied, 'How regrettable that you have not come sooner. I have already partaken of the food of Yomi. Nevertheless, since my beloved husband has come here, I will discuss the matter with the *kami* of Yomi to see about going back with you. My beloved, please do not look upon me.' Having said this, she went back inside the palace; having been gone a long time, Izanagi could wait no longer. ... Izanagi lit one torch, and when he went inside, he saw that Izanami's body was swollen like the tide, and she was covered with maggots. ... There resided the eight gods of thunder. Izanagi was greatly surprised and when he began to flee, he said, 'Our bond is severed!' And he spit on the ground. The *kami* formed from the spit was named Hayatamanoo. The *kami* that formed when Izanagi fled was called Yomotsu Kototoke no O. Izanami said, 'You have not kept your promise, and have brought me to shame!' ... And (the gods of thunder) pursued after Izanagi. When Izanagi reached the Even Pass of Yomi, he attacked the on-comers with three peaches that grew on a peach tree near the pass; having been attacked, the army of the gods of thunder all fled. Izanagi commanded the peaches, 'So-and-So.' Saying this, he gave them the name of Ōkamutsumi. ... Thus, his wife, Izanami, arriving late, was the last person to arrive at the Even Pass of Yomi. Izanagi blocked the passageway with a rock that was so large it would take one thousand people to move it. With the rock in the middle, Izanagi and Izanami stood opposite each other. Here Izanagi commanded, 'Come no further.' Thus, he threw down his staff. The name of the *kami* born from the staff was called Kunado. Izanami declared, 'My beloved husband, I proclaim that I will strangle the throats of one thousand of your subjects a day.' To this Izanagi replied, 'My beloved wife, I proclaim that I will give birth to fifteen hundred people a day.' ... Izanagi stated, 'I was weak to have felt anguish and longing for you in the beginning.' ... At that time, Izanami gave the guard of the road to Yomi a message to deliver. 'You and I have already produced the country. Why do you desire to produce more? I will thus stay in this land (Yomi) and will return with you.' Izanagi listened and agreed with what was said. The *kami* then withdrew. Thus, Izanami is called the great *kami* of Yomi. ... And the great boulder that was used to block the Even Pass of Yomi is known as the great *kami* Chigaeshi. Some say that the Even Pass of Yomi is now Ifuya hill in Izumo."

Izanami's words "I have already partaken of the food of Yomi" demonstrates that when her husband, Izanagi, arrived, she had found it hard to divorce him, and still had the desire to return with him to the upper land; however, because she had already tasted the food of Yomi, she was saddened, realizing she could no longer return with Izanagi. And this is exactly how our master, Motoori, explained this section. Let us now ponder the reason why Izanami could no longer return to the upper land. First, when Izanagi killed the fire *kami*, blood spurted out from the body, and stained the clusters of boulders, shrubs, and trees, and that is why plants, trees, and rocks naturally contain the element of fire. And considering that even that which congealed and formed the bottom of the ocean contains the element of fire, we believe that this fire penetrates down to the lower land, and so fire also first appeared at the time the fire *kami* was created.

On the other hand, since Yomi is an extremely polluted place, it is quite possible that the fire of Yomi is also very defiled. And since Izanami had partaken of something cooked in that fire, then her very being had become defiled, and that is why she could not return with Izanagi. If she had returned to this land in her defiled state through contact with the polluted fire of Yomi, then her violent child (the fire *kami*) would have become riotous, and various calamities would have occurred in this land. …

Now the fire of Yomi and this land (Japan) were originally from the same extraction, so why should the fire of Yomi be avoided? The answer to this question is multifaceted: there is the fact that the fire of Yomi has been defiled by the pollution from the land. Also, as mother of the fire *kami*, Izanami retired to Yomi because she gave birth to that *kami*, and then [Izanagi] killed the fire *kami*. Thus, Yomi is a place that was utterly abhorred. And that is why it is believed that the fire of Yomi was avoided and abhorred so much. To take this a step further, this polluted fire of Yomi is not only incapable of producing life, but will instead become angry and cause horrible disasters to occur, preventing the fire *kami* to bestow blessings on this land. (In relation to everything in the world, if the spirit of the fire *kami* does not bestow his blessing, then nothing can be created; as all defilement is connected to the land of Yomi, the fire *kami* does not bestow his blessing. For example, if one is to forge something out of iron, or is going to dye a cloth blue and red, it is clear that a pure fire must be employed, and it is difficult to argue about avoiding a polluted fire; thus, the reader should realize that one cannot ignore the defilement of fire. Whether one forges something or dyes a cloth a color, these actions all relate to the works of humans, but whether something is given life or not is the doing of the will of the *kami*. Taking this fact together, the reader may know that the words of our master, Norinaga, "*Kami* are like people who use puppets, and humans are the puppets" are very profound indeed. …) The theory of our master, Norinaga, that all calamity is due to the workings of the spirit of Magatsubi is inadequate.[10]

From this time forth, the great *kami* Izanami has ruled the land of Yomi. In this section Izanami said, "I will discuss the matter with the *kami* of Yomi." It is clear that since the creation of the land of Yomi the two *kami* Kunino Soko Tachi and Toyo Kumunu resided in Yomi, but it is unclear which *kami* Izanami went to have her discussion with. … But before Izanami became the great *kami* in charge of the land of Yomi, perhaps these *kami* governed Yomi, and that is why Izanami told Izanagi that she had to discuss the matter with them. …

---

10. See *Kojiki-den*, pp. 425, 431, 434–35 in this volume.

As we are told in *Sandaikō*, the Even Pass of Yomi is the border of Yomi. Nevertheless, it is unclear whether this pass is located on the edge of our country and the earth, or within the earth, or between Yomi itself and the earth. As the ancient tradition states, the Ifuya hill in Izumo was believed to have been this pass.

In this section, the two *kami* made vows to have Izanagi remain in Japan and have Izanami remain in Yomi; this is a mysterious and significant passage. I have some thoughts on this, but will not voice them here.

The ancient records say, "Hereupon, Izanagi stated, 'I have gone to a severely defiled place. I must purify myself.' … He arrived in Ahagihara of Odo in Tachibana in the province of Hyūga where he performed purification. … When he washed himself in the center flow of the water, he blew his breath out, and the *kami* that was formed was called Yaso Magatsubi and then Ōmagatsubi. These two *kami* were created from the pollution that tainted Izanagi when he went to Yomi. … Next, the *kami* created when Izanagi expelled his breath was called Kamu Naobi, and he rectified the evil. Next appeared Ōnaobi. … After this, the *kami* born when Izanagi washed his left eye was named Amaterasu no Ōmikami, also known as Amaterasu Ōhirume. The *kami* produced when he washed his right eye was called Tsukuyomi, also known as Takehaya Susanoo.[11] Izanagi was filled with joy and issued a decree, declaring, 'I have given birth to two noble children this last time that I have produced offspring.'[12] Thus, the form of Amaterasu was illustrious and beautiful, and she shines behind heaven and earth. Izanagi said, 'I have produced many children, but none have been as mysterious as this one. She should not remain here.' With these words, his necklace jingled as he took it off and gave it to Amaterasu no Ōmikami. He decreed to Amaterasu no Ōmikami, saying, 'You will rule the High Plain of Heaven.' At this time heaven and earth were not distantly separated. Izanagi had the sun goddess ascend up to heaven via the heaven pillar. … To Susanoo he decreed, saying, 'You will rule over the blue ocean plain and the many folds of the tide.' Susanoo did not fulfill his father's command and did not rule over the area he had been given. … Izanagi questioned Susanoo, saying, 'Why is it that you do not rule over the country given you, but cry all the time?' Susanoo replied, 'I weep because I desire to follow my mother to the Distant Land.' Izanagi was greatly angered at these words and declared, 'Thus, you will no longer dwell in this land! Do as your heart desires and proceed to the Distant Land!' Hereupon, Susanoo said, 'But I desire to make a petition to Amaterasu Ōmikami.' And so he ascended to heaven. Izanagi's mission was fulfilled, and his virtue was

11. It is interesting that Atsutane ignores the story in *Kojiki*, where Amaterasu is born from Izanagi's left eye, the moon *kami* from his right eye, and Susanoo from his nose.

12. *Kojiki* has Izanagi say, "I have given birth to *three* noble children."

> great. His divine task had been completed, and he returned to heaven to make his report. Izanagi now resides in the Lesser Palace of the Sun."

The *kami* Magatsubi and Noabi are the violent and meek spirits of Amaterasu and Susanoo. There is the mysterious tradition that the meek spirit, Naobi, belongs to Amaterasu while the violent spirit, Magatsubi, belongs to Susanoo. The diagram here has been drawn to reflect this thinking. ... This is the tradition about the birth of these two *kami* [Magatsubi and Naobi], but as a token that Izanagi had beheld a terribly defiled land, had despised it, and had thought deeply about quickly being able to perform ablutions to purify himself of the defilement, Magatsubi was born first when the defilement had been washed away from Izanagi's body. With this, Magatsubi deeply hates pollution, and becomes violent when defilement is close. ... Now, when the great *kami* Izanagi had purified himself of the pollution, he gave birth to Magatsubi, a violent *kami* who suddenly becomes angry if things do not go his way, so Izanagi felt regret for this action, as Magatsubi would spell disaster for the country; in order to rectify the evil that this *kami* created, Izanagi gave birth to Noabi. (When we remember that Izanami gave birth to the earth and wind *kami* to quench the violent nature of the fire *kami*, we understand the reason for this.) Therefore, Naobi is a *kami* who rectifies the evil in the world, transforming bad into good. The divine forms of these two *kami* are divided between heaven and Yomi, but the influence of their spirits has an effect on this country just as wind and fire can penetrate to the core of anything. Therefore, evil occurs after something good has happened, and good occurs after evil has taken place. And this is not only true of the country, but *kami* and humanity alike all receive some influence from both of these *kami*. ... There is not a person alive who does not despise filth and evil, and there are those people who are violent when they are angered. This is because their nature is influenced by Magatsubi. But on the other hand, there are those who are appeased of their anger, and change their way of thinking, and this state is influenced by the spirit of Naobi. Those who do not change their thinking but grow all the more violent are sucked into the calamity of the evil which Magatsubi creates, and then that person sees eye to eye with this evil *kami*. In other words, you agree with what he does. (The liturgy of the Great Palace Festival praises Yabune, but within those words is the phrase, "If there is any omission or any oversight, then we beseech that the *kami* Kamu Naobi and Ōnaobi may hear and rectify, and see and correct these." One should ponder these words. This means that humans and *kami* alike have the spirit of Magatsubi in them, which is angered at errors and blunders, and since there also exist the spirit of Noabi, which observes such mistakes and rectifies them, the liturgy was pronounced in this manner. People should realize that this is the reasonable state of all things. There is a deficiency in the theory of our master, Norinaga, and there are even places where he has argued incorrectly.[13]) However, there is a mysterious import in this tradition about these two spirits, which are like, for example, the wheels on a cart, being necessary, no matter who you are. I have discussed this necessity in *Koshi-den*.

The High Plain of Heaven is the land in heaven. (The minute discussion in *Kojiki-den* is satisfactory.) Amaterasu was born from the praiseworthy spirit of Izanagi, and her form is of unparalleled illuminance and beauty. Since she shines in space between heaven and earth, her father, the great *kami* [Izanagi], felt that she was a worthy ruler for the land in the High Plain of Heaven, and that is why she was established where she is. ...

The presentation of the necklace to Amaterasu is likely a symbol that Izanagi had transferred the right to bestow blessings upon the world to her because he [Izanagi] was delighted with having completed his work, having now finished giving birth to the land, and the *kami* that pour blessings upon the land. (And that is also the reason why Izanagi retired to the Lesser Palace of the Sun.) And the reason that Izanagi produced the beautiful sound with the jewels on the necklace was the act of praying for long life. (That is why in the liturgy of appeasing the spirit of the emperor where the ten heavenly symbols are given we see the following, "Then move and dance about! Sway back and forth. If you do this, the dead will return to life."[14] From this the reader may know the truth of these things. It is insufficient to believe that there was no meaning to the ancient custom of wearing jewels. The case here with Izanagi giving the necklace to Amaterasu shows he wants to pray for long life. ... Anciently, when one wanted to live a long life he put many jewels on a string and wore it around his neck, so the breaking of the necklace was a symbol of death. Taking this all into consideration, the reader will realize that Izanagi's presentation of the necklace to Amaterasu was the act of bestowing all blessings of fortune upon her. ... And the words of our master, Norinaga, are completely reasonable when he said, "All usages of the word *tamafu* 'to bestow' come

13. Atsutane continues to take issue with Norinaga's view in the sixth chapter of *Kojiki-den*, where he says, "Now, all the evil, wicked events in the world have their origins in the spirit of Magatsubi." It would seem that Atsutane does not agree with Norinaga's assessment that Magatsubi is *specifically* evil.

14. This is seen in *Kujiki*. See Bentley (2006:156).

from the jewels (*tama*) that were worn around the neck. And that is why gifts were known as *tamamono*." Furthermore, that does not only mean objects, but also points to the spirits (*tama*) that were bestowed upon human beings by the *kami*. …)

Thus, these jewels are symbols that Izanagi had bestowed the revered spirit of fortune upon Amaterasu and that is why these jewels have been worshipped as Mikuratana. Now, Amaterasu became the ruler over the High Plain of Heaven as her father had commanded, and she is called Amaterasu Ōmikami "the great *kami* which shines in heaven" because she sends her rays down upon the entire world. And as has been stated above, heaven also refers to the sun, so the *kami* that rules over this place should be known as the sun goddess. Now, as our master, Norinaga, stated, there is a country in heaven just like there is a country on this earth, and that country is known as the High Plain of Heaven; however, in contrast to all the countries on earth existing on the surface, it is believed that the High Plain of Heaven exists below the surface. The reason for this belief is because when Ame Waka Hiko shot the pheasant with his arrow, and when that arrow arrived at the place where Takaki dwelt, the *kami* took the arrow and threw it back down through the hole it had made when it came up. …

The "blue ocean plain" is an ancient usage that refers to this entire place [Japan], but when the text says "the many folds of the tide," it then refers to the entire ocean, being the same usage as is seen in the liturgies of the indigenous religion, "to the very bounds of the foam and the tide." … Now, the command given to Susanoo to rule over the blue ocean plain and the many folds in the tide was given in contrast to that command bestowed upon Amaterasu, "Rule over the High Plain of Heaven." This shows that the sphere of jurisdiction was divided between heaven and earth, and because these two praiseworthy *kami* were born from different eyes of Izanagi, it is only proper that the division be done in this manner.[15] Nevertheless, Susanoo went contrary to the command, and his father, the great *kami*, thought him an extremely filthy soul, and it is only reasonable that Izanagi should have been so angered, since Susanoo wanted to go to the despicable Distant Land, and always was weeping and wailing. … And yet, when we fully consider the fact that Susanoo really just wanted to go to the Distant

---

15. It needs to be noted that this storyline is created by Atsutane and does not represent the orthodox texts. *Nihon shoki* has twelve versions here, the orthodox and eleven variations. Of these, only one mentions Amaterasu and Tsukuyomi being born from the eyes and Susanoo from the nose of Izanagi, which may reflect the version found in *Kojiki*. On the other hand, *Kujiki* only notes that these *kami* were born, not in what manner. There is no account in *Kujiki* where only Amaterasu and Susanoo are born from the eyes of Izanagi.

Land where his mother was, then there was nothing that could have been done with Susanoo's plight. Izanagi and Izanami gave birth to the country in the beginning according to the command of the heavenly *kami*, and even though there was a deep bond between Izanagi and Izanami when they exchanged their wedding vows, Izanagi went to Yomi and beheld the pollution there, cut his ties with Izanami, spit on the ground to expel her, and then went and purified his body. Thus, perhaps Susanoo was created as a symbol of expiation of the deep affection that Izanagi had carried for Izanami. And that is why this *kami* could not govern the land he had been assigned, but wished to go to the Distant Land where his mother was, and in the end, departed for that place. (The student should ponder this. Amaterasu is a female but served Izanagi and was given charge over the sun in heaven; Susanoo is a male but served his mother, and was given charge over the place of night. This is a mysteriously profound tradition that is unequaled in the world. …) Now, even though Susanoo wished to go to the land where his mother resided, he did not go right away, but started to fulfill the command of his father. He spent a long time in Japan, accomplishing many respectable things, and in the end, as was reasonable, he went to the Distant Land and became Tsukuyomi.

Since Izanagi first accomplished the task given him from the heavenly *kami* of creating and forming the country, naturally it should be his final duty to return to heaven and make his report. I fully agree with Hattori Nakatsune, who states that there is no problem in theorizing that this Lesser Palace of the Sun was located in heaven because of the usage in the text of "thus, he resided there." I believe that this palace refers to Izanagi quietly retiring indefinitely, and the name is in contrast with the residence of Amaterasu, who resides in the Greater Palace. (There is something I have pondered in relation to this. Izanagi went so far as to give the jeweled necklace to Ōhirume, and caused her to rule over heaven, and then he retired to the palace in heaven, while Izanami retired to the land of Yomi, where Tsukuyomi had been given the right to rule. Thus, this shows the reasonable logic that the *kami* of the sun and moon inherited the authority to rule from Izanagi and Izanami. And there is profound meaning in the fact that the offspring of the sun and moon *kami* became the rulers of this land.)

> The ancient legends go on to say, "Because of the strength and superiority of Susanoo's divine nature, the seas thrashed and raged, and the mountains moaned and bellowed when Susanoo proceeded to heaven. When Amaterasu heard about the manner in which Susanoo had reached heaven, she

was filled with amazement … Susanoo said, 'Let us together make a vow, and within that vow we will give birth to children. If those children that I produce are sons, then you may know that I have pure intentions. However, if I produce daughters, then you may know that I have evil intentions.' … The myriad jewels were asked for. … Male *kami* were produced in the mist when the blade of the sword was chewed up with a crunching sound, and blown out. Hereupon, Susanoo raised his voice and said, 'Truly, I am victorious.' And that is why the name of that child was called Masaka Akatsukachi Hayahi Ama no Oshihowake. … Hereupon, Amaterasu … declared, 'The original essence of those jewels from which these *kami* were produced are mine. That means that these male *kami* that were produced are all my children. …' Hereupon, Susanoo addressed Amaterasu, 'Since I have come up here with pure intentions, I have produced male *kami*. Therefore, I am the victor.' Having said this, he became violent, gloating in his victory. With this, Amaterasu said, 'There is a *kami* named Ukemochi that resides in the central land of Ashihara. You, Susanoo, will go and see him.'[16] Susanoo went down to where Ukemochi dwelt. … Thus, Susanoo was enraged and declared, 'How filthy! How disgusting! You intend to serve me things that you have vomited from your mouth?' Having said this, he drew his sword and slew Ukemochi. … Various grains were produced from the dead body of Ukemochi. … Amaterasu was filled with joy, proclaiming, 'These are the things that the common man will use to subsist.' … The sun goddess had fields called Amasata and Nagata in which her grain was planted. … In the spring, Susanoo destroyed the divisions of the rows. … Amaterasu was stunned, and entered into the heavenly cave and shut the door of rock. Thus all of the High Plain of Heaven was without light, and the central land of Ashihara was in constant darkness, the people not being able to tell when it was day or night. … At that time, the multitude of *kami* were severely grieved, and gathered themselves together, and thought of a way to coax the sun goddess out of the cave. … When Amaterasu came forth from the heavenly cave, light illuminated the High Plain of Heaven and the central land of Ashihara again … The myriad of *kami* counseled among themselves, and levied a punishment for defilement of one thousand tables upon Susanoo. … The myriad of *kami* said to Susanoo, 'Your actions have been extremely rude. You may not remain in heaven! You will go immediately to the Distant Land!' With this they threw Susanoo out of heaven … Thus, Susanoo led his son, Itakeru, and descended

16. Ukemochi appears in one variant tradition in *Nihon shoki*, where Amaterasu commands Tsukuyomi to go down and observe. Atsutane has dovetailed Susanoo and Tsukuyomi together apparently to give Susanoo more authority and privilege than the existing legends contain. *Kujiki* (Bentley 2006:145–46) contains a related version of this story, but again the moon *kami* is the actor.

from heaven, and went around the farthest wall of heaven, and came to the land of Silla. … They crossed over to the east … and said, 'This island of Kara[17] is an island of gold and silver. My son will rule it, and the ships filled with treasure will never cease.' … And his eyebrows became camphor trees. Hereupon, Susanoo proclaimed, 'So on and so forth.' … Thus, Susanoo arrived at the upper part of the river Hi in the province of Izumo … and when he slew the great serpent … he found the sword Tsumugari.[18] Taking the sword, and feeling that it had a mysterious power, Susanoo put it near him. … Susanoo placed Kushinada Hime in the wedding cottage that he built, and she gave birth to a *kami* named Yashimajinumi. … Thus, Susanoo took the heavenly Murakumo sword, and said, 'This is a mysterious sword. How can I keep it peacefully?' So he had Ame no Fukine, a descendant of Susanoo in the fifth generation, take the sword up to heaven and after presenting it to Amaterasu, Susanoo went to Kumanasu Peak, and then proceeded to the Distant Land, and ruled over the land of the night. … And Ōkuninushi had eight brothers. … Hereupon, Ōkuninushi … was finished with the organization of the land. … When Ōkuninushi was at the cape of Miho in the land of Izumo, he saw that there a heavenly *kagami*[19] boat came riding on the crest of the waves. Within it rode a dwarf who had made the boat out of the skin of the *kagami* fruit and wore a robe made of wren feathers. Ōkuninushi asked the dwarf his name, but he did not answer. … Kamu Musubi replied, 'Truly, this is my son.' … Thus, Ōnamochi and Sukuna Bikona worked together and formed the land. When these two *kami* traveled around the divine land. … Ōkuninushi said to Sukuna Bikona, 'Would you not say that the country that we have created is well done?' Sukuna Bikona replied, 'Some places have been completed, and some others have not.' Later, Sukuna Bikona was traveling, and came to the cape of Kumano, and finally went off to the Distant Land."

It is only sensible that Susanoo would wish to ascend to heaven and beg to have an audience with Amaterasu, but the reason that he boasted when they gave birth to children, and then became extremely violent is because

17. Here written as 韓, referring to the Korean Peninsula.

18. The sword is called Kusanagi in *Nihon shoki*. *Kujiki* calls the sword produced from the serpent's tail "Ama no Murakumo" (cf. Bentley 2006:178). The Kusanagi sword is also mentioned in *Kujiki*, but as one of the three imperial regalia (2006:173), thus keeping the two names separate. There is some confusion in the *Kojiki* texts, where the name of the sword is written as 都牟羽之大刀, the great sword *tumupa*, but this orthography does not fit the standard of *Kojiki*, where 羽 is a *kungana*. Some texts, however, have 都牟刈, which is what Atsutane has based his reading on.

19. A plant known as *Metaplexis japonica*, which is native to China and Japan. The fruit is somewhat elongated, and when split open resembles a small boat.

the violent spirit of Magatsubi was with him at the time. (In other words, this is Susanoo's son, Itakeru, regardless that the fact that Susanoo brought Itakeru with him when he ascended to heaven has vanished from the ancient records. This is clear from the usage of "Susanoo led his son, Itakeru, and descended from heaven.") Susanoo became violent according to the spirit of Magatsubi. Since Magatsubi is a *kami* who despises any kind of defilement, when Ukemochi presented things to Susanoo produced from the mouth and buttocks, he became violent. … However, because of the symbol of purification, Susanoo's heart was not only pacified, but Itakeru also became a *kami* of great virtue. And this shows that the spirit of expiation is very mysterious. … Now, Susanoo descended from heaven and went around the farthest wall of heaven; this means that when Izanagi gave Susanoo the command to rule over the blue ocean plain and the many folds of the tide, Susanoo did as he was commanded, and went as far as the tide went, and looked out upon the various foreign countries that existed on the boundaries. However, he returned to Japan, saying that "There is an island called Kara that has gold and silver. My son will rule this land, and the ships filled with treasure will never cease." And so he grew camphor trees with which to construct ships. This entire string of events is very profound, and the results of his work are finally realized for the first time during the reign of Okinaga Tarashi Hime.[20] However, Susanoo went to plant and grow various other kinds of trees, and obtained the Murakumo sword from cutting the tail of the great serpent, and his descendants up to the fifth generation resided in the province of Izumo, watching over the creation of the land by the *kami*. After Ōkuninushi who was born in the sixth generation came on the scene,[21] Susanoo was able to finally realize his desire and then went off to the Distant Land. (The word *finally* must not be looked upon lightly. It carries the same profundity that the *finally* used in relation to Izanagi who retired to the Lesser Palace of the Sun had.) When it was time for Susanoo to proceed to the Distant Land, he gave the sword to Ame no Fukine, his grandson in the fifth generation, and had him present it to Amaterasu, and this also was an act in which Susanoo had deep feeling.

Our master, Norinaga, theorized that this Kumanasu peak to which Susanoo proceeded was really Kumano, and that is a most reasonable idea.

---

20. Emperor Jingū. The "results" that Atsutane is referencing is the legend of the subjugation of the Korean Peninsula by Jingū.

21. *Kojiki* makes Ōkuninushi a descendant of Susanoo in the sixth generation. *Kujiki*, which contains a detailed genealogy of Susanoo down to the eleventh generation, records Ōnamuji (another name for Ōkuninushi) as a son of Susanoo (Bentley 2006:191), not a great-great-grandson.

When Susanoo entered Yomi, his spirit stayed there. This is the spirit of Kumano, Kushimikenu, and when Ōkuninushi and Sukuna Bikona were completing the land, Kushimikenu gave them many plows, and this shows his desire to participate in the creation of the land. Now, this great *kami*, Susanoo, had no other choice but to join his mother in the land below. However, when we examine the behavior of this *kami* from his conception till he went to the Distant Land, we see that he gave heed to the words of his father, and it is simply not enough to say that he paid reverence to the will of his father. It is likely because his existence was due to the purification ceremony that Susanoo was possessed with such intentions. There is Haya Sasurahime mentioned in the Great Purification liturgy, which says, "And there will be no sin remaining. … Haya Sasurahime who resides in the Distant Land will then take these sins and wash them away" and this is actually Susanoo, mentioned under another name because he was banished and sent away.[22] (Norinaga's theory that Sasurahime was Suserihime is mistaken.[23] There are many other examples where a male *kami* is later mentioned as a female, like this one with Susanoo being mentioned as Sasurahime. This is a very mysterious legend. I have dealt with this in detail in *Koshi-den*.) The reader should understand the workings of this mysterious power of reason by considering the actions of Susanoo from beginning to end, and this purification ceremony. … And since Susanoo rules over the underworld, he has been given the name Tsukuyomi. (The fact that Susanoo and Tsukuyomi are the same *kami* is also seen in *Kojiki-den* and *Sandaikō*, and this theory has now become entrenched in society.[24])

Ukemochi, Ōgetsuhime, and Toyouke Hime are one and the same, and the spiritual power of this *kami* in producing trees is known as Kukunochi, and the power to produce plants is known as Kayanohime. Taking these two spiritual powers together, they are known by the name Yabune, and the fact that Toyouke Hime is the *kami* of food, lodging, and clothing is explained in detail in *Koshi-den*. … A person should not forget the blessings of this *kami* even for a short time.

One person asked me, "You said that in the beginning the sun in the heavens came from the luminous object that sprouted and grew upward, becoming brighter when fire came close, and then it grew even brighter

22. In other words, he is a fitting character to dispose of the defilement being purged during the Great Purification.

23. This theory appears in *Ōharae no Kotoba Kōshaku* (MNZ 1976, 7:159).

24. Norinaga states that there is a possibility that Susanoo and Tsukuyomi were actually the same actor in the legend (MNZ 1976, 9:388). He concludes by saying, "It is not easy to claim this, however."

when Amaterasu Ōmikami was given reign over the land. This is proper because that is how the ancient legends describe the events; however, when Amaterasu hid herself in the Iwato cave, why would the High Plain of Heaven and the central land of Ashihara be cast into darkness?"

I replied that at the time, Magatsubi was very violent, and the ruler of the High Plain of Heaven, in other words even the sun goddess, could not endure the violence and hid herself in the Iwato cave. Thus we may know that the other myriad *kami* were at a loss to what to do. But as it was the creative spirit of the *kami* that formed heaven and made the object that sprouted and grew upward luminous and clear in the beginning, so these things were resplendent because of this spiritual power. And the brightness increased when fire grew close, and this is due to the spiritual power of the fire *kami*, Ho Musubi. However, because of Magatsubi's violence, the spiritual workings of these *kami* ceased, so why should there be any doubt about everything being cast into darkness? Through these events, one should ponder the great virtue of Amaterasu Ōmikami. The myriad *kami* grieved for her, and even Takami Musubi was beside himself with worry about getting Amaterasu out of the cave. The reader should ponder the words of the great *kami*, Izanagi, who said that he had no other children who were as splendid as Amaterasu. Also, one should think about the fearsome nature of Susanoo and all the violent spiritual power of Magatsubi. Even a splendid, mysterious, and praiseworthy *kami* like Amaterasu could not endure the violence of Magatsubi. Nevertheless, the spirit that was created to rectify such evil is Ōnaobi, who is the sweet spirit of Amaterasu, and in the end, the violence of Magatsubi was rectified and Magatsubi was labeled a meritorious *kami*. Is this not the epitome of miraculous? ... (NST 50:46–64).

In other words, this is the great Way of governing our land by the emperor, an ancient Way that has been transmitted down to us from the divine age using the actual liturgical words of the *kami* Takami Musubi and Kamu Musubi. (I shall describe in the next diagram about the transmission of the ancient Way from the divine age on according to the liturgical words of these two creative *kami*. The usage of *ancient Way* is first seen in the reign of Emperor Kōgyoku within *Nihon shoki*, where it states, "The emperor pondered and followed the ancient Way, and governed thus."[25] We know that governing the country according to the ancient Way meant that

25. It would no doubt ruffle Atsutane's feathers, but this sentence appears to have been modeled after a passage in the *Wei zhi* where it says, "Yao pondered and followed in the traditions of the ancient way, acting accordingly" (Ienaga et al. 1967, 2:236, n. 6).

when Soga no Iruka prayed for a sign of rain according to Buddhism rites, the emperor put a stop to this, and went out in person to the Nabuchi River, and prayed for rain. Rain then fell for five days, and the five grains grew in abundance; the farmers were filled with joy and called the emperor the most virtuous sovereign.)

The theory of our master, Motoori Norinaga, that the various foreign lands were created by Sukuna Bikona is correct, and the reason that he went to the Eternal Land is because of what he said, "Some places are not complete." So he went to complete those areas. (Norinaga stated, "The naming of this place as the Eternal Land does not mean that there is one place like this. No matter where, it means a place separated from Japan, a place generally known because it is not easy to get there. Thus the characters for Eternal Land are merely borrowed, and the meaning of the word is *sokoyori*, which means a place very distant. Thus, all foreign lands are considered part of the Eternal Land."[26]) But when we consider that Susanoo gave this *kami* plows, we then know that when Susanoo went around the farthest wall of heaven, he noticed that there were countries that were not yet completed. Thus, Sukuna Bikona's work of completing the various foreign countries was not accomplished just because of a command from Kamu Musubi. After this time, Ōkuninushi followed after Sukuna Bikona and traveled to the Eternal Land (reasonably, it was not Ōkuninushi who traveled over to the Eternal Land, but it was his spirit) and it can be seen that these two *kami* combined their spiritual energies and created these foreign countries so that they could rely on and serve the imperial country. In reply to the question, "What proof are you using to declare this?" there is the usage of "I will conceal myself in the eighty folds." The expression "eighty folds" was understood to refer to the Eternal Land (this expression will be explained in the next section), and Ōkuninushi's statement that he would go to that far-off place and be concealed demonstrates that he was concerned, and he said if there was something the *kami* wished to convey, he would listen. This is also clear from the record in the twelfth month of Seikō 3 [856] when a person like a *kami* appeared and said, "I am the *kami* Ōnamochi and Sukuna Bikona. Anciently I completed creating this land and then departed for the eastern sea. But now I have returned again to save people."[27] Also, the usage of "returned again to save people" means

26. See *Kojiki-den* (MNZ 1976, 10:8–10).

27. Quoted from *Montoku jitsuryoku*, 856.12.29. The text says, "The province of Hitachi reported, 'A *kami* newly appeared (by the beach) in Isosaki of Ofoarai in Kashima District. A person of the district who was making salt one night saw a light out in the ocean coming

that while the spiritual influence of this *kami* is over the Eternal Land, his words show that he still has the intention of protecting the imperial land, and it clearly agrees with the words, "I will conceal myself in the eighty folds." And since he said, "Anciently I completed creating this land and then departed for the eastern sea," there is no problem with the theory that Ōkuninushi followed after Sukuna Bikona and traveled to the Eternal Land. …

Now, when we think about these things in detail, the various foreign countries send a variety of treasures to our court as tribute, and I feel that there is a reason to open relations with these countries. The reason for this is because the spirits of Ōnamochi and Sukuna Bikona reside in the foreign countries, and these countries exist to serve Japan. (… However, among the tribute that is brought to our country from foreign lands, medical skills are very useful for the imperial country, and this is because these two *kami* are in reality the creators of the medical profession. The reason that medicine has long been practiced in foreign countries, those doctors being very knowledgeable in the ways of medicine, is because there is so much evil disease in foreign lands, and these two *kami* have used their powers to develop cures for those diseases. Thus, students who have their Japanese spirit firmly grounded and understand these concepts must study the foreign ways of medicine. However, there are many evil practices in this profession, and this is due to the fact that originally these two *kami* belonged to Susanoo's group, especially Sukuna Bikona, who fell between the spaces in the fingers of Kamu Musubi and got away. And foreign countries are located below the imperial country, thus they have some remains from the distant land, and pollution has formed within their lands, causing the great amount of evil in these lands. And that is why there is no way around having evil mixed in with the things that come from abroad, so the student must be prudent, and discard those areas that are evil. Everything in relation to medicine has been dealt with in detail in my work, *Shizunoiwaya*[28] … (NST 50:65–69).

---

down from heaven. The next day on the beach there were two mysterious stones, each about three feet in height. The shapes were not made by man, but appeared to be divine in origin. These did not belong to the salt man, so he let it be. The next day [after that] these two mysterious stones were surrounded by twenty or so smaller rocks, arranged as if paying respect [to the two larger stones]. The color was unearthly and the shapes were like monks, without ears or eyes. At the time a *kami* spoke through a medium, saying, "I am Ōnamochi and Sukuna Bikona. Anciently I completed creating this land and then departed for the eastern sea. But now I have returned again to save people"'" (Kuroita 1984:86).

28. More commonly known as *Idō taii*, "A treatise on the Way of Medicine."

PART TWO

The ancient record states, "Amaterasu commanded, saying, 'The Land of Ashihara of Endless Autumns and Precious Ears of Rice will be ruled over by my son, Masaka Katsukachi Hayahi Ameno Oshihomimi.' … Hereupon, Take Mizukachi descended to the small beach in Itasa in the province of Izumo. … He inquired of Ōkuninushi … and he replied, '… I will give this land of Ashihara to the son of the sun goddess and he may do as he sees fit. … I will conceal myself in the eighty folds of the road.' … Take Mizukachi asked again … and Ōkuninushi replied, 'The decree of the Heavenly *kami* is thus generous, so how can I not accept it? The authority over the political body I now control will be transferred to the imperial grandson. I will retreat and govern hidden things.' … Also, if Yafe Koto Shironushi is made the leader of the *kami*, then my one hundred and eighty sons will follow in serving the heavenly son, and surely there will not be a disobedient one among them. …'

"Hereupon, the crown prince, Masaka Katsukachi Hayahi Ameno Oshihomimi, stated, 'The child, Hiko Honinigi, who was born while I was preparing to descend should be sent down in my place.' Thus, the imperial grandson [Ninigi] was put on the high throne of heaven according to the command. … The liturgy was recited, and the two treasures, the Yata mirror and the Ame Murakumo sword, were thus made the eternal symbols of the throne. Then, with another liturgy, they presented the divine jewels to him. They also presented the broad spear used to subdue the land. Amaterasu took the Yata mirror and presented it to Ninigi saying, 'The Precious Rice Ear Land of Ashihara is the land over which my posterity will rule. You, imperial grandson, will go down, and subdue and pacify that land, and rule from this heavenly inherited high throne. …' Thus, the *kami* Kamurogi and Kamuromi were given charge over the heavenly liturgy, and said, '…You, Ame no Koyane and Futodama, … will lead the various *kami* of the families in their duties, and will have charge over the ceremonies in heaven.' … Thus, the command was given to Ninigi to descend, and he left the rock throne. …"

As I said before, this land was originally ruled over by Ōkuninushi, but Amaterasu gave the command, "The Land of Ashihara of Precious Ears of Rice will be ruled over by my son." This one section is incomprehensible for everyone. But if you ponder deeply the meaning, you will find that there is deep significance in these words. Now, that significance is as follows: The wise and awe-inspiring great *kami* Izanagi decreed that this land be given to Take Susanoo to govern forever, but Susanoo wished to go to the distant land where his mother resided. There was nothing that could be done [to dissuade] Susanoo from going to the distant land, and so he proceeded there; however, when he proceeded there, he ascended to heaven, and gave birth to children from the vows that he exchanged with Amaterasu. After this, Susanoo returned to Japan and accomplished many great deeds, and then he went to the distant land. Ōkuninushi was the successor of Susanoo, and he solidified the land. When the imperial grandson descended, Ōkuninushi retired. When we consider this chain of events, as our master stated, the children born from the vow would view Amaterasu as their father and Susanoo as their mother. And these children were given authority to rule over Japan, similar to how Izanagi gave Susanoo the same right. (And one can perceive the mysterious reasoning, which cannot be expressed in words, according to the statement of Susanoo, "The island country of Kara is a land of gold and silver. It will be ruled over by my son, and the ships filled with treasure will never cease," prophetic words that finally materialized during the reign of Emperor Chūai.[29]) And it is believed that the words of Amaterasu, "The Land of Ashihara of Endless Autumns and Precious Ears of Rice will be ruled over by my son," were uttered based upon what Susanoo had declared. If you do not think of it that way, then the reason for the words "the country my son will rule over" remain unclear. (The sword Susanoo presented to heaven when he was about to leave for the land of Yomi was given to the imperial grandson as an imperial symbol along with the Yata mirror, and the reason for this is also made clear by what has been said above. Of these two symbols, one represents the sun goddess, who is connected to Izanagi, and the other is the symbol of the moon, which is connected to Izanami. Thus, this act fits perfectly with the logic that the land be governed by Izanagi and Izanami. And there is a profound significance in the children being connected to Amaterasu, who is the father, and connected to Izanagi and the moon *kami,* who is the mother and connected with Izanami.)

Therefore, the words of Amaterasu, who only said "the Land of Ashihara of Precious Ears of Rice" refer to the land where the capital would be established, and these words are consistent with "the blue ocean plain and many folds of the tide" uttered by Izanagi. These are great words to which one can only say, "How awe-inspiring!" Taking this all into consideration, the emperor of our country is the posterity of the creative *kami* and Amaterasu, and since this is the origin of things, it now gradually becomes evident that he is the great ruler of all the countries that extend as far as the blue ocean plain and the many folds of the tide.

Behold and remember, all the rulers of the foreign countries now reign

---

29. Referring to the legend that Jingū invaded and conquered the Korean Peninsula for the first time.

over their individual countries as true leaders, but the existence of the history mentioned above cannot be ignored, and as Ōanamuchi and Sukuna Bikona arranged things so that the various foreign countries would offer homage to the imperial country, it is clear that at last, things should be as they were originally established, and all the rulers of foreign countries should be called servants, bowing before the emperor and offering submission, sending many ships to offer tribute and their respectful service. Oh, how pleasant that would be. How joyful it would be. And people do not realize that the bud has already appeared within the flow of time, and this is profoundly sad. (There are many scholars in the world who are bothersome like flies in the spring, and they are lost, drowning in the blind theories of foreign learning. They do not attempt to come to terms with, nor elucidate the noble history of the imperial country. Sometimes when they hear these things, they do not only wonder and doubt, but on the other hand, they spend their energies trying to deny the truth. What kind of perverted thinking is this? Therefore, even though I explain these things, there is not a single scholar right now who believes me, but people who will live a thousand years from now will for the first time be filled with wonder at these words, thinking that these ideas have been well explained with foresight during an era of culture. It will be as if one were waiting to see the other side.)

In relation to the place where Ōkuninushi went after he retired from this world, he concealed himself in the eternal palace of Kizuki. The words "I will conceal myself in the eighty folds of the road" do not point to any place in particular. And though he has retired to the Kizuki Palace, this usage is adjectival in showing that Ōkuninushi's form is not visible in this world, and it is unknown where he resides; he has concealed himself. This usage of "eighty folds" is the same in nature as the name of distant land. (Our master stated the following [in *Kojiki-den*] regarding the usage of "I will conceal myself in the eighty folds of the road," "Since the posterity of Susanoo could not remain in this land, they went to Yomi and that is why these words were uttered."[30] However, this belief is mistaken. Our master also quoted the following poem from *Man'yōshū*:

momotarazu	If you have traversed
yasokumazaka ni	the pass of the eighty folds
tamuke seba	and offered your prayers,
suginisi fito ni	then perhaps you also will
kedasi afamu kamo	encounter someone who is dead.

[MYS 427]

30. MNZ 1976, 10:118.

Nevertheless, the meaning of this poem is that since no one knows where the spirit of the dead goes, if a person offers prayers in the direction of that road of eighty folds, then perhaps he can meet someone who has passed from this life. Thus, this poem does not actually refer to the road that leads to the land of Yomi. Before this event, both Izanagi and Ōkuninushi had already traveled down the road to Yomi, and there is no description of it being a winding way; it is completely straight.[31] However, in *Nihon shoki*, the road down to the palace of the Sea *kami* is described by the same person as "and though you have passed through the eight layered folds." One may think of this as the same as above, but there is a great difference between the numbers "eighty" and "eight." "Eighty" is much the same as "eighty families," or "eighty islands," representing a large number, while "eight layered" refers to something thick, having had many layers applied. This is analogous to words such as "eight-layered mat," or "eight-layered trailing clouds." The student should not confuse the two. If Ōkuninushi had gone off to the land of Yomi, then he would have said, "I will conceal myself down past the eight-layered road." I will deal with these things at the end of this work.) …

Now, they constructed a palace for Ōkuninushi as he had desired, and he accepted the decree from the two procreative *kami*, Takami Musubi and Kamu Musubi, that he be granted authority over the affairs of hidden things, and the authority to govern in political affairs was entrusted to the imperial grandson. Then Ōkuninushi retired to the palace, and he retains authority over the affairs of the underworld.[32] (The word "retire" does not mean that he has removed himself to some other place, but implies that he stays in that place. The words *sidumari* and *todomari* mean the same thing. …) In relation to the affairs of the underworld, our master correctly stated, "In contrast to the political affairs the imperial grandson has authority and exercises among the men who live in this world, the affairs of the underworld refer to the acts of the *kami* that no human can see or participate. All events in this world are due to the workings of the *kami*, but the affairs of men in this world and the affairs of the *kami* are here separated, and the latter is called divine affairs in relation to the former. The divine affairs that Ōkuninushi has jurisdiction over quietly assist in the political affairs of the

31. The word *yasokumade* has been translated as "eighty folds," but it can also mean "eighty turns." Thus, Atsutane is taking the name literally, saying that this description is of a winding path, while the path to Yomi is straight.

32. Atsutane uses the Chinese characters 幽冥事 "dark world, underworld," and yet he has the interlinear reading of *kamigoto*, "affairs of the *kami*."

imperial court, and that is why the humble usage of *samorawamu* was used."[33] (However, Ichijō Kaneyoshi said in *Nihon shoki sanso*, "When a person commits evil in the land of humans, he [does things such as] murders the emperor. When evil is committed in the underworld, the spirits and *kami* are punished. It is the same when one does a good deed and is rewarded. Divine affairs refer to the affairs in the underworld." In other words, Ōkuninushi resides in the Kizuki Palace and has authority over the so-called affairs of the dark world. But in reality, I believe that it is not Ōkuninushi who is performing this function, but his son, Koto Shironushi. The reason for this is because one must take into consideration that when Emperor Jingū subjugated Korea, or when Emperor Tenmu battled [the forces of] Prince Ōtomo, Ōkuninushi did nothing, but left everything up to his son. When we reflect upon the words of Ōkuninushi, "If Yafe Koto Shironushi is made the leader of the *kami*, then my one hundred and eighty sons will follow in serving the heavenly son, and surely there will be no disobedient *kami*," we realize that with the assistance given by Koto Shironushi when he led the *kami*, the seventeen generations[34] of *kami* who were the posterity of Ōkuninushi as well as all the families of *kami* who were related to him rendered assistance to the court. When we ponder this state of affairs in relation to the present state of society, it resembles the condition we now have where the emperor resides in Yamashiro Province and has authority over the affairs of men, but the men of the Shōgun family [Tokugawa] have taken concrete control in place of the emperor and lead the various feudal lords. And this has profound meaning. Now, it is possible that because Koto Shironushi has strong spiritual powers, he was included in the list of the eight *kami* who are especially worshipped.[35] Also, because he is in charge of the affairs of hidden things, he appeases the spirit of the emperor much like the other *kami* Ikumi Musubi, Tarumi Musubi, and Tamarumi[36] Musubi, so perhaps that is why he was included in this list. When Koto Shironushi lent assistance to Emperor Tenmu, we should understand that he offered that assistance concurrently with Ikumi Musubi.

33. MNZ 1976, 14:120.

34. *Kojiki* only records fifteen generations. It is possible that Atsutane is counting names differently.

35. Noted in the ninth chapter of *Engi shiki*. These eight *kami* were thought to dwell in the palace and were there to protect the emperor. Therefore, they were worshipped and appeased. These eight *kami* are Kamu Musubi, Takami Musubi, Tamarumi Musubi, Ikumi Musubi, Tarumi Musubi, Ōmiya Hime, Miketsu, and Koto Shironushi.

36. Atsutane writes this name as Tamatsume, but the *Engi shiki* manuscripts agree that the original reading was Tamaru.

There is a mistake in the theory of our master in relation to this list of eight *kami*, but I have dealt with it in detail in *Koshi-den*.[37]

If we ponder thoroughly the difference between the affairs of this world and the hidden world, as long as a person is alive on this earth, then he is a servant of the emperor, but when he dies, his spirit becomes a *kami*, and like a ghost or apparition, he returns to the underworld. Thus, he is under the jurisdiction of that great *kami* in the hidden world; in other words, he becomes a subject of Ōkuninushi, and is subject to the laws of that sphere. And while a person's spirit is in the underworld, his act of protecting the ruler, parent, or posterity in the present world is just like Ōkuninushi who retired but continues to protect the world.)

Now, while Ōkuninushi resided peacefully forever in the Kizuki Palace, he sent his spirit to the distant land where Sukuna Bikona had crossed, and they finished creating the various foreign lands. Since the various lands were created from the foam of the tide after it hardened, these countries are located across the ocean here and there, but all belong to the same ocean, and as I stated above, they are all countries under the jurisdiction of Susanoo's rule. However, Susanoo went off to the underworld, so the lands that Susanoo originally had inspected were given to his posterity, because there was an order in finishing the work of Susanoo … (NST 50:70–78).

When Ōkuninushi retired from the world, he handed the spear to the representative of the imperial grandson. This was done because Ōkuninushi's other names are Yachihoko "eight thousand spears" and Ashihara Shikoo "the ugly male of Ashihara." He was an extremely intrepid *kami*, and beginning with subjugating the eighty *kami*, he also pacified the northern territories, during which he finished creating the country and then governed it. With the spear he subjugated many unruly *kami*, and that is why he presented it with the words, "If you govern the land with this spear, then you will surely subdue it." Since this was an awe-inspiring spear, it was prepared as one of the imperial regalia along with the mirror

37. In Book 22 of *Koshi-den*, paragraph 117, it says, "Now, in relation to the fact that Ōkuninushi is not seen in the list of the eight *kami* worshipped by the priests in the Japanese cult, our master says, 'The remaining seven *kami* (aside from Koto Shironushi) of these eight *kami* who reside within the palace were prepared to protect and bless the being of the emperor. When we consider this fact taken with the words of Ōkuninushi who said, "If Yahe Koto Shironushi is made the leader of the *kami*, then surely there will not be a disobedient *kami*," then Koto Shironushi should also be looked upon as a *kami* who protects the emperor.'" In point of fact, there actually seems to be general agreement between Norinaga and Atsutane.

and the sword to be given to the imperial grandson. (Natsume Mikamaro[38] stated, "When we ponder the words pronounced when the spear was presented, we find that the symbols of governing the country were the mirror and the sword, but as the spear subjugated the unruly *kami*, it is a national treasure without peer. When we think back on this era, Ōkuninushi, who had ruled the land in peace after a period of trouble, presented the sword with the words 'If you govern the land with this spear, then it shall surely be subdued'; because of these words, the spear had to be included among the other imperial symbols when the imperial grandson descended from heaven." I agree with this statement. When Yamato Takeru was ready to head off to and subjugate the eastern countries, [his father] presented him with the Yahiro spear of Hiiragi, and this should be taken into consideration, also.) It appears that anciently it was the will of the *kami* that this spear be presented. Master Agatai noted, "Emperors in the ancient past worshipped the ancestral *kami* within the palace, and wielded strong authority in governing the country on the outside. They subjugated disobedient countries, tamed violent individuals, uniting heaven and earth by governing from a noble and pure way. Above this, they corrected even small things they found deficient, rectifying things they heard. … Because of this, even the commoner revered the imperial *kami*, avoiding the hypocritical state of having two hearts. They revered the commands of the emperor, and no one committed crimes. Furthermore, the servants who were in the service of the emperor were known by the phrase 'even if I die at sea and am buried there, or die in the mountains and am buried there, I will die by my emperor.' They had masculine, sincere hearts and served the emperor in like manner."[39]

So, the heart of the ancient people of our land originally was brave and fearless, but after foreign beliefs entered the country, the Yamato heart turned evil and feminine. Nevertheless, presently, ancient studies have flourished, and the time has come when the hearts of the Japanese will gradually return to that masculine state of antiquity. This spear is now enshrined in the province of Kii, and is known as Kunikakasu. (In relation to this, Mikamaro has done detailed research that has been published. I have more I would like to say about this spear, but I have already made mention of it in *Koshi-den*.)

The reason that Ōkuninushi referred to the imperial ancestor as a "heavenly *kami*" is because, as our master has already stated, Ninigi was

38. Natsume Mikamaro (1773–1859) was a student of Mabuchi's.

39. From Mabuchi's *Man'yōshū daikō* (Yamamoto 1942:148–49).

the son of Oshihomimi, the son of Amaterasu. Thus, Ōkuninushi realized that he was different from the other earthly *kami* and employed this title to make a clear, praiseworthy distinction. Also, the reason that the successive emperors are known as the sons of the heavenly *kami* is because the throne is to be inherited by the son of Amaterasu, who was commanded to rule over the Land of Endless Autumns and Precious Ears of Rice, so those who ascend the throne are denoted as the posterity of the successive heavenly *kami*. The reason that the throne is referred to in such a way is because all of the emperors are descendants of Amaterasu … (NST 50:80–82).

Kamurogi and Kamuromi are the names the emperor calls the procreative *kami* Takami Musubi and Kamu Musubi. … The way each successive imperial grandchild follows the commands [of the heavenly liturgy] and takes the reign of government without adding any knowledge from his own intellect is called the Way of *kamunagara*. (The record of Emperor Kōtoku in *Nihon shoki* states, "*Kamunagara* means to follow the will of the *kami*. It also means that one has entered that way." …) Truly our ancient traditions have transmitted down to us properly and truthfully, and the ancient lexicon is beautiful; the voices of the people as well as the ancient words in society are elegant; our land is without parallel in the world. There is no doubt that the words of Takami Musubi and Kamu Musubi were handed down to Izanagi and Izanami; also, the command was then given to the imperial grandson from Amaterasu. (However, since the myriad countries in the world were fashioned by Ōnamuchi and Sukuna Bikona, the exact same words should have been transmitted to all of these countries, also. However, when certain traditions have the same origin, on the whole they tend to deviate greatly. And even the ancient words can become the prattle of slaves, and all of the languages of the world, starting with Chinese, are the so-called ear-grating mumblings of barbarians. As our master stated in minute detail within *Kanji san'onkō*, there are sounds that originated from nasalization or the interaction of the tongue and chin,[40] and that the cause and effect of declinable and indeclinable morphemes have been mistaken. The present theories do not suit the spiritual origins of the Japanese language. It was incomprehensible as to why the conjugation of foreign phonemes had become so very bothersome and chaotic. However, there is a principle of the way things should be for this phenomenon, and it is beyond debate to say that it was the will of the *kami* that things turn out this way. Only the reasoning is unclear. …)

40. Norinaga's (and Atsutane's) very rudimentary knowledge of phonetics is demonstrated by the vague use of "tongue and chin," which I interpret to be the interaction of labials and dentals.

Looking at the details in all the ancient works about the floating bridge of heaven, it was not the kind of bridge that we think of now—one extending from bank to bank, spanning the space between heaven and earth. Also, it was not a straight line connecting heaven with earth. It was constructed according to the way that the *kami* think, being an object that at some time was a vehicle allowing one to fly through the sky; to compare it to something on the earth, it was like a boat sailing upon the surface of the water. It was called a floating bridge because a person rode in it and floated here and there through the sky. (If, as *Sandaikō* points out, there was one line that connected heaven and earth, then why would this have been labeled the *floating* bridge?[41]) When Izanagi and Izanami first stood and created the land, they did so by riding in this object, but the details are not alluded to in the record. … However, the appearance of this object is explained in detail when the imperial grandson descends to Japan, so we know what the object was. The record says that the imperial grandchild "departed, riding within the floating bridge of heaven." *Ukijimari* is an epithet for the word *sori*. The word *soritatu* means the same as "to be carried off" as it is used in *Man'yōshū*.[42] Thus, this is a wondrous explanation of the authority of the imperial grandchild who rode in the floating bridge and descended down to our land. The same word usage is seen in the following *Man'yōshū* poem:

siro kumo no	Pushing asunder
tife wo osiwake	the many folds of white clouds,
ama sosori	it soars loftily,
takaki tatiyama	that peak of Tachiyama. …[43]

The imperial grandchild soared aloft in the sky like a high peak, and this usage of *soritatasite* illustrates the strong power of his authority which opened the way as he descended from heaven. …

Now, this floating bridge is like a boat in the present, one rides in it and may stop where he wishes, so it is also referred to as a rock boat. (It is difficult right now to say if *ifa* "rock, boulder" refers to the boat being actually made of rock, or if it was sturdy and sound as a rock.) We realize this from the following passage in *Kujiki*, "Nigi Hayahi rode in the heavenly rock boat, and descended to Ikaruga Peak in Kawakami in the province of Kawachi. He then moved to Mount Shiraniwa in Yamato and there resides.

41. MNZ 1976, 10:310.
42. For example in MYS 475.
43. Partial quote of MYS 4003.

... The so-called heavenly rock boat descended and flew around the sky. A village was spotted, and the boat descended. The words *sora mitu yamato no kuni* probably originate from this event."[44] (It says basically the same thing in *Nihon shoki*. I have quoted from *Kujiki* because it goes into greater detail. ...) The student may be suspicious, wondering if this bridge was actually like present-day boats, but among the people who were sent to accompany Nigi Hayahi in his descent was the captain of the boat, Amatsu Habara, the distant ancestor of the rulers of the Atobe. We also notice that there was a navigator, so we may know that this was exactly the same as contemporary boats. Now, there may also be some who do not believe that the rock boat and the floating bridge are the same object, so I would direct the student's attention to the following passage from *Kojiki*, "The imperial grandchild left the floating bridge, which was on the twin peaks of Mount Kushibi located in So, and departed. He looked out over the barren land from a small hillock." Thus, while riding in the floating bridge he landed on the twin peaks of Mount Kushibi, left the bridge and went in search of a place where he could establish his capital. ... This is just like a boat lowering anchor and the sailors coming ashore, and that is one more piece of evidence to show that we should think of the rock boat and the floating bridge as the same object.

Therefore, when Ame no Hohi flew over heaven and earth, he flew in the same object. Also, (when the imperial grandchild descended to Japan) Ame no Oshikumone climbed up the two points of heaven and rode on the floating cloud of heaven; this is likely the same rock boat. Also, [in the reign of Jinmu] Kamo Taketsunumi came down from the peak of Futanobori in the same vehicle. (Nevertheless, in *Sandaikō* it says, "The floating bridge of heaven was one passage that connected heaven and the earth. As heaven and earth gradually separated, this passage slowly narrowed; when the imperial grandchild descended to earth, this passage still existed, but after the descent, the passage was severed, and heaven and earth have been separated for eternity, and no one can come or go."[45] This sounds very reasonable, but if things were exactly as Nakatsune stated, how does he explain the fact that *kami* continue to descend from heaven or ascend back up even after the imperial grandchild had come to earth? Even the event of Kamo Taketsunumi coming down occurred ten million years after the descent of the imperial grandchild. These kinds of errors encountered in *Sandaikō* are like a person striking a rock while rowing a large boat, or a hunter chasing a deer and not seeing the mountain.) ...

44. For an explanation of this, see Bentley (2006:196).
45. MNZ 1976, 10:310.

In the beginning, the three spheres of heaven, earth, and the Yomi were strung together like beads, with heaven above and Yomi below; however, heaven was separated early on, and the fact that earth and Yomi were connected together for a long time was noted above. Now, in response to the question about when earth and Yomi were separated, we are not sure, but we can get a general idea from the ancient records. First, I have already stated above that Ōkuninushi went back and forth between Yamato and Yomi while he still resided in Japan, so there is no doubt that Yomi was still connected to the earth at this time. It thus appears that Yomi separated from the earth sometime during the descent of the imperial grandchild. Since this is the time when the heaven, earth, and Yomi were finally finished, Izanagi and Izanami had given birth to the land, Amaterasu had given birth to the ruler over the land and had given him authority, the imperial grandchild had descended, and Susanoo's posterity starting with Ōkuninushi had all departed, this is the most reasonable time when the earth and Yomi separated. After the three spheres were clearly separated, the sun in the heavens did not change from its appointed movement, and the earth continued to float about as it had since its creation, and perhaps this is why even though Yomi was separated from the earth, it continued to revolve around it, Yomi having originally been created below the earth, moving in rhythm with the movement of the earth. This state is just as we see today. …

Everything has come about in this manner through the mysterious, spiritual workings of the procreative *kami*, and these things cannot be discovered with man's puny knowledge. Now, heaven refers to the sun and Yomi refers to the moon; the reason that people do not believe this is because, as was pointed out in *Sandaikō*, people still think that heaven is above and Yomi beneath as they were before they were severed. After these were severed, people called the objects they could actually see with their eyes *fi* "sun" and *tuki* "moon" and thought that these two objects were different from heaven and Yomi. It is clear that heaven is the sun because we call the *kami* who resides there Amaterasu Ōmikami "great *kami* who illuminates the heavens." It is also unmistakable from the words of Emperor Jinmu's older brother, Itsuse, who said, "It is not good that I, a descendant of the sun goddess, should wage war facing the sun." This means that even though it is clear that the emperor is the descendant of the heavenly *kami*, these words make heaven the sun, saying that he is related to the sun goddess. So from this point, it is evident that heaven is the sun … (NST:83–90).

The sun and moon appeared either from within that thing which sprouted and rose upward, or from within that which descended downward. In spite of this uncertainty, one variation in *Nihon shoki* states, "The sun and moon were already created." And in the present generation, sometimes there are those who interpret things by saying that the two creative *kami* gave birth to the sun and moon that we see before us. (Even in foreign countries, there are many examples where some say that the sun and moon were created from both eyes of Pan Ku, while others state that these heavenly bodies were created first by ministers Xi and He.) In truth, the *kami* that govern the sun and the moon gave birth to these orbs, and this usage in the records points to the country where these *kami* dwell; people later misinterpreted this usage, and this is how it has been transmitted down through the ages. (There are many examples in the ancient past as well as the present, where *kami* and people are called by the place where they reside. Please look at what has been said on this subject in my *Kishin Shinron.*[46]) Amaterasu Ōmikami is not the sun itself, and it is clear from the words of Itsuse noted above that she is the *kami* who governs the sun.[47] In the same vein, Tsukuyomi is not the moon, but the *kami* who rules over the moon, and one may appreciate this by considering the various ideas noted above as well as the poem in *Man'yōshū*:

sora no umi ni	Behold the moon floating
tuki no fune uke	in the ocean of heaven;
katurakadi	the man in the moon
kakete kogumiyu	steers the boat with the rudder
tuki fito wotoko	made from the *katsura* tree.
	[MYS 2223][48]

(This poem truly makes a distinction between the *kami* of the sun and moon. The idea that the sun refers to the heavens and the moon is *yomi* was first introduced by Hattori Nakatsune; this idea is unalterable from ages to ages. My own explanation has also expounded minutely upon this.)

A person once asked the following. "I am still not convinced that the imperial country is the top of the great continent and directly faces the heavens. If this were true, then during the vernal and autumnal equinoxes, the sun should be visible from directly above, but the sun is always to the

46. Literally, "A New Treatise on Demons and *Kami*." It was finished in 1819. The usage of *new* is in response to Arai Hakuseki's *Kishinron* "Treatise on Demons and *Kami*." The passage in question appears in Tahara (1973:139).

47. This statement goes against what Norinaga said, when he stated that Amaterasu is the sun itself (see p. 433 in *Kojiki-den* in this volume).

48. I have followed Atsutane's readings. Modern scholarship reads the first line as *ame no umi ni.*

south. Considering that we view the sun from this angle, it is hard to believe that Japan is at the top of the continent. How do you respond?" I replied that this physical location is the same as the placement on the face of man, which is not located on the top of the head, but the eyes, nose, and mouth are on the front side of the head. The world is round, and it may appear that there is no difference between front and back, but in reality, there is such a distinction. The earth always rotates from east to west, not north to south. Therefore, there are countries that only see the sun from the side. Since there is a difference between east–west and north–south, they cannot be the same. Taking this into consideration, we realize that there is a distinction between front and back. In this way, the imperial country is located on the front, south being front and north being back, south being left and north being right. Thus, seeing the sun slightly to the south is the same as one's face being in the front, and so it becomes clear that the imperial country is located on the top of the continent because Japan faces the sun directly. (This theory is in reality my master's, as contained in *Sandaikō*. However, Motoori stated that earth does not move, but the sun revolves around it, and I have replied to this question adding this slight correction. You will see the difference if you read *Sandaikō*.[49])

There was a follow-up question. "If what you have said is true, does that mean that all countries that view the sun and moon somewhat to the south are located at the top? How can you limit Japan to being the only country located on the top?" I responded by saying that Japan is not located on the top simply because it views the sun and moon to the south. Conversely, since Japan was located on the top, it views the sun and moon to the south. Therefore, countries that view the sun and moon in like manner as the imperial country just happened to be located in the east–west region like Japan … (NST 50:91–92).

Let us think deeper about the condition of heaven, the earth, and Yomi, and about the mysterious nature of the underworld. First, I have taught a variety of things about heaven: as the substance from the object that sprouted and rose upward was clear and beautiful, the eight million good *kami* starting with the five heavenly *kami*, Izanami and Amaterasu were appeased (this does not only apply to the *kami* born in heaven, but also applies to those *kami* who were born on the earth; thus, I have included all good *kami* in this group. …), and when a violent *kami* appeared, he was driven out and sent to the nether land; thus, only good *kami* reside in heaven. Since the land of Yomi was created from the heavy and dirty sub-

49. MNZ 1976, 10:310.

stance that sank down and became land, we know that it was formed from the heaviest and dirtiest parts that coagulated together. Perhaps because of this, my master stated that Yomi is the place where all the calamities and evil actions end. …[50] And that is why Yomi is the place where the violent *kami* remain. (This is clearly explained in diagram number nine [of *Sandaikō*] in conjunction with the truth from the ancient past.[51]) And there is a reason why the violent *kami* are required to remain in Yomi. (The idea of foreign countries is that below this country is a very terrible place known as *Naraku* "hell," and this is where the spirits of the evil go. Also, the idea that there are evil *kami* there who torment the spirits of the evil is proof that the traditions of Japan have been transmitted incorrectly to other countries, having various additions attached.)

However, this land that is located between heaven and Yomi was created when the pure elements of heaven and the dirty elements of the underworld separated, and so it is composed of some residue of the pure elements of the clear object that sprouted and rose upward, and the defiled elements that remained when the dirtier parts settled downward. Thus, it is obvious that there is a mixture of the good elements of heaven and the evil disposition of Yomi. (As has been described above, there is a division on the earth, too. The imperial country is located on the top; if we used the allegory of the human body, then Japan is like the forehead. Therefore, our land is an unparalleled, wonderful place on the earth. This fact about the imperial land is clear from the evidence that heaven was first created from the pure element that sprouted and rose upward. And since the islands south were created from the lower substance, one may know that there are many polluted and evil countries in that direction. By the way, there is an old tradition in China that states that in the beginning, heaven and earth were like a confused mixture analogous to an egg. The purer elements floated upward and became heaven and the heavier elements sank down and became the earth. This is the manner in which the ancient Japanese tradition was transmitted. …) Now, even after heaven, earth, and Yomi were divided into three different spheres, there is sufficient proof that the *kami* still journeyed back and forth between heaven and earth … , but after Ōkuninushi made his voyage to the nether land, which, needless to say, he did as a spirit, there is no evidence whatsoever that even spirits have made the trip between earth and Yomi any longer. I feel that this is because Izanagi despised Yomi so much that he prohibited passage between that land and this. It is truly an awe-inspiring principle. (Now, it is a different

50. MNZ 1976, 9:294–95.
51. MNZ 1976, 10:310.

matter when we deal with Magatsubi, who dwells in the nether land and causes catastrophe in this land.)

In spite of this, in the ancient past as now, there are those who declare that when a person dies, his spirit goes to Yomi regardless. This type of thinking ignores the infinitely wise principles of Izanagi … , and disregards the mysteriously profound promise of Ōkuninushi, who governs the underworld; this thinking is terribly mistaken.[52] It is truly deplorable. I will take this incorrect thinking apart and comment upon it in detail. Having spent great time thinking about why this perverted idea came about, I believe it is because the Chinese characters 黄泉 "yellow spring" have been given the reading of Yomi.[53] (This is seen early on in *Kojiki*, telling us that the usage is indeed ancient. When Chinese literature was imported into Japan, I believe the Japanese put this Chinese reading onto a Japanese word. When such usages become customary after a long time, people begin to believe that this is truly the pure and ancient tradition of Japan; thus, it is only logical that people have been making this mistake for over a thousand years. …)

First, in *Nihon shoki*, in the reign of Emperor Kōtoku, Soga no Kurayamada uttered the following words when he committed suicide, "I have now been slandered by Muzashi and fear I will be put to death unfairly. I desire to proceed even to Yomi with my loyalty intact." These are the words of Kurayamada at the time, and when he said, "I will die with my loyalty intact." The compilers used a Chinese notion to make the words more ornate. There is no doubt that this usage of "with my loyalty intact" shows that Kurayamada's heart will remain unchanged though he die, so the record insinuates that even though a person will go to the yellow spring, his heart will remain faithful to the emperor, and this Chinese usage differs from the way the ancient Japanese thought. (The thinking in Chinese works is that when a person dies, his spirit and corpse go to Hades together. …) However, in later eras, people did not understand the true meaning of "yellow spring" (黄泉), but gradually grew accustomed to the usage. Even in *Man'yōshū* … the usage of

iyasiki wa ga yuwe	Since I am of no social rank,
masurawo no	when I gaze upon
arasofu mireba	the fight of these noble men,

52. This appears to be a veiled criticism of Norinaga (see *Kojiki-den*, p. 429 in this volume).

53. The yellow spring in Chinese was essentially Hades, the place where the spirits of the dead went.

ikeritomo
afu beku are ya
sisikusiro
yomi ni matamu to
kakurenu no[54]
sitabafe okite
utinageki
imo ga inureba

I think to myself—
could I ever be married,
even if I should live?
"I will be waiting for you
in the nether land,"
she said with the promise in her heart.
And she slipped away from this life
while she wept tears of grief. …

[MYS 1809]

This demonstrates that the poet was thinking of a Chinese notion when he composed the poem: the spirit went to the "yellow spring" (黄泉尓将待跡). This is distinctly different from the ancient Japanese tradition about Yomi. In addition to this ancient mistaken usage is the notion of hell found in the Buddhist scriptures. Consider a poem like the following:

wakakereba
miti yukisirani[55]
mafifasemu
sitabe no tukafi
ofite toforase

As he is still young,
the way there will be unclear to him.
I will give him a present.
Messenger from below,
carry me to that world.

[MYS 905]

It was written based on the Buddhist idea that a servant from beyond would guide one to the other side. …

Thus it is only natural that people would have mistaken ideas since the original ancient tradition has become confused with these other ideas. And even my own master did not notice this fact; he mentioned the poem above and said, "*Kami* and people alike, whether they be good or evil will all go to the land of Yomi."[56] This is a mistake that came from not thinking deeply about this issue. (Even Master Agatai Nushi [Mabuchi] did not understand this problem because he wrote the following poem about death:

wa ga miti mo
sasofamu fito wo
nubatama no
yomi ni okurite

I find myself
at such a terrible loss,
having sent my friend—
a fellow scholar of the Way —

54. Omodaka proposes the reading of *komorinu no* for the stanza 隠沼乃 (1983, 9:258).

55. Atsutane must have read the text wrong, or he had a variant text before him. The common reading is *yukisirazi*.

56. MNZ 1976, 9:239.

madofu koro kana to the dark land of Yomi.

However, in saying this, not all poetry deals with reality, so there may be some people who say that this poem was composed for this or that reason, and this can be said about the average student of learning. But we, the students of ancient learning, think about the true foundation of everything, and are engaged in letting the rest of the world know about these correct ideas. Because of this, knowing that it was merely a casual mistake, who would trust this person's scholarship if he taught such mistaken ideas? This kind of learning is very confusing and can hardly be labeled ancient learning. Ancient learning refers to the study of elucidating the facts of the ancient, and using such facts as a standard by which to correct life in the present. Thus, even if one were to use *Man'yōshū* as his model in composing poetry, he should compose such poetry without forgetting that he is a student of ancient learning. …)

Thus, the idea that when a person dies his spirit goes to Yomi originated from foreign countries, and there is no proof of such thinking in ancient Japan, but people state that when the earth and Yomi were barely separated, Izanami died and went to Yomi, so why not others? However, the reason that Izanami went to Yomi is due to the fact that she had given birth to the *kami* of fire, and she was ashamed because her husband had seen her in such terrible shape. Thus, she said in her heart that she would never meet her husband again and left the presence of Izanagi; thus, it does not mean that only her spirit went to Yomi. So, why should all the spirits of men on this earth go to Yomi when Izanami went for that reason? … (NST 50:95–100).

However, the spirits of men were originally endowed from the procreative spirit-*kami*, so if you look at things from this point of view, then the spirits of the dead should return whence they came. Thus, they should return to heaven. However, there is no proof in the records that all the spirits of men return to heaven. (But there are the words from the emperor, who upon hearing the name *faya saagari* in the Chūai section of *Nihon shoki*, replied, "That sounds evil." To this my master added the following interpretation, "This was said due to the fact *fayaku agaru* was something to be despised, since *agaru* refers to death. The meaning of *agari* is seen in *Man'yōshū* poetry when a prince passed away, for it is noted as 'going to rule in heaven.' The same kind of usage was employed even when a person of little rank passed away. Since dying is the same event regardless of rank, it was labeled as *agari* 'to ascend up,' because the person went to heaven after he had died. Agatai Nushi once said, 'Even now, people in Tōomi call the three-day period observed after a person has passed away as *Mikka*

Agari.' This has the same meaning as sending a person up to heaven."[57] Thus, since ancient times, people have believed that when the body dies, the spirit ascends up to heaven, so perhaps that is exactly what happens. Ōgetsuhime was put to death, and Nuzuchi, who was the spirit of fortune, was present when the spirits gathered together in front of the heavenly cave where the sun goddess had hidden.[58] Also, Ōkuninushi and Koto Shironushi hid themselves in the eighty corners of the road, but their spirits were gathered together at the marketplace of heaven. Add to this that *kami* were gathered together in heaven to worship these spirits. And even when we come to the age of human rulers, Yamato Takeru's spirit is noted as "rising up to heaven and flying away," and "it ascended up to heaven." So it cannot be said that there are no examples in the records of spirits rising up to heaven …).

If the spirit traveled to Yomi and was invited to be worshipped, or was called back to earth in order to be worshipped, then there should not be the strict observation of the defilement from fire. Even if the fire of this earth was only slightly defiling, there should be no problem in comparing that to the defilement from the fire of the underworld. … But it is clear that once in Yomi a person cannot return to this place from the fact that Izanami could not return to this world simply because she had eaten of the food of Yomi just once. In spite of this, it is a horribly unthinkable idea to state that a spirit from Yomi could be invited back to this world in order to be worshipped and entreated, but if this actually were the case, then there would be nothing less than a traveling entity announcing himself as a *kami* from Yomi who had come to be worshipped. Yet, I believe that such a thing is impossible. (My master explained that even though one worships spirits here and there, each spirit has its own spiritual power, much like fire does not disappear nor change though it is moved from place to place—it continues to burn brightly.[59] This is correct, and a person could try to use this as proof that spirits had come from Yomi, but my master's explanation is an excellent allegory about worshipping spirits in this world, and even though we may worship them wherever, their spiritual power does not diminish in the least; therefore, this cannot be used as proof that the spirits had come from Yomi. Since it appears that the spirits of people who had died and were not worshipped, but went to Yomi immediately, then as has been noted above, there is no way for them to return to this world. If a spirit has

57. MNZ 1976, 11:355.

58. Apparently demonstrating that Ōgetsuhime's spirit had returned to heaven.

59. MNZ 1976, 11:387.

gone to Yomi, then to worship that spirit here in this world becomes an act of ostentation, and it is not a correct form of worship. Why should there have been such an incorrect form of conduct in ancient Japan? My master also made the following observation. "The only way that a spirit that had gone to Yomi could remain in this world would be if when fire was being moved to another place, the light from the flames reached back to the original place and lit it up for a short time. But as the fire is withdrawn, the light gradually fades. And as the light disappears, after many months and years, the spirit also disappears from this world. Only in the case of the noble spirits of *kami* who have gone down to Yomi, their spiritual presence does not decrease, but continues on indefinitely. The reason for this is because the flame of that spirit is large, and even though the flame is deposited in another place, the light continues to reach the original place, and there is thus no change in the spirit."[60] This explanation may sound reasonable, but it is mistaken. If the reader will look carefully at what I have said in this work and think about the problem, he will understand what I mean. For now, it may be difficult to comprehend, so I desire the reader to await the publication of *Koshi-den* and then read it. …) Therefore, the idea that the ancient Japanese felt that the spirit after death went to Yomi does not hold water.

Now, to answer the question about where the spirit goes after death, they remain upon this earth forever. This is clear from the ancient records and other evidence presently at hand. And it is clear from the following *Man'yōshū* poem that it is difficult for people to ascertain where they are even in this present life.

momotarazu	If you have traversed
yasokumazaka ni	the pass of the eighty folds
tamukeseba	and offered your prayers,
suginisi fito ni	then perhaps you also will
kedasi afamu kamo	encounter someone who is dead.
	[MYS 427]

(… And that is why before foreign ideas were imported into Japan, the people of ancient times were generous and did not take issue with problems like where the spirit went after death.) Now, the reason that people cannot know for a surety about these things is because these spirits belong to the nether land, which is governed by Ōkuninushi, who hid himself in

60. MNZ 1976, 11:388.

the eighty folds of the way according to the great command of the two procreative *kami* in the ancient divine age … (NST 50:105–9).

Now, when a person dies, he goes to the nether land, so like Ōkuninushi who hid himself in the eighty folds of the way, it is impossible to know where to go and make one's offering nor where one may meet someone who has passed on. Yet if you study the divine age and understand that while the form of the *kami* is not visible to men, hidden away in the shrines of the land, and if you think about the person, then you will come to an understanding about these things. First, there is the tradition that the great *kami* who is enshrined in Tachino of Tatsuta[61] was created from the breath of Izanagi, and there was no shrine nor festival for him; however, in the reign of Emperor Sujin, there was a revelation, and for the first time the court established a shrine to this *kami*. Also, there is the tradition that Izanagi gave birth to the great *kami* of Sumiyoshi when he purified himself at Ahagihara, and there was no shrine or festival for this *kami* until the reign of Emperor Jingū. But with a command from her court a shrine was built and the *kami* was enshrined. These *kami* were both born in the ancient period of the divine age, but they did not appear here until the age of men. Since this great *kami* of Sumiyoshi is known as the one who resides on the bottom of the river in Tachibana, it is clear that he was created when Izanagi performed his ablutions there and then he resided there. And it is unclear where the wind *kami* resided, but as has been mentioned above, the court established shrines for both of these at a later time, and after the shrines were built these *kami* moved in and it goes without saying that they have been enshrined there ever since. …

Naturally, it is not just these two *kami* that have been dealt with in this manner. Whenever *kami* from the divine age are enshrined somewhere, they reside in the shrine without showing their form to men, like the case with the two *kami* above. Also it goes without saying that heaven and earth are boundless. (I now would like to consider the place where Ōkuninushi who was mentioned above resides. My master stated, "The *kami* in heaven do not suffer death but exist forever; however, all *kami* on this earth do experience death."[62] What evidence has Master Motoori used in making this statement? If they had died, then the two *kami* mentioned above would

61. Known as Shinatsu Hiko, the wind *kami*.

62. This appears in *Tōmonroku*, no. 6. Norinaga actually said, "The *kami* that reside in the High Plain of Heaven do not suffer death but exist eternally. Every single *kami* on the earth experiences death. And even though they are known as heavenly *kami*, if they come down to the earth, they cannot escape death. One should judge death by thinking about [the significance of] heaven and earth" (MNZ, 1976, 1:522).

have graves and we would know about it. And even from that fact they only have shrines where they are worshipped and have no graves, I desire that people stop mentioning this mistaken theory, especially from those colleagues who believe the work of my master. The only thing that is beyond doubt is the fact that these *kami* have concealed themselves and have been enshrined forever. Those who doubt these things have as yet not made firm their Japanese hearts.) Hereupon, there are times when these *kami* show themselves and clearly perform their work … (NST 50:109–11).

While men are alive on this earth, things occur in this manner, but when a person dies and becomes attached to the nether land, his spirit becomes a *kami*, and the spiritual classification follows the nature of the individual, some being noble, others base, some good, others evil, some strong, and others weak. And among these, those spirits that are superior perform the same sort of work that the *kami* from the divine age are engaged in, there being nothing different from them and the *kami* from the divine age who gave warning about occurrences before they happened. … In the same vein that there are attending spirits for Ōkuninushi while he is concealed who protect this world, there are spirits whose protective power extends from the nether land and protects lords, parents, wives, and children. Now, if these spirits do not go to Yomi, where do they reside so that they may protect this world? That is why we build shrines and sacred edifices to worship these *kami*. For those who are not treated in like manner, the spirits are enshrined by the grave. Even in this case, these spirits are eternally enshrined with heaven and earth just like the *kami* who are enshrined in shrines and sacred edifices. As an example of a person who was enshrined at the grave, we see that when Yamato Takeru died and was buried in Nobonu in Ise, his spirit became a white bird and flew off, landing in Shiki in the province of Kawachi. Thus, a grave was also built there, and the record says, "He was enshrined." … This is an example of the spirit being enshrined right there at the grave. In ancient times, all graves were built as places of enshrinement for the spirit, and this is seen in the fact that when Yamato Takeru's spirit became a white bird and flew to another place, another grave was constructed … (NST 50:112–13).

The students of ancient learning in the present world appear on the surface to possess a Yamato spirit, being cold to Buddhism, despising it as dung, but is this actually the case? My master stated, "It is the common concern of man to want to know about life before and after he is born into this world."[63] He also said, "Every man is worried about what will happen

63. Bentley (2013:278).

to him after death, and this is natural from an emotional point of view."[64] Surely, this type of doubt cannot be avoided as long as we live in this world, and everyone desires a clear answer to the question. However, since the hearts of men are such, they do not comprehend the fact that the old idea that the spirits of men go to Yomi does not agree with the ancient tradition that has been incorrectly transmitted down to us. And even when they do dubiously wonder if spirits actually go to such a putrid and polluted place, there is not a single person who does not believe that the spirits go to Yomi at some time or another. … O even such people as students of ancient learning, when they are young and vigorous, speak evil of Buddhism, but when they are old, or possessed of some terrible disease and believe that their time has come, most will call upon the name of Buddha in their hearts; I, Atustane feel uneasy about the entire affair … (NST 50:116–17).

O, you people, how I wish you would cease believing that your spirit at death will ride upon a large and blessed boat and sail off to that polluted land of Yomi. [I say this] because as I have mentioned above, there is no evidence in the ancient records or even now that the spirits of men go to Yomi. Even my master made the casual mistake of thinking that spirits go to Yomi, but his spirit has not gone off to Yomi. Atsutane knows for sure where his spirit has departed. His spirit has calmly and quietly been enshrined, and is in the company of our other colleagues who have passed from this life. And while they compose poetry and write prose, they change their thinking from those things that they missed or mistook while in this life. This point is without doubt certain, as clear as those things we behold with our eyes in the present; they are talking about these things because So-and-So has a strong desire to seek for the Way. …

The answer to the question about where Motoori Norinaga's spirit has gone to dwell is Mount Yamamuro. He spent the long years of his life expounding the mistaken idea that the spirits of men go to Yomi, and could not quickly correct his thinking; however, since he knew that the grave was constructed from ancient times on to enshrine the spirit of man, he had his grave selected before he left the world. Thus he wrote the following poems about that mountain.

yamamuro ni	I set up markers
titose no faru no	on Mount Yamamuro
yado simete	for my eternal, spring lodging.
kaze in sirarenu	Unknown to the wind,
fana wo koso mime	but I do want to view the blossoms.

64. MNZ 1976, 1:526.

ima yori fa
fakanaki mi tofa
nagekazi yo
tiyo no sumi ka wo
motome etureba

What does it mean
that my body is ephemeral?
It should not be lamentable,
when I have been able to find
and obtain my eternal dwelling.[65]

These show that Norinaga knew that by selecting the place, his spirit would be enshrined and appeased there. Since this beautiful mountain is the place that he selected before he died for his spirit to be eternally enshrined, there is no room for doubt that that is where his spirit now resides ... (NST 50:118–20).

Students of ancient learning, for the most part, in the present believe everything regarding the theories of my master, and cannot comprehend any of the foreign ideas. Thus, there are many who when they encounter a foreign idea they have never heard before, immediately agree with it and are led into evil paths. And those who are not led into evil paths, which in and of itself is something good, possess only shallow views and ideas, respecting my master much like an old woman reveres the Buddha. In other words, these people do not respect Norinaga because he was the only true scholar in the world. From this, they proclaim foolish ideas because the foundations of their hearts are not firmly set. It is truly deplorable. And once in a blue moon, there are some who attack the theories of others, but since they do not understand their own position very well, and they have not listened carefully to the theory they are criticizing, they merely raise their voices and argue. A scholar who agrees with the person watches in vexation. ...

I, Atsutane, of humble birth have been born in a blessed era, and am fortunate to reside in Edo where the shogun dwells, ruling the boundless world. I have studied diligently about the ancient Way, examining foreign ideas as I need to, and have composed *Tama no mihashira*, expounding upon the basics of the spirit. To you students who desire to be engaged in the study of ancient learning, remember that even the Chinese say 無固無我,[66] which means to avoid sticking to theories and avoid setting yourself up; thus, rid yourselves of meaningless defeatism and firmly ground the pillar of your spirit and construct your large palace. Then when you view foreign theories, you will be able to comprehend that our country is

65. Both appear in MNZ 1976, 8:151.

66. Meaning "Be not obstinate or egotistical." From *The Analects*, "The Master absolutely eschewed four things: capriciousness, dogmatism, willfulness, self-importance" (Nylan 2014:23).

the father of all other countries; our sovereign is the ruler of the world, and Motoori Norinaga was the only true scholar among the myriad countries. And you will also come to see that the knowledge of foreign countries is nothing but sundry forms of noisy confusion and there is really nothing worth taking into consideration. When you have done this, then your study into the ancient Way will for the first time come to fruition. How noble and pleasant!

I finished writing this on the fifth day of the twelfth month.

[NST 50:130–31].

ଔ

TSUKI NO SAKAKI

Suzuki Masayuki | ca. 1867

[It is unclear when this work was written, but it must have been finished by the end of 1867. The title is taken from the name the sun goddess used when she revealed herself to Jingū: "The emperor … prayed, 'Which *kami* gave the great ruler instructions the other day?' … After seven days and seven night a *kami* replied, '… My name is the lone-standing *sakaki* tree (**tuki sakaki**) with the solemn spirit who left heaven, Mukatsuhime'" (Kojima et al. 2002, 1:418). Here the *sakaki* tree signifies a sacred place where the spirit of the *kami* may come down to communicate with humanity. The belief was that when the spirit of the *kami* had come down, however, the tree then became the actual being. Masayuki was also influenced by *Sandaikō*, and used this essay to develop his own ideas about the afterlife. His purpose is to elucidate the Way leading to human truth and fulfillment. The work is written in five *maki*: (a) general outline, (b) heavenly *kami*, (c) Susanoo, Magatsubi, Naobi, and Ōnamuchi, (d) spirit, mind, life, death, and the afterlife, and (e) lord, parent, heaven, earth, Yomi, the imperial land, foreign countries, Confucianism, and Buddhism. The following translation comes from the first *maki*.

Masayuki constructs his text with three different, layered types of argument. The first is an overall statement of the ancient Japanese tradition, set one character higher than the rest of the text. This appears in my translation in 11-point font. Following this is Masayuki's explanation, which I have put in 9-point font. He then adds further clarification in characters half the size of the rest. I have placed these in parentheses. Clarifications from the translator appear in square backets.]

INTRODUCTION

The key to the Way of scholarship is to understand the truth of humanity, do your best as a human, and perfect your innate virtues. To achieve this people must understand the primary aspects. I mean that our business in this world is hectic, with various demands, public and private, and if the individual does not understand some basic principles, then we tend to fall into arrogance because of our frenetic lives. Then we are apt to commit transgressions, some of us may even commit serious crimes, and there are many who then lose those innate virtues. Therefore, people should first understand well the basics, and then do their best to do their duty. This then is the true Way to scholarship, where people do not commit serious crimes, but do their best as humans and perfect their innate virtues.

Concerning the basics, while our lives are busy and stressed, if you investigate the foundation of our lives, you will find that it is the body. If you investigate the foundation of the body, you will find it is your parents. If you investigate the foundation of your parents, you will find it is the *kami*. Thus, the *kami* existed first, then came our parents, and that is why we have bodies. The earth supports and nourishes our bodies. Our lord governs and nourishes our bodies. But it is the *kami* that have created the earth and our lord. Thus, the *kami* are the foundation of things above and below heaven. These are the four basic principles of our existence: the *kami*, our lord, our parents, and the earth. Because these are the foundation from which spring the many and varied humans, people cannot go about their lives ignorantly. In spite of scholars in the present having superior talents, their scholarship reaching the highest levels of achievement, as their fame thunders in every ear, none of these scholars can give an answer about the basics of life. How lamentable that people in the present only search after unfounded theories and unsubstantiated works, and there are very few people who seek the true Way and fruitful scholarship. Thus, it is not natural that there are so many examples of people who meet fortunate people or circumstances without realizing they have things backward, and lose their innate virtues through confusion in the chaos of life, and go on to commit grave crimes; these then lead to the weakening or destruction of the state. This is due to everyone fumbling in the dark, feeling after foreign and evil beliefs. I have little talent or learning, but because I understand the basics, and though I may not know myself well I desire to proclaim here the fundamental teachings of the true Way,[1] and wake people from their fog of confusion, so together we can do our best as people, and perfect our innate virtues. I hope you will read the following words with this intention in mind.

(1)

All living things born into this world (needless to say man is included among the beasts, birds, insects, and fish) are born within a Way (I will define "the Way" below). Because the Way exists [beforehand], all living things are

1. "Fundamental teachings" is a translation of 本教, a usage that appears in the beginning of the preface to *Kojiki*, "Thus, while the circumstances of the beginning of creation are shrouded in mystery, through the fundamental teachings we may know the timing of when (these two *kami*) gave birth to our islands" (Kōnoshi et al. 2007:17).

born into the Way. The Way was *not* created because living things were first created. The Way has a foundation and a limit and life responds within these parameters. Actions within this Way thus caused the creation of life. It is a mistake to believe that the Way was first created after living beings came into existence (People in China claim that the Way is based on human morality, but this is a peripheral Way willfully created by humans, so readers should not be confused).

All living things act within a Way and that allows them to function within life. The more a being acts in this life, the greater the necessity that this being not depart from the Way (I will explain why below).

We do not live *and then* act within the Way. Humans initially exist because they fulfill their duty within the Way. It is an inside-out mistake to think that because humans are alive that they perform the Way. (Because of this mistaken thinking people drift away from the Way and the two become separated. But the relationship of people and the Way is not such that they can actually become separated. There are those who perfectly perform the Way and those who do it imperfectly, but as long as we live, we are subconsciously performing the Way. It is impossible for a human to completely abandon the Way and continue to live. I will explain more below.)

Our death means that we have completed our work within the Way. Death comes because of the Way. However, there are two types of death. One is destiny and the other is nondestiny (There are actually two divisions within the category of nondestiny. I mention this under the section on death).[2] Here I am referring to death because of destiny, not the other one.

The Way does not end because of death. We fulfill the Way of humanity, refining our innate virtues, and the reward for this accomplishment is that our spirits depart from this seen world for the unseen world, and ascend to heaven. This is a destined death. However, not everyone fulfills their duty within the Way to perfect their innate virtues, but in general humanity is granted a time to achieve their merits in this life, and when the time [to depart] comes, even those who have not yet perfected their innate virtues still die. Now, even when a person dies, the Way does not end.

Now, what is the Way? The Way is not a perverted version like a variety of philosophies, such as Confucianism or Buddhism. In general people in society imagine Confucianism or Buddhism when they hear the word "Way." But these so-called Ways were willfully created at various times, fabricated according to the qualifications of the human heart or expounded in an especially convincing manner. Within these peripheral Ways many have evil and impetuous teachings that stir up issues dealing with morality. These are not the correct Way. (In general many of the

2. This terminology ultimately goes back to Mencius. My translation is based on Bloom and Ivanhoe (2009:144).

foreign teachings are evil and damage the true Way, causing harm to the morale fiber between sovereign and subject, and parent and child. By which I mean that all these foreign Ways are built on the selfish teaching of taking over the country and trying to unite the minds of the people, or are built on the thinking that they will establish laws to prevent others from stealing their country, while others fabricate a Way and teach people to respect them. There are many malevolent Ways like these. However, since all foreign countries were created when the *kami* congealed the foam of the tide and mud, their national character is inherently evil, the hearts of the people cunning, and since there have been many people who have committed crimes against their Way, people appeared teaching doctrine that attempted to correct their Way by leading people in the proper direction; however, people in later eras again taught their own ideas and this created the problem we see now. These Ways were originally incorrect, fabricated to persuade even those who were cunning, and these philosophies [later] came to our shores, and for over a thousand years our people have believed what they taught. It is thus regrettable that people think of these things when they hear the phrase "the Way." In the life of a person there are three pivotal events: their birth, their life, and their death. There are people who do not know the facts I have expounded above that these three events are all determined by the Way, but rejoice in the tenets of a malevolent [foreign] Way fabricated by man, exerting themselves to learn these tenets. This is a terrible misconception. These tenets turn a person's heart, so that they are like a child who wants some other, evil parent, forgetting that their parents are good people. The extreme example of this confusion is when these people turn against their lord, rebel against their parents, lose their morality, and damage their virtue, which leads to the weakening and destruction of the country and a generation of chaos in the land. Thus, it is clearly the duty of scholars to elucidate and expound, demonstrating the true Way, criticizing and refuting the heretical and evil, and awakening society from their stupor. So I exert all my faculties and cheer up my heart, and proclaim that all heretical and evil philosophies that stand in the way of the true Way are those beginning with Confucianism and Buddhism. People tainted by vulgar customs are struck with wonder and amazement when they first hear these words, and certainly they become angered. But I do not do this because I recklessly enjoy disputations. My desire comes from the fact that there is no other method, and those who realize that my heart is right, and my understanding sound will not resent me that much. My reasoning is sound, and those who peruse the evidence contained in my works, *Daigaku-ben*, *Chūyō-ben*, *Rongo-ben*, *Mōshi-ben*[3] should understand clearly.) Why should a Way be so deplorable?

A definition of the Way is that it believes that the heavenly *kami* reside

3. Of these four titles, only *Daigaku-ben* and *Mōshi-ben* have survived to the present. These four works all appear to have been critiques of problems and irrational arguments concerning the philosophy of Confucianism.

graciously in the High Plain of Heaven ("heaven" is a word that refers to a place from the point of view of this country. Heaven is the solar orb), a Way that we fulfill for our lives.

The heavenly *kami* refer to the four divine pillars: Ame no Minakanushi, Takami Musubi, Kamu Musubi, and Amaterasu Ōmikami (I will expound later in detail regarding the meaning of the names of the great *kami* and their virtues). These are all called the heavenly *kami*, and some are called that in relation to only one or two of these names. (The meaning of this is found under the section on the heavenly *kami*.) The Way of life is fulfilled by these *kami* through their procreative powers to produce all things, achieving their purposes by increasing, nurturing, and prospering their creations. I direct the reader to search later pages in this work to understand the significance of this. The definition of the Way is the workings of the august spirit and will of the heavenly *kami*. As these are definitely the workings of the spirit and will of the *kami* it should not be labeled "the Way," but we call it thus because humans use their conjecture based on their experiences to understand things. First, a *way* is originally a path someone follows, and we label it thus based on our experience. What we presently call the Way of life is human reasoning, which we follow according to good conduct, analogous to a person proceeding down a road. The reason that the work of creating life through the heavenly *kami* who demand reverence has not changed through time is analogous to humanity fulfilling their duty in the Way, because these *kami* also have a Way that they must fulfill. I have stated that people have a Way to fulfill [to follow reason and do acts of good], but as I have already stated, we as humans are granted a portion of the spirit of the heavenly *kami* in fulfilling our life duties. Thus the procreative activities of the heavenly *kami* are the great foundation. It goes without saying that what we call the Way that humans fulfill is named after the great foundation of the achievements of the heavenly *kami*, but I thought that someone who heard about this for the first time would have doubts, which is why I have provided a detailed explanation. (We call it the "true Way" when people follow reason and act accordingly, and anything that goes against reason we label "an evil Way." This is both a correct and a perverse Way. You must select the "true Way.")

(2)

Because the Way is the achievements of the procreative work of the heavenly *kami*, and the bodies of people are endowed with their [divine] power, as long as people fulfill their duty according to this endowed influence and do not commit any grave crimes, there is no necessity for any special teachings in this Way. Thus, anciently in our country there was nothing specially labeled the Way or our doctrine. We were endowed with this influence and that is why our country has had few wicked people, our land being well governed. Why would there be a need to set up a special Way or doctrine? Contrary to that, those corrupt Confucian scholars are apt to say that anciently we had no Way and greatly despised our land. How fearful. They live life walking this path and are unaware of the great blessings they receive. It should be labeled an extreme example of evil. The hearts of people fumbling lost in an evil Way in general are all similar. It is something to fear. …

Here I introduce Master Motoori, an individual of unparalleled talent, who demonstrated to society the true Way after reestablishing the original Way from a thousand years before. This is truly a historic event since the creation of the world. However, because Master Motoori strongly criticized and refuted the need for any doctrine many of the students who have followed him have drifted away, chasing the elegance of poetic vocabulary, and it is regrettable that they despise the idea of a doctrine. If it simply was that the hearts of the ancient people were simple and affectionate, would the Way be able to exist without doctrine in later eras where heretical and evil teachings flourished? Furthermore, if there were no doctrine anciently because there were few diabolical people, then are we not obligated to have doctrine when we establish the Way in the present when there are so many wicked people? This would allow people to do good, fulfill the Way, and perfect their innate virtues, accomplishing the great commands of the heavenly *kami* (I will discuss this "great command" later). If true, then when people scorn doctrine it allows evil to increase and this goes against the will of the heavenly *kami*. (Master Motoori despised doctrine because it had a connection to evil philosophies. That does not mean that he despised the true doctrine of our Way. It is not the fault of Master Motoori that many of his students loathe the idea of doctrine, but the fault of those who entered his school. If they heard me say this, they would laugh me to scorn and censure me by saying I am infected with the Chinese heart. On the other hand, it demonstrates that they are unaware that they themselves are stained with the Chinese heart, composing poetry with false emotions, writing fake prose, enjoying old vessels and antiques, and amusing themselves with counterfeit styles of paintings. It shows they do not know the Yamato heart. I want to declare this fact to this group.)

(3)

Someone asked me, "There is nothing created between heaven and earth that decays away. So why is this so with the Way of life?" I answered that this misconception stems from the misunderstanding that all things created in the Way of life have an end, but this does not mean that they "decay away." This is based on the Buddhist teaching of *nirvana* [or annihilation]. Humans and other living things die or wither away as a process of accomplishing their existence. (People as well as birds, beasts, insects, and fish all die and plants and shrubbery wither away, but this is not considered "decaying away," so the reader should not fall into the trap of misjudging what I am saying.)

The Way of life begins with the relationships of sovereign and subject, parent and child, husband and wife, brothers and friends. Parents are the origin of life, and the sovereign controls the management of this life. All others, subjects, children, husbands, wives, brothers, and friends are born through parents, and the sovereign accomplishes his purpose by governing these people. These various groups follow each other, and fulfill the duty of the Way by helping each other. This is the common situation in society, all due to the profound thinking and mysterious creative power of the heavenly *kami.* (All things created in the world start by helping each other, which allows them to fulfill their work, and their purposes are fulfilled. In general there are no living things that work and fulfill their purposes based on their own individual strength. To give an allegory, the body has various organs, and each has a function: the eyes see, the ears hear, the mouth speaks, the hands hold things, and the legs carry the entire body. These organs work in concert to assist the living being to accomplish its purpose in life. Speculating on this, regardless of how small or insignificant something is, if a number are gathered together and work together, there is no difference in their being able to fulfill their purpose. It is all due to the profound thinking and mysterious creative power of the heavenly *kami.* This represents the condition in society).

Therefore, when people go against this Way the country is thrown into chaos and it becomes difficult for people to fulfill their duty to accomplish their purpose in life. (When people break this moral law everything under heaven immediately is thrown into chaos and for a while it is difficult to govern the land. You may know this by looking at the tradition in China where a subject kills his sovereign and steals the throne. Examining history through time, there are few eras that were easy to govern, and there were many periods in disorder. Even in our country, insurgents accepted the teachings of the sages and the hearts of the people gradually became stained with the philosophy of these evil doctrines. Our customs turned to denigrating the sovereign, and it is terrifying to think that there are many people who now make light of the imperial court. Thus, after the Hōgen and Heiji eras there have been many years of tumult and few periods of peace. There have been many miserable instances that resemble the situation in China. This is the result of malicious doctrine becoming popular and people breaking moral rules. Is this not truly lamentable? I have provided a detailed account of this in *Chian-saku.*[4]) …

This is a Way where everything is bestowed by the heavenly *kami*, food

4. Masayuki argues for the government to work to unite the minds of the people by having the ruler espouse and demonstrate the value of hard work and diligence.

and drink, men and women. Food is provided to nourish the body, and men and women are provided to give birth to children, and each of these has a great work to do within the Way of life. (If people do not eat and drink then they cannot support life, and if men and women do not have sexual relations, then the race will die out. That is why food and drink, and men and women perform a great work within the Way of life.)

Some people censure me by saying that if food and drink, men and women, are part of the Way, then are not gluttony, drunkenness, and sensual pleasures also part of the Way? [This reasoning] is difficult to comprehend. I answer that food and drink, men and women are part of the Way. Thus eating and drinking sustain the body, and relations between men and women produce children. Is this not the way to fulfill one's duty within the Way? However, there is a force that compels some to fall into riotous living and damage their own health, based on the principle that within good the seeds of evil are sown. (All examples of evil sprout from the soil of goodness. Magatsubi is the author of this evil, and he tries to obstruct the Way of life. Those who fall into riotous living and ruin their health are possessed by this *kami*. Do not blame the fault of food and drink, or men and women. I wish people would ponder this and come to an understanding.)

Cultured individuals understand this principle and should always beware. (People should make sure they are not tempted by Magatsubi. I will say more about this later.) So even if this kind of evil temptation exists, food and drink, men and women, still are able to fulfill their duty within the great Way of life. This is how people continue to live, but if someone were to doubt me, it is because they are lost within the fog of false logic and perverted doctrine. If someone still has reservations, then try accomplishing your duty within the Way of life by abandoning these two important things [food and drink and sexual relations]. You will figure it out almost immediately. (Foreign doctrine holds these two things in great contempt, but this belief is excessive, because these people are going against the heavenly *kami*. If people do not argue from a well-grounded position, but only talk about evil influences, would there be anything without an evil influence? It is the duty of men to know which are evil influences and use caution to prevent these. Food and drink and relations between men and women are two critical parts of the Way of the heavenly *kami*, so people should realize that when people connected with Buddhism despise and try to prohibit these, it only causes harm to society and has absolutely no value. The sins of the founder of the evil doctrine of Buddhism are so great that they cannot be expunged, even if someone were to cut his finger and toenails and beard.[5] Among

5. A reference to the price Susanoo was ordered to pay for throwing the High Plain of Heaven into chaos because of his unruly behavior. *Kojiki* records, "The eight million *kami* held council together and levied a fine of one thousand tables on Susanoo, and they cut his

the followers of Buddha are some fools who eschew grain, and eat only the fruit of trees [known as *mokujiki*] to sustain themselves, claiming it is an act of virtue. When a person dies having committed a sin against the heavenly *kami*, it does not matter how one dies, be it drowning, or by starvation—there are many methods. I would not want to lose my life just by subsisting on the fruit of trees. In spite of that, why would someone who should be sustaining and nourishing their bodies refuse to eat? It is a miserable state of confusion. This state is because these people do not know the truth).

Receiving this power from the heavenly *kami*, our spirits fulfill their duty in the Way. Our spirits are *kami* that reside within our bodies. (The spirits of our bodies are divided from our parents, and their spirits originally came from the heavenly *kami*.) This spirit is not a *yang* element as taught by the Chinese. You may know the truth of this by reading our old works. (Our language has simply borrowed the character 魂 "spirit," but the Japanese word *tamasifi* means "a divine spirit."[6] Even in some dictionaries it says that 魂 refers to a *kami*, a proper definition. This is different than what Chinese people say when referring to 魂 as a *kami* who performs the function of *yin* and *yang*. Since Chinese people always claim there is no such thing as a *kami*, there is no way their definition would match that in our country.) The meaning of "receiving this power from the heavenly *kami*, our spirits fulfill their duty" is that everything that people do within life is also done by the spirit. (The mind and the body function together in fulfilling one's duty in life, but in the end this is all the spirit, because the spirit has created both the mind and the body.) The spirit functions because it has received the great command of the heavenly *kami*. Read the passages after this to gain an understanding of this.

This refers to the beginning of the world when the two great *kami* Izanagi and Izanami received the decree to give birth to the heavenly *kami*. This is described in detail in *Kojiki* and *Nihon shoki*. In the beginning the spirits of everyone came from the heavenly *kami* and then were divided into thousands and tens of thousands of spirits. (Because these spirits are *kami*, no matter how many times they are divided the original spiritual essence does not decrease. This is based on the same reasoning that no matter how many times we divide up one *kami* and worship him here and there [throughout the country] the original entity does not diminish. It is the same reason that no matter how many children parents give birth to and share their own spirits with these new bodies, the original spirit does not decrease.) The spirits of these two *kami* [Izanagi and Izanami] also came from the

---

beard, finger, and toenails as a price of expiation. Then they expelled him" (Kōnoshi and Yamaguchi 2007:67).

6. The Old Japanese word **tamasipi** is of unclear etymology, but it may be composed of *tama* "spirit" and *sipi* "strength" (cf. Martin 1987:540).

heavenly *kami*. (The reason for this is mentioned below.) Thus, "spirit" acknowledged from the beginning that it would participate in procreation (this is a hidden mystery), and it received the decree to procreate (this is a visible mystery).

First the *kami* created the land as a sphere in which the myriad objects could be placed. This design is also described in detail in *Kojiki* and *Nihon shoki*. Through sexual intercourse the two *kami* gave birth to the land, and they gradually created the earth, the waters and land were separated, and then they created the various foreign countries.

Next, they gave birth to the various *kami*. First they gave birth to the land where the myriad objects could be located, and then they gave birth to the myriad *kami* who form the foundation *kami* of each of the myriad objects. The reader should ponder this Way of creation that increases and helps the myriad things in this world prosper. You must not be negligent and overlook this.

From this point the spirit was divided into hundreds and thousands of other spirits, and this has been transmitted from parent to child through the ages down to the present. The spirits of these two *kami* divided and became the other various *kami*, and the spirits of the various *kami* then divided and became the spirits of the eight million *kami* and became the spirits of the billions of people. It has been transmitted from parent to child, from child to their children, and there is no end to this creation. Now, since the spirits of these two *kami* was divided from the heavenly *kami*, our own spirits are all originally the spirits of the heavenly *kami*. It is not a personal belonging! Thus, it is the height of the Way of humanity that while we are alive we should fulfill our duty in the Way (the Way of life), perfect our innate virtues (the virtues of life), ascend to heaven (death), and make a report on our lives (our achievements).

(Since humanity originated from these *kami*, it is the natural course for people to follow the Way of the *kami* and fulfill their duty. Why should there be another reason other than the Way of the *kami* where someone would treat the spirit from the heavenly *kami* as a personal belonging? I desire that anyone who is discerning ponder this point. As both the *kami* and humanity have shared in the same spirit, this is the same logic. There is a difference between those with a supernatural power and those without, but this disparity is due to a difference in the wisdom, strength, and the density of these spirits. The reason people in society become surprised or suspicious when they read the ancient traditions from the divine age, which leads them to disbelieve these traditions, is because they do not comprehend this reasoning. When there is the same kind of disparity in wisdom relating to the same kind of people in the present there is a difference in their actions as great as heaven and earth. By this you may know that while *kami* and men operate on the same kind of reasoning, their actions can be vastly different. And scholars of the ancient Way believe that *kami* are only mysterious, and they do not realize that they operate on the same principles as humans. Thus their discussions are vague and circuitous, and have no direct influence on the actual condition in this world. Is this not lamentable? It is because their theories are lacking in precise investigation of the principles of the practical. In spite of this, it is not easy to be cognizant of the actual principles. We have the examples of the students of Yamazaki Ansai[7] who have demonstrated the tendency to fall prey to the empty logic of the Chinese heart. The reader should not think casually about this.)

In spite of this, the people in this world think of their lives as their own, (They do not realize that the spirit creates and sustains life) treating the spirit as a personal belonging, (They do not understand the meaning of their spirits being interconnected with the spirit of the heavenly *kami*) and failing to follow the Way of the heavenly *kami* (they do not follow the Way of life). It is unspeakably distressing that these people drown in heretical and evil philosophies, breaking moral principles, or losing their innate virtues, committing great crimes, and consigned to receive punishment in the visible and invisible worlds. (I explain this later.)

A certain person rebuked me when he asked, "According to your theory, if the spirit governs the body and is interconnected with the spirit of the heavenly *kami*, then why does this spirit fail to serve the Way of the *kami*, failing to protect the body from drowning in heresies and refining its innate virtues? And if this spirit is interconnected with the *kami*, then people naturally would perceive that relationship; why is it that no one is aware of this relationship?" I responded that the reason that the spirit cannot rescue a person from falling into heresies even though it governs the body is analogous to a parent being unable to prevent a child from being foolish. First, the spirit is a *kami*, making it an unseen entity, so it is unable to work in this visible world. Thus, it produces the mind and oversees the work in the visible realm, and the spirit withdraws and generates the government of the unseen.

(Work in the visible realm refers to all work that can be seen, while the government of the unseen refers to all the work that is not visible. Everything in this world belongs to these two realms and nothing else. Order and disorder in society, as well as success and failure originate from these two realms.)

While we say that the spirit produces the mind, once it has come into existence it controls what happens in the visible realm, and when it becomes another type of spiritual manifestation it is difficult to control freely by the spirit. Parent and child originally were of one body, but as the one grows, the child becomes a separate entity from the parent, and as the talent of the child comes into his own, it is difficult for the parent to freely control the behavior of the child. This is the same principle. Therefore, if the

7. Yamazaki Ansai (1619–82) was a Neo-Confucian scholar who is also well known as a founder of *Suika Shintō*, where he established a "living shrine" to worship 心神 "the *kami* of one's mind" (cf. Inoue et al. 1999:538).

mind becomes confused and drowns [in some philosophy], [causing] the body to make a mistake, the spirit laments and weeps, but it cannot save the body. (Now if a person is deceived by an evil philosophy or commits a crime, the fault lies with the mind, and the spirit is blameless. A person may then wonder if the person will be punished in the afterlife; it is true that the mind will be punished for the action, and since the mind is a product of the spirit, the spirit cannot avoid some responsibility. It is the same principle where an attendant is punished when his master is [actually] at fault.) Another reason it is difficult for your own mind to perceive that your spirit is interconnected with the *kami* is due to the distinction between the visible and invisible. It is difficult for the visible mind to use its wisdom to perceive the invisible spirit. (This is the same principle where it is difficult for human wisdom to perceive the existence of the *kami* enshrined at the various shrines.)

Another person asked, "I have heard you explain that the spirit and the mind are the same thing, so it is extremely strange to now hear you say that these are separate entities. Do you have proof of this assertion?" I responded that there is a place in *Kojiki* and *Nihon shoki* where Ōnamochi participated in a question-and-answer exchange, demonstrating that he did not perceive his own spirit (the spirit of fortune and the spirit of wonder).[8] This passage is proof that the spirit and the mind are separate. (While it is a spirit that has come from the *kami*'s own body, it still cannot be easily perceived by the wisdom of the mind connected with the visible world, so that is why he asked, "And who are you?" Pondering this fact, we see that the same principle operating in the visible and invisible world is valid for this great *kami* as well as humans. However, this scene also demonstrates the superior wisdom that exceeds our human wisdom, because as soon as the spirit that left his body spoke its name, he realized who it was). When the spirit leaves the body, the body dies. Even when someone wishes for the spirit to remain in the soul for a thousand, ten thousand years, it is not up to our own will whether the spirit stays or departs. [The festival known as *Chinkonsai* originated from this desire.[9] Ancient people knew there was a difference between the spirit and the body, so they conducted this ritual to prevent the spirit from leaving the body. If the spirit and the mind were the same, would there be times when the spirit would do something the mind did not want?] This is a second piece of evidence. If the mind gets tired, the body can sleep, then the mind can cease its labors. However, breathing and circulation remain unchanged, because the spirit is still in control. This is the third piece of evidence that the spirit and the mind are separate. Children have very immature minds and cannot discern things well, but the function of

8. This actually only appears in *Nihon shoki*, at the end of Book 1 of the divine age.

9. 鎮魂祭, known as "the settling of the soul ritual." "According to the 'Explanations of the Prescriptions' (in *Ryō no gige*), the rite is intended to 'call back' and 'pacify' a soul that is trying to depart from someone's body" (Inoue et al. 1999:229).

breathing and circulation are no different than an adult's. This is a fourth piece of evidence. By these you may know that the spirit and the mind are distinct. (I could give more evidence, but these are more complex, so I set these aside for the moment. A detailed account is given later, or is given in a different work.)

The heavenly *kami* are generously and profoundly concerned with the Way of life, and mysteriously bestow their spirits [on us], spirits endowed with fortune. Before heaven and earth were created, Ame no Minakanushi resided in the void and divided his mysterious and incomprehensible spirit, giving birth to the two *musubi kami*.[10] Thus, the spirits of the *musubi kami* were endowed with fortune, so when their spirits were divided it became the matter of heaven and earth, and also created the two male and female *kami* [Izanagi and Izanami]. Every form of life was created through the mysterious work of the divine spirit, which also imparted fortune to heaven and earth.

So heaven, earth, and Yomi appeared.[11] "Heaven" refers to the solar orb, which is the land where the heavenly *kami* reside, an incomparably good place. "Earth" refers to this world. "Yomi" refers to the lunar orb, which is the land where evil *kami* reside, an extremely wicked place. It was not through frivolous amusement that the *kami* caused the matchless and grand sphere of heaven, earth, and Yomi and the countless living entities to come into being. All these things are due to the profound deliberation of the *kami*, and no matter how much we bow in reverence and worship them we can never repay the *kami* for their great benevolence. Any sensitive person should think on these things. Fools and those who are deceived by evil philosophies believe that all these things were spontaneously created. First, since these three objects, heaven, earth, and Yomi are suspended in space there must be something that supports them (so how would that be possible if these were spontaneously created?). Also in the thousands and tens of thousands of years that these objects have moved in their respective spheres, there has not been the slightest change in movement, but they continue to orbit the same, through spring and autumn, day and night. This is because of the government of life conducted by the heavenly *kami* for all creation, humans, and animals. This is also true of our lives. If there was no one to give me birth and life, then why am I here in the present? There should be no person who fails to realize this principle that his existence, his being able to eat and drink in the present, is due to being born of a father and mother. Even if someone were to assert that his existence was not due to a father and mother, not due to eating and drinking, who would believe this? If people understand that their existence is due to parents and food and drink, and not because of some spontaneity, then why do they not seek the origin? If they would seek the origin they

10. Being Takami Musubi and Kamu Musubi.

11. This is based on the fourth diagram of *Sandaikō*. Atsutane has altered this diagram slightly.

would realize, as I have argued above, that everything goes back to the heavenly *kami*. People who believe in some spontaneous creation are either fools or lost in [the fog of] an evil philosophy. (I address this later).

Thus, the spirit first will discern and understand this Way (of life). While the origin of these successive spirits is in the ancient past, because all spirits have come from the heavenly *kami*, the spirits do discern and understand this Way. Thus, no matter how violent and evil a person may be, he is not able to completely discard or abandon this Way. This kind of person indeed cannot abandon the morality of sovereign and subject, parent and child, husband and wife, brothers and friends. Their attempt to do it is simply superficial. (Even bandits and villains call their master *oyabun* "boss," treating their ruler as if he was a parent (*oya*) or a ruler. And among themselves they call each other *anibun* "brother" or *kyōdai* "brother," creating a society where they emulate the form of brothers and friends. Rather than viewing these people as having been evil from the beginning, they actually have aligned themselves with Magatsubi and *became* evil, but even after becoming evil they still cannot completely abandon the Way bestowed by the heavenly *kami*. How much more is this true of people who are not that wicked.) How much less can people abandon the Way of food and drink and male and female relations? (People cannot completely cut themselves off from these two things.)

And we rely on the fortune of the heavenly *kami*. This is through the blessings of the heavenly *kami*. In the first place, the heavenly *kami* actually reside in heaven at this time, blessing the spirits of the myriad creations even as they cause the myriad creations to live. We should look up and acknowledge the light of Amaterasu Ōmikami, and below we should acknowledge the prosperity of all things. (Because the life of all things is according to the will of the heavenly *kami*.) If the blessings from the heavenly *kami* were to cease heaven and earth would be extinguished and people and animals would perish. How awe-inspiring, how wondrous! (We should reverently serve with esteem, and without shame.)

Through the mysterious work of that spirit the body was created and the mind produced, giving vigor to these to perform their duty in the Way of life. From the beginning the spirit has performed work that is mysterious and cannot be comprehended, but now through the power of the blessings of the heavenly *kami* we participate. Our spirits divided from our fathers and mothers, and came together as one entity in our bodies, and through its mysterious functions this creates the body and the mind, and through this we perform the Way of life. To give an outline of the process, first the mind is produced to deal with all other things. Then it creates ears, eyes, mouth, nose, the genitals, and the four limbs, and prepares these to function. The spirit is already managing the core, causing respiration and circulation, nourishing the body and sustaining life. Is it not wondrous?

A certain person asked, "This idea that the spirits of our father and mother come together as one to create our body and mind is different than what I have heard before. Do you have any proof?" I responded that the spirit is like a fire, (You should reference the theory from Master Motoori[12]) and the parts coalesce freely. There are times when both spirits move with emotion, (when father and mother are moved with sympathy[13]) and the spirits that separate from each parent then come together and form the body, but [this body] resides in the body of the mother, having created the new body. (After completing the creation of this body, it temporarily resides within the body of the mother.) The proof for this idea is in this section on life, and should be read. The theory that the questioner has heard likely is generally something from Confucianism or Buddhism. It is only natural that their conjecture should differ from my teachings, which are based on actual principles from the ancient traditions. How can fabricated ideas of *yin* and *yang*, or the ridiculous teachings of the twelve *nidānas*, compare with the expounding of the profound and mysterious Way of life?[14] I will give a detailed exposition on this below.

A certain person asked me, "What do you mean that the spirit produces the mind?" I responded that the mind grows along with the body. Thus, when one is a child, both the body and the mind are immature, and at the peak of one's life, the body and the mind are at their height. When one is elderly and weak, the body and the mind are also aged. If the body changes with the rise and fall of life, then we know that life follows like the body. In other words, is it then not clear that the spirit is a product of the spirit?

Thus, this is born through the Way and is given life by fulfilling the Way. This is the principle of life for humanity. One should not neglect this.

Thus we serve our sovereign and our parents, giving birth to children, producing and finalizing all things of life within society. All principles such as food and drink, relations between men and women, sovereign and subject, parent and child, husband and wife, brothers and friends, and all other things for the management of life are produced and finalized. When one has fulfilled this work, the spirit ceases its work of production and departs from the body, resulting in death. The principle of human death is like this, according to what I have already stated. A person asked, "Death has different circumstances and is not the same for each person. Are all these different types the same where the spirit leaves the body?" I answered that when you reach that period where you have lived meritoriously, first the spirit leaves

12. Perhaps he means the theory found in *Kojiki-den* (MNZ 1976, 9:129–30). Atsutane also taught that Izanami was responsible for the creation of the *kami* of fire, water, earth, and wind. When she died, water and earth decayed as her body, while fire and wind departed as her spirit (cf. *Tama no mihashira*).

13. This is a euphemistic saying for intercourse.

14. This is a doctrine found in a number of Buddhist sutras. The twelve *nidānas* refers to the origin of suffering, and this can be overcome by eradicating ignorance.

the body and then the body dies. This is the common death. An uncommon death is where that time has not yet come, but the body is injured and the spirit loses its lodging in the body and so departs. The principle for these deaths is not the same. The common death is as I discussed above. An uncommon death is because of the influence of Magatsubi. Because I am explaining the common death here, I will explain an uncommon death at a later point. Please do not doubt. (I have explained this in depth in the section on death.)

Does one not experience death because the person has been able to fulfill his duty within the Way? Reading the above explanation, you should realize that birth, life, and death are all according to the Way. When you realize this principle the truth and deceit, the correct and evil, the advantage and harm in relation to the Way will naturally become clear to you. (Evil philosophies like Confucianism and Buddhism are all evil and deceptive and result in great harm.) This realization is actually a step on the ladder to perfecting the Way of humanity and realizing one's innate virtues, and this is the great foundation of learning. The sensitive person will want to read deeply, investigating and debating these things, pondering these deeply, and spread the true Way throughout society, teaching people.

In this way, all people who survive in this world do so because of this Way, entirely due to the blessings of the heavenly *kami*. There is no one, regardless of their nationality or ethnicity, who stands outside the sphere of the blessings of the heavenly *kami*. (People other than those in our august land all receive blessings through this Way and exist in this world because of divine blessings.) Regardless of one's social status or intellect, every person lives in his world through the Way, but people drown in heretical and evil philosophies and fail to receive the true doctrine of the ancient traditions, and they are apt to treat lightly and despise the *kami*. What kind of foolish and crazed state of mind is this? Even if we were to allow that the *kami* have no virtues, are they still not our fathers? Are we not living based on their divine blessings? (Those people who advocate the investigation of knowledge for a complete understanding[15] ignore the great trunk and search after branches and leaves, unaware that they are here [on earth] because of this truth. Others diligently seek after the true Way, but failing to understand truth they wander lost in evil and vapid philosophies. For example, even if one has a vast understanding of things, and has experienced much, how can that be labeled "a complete understanding," or an investigation into knowledge? And while these people are labeled sages or wise men in their respective fields, how will people in later eras view them? Is it not something terribly shameful?)

15. 格物致知, a phrase based on a line in *Liji*, "The Great Learning" section, "Such extension of knowledge lay in the investigation of things. Things being investigated, knowledge became complete" (Legge 1967, 2:412).

One must look up and feel veneration. One must not forget this reverence for even a moment.

If we return to the principle of life and reconsider [my argument], then first we will establish parent, sovereign, and earth as the three essences, and make these three the foundation of all things. Establishing these as the three essences, the *kami* control all things in the universe. Parents preside over their children, and the sovereign governs his subjects, and the earth provides space and order to all things. This arrangement is not accidental, but is based on the profound thinking of the heavenly *kami*. Thus, if the parent does not govern his children, and the sovereign does not govern his subjects, then the state falls into chaos. (This is due to self-interest burning hot without anyone to restrain it.) If the earth does not provide space and order to all things, how would we be able to live? Parents preside over their children in the private sphere, while the sovereign governs his subjects in the public sphere, and the earth provides space for the myriad objects, and this is how the world is established. Thus, the heavenly *kami* mysteriously created these three essences and made these the foundation of all things. These have remained unchanged for eternity.

Parents obtain the foundation of life, the sovereign fulfills the foundation of livelihood, and the earth sustains the cycle of life. These are all the foundations of life.

I will expound on this in greater detail. While we say that the spirit is mysterious if it has nothing to rely on, it cannot fulfill life. Because there is a difference between the hidden and visible, in order to do its work in the visible world the spirit must rely on the visible form.

Thus, the heavenly *kami* are the parents of all. The mysterious *kami* are thus. How much more is this true for people in later eras [from the divine age]. A certain person asked me, "The *kami* in the divine age should belong to the invisible world, so why should there be a visible form?" I replied that [this assumption] was incorrect. Even in the divine age there was a distinction between visible and invisible. You should understand this based on the words of decree by Kamu Musubi to Ōnamochi, "You will have control over the affairs of the visible world. ..." (I will explain this in greater detail below.)

Because we receive our bodies from our parents, they become the foundation of life. It is the work of the spirit to provide a soul and body to the child. The mind of the parents has nothing to do with this function. As I have already explained about the principle of life, as the spirit of the parents divides and then comes together to produce the body of the child, the foundation of the parent and the child is the same. However, as the spirit divides to create life they are essentially different entities and we cannot say they are the same. As this separate body is received from our parents, it becomes the foundation of life. We should not make light of our parents. (We should never treat our parents roughly, claiming that they and we are of the same body. While we may claim it is our body, it is not a personal belonging, but is a gift from the heavenly *kami*. It is the Way of humanity to take good care of our bodies. How much more should we treat our parents from whom our bodies originate? We should not treat them roughly. As I have argued about the foundation of various things, do not misunderstand the distinction between "same body" and "separate bodies".)

Therefore, if there are no parents, then we are not. Even if we were to spend our entire lives trying to repay our parents for this great blessing, it is not possible to repay them. This is true while our parents are still in the world. Even if your parents are dead presently, you should not forget the debt you owe them as long as you live, because you have your present body due to your parents. The saying "out of sight, out of mind" is human nature. No one would treat their parents lightly while they are still alive, but once they have passed on we naturally become negligent and do not act as principle dictates. This is especially true in the present, where many people are blind to the truth and there is undutiful conduct within what people consider to be filial conduct toward their parents, whether they are still alive or not. As an example, there are some who follow the intention of their parents without protesting the unvirtuous conduct of the parent (The words in *Liji* where it says if a son protests [the acts] of his parents and they do not give ear, he should follow them with crying[16] are extremely wicked in certain circumstances) or others who become lost in an evil philosophy and leave the world. (There are some who believe the words of that wicked doctrine, "If one son takes the tonsure, nine relatives are born in heaven," and take the tonsure, or force their son to take the tonsure. These actions all result in discarding the Way of life of the heavenly *kami*, which resembles a filial act, but which is actually highly undutiful.) Others pay alms to a Buddhist priest, (This act is the foundation for encouraging panhandling and laziness) while others recite the sutras (an extremely foolish distraction). In the end, true filial conduct is fulfilling the principle of life, and true unfilial conduct is spoiling the principle of life. In other words, because of the principle of life we have parents. Fulfilling the principle of life includes acts such as both parents and children devoting themselves to the Way of life, conducting themselves within the sphere of morality, making a name for themselves, and causing their houses to be prosperous. Spoiling the principle of life is the opposite of this. These are all heretical and evil philosophies that people accept, and there are not a few who have experienced great failure [because of this]. Especially within the important matter of loyalty and duty, people are committing great errors. Arguing from the point of view of truth, the idea of loyalty and duty as currently prac-

16. Part Two of the "Qu li" section of *Liji* says, "In the service of his parents by a son, if he have thrice remonstrated and is still not listened to, he should follow (his remonstrance) with loud crying and tears" (Legge 1967, 1:114).

ticed in our society is actually disloyal and undutiful. What we now label as disloyal and undutiful is not necessarily so. However, since evil philosophies have blinded the eyes and stopped the ears of people in society, no matter how diligently we discuss and criticize these mistakes there are few people who quickly come to this realization. In spite of this we cannot stop trying to open people's eyes. I give a detailed account in the section about parents. (Chinese people often debate about serving their parents, and they even have a work titled "Classic of Filial Piety," but it is filled with examples of worthless logic and superficial reasoning. It is extremely rare that any principle suits reason. Of the examples of filial piety in the twenty-four sections in the book there are even examples that are actually unfilial.)

Thus as we fulfill the Way of life evil practices also become intermixed in what we do. All examples of evil spring forth from good. As the Way of life is good, evil practices spring from this [intermixed with the good].

Magatsubi waits for us and then causes evil to spring forth so that he can obstruct the Way of life. While we can say that evil springs forth from good, it is the work of Magatsubi to cause this to happen. (In general the theories about good and evil proclaimed by foreigners are reckless lies. The student should study and learn the truth from our ancient traditions. Also, the theory from Master Motoori about good and evil originating from a common source is mistaken.[17] I give a detailed exposition about this under the sections on Magatsubi and Naobi.)

This state originates from the will of Izanami, in case humanity was to be lost. The actions of Magatsubi are a result of the words of Izanami, when she said, "I will kill a thousand people per day." This event is seen in *Kojiki* and *Nihon shoki*.

Izanagi was saddened that it had thus become difficult for people to fulfill the Way of life, and he gave birth to Naobi to try and rectify this evil. (This event appears in *Kojiki* and *Nihon shoki*. One should consider these things related to these *kami* from the information below.) Evil that the power of Naobi cannot rectify is punished by men. (The action of Naobi to rectify the evil belongs to the invisible world, while the punishing of evil men by the sovereign belongs to the visible world; thus the visible and invisible worlds assist each other in fulfilling the Way of life.)

The august child of the heavenly *kami* [Ninigi] was granted this great responsibility. "Great responsibility" refers to punishing evil and encouraging good, and this is the stewardship of the sovereign in this life.

---

17. In *Kojiki-den*, Norinaga says, "Thus, if the reader digests well this order of things he will comprehend the principle that in all things in the world, evil is produced from good ... and good is produced from evil, and they change in tandem with each other" (MNZ 1976, 9:295).

Ninigi received this responsibility with the words of a decree, "Rule over heaven and earth for eternity" and he descended down to this imperial land (This is recorded in detail in *Kojiki, Nihon shoki, Kogo shūi*, and the various liturgies), and he is the ancestor of our imperial family. Thus, our emperor is a child of the heavenly *kami*. (Anciently one called his ancestors "parent," and the descendant was called "child," no matter how many generations removed. These words are filled with tremendous affection, and this is exactly how things reasonably should be. Later eras imitated the learning of China, using their kinship terms, and the distance between a parent and child grew much greater, which has been a source of extreme harm to the Way.) The emperor is also the great ruler of all the countries of the earth.

There is the great command of the heavenly *kami* who created heaven, earth, and all things, and who supports these, through which authority was bestowed on the imperial son to govern things in the visible world. It is clear what the principle is upon which the visible world should be governed. Does that not make him the great ruler of all countries? Since that truth is not apparent in the world, and there are countries that are not submissive or obedient to our ruler, but if all people were to break the hold of heresies and evil philosophies and accept the true Way the result of accepting the great decree would become evident.

Since the sovereign has authority over life it is silly to claim he is worthy of awe, but there are no words to describe the profundity or loftiness of the blessing of this authority. Our current emperor is a descendant of the imperial grandchild who shrewdly cut ties with the blessings of the heavenly *kami* and descended from heaven to Japan for our lives, leaving the land of heaven, which was of unparalleled beauty, taking leave of his divine father and mother, and descending to Japan. He immediately received the "heavenly-sun-inheritance" (referring to inheriting the position of Amaterasu Ōmikami), so he is worthy of unbounded respect, and our obligation to him is truly profound and lofty. That is why anciently he was labeled a visible *kami* (which means that he is a *kami* that is visible to the human eye), someone categorized as different from mere mortals. A poem in *Man'yōshū* Book 18 even describes him as:

umi yukaba	We will promise to die
miduku kabane	by the side of our Great Lord!
yama yukaba	Even if we travel by sea
kusa musu kabane	and our corpses are soaked in sea water
ofokimi no	or even if we travel over mountains
fe ni koso siname	and our corpses are overgrown with weeds.
kaferimi fa	We will make a vow with the words
sezi to kotodate	that we will disregard our lives for him.

[MYS 4094]

We pledge to serve him with our lives. This is truly the great responsibility of humanity. However, in later eras the families of the Hōjō and Ashikaga appeared on the scene, and a spirit of rebellion emerged from their arrogance, and because they became hostile toward the emperor society was thrown into chaos, and there was no peace for a time. This result came about because these families turned their back to the Way of the heavenly *kami*, treated lightly and despised the master of the foundation of life, as if there were no emperor. Society was in chaos, like cutting the thread on a string of jewels, and it became difficult to fulfill one's duty of the Way of life. If one researches into the root cause of this lamentable decline in the world, you will find that the ruler who is the descendant of the heavenly *kami* has become a slave of the despicable three treasures,[18] or because those radical sages who throw the truth into confusion are now revered above everything else, and this has tilted the hearts of all the people toward the Chinese Heart and the Buddhist Heart. People forget the original sayings, and their thoughts and actions generally are turned away from the Way of the heavenly *kami*, and that is the origin of society being thrown into confusion. (I have made this argument in detail in *Chian-saku* and other of my works.)

In Master Motoori's work, *Tama kushige*, he states that people in general believe that the reason that the imperial court in middle antiquity experienced such a severe decline was due to the unrest at the time, but he states that because the imperial court went into decline,[19] society was then thrown into confusion (and not the other way around). These words are true. Sensitive individuals will research these principles deeply, come to a thorough understanding, and when they have made the mind of the heavenly *kami* their own, they will realize that they must not disturb this great responsibility. Being thankful and revering this imperial blessing is in unity with the mind of the heavenly *kami* and forms the foundation of stability of the nation. (Nothing good comes from turning one's back on the mind of the heavenly *kami* and going against their Way. How much more severe it will be for those who destroy this Way of morality. However, foreign countries have not had a firm foundation from ancient times in relation to this Way of the sovereign, and it is lamentable that they have treated lightly and despised their ruler continually. This is especially true of China, where they have labeled themselves 中華 "the central flower"[20] and 中国 "the central country," or the land of the sages, so they may brag about themselves to other countries, but in actuality it is a very inconsequential and vulgar country, and the hearts of the people have always been fickle. If someone simply has the power,

---

18. The label "three treasures" (Buddha, Dharma "the Law," and Sangha "the monk") is a euphemism for Buddhism.

19. Norinaga gives a detailed account of this argument in *Tama kushige* (MNZ 1976, 8:317–19).

20. It appears that *hua* 華 in 中華 is actually an ancient place name, and the idea of "flower" or "splendid" is a later interpretation.

yesterday's subject is today's ruler: disposing of the current ruler, and making himself the emperor. Through this China has become a highly chaotic country. Naturally there is an insightful reason for why they cannot preserve a stable ruling lineage, so it is useless to censure them. So what kind of reckless mind do these Confucian scholars and citizens stained in Confucian learning from our imperial country have when they covet things from this evil country, imitating it, despising and belittling our own ruler? As the owner of such a misguided and drowning heart will openly argue from evil works and theories and attract younger people to their theories, those who study from Confucian works will never follow the true ruler or understand and follow the true Way. And that is why so many people make self-interest central in their lives, and the country has always been in chaos, because there is no unity. Is this not distressing? What kind of hearts do these government officials have, allowing the blind to instruct the masses and guide everyone to fall into a deep gorge? It is very lamentable.

And in the West they have something called "republican government," and because their politicians claim that this better suits reason, they become entranced by their own principles; however, it is a great mistake when people blindly follow these principles. And no matter how many foreign countries there may be which are governed by a temporary ruler, and not the true ruler, the reader must not amuse himself with vain philosophies about our imperial land. You should exercise extreme caution.)

(4)

As I have argued above, our imperial court became disoriented by the parasitic teachings of Confucianism and Buddhism, and they were swayed by vain embellishments (It is due to the influence of the Chinese Heart and the Buddhist Heart that they made their rooms and clothing very ostentatious, taking a posture of great reverence and showing their authority) and empty logic, and before anyone knew it the court was in decline. Through this the distinction between sovereign and subject, master and subordinate became clouded, and our society passed through a time where the Way was obscured, and we had war and chaos; still the true teachings have not spread. Because truth is not made clear in the world, people in general struggle to understand these things, and there are many whose actions are based on an inverted idea of loyalty and treachery. This originates from the confusion of who is sovereign or subject, and who is master or subordinate.[21] This is due to the transmission of old traditions born of a society steeped in war and chaos and the loss of the Way, as well as

21. Masayuki's original is: 是君を主と相混ひ、臣と従者とまがふ故なり, which

everyone studying heresies and evil philosophies. Thus, the confusion of people in the present is not their fault. Why should we lay the blame at the feet of people in the present when this state is actually an accretion of a thousand years of evil practices? And that is why I investigate the origin of these things, criticize Confucianism and Buddhism, argue for proper conduct, write historical criticism, refuting these evil practices, and stir people from this slumber of confusion. These things are actually greater than my ability, but when I think about the Way of the heavenly *kami*, and the blessings of life, I find that I am compelled to do this as a scholar. Thus, I will debate as far as I have strength. ... I will discuss the Way in relation to sovereign and subject, master and subordinate later.

Now everything in the world fulfills its purpose in life on this great earth. And while birds fly in the sky they are not able to exist if they completely separate themselves from the earth. Is this not that much truer of all others?

Thus the earth is the place of life from beginning to end, and no matter how evil a place a person may be in, he should not forget the blessings of life. Because we cannot exist without this earth—no matter how extreme the heat or cold of that specific place—we should not forget these blessings. However, the earth is one type of "organism" because the heavenly *kami* created it and placed humans and animals upon it, but it does not have consciousness, so while people reside on the earth they do not consider the blessing of this earth. Consider that while the earth does not have consciousness, its value is greater than the ruler or parents because we cannot exist without being on it. (The ruler and parents have their status because they are on the earth, so the blessing of the earth is actually very great. That is why the first thing the heavenly *kami* created was this earth. The student should deeply ponder this fact. People in China also make recurrent mention of heaven and earth, and it is proper that they pay respect to these. But they speak of the earth as if it has consciousness, based on their empty logic and conjecture, creating a great error in bestowing thanks only on the earth.)

If you look into this principle, you see that the earth is supported by the *kami* (because the *kami* gave birth to and support the earth). Thus, while it is the blessing of the earth we consider, in reality it is not the blessing of the earth, but the blessing of the *kami*. And it would appear that we cannot compartmentalize the blessing of our own land [of Japan] separate from the earth, but our land is a distinct entity, so we must talk about the blessing of this land. Thus, if you consider the blessing of our land, then you would look up to the *kami*. That is how you show gratitude for the blessing of this land. (The land is like shrubbery and trees, water and fire, where it has life but does not have consciousness. So while we benefit from the blessing of these things, using

---

must be an error, as it is backward from what he is arguing. I have translated it with the second constituent of each pair switched.

shrubbery and trees, water and fire every day, we are ungrateful if we do not consider the blessing of the existence of these things. Since the *kami* originally created these things for the use of man and beast, we must thank the *kami*, even if we do not put much thought into the purpose of these objects. It is impossible for the land to be simply that, and this is true of shrubbery and trees, water and fire. These things are all from the *kami* to support life, so the land can fulfill its purpose as the land, as well as shrubbery and trees, water and fire fulfill their purpose. People in society generally think only of Toyo Ukehime, also known as the great *kami* Inari, when they think of the ancestor of grain, or the *kami* of grain, so I wonder why people do not consider the blessing of other things. I point this out so people will appreciate their error.)

How can people fail to consider the blessing of having been born in the precious land of the great ruler of the world, where they can live their lives in peace and tranquility? How grateful we should be to have been born in the ancestral land of the myriad countries (The foreign countries were created through the force of creation when our imperial land was first created, so it goes without saying that ours is the ancestral land), a land that is neither too hot nor too cold, where the climate is moderate, and grain and fruit are produced in abundance, a delightful land.

Based on the above evidence, we received these blessings from the *kami* before we were born. It is the work of the spirit to create life, but again, this is because of the blessings of the heavenly *kami*; thus, we received the blessings of the *kami* before we were born.

After we were born into this world, we receive the four blessings (blessings of the *kami*, of our parents, of our ruler, and of our country) and are established in the world. Through our sovereign and parents we are born and raised, and on the earth we are allowed to grow. The origin of all these comes through the *kami*. Thus, in the end all these blessings come back to one blessing of the *kami*, but the *kami* belong to the invisible world, while our sovereign and parents belong to the visible world, and that is why I have divided these [into four groups].

(5)

These three—the sovereign, parents, and the earth—were established by the heavenly *kami* to promote life in the visible world, and that is why I already stated that if one were to be separated from this one cannot exist. However, self-interest is rabid, so it is lamentable that people forget the origin of these things, and fail to look back on these blessings. When people turn their backs on the Way of the heavenly *kami* and perform immoral acts, the country will always be thrown into chaos, and that puts the lives of people in danger. The reader should carefully consider this and not take these things lightly.

If there are any who doubt these things, then separate yourself from these things and try to live your life. There is no way one could live even one day, even part of a day, having separated himself from these four blessings. There is no one who has been able to live life apart from these four blessings. That is why I label these the "four great blessings." (Another name for this work is the four great blessings, based on this statement. While Buddhist scholars also claim to have "four kinds of grace,"[22] these are simply private words based on an empty argument and cannot be taken seriously. You should not take the flippant attitude of thinking that I have based my own theory on this Buddhist theory. If I have an opportunity later I will expound on this thought.) How noble and profound, how great and expansive are the blessings of the *kami* who created heaven and earth, gave birth to and cultivate all things under heaven, and support the world. With my limited vocabulary I cannot express how boundless, how limitless these blessings are.

There are ungrateful people, regardless that they receive these great blessings; perhaps they have allowed themselves to be deceived and drowned in heresies and evil philosophies, denying the *kami* and not following the true Way. The concern of those people who disseminate these foreign heresies and evil philosophies is roughly in direct opposition to the true Way. (They make evil teachings the correct Way, and make the correct Way evil teachings.) If they presently were people who would put straw sandals on their head and walk on a crown, who would not think that they were irrational? Thus, those who do not welcome and believe these upside-down theories are treated as if an insane person were sane, and the sane were labeled insane. Nevertheless, these people are all living according to the Way that I have explained. In spite of this, their words and actions do harm to the true Way. To say it in a vulgar way, it is much like a parasite inside a lion. Is it not an extreme example of deception? Life and death are the limits of human life, and pursuing one's life is the great foundation of fulfilling the Way. If people have no life, what other Way is there? How can anyone journey to the end of this path without knowing the foundation of their body, without showing gratitude for the blessing of life?

What is wrong with people when some desire easiness and become lazy in relation to their profession in life and do not think about doing something worthy? Working at one's life profession and doing good according to one's belief in the *kami* and through the Way is how we refine virtue in this life and fulfill our duty in the Way, and this is exactly how we show gratitude for the virtue we are born with. Regardless that there is a logical reason why people who certainly do this, why do

22. Muller's *Digital Dictionary of Buddhism* notes there are two interpretations of this: (i) According to the *Dasheng ben shengxin di guan jing* 大乘本生心地觀經: the compassion of parents 父母恩; the compassion of sentient beings 衆生恩; the compassion of rulers 國王恩; the compassion of the Three Treasures 三寶恩. (ii) Four benefactors: the Buddha, the head of state, one's parents, and all other people.

people allow themselves to be deceived by evil philosophies, upon which they fail to do these things?

If people think about repenting of these transgressions, fulfilling their life duty, and refining their innate virtues, they must first abandon these baseless, evil teachings, come to their original senses, then abandon the practices of society and search the ancient meaning [of our culture], and align with the truth. If you do not abandon these baseless, evil teachings then you cannot come to your original senses. If you do not abandon the practices of society, then you cannot know the ancient meaning, and without knowing that you cannot align yourself with the truth.

(6)

Truth is the logic of life through the heavenly *kami*. All principle is connected to a specific object, so if an object exists then so does that principle. Fire has the principle of fire, and water has the principle of water. Shrubbery and trees have the principle of foliage. Thus, the sovereign has the principle of the sovereign, and parents have the principle of parents, and subjects and children have their own principle. The foundation of principles is the object. The foundation of each object is the heavenly *kami*. Thus, pondering the intention behind the creation of each object by the heavenly *kami*, you understand the principle of each object. It is truth to follow the principle of each object. …

(7)

The ancient meaning refers to abandoning personal wisdom and following the Way of the *kami*. The hearts of the ancient people were generous and sincere, and while they had no word for the Way, there is no doubt that they believed in it. They served with their will aligned with the will of the *kami*, obeying the *kami* in all things; they prevented evil and sought after fortune, and were careful in general to worship the *kami*. As they did not rely on personal wisdom, society was tranquil and the hearts of the people were peaceful. This means they learned after the manner of the *kami*. All things were created by the *kami* and supported by the same, so it is reasonable that they acted in tandem with the *kami*. (In relation to the heavenly *kami*, it goes without saying that we must worship the worthy *kami* who give assistance to the Way of life as well as those *kami* who do not. Not only do we pray to the good *kami* for fortune, but we should not despise and belittle the evil *kami*; we should do everything in our power to soften their hearts. We do that to fulfill our duty in the Way.) The [current] customs of people in society are generally Chinese in origin or influenced by

Buddhism, and many are in opposition to the ancient traditions, be they words or actions. These customs belittle the *kami*, (People educated in Confucianism despise nonpublic shrines by calling them "perverted ceremonies," and people connected to Buddhism demean the *kami* by saying that they are servants of the Buddha. Others claim that there are no *kami*, but all these people say disrespectful and insolent things because they are lost in a fog of personal wisdom, stained with evil insight. It leaves one speechless.) and they laugh at the true Way, believing that this very attitude of mockery is educated. Thus, they pay lip service to the Way, and noisily proclaim the teachings (because it is an evil Way with evil teachings), but there is absolutely no value in this; it only leads to daily acts of evil. That is why it is difficult to know the ancient meaning without separating oneself from popular customs of our day; it is difficult to align oneself with the truth.

(8)

The "original mind" of the ancients refers to a refreshing *Yamato kokoro* "Yamato Heart." This person always is aware of benevolence and charity, and we call this "the heart of Japan" when circumstances call for it and the person reacts valiantly, bravely, and without guile. This is the heart created through the mysterious portion of spirit of the heavenly *kami*, having not the slightest blemish of the Confucian Heart or the Buddhist Heart. In general the hearts of people in society are tainted with heresies and evil philosophies and bound up with these ideas, and the original, good heart of people becomes clouded and grubby. As these people cannot discern evil and truth, when they want to fulfill the Way of humanity they need to be washed clean of the filth and grime of Confucianism and Buddhism, discard the muck of evil philosophies, and return to the state of the original heart. If they do not do this they cannot enter into the true Way.

To arouse this heart and act in accordance with truth is to fulfill the Way of humanity. Fulfilling the Way of humanity means to arouse one's conscience, search the ancient texts, and do one's life profession according to the truth.

The Way of humanity is the so-called Way of life of the heavenly *kami*, which is the principle of sovereign and subject, parent and child, husband and wife, brothers and friends. As everyone is born through the Way of life of the heavenly *kami*, fulfilling the duty of that Way is the Way of humanity. I have already noted that the morality of sovereign and subject, parent and child, and others is the Way of life of the heavenly *kami*. I will now give an outline of what we need to do to fulfill our duty. It is quite a terrifying act to put forth what the sovereign should do, but I am obligated to say something, because it is a great omission to talk about the Way of the heavenly *kami* and yet not say anything here. I feel ashamed if I come on too strongly in what I myself say, but as we are talking about the Way of the heavenly *kami*,

I believe you will forgive me as I am not giving my personal opinion. Now, as the ruler receives his great responsibility from the heavenly *kami*, holding authority to encourage good and punish evil, this responsibility truly is not easy to fulfill. He functions according to the will of the heavenly *kami*, [determining] never to be swayed by self-interest (enjoying Confucianism and Buddhism are self-centered actions), has wise men in his employ, finding good men and avoiding men with twisted hearts. He punishes rebels and puts his heart into pursuing government of life, having mercy on the people, causing the world to be prosperous, and avoiding tormenting the people. He causes the light of the influence of the country to shine brightly, spreads truth, and causes the people to do good as far as he can influence.

(9)

The responsibility of the subject is to follow the will of the sovereign. He will strive to fulfill the responsibility of life, avoiding self-interest, working toward justice, aiding the ruler in his work, and helping make the ruler's job complete. Thus, the subject should always respect the commands of the ruler, and if there is a grave mistake committed by the ruler, he remonstrates with the ruler, even at the peril of his own life. It is a grave mistake to take the tonsure through the Buddhist heart or to retire because of the Confucian Heart.

(10)

The responsibility of parents is to have the mind of life and work hard in the home, teaching their children so they do not enter the wrong path, working to keep the work of parents and ancestors from deteriorating, preventing the family lineage from dying out. It is a grave error to fail to work at one's profession, fail to teach one's children, or forget that you yourself have parents (if they have passed away, pretending you have no parents), or claiming that you are the elder of the family, doing as you please, tormenting your grandchildren, or failing to recognize that you are letting the family lineage die out.

(11)

The responsibility of children is to have the mind of one's parents in fulfilling your duty in life, obeying the teachings of your parents, not entering the wrong path, working hard at your profession, and causing your house to prosper. You should make a name for yourself, so that the world will know about your parents and ancestors. It is a grave error to disobey your parents, not obey the principles of the Way, be indolent at work, indulge in alcohol and lust, be consumed with gambling and lose your property, and bring shame to your ancestors.

(12)

The responsibility of husbands is to teach and guide his wife well, prevent an evil heart from arising, and make sure he does not go astray from the Way of life. It is an extreme mistake for the husband to be trammeled by lust, be so overtaken with devotion to his wife that he becomes henpecked, to abandon an innocent wife and take a new woman to wife, or to commit adultery with someone's wife.

(13)

The responsibility of wives is to obey the teachings of her husband, follow these teachings and keep peace with father and mother, not getting into arguments with people, or being jealous, working hard to nurture her children, and helping around the house. It is a grave mistake to go against these things.

(14)

The responsibility of brothers is first, the older brother will love his younger brother and guide him in the way of right. The younger brother will respect his older brother and be obedient to his teachings, and both will work hard at home, both assisting their father and mother. This is how they should fulfill their duty in life. It is wrong for brothers to become competitors and fight for the inheritance, always fighting and causing their parents to worry.

(15)

The responsibility of friends is to engender trust, avoid lying or deceiving others, imparting wisdom, and giving ear to advice. He will lend to those in need, remonstrate with those in error, respect those who are wise, and have sympathy for the intellectually impaired. In all things he will assist in fulfilling the duty of life. It is not the Way of friendship to deceive or entrap each other, or withhold one's wisdom through malice, or be ashamed at one's lack of knowledge and failing to ask for advice, or save up several thousand ounces of gold while refusing to lend some to those in need, or fail to remonstrate someone when the fault is clear, being jealous of those who are wise, despising those with inferior intellect, or ignoring the plight of others because you yourself are sufficiently well-off.

Moral principles are divided into five categories, and human behavior is divided into ten grades,[23] but the five categories as subsumed under the heading of sovereign and subject, and the ten grades subsumed under the heading of life. What we call the sovereign is the singular person who is the emperor, and the others are all subjects, in spite of our categorizing these as noble or base, old or young, kin or unrelated. In our service to the ruler there is no difference between parent, child, husband, wife, older, or younger brother. Thus, the five categories of human morality are all connected to the two groups, the sovereign and the subject. While there are differences in the ten grades of human behavior, each is something bestowed by the heavenly *kami* to help us fulfill the Way of life, so these actually belong to the same group of life. Thus, when all people serve the ruler according to the Way of life, and when the ruler governs his subjects according to the Way of life, there is only one Way of life, regardless how broad the area of everything under heaven—there are not two Ways. Though there are ten grades of human behavior, we all have one heart, not two. It thus follows that while we divide society into noble and base, old and young, kin and unrelated, wise and foolish, we are united and have the same heart. When all people are united and have the same heart, then a time when the world is not well governed does not exist. This then is the mysterious Way of the heavenly *kami*. We must modestly and reverently work hard to fulfill our duty.

Now, if people thus study the truth and fulfill their duty in the Way of humanity with all their hearts, then the heavenly *kami* will smile down upon us and bestow blessings on us. If people obey the will of the heavenly *kami* and strive to make perfect their innate virtues, why would the *kami* not smile down upon us? Would they not grant happiness to us? The good *kami* grant happiness, and if we soothe the hearts of the evil *kami*, why should evil occur?

The sovereign will also be pleased with us, and have joy. The ruler then would generously serve.

23. The five categories of moral principles refers to that found in *Bai hu tong*, "What are the five constants? They are humanness, righteousness, proper behavior, knowledge, and trust." The ten grades of human behavior refer to the line in *Liji*, "Kindness on the part of the father, and filial duty on that of the son; gentleness on the part of the elder brother, and obedience on that of the younger; righteousness on the part of the husband, and submission on that of the wife; kindness on the part of elders, and deference on that of juniors; with benevolence on the part of the ruler, and loyalty on that of the minister—these ten are the things which men consider to be right" (Legge 1967, 1:379–80).

People of the world will also praise this situation and make a lasting name for themselves. The good name of loyal subjects and filial sons will last forever, remaining in the memory of the people.

When our time has come, our spirits will leave our bodies and immediately climb to heaven and return to the presence of the heavenly *kami*. There are no examples where someone fails to return to his place of origin. Thus, since the spirit originated from the heavenly *kami* there is an established principle that it should return to heaven. The reader will realize this through the event where the great *kami* Izanagi finished his work and climbed to heaven, made his report to the heavenly *kami*, and then resided in the Lesser Palace of the Sun. (I will explain this in detail later.)

There are vast differences in people, those who are noble or base, wise or foolish, having great or little success, with some who serve close or serve far, who live in houses far more established and beautiful than in our land, wear fine apparel, and eat fine food. Heaven is one land, blessed with mountains, rivers, shrubbery, trees, mansions, dwellings, food, clothing, utensils, all things that are far superior to anything we now have. The student should read *Kojiki* and *Nihon shoki* to comprehend this. There is no doubt that if you journey there, everything is boundlessly more superior to anything we have.

People [in heaven] live eternally in joy and peace without change. The spirit is a *kami*. People know that the *kami* cannot be destroyed, and we should understand this based on the fact that the spirit of Emperor Ōjin appeared as Hachiman, and the spirit of Minister Sugawara [Michizane] appeared as Tenman. Is it not proof that the spirit cannot be destroyed because the spiritual manifestations of these two *kami* continue to appear? If it cannot be destroyed, then it also does not change.

Our reward for this is our gratitude to the heavenly *kami* as we follow the Way, doing good, trying to recompense for the blessings of life. The reward for promoting good is as I have described. Sensitive people must definitely strive to fulfill their duty.

These are the two sides to what people do, but for that group of people who do not accept the truth, will not enter the true Way, are deceived by evil teachings and fail to repent of their errors, consumed by self-interest, engaging in deceptive practices, failing to stop their filthy hearted and malicious activities, refusing to acknowledge the blessings of the heavenly *kami* even while they are the recipients of those blessings (many of these people are possessed by Magatsubi and thus act wickedly), these people will be punished by both the sovereign and the *kami* (Punishment will be meted out by the *kami* in the invisible world, and by the sovereign in the visible world).

People of the world will also hate and censure these people. (They will leave an ignominious name for their evil acts, and people will revile and censure them.) These people will die, but their spirits cannot ascend back to heaven.

These receive punishment from the heavenly *kami*. Those who do not follow the Way of life, but engage in evil activities will be detested and hated by the heavenly *kami*. You may know this by how the *kami* banished Susanoo from heaven.

These people will be led away by others and endure anguish. The spirits of those who are deceived by evil philosophies or have joined foreign teachings wander lost, enduring pain, unable to find peace.

These people are banished to the land of Yomi, where they live in dilapidated houses, wear poor clothing, and eat filthy food, enduring eternal suffering. The land of Yomi is extremely filthy and evil, the land where the rebellious *kami* dwell. It is a very frightening place. Ōnamochi dwells there, and we see in *Kojiki* and *Nihon shoki* that he was reprimanded in a dwelling where there were serpents, centipedes, and bees. This shows how many miserable and disgusting things happen to these people. Many of the evil people will be banished to this place, because they were overtaken by Magatsubi while they were still alive, experiencing an increasingly wicked heart, leading them to do evil act upon evil act, committing heinous crimes, resulting in their being put to death. If one were to be banished to this evil land where wicked *kami* dwell, try imagining the anguish and hardship you would endure. If you were worthy of censure, how oppressive would the agony be!

A person asked me, "Do you claim that when we die that the spirit still has form, because you mention clothing, food, and a dwelling?" I replied that if it had no form, why would it need clothing, food, or a dwelling? However, the form is not the same as our physical body in the present world, but it is a transformative shape, one that is mysterious and unseen. Read the section on the spirit so you will understand. Now, it is true that the reason humans have clothing, food, and shelter is because we have a physical body, but in reality this is the work of the spirit, because warmth or cold, hunger or satisfaction, generally occur through the spirit. (You may know this because babies in the beginning are born innocent but still crave milk when they are hungry). You should thus realize that having a body without a spirit (at death the spirit leaves the body) means you do not need clothing, food, or shelter.

This individual asked another question, "You claim that the spirit and the *kami* are the same entities, so the spirit has clothing, food, and shelter, but the *kami* have shrines for shelter but do not dwell there. Though we give them clothing and food [as offerings] they do not partake. Why is this?" I responded that there are likely a number of reasons why the *kami* do not partake even though we offer them food. Would it not be that the food is defiled or filthy, or a dish that they dislike? Or it might be that the food presented to the *kami* remains the same because people *think* the *kami* have not eaten it. It could be that we do not understand the principles of food. First, regardless of the type of food, it has a flavor based on its essence, and if you consume its essence, even if you have not partaken of the actual object, you still have eaten it. You may know this because when a patient smells a medicinal herb, they have inhaled its essence, and they get better. Even if the food presented to the *kami* remains in its presented state how can we determine that the *kami* have not partaken of it? We should not doubt these things based on our personal wisdom. An explanation about clothing and dwellings will require more pages to argue, so I will argue that later.

This is the reward for those who have committed the crime of turning their backs on the great will of the heavenly *kami*, opposing the Way, and obstructing life. The reward for engaging in evil activities is thus. Sensitive people should be terrified of these consequences. Another person asked, "If we accept your premise that the spirit was divided and separated from the heavenly *kami*, and we then know that the reward for doing good is this, while the reward for doing evil is that, then why is it that we cannot cause people to avoid committing evil?" I answered that while our spirits comprehend this, people differ in their intellect and fortitude, and also the mind must be seduced [to achieve this aim], so though people understand that they should do good and shun evil, we still find that people commit evil. (Rather than saying that the spirit gets deceived, this state [of committing evil] simply occurs, as I noted above.)

There are those who sometimes avoid being punished in this visible world. This likely happens through the assistance of Magatsubi. In other words, he lends aid to those evil people in obstructing life.

Even if people go through life in this world without getting caught, the spirit will be banished for eternity and endure the kind of punishment I mentioned above. Sensitive people deeply fear this and think on it, ridding themselves of self-interest, so they can fulfill their duty in the Way of humanity according to the truth. Reward and punishment are meted out in both the visible and invisible worlds. These are not based on a capricious standard. People will receive many forms of reward or punishment based on their own actions. Surely sensitive people desire fortune [as a reward]. Whether you receive a reward or a punishment is all determined by which path you follow. Following the true Way results in fortune, but following an evil Way results in punishment. If a sensitive person desires fortune, then why would he not follow the true Way? People who try to obtain fortune but do not follow the true Way are like people who dive in the water in search for beasts of the land. They not only fail to find what they are looking for, but place themselves in danger. People should immediately come out of the fog of confusion and follow the true Way.

(16)

A certain person rebuked me, saying, "The argument in this chapter on principles is in large measure based on reason. It is true that these arguments will supplement the teachings in society. However, on the surface his argument attacks the teachings of Confucianism, Buddhism, and the various foreign countries, but in the background he actually adheres to these teachings. People will find this disingenuous of him. Why does he not take a step back and soften his stance?" I will reply that this kind of criticism is typical of people in the world. I have pondered this and realize that some of what I have argued does actually have some parallels in foreign countries, so I cannot claim that this criticism is baseless. However, my argument is based on the ancient traditions of our country in searching for the truth, so it is not the same as the many pointless and deceptive philosophies found in foreign teachings. … As the logic and evidence of my argument is clear, a person who has *magokoro* "the true sincere heart" and is discerning will see the truth in my words. Why should I fear the barbs of ridicule from someone drowning in confusion and not speak the truth? Is it not the responsibility of a scholar to lecture on the correct Way, and teach true words? If foreign teachings resemble things in our country, it is because these foreign teachings contain vestiges of our ancient traditions. It is not because my teachings are based on their teachings. And why should anyone detest the fact that there are similarities? Our teachers, Master Motoori and Master Hirata have argued this, and the reader should read their words.

[Ogasawara 1988:331–55]

☙

BIBLIOGRAPHY

All works in Kokugaku Sources and Other Japanese Sources published in Tokyo unless otherwise noted.

Abbreviations used in this work:

GSS	*Gosenshū*
HAZ	*Hirata Atsutane zenshū*
KJK	*Kojiki*
KKS	*Kokinshū*
KKWS	*Kinkai wakashū*
MNZ	*Motoori Norinaga zenshū*
MYS	*Man'yōshū*
NKBT	*Nihon koten bungaku taikei*
NKBZ	*Nihon koten bungaku zenshū*
NKT	*Nihon kagaku taikei*
NS	*Nihon shoki*
NST	*Nihon shisō taikei*
SKKS	*Shin Kokinshū*
SNKBT	*Shin Nihon koten bungaku taikei*
SS	*Shūishū*
ST	*Shintō taikei*

KOKUGAKU SOURCES

Abe Akio and Taira Shigemichi, eds. 1972. *Keichū: Zassetsu. Manyō daishō*ki *sōshaku.* Contained in *Zenki kokugaku.* Volume 39 of NST, Iwanami Shoten. This volume also contains Mabuchi's Five Treatise (*Bunikō, Goikō, Kaikō, Kokuikō,* and *Shoikō*), Azumamaro's *Sōgakkō kei* (Petition), and Andō Tameakira's *Shika shichiron.*

Hashimoto Fumio, Ariyoshi Tamotsu, and Fujihira Haruo, eds. 1975. *Karonshū.* Volume 50 of NKBZ, Shōgakkan. This contains *Kokka hachiron* and *Nifimanabi iken.*

Katō Totsudō (Kumaichirō), ed. 1929. *Kokumin shisō sōsho*, Shintō-hen. Daitō Shuppansha.

Motoori Toyokai, Kimura Masakoto, Inoue Yorikuni, and Muromatsu Iwao, eds. 1910. *Kokubun chūshaku zensho*, Volume 3. Kokugakuin Daigaku Shuppan.

Nakamura Yukihiko, ed. 1966. *Kokka hachiron*. Contained in volume 94, NKBT, Iwanami Shoten.

Ogasawara Haruo, ed. 1988. *Shoka Shintō, jō*. Ronsetsu-hen, Volume 27 ST. Shintō Taikei Hensankai.

Ōkubo Tadashi and Ōno Susumu, eds. 1976. Volume 1 of MNZ. Chikuma Shobō. This contains *Tamagatsuma* and *Uiyamabumi*.

______. 1976. Volume 2 of MNZ. Chikuma Shobō. This contains *Ashiwake obune*, *Isonokami sasamegoto*.

______. 1976. Volume 4 of MNZ. Chikuma Shobō. This contains *Genji monogatari: tama no ogushi* and *Shibun yōryō*.

______. 1976. Volume 6 of MNZ. Chikuma Shobō. This contains *Man'yōshū: tama no ogoto*.

______. 1976. Volume 8 of MNZ. Chikuma Shobō. This contains *Kagaika* and *Kokugōkō*.

______. 1976. Volumes 9 through 12 of MNZ. Chikuma Shobō. This contains *Kojiki den*. *Naobi no mitama* is contained in volume 9, part of Norinaga's introduction to *Kojiki den*.

______. 1976. Volume 14 of MNZ. Chikuma Shobō. This contains *Kogo shinan*.

Tahara Tsuguo, ed. 1973. Volume 50 of NST, Iwanami Shoten. This contains *Kodō taii* and *Tama no mihashira*.

Yamamoto Yutaka, ed. 1942. *Kōhon Kamo Mabuchi zenshū*. Kōbundō Shobō.

OTHER JAPANESE SOURCES

Araki Yoshio. 1943. *Kamo Mabuchi no hito to shisō*. Kōseikaku.

Denki gakkai. 1943. *Kokugakusha kenkyū*. Hokkai Shuppansha.

Furuta Tōsaku. 1973. "Yamada Yoshio." Entry in Sōga, Tetsuo, ed. *Encyclopedia Japonica*, 23 volumes. Shōgakkan.

Haga Noboru and Matsumoto Sannosuke, eds. 1971. *Kokugaku undō no shisō*. Volume 51 of NST, Iwanami Shoten.

Haga Yaichi. 1904. "Kokugaku to ha nani zo ya." *Kokugakuin zasshi* 10.1:1–13 and 10.2:1–16.

Hisamatsu Sen'ichi. 1942. *Keichū no shōgai*. Sōgensha.

Ienaga Saburō, Inoue Mitsusada, Ōno Susumu, and Sakamoto Tarō, eds. 1967. *Nihon shoki*. Vols. 67–68 of NKBT. Iwanami Shoten.

Iida Mizuho, ed. 1986. *Kogo shūi*. Volume 5 of Koten-hen, ST. Shintō Taikei Hensankai.

Inoue Mitsusada, Seki Akira, Tsuchida Naoshige, and Aoki Kazuo, eds. 1985. *Ritsuryō*. Volume 3 of NST, Iwanami Shoten.

Inoue Nobutaka, Okada Shōji, Sakamoto Koremaru, Sugiyama Shigetsugu, and Takashio Hiroshi, eds. 1999. *Shintō jiten*. Kōbundō. All English translations are from http://eos.kokugakuin.ac.jp/modules/xwords/

Kamochi Masazumi. 1891. *Man'yōshū kogi*. Kunaishō. Each volume is divided into subvolumes. So 1.6 refers to the sixth part of Volume 1.

Kanamoto Takuji. 2013. "Kindai Nihon no reikonkan: Hirataha Kokugakusha Suzuki Masayuki *Tsuki sakaki* o tōshite." *Gendai mikkyō*, no. 24, pp. 143–60.

Katakiri Yōichi, ed. 1990. *Gosen wakashū*. Volume 6 of SNKBT. Iwanami Shoten.

Katsurajima Nobuhiro. 1992. *Bakumatsu minshū shisō no kenkyū*. Bunrikaku.

Kiyohara Sadao, ed. 1981. *Kokugaku hattatsu shi*. Kokusho Kankōkai.

Kojima Noriyuki and Arai Eizō, eds. 1989. *Kokin wakashū*. Volume 5 of SNKBT, Iwanami Shoten.

Kokugakuin daigaku dōgi gakkai, 1936. *Motoori Norinaga kenkyū*. Seinen kyōiku Fukyūkai Hakkō.

Komachiya Teruhiko, ed. 1990. *Shūi wakashū*. Volume 7 of SNKBT. Iwanami Shoten.

Kōnoshi Takamitsu and Yamaguchi Yoshinori, eds. 2007. *Kojiki*. Volume 1 of Shinpen Nihon koten bungaku zenshū. Shōgakkan.

Koyama Tadashi. 1938. *Kamo Mabuchi den*. Shunshūsha.

Kurano Kenji and Takeda Yūkichi, eds. 1985. *Kojiki/Norito*. Volume 1 of NKBT. Iwanami Shoten.

Kuroita Katsumi, ed. 1982. *Nihon sandai jitsuroku*. Shintei zōho Kokushi Taikei. Yoshikawa Kōbunkan.

______. 1983. *Shoku Nihon kōki*. Shintei zōho Kokushi Taikei. Yoshikawa Kōbunkan.

______. 1984. *Montoku jitsuroku*. Shintei zōho Kokushi Taikei. Yoshikawa Kōbunkan.

Maruyama Kiyoko. 1986. "*Genji monogatari* narabi no maki ni tsuite." *Chūko bungaku*, no. 36, pp. 1–10.

Matsuo, Sutejirō. 1936. "Motoori Norinaga no kokugogaku." In Kokugakuin Daigaku Dōgi Gakkai, ed. *Motoori Norinaga kenkyū*. Seinen Kyōiku Fukyūkai, pp. 16–32.

Matsushita Kōnosuke. 1977. "Kankō no kotoba." Shintō Taikei Geppō, no. 1. Shintō Taikei Hensankai (December).

Miyajima Katsuichi. 1943. *Norinaga no tetsugaku*. Takayama Shoin.

Muraoka Tsunetsugu. 1928. *Motoori Norinaga*. Iwanami Shoten.

______. 1981. *Norinaga to Atsutane*. Sōbun Shahan.

Nakanishi Masayuki. 1998. *Ise no miyabito*. Kokusho Kankōkai.

Nakanishi Susumu, ed. 1989. *Kakinomoto Hitomaro: hito to sakuhin*. Baifūsha.

Nihon koten bungaku jiten henshū iinkai, 1986. *Nihon koten bungaku jiten*. Iwanami Shoten.

Nishide Naho. 2010. "*Koyōryaku ruijūshō* no dokujisei to hensan ito—bunrui oyobi seiritsu haikei kara no kōsatsu." *Josetsu* (Nara Joshi Daigaku Kokugo Kokubungakkai), Volume 37, pp. 290–304.

Ogata Hiroyasu. 1944. *Kamochi Masazumi*. Chūō Kōronsha.

Ogihara Asao and Kōnosu Hayao, eds. 1973. *Kojiki/Jōdai kayō*. Volume 1 of NKBZ. Shōgakkan.

Ōishi Arata. 1942. *Kamo Mabuchi*. Yanagihara Shoten Kankō.

Ōkawa Shigeo, Minami Shigeki, Ueda Kazutoshi, and Haga Yaichi, eds. 1934. *Kokugakusha denki shūsei*. Kunimoto Shuppansha.

Ōkubo Tadashi. 1964. *Edo jidai no kokugaku*. Shibundō.

Omodaka Hisataka. 1983. *Man'yōshū chūshaku*. Chūō Kōronsha.

Onoda Mitsuo, ed. 1977. *Kojiki*. Volume 1 of Koten-hen, ST. Shintō Taikei Hensankai.

______. 1986. *Shaku Nihongi*. Volume 5 of Koten Chūshaku-hen, ST. Shintō Taikei Hensankai.

Orikuchi Shinobu. 1956a. "Kokugaku to wa nani ka?" Contained in Volume 20 of *Orikuchi Shinobu zenshū*. Chūō Kōronsha.

______. 1956b. "Hirata kokugaku no dentō." In Volume 20 of *Orikuchi Shinobu zenshū*. Chūō Kōronsha.

Saigusa Yasutaka. 1962. *Kamo Mabuchi*. Yoshikawa Kōbunkan.

______. 1966. *Kokugaku no undō*. Kazama Shobō.

Saitō Mokichi. 1980. *Kinkai wakashū*. Iwanami Shoten.

Sakamoto Tarō, Ienaga Saburō, Inoue Mitsusada, and Ōno Susumu, eds. 1986. *Nihon shoki*. Volumes 67–68 of NKBT, Iwanami Shoten.

Sano Kazuhiko. 1944. *Kokoro to michi*. Seibunsha.

Sasaki Nobutsuna. 1934. *Sotei Kamo Mabuchi to Motoori Norinaga*. Kobunsha.

Sasazuki Kiyomi. 1944. *Motoori norinaga no kenkyū*. Iwanami Shoten.

Shimizu Yasuyuki. 1994. "Yamada Yoshio," entry in *Nihon daihyakka zensho*, 25 volumes. Shōgakkan.

Takahashi Toshikazu. 1993. "Norinaga no shin kokin shugi." *Kokugo tokokubungaku*. 70.3, 26–41.

Takaki Ichinosuke, Gomi Tomohide, and Ōno Susumu, eds. 1974 *Man'yōshū*. Volumes 4–7 of NKBT, Iwanami Shoten.

Takeda Munetoshi. 1954. *Genji monogatari no kenkyū*. Iwanami Shoten.

Takeuchi Rizō, Yamada Hideo, and Hirano Kunio, eds. 1962. *Nihon kodai jinmei jiten*. Yoshikawa Kōbunkan. In seven volumes.

Tanaka Yoshitō. 1942. *Shintō gairon*. Meiji Shoin.

Tanaka Yutaka and Akase Shingō, eds. 1992. *Shin kokin wakashū*. Volume 11 of SNKBT, Iwanami Shoten.

Tōdō Akiyasu. 1978. *Gakken Kanwa daijiten*. Gakken Kenkyūsha.

Umezawa Isezō. 1976. *Zoku Kiki hihan*. Sōbunsha.

Yamada Yoshio. 1942. *Kokugaku no hongi*. Unebi Shobō.

SECONDARY SOURCES

Aston, William George. 1972. *A History of Japanese Literature*. First published in 1899. Rutland, Vermont: Tuttle Publishing. Paperback edition.

Baxter, William H., and Laurent Sagart. 2014. *Old Chinese: A New Reconstruction*. Oxford: Oxford University Press.

Bentley, John R. 2002. *Historiographical Trends in Early Japan*. Lewiston, NY: Edwin Mellen Press.

______. 2006. *The Authenticity of* Sendai Kuji Hongi*—A New Examination of Texts. With a Translation and Commentary*. Leiden: E. J. Brill.

______. 2013. *Tamakatsuma—A Window into the Scholarship of Motoori Norinaga*. Ithaca, NY: Cornell University East Asia Program.

Bloom, Irene, and Philip J. Ivanhoe, trans. 2009. *Mencius*. New York: Columbia University Press.

Bodart-Bailey, Beatrice M. 1988. "Kaempfer Restor'd." *Monumenta Nipponica* 43.1: 1–33.

______. 1999. *Kaempfer's Japan: Tokugawa Culture Observed*. Honolulu: University of Hawai'i Press.

Bock, Felicia G. 1972. *Engi-shiki: Procedures of the Engi Era*. Tokyo: Sophia University.

Bowring, Richard. 1996. *The Diary of Lady Murasaki*. London: Penguin.

Burns, Susan L. 2003. *Before the Nation: Kokugaku and the Imagining of Community in Early Modern Japan*. Durham: Duke University Press.

Caddeau, Patrick W. 2006. *Appraising "Genji": Literary Criticism and Cultural Anxiety in the Age of the Last Samurai*. Albany: State University of New York Press.

Coblin, W. South. 1994. *A Compendium of Phonetics in Northwest Chinese*. *Journal of Chinese Linguistics* monograph 7.

Flueckiger, Peter. 2008. "Reflections on the Meaning of Our Country: Kamo no Mabuchi's *Kokuikō*." *Monumenta Nipponica* 63.2:211–63.

______. 2010. *Imagining Harmony: Poetry, Empathy, and Community in Mid-Tokugawa Confucianism and Nativism*. Stanford: Stanford University Press.

Forke, Alfred. 1962. *Lun-hêng: Philosophical Essays of Wang Ch'ung*. Parts 1 and 2. New York: Paragon.

Frellesvig, Bjarke, and John Whitman, eds. 2008. *Proto-Japanese: Issues and Prospects*. Amsterdam: John Benjamins Publishing Company.

Hansen, Wilburn. 2008. *When Tengu Talk: Hirata Atsutane's Ethnography of the Other World*. Honolulu: University of Hawai'i Press.

______. 2013. Review of *Imagining Harmony: Poetry, Empathy, and Community in Mid-Tokugawa Confucianism and Nativism*. In *Japanese Language and Literature* 47.2:286–91.

Harootunian, H. D. 1988. *Things Seen and Unseen: Discourse and Ideology in Tokugawa Nativism*. Chicago: The University of Chicago Press.

Heldt, Gustav. 2014. *The Kojiki: An Account of Ancient Matters*. New York: Columbia University Press.

Huang, Junjie. 2001. *Dong ya ru xue shi de xin shi ye* (A new look into the historical influence of Confucian studies in Asia). Taipei: Cai tuan fa ren Ximalaya yanjiu fazhan jijin hui.

Keene, Donald, 1976. *World Within Walls: Japanese Literature of the Pre-Modern Era, 1600–1867*. New York: Holt, Rinehart, and Winston.

Kinney, Anne Behnke. 2014. *Exemplary Women of Early China: The Lienü zhuan of Liu Xiang*. New York: Columbia University Press.

Lau, D. C, tr. 1979. *The Analects* (*Lun yü*). Harmondsworth: Penguin Books.

Ledyard, Gari. 1975. "Galloping Along with the Horseriders: Looking for the Founders of Japan." *Journal of Japanese Studies* 1.2:217–54.

Legge, James. 1960. *Book of Odes*. Hong Kong: Hong Kong University Press.

______. 1967. *Li chi: Book of Rites—An Encyclopedia of Ancient Ceremonial Usages, Religious Creeds, and Social Institutions*. New Hyde Park: University Books.

______. 1970. *The Works of Mencius*. New York: Dover Publications.

Li, Fang Kuei. 1971. "Studies on Archaic Chinese phonology" (in Chinese). *Tsing Hua Journal of Chinese Studies* 9:1–61.

Lynn, Richard John. 1994. *The Classic of Changes: A New Translation of the I Ching As Interpreted by Wang Bi*. New York: Columbia University Press.

Major, John S. 2010. *Huainanzi: A Guide to the Theory and Practice of Government in Early Han China*. New York: Columbia University Press.

Martin, Samuel E. 1987. *The Japanese Language through Time*. New Haven: Yale University Press.

Matsumoto, Shigeru. 1970. *Motoori Norinaga: 1730–1801*. Cambridge: Harvard University Press.

McCullough, Helen Craig. 1985. *Kokin Wakashū: The First Imperial Anthology of Japanese Poetry*. Stanford: Stanford University Press.

McCullough, Helen C., and William and H. 1980. *A Tale of Flowering Fortunes: Annals of Japanese Aristocratic Life in the Heian Period*. Stanford: Stanford University Press.

McNally, Mark. 2005. *Proving the Way: Conflict and Practice in the History of Japanese Nativism*. Cambridge, MA: Harvard University Asia Center.

Miyake, Marc Hideo. 2003. *Old Japanese: A Phonetic Reconstruction*. London: Routledge Curzon.

Muller, A. Charles. 1995. "Digital Dictionary of Buddhism." Internet Resource accessed 2015/2016. http://www. buddhism-dict.net/ddb/

Najita, Tetsuo, and Irwin Scheiner. 1978. *Japanese Thought in the Tokugawa Period: 1600–1868*. Chicago: The University of Chicago Press.

Nakai, Kate Wildman. 1989. "Review of *Things Seen and Unseen* by H. D. Harootunian." In *Monumenta Nipponica* 44.2:224–28.

Nienhauser, William H., Jr., ed. 2006. *The Grand Scribe's Records.* Volume 5, *The Hereditary Houses of Pre-Han China, Part I.* Bloomington: Indiana University Press.

______. ed. 2008. *The Grand Scribe's Records.* Volume 8, *The Memoirs of Han China, Part I.* Bloomington: Indiana University Press.

Nosco, Peter. 1978. "Remembering Paradise, Nostalgic Themes in Japanese Nativism." Diss. New York, Columbia University.

______. 1980. "Keichū (1640–1701): Forerunner of National Learning." *Asian Thought and Society* 5.1:237–52.

______. 1981. "Nature, Invention and National Learning." *Harvard Journal of Asiatic Studies* 41.1:75–91.

______. 1990. *Remembering Paradise: Nativism and Nostalgia in Eighteenth-Century Japan.* Cambridge, MA: Harvard University Asia Center.

Nylan, Michael, ed. 2014. *The Analects—The Simon Leys Translation, Interpretations.* New York: W. W. Norton and Company.

Odronic, Walter John. 1967. "Kodo taii (An outline of the ancient Way). An annotated translation with an introduction to the Shinto revival movement and a sketch of the life of Hirata Atsutane." Ph.D. diss., University of Pennsylvania.

Ōkubo Tadashi. 1973. "The Thoughts of Mabuchi and Norinaga." *Acta Asiatica* 25: 68–90.

Philippi, Donald L. 1968. *Kojiki.* Tokyo: University of Tokyo Press.

Pulleyblank, Edwin G. 1962. "The Consonantal System of Old Chinese," *Asia Major* 9:58–144, 206–65.

______. 1992. "How Do We Reconstruct Old Chinese?" *Journal of the American Oriental Society* 112:365–82.

______. 1999. "Chinese Traditional Phonology." *Asia Major,* Third Series 12:101–37.

Schuessler, Axel. 2007. *ABC Etymological Dictionary of Old Chinese.* Honolulu: University of Hawai'i Press.

Teeuwen, Mark. 2006. "Kokugaku vs. Nativism." *Monumenta Nipponica* 61.2:227–42.

Tyler, Royall, trans. 2001. *The Tale of Genji.* Two volumes. New York: Viking.

Unger, J. Marshall. 1993. *Studies in Early Japanese Morphophonemics.* Bloomington: IULC—Indiana University Linguistics Club.

______. 2008. "Early Japanese Lexical Strata and the Allophones of /g/." In Bjarke Frellesvig and John Whitman, eds. 2008. *Proto-Japanese: Issues and Prospects,* pp. 43–53. Amsterdam: John Benjamins Publishing Company.

Vovin, Alexander. 2005. *A Descriptive and Comparative Grammar of Western Old Japanese: Part 1: Sources, Script and Phonology, Lexicon and Nominals.* Folkestone, Kent: Global Oriental.

Wachutka, Michael. 2013. *Kokugaku in Meiji-period Japan—The Modern Transformation of 'National Learning' and the Formation of Scholarly Societies.* Leiden: Global Oriental.

Wagner, Rudolf G. 2003. *A Chinese Reading of the Daodejing: Wang Bi's Commentary on the* Laozi *with Critical Text and Commentary.* Albany: State University of New York Press.

Wakabayashi, Bob Tadashi. 1990. Review of *Remembering Paradise: Nativism and Nostalgia in Eighteenth-Century Japan*, by Peter Nosco. *Monumenta Nipponica*, 45:3.372–75.

Watson, Burton. 1995. "Chinese History." In Chan Sin-wai and David E. Pollard, eds., *An Encyclopedia of Translation: Chinese-English, English-Chinese.* Hong Kong: The Chinese University Press, pp. 347–36.

ঌ

INDEX

ଓ

CORNELL EAST ASIA SERIES

4 Fredrick Teiwes, *Provincial Leadership in China: The Cultural Revolution and Its Aftermath*
8 Cornelius C. Kubler, *Vocabulary and Notes to Ba Jin's Jia: An Aid for Reading the Novel*
16 Monica Bethe & Karen Brazell, *Nō as Performance: An Analysis of the Kuse Scene of Yamamba.* Available for purchase: DVD by Monica Bethe & Karen Brazell, "Yamanba: The Old Woman of the Mountains"
18 Royall Tyler, tr., *Granny Mountains: A Second Cycle of Nō Plays*
23 Knight Biggerstaff, *Nanking Letters, 1949*
28 Diane E. Perushek, ed., *The Griffis Collection of Japanese Books: An Annotated Bibliography*
37 J. Victor Koschmann, Ōiwa Keibō & Yamashita Shinji, eds., *International Perspectives on Yanagita Kunio and Japanese Folklore Studies*
38 James O'Brien, tr., *Murō Saisei: Three Works*
40 Kubo Sakae, *Land of Volcanic Ash: A Play in Two Parts,* revised edition, tr. David G. Goodman
44 Susan Orpett Long, *Family Change and the Life Course in Japan*
48 Helen Craig McCullough, *Bungo Manual: Selected Reference Materials for Students of Classical Japanese*
49 Susan Blakeley Klein, *Ankoku Butō: The Premodern and Postmodern Influences on the Dance of Utter Darkness*
50 Karen Brazell, ed., *Twelve Plays of the Noh and Kyōgen Theaters*
51 David G. Goodman, ed., *Five Plays by Kishida Kunio*
52 Shirō Hara, *Ode to Stone,* tr. James Morita
53 Peter J. Katzenstein & Yutaka Tsujinaka, *Defending the Japanese State: Structures, Norms and the Political Responses to Terrorism and Violent Social Protest in the 1970s and 1980s*
54 Su Xiaokang & Wang Luxiang, *Deathsong of the River: A Reader's Guide to the Chinese TV Series* Heshang, trs. Richard Bodman & Pin P. Wan
55 Jingyuan Zhang, *Psychoanalysis in China: Literary Transformations, 1919–1949*
56 Jane Kate Leonard & John R. Watt, eds., *To Achieve Security and Wealth: The Qing Imperial State and the Economy, 1644–1911*
57 Andrew F. Jones, *Like a Knife: Ideology and Genre in Contemporary Chinese Popular Music*
58 Peter J. Katzenstein & Nobuo Okawara, *Japan's National Security: Structures, Norms and Policy Responses in a Changing World*
59 Carsten Holz, *The Role of Central Banking in China's Economic Reforms*
60 Chifumi Shimazaki, *Warrior Ghost Plays from the Japanese Noh Theater: Parallel Translations with Running Commentary*

61 Emily Groszos Ooms, *Women and Millenarian Protest in Meiji Japan: Deguchi Nao and Ōmotokyō*
62 Carolyn Anne Morley, *Transformation, Miracles, and Mischief: The Mountain Priest Plays of Kyōgen*
63 David R. McCann & Hyunjae Yee Sallee, tr., *Selected Poems of Kim Namjo*, afterword by Kim Yunsik
64 Hua Qingzhao, *From Yalta to Panmunjom: Truman's Diplomacy and the Four Powers, 1945–1953*
65 Margaret Benton Fukasawa, *Kitahara Hakushū: His Life and Poetry*
66 Kam Louie, ed., *Strange Tales from Strange Lands: Stories by Zheng Wanlong*, with introduction
67 Wang Wen-hsing, *Backed Against the Sea*, tr. Edward Gunn
69 Brian Myers, *Han Sŏrya and North Korean Literature: The Failure of Socialist Realism in the DPRK*
70 Thomas P. Lyons & Victor Nee, eds., *The Economic Transformation of South China: Reform and Development in the Post-Mao Era*
71 David G. Goodman, tr., *After Apocalypse: Four Japanese Plays of Hiroshima and Nagasaki*, with introduction
72 Thomas Lyons, *Poverty and Growth in a South China County: Anxi, Fujian, 1949–1992*
74 Martyn Atkins, *Informal Empire in Crisis: British Diplomacy and the Chinese Customs Succession, 1927-1929*
76 Chifumi Shimazaki, *Restless Spirits from Japanese Noh Plays of the Fourth Group: Parallel Translations with Running Commentary*
77 Brother Anthony of Taizé & Young-Moo Kim, trs., *Back to Heaven: Selected Poems of Ch'ŏn Sang Pyŏng*
78 Kevin O'Rourke, tr., *Singing Like a Cricket, Hooting Like an Owl: Selected Poems by Yi Kyu-bo*
79 Irit Averbuch, *The Gods Come Dancing: A Study of the Japanese Ritual Dance of Yamabushi Kagura*
80 Mark Peterson, *Korean Adoption and Inheritance: Case Studies in the Creation of a Classic Confucian Society*
81 Yenna Wu, tr., *The Lioness Roars: Shrew Stories from Late Imperial China*
82 Thomas Lyons, *The Economic Geography of Fujian: A Sourcebook*, Vol. 1
83 Pak Wan-so, *The Naked Tree*, tr. Yu Young-nan
84 C.T. Hsia, *The Classic Chinese Novel: A Critical Introduction*
85 Cho Chong-Rae, *Playing With Fire*, tr. Chun Kyung-Ja
86 Hayashi Fumiko, *I Saw a Pale Horse and Selections from Diary of a Vagabond*, tr. Janice Brown
87 Motoori Norinaga, *Kojiki-den, Book 1*, tr. Ann Wehmeyer
88 Chang Soo Ko, tr., *Sending the Ship Out to the Stars: Poems of Park Je-chun*
89 Thomas Lyons, *The Economic Geography of Fujian: A Sourcebook*, Vol. 2

90 Brother Anthony of Taizé, tr., Midang: *Early Lyrics of So Chong-Ju*
92 Janice Matsumura, *More Than a Momentary Nightmare: The Yokohama Incident and Wartime Japan*
93 Kim Jong-Gil tr., *The Snow Falling on Chagall's Village: Selected Poems of Kim Ch'un-Su*
94 Wolhee Choe & Peter Fusco, trs., *Day-Shine: Poetry by Hyon-jong Chong*
95 Chifumi Shimazaki, *Troubled Souls from Japanese Noh Plays of the Fourth Group*
96 Hagiwara Sakutarō, *Principles of Poetry (Shi no Genri),* tr. Chester Wang
97 Mae J. Smethurst, *Dramatic Representations of Filial Piety: Five Noh in Translation*
99 William Wilson, *Hōgen Monogatari: Tale of the Disorder in Hōgen*
100 Yasushi Yamanouchi, J. Victor Koschmann and Ryūichi Narita, eds., *Total War and 'Modernization'*
101 Yi Ch'ŏng-jun, *The Prophet and Other Stories,* tr. Julie Pickering
102 S.A. Thornton, *Charisma and Community Formation in Medieval Japan: The Case of the Yugyō-ha (1300–1700)*
103 Sherman Cochran, ed., *Inventing Nanjing Road: Commercial Culture in Shanghai, 1900–1945*
104 Harold M. Tanner, *Strike Hard! Anti-Crime Campaigns and Chinese Criminal Justice, 1979–1985*
105 Brother Anthony of Taizé & Young-Moo Kim, trs., *Farmers' Dance: Poems by Shin Kyŏng-nim*
106 Susan Orpett Long, ed., *Lives in Motion: Composing Circles of Self and Community in Japan*
107 Peter J. Katzenstein, Natasha Hamilton-Hart, Kozo Kato, & Ming Yue, *Asian Regionalism*
108 Kenneth Alan Grossberg, *Japan's Renaissance: The Politics of the Muromachi Bakufu*
109 John W. Hall & Toyoda Takeshi, eds., *Japan in the Muromachi Age*
110 Kim Su-Young, Shin Kyong-Nim, Lee Si-Young; *Variations: Three Korean Poets;* trs. Brother Anthony of Taizé & Young-Moo Kim
111 Samuel Leiter, *Frozen Moments: Writings on* Kabuki, *1966–2001*
118 Mae J. Smethurst and Christina Laffin, eds., *The Noh* Ominameshi*: A Flower Viewed from Many Directions*
112 Pilwun Shih Wang & Sarah Wang, *Early One Spring: A Learning Guide to Accompany the Film Video* February
113 Thomas Conlan, *In Little Need of Divine Intervention: Scrolls of the Mongol Invasions of Japan*
114 Jane Kate Leonard & Robert Antony, eds., *Dragons, Tigers, and Dogs: Qing Crisis Management and the Boundaries of State Power in Late Imperial China*
115 Shu-ning Sciban & Fred Edwards, eds., *Dragonflies: Fiction by Chinese Women in the Twentieth Century*
116 David G. Goodman, ed., *The Return of the Gods: Japanese Drama and Culture in the 1960s*

117 Yang Hi Choe-Wall, *Vision of a Phoenix: The Poems of Hŏ Nansŏrhŏn*
119 Joseph A. Murphy, *Metaphorical Circuit: Negotiations Between Literature and Science in Twentieth-Century Japan*
120 Richard F. Calichman, *Takeuchi Yoshimi: Displacing the West*
121 Fan Pen Li Chen, *Visions for the Masses: Chinese Shadow Plays from Shaanxi and Shanxi*
122 S. Yumiko Hulvey, *Sacred Rites in Moonlight: Ben no Naishi Nikki*
123 Tetsuo Najita and J. Victor Koschmann, *Conflict in Modern Japanese History: The Neglected Tradition*
124 Naoki Sakai, Brett de Bary, & Iyotani Toshio, eds., *Deconstructing Nationality*
125 Judith N. Rabinovitch and Timothy R. Bradstock, *Dance of the Butterflies: Chinese Poetry from the Japanese Court Tradition*
126 Yang Gui-ja, *Contradictions*, trs. Stephen Epstein and Kim Mi-Young
127 Ann Sung-hi Lee, *Yi Kwang-su and Modern Korean Literature:* Mujŏng
128 Pang Kie-chung & Michael D. Shin, eds., *Landlords, Peasants, & Intellectuals in Modern Korea*
129 Joan R. Piggott, ed., *Capital and Countryside in Japan, 300–1180: Japanese Historians Interpreted in English*
130 Kyoko Selden and Jolisa Gracewood, eds., *Annotated Japanese Literary Gems: Stories by Tawada Yōko, Nakagami Kenji, and Hayashi Kyōko* (Vol. 1)
131 Michael G. Murdock, *Disarming the Allies of Imperialism: The State, Agitation, and Manipulation during China's Nationalist Revolution, 1922–1929*
132 Noel J. Pinnington, *Traces in the Way: Michi and the Writings of Komparu Zenchiku*
133 Charlotte von Verschuer, *Across the Perilous Sea: Japanese Trade with China and Korea from the Seventh to the Sixteenth Centuries*, tr. Kristen Lee Hunter
134 John Timothy Wixted, *A Handbook to Classical Japanese*
135 Kyoko Selden and Jolisa Gracewoord, with Lili Selden, eds., *Annotated Japanese Literary Gems: Stories by Natsume Sōseki, Tomioka Taeko, and Inoue Yasushi* (Vol. 2)
136 Yi Tae-Jin, *The Dynamics of Confucianism and Modernization in Korean History*
137 Jennifer Rudolph, *Negotiated Power in Late Imperial China: The Zongli Yamen and the Politics of Reform*
138 Thomas D. Loooser, *Visioning Eternity: Aesthetics, Politics, and History in the Early Modern Noh Theater*
139 Gustav Heldt, *The Pursuit of Harmony: Poetry and Power in Late Heian Japan*
140 Joan R. Piggott and Yoshida Sanae, *Teishinkōki: The Year 939 in the Journal of Regent Fujiwara no Tadahira*
141 Robert Bagley, *Max Loehr and the Study of Chinese Bronzes: Style and Classification in the History of Art*
142 Edwin A. Cranston, *The Secret Island and the Enticing Flame: Worlds of Memory, Discovery, and Loss in Japanese Poetry*
143 Hugh de Ferranti, *The Last Biwa Singer: A Blind Musician in History, Imagination and Performance*

144 Roger des Forges, Minglu Gao, Liu Chiao-mei, Haun Saussy, with Thomas Burkman, eds., *Chinese Walls in Time and Space: A Multidisciplinary Perspective*
145 Hye-jin Juhn Sidney & George Sidney, trs., *I Heard Life Calling Me: Poems of Yi Sŏng-bok*
146 Sherman Cochran & Paul G. Pickowicz, eds., *China on the Margins*
147 Wang Lingzhen & Mary Ann O' Donnell, trs., *Years of Sadness: Autobiographical Writings of Wang Anyi*
148 John Holstein, tr., *A Moment's Grace: Stories from Korea in Transition*
149 Sunyoung Park in collaboration with Jefferson J.A. Gatrall, trs., *On the Eve of the Uprising and Other Stories from Colonial Korea*
150 Brother Anthony of Taizé & Lee Hyung-jin, trs., *Walking on a Washing Line: Poems of Kim Seung-Hee*
151 Matthew Fraleigh, trs., with introduction, *New Chronicles of Yanagibashi and Diary of a Journey to the West: Narushima Ryūhoku Reports from Home and Abroad*
152 Pei Huang, *Reorienting the Manchus: A Study of Sinicization, 1583–1795*
153 Karen Gernant & Chen Zeping, *White Poppies and Other Stories by Zhang Kangkang*
154 Mattias Burell & Marina Svensson, eds., *Making Law Work: Chinese Laws in Context*
155 Tomoko Aoyama & Barbara Hartley, trs., *Indian Summer by Kanai Mieko*
156 Lynne Kutsukake, tr., *Single Sickness and Other Stories by Masuda Mizuko*
157 Takako U. Lento, tr. with introduction, *Tanikawa Shuntarō: The Art of Being Alone, Poems 1952–2009*
158 Shu-ning Sciban & Fred Edwards, eds., *Endless War: Fiction & Essays by Wang Wen-hsing*
159 Elizabeth Oyler & Michael Watson, eds., *Like Clouds and Mists: Studies and Translations of Nō Plays of the Genpei War*
160 Michiko N. Wilson & Michael K. Wilson, trs., *Of Birds Crying by Minako Ōba*
161 Chifumi Shimazaki & Stephen Comee *Supernatural Beings from Japanese Noh Plays of the Fifth Group: Parallel Translations with Running Commentary*
162 Petrus Liu, *Stateless Subjects: Chinese Martial Arts Literature and Postcolonial History*
163 Lim Beng Choo, *Another Stage: Kanze Nobumitsu and the Late Muromachi Noh Theater*
164 Scott Cook, *The Bamboo Texts of Guodian: A Study and Complete Translation, Volume 1*
165 Scott Cook, *The Bamboo Texts of Guodian: A Study and Complete Translation, Volume 2*
166 Stephen D. Miller, translations with Patrick Donnelly, *The Wind from Vulture Peak: The Buddhification of Japanese Waka in the Heian Period*
167 Theodore Hughes, Jae-yong Kim, Jin-kyung Lee & Sang-kyung Lee, eds., *Rat Fire: Korean Stories from the Japanese Empire*
168 Ken C. Kawashima, Fabian Schäfer, Robert Stolz, eds., *Tosaka Jun: A Critical Reader*
169 John R. Bentley, *Tamakatsuma—A Window into the Scholarship of Motoori Norinaga*
170 Dandan Zhu, *1956: Mao's China and the Hungarian Crisis*
172 Sherman Cochran, ed., *The Capitalist Dilemma in China's Cultural Revolution*

173 Eunju Kim, tr., *Portrait of a Suburbanite: Poems of Ch'oe Seung-ja*
174 Christina Laffin, Joan Piggott & Yoshida Sanae, eds., *The Birth of a Monarch 1103: Selections from Fujiwara no Munetada's Journal* Chūyūki
175 J. Marshall Unger, Sangaku *Proofs: A Japanese Mathematician at Work*
176 Naoki Fukumori, *In Spring the Dawn: Sei Shōnagon's Makura no sōshi (The Pillow Book) and the Poetics of Amusement*
177 John B. Weinstein, *Voices of Taiwanese Women: Three Contemporary Plays*
178 Shu-ning Sciban & Ihor Pidhainy, eds., *Reading Wang Wenxing: Critical Essays*
179 Hou Xiaojia, *Negotiating Socialism in Rural China: Mao, Peasants, and Local Cadres in Shanxi, 1949–1953*
180 Joseph Esherick & Matthew Combs, eds., *1943: China at the Crossroads*
181 Rebecca Jennison & Brett de Bary, eds., *Still Hear The Wound: Toward an Asia, Politics, and Art to Come*
182 Nicholas Morrow Williams, *The Residue of Dreams: Selected Poems of Jao Tsung-i*
183 Bishop D. McKendree, *Barbed Wire and Rice: Poems and Songs from Japanese Prisoner-of-War Camps*
184 John R. Bentley, *An Anthology of* Kokugaku *Scholars, 1690 to 1898*
185 Elizabeth Markham, Naoko Terauchi, Rembrandt Wolpert, eds., *What the Doctor Overheard: Dr. Leopold Müller's Account of Music in Early Meiji Japan. Einige Notizen über die japanische Musik.* 日本音楽に関するノート *(1874–1876)*
186 Glynne Walley, *Edification, Entertainment, and Kyokutei Bakin's* Nansō Satomi hakkenden
187 Yung-Hee Kim, *Gendered Landscapes: Short Fiction by Modern and Contemporary Korean Women Novelists*

eap.einaudi.cornell.edu/publications

CPSIA information can be obtained
at www.ICGtesting.com
Printed in the USA
LVHW092346291119
638472LV00007BB/23/P